437

Colin Wilson is one of the most [...]
at work today. He was born i[...]
sixteen. After he had spent y[...]
laboratory, a plastics factory [...]
Outsider was published in 19[...]
acclaim and was an immediate bestseller.

Since then he has written many books on philosophy, the occult,
crime and sexual deviance, plus a host of successful novels which
have won him an international reputation. His work has been
translated into Spanish, French, Swedish, Dutch, Japanese, German,
Italian, Portuguese, Danish, Norwegian, Finnish and Hebrew.

huge

- very Euro-centred

- p601 - a great man theory
(yet he forgets: the will of
great man must be
reflected in the will of
the people.)

By the same author

NON-FICTION

The Outsider cycle:
The Outsider
Religion and the Rebel
The Age of Defeat
The Strength to Dream
Origins of the Sexual Impulse
Beyond the Outsider
Introduction to the New
    Existentialism

Books on the occult and paranormal:
The Occult
Mysteries
Poltergeist
Psychic Detectives
Strange Powers
The Geller Phenomenon
A Dictionary of Possibilities (with
    John Grant)

Other Non-Fiction:
An Encyclopedia of Murder
    (with Pat Pitman)
An Encyclopedia of Modern Murder
    (with Donald Seaman)
A Casebook of Murder
Order of Assassins
Rasputin and the Fall of the
    Romanovs
Bernard Shaw – A Reassessment
New Pathways in Psychology
The Quest for Wilhelm Reich
The War Against Sleep – The
    Philosophy of Gurdjieff
The Lord of the Underworld – A
    Study of Jung

The Craft of the Novel
The Strange Genius of David
    Lindsay
Frankenstein's Castle
Access to Inner Worlds
Eagle and Earwig (Essays on books
    and writers)
Poetry and Mysticism
A Book of Booze
Starseekers
Brandy of the Damned (Essays on
    Music)
Anti-Sartre

AUTOBIOGRAPHY

Voyage to a Beginning

FICTION

The 'Sorme Trilogy':
Ritual in the Dark
The Man Without a Shadow (retitled
    The Sex Diary of Gerard Sorme)
The God of the Labyrinth

Other Fiction:
Adrift in Soho
The World of Violence
Necessary Doubt
The Glass Cage
The Mind Parasites
The Killer
The Philosopher's Stone
The Black Room
The Space Vampires
The Schoolgirl Murder Case
Rasputin: A Novel

COLIN WILSON

A Criminal History of Mankind

PANTHER
Granada Publishing

Panther Books
Granada Publishing Ltd
8 Grafton Street, London W1X 3LA

Published by Panther Books 1985

First published in Great Britain by
Granada Publishing 1984

Copyright © Colin Wilson 1984

ISBN 0-586-05486-3

Reproduced, printed and bound in Great Britain by
Hazell Watson & Viney Limited,
Aylesbury, Bucks

Set in Plantin

CONTENTS

PART THREE: **THE AGE OF MASS MURDER**

ANALYTICAL TABLE OF CONTENTS

Introduction
Optimism of Wells's *Outline of History* and pessimism of his postscript to *A Short History of the World*. The need to understand crime as an integral part of history.

PART ONE: THE PSYCHOLOGY OF HUMAN VIOLENCE

1. Hidden Patterns of Violence
Changing types of crime: from country to country and century to century. The 'motiveless murder'. Gide's 'gratuitous act'. Herbert Mills. Norman Foose. Penny Bjorkland. Norman Smith. Robert Smith of Arizona. The desire to 'become known'. Becker's *Denial of Death*. The child's need to be the centre of the world. The development of realism. Maslow's theory of the 'hierarchy of needs'. The five levels. The 'hierarchy of needs' applied to crime. The emergence of 'self-esteem' crimes in the twentieth century. Frazier and the murder of the Ohta family. Maslow in the Bronx zoo. Dominance behaviour. Maslow's studies in female dominance. The 'dominance gap' theory applied to partnerships in crime: Albert Patrick and Charles Jones, Fernandez and Beck, Leopold and Loeb, the Moors murder case. Psychology of Myra Hindley. The Heidelberg hypnosis case. Janet's experiments in hypnotic domination. The hypnosis of animals. 'Battle of wills' between a toad and a snake. Explanation of hypnosis. Stagefright. Case of Pauline. Hudson's *The Law of Psychic Phenomena*. The Sala case. Arrest of Dr Sigvard Thurneman. Durkheim's study of suicide. Is suicide 'mechanical'? Suicide as a deficient sense of reality.

2. A Report on the Violent Man

The Japanese 'rape of Nanking'. The discovery of Peking man. Was early man a cannibal? Raymond Dart's 'killer ape' theory of human violence. Man's use of weapons. The Piltdown hoax. Ardrey and Lorenz on human aggression. Koestler on nature's 'evolutionary blunders'. The reactions against the 'killer ape' theory. Fromm's *Anatomy of Human Destructiveness*. 'No evidence that our ancestors were basically warlike and aggressive.' Wells on human destructiveness. The city as the origin of crime. Is fellow-feeling 'natural' to man? Colin Turnbull's *The Mountain People*. The Ik. Xenophobia – dislike of the foreigner. Natural size of animal groups. Indifference of Nazis to concentration camp victims. The deer population on James Island. Overcrowding. John Calhoun's observation on over-crowded rats. Augustus Kinzel's experiment in 'personal space'. Mass suicide in lemmings. American prisoners die of 'give-up-itis'. Force C and Force T. The release of adrenalin. Tension and illness. The criminal and 'stress resistance'. Stanley Milgram's experiments in torture. Japanese traditionalism. Freud's 'death-wish' theory. Fromm on necrophilia. The 'Right Man'. Men who refuse to admit they are ever in the wrong. Insane jealousy. How the Right Man can be destroyed. Peter Sellers as a Right Man. The 'decision to be out of control'. Aksakov's grandfather. His insane rages. Sartre's concept of 'magic'. Wishful thinking. Elizabeth Duncan: a Right Woman. Human dominance – the dominant five per cent.

3. The Psychology of Self-Destruction

Jack Henry Abbott's *In the Belly of the Beast*. Abbott's murder of Richard Adan. Abbott's self-justification. Romanticizing the criminal. The ostrich reaction. The career of Carl Panzram. His sense of injustice. His career of mass murder. He writes his autobiography. Panzram's execution. 'Society' does not exist. Why Panzram's death was a form of suicide. Resentment. John Haigh, the acid bath murderer. Gorky's story of Merkhouloff. Steven Judy and his demand to be executed. The paradox of human self-destruction. The 'two selves'. 'Long-term' needs and 'short-term' needs. The microscope and the telescope. Hypnosis: using the mind's power against itself. 'The mind is the slayer of the real.' Dan MacDougald's experiments in rehabilitating 'hard-core psychopaths'. The Harvard cat experiment. Alfred Reynolds and 'de-nazifying' young Nazis. Abram Hoffer and alcoholism. Werner Erhard and *est*. The ego is the director of consciousness. The 'robot' which does our living for us. Mrs Marva Drew types out every number from one to a million. The defiance of authority.

4. How Man Evolved

Two examples of sadism: the old man thrown into the furnace. Juliette's murder of an 'unfortunate'. Sadism as 'an inflated ego'. Yochelson and Samenow study criminals in St Elizabeth's hospital. Their increasing disillusionment. Criminals unable to escape the 'pattern'. Criminality and sex. Crime is a combination of egoism, infantilism and sex. The hardships of ancient Greece and Rome. The dwellings of medieval labourers. The crimes of a luxury society. Is war as old as humanity? Louis Mumford denies it. The foundation of the cities. The earliest wars: boundary disputes. The early civilizations seem devoid of cruelty. The early pharaohs. Sargon of Akkad, the first empire builder. Oscar Maerth's theory of brain-cannibalism. Elaine Morgan's *Descent of Woman*. Her theory of human violence. Ardrey's hunting 'hypothesis'. Man as an out-of-work hunter. Ardrey and Leakey on the origin of war. The feeling of 'non-fellowship'. Primitive violence: the Pishaukos and the Taulipang. Social instinct and killer instinct. The Fort Ternan evidence that man has been a meat eater for three million years. Man's ancestor Ramapithecus. Australopithecus. *Homo habilis*. Man's emergence during the Pleistocene. *Homo erectus*. The expanding brain. Was the 'brain explosion' triggered by reversal of the earth's polarity? Neanderthal man – was he exterminated by Cro-Magnon man? The invention of long-distance weapons. The bow and arrow theory of evolution. The sex theory of evolution. 'Romantic sexual selection'. What did man *do* with his increased brain? The world's earliest engraving. Cro-Magnon art. Alexander Marshack and the 'earliest writing'. Extra-sensory perception as a basis for religion. Dowsing. The earth's magnetic field. Ancient man and the 'forces of nature'. Why did man lose his sense of involvement with the gods?

5. The Disadvantages of Consciousness

Klaus Gosmann, the 'midday murderer'. The need to 'strength identity'. Crime and the sense of identity? Julian Jaynes a theory of the 'bicameral mind'. Did ancient man lack co ness? The double brain – the left and right hemispheres. Th

PART TWO: A CRIMINAL OUTLINE OF HISTORY

1. Pirates and Adventurers

2. No Mean City

The foundation of Rome by slaves and murderers. The Roman Republic. The first strike in history. Spurius Cassius executed for befriending the poor. Murder of Spurius Maelius. Condemnation of Marcus Manlius. Rome and Carthage become allies. The takeover of Messana. Messanian pirates appeal to Rome for aid. The first war against Carthage. MacArthur's *No Mean City*. Rome as the 'razor king' of the Mediterranean. Hamilcar invades Spain. Hannibal invades Italy. The Roman destruction of Carthage. The Roman taste for luxury. The Romans conquer the Mediterranean. Increasing corruption of Rome. Murder of Tiberius Gracchus. Murder of Gaius Gracchus. Marius becomes dictator. Revolt of Mithridates. Sulla becomes master of Rome. Marius becomes a paranoid maniac. Slaughter of Marius's troops. Sulla as dictator. King Asoka in India: conquest by religion. The religious revolution of the fifth century B.C. Roman lack of religious sense. Later development of the east. Athenian destruction of Melos. Revolt of Spartacus. Destruction of the slave army. Rise of Pompey. The Mediterranean pirates destroyed by Pompey. Pompey's triumphs. Rise of Julius Caesar. Caesar crucifies the pirates. The 'three-headed monster'. Caesar crosses the Rubicon. Murder of Pompey. Augustus becomes Caesar. Sexual misdemeanours of ancient Rome. Tiberius as emperor. His sexual perversions. Caligula as Caesar. Assassination of Caligula. Accession of Claudius. Claudius's sadism. Killing of Messalina. Revolt of Queen Boudica. Boudica's army destroyed by Romans.

3. From Nero to Constantine

The emperor Nero. His taste for applause. His murder of his mother. The marriage with Poppaea. The fire of Rome. Murder of Nero. Was Nero a criminal type? His inability to resist the 'destabilizing force'. The rise of Christianity. The agitator Jeshua. Original description of Jesus. The Jews in the time of Jesus. Jewish religion. Teachings of Jesus. Reasons for the triumph of Christianity. Healing powers. St Paul's version of Christianity. The new evolutionary promise. Trajan, Hadrian and Marcus Aurelius. The 'barrack emperors'. Heliogabalus and his peculiar vices. Sex and practical jokes. The emperor Diocletian. Constantine and the triumph of Christianity.

4. End of the Roman Empire

5. Europe in Chaos

6. Assassins and Conquerors

husband. Cesare's downfall. Machiavelli. *The Prince*. The problem of human purpose. The Cathars. Wycliffe and Hus. The Council of Constance. Crime in Italy. The Jubilee as a money-making device. Martin Luther visits Rome. Luther begins lecturing. Justification by faith. Sale of indulgences. The ninety-five theses. 'Luther is just a drunken German.' The debate of Leipzig. The Diet of Worms. The Protestant revolt. Luther's opposition to the peasants. Henry VIII. Another sack of Rome. Henry's break with Rome. Ulrich Zwingli. Müntzer and the Anabaptists. Massacre of the Anabaptists. Loyola and the Counter-Reformation. Charles V. The Duke of Alva and the massacres in the Netherlands. Death of Charles V. Bloody Mary. More persecutions in the Netherlands. The Spanish Armada. French Protestantism and the Huguenots. The massacre of St Bartholomew.

9. History Changes its Rules
The murder of Christopher Marlowe. Torture of Kyd. The Elizabethan mentality. Copernicus and his *Revolutions of the Heavenly Bodies*. Tycho Brahe. Galileo and the telescope. Galileo's downfall. The witchcraft craze. How it originated. The Cathars. The climax of the craze. Matthew Hopkins. The Salem witchcraft case. The Chambre Ardente affair. The Louviers nuns. The crimes of Marie de Brinvilliers. A backward look at history. The new Athenian age. Francis Bacon. Hobbes and Locke. Wells's 'imprisoned sleeper'. The last world conqueror, Babur. Akbar the Great Mogul. The Ming dynasty in China. The mistakes of Philip II of Spain. The Turks. James I. Richelieu and Louis XIII. The Thirty Years War. The changing rules of history. The original Dracula. Ivan the Terrible. Gilles de Rais. The diary of the Nuremberg executioner. The Elizabethan novel. The new Puritanism. *The Pilgrim's Progress*. The invention of gin. The crime wave of the eighteenth century. Eighteenth-century crime compared to Elizabethan. Punishments. Execution of Damiens. 'Gallows days'. *The Lives of the Most Remarkable Criminals*. The Catherine Hayes case.

10. From Individualism to Rebellion
Robinson Crusoe. Life of Defoe. Defoe as a criminal type. Foundation of the British Secret Service. Defoe's downfall. His Machiavellianism. Importance of the novel. Samuel Richardson and *Pamela*. Rousseau and *The New Héloïse*. Goethe's *Young Werther*. *The Man of*

boys' gang. The Chowchilla kidnap of a school bus. 'Son of Sam'. Mutilation rape of Mary Vincent. The Hillside Strangler. Gacy. The Yorkshire Ripper. Ted Bundy. Crimes of 1983.

6. The Sense of Reality

Parson Grimshaw and his flock. Religion in the eighteenth century. The rise of self-indulgence. Breakdown of social prohibitions. Is Western civilization in decline? The need for 'objectivity'. The two modes of perception. *Nausea*. *The Dam Busters*. Summary of human history. Man's attempt to develop 'stilts'. The death of romanticism. Existentialism. Husserl and intentionality of consciousness. The consciousness explosion. 'Completing', the basic mechanism of perception. Shelley and Proust. Sex crime as a method of 'focusing'. Crime as an attempt at personal evolution. The problem of 'leakage'. Stopping the 'leaks'. The identity crisis. The ego's ignorance of its own powers. Maslow's students and the peak experience. 'Clenching'. Dan MacDougald and the cure of criminality. The criminal as a 'collective nightmare'.

Selected Bibliography

Index

A CRIMINAL HISTORY
OF MANKIND

INTRODUCTION

I was about twelve years old when I came upon a bundle of magazines tied with string in a second-hand bookshop – the original edition of H. G. Wells's *Outline of History*, published in 1920. Since some of the parts were missing, I got the whole pile for a few shillings. It was, I must admit, the pictures that attracted me – splendid full-page colour illustrations of plesiosaurs on a Mesozoic beach; Neanderthal men snarling in the entrance to their cave; the giant rock-hewn statues of Rameses II and his consort at Abu Simbel. Far more than Wells's text, these brought a breathless sensation of the total sweep of world history. Even today I feel a flash of the old magical excitement as I look at them – that peculiar delight that children feel when someone says, 'Once upon a time . . . .'.

In 1946, Penguin Books republished ten volumes of Wells to celebrate his eightieth birthday, including the condensed version of the *Outline*, *A Short History of the World*. It was in this edition that I discovered that strange little postscript entitled 'Mind at the End of Its Tether'. I found it so frustrating and incomprehensible that I wanted to tear my hair: 'Since [1940] a tremendous series of events has forced upon the intelligent observer the realization that the human story has already come to an end and that *Homo sapiens*, as he has been pleased to call himself, is in his present form played out.' And this had not been written at the beginning of the Second World War – which might have been understandable – but after Hitler's defeat. When I came across the earlier edition of the *Short History* I found that, like the *Outline*, it ends on a note of uplift: 'What man has done, the little triumphs of his present state, and all this history we have told, form but the prelude to the things that man has yet to do.' And the *Outline* ends with a chapter predicting that mankind will find peace through the League of Nations and world government. (It was Wells who coined the phrase 'the war to end war'.)

What had happened? Many years later, I put the question to a friend of Wells, the biblical historian Hugh Schonfield. His answer was that Wells had been absolutely certain that he had the solutions to all the problems of the human race, and that he became embittered when he realized that no one took him seriously. At the time, that seemed a plausible explanation. But since then I have come upon what I believe to be the true one. In 1936, Wells produced a curious short novel called *The Croquet Player*, which is startlingly different from anything he had written before. It reveals that Wells had become aware of man's capacity for sheer brutality and sadism. *The Outline of History* plays down the tortures and massacres; in fact, it hardly mentions them. Wells seems totally devoid of that feeling for evil that made Arnold Toynbee, in his *Study of History*, speak of 'the horrifying sense of sin manifest in human affairs'. Wells's view of crime was cheerfully pragmatic. In *The Work, Wealth and Happiness of Mankind* he spoke of it as 'artificial', the result of 'restrictions imposed upon the normal "natural man" in order that the community may work and exist.' He seems quite unaware that the history of mankind since about 2500 B.C. is little more than a non-stop record of murder, bloodshed and violence. The brutalities of the Nazi period forced this upon his attention. But it seems to have been the horrors of Hiroshima and Nagasaki, and the revelations of Belsen and Buchenwald, which convinced him that man was bound to destroy himself from the beginning, and that 'the final end is now closing in on mankind'.

I am not suggesting that Wells's view of history was superficial or wrong-headed; as far as it went, it was brilliantly perceptive. As a late Victorian, he was aware of the history of mankind as a marvellous story of invention and achievement, of a long battle against danger and hardship that had resulted in modern civilization. And it is certainly true that man's creativity is the most centrally important fact about him. What Wells failed to grasp is that man's intelligence has resulted in a certain lopsidedness, a narrow obsessiveness that makes us calculating and ruthless. It is this ruthlessness – the tendency to take 'short-cuts' – that constitutes crime. Hitler's mass murders were not due to the restrictions imposed on natural man so the community can exist. They were, on the contrary, the outcome of a twisted kind of idealism, an attempt to create a 'better world'. The same is true of the destruction of Hiroshima, and of the terrorist bombings and shootings that have become everyday occurrences since the 1960s. The frightening thing about the members of the Japanese Red Brigade who machine-gunned passengers at Lod airport, or the Italian terrorists who burst into a university classroom and shot the professor in the legs – alleging that he was teaching his students 'bourgeois values' – is that they were not criminal lunatics but sincere idealists. When we realize this we recognize that criminality is not the reckless aberration of a few moral delinquents but an inevitable consequence of the development of intelligence, the 'flip side' of our capacity for creativity. The worst crimes are not committed by evil degenerates, but by decent and intelligent people taking 'pragmatic' decisions.

It was basically this recognition that plunged Wells into the nihilism of his final period. He had spent his life teaching that human beings can be guided by reason and intelligence; he had announced that the First World War had been fought to end war and that the League of Nations and world government would guarantee world peace. And at that point, the world exploded into an unparalleled epoch of murder, cruelty and violence: Stalin's starvation of the kulaks, the Japanese 'rape' of Nanking, Hitler's concentration camps, the atomic bomb. It must have seemed to Wells that his whole life had been based on a delusion, and that human beings are incorrigibly stupid and wicked.

If Wells had understood more about the psychology of violence, he would not have allowed this insight to plunge him into despair. Criminality is not a perverted disposition to do evil rather than good. It is merely a childish tendency to take short-cuts. All crime has the nature of a smash and grab raid; it is an attempt to get something for nothing. The thief steals instead of working for what he wants. The rapist violates a girl instead of persuading her to give herself. Freud once said that a child would destroy the world if it had the power. He meant that a child is totally subjective, wrapped up in its own feelings and so incapable of seeing anyone else's point of view. A criminal is an adult who goes on behaving like a child.

But there is a fallacy in this childish morality of grab-what-you-want. The person who is able to indulge all his moods and feelings is never happy for more than a few moments together; for most of the time, he is miserable. Our flashes of real happiness are glimpses of *objectivity*, when we somehow rise above the stifling, dreamlike world of our subjective desires and feelings. The great tyrants of history, the men who have been able to indulge their feelings without regard to other people, have usually ended up half insane; for over-indulged feelings are the greatest tyrants of all.

Crime is renewed in every generation because human beings *are* children; very few of us achieve anything like adulthood. But at least it is not self-perpetuating, as human creativity is. Shakespeare learns from Marlowe, and in turn inspires Goethe. Beethoven learns from Haydn and in turn inspires Wagner. Newton learns from Kepler and in turn inspires Einstein. But Vlad the Impaler, Jack the Ripper and Al Capone leave no progeny. Their 'achievement' is negative, and dies with them. The criminal also tends to be the victim of natural selection – of his own lack of self-control. Man has achieved his present level of civilization because creativity 'snow-balls' while crime, fortunately, remains static.

We may feel that Wells must have been a singularly naive historian to believe that war was about to come to an end. But this can be partly explained by his ignorance of what we now call sociobiology. When Tinbergen and Lorenz made us aware that animal aggression is largely a matter of 'territory', it suddenly became obvious that all wars in history have been fought about territory. Even the murderous behaviour of tyrants has its parallels in the animal world. Recent studies have made us aware that many dominant males, from lions and baboons to gerbils and hamsters, often kill the progeny of their defeated rivals. Hens allow their chicks to peck smaller chicks to death. A nesting seagull will kill a baby seagull that wanders on to its territory from next door. It seems that Prince Kropotkin was quite mistaken to believe that all animals practise mutual aid and that only human beings murder one another. Zoology has taught us that crime is a part of our animal inheritance. And human history could be used as an illustrative textbook of sociobiology.

Does this new view of history suggest that humankind is likely to be destroyed by its own violence? No one can deny the possibility; but the pessimists leave out of account the part of us that Wells understood so well – man's capacity to evolve through intelligence. It is true that human history has been fundamentally a history of crime; but it has also been the history of creativity. It is true that mankind could be destroyed in some atomic accident; but no one who has studied history can believe that this is more than a remote possibility. To understand the nature of crime is to understand why it will always be outweighed by creativity and intelligence.

This book is an attempt to tell the story of the human race in terms of that counterpoint between crime and creativity, and to use the insights it brings to try to discern the next stage in human evolution.

Part One

THE PSYCHOLOGY OF HUMAN VIOLENCE

One
HIDDEN PATTERNS OF VIOLENCE

During the summer of 1959, my study was piled with books on violent crime and with copies of *True Detective* magazine. The aim was to compile an Encyclopedia of Murder that might be of use to crime writers. But I was also moved by an obscure but urgent conviction that underneath these piles of unrelated facts about violence there must be undiscovered patterns, certain basic laws, and that uncovering these might provide clues to the steadily rising crime rate.

I had noted, for example, that types of murder vary from country to country. The French and Italians are inclined to *crime passionel*, the Germans to sadistic murder, the English to the carefully-planned murder – often of a spouse or lover – the Americans to the rather casual and unpremeditated murder. Types of crime change from century to century, even from decade to decade. In England and America, the most typical crimes of the 1940s and '50s had been for gain or for sex: in England, the sadist Neville Heath, the 'acid bath murderer' Haigh; in America, the red-light bandit Caryl Chessman, the multiple sex-killer Harvey Glatman.

As I leafed my way through *True Detective*, I became aware of the emergence of a disturbing new trend: the completely pointless or 'motiveless' murder. As long ago as 1912, André Gide had coined the term 'gratuitous act' to describe this type of crime; the hero of his novel *Les Caves du Vatican* (which was translated as *Lafcadio's Adventure*) suddenly has the impulse to kill a total stranger on a train. 'Who would know? A crime without a motive – what a puzzle for the police.' So he opens the door and pushes the man to his death. Gide's novel was a black comedy; the 'motiveless murder' was intended as a joke in the spirit of Oscar Wilde's essay about the forger who murdered his sister-in-law because she had thick ankles. Neither philosophers nor policemen seriously believed that such things were possible. Yet by 1959 it was happening. In 1952, a nineteen-year-old clerk named Herbert Mills sat next to a forty-eight-year-old housewife in a Nottingham cinema and decided she would make a suitable victim for an attempt at the 'perfect murder'; he met her by arrangement the next day, took her for a walk, and strangled her under a tree. It was only because he felt the compulsion to boast about his 'perfect crime' that he was caught and hanged. In July 1958, a man named Norman Foose stopped his jeep in the town of Cuba, New Mexico, raised his hunting rifle and shot dead two Mexican children; pursued and arrested, he said he was trying to do something about the population explosion. In February 1959, a pretty blonde named Penny Bjorkland accepted a lift from a married man in California and, without provocation, killed him with a dozen shots. After her arrest she explained that she wanted to see if she could kill 'and not worry about it afterwards'. Psychiatrists found her sane. In April 1959, a man named Norman Smith took a pistol and shot a woman (who was watching television) through an open window. He did not know her; the impulse had simply come over him as he watched a television programme called 'The Sniper'.

The *Encyclopedia of Murder* appeared in 1961, with a section on 'motiveless murder'; by 1970 it was clear that this was, in fact, a steadily increasing trend. In many cases, oddly enough, it seemed to be linked to a slightly higher-than-average IQ. Herbert Mills wrote poetry, and read some of it above the body of his victim. The 'Moors murderer' Ian Brady justified himself by quoting de Sade, and took pains in court – by the use of long words – to show that he was an 'intellectual'. Charles Manson evolved an elaborate racialist sociology to justify the crimes of his 'family'. San Francisco's 'Zodiac' killer wrote his letters in cipher and signed them with signs of the zodiac. John Frazier, a drop-out who slaughtered the family of an eye surgeon, Victor Ohta, left a letter signed with suits from the Tarot pack. In November 1966, Robert Smith, an eighteen-year-old student, walked into a beauty parlour in Mesa, Arizona, made five women and two children lie on the floor, and shot them all in the back of the head. Smith was in no way a 'problem youngster'; his relations with his parents were good and he was described as an excellent student. He told the police: 'I wanted to get known, to get myself a name.' A woman who walked into a California hotel room and killed a baseball player who was asleep there – and who was totally unknown to her – explained to the police: 'He was famous, and I knew that killing him would make me famous too.'

It is phrases like this that seem to provide a clue. There is a basic desire in all human beings, even the most modest, to 'become known'. Montaigne tells us that he is an ordinary man, yet that he feels his thoughts are worthy of attention; is there anyone who can claim not to recognize the feeling? In fact, is there anyone in the world who does not secretly feel that he is worthy of a biography? In a book called *The Denial of Death*, Ernest Becker states that one of the most basic urges in man is the urge to heroism. 'We are all,' he says, 'hopelessly absorbed with ourselves.' In children, we can see the urge to self-esteem in its least disguised form. The child shouts his needs at the top of his voice. He does not disguise his feeling that he is the centre of the world. He strenuously objects if his brother gets a larger piece of cake. 'He must desperately justify himself as an object of primary value in the universe; he must stand out, be a hero, make the biggest possible contribution to world life, show that he *counts* more than anyone else.' So he indulges endless daydreams of heroism.

Then he grows up and has to learn to be a realist, to recognize that, on a world-scale, he is a nobody. Apparently he comes to terms with this recognition; but deep down inside, the feeling of uniqueness remains. Becker says that if everyone honestly admitted his desire to be a hero, and demanded some kind of satisfaction, it would shake society to its foundations. Only very simple primitive societies can give their members this sense of uniqueness, of being known to all. 'The minority groups in present-day industrial society who shout for freedom and human dignity are really clumsily asking that they be given a sense of primary heroism . . .'

Becker's words certainly bring a flash of insight into all kinds of phenomena, from industrial unrest to political terrorism. They are an expression of this half-buried need to *be* somebody, and of a revolt against a society that denies it. When Herbert Mills decided to commit a 'perfect murder', he was trying to provide himself with a reason for that sense of uniqueness. In an increasing number of criminal cases, we have to learn to see beyond the stated motivation – social injustice or whatever – to this primary need. There was a weird, surrealistic air about Charles Manson's self-justifications in court; he seemed to be saying that he was not responsible for the death of eight people because society was guilty of far worse things than that. Closer examination of the evidence reveals that Manson felt that he had as much right to be famous as the Beatles or Bob

Dylan (he had tried hard to interest record companies in tapes he had recorded); in planning Helter Skelter, the revolution that would transform American society, he was asserting his primacy, his uniqueness.

I was struck by the difference between these typical crimes of the late sixties – Manson, the Moors murders, Frazier, Zodiac – and the typical crimes of ten or twenty years earlier – Haigh, Heath, Christie, Chessman, Glatman. John Christie killed girls for sexual purposes – he seems to have been impotent if the woman was conscious – and walled them up in a cupboard in his kitchen. The cupboard is somehow a symbol of this type of crime – the place where skeletons are hidden by people who are anxious to appear normal and respectable. Manson's 'family' sat around the television, gloating over the news bulletin that announced the killings in Sharon Tate's home. The last thing they wanted was for their crimes to be hidden.

Clearly, there is some sort of pattern here. But what are the underlying laws that govern it? In the mid-1960s, the psychologist Abraham Maslow sent me his book *Motivation and Personality* (1954), and it was in the fourth chapter, 'A Theory of Human Motivation', that I thought I saw the outline of some kind of general solution to the changing pattern. The chapter had originally been published in 1943 in the *Psychological Review*, and had achieved the status of a classic among professional psychologists; but for some reason it had never percolated through to the general public. What Maslow proposed in this paper was that human motivation can be described in terms of a 'hierarchy of needs' or values. These fall roughly into four categories: physiological needs (basically food), security needs (basically a roof over one's head), belongingness and love needs (desire for roots, the need to be wanted), and esteem needs (to be liked and respected). And beyond these four levels, Maslow suggested the existence of a fifth category: self-actualization: the need to know and understand, to create, to solve problems for the fun of it.

When a man is permanently hungry, he can think of nothing else, and his idea of paradise is a place with plenty of food. In fact, if he solves the food problem, he becomes preoccupied with the question of security, a home, 'territory'. (Every tramp dreams of retiring to a country cottage with roses round the door.) If he solves this problem, the sexual needs become urgent – not simply physical satisfaction, but the need for warmth, security and 'belonging'. And if this level is satisfied, the next emerges: the need to be liked and admired, the need for self-esteem and the esteem of one's neighbours. If all these needs are satisfied, the 'self-actualizing' needs are free to develop (although they do not always do so – Maslow recognized that many people never get beyond level four.)

Now, as I worked on a second study in criminology, *A Casebook of Murder*, it struck me that Maslow's hierarchy of needs corresponds roughly to historical periods of crime. Until the first part of the nineteenth century, most crimes were committed out of the simple need for survival – Maslow's first level. Burke and Hare, the Edinburgh body-snatchers, suffocated their victims and sold the corpses to the medical school for about £7 each. By the mid-nineteenth century the pattern was changing; the industrial revolution had increased prosperity, and suddenly the most notorious crimes are 'domestic murders' that take place in respectable middle-class homes: Dr Palmer, Dr Pritchard, Constance Kent, Florence Bravo. (American parallels would include Professor Webster and Lizzie Borden.) These people are committing crimes to safeguard their security. Charlie Peace, housebreaker and murderer, practised burglary to subsidize a respectable middle-class existence that included regular churchgoing and musical evenings with the neighbours.

But even before the end of the century, a new type of crime had emerged: the sex crime. The Jack the Ripper murders of 1888 were among the first of this type, and it is significant that the killer's contemporaries did not recognize them as sex crimes; they argued that the Ripper was 'morally insane', as if his actions could only be explained by a combination of wickedness and madness. The Ripper is the first in a long line of 'maniac' killers that extends down to Heath and Glatman, and that still throws up appalling examples such as Dean Corll, John Wayne Gacy and Ted Bundy. To the crime committed for purely sexual reasons we should also add the increasing number of crimes committed out of jealousy or the desire to get rid of a spouse in favour of a lover – Crippen, Bywaters and Thompson, Snyder and Gray.

So what I had noticed in 1959 was a transition to a new level in the hierarchy: to the crime of 'self-esteem'. From then on, there was an increasing number of crimes in which the criminal seemed to feel, in a muddled sort of way, that society was somehow to blame for not granting him dignity, justice and recognition of his individuality, and to regard his crime as a legitimate protest. When, in October 1970, Victor Ohta and his family were found murdered in their California home, a note on the doctor's Rolls-Royce read: 'Today World War III will begin, as brought to you by the people of the free universe . . . I and my comrades from this day forth will fight until death or freedom against anyone who does not support natural life on this planet. Materialism must die or mankind will stop.' The killer, the twenty-four-year-old drop-out John Linley Frazier, had told witnesses that the Ohta family was 'too materialistic' and deserved to die. In fact, Frazier was reacting with the self-centred narcissism of the children described by Becker. ('You gave him more juice.' 'Here's some more then.' 'Now *she's* got more juice than me . . .') He felt he had a long way to go to achieve 'security', while Ohta had a swimming pool and a Rolls-Royce parked in the drive.

The irony is that Ohta himself would serve equally well as an example of Becker's 'urge to heroism'. He was the son of Japanese immigrants who had been interned in 1941; but Ohta had finally been allowed to join the American army; his elder brother was killed in the fighting in Europe. Ohta had worked as a railway track-layer and a cab driver to get through medical school, and his success as an eye surgeon came late in life. Ohta achieved his sense of 'belonging-ness' through community work; he was one of the founders of the Dominican Hospital in Santa Cruz – a non-profit-making hospital – and often gave free treatment to patients who could not afford his fees. Frazier was completely unaware of all this. But it would probably have made no difference anyway. He was completely wrapped up in his own little world of narcissism.

Clearly there are many ways in which human beings can satisfy the narcissistic craving for 'being first'. Ohta's was balanced and realistic, and he was therefore a valuable member of the community. Frazier's was childish and unrealistic, and his crimes did no one any good, least of all himself.

Maslow's theory of the hierarchy of needs developed from his observation of monkeys in the Bronx zoo in the mid-1930s. He was at this time puzzling about the relative merits of Freud and Adler: Freud with his view that all neurosis is sexual in origin, Adler with his belief that man's life is a fight against a feeling of inferiority and that his mainspring is his 'will to power'. In the Bronx zoo, he was struck by the dominance behaviour of the monkeys and by the non-stop sex. He was puzzled that sexual behaviour seemed so indiscriminate: males mounted females or other males; females mounted other females and even males. There was also a distinct 'pecking order', the more dominant monkeys bullying the less dominant. There seemed to be as much evidence for Freud's theory as for Adler's. Then, one day, a revelation burst upon Maslow. Monkey sex *looked* indiscriminate because the more dominant monkeys mounted the less dominant ones, whether male or female. Maslow concluded, therefore, that Adler was right and Freud was wrong – about this matter at least.

Since dominance behaviour seemed to be the key to monkey psychology, Maslow wondered how far this applied to human beings. He decided to study dominance behaviour in human beings and, since he was a young and heterosexual male, decided that he would prefer to study women rather than men. Besides, he felt that women were usually more honest when it came to talking about their private lives. In 1936, he began a series of interviews with college women; his aim was to find out whether sex and dominance are related. He quickly concluded that they were.

The women tended to fall into three distinct groups: high dominance, medium dominance and low dominance, the high dominance group being the smallest of the three. High dominance women tended to be promiscuous and to enjoy sex for its own sake – in a manner we tend to regard as distinctly masculine. They were more likely to masturbate, sleep with different men, and have lesbian experiences. Medium dominance women were basically romantics; they might have a strong sex drive, but their sexual experience was usually limited. They were looking for 'Mr Right', the kind of man who would bring them flowers and take them out for dinner in restaurants with soft lights and sweet music. Low dominance women seemed actively to dislike sex, or to think of it as an unfortunate necessity for producing children. One low dominance woman with a high sex-drive refused to permit her husband sexual intercourse because she disliked children. Low dominance women tended to be prudes who were shocked at nudity and regarded the male sexual organ as disgusting. (High dominance women thought it beautiful.)

Their choice of males was dictated by the dominance group. High dominance women liked high dominance males, the kind who would grab them and hurl them on a bed. They seemed to like their lovers to be athletic, rough and unsentimental. Medium dominance women liked kindly, home-loving males, the kind who smoke a pipe and look calm and reflective. They would prefer a romantic male, but were prepared to settle for a hard worker of reliable habits. Low dominance women were distrustful of all males, although they usually wanted children and recognized that a man had to be pressed into service for this purpose. They preferred the kind of gentle, shy man who would admire them from a distance for years without daring to speak.

But Maslow's most interesting observation was that *all* the women, in all dominance groups, preferred a male who was slightly more dominant than themselves. One very high dominance woman spent years looking for a man of superior dominance – meanwhile having many affairs; and once she found him, married him and lived happily ever after. However, she enjoyed picking fights with him, provoking him to violence that ended in virtual rape; and this sexual experience she found the most satisfying of all. Clearly, even this man was not *quite* dominant enough, and she was provoking him to an artifically high level of dominance.

The rule seemed to be that, for a permanent relationship, a man and woman needed to be in the same dominance group. Medium dominance women were nervous of high dominance males, and low dominance women were terrified of medium dominance males. As to the males, they might well show a sexual interest in a woman of a lower dominance group, but it would not survive the act of seduction. A medium dominance woman might be superficially attracted by a high dominance male; but on closer acquaintance she would find him brutal and unromantic. A high dominance male might find a medium dominance female 'beddable', but closer acquaintance would reveal her as rather uninteresting, like an unseasoned meal. To achieve a personal relationship, the two would need to be in the same dominance group. Maslow even devised psychological tests to discover whether the 'dominance gap' between a man and a woman was of the right size to form the basis of a permanent relationship.

It was some time after writing a book about Maslow (*New Pathways in Psychology*, published in 1972) that it dawned on me that this matter of the 'dominance gap' threw an interesting light on many cases of partnership in crime. The first case of the sort to arouse my curiosity was that of Albert T. Patrick, a scoundrelly New York lawyer who, in 1900, persuaded a manservant named Charles Jones to kill his employer with chloroform. Jones had been picked out of the gutter by his employer, a rich old man named William Rice, and had every reason to be grateful to him. Yet he quickly came under Patrick's spell and took part in the plot to murder and defraud. The plot misfired; both were arrested. The police placed them in adjoining cells. Patrick handed Jones a knife saying 'You cut your throat first and I'll follow . . .' Jones was so completely under Patrick's domination that he did not even pause to wonder how Patrick would get the knife back. A gurgling noise alerted the police, who were able to foil the attempted suicide. Patrick was sentenced to death but was eventually pardoned and released.

How did Patrick achieve such domination? There was no sexual link between them, and he was not blackmailing Jones. But what becomes very clear from detailed accounts of the case is that Patrick was a man of extremely high dominance, while Jones was quite definitely of medium dominance. It was Patrick's combination of charm and dominance that exerted such a spell.

It struck me that in many cases of double-murder (that is, partnership in murder), one of the partners is high dominance and the other medium. Moreover, it seems that this odd and unusual combination of high and medium dominance actually *triggers* the violence. In 1947, Raymond Fernandez, a petty crook who specialized in swindling women, met Martha Beck, a fat nurse who had been married three times. Fernandez picked up his victims through 'lonely hearts club' advertisements, got his hands on their cash, and vanished. When Martha Beck advertised for a soul-mate, Fernandez picked out her name because she was only twenty-six. His first sight of her was a shock: she weighed fourteen and a half stones and had a treble chin and a ruthless mouth. She also proved to have no money. But when Fernandez succumbed to the temptation to sleep with her, he was caught. She adored him; in spite of his toupée and gold teeth, he was the handsome Latin lover she had always dreamed about. Their sex life was a non-stop orgy. When Fernandez attempted to leave her, she tried to gas herself. And when he finally explained that he had to get back to the business of making a living, and that his business involved seducing rich women, her enthusiasm was unchecked. She offered to become a partner in the enterprise. But she suggested one refinement: that instead of merely abandoning the women, Fernandez should kill them. During the next two years, the couple murdered at least twenty women. Their final victims were Mrs Delphine Dowling of Grand Rapids, Michigan and her two-year-old daughter Rainelle; the police became curious about Mrs Dowling's disappearance, searched the house, and found a spot of damp cement in the cellar floor. Under arrest, Fernandez and his 'sister' admitted shooting Mrs Dowling and drowning the child in a bathtub two days later when she would not stop crying. Further investigation slowly uncovered a two-year murder spree. Both were executed.

The evidence makes it clear that the sexually insatiable Martha was an altogether more dominant character than Ray Fernandez, who, at the time of their meeting, was only a rather unsuccessful petty crook. Almost certainly, he qualifies as medium dominance; certainly, Martha was high dominance. Then why were they drawn together? From Martha's point of view, because Fernandez was a fairly personable male with a high sex drive. From his point of view, because the frenzied adoration of this rather frightening woman was flattering. A revealing glimpse into their relationship was afforded by an episode in court; Martha came into court wearing a silk dress, green shoes and bright red lipstick; she rushed across the court, cupped Fernandez's face in her hands, and kissed him hungrily again and again. Sexually speaking, she was the one who took the lead.

It seems evident that Fernandez would have never committed murder without Martha's encouragement. It was the combination of the high dominance female and medium dominance male that led to violence.

Again and again, in cases of 'double murder', the same pattern emerges. It explains one of the most puzzling crimes of the century – the murder by Nathan Leopold and Richard Loeb of fourteen-year-old Bobbie Franks in May 1924. Both came from wealthy German-Jewish homes; both were university graduates. They became lovers when Loeb was thirteen and Leopold fourteen. Loeb was handsome, athletic and dominant; Leopold was round shouldered, short-sighted and shy. Loeb was a daredevil, and in exchange for submitting to Leopold's desires, made him sign a contract to become his partner in crime. They committed a number of successful petty thefts and finally decided that the supreme challenge was to commit the perfect murder. Bobbie Franks – a friend of Loeb's younger brother – was chosen almost at random as the victim. Franks was picked up when he came out of school and murdered in the back of the car by Loeb, while Leopold drove; then his body was stuffed into a culvert. Then they tried to collect ransom money from the boy's family, but the body was discovered by a railway worker. So were Nathan Leopold's spectacles, lying near the culvert. These were traced to Leopold through the optician. The trial was a sensation; it seemed to be a case of 'murder for fun' committed by two spoilt rich boys. Leopold admitted to being influenced by Nietzsche's idea of the superman. Both were sentenced to life imprisonment.

Yet the key to the case lies in their admission that Leopold called Loeb 'Master' and referred to himself as 'Devoted Slave'. Loeb derived his pleasure from his total dominance of Leopold. Leopold might be far cleverer than he was, but he was obedient to Loeb's will. It was Loeb who made Leopold sign a contract to join him in a career of crime, in exchange for permitting sodomy. Loeb was the one who got his 'kicks' out of crime; Leopold preferred bird-watching. Left to himself, Loeb would never have committed murder. But his deepest pleasure came from his dominance of Nathan Leopold, and to enjoy that dominance to the full he had to keep pushing Leopold deeper and deeper into crime.

One of the clearest examples of the dominance syndrome is the Moors murder case. Ian Brady and Myra Hindley were arrested in October 1965, as a result of a tip-off to the police that they were concealing a body in their house. A cloakroom ticket concealed in a prayer book led to the discovery of two suitcases in the railway left luggage office at Manchester, and to photographs and tapes that connected Brady and Hindley to the disappearance of a ten-year-old girl, Lesley Ann Downey, who had vanished on Boxing Day 1964. A police search on the moors revealed the body of Lesley Ann, and also that of a twelve-year-old boy, John Kilbride. The body found in their house was that of a seventeen-year-old youth, Edward Evans, who had been killed with an axe. Charged with the three murders, both were found guilty and sentenced to life imprisonment.

It was the actor-playwright Emlyn Williams who revealed the curious psychological pattern behind the murders. Ian Brady and Myra Hindley first set eyes on each other on 16 January 1960, when she became a typist at Millwards, a chemical firm in the Gorton district of Manchester. Myra was a typical working-class girl, a

Catholic convert who loved animals and children. Brady was a tough kid from the Clydeside district of Glasgow. Born in 1938 – four years before Myra – he had been in trouble with the police since he was thirteen and had spent a year in Borstal. He read gangster novels and books about the Nazis, whom he admired. He also read de Sade's *Justine* and was impressed by de Sade's philosophy of 'immoralism' and crime.

Brady ignored Myra; she was just another working-class typist. As the months passed, she became increasingly intrigued. He looked like a slightly delinquent Elvis Presley, and rode a motor bike dressed in leather gear; but underneath this he wore his well-pressed business suit. By 23 July she was confiding to her diary: 'Wonder if Ian is courting. Still feel the same.' Four days later she records that she spoke to him, and that he smiled as though embarrassed. A few days later: 'Ian isn't interested in girls.' On 8 August she records: 'Gone off Ian a bit.' No reason is mentioned, but it may have been his bad language, which shocked her; she mentions later: 'Ian swearing. He is uncouth' – the typical reaction of the romantic, medium-dominance female to a high-dominance male. And her romanticism emerges obviously in the diary, which Emlyn Williams quotes: 'I hope he loves me and will marry me some day.' But he seems to ignore her: 'He hasn't spoken to me today.' For months the entries swing between hope and misery: 'He goes out of his way to annoy me, he insults me . . .' / 'I hate Ian, he has killed all the love I had for him.' / 'I'm in love with Ian all over again.' / 'Out with Ian!'

Williams is almost certainly right when he suggests that Brady revelled in his feeling of power over Myra, his ability to make her happy or miserable. On New Year's Eve 1961, Brady took her to the cinema, then back to her parent's home to see in the New Year with a bottle of whisky. Myra was living round the corner in the home of her grandmother; Brady took her back there at midnight and, on the divan bed in the front room, deflowered her. And in her diary the next day she recorded: 'I have been at Millwards for twelve months and only just gone out with him. I hope Ian and I will love each other all our lives and get married and be happy ever after . . .' However, it is not marriage that interests Brady but the power game. He has asserted his dominance by taking her virginity on their first date; what now?

The process of conversion begins. Myra is persuaded to share his admiration for the Nazis – he had a large collection of books about them – and de Sade. Most people who buy de Sade read him for sex; Brady read him for the ideas. Society is utterly corrupt. Human life is utterly unimportant; nature gives and takes with total indifference. We live in a meaningless universe, created by chance. Morality is a delusion invented by the rulers to keep the poor in check. Pleasure is the only real good. A man who inflicts his sexual desires by force is only seizing the natural privilege of the strong . . . And Myra, who regards him as a brilliant intellectual (he is learning German to be able to read *Mein Kampf* in the original), swallows it all – without enthusiasm, but with the patience of the devoted slave who knows that her master is seldom wrong.

How can he push her further, savour his dominance? He tells her he is planning a bank robbery, a big job. She is shocked – at first – then, as usual, she accepts it as further evidence of his resourcefulness and self-reliance. He persuades her to join a rifle club and buy a gun.

He begins to take a popular photography magazine and buys a camera with a timing attachment. He persuades her to dress in black panties without a crotch and pose for photographs. Then the timing attachment allows him to take photographs of the two of them together, navel to navel, engaged in sexual intercourse – with white bags over their heads. In others, she has whip marks on her buttocks. Brady apparently hoped to sell the photographs (for these were the days before pornography could be bought in most newsagents) but was apparently unsuccessful.

At this stage, there is only one possible way in which Brady can push her further into total acquiescence: by finally putting the daydreams of crime into practice and ordering her to be his partner. But bank robbery is a little too dangerous. In fact, most crime carries the risk of being caught. Perhaps the crime that carries least risk is the kind committed by Leopold and Loeb: luring a child into a car . . .

Myra Hindley bought a small car – a second-hand green Morris – in May 1963, having taken driving lessons. (Brady had given up his motor cycle after an accident.) Two months later, on 12 July 1963, a sixteen-year-old girl named Pauline Reade, who lived around the corner from Myra and knew her by sight, vanished on her way to a dance and was never seen again. When police began investigating the moors murders, they started with the file on Pauline Reade. It seemed probable that she had been picked up by a car. Since she was unlikely to get into a car with a strange man, it may have contained someone she knew. The disappearance of the body suggests that she was buried – and casual rapists seldom bother to bury a body. It is conceivable then, that Pauline Reade was their first victim.

On Saturday afternoon, 23 November, they drove out to Ashton-under-Lyne and offered a lift to a twelve-year-old boy, John Kilbride, who was about to catch a bus home. He climbed in and was never again seen alive. Nearly two years later, his corpse was dug up by police on Saddleworth Moor. His trousers and underpants had been pulled down around his knees. Myra Hindley had allowed Brady to take a photograph of her kneeling on the grave.

On 16 June 1964, twelve-year-old Keith Bennett set out to spend the night at his grandmother's house in the Longsight district of Manchester – where Brady had lived until he moved in with Myra and her grandmother. Bennett vanished, like Pauline Reade. Brady still visited the Longsight district regularly to see his mother.

On 26 December 1964, Brady and Hindley drove to the fairground in the Ancoats district of Manchester and picked up a ten-year-old girl, Lesley Ann Downey. They took her back to their house – they had now moved to Hattersley, where Gran had been assigned a council house – made her strip, and took various photographs of her. They also recorded her screams and pleas to be released on tape. Then she was killed and buried on the moor near the body of John Kilbride. Later, they took blankets and slept on the graves. It was part of the fantasy of being Enemies of Society, dangerous revolutionaries.

Nine months later, Brady made the mistake that led to his arrest. A sixteen-year-old named David Smith had become a sort of disciple. He had married Myra's younger sister Maureen when she became pregnant. Like Myra, David Smith was easy to convert; he had also had his troubles with the police, and was eager to swallow the gospel of revolution and self-assertion. Smith was an apt pupil, and wrote in his diary: 'Rape is not a crime, it is a state of mind. Murder is a hobby and a supreme pleasure.' / 'God is a superstition, a cancer that eats into the brain.' / 'People are like maggots, small, blind and worthless.' Smith also listened with admiration as Brady talked about his plans for bank robbery. Brady told him that he had killed three or four people, whose bodies were buried on the moor, and that he had once stopped the car in a deserted street and shot a passer-by at random. On 6 October 1965, Brady decided it was time for Smith's initiation. In a pub in Manchester he and Myra picked up a seventeen-year-old youth, Edward Evans, and drove him back to the house in Hattersley. At 11.30, Myra went to fetch David Smith. As he was in the kitchen, he heard a loud scream and a shout of 'Dave, help him.' He found Brady striking Evans with an axe. When Evans lay still, Brady strangled him with a cord. He handed Smith the hatchet – 'Feel the weight of it' – and took it back with Smith's fingerprints on the bloodstained handle. The three of them cleaned the room and wrapped the corpse in polythene – as they lifted it, Brady joked 'Eddie's a dead weight.' They drank tea, and Myra reminisced about the time a policeman had stopped to talk to her as she sat in the car while Brady was burying a body. Then Smith went home, promising to return with a pram to transport the body to the car. At home, he was violently sick, and told his wife what had happened. She called the police. At 8.40 the next morning a man dressed as a baker's roundsman knocked at Brady's door, and when he opened it – wearing only a vest – identified himself as a police officer. In a locked bedroom, the police found the body of Edward Evans. Brady was arrested and charged with murder.

There was no confession. Brady stonewalled every inch of the way. He insisted that Lesley had been brought to the house by two men, who also took her away. The tape was played in court, and provided the most horrifying moment of the trial. Myra later said she felt ashamed of what they had done to Lesley (although she would only confess to helping to take pornographic photographs); Brady remained indifferent. He explained at one point that he knew he would be condemned anyway. On 6 May 1966, he was sentenced to three concurrent terms of life imprisonment; Myra Hindley was sentenced to two. Since then, there has been occasional talk of releasing Myra from prison; but the public outcry reveals that the case still arouses unusual revulsion. No one has even suggested that Brady should ever be released.

The central mystery of the case remains: how a perfectly normal girl like Myra Hindley could have participated with a certain enthusiasm in the murders. At the time I was studying the case (for a book called *Order of Assassins*) I had long discussions with Dr Rachel Pinney, who had met Myra in jail and had become convinced of her innocence. In her view, Myra had been 'framed'. 'I still think Myra had no part in the killings or torture,' she wrote in a letter to me, 'and the end result of my work will be a fuller study of the psychology of being "hooked" – e.g. Rasputin and the Tsarina, Loeb and Leopold, Hitler and his worshippers.' This seems to me a penetrating comment; but it still leaves us no clue as to how a girl who loved animals and children became involved in such appalling crimes.

Her early background suggests that the answer may be partly that she was not as 'normal' as she seemed. Daughter of a mixed Catholic-Protestant marriage, she had been sent to live with her grandmother from the age of four – her father was something of an invalid after an accident. Myra undoubtedly felt that she had been rejected in favour of her younger sister Maureen. Moving between two homes a few hundred yards apart, Myra knew little of parental discipline; her grandmother adored her and spoiled her. She had a forceful personality, which manifested itself in her large, firm chin and her share of Lancashire commonsense and hard-headedness. Her school report described her personality as 'not very sociable', although her classmates remembered her as something of a comedienne. Then, shortly before her fifteenth birthday, she received a severe psychological shock. She was friendly with a thirteen-year-old boy named Michael Higgins; he was shy and delicate and seems to have aroused maternal feelings in her. On a hot June afternoon he asked her to go swimming in a disused reservoir; she declined. The boy was seized with cramp and drowned; Myra, going along to see why Michael had not returned home, found police standing around his body. She was shattered. She spent days collecting money for a wreath and attended the funeral. She wore black clothes for months afterwards and became gloomy and silent. Then she reacted to the shock of the death by becoming a Roman Catholic. She left school a few weeks after the funeral and took a succession of office jobs. She found them utterly boring, and made a habit of absenteeism; the result was that they never lasted for more than a month or so. She went to dances and changed the colour of her hair repeatedly; but she never allowed boys any liberties. In fact, she was a prude. Engaged briefly at seventeen, she broke it off because 'he is too childish'. When her dog was killed by a car, she again went into a state of traumatic gloom.

Myra's problem was that of many strong-willed girls. Where males are concerned, determination is not a particularly alluring feminine characteristic. The male image of the eternal feminine is of softness, gentleness. But the strong-minded girl cannot help being strong-minded, and feeling a certain impatient contempt for most of the males of her acquaintance. So most men find her off-putting and she finds most men off-putting. This does not prevent her longing for the right man – particularly if, like Myra, she has strong nest-building instincts. It only prevents her being experimental, from having the kind of experience that weaker and sillier girls have every night of the week. Even if she finds a man attractive, it is difficult for her to send out the signals that might attract him – the yielding look, the lowered eyelids. Sheer cussedness makes her glare defiantly, or say something that implies she knows better than he does. She is her own worst enemy.

Brady's first impression of Myra was probably that she was a hard-looking bitch, the kind who would want to cut him down to size. Then, as it became clear that this big-chinned female was 'gone on him', the vague dislike would be replaced by pleasure; we all find it hard not to see the best side of people who approve of us. He notices she looks rather Germanic – a bit like one of those concentration camp guards. He begins to enjoy the game, like an angler playing a salmon; he wants it to go on as long as possible. She speaks to him in July and he looks embarrassed. In August she notices that 'Ian is taking sly looks at me.' And from then on, it is all ups and downs; one day he has got a cold and she wants to mother him, the next he has been rude to her and she hates him. But although it is sweeter to travel than to arrive, these preliminaries cannot go on for ever, and five months later, he takes her out. And, like Martha Beck, she has suddenly found the lover of her daydreams.

The next stage is the difficult one to understand. How does he turn her into a murderess? The earlier trauma about the death of Michael Higgins must have played its part. It remains a psychological scar; but Brady's tough-minded attitude towards death acts as a catharsis. The books about concentration camps, the Nazi marching music, the records of Hitler making speeches, all seem to launch her on to a level of vitality where the tragedy ceases to depress her.

If she had been a quiet, efficient girl who enjoyed office work, all this would have been impossible. But it bored her silly; she had lost job after job through absenteeism.

Brady had been through the same stage. He had also lost job after job; but these had all been hard manual jobs, and the position as a stock clerk must have seemed a pleasant change. Now the only sign of his earlier instability was his constant unpunctuality, and his tendency to slip out of the office to place bets. There were always books about the Nazis in the office drawer. He seldom spoke to the other employees. He spent his lunch breaks reading his books on war crimes. He had successfully withdrawn into his own fantasy world. In due course, he found no difficulty in fitting Myra into the fantasy. He called her 'Hessie', not just because her name was Myra, but because he admired Hitler's deputy Rudolf Hess.

All this helps to explain how Myra became his devoted slave. But none of these factors was crucial. The fundamental explanation lies in the recognition that she was medium dominance and Brady was high. She, in spite of her hard-headedness, was a typical romantic typist longing to be embraced by a masterful but gentle male. But for Brady, she was the catalyst that turned him from a fantasist into a killer. For him it was not a love game but a power game. No doubt this is a simplification: all male sexuality contains an element of the 'power game'. But when the male belongs to a higher dominance group, then the sense of power provides the chief pleasure in the relationship.

These observations afford important insights into crime on Maslow's fourth level, the level of 'self-esteem'. But there is still a question that remains unexplained: the psychology of the 'submissive' part-ner. In the case of Leopold and Loeb, or Brady and Hindley, the question is blurred by the sexual relationship between the partners, which suggests a kind of equality of responsibility. But in the Albert T. Patrick case, there was no such relationship and the question becomes insistent. When Patrick first called on Charles Jones, he was looking for information that he could use against Jones's employer, William Rice. Jones indignantly refused: yet for some reason, he did not tell Rice. Already, Patrick had established some subtle dominance. He called again; Jones weakened, and allowed Patrick to persuade him to forge his employer's signature to a letter to be used against Rice in a law suit. Six months later, Jones was administering poison to his employer, the man to whom he owed everything. We may object that perhaps Jones had reason to dislike his employer; perhaps the old man was a bully. But this would still not explain the ascendancy that made Jones agree to cut his throat in prison. This brings to mind another curious criminal case of the mid-1930s. A woman on a train to Heidelberg – where she intended to consult a doctor about stomach pains – fell into conversation with a fellow passenger who claimed to be a nature healer. This man, whose name was Franz Walter, said he could cure her illness, and when the train stopped at a station, invited her to join him for coffee. She was unwilling, but allowed herself to be persuaded. As they walked along the platform he took hold of her hand 'and it seemed to me as if I no longer had a will of my own. I felt so strange and giddy.' He took her to a room in Heidelberg, placed her in a trance by touching her forehead, and raped her. She tried to push him away, but she was unable to move. 'I strained myself more and more but it didn't help. He stroked me and said: "You sleep quite deeply, you can't call out, and you can't do anything else." Then he pressed my hands and arms behind me and said: "You can't move any more. When you wake up you will not know anything of what happened."'

Later, Walter made her prostitute herself to various men, telling her clients the hypnotic word of command that would make her unable to move. And when she married, he made her attempt to kill her husband by various means. The latter became suspicious after her sixth attempt at murder – when his motor cycle brake cable snapped, causing a crash – and when he learned that she had parted with three thousand marks to some unknown doctor. The police came to suspect that she had been hypnotized, and a psychiatrist, Dr Ludwig Mayer, succeeded in releasing the suppressed memories of the hypnotic sessions. In due course, Walter received ten years in prison.

How did Walter bring her under his control so quickly and easily? Clearly, she was a woman of low vitality, highly 'suggestible'. Yet holding her hand hardly seems to be a normal means of inducing hypnosis. In fact, there is a certain amount of evidence to suggest that hypnosis can be induced through a purely mental force. In 1885, the French psychologist Pierre Janet was invited to Le Havre by a doctor named Gibert to observe his experiments with a patient called Léonie. Léonie was an exceptionally good hypnotic subject, and would obey Gibert's mental suggestions *at a distance*. Gibert usually induced a trance by *touching Léonie's hand*, but Janet confirmed that he could induce a trance by merely thinking about it. On another occasion he 'summoned' Léonie from a distance by a mental command. Gibert discovered that he had to concentrate hard to do these things; if his mind was partly on something else, it failed to work – which suggests that he was directing some kind of mental 'beam' at her. In the 1920s, the Russian scientist L. L. Vasiliev carried out similar experiments with a patient suffering from hysterical paralysis of the left side. She was placed under hypnosis and then mentally ordered by Vasiliev to make various movements, including movements of the paralysed arm; she obeyed all these orders. (In the 1890s, Dr Paul Joire had conducted similar experiments in which the patients were not hypnotized but only blindfolded, and again he discovered that the mental 'orders' would only be obeyed if he concentrated very hard.) J. B. Priestley has described how, at a literary dinner, he told his neighbour that he proposed to make someone wink at him; he then chose a sombre-looking woman and concentrated on her until suddenly she winked at him. Later she explained to him that she had experienced a 'sudden silly impulse' to wink.

Whether or not we accept the notion that hypnosis is, to some degree, 'telepathic', there can be no doubt about the baffling nature of the phenomenon. Animals are particularly easy to hypnotize, a fact that first seems to have been recorded by a mathematician named Daniel Schwenter in 1636. Schwenter noted that if a small bent piece of wood is fastened on a hen's beak, the hen fixes its eyes on it and goes into a trance. Similarly, if the hen's beak is held against the ground and a chalk line is drawn away from the point of its beak, it lies immobilized. Ten years later, a Jesuit priest, Fr Athanasius Kircher, described similar experiments on hens. All that is necessary is to tuck the hen's head under its wing and then give it a few gentle swings through the air; it will then lie still. (French peasants still use this method when they buy live hens in the market.) A doctor named Golsch discovered that frogs can be hypnotized by turning them on their backs and lightly tapping the stomach with the finger. Snapping the fingers above the frog is just as effective. Crabs can be hypnotized by gently stroking the shell from head to tail, and unhypnotized by reversing the motion. In *Hypnosis of Men and Animals* (published in 1963), Ferenc András Völgyesi describes how Africans hypnotize wild elephants. The elephant is chained to a tree, where it thrashes about savagely. The natives then wave leafy boughs to and fro in front of it and chant monotonously; eventually, its eyes blink, close, and the elephant becomes docile. It can then be teamed with a trained elephant and worked into various tasks. If it becomes unmanageable, the treatment is repeated, and usually works almost immediately.

Völgyesi also discusses the way that snakes 'fascinate' their victims. Far from being an old wives' tale, this has been observed by many scientists. Toads, frogs, rabbits and other creatures can be 'transfixed' by the snake's gaze – which involves expansion of its pupils – and by its hiss. But Völgyesi observed – and photographed – a large toad winning a 'battle of hypnosis' with a snake. Völgyesi observed two lizards confronting each other for about ten minutes, both quite rigid; then one slowly and deliberately ate the other, starting at the head. It was again, apparently, a battle of hypnosis. What seems to happen in such cases is that one creature subdues the will of the other. Völgyesi observed that hypnosis can also be effected by a sudden shock – by grabbing a bird violently, or making a loud noise. He observes penetratingly that hypnosis seems to have something in common with stage fright – that is, so much adrenalin is released into the bloodstream that, instead of stimulating the creature, it virtually paralyses it. (We have all had the experience of feeling weakened by fear.)

How can hypnosis be explained? We know that we are, to a large extent, machines; but the will drives the machine. In hypnosis, the machine is taken over by the will of another. When I am determined and full of purpose, I raise my vitality and *focus* it. In hypnosis, the reverse happens; the vitality is suddenly reduced, and the attention is 'unfocused'. The 'machine' obeys the will of the hypnotist just as a car will obey the will of another driver.

There is another part of the mechanism that should be mentioned here. If I am concentrating on some important task, I direct my full attention towards it like a fireman pointing his hosepipe at the blaze. I permit no self-doubt, no relaxation, no retreat into my inner world; these would only weaken the force of the 'jet'. If we imagine the snake confronted by the toad, or the two lizards, we can see that they are like two firemen directing their jets at each other. The first to experience doubt, to retreat into his inner world, is the victim. Another authority on hypnosis, Bernard Hollander, remarks in his book *Hypnosis and Self-Hypnosis* (published in London in 1928), that 'the hypnotic state . . . is largely a condition of more or less profound *abstraction*.' So when a bored schoolboy stares blankly out of the window, thinking of nothing in particular, he is in a mildly hypnotic state, and the schoolmaster is quite correct to shout: 'Wake up, Jones!' The boy has retreated into his subjective world, yet without *focusing* his attention, as he would if he were trying to remember something. Hypnosis seems to be a state when the mind is 'elsewhere', and yet nowhere in particular.

Völgyesi's book brings out with great clarity that there is something *very* strange about the mind. A wild elephant trumpeting and rearing – that seems natural. The same elephant becoming completely docile after branches have been waved in front of its eyes seems highly unnatural. And the notion that lizards – or even crocodiles – can be reduced to immobility by a gentle pressure on the neck seems somehow all wrong. What on earth is nature doing, making them so vulnerable?

The answer would seem to be that the vulnerability is not 'intentional'. Like crime itself, it is a mistake, a disadvantage that has emerged in the process of developing other advantages. In order to build up a certain complexity – which seems to be its basic aim – life had to create certain mechanisms. The more complex the 'works', the easier it is to throw a spanner in them. A big car uses a lot of fuel; a big biological mechanism uses a lot of vitality. If this vitality can suddenly be checked or diminished, the creature ceases to have free will.

Human beings, as Völgyesi points out, are far more complex than birds and animals. Yet the same principles apply. He noticed that the easiest people to hypnotize were those of a 'nervous constitution'. Clever, *sensitive* people are far more easily hypnotized than stupid, insensitive ones. He noticed that these highly sensitive people usually had damp hands, so that he could tell by shaking hands whether a person would be a good hypnotic subject. He refers to such people as 'psycho-passive'. People with dry handshakes are 'psycho-active'. They can still be hypnotized, but far more co-operation is needed from the patient, and sometimes the use of mild electric currents.

This is an observation of central importance. It means that clever, sensitive people are usually under-vitalized. They *allow* themselves to sink into boredom or gloom more easily than others. There is not enough water to drive the watermill, so to speak. Because their vitality is a few notches lower than it should be, it is easy to reduce it still lower by suggestion, and plunge them into a hypnotized state. In *Hypnotism and Crime*, Heinz Hammerschlag quotes a psychotherapist who got into a discussion about hypnotism in a hotel. He turned to glance casually at a young man sitting beside him on the couch; the young man said, 'Don't look at me like that – I can't move my arms any more', and sank with closed eyes sideways. This was pure auto-suggestion. Hammerschlag also has an amusing story of some practical joker – probably a medical student – who hypnotized a hysterical girl named Pauline in a hospital ward and ordered her to go and embrace the Abbé in charge of the hospital at four that afternoon. When the girl tried to leave the ward at four o'clock, nurses restrained her and she fought frenziedly. A doctor who suspected that the trouble was hypnotic suggestion placed her in a trance and got the story out of her. The original hypnotist was sent for to remove the suggestion. And even then she continued to have relapses until she was allowed to embrace the Abbé.

In a case like this the problem is that the girl's normal mental condition is close to sleep. She exists in a borderland between sleeping and waking. Above all, she is 'under-vitalized'. Because of this, she lives in a permanent state of unreality, and her failure to embrace the Abbé reduces her to neurotic anxiety. Unless she can somehow be persuaded to make an effort to raise her own vitality, she is trapped in a kind of vicious circle. Neurotic anxiety lowers her vitality and makes the world unreal; her sense of unreality makes her feel that nothing is worth doing, and so increases the unreality and the anxiety.

The schoolmaster who shouts: 'Wake up, Jones!' is, in fact, ordering Jones to increase his mental energy – to raise his vitality. Völgyesi achieved the same effect by sprinkling hypnotized frogs with a little sulphuric acid. And what precisely happens when a hypnotized subject is awakened? A vicious circle is broken; the critical self, the self that copes with the outside world, suddenly jumps to attention.

This matter can be made clearer by borrowing the terminology of Thomson J. Hudson, who in 1893 produced a remarkable book called *The Law of Psychic Phenomena* (psychic here means simply 'mental'.) Hudson was a student of hypnotism and he advanced the interesting notion that we all possess two minds or 'selves': the objective and the subjective. The objective mind is the practical part of us, the part that copes with external problems. The subjective minds looks inward, and copes with internal problems; it also 'summons' energy when we need it. (As we shall see later, modern research suggests that these two 'selves' are located in the left and right cerebral hemispheres of the brain.) Under hypnosis, Hudson says, the objective mind is put to sleep and the subjective mind takes over. In effect, the hypnotist himself becomes the 'objective mind' of the patient, and the patient obeys him just as if he *were* his own objective mind.

When the schoolboy goes into a daydream, he has descended into the subjective mind. The schoolmaster's shout of 'Wake up!' jerks him back into the real world – wakes up the objective mind.

And here we come to one of the most crucial points in the argument. You do not need to be in a state of 'abstraction' or daydreaming to be 'hypnotized'. Consider the following hypothetical case. You are in a hurry to get to work and there is an unusual amount of traffic on the road. Every light is against you, and you get more and more angry. The traffic light changes to green, but the car in front of you does not move. You are just about to lean out of the window and shout something insulting when the man turns his face. You recognize your boss. Instantly, your rage dissolves . . .

What has happened? The anger and tension have trapped you in a vicious circle of rising irritation, in which your values have become exaggerated, subjective. Your rage against the traffic is quite irrational, for the other cars have as much right to be on the road as you have. And traffic lights are mechanical; they do not *really* turn red because they see you coming.

When you spot your boss, realism breaks in like the snap of the hypnotist's fingers. The circle is broken. Your objective mind once again takes over. You came very close to getting yourself the sack, or at least losing your chance of promotion. And all for a momentary flash of rage. You heave a sigh of relief that you recognized him in time. It is as if you had been woken up.

Hypnosis, then, is not simply a trance state. It is, as Hollander says, basically a state of abstraction – to be trapped in the subjective vicious circle, having *lost contact* with reality.

There is an obvious analogy between such a state and the blind resentment of a Charles Manson, a John Frazier, or an Ian Brady, and this leads to the interesting recognition that the 'hypnotic domination' that Manson exercised over his followers, and that Brady seemed to exercise over Hindley, emanated from a person who was himself hypnotized. Like the hysterical girl in the hospital, Manson was trapped in a world of unreality.

Is this equivalent to saying that the criminal is 'not responsible'? Hardly. For the vicious circle is, in a basic sense, self-chosen. When you get angry in a traffic jam, you are *giving way* to your anger instead of telling yourself realistically that you are only wasting energy. A part of you remains detached. But if the anger becomes habitual, this detached part gradually loses strength, becomes involved in the anger. The mechanism can be seen clearly in Dostoevsky's *Crime and Punishment*. Raskolnikov's increasing resentment at his poverty, his sense of dependence on his family, slowly builds up into the vicious-circle mechanism – at which point it seems to him reasonable and logical to murder the old pawn-brokeress for her money. The essence of the 'hypnotic' reaction is to 'block out' part of the real world, to refuse to recognize its existence – in this case, the fact that the old woman is a human being like himself. The novel shows Raskolnikov being slowly awakened to this realization.

This leads to the crucial recognition that all crime contains this element of 'hypnosis'. In his study in modern totalitarianism, *The Tower and the Abyss*, Erich Kahler cites the massacre carried out in the French village of Oradour-sur-Glane in June 1944 by Hitler's SS. In reprisal for Resistance activity in the area, the Germans rounded up all the inhabitants and made them go to the market place. The women and children were herded into the village church. No one was alarmed at this stage – the Germans were laughing and joking, and playing with the babies. Then, at a signal from a captain, the soldiers in the square opened fire on the men and massacred them all. The church was set on fire and the women and children burned alive. The children who managed to stumble out were thrown back into the fire. A Swiss who described the massacre remarked, 'I am convinced that these Elite Guards did not feel the slightest shade of hatred against the French children when they held them in their arms. I am equally convinced that, if a counter order had arrived . . . they would have continued to play daddy.' But the SS men were 'under orders', and the order had the effect of a hypnotist's command. They 'blocked out' the reality of the women and children, and 'did their duty'. A confidence trickster swindles his victims in much the same way; he may actually feel genuinely friendly towards them as he lulls them into a state of trustfulness, yet the basic intention remains unchanged. Manson's 'family' killed Sharon Tate and her guests in the same 'blocked out' state. And Myra Hindley helped Brady to murder children yet continued to strike her family as a person who loved children. When she heard that her dog had died under anaesthetic when in the hands of the police she burst out: 'They're just a lot of bloody murderers.' For practical purposes, she had become two people.

Yet although crime – particularly violent crime – contains this element of 'dissociation', of 'alienation', there is another sense in which it is an attempt to break out of this state. The sex murderer John Christie remarked that after strangling and raping one of his victims, 'once again I experienced that quiet, peaceful thrill. I had no regrets.' The killing had removed the tension that kept him trapped in the vicious circle of his own emotions and desires; he was awake again.

We can discern the same factor in the petty crimes committed by Leopold and Loeb before they killed Bobby Franks. Loeb was the one who 'got a thrill' from crimes; it was like a game of Russian roulette in which he experienced relaxation and relief every time he 'won'. (After all, to be caught in a burglary would mean social disgrace.) Crime was Loeb's way of discharging tension, of waking himself up.

This is also quite plainly the key to the Moors case. When he murdered Edward Evans, Brady was trying to involve David Smith, with the intention of making him a part of a criminal gang; his aim was to commit bank robberies. We may assume that, since he had been planning bank robberies from the beginning, he regarded his murders as some form of training for the 'bigger' crime. It was Brady's intention to become a kind of all-round enemy of society, the English equivalent of Public Enemy Number One – with the difference that, like Charlie Peace, he hoped to remain undiscovered and live happily ever after on his gains. Crime would become a way of life involving continual stimulation and excitement.

And in this we can note another interesting aspect of the 'pattern'. At any given level, crime contains an element that reaches towards the next level of the hierarchy. Charlie Peace's crimes are crimes of 'subsistence' (to make a living), but he shows a powerful urge towards security and domesticity. Many 'domestic' crimes – Dr Pritchard, Constance Kent, Adelaide Bartlett – contain a strong element of sadism, reaching towards the sexual level. Jack the Ripper's sex crimes contain a strong element of exhibitionism – in the lay-out of the corpses, the letters to the police – reaching towards the self-esteem level. And the crimes of Manson and Brady contain a distorted element of self-actualization, reaching towards the creative level. (In my *Order of Assassins* I have labelled such killers 'assassins'

– those who kill as a violent form of self-expression; we can see a clear relationship between such crimes and the 'violent' art of painters such as Munch, Ensor, Soutine or Pollock.)

The case that, above all others, embodies this notion of crime as a 'creative act' is scarcely known outside the country in which it took place, Sweden, and may serve as a demonstration of the main threads of the preceding argument. It concerned a real-life Professor Moriarty, Dr Sigvard Thurneman, who came rather closer than Charles Manson to the dream of one-man Revolution.

In the early 1930s, the small town of Sala, near Stockholm, was struck by a minor crime wave. It began on 16 November 1930, when the body of a dairy worker, Sven Eriksson, was discovered in a half-frozen lake near Sala; Eriksson had vanished two days before, on his way home from work. He had been shot in the chest – apparently after a fierce struggle, for his clothes were torn and his face bruised. He had been alive when thrown into the lake. The motive was clearly not robbery, since he was still carrying his week's wages in his wallet. Mrs Eriksson said her husband had been suffering from a certain amount of nervous stress – he had even seen a doctor about it – but she could think of no reason why anyone should wish him dead. The police could not find a single clue to the murder.

During the next two years there was an unusual number of crimes in the Sala area, including three burglaries and two car thefts. Either the criminal was incredibly careful or he had incredible luck, for again the police could find no leads.

In the early hours of the morning of 15 September 1933, firemen were called to a house near the centre of Sala. It belonged to a wealthy mining official, Axel Kjellberg. The flames were already too fierce for any attempt at rescue. Two charred bodies – that of Kjellberg and his housekeeper – were recovered. Both had been shot in the head. The motive was robbery. Kjellberg had collected the wages for his mine on the previous day and had kept them in his safe overnight. Evidently the intruder, or intruders, had forced him to open the safe. A forced strongbox was found in the ruins.

During the next year there were a few more burglaries, but no serious crimes. Citizens formed vigilante groups to patrol the town at night. And on 12 October 1934, such a group observed that the house of Mrs Tilda Blomqvist was on fire. The vigilantes raised the alarm, as a result of which Mrs Blomqvist's chauffeur and his wife escaped from the burning house. This time, it was possible to enter the house before it was seriously damaged. Mrs Blomqvist's body was in her bedroom. She was dead, but there were no marks of violence. Medical examination failed to reveal cause of death. She had not inhaled smoke so it seemed conceivable that she had been suffocated before the fire began. Again, the motive was robbery. Mrs Blomqvist was a rich widow of sixty, and her cash and jewellery had vanished. Friends of the dead woman said she had been in poor health, and had been interested mainly in spiritualism and yoga. Once again, the police found themselves facing a blank wall.

Their luck began to change on 19 June 1936, when a quarry-worker named Elon Petterson was shot on the outskirts of Sala. He was bicycling back to the quarry with the week's payroll. This time, there had been a witness. An elderly man was sunning himself on his lawn as Petterson rode past, and a few moments later, he heard the sound of shots. He walked to the road and saw two men dragging Petterson towards the ditch. They then climbed into a black American car and drove away. The man noted down the car's number. A few hours later, Petterson died without recovering consciousness; he had been shot in the chest and stomach.

It soon became clear that the car's number was not going to provide an easy solution. The car of that number was not American, and it had been in a garage all day; the owner had an unshakable alibi. But an American sedan with a very similar number had been stolen recently from another town. It was conceivable its licence plate had been altered. The police decided to attempt to alarm the thieves. They told the newspapers that they were looking for a black Chevrolet whose licence plate had recently been altered – giving the number – and announced that they intended to search all garages. The next day, the missing car was found parked by the roadside near Sala. The licence plate *had* been skilfully changed, obviously by a man who knew his job. That seemed to argue that he was not a professional criminal, since few criminals spend years becoming expert metal workers. The police began a slow, thorough check of all garages and metal-working shops. Finally, they discovered what they were looking for. A young worker admitted that it was he who had altered the plate. At the time, he had been working for a garage owner named Erik Hedstrom, who had a business in the nearby town of Köping. According to this witness, he had only been working for Hedstrom for a few days when he was asked to alter the plate. He did it without question. But shortly after that Hedstrom had asked him whether he was willing to take part in the robbery of a bank messenger. The man asked for time to think it over, and rang back the next day to say that he had found another job.

Questioned about all this, Hedstrom – a good-looking young man of excellent reputation – flatly denied everything. But the moment the police left his home, Hedstrom picked up the telephone and asked the operator for a Stockholm number. The police checked with the operator and discovered that it was the number of Dr Sigvard Thurneman, a doctor specializing in nervous disorders. The Sala constable who had investigated the first murder – of Sven Eriksson – recalled that *he* had been consulting a doctor about nervous tension shortly before his death. A call to Eriksson's wife revealed that the doctor was Sigvard Thurneman.

A Stockholm detective called on Thurneman the next day, claiming that he was involved in a routine investigation about neurosis and crime. Thurneman proved to be a small, pale man with a thin, firm mouth, a receding chin and a receding hairline that made his high forehead seem immense. He was in his late twenties. With considerable reluctance, Thurneman allowed the detective to glance into his files, standing at his elbow. But the detective was able to confirm that Sven Eriksson had been a patient. So had Mrs Blomqvist.

Hedstrom was brought in for questioning, while police searched his house. He insisted that he only knew Thurneman slightly. They had been at college together, and he had occasionally consulted him since then. But while he was being questioned, a phone call revealed that the police had found a gun in his garage – of the calibre that had shot Eriksson. Hedstrom suddenly decided to confess. Thurneman, he said, was the man behind all the crimes. They had become acquainted at the university of Uppsala, when both had been interested in hypnotism. He had found Thurneman a fascinating and dominant character, a student of occultism, theosophy and philosophy. This had been in the mid-1920s. Thurneman was also fascinated by crime. One of his favourite pastimes was to devise 'perfect crimes'. Hedstrom had joined in the game. Then, in 1929, Thurneman had proposed that it was time to try out one of the crimes they had planned so thoroughly in imagination. It was to be a robbery at the dairy where Eriksson worked. Eriksson was a patient of Thurneman's, and Thurneman had been treating him through hypnosis.

Eriksson had agreed to be the 'inside man' in the robbery. Then, at the last minute, he had changed his mind. Thurneman was afraid he might go to the police, or at least tell his wife. So Hedstrom, together with two other men, was delegated to kill him. From then on, said Hedstrom, Thurneman had made them continue to commit crimes that he had planned in detail. Thurneman actually took part in the robbery and murder of Axel Kjellberg – he and Hedstrom wore policemen's uniforms (which Thurneman had had made by a theatrical costumier) to persuade the old man to open his door in the early hours of the morning. Then Kjellberg and his wife were murdered in cold blood, and the house set on fire.

Tilda Blomqvist had been chosen because she had told Thurneman where she kept her jewels while under hypnosis. Her murder had been a masterpiece of planning. They had bored a hole in the wall of her bedroom (the house was made of wood, like so many in Scandinavia), inserted a rubber hose attached to the car's exhaust and gassed her in her sleep. Then they had stolen the jewels and set fire to the house.

Faced with Hedstrom's signed confession, Thurneman decided to tell everything. In fact, he wrote an autobiography while in prison. As a child, Thurneman had had an inferiority complex because of his small build and poor health. He was a solitary, deeply interested in mysticism and the occult. At thirteen – in 1921 – he had begun to experiment in hypnotism and thought-transference with school-mates. He also read avidly about mysticism and occult lore. Then, at sixteen, he had met a mysterious Dane who was skilled in yoga. In 1929, he claimed, he had been to Copenhagen and joined an occult group run by the Dane. On his return to Stockholm he had started his own magic circle, gathering together all kinds of people and making them swear an oath of obedience and secrecy.

The position of cult-leader seems to have given Thurneman a taste of the kind of power he had always wanted. He used hypnosis to seduce under-age girls, and then – according to his confession – disposed of them through the white slave trade. Other gang members were also subjected to hypnosis and 'occult training' (whatever that meant). Thurneman was bisexual, and became closely involved with another gang member who was a lover as well as a close friend. When this man got into financial difficulties, Thurneman became worried in case he divulged their relationship – which, in 1930, was still a criminal offence. He claimed that, by means of hypnotic suggestions over the course of a week, he induced the man to commit suicide. In 1934, he placed another member of the gang in a deep trance and injected a dose of fatal poison.

Thurneman's aim was to make himself a millionaire and then leave for South America. The two Sala murders – of Axel Kjellberg and Tilda Blomqvist – brought in large sums of money. But the 'big job' he was planning was the robbery of a bank housed in the same building as the Stockholm Central Post Office. The gang had stolen large quantities of dynamite – thirty-six kilos – and the plan was to blow up the post office with dynamite and rob the bank in the chaos that followed. Thurneman had also become involved in drug smuggling.

Thurneman was brought to trial in July 1936, together with Hedstrom and three accomplices who had helped in the killing of Eriksson and Petterson. All five were sentenced to life imprisonment; but after six months in prison, Thurneman slipped into unmistakable insanity and was transferred to a criminal mental asylum.

The Thurneman case throws a powerful light into the innermost recesses of the psychology of the self-esteem killer. He was the kind of criminal that Charles Manson and Ian Brady would have liked to be. His dominance over his 'family' was complete. Men accepted him as their unquestioned leader; women submitted to him and were discarded into prostitution. His life was a power-fantasy come true. He was indifferent to all human feeling. When his closest friend became a potential danger, he was induced to commit suicide; when a gang-member's loyalty became suspect, he was killed with an injection like a sick dog. When the gang committed robbery, witnesses were simply destroyed, to eliminate all possibility of later recognition and identification. (Thurneman must have reflected with bitter irony that it was Hedstrom's failure to observe this rule that led to discovery.) Thurneman had found his own way to the 'heroic', to a feeling of uniqueness; by the age of twenty-eight he had achieved his sense of 'primary value'.

But why, if he was such a remarkable individual, did he choose crime? No doubt some deep resentment, some humiliation dating from childhood, played its part. Yet we can discern another reason. As a means of achieving uniqueness, crime can *guarantee* success. Thurneman might have aimed for 'primacy' in the medical field; he might have set himself up as a guru, a teacher of occult philosophy;

he might have attempted to find self-expression through writing. But then, each of these possibilities carries a high risk of failure and demands an exhausting outlay of energy and time. It is far easier to commit a successful crime than to launch a successful theory or write a successful book. All this means that the 'master criminal' can achieve his sense of uniqueness at a fairly low cost. Society has refused to recognize his uniqueness; it has insisted on treating him as if he were just like everybody else. By committing a crime that makes headlines, he is administering a sharp rebuke. He is making society aware that, somewhere among its anonymous masses, there is someone who deserves fear and respect . . .

There is, of course, one major disadvantage that dawns on every master criminal sooner or later. He can never achieve public recognition – or at least, only at the cost of being caught. He must be content with the admiration of a very small circle – perhaps, as in the case of Leopold and Loeb, Brady and Hindley, just one other person. This explains why so many 'master criminals' seem to take a certain pleasure in being caught; they are at last losing their anonymity. Thurneman not only wrote a confession; he turned it into an autobiography, in which he explained with pride the details of his crimes. This is the irony of the career of a 'master criminal'; unless he is caught, he feels at the end the same frustration, the same intolerable sense of non-recognition, that drove him to crime in the first place. It may have been the recognition of this absurd paradox that finally undermined Thurneman's sanity.

The Thurneman case illustrates in a particularly clear form the problem that came to fascinate me as I worked on the *Encyclopedia of Murder* and its two successors. Thurneman was convinced he was acting out of free will, and thus demonstrating his 'uniqueness'. But to see him as part of a 'pattern' of crime implies that he was neither unique nor free. Which is the truth? It only begs the question to point out that we can also see Shakespeare or Beethoven as part of the historical pattern of their time, for, as Shaw points out, we judge the artist by his highest moments, the criminal by his lowest. Creativeness involves a certain mental effort; destructiveness does not.

The question was raised in the 1890s by the sociologist Emile Durkheim in his study of suicide. Fellow sociologists were doubtful whether suicide *could* be treated scientifically, since every suicide has a different reason. Durkheim countered this by pointing out that the rates of suicide in individual countries are amazingly constant; therefore it cannot depend on individual choice. There must be hidden laws, underlying causes. Besides, there are quite recognizable patterns. 'Loners' kill themselves more often than people who feel they belong to a group. Free thinkers have a higher suicide rate than Protestants, Protestants than Catholics, and Catholics than Jews – who, at least in the 1880s, had the lowest suicide rate of all because Jews have such a powerful sense of social solidarity.

Durkheim also observed a type of suicide that corresponds roughly to 'motiveless murder'; he called it *suicide anomique*, suicide due to lack of norms or values. Bachelors have a higher suicide rate than married men. Moreover, during times of war, the suicide rate drops; it rises again in times of peace and prosperity. (In 1981, the Lebanon Hospital for Mental Disorders recorded that admissions rise during the cease-fires and drop when the shooting starts.) From this, Durkheim deduced that people need social limits to keep them balanced and sane. Suicide is, therefore, a 'social act' not an individual one. He concludes that there are 'suicidal currents' in society that act mechanically on individuals and force a number of them to commit suicide. The same argument could obviously be applied to *crime anomique*, the type of crime committed by socially rootless individuals such as Thurneman, Manson, Brady, Frazier.

The arguments of this chapter have placed us in a position to see precisely where Durkheim was mistaken. He believed that it is the individual's *social* orientation that leads to suicide (or crime – as we shall see later, there is a close connection). But our study of the relation between crime and 'hypnosis' has shown that this fails to get to the heart of the matter. It is true that society provides norms and values; but these in turn provide a *sense of reality*, the essential factor in preventing both suicide and crime. The most amazing realization that emerges from the study of hypnosis is that our sense of reality is so easily undermined. In chickens it can be done with a chalk line or a bent piece of wood on the beak; in frogs, with a few taps on the stomach. In human beings that process is slightly more complicated, but not much. Völgyesi talks about the 'law of point reflexes', which states that any monotonously repeated stimulus of the same point in the cerebral cortex produces compulsive sleepiness. Similarly, our eyes cannot focus for long on unmoving objects; they keep de-focusing. It takes a sudden movement to shake the 'controlling ego' awake again, to 'restore us to reality'.

It is this sense of reality that makes the difference between suicide or non-suicide. Durkheim was therefore mistaken. The 'social currents' certainly exist; but they are only the secondary cause of crime or suicide. The primary cause must be sought in the psychology of the individual.

Does this mean that Durkheim's opponents were right? No, for they argued that suicide can *only* be understood in psychological terms, and Durkheim proved them wrong. It must be understood in social *and* psychological terms. And if we are to understand the basic patterns of criminal behaviour – and therefore how to combat it – the search for patterns must be continued on both levels.

Two

A REPORT ON THE VIOLENT MAN

On 13 December 1937, the Imperial Japanese Army marched into Nanking, in Central China, and began what has been described as 'one of the most savage acts of mass terror in modern times' – a campaign of murder, rape and torture that lasted for two months. Chinese soldiers had divested themselves of their uniforms and mixed with the civilian population, in the belief that the Japanese would spare them if they were unarmed. The Japanese began rounding them up and shooting them in huge numbers, using machine-guns. The bodies – some twenty thousand of them – were thrown into heaps, dowsed with petrol, and set alight; hundreds who were still alive died in the flames. Because they were indistinguishable from the soldiers, male civilians were also massacred. Women were herded into pens which became virtually brothels for the Japanese soldiers; more than twenty thousand women between the ages of eleven and eighty were raped, and many disembowelled. Many who were left alive committed ritual suicide, the traditional response of Chinese women to violation. Boys of school age were suspended by their hands for days, and then used for bayonet practice. Rhodes Farmer, a journalist who worked in Shanghai, came into possession of photographs of mass executions of boys by beheading, of rapes of women by Japanese soldiers, and of 'slaughter pits' in which soldiers were encouraged to develop their killer-instinct by bayoneting tied prisoners. When published in the American magazine *Look*, they caused worldwide condemnation, and the Japanese commander was recalled to Tokyo. The odd thing was that these photographs were taken by the Japanese themselves; for they regarded the atrocities as simply acts of revenge. In two months, more than fifty thousand people died in Nanking, and towards two hundred thousand in the surrounding countryside. (In 1982 – when the Chinese were quarrelling with the Japanese about their 'rewriting' of history – the official Chinese figure was three hundred and forty thousand.)

Some six hundred miles to the north-west of Nanking, the city of Peking was already in Japanese hands. But the village of Chou-kou-tien, thirty miles to the south-west, was still held by Chinese Nationalists, and there a team of international scientists were collaborating on a project that had created immense excitement in archaeological circles. In 1929, a young palaeontologist named Pie Wen-Chung had discovered in the caves near Chou-kou-tien the petrified skull of one of man's earliest ancestors. It looked more like a chimpanzee than a human being, and the Catholic scientist Teilhard de Chardin thought the teeth were those of a beast of prey. It had a sloping forehead, enormous browridges and a receding chin. But the brain was twice as big as that of a chimpanzee. And as more skulls, limbs and teeth were discovered, it became clear that this beast of prey had walked upright. At first, it looked as if this was a cross between ape and man – what earlier anthropologists such as Haeckel had called 'the missing link'. Nearly half a century earlier the missing link theory had apparently been confirmed when the bones of an 'ape-man' had been discovered in Java. The ape-man of Peking clearly belonged to the same species. But the caves of the Chou-kou-tien hills yielded evidence that this was no missing link. Peking man had constructed hearths and used fire to roast his food – his favourite meal seems to have been venison. He was therefore more culturally advanced than had been supposed. This creature, who lived more than half a million years ago, was a true human being.

He was also, it seemed, a cannibal. All the forty skulls discovered at Chou-kou-tien were mutilated at the base, creating a gap into which a hand could be inserted to scoop out the brains. Franz Weidenreich, the scientist in charge of the investigation, declared that these creatures had been slaughtered in a body, dragged into the caves and there roasted and eaten. By whom? Presumably by other Peking men. In other caves in the area, bones of Cro-Magnon man were discovered, and here too there was evidence of cannibalism; but Cro-Magnon man came on the scene more than four hundred thousand years later; he could not have been the culprit. The evidence of the Chou-kou-tien caves revealed that Peking man had fought against the wild beasts who occupied the caves and had wiped them out; after that, he had fought against his fellow men and eaten them. While editorials around the world were asking how civilized men could massacre the population of a large city, the Peking excavations were suggesting an unpalatable answer: that man has always been a killer of his own species.

Nowadays, that view seems uncontroversial enough; the threat of atomic annihilation has accustomed us to take a pessimistic view of the human race. But in 1937, the 'killer ape' idea met with strong resistance among scientists. According to the theory that had been current since the 1890s, *homo sapiens* had evolved because of his intelligence. He started life as a gentle, vegetarian creature, like his brother the ape, then slowly learned such skills as hunting and agriculture and created civilization. In his book on Peking Man, Dr Harry L. Shapiro, one of the scientists at Chou-kou-tien, does not even mention the mutilations in the base of the skulls; he prefers to believe they were damaged by falling rock and layers of debris. But new evidence continued to erode the older view. As early as 1924, the palaeontologist Raymond Dart had discovered an even older species of 'ape-man', which he called Australopithecus (or southern ape-man). In the late 1940s, examining an Australopithecus site near Sterkfontein, Dart found many shattered baboon skulls. Looking at a club-like antelope thighbone, he was struck by a sudden thought. He lifted the bone and brought it down heavily on the back of one of the baboon skulls. The two holes made by the protuberances of the leg joint were identical with similar holes on the other skulls. Dart had discovered the weapon with which the 'first man' had killed baboons. It seemed to verify that similar thighbones found in the caves of Peking man had also been weapons . . .

In 1949, Dart published a paper containing his claim that Australopithecus – who lived about two million years ago – had discovered the use of weapons. Fellow scientists declined to take the idea seriously. In 1953, he repeated the offence with a paper called *The Predatory Transition from Ape to Man*, which so worried the editor of the *International Anthropological and Linguistic Review* that he prefaced it with a note disclaiming responsibility for its opinions. For in this paper Dart advanced the revolutionary thesis that 'southern ape-man' had emerged from among the apes for one reason only: because he had learned to commit murder with weapons. Our remote ancestors, he said, learned to stand and walk upright because they needed their hands to carry their bone clubs. Hands replaced teeth for tearing chunks of meat from animal carcases, so our teeth became smaller and our claws disappeared to be replaced by nails. Hitting an animal with a club – or hurling a club or stone at it from a distance – meant a new kind of co-ordination between the hand and eye; and so the brain began to develop.

At the time Dart was writing his paper, there was one remarkable piece of evidence for the older view that 'intelligence came first'. This was the famous Piltdown skull, discovered in a gravel pit in 1913. It had a jaw like an ape but its brain was the same size as that of modern man. Then, forty years later, tests at the British Museum revealed that the Piltdown skull was a hoax – the skull of a modern man and the jawbone of an ape, both stained by chemicals to look alike. The revelation of the hoax came in the same year that Dart's paper was published, and it went a long way towards supporting Dart's views. The brain of Australopithecus *was* larger than that of an ape, but it was far smaller than that of modern man.

In the early 1960s, two remarkable books popularized this distur-bing thesis about man's killer instincts: *African Genesis* by Robert Ardrey and *On Aggression* by Konrad Lorenz. Both argued, in effect, that man became man because of his aggressiveness, and that we should not be surprised by war, crime and violent behaviour because they are part of our very essence. Ardrey's final chapter was grimly entitled: 'Cain's Children'. Yet both Ardrey and Lorenz were guardedly optimistic, Lorenz pointing out that man's aggressions *can* be channelled into less dangerous pursuits – such as sport and exploration – while Ardrey declared, with more hope than convic-tion, that man's instinct for order and civilization is just as powerful as his destructiveness. Ardrey even ends with a semi-mystical passage about a mysterious presence called 'the keeper of the kinds', a force behind life that makes for order. Yet the overall effect of both books is distinctly pessimistic.

The same may be said for the view put forward by Arthur Koestler in *The Ghost in the Machine* (1967). Koestler points out: '*Homo sapiens* is virtually unique in the animal kingdom in his lack of instinctive safeguards against the killing of conspecifics – members of his own species.' (He might have added that he is also one of the few creatures who has no instinctive revulsion against cannibalism – dogs, for example, cannot be persuaded to eat dog meat.) Koestler's explanation is that the human brain is an evolutionary blunder. It consists of three brains, one on top of the other: the reptile brain, the mammalian brain and, on top of these, the human neo-cortex. The result, as the physiologist P. D. Maclean remarked, is that when a psychiatrist asks the patient to lie down on the couch he is asking him to stretch out alongside a horse and a crocodile. The human brain has developed at such an incredible pace in the past half million years that physiologists talk about a 'brain explosion' and compare its growth to that of a tumour. The trouble, says Koestler, is that instead of *transforming* the old brain into the new – as the forelimb of the earliest reptiles became a bird's wing and a man's hand – evolution has merely superimposed a new structure on top of the old one and their powers overlap. We are a 'mentally unbalanced species', whose logic is always being undermined by emotion. 'To put it crudely: evolution has left a few screws loose between the neo-cortex and the hypothalamus', and the result is that man has a dangerous 'paranoid streak' which explains his self-destructiveness.

Inevitably, there was a reaction against the pessimism. In *The Anatomy of Human Destructiveness* (1974), the veteran Freudian Erich Fromm flatly contradicts Dart, Ardrey and Lorenz, and argues that there is no evidence that our remote ancestors were basically warlike and aggressive. 'Almost everyone reasons: if civilized man is so warlike, how much more warlike must primitive man have been! But [Quincy] Wright's results [in *A Study of War*] confirm the thesis that the most primitive men are the least warlike and that warlikeness grows in proportion to civilization.' And in a television series called *The Making of Mankind* (broadcast in 1981), Richard Leakey, son of the anthropologist Louis Leakey (whose investigations into 'southern ape-man' had been widely cited by Ardrey to support his thesis) left no doubt about his opposition to the killer ape theory. Everything we know about primitive man, he said, suggests that he lived at peace with the world and his neighbours; it was only after man came to live in cities that he became cruel and destructive. This is also the view taken by Fromm in *The Anatomy of Human Destructiveness*.

Yet even the title of Fromm's book suggests that Ardrey, Lorenz and Koestler were not all that far from the truth. 'Man differs from the animal by the fact that he is a killer,' says Fromm, 'the only primate that kills and tortures members of his own species without any reason . . .' And the book is devoted to the question: *why* is man the only creature who kills and tortures members of his own kind?

Fromm's answer leans heavily upon the views of Freud. In *Civilization and its Discontents* (1931), Freud had argued that man was not made for civilization or civilization for man. It frustrates and thwarts him at every turn and drives him to neurosis and self-

destruction. But Freud's view of our remote ancestors implied that
they spent their time dragging their mates around by the hair and
hitting their rivals with clubs, and that it is modern man's inhibitions
about doing the same thing that make him neurotic. Fromm, in fact,
is altogether closer to the views that had been expressed thirty years
earlier by H. G. Wells. In one of his most interesting – and most
neglected – books, *'42 to '44*, written in the midst of the Second
World War, Wells tried to answer the question of why men are so
cruel and so destructive. 'We now know that the hunters of the great
plains of Europe in the milder interglacial periods had the character of
sociable, gregarious creatures without much violence.' Like Fromm
and Leakey, Wells believed that the trouble began when men moved
into cities, and were 'brought into a closeness of contact for which
their past had not prepared them. The early civilizations were not
slowly evolved and adapted *communities*. They were essentially
jostling *crowds* in which quite unprecedented reactions were possible'.
Ruthless men seized the power and wealth and the masses had to live
in slums. This is Wells's explanation of how man became a killer.

What puzzles Wells is the question of human cruelty. He makes the
important observation that when we hear about some appalling piece
of cruelty our reaction is to become angry and say, 'Do you know what
I should like to do to that brute?' – a revelation 'that vindictive
reaction is the reality of the human animal.' When we hear of cruelty,
we instantly feel a sense of the *difference* between ourselves and the
'brute' who is responsible. And it is precisely this lack of fellow-
feeling that made the cruelty possible in the first place.

It has to be acknowledged that 'fellow-feeling' is *not* the natural
response of one human being to another. We feel it for those who are
close to us; but it requires a real effort of imagination to feel it for
people on the other side of the world – or even the other side of the
street. Sartre has even argued, in his *Critique of Dialectical Reason*,
that all men are naturally enemies and rivals. If a man goes for a
country walk, he resents the presence of other people; nature would
be more attractive if he was alone. When he joins a bus queue, every
other person in it becomes a rival – the conductor may shout 'No more
room' as he tries to climb on board. A crowded city or supermarket is
an unpleasant place because all these people want *their* turn. If a man
could perform magic by merely thinking, he would make others
dissolve into thin air – or perhaps, like Wells's 'man who could work
miracles', transport them all to Timbuktu.

This is a point that was made with brutal explicitness in Colin Turnbull's study of a 'dispossessed' African tribe, *The Mountain People*. Since the Second World War, the Ik have been driven out of their traditional hunting grounds by a government decision to turn the land into a game reserve. They became farmers in a land with practically no rain. The result of this hardship is that they seemed to lose all normal human feelings. Children were fed until the age of three, then thrown out to fend for themselves. Old people were allowed to starve to death. In the Ik villages, it was every man for himself. A small girl, thrown out by her parents, kept returning home, looking for love and affection; her parents finally locked her in and left her to starve to death. A mother watched with indifference as her baby crawled towards the communal camp fire and stuck its hand in; when the men roared with laughter at the child's screams, the mother looked pleased at providing amusement. When the government provided famine relief, those who were strong enough went to collect it, then stopped on the way home and gorged themselves sick; after vomiting, they ate the remainder of the food. One man who insisted on taking food home for his sick wife and child was mocked for his weakness.

Some writers – like Ardrey – have drawn wide conclusions from the Ik – such as that human values are superficial and that altruism is not natural to us. This is illogical. We could draw the same conclusions from the fact that most of us get bad tempered when we become hungry and tired. In the case of the Ik, the 'culture shock' was particularly severe; as hunters, they practised close co-operation, involving even the women and children; to be suddenly deprived of all this must have left them totally disoriented. But then, the important question about human beings is not how far we are capable of being disoriented and demoralized – losing self-control – but how far we are capable of going in the opposite direction, of using our intelligence for creativity and organization. Negative cases, like the Ik, prove nothing except what we already know: that human beings are capable of total selfishness, particularly when it is a question of survival. In fact, many primitive peoples practise infanticide and gerontocide. In *The Hunting Peoples* (p. 329) Carleton S. Coon describes how, among the Caribou Indians of Hudson Bay, old people voluntarily commit suicide when the reindeer herds fail to appear and starvation threatens. When the old people are all dead, girl babies will be killed. 'This is a heartrending business because everybody loves children.' John Pfeiffer, the author of *The Emergence of Man*, describes (p. 316) how, among the aborigines of Australia, infanticide is the commonest form of birth control, and that between 15 and 50 per cent of infants are killed; it is the mother's decision and the mother's job, and she kills the baby about an hour after birth as we drown unwanted kittens.

There is another, and equally instinctive, element that helps us to understand human criminality: xenophobia, dislike of the foreigner. In *The Social Contract*, Ardrey points out that xenophobia is a basic instinct among animals, and that it probably has a genetic basis. All creatures tend to congregate in small groups or tribes and to stick to their own. Darwin even noticed that in a herd of ten thousand or so cattle on a ranch in Uruguay the animals naturally separated into sub-groups of between fifty and a hundred. When a violent storm scattered the herd, it re-grouped after twenty-four hours, the animals all finding their former group-members. And this instinctive tendency to form 'tribes' is probably a device to protect the species. If some favourable gene appears, then it will be confined to the members of the group and not diluted by the herd. A study by Edward Hall of the black ghetto area of Chicago revealed that it was virtually a series of independent villages. And even in more 'mobile' social groups the average person tends to have a certain number of acquaintances who form his 'tribe' – Desmond Morris suggested in *The Human Zoo* the number of between fifty and one hundred, figures that happen to agree with Darwin's observation about cattle. The group may adopt his own modes of dress, catch-phrases, tricks of speech. (Frank Sinatra's 'in-group' was significantly known as 'the rat pack'.) They enjoy and emphasize the privilege of belonging, and adopt an attitude of hostility to outsiders. Hall's study of Chicago showed that there was often gang warfare between the ghetto communities.

This helps to explain how the Nazis could herd Jews into concentration camps. Hitler's racist ideology would not have taken root so easily were it not for the natural 'animal xenophobia' that is part of our instinctive heritage. In his book on the psychology of genocide *The Holocaust and the German Elite*, Professor Rainer C. Baum remarks on the *indifference* of the German bureaucrats who were responsible for the concentration camps and the banality of the whole process. They were not frenzied anti-semites, lusting for blood; what was frightening about them was that they had no feeling about the women and children they herded into cattle trucks. And if we assume that this was due to the evil Nazi ideology, we shall be oversimplifying. Human beings do not need an evil ideology to make them behave inhumanly; it comes easily to us because most of us exist in a state of self-preoccupation that makes our neighbour unreal. The point is reinforced by the massacre of Palestinians that took place in two refugee camps, Sabra and Shatila, in September 1982. Palestinian fighters had agreed to be evacuated from Beirut – after a siege – on the understanding that their women and children would be safe. On Saturday, 18 September the world became aware that Christian phalangists had massacred hundreds of women and children – as well as a few male non-combatants – in the camps, and that the phalangists had been sent into the camps by the Israelis. While the slaughter was going on, the US envoy sent Israel's General Sharon a message: 'You must stop this horrible massacre . . . You have absolute control of the area and are therefore responsible . . .'

What shocked the world – including thousands of Israelis, who demonstrated in Tel Aviv – was that it should be Jews, the victims of the Nazi holocaust, who apparently countenanced the massacre. But Baum's analysis applies here as well as to Belsen and Buchenwald; it was not a matter of 'evil' but of indifference. Most of the mass-murderers in history have simply placed their victims in a different category from their own wives and children, just as the average meat eater feels no fellowship for cows and sheep.

In our humanitarian age, these horrors stand out, and we draw the lesson: that to be truly human demands a real effort of will rather than our usual vague assumption of 'mutual concern'. Five thousand years ago, no one made that assumption; they were governed by the law of xenophobia and recognized that mutual concern only exists between relatives and immediate neighbours.

As we shall see, there is evidence of a slowly increasing criminality from about 2000 B.C. The old religious sanctions began breaking down at this period; the force that made men come together into cities in the first place was unable to withstand the new stresses created by these 'jostling crowds'. In his book on *Animal Nature and Human Nature*, Professor W. H. Thorpe comments on the rarity of inter-group aggression between chimpanzees and gorillas, and speculates on why human beings are so different. But he then answers his own question by pointing out that, while there is very little violence between groups of animals in the wild, this alters as soon as they are kept in captivity and subjected to unnatural conditions such as shortage of food and space; then, suddenly, they become capable of killing one another. This is what happened to man when he became a city dweller. The need to defend food-growing 'territory' from neighbours in nearby cities made man into a warlike animal. Moreover, cities had to be defended by walls, and this eventually introduced an entirely new factor: overcrowding. And this, it now seems fairly certain, was the factor that finally turned man into a habitual criminal.

It is only in recent years that we have become aware of the role of overcrowding in producing stress and violence. In 1958, a scientist named John Christian was studying the deer population on James Island, in Chesapeake Bay, when the deer began to die in large numbers. There were about three hundred on the island; by the following year, two hundred and twenty of these had died for no apparent cause. Post mortems revealed that the deer had enlarged adrenal glands – the gland that floods the bloodstream with the hormone called adrenalin, the stress hormone. James Island is half a square mile in size, so each deer had more than five thousand square yards of territory to itself. This, apparently, was not enough. The deer needed about twenty thousand square yards each. So when numbers exceeded eighty, they developed stress symptoms, and the population automatically reduced itself.

A psychologist named John B. Calhoun has made a similar observation when breeding wild Norwegian rats in a pen. The pen was a quarter of an acre and could have held five thousand rats. With a normal birthrate, this could have swelled tenfold in two years. Yet the rat population remained constant at a mere two hundred.

Calhoun was later to perform a classic experiment with his Norwegian rats. He placed a number of rats into four interconnecting cages. The two end pens, which had only one entrance, were the most 'desirable residences' – since they could be most easily defended – and these were quickly taken over by two highly dominant rats with their retinue of females. All the other rats were forced to move into the two centre cages, so that these soon became grossly overcrowded. There were also dominant males in these two centre cages (it was Calhoun who observed that the number of dominant rats was one in twenty – five per cent), but because of the overcrowding, they could not establish their own territory. And as the overcrowding became more acute, the dominant rats became criminals. They formed gangs and indulged in rape, homosexuality and cannibalism. In their natural state, rats have an elaborate courting ritual. The criminal rats would force their way into the female's burrow, rape her and eat her young. The middle cages became, in Calhoun's words, a 'behavioural sink'.

Ever since Lorenz's *On Aggression*, ethologists have warned about the dangers of drawing conclusions about human behaviour from animal behaviour; but in this case, it is impossible to see how it can be avoided. We have always known that our overcrowded slums are breeding grounds of crime. Calhoun's experiment – performed at the National Institute of Mental Health in Maryland – shows us why: the dominant minority are deprived of normal outlets for their dominance; it turns into indiscriminate aggression. Desmond Morris remarks in *The Human Zoo*: 'Under normal conditions, in their natural habitats, wild animals do not mutilate themselves, masturbate, attack their offspring, develop stomach ulcers, become fetishists, suffer from obesity, form homosexual pair-bonds, or commit murder. Among human city dwellers, needless to say, all of these things occur.' Animals in captivity also develop various 'perversions' – which leads Morris to remark that the city is a human zoo. And the reason that a 'zoo' breeds crime is that dominance is deprived of its normal outlets and turns to violence. As William Blake says: 'When thought is closed in caves, then love shall show its root in deepest hell.'

Yet the warning about extrapolating from animal to human behaviour deserves serious consideration. Why is not every large city in the world a 'sink' of violence and perversion? It is true that many of them are; yet others, such as Hong Kong, where you would expect to find the 'dominant rat syndrome', have a reasonably low crime rate.

Ardrey provides one interesting clue in the chapter on 'personal space' in *The Social Contract*. He describes an experiment carried out by the psychiatrist Augustus Kinzel in 1969. Prisoners in a Federal prison were placed in the centre of a bare room, and Kinzel then advanced on them slowly, step by step. The prisoner was told to call 'Stop!' when he felt that Kinzel was uncomfortably close. Non-violent prisoners seemed to need a 'personal space' of about ten square feet. But prisoners with a long record of violence reacted with clenched fists long before Kinzel was that close; these prisoners seemed to need a 'personal space' of about forty square feet.

This seems to support the 'personal space' theory. But it still leaves unanswered the question: why do some criminals need more than others? And the answer, in this case, requires only a little common-sense. When I am feeling tense and irritable, I tend to be more 'explosive' than when I am relaxed; so much is obvious. My tension may be due to a variety of causes – hunger, overwork, a hangover, general frustration and dissatisfaction. The effect, as John Christian discovered with his Sika deer, is to cause the adrenal glands to overwork; the result of long-term stress in animals is fatty degeneration of the liver and haemorrhages of the adrenals, thyroid, brain and kidneys. The tension causes fear-hormones to flood into the bloodstream. In *The Biological Time Bomb* (p. 228) Gordon Rattray Taylor mentions that this is what causes the mass-suicide of lemmings, who are also reacting to over-population. He also describes how American prisoners in Korea sometimes died from convulsive seizures or became totally lethargic; the disease was named 'give-up-itis'.

But then, we are all aware that our attitudes determine our level of tension. I *allow* some annoyance to make me angry or impatient. When the telephone has dragged me away from my typewriter for the fifth time in one morning, I may say: 'Oh dammit, NO!' and experience rising tension. Or I may take the view that these interruptions are tiresome but unavoidable, and deliberately 'cool it'. It is my decision.

It seems, then, that my energy mechanisms operate through a force and counter-force, like garage doors on a counterweight system. Let us, for convenience, refer to these as Force T – the T standing for tension – and Force C, the C for control. Force T makes for destabilization of our inner being. Force C makes for stabilization and inhibition. I experience Force T in its simplest form if I want to urinate badly; there is a force inside me, making me uncomfortable. And if I am uncomfortable for too long, the experience ceases to be confined to my bladder; my heartbeat increases, my cheeks feel hot. My *energies* seem to be expanding, trying to escape.

Consider, on the other hand, what happens when I become deeply interested in some problem. I deliberately 'damp down' my energies, I soothe my impatience, I focus my attention. I *actively apply a counter-force* to the force of destabilization. And if, for example, I am listening to music, I may apply the counter-force until I am in a condition of deep 'appreciation', of hair-trigger perception.

When we look at it in this way, we can see that the two 'forces' are the great governing forces of human existence. From the moment I get up in the morning, I am subjecting myself to various stimuli that cause tensions, and I am continually monitoring these tensions and applying 'Force C' to control them and – if possible – to canalize them for constructive purposes. Biologists are inclined to deny the existence of free will; yet it is hard to describe this situation except in terms of a continuous act of choice. The weak people, those who make little effort of control, spend their lives in a permanent state of mild discomfort, like a man who wants to rush to the lavatory. Blake says in *The Marriage of Heaven and Hell*: 'Those who restrain their desire do so because theirs is weak enough to be restrained', and this is one of the few statements of that remarkable mystic that is downright wrong-headed. (Admittedly, he is putting it into the mouth of the devil.) Beethoven was notoriously explosive and irascible; but his 'inhibitory force' was also great enough to canalize the destabilizing force into musical creation.

It is obvious that Sika deer, Norwegian rats, lemmings, snow-shoe hares and other creatures that have been observed to die of stress, lack control of the inhibitory force. Certainly all creatures must possess some control of this force, or they would be totally unable to focus their energies or direct their activites. But in animals, this control is completely bound up with external stimuli. A cat watching a mouse hole, a dog lying outside the house of a bitch on heat, will show astonishing self-control, maintaining a high level of attention (that is, focused consciousness) for hours or even days. But without external stimuli, the animal will show signs of boredom or fall asleep. Man is the only animal whose way of life demands almost constant use of the inhibitory faculty.

We can see the problem of the Ik: they had no reason to develop the inhibitory faculty where personal feelings were concerned. As hunter-gatherers, their lives had been very nearly as uncomplicated as those of the animals with whom they shared their hunting grounds. Placed in a situation that required a completely different set of controls, they became victims of their own destabilizing forces.

All of which suggests that, in the case of Kinzel's prisoners, 'personal space' was not the real issue. This can be grasped by repeating his experiment. The co-operation of a child will make the point even clearer. Ask the child to stand in the centre of the room, then go on all fours and advance towards him, making growling noises. The child's first reaction is amusement and pleasurable excitement. As you get nearer, the laughter develops a note of hysteria and, at a certain distance, the child will turn and run. (It may be an idea to conduct the experiment with the child's mother sitting right behind him, so that he can take refuge in her arms.) More confident children may run *at* you – a way of telling themselves that this is really only daddy.

Now reverse the situation, and take his place in the centre of the room, while some other adult crawls towards you and makes threatening noises. You will observe with interest that although you have set up the experiment, you still feel an impulse of alarm, and a release of adrenalin. To a large extent, the destabilizing mechanism is automatic.

You will also have the opportunity to note the extent to which you can apply the control mechanism. The imagined threat triggers a flight impulse and raises your inner tension. One way of releasing this tension is to give way to it. If you refuse to do this, you will be able to observe the attempts of your stabilizing mechanism – the C Force – to control the destabilizing force. You will observe that you still have a number of alternatives, depending on *how far* you choose to exert control. You can allow yourself to feel a rush of alarm, but refuse to react to it. You can actively suppress the rush of alarm. You may even be able, with a little practice, to prevent it from happening at all.

I had a recent opportunity to observe the mechanism at an amusement park, where a small cinema shows films designed to induce vertigo. The audience has to stand, and the screen is enormous and curved. Carriages surge down switchbacks; toboggans hurtle across the ice and down ski-slopes; the watchers soon begin to feel that the floor is moving underneath their feet. After twenty minutes or so I began to feel that I'd got the hang of it, and could resist the impulse to sway. Even so, the end of the film took me unaware; a car hurtles off a motorway at a tremendous speed and down the exit lane, ramming into a vehicle waiting to pull out into the traffic. My foot went automatically on the brake, and I staggered and fell into the arms of the unfortunate lady standing behind me.

What had happened is that the suddenness of the final crash pushed me beyond the point at which I had established control. Yet for the previous twenty minutes I had been establishing a higher-than-usual degree of control. Under circumstances like this – and something similar happens to city dwellers every day – we are inclined to feel that all control is 'relative' and perhaps therefore futile. And this mistake – which is so easy to make – is the essence of the criminal mentality. The criminal makes the *decision* to abandon control. He can see no sound reason why he should waste his time establishing a higher level of self-control. Let other people worry about that. The result is bad for society, but far more disastrous for himself. After all, society can absorb a little violence, but for the destabilized individual it means ultimate self-destruction.

When we observe this continual balancing operation between Force T and Force C, we can grasp its place in the evolution of our species. When deer and lemmings are overcrowded, the result is a rise in the destabilizing force which causes the adrenal glands to overwork; beyond a certain point of tension, this results in death. There is no alternative – no possibility of developing the stabilizing force. They lack the motivation. When men came together to live in cities, their motive was mutual protection. One result was the development of the abnormalities listed by Desmond Morris and the creation of the 'criminal type'. But it also led to an increase in the stabilizing force, and to a level of self-control beyond that of any other animal.

It was through this development that man made his most important discovery; that control is not simply a negative virtue. Anyone who has been forced to master some difficult technique – such as playing a musical instrument – knows that learning begins with irritation and frustration; the task seems to be as thankless as breaking in a wild horse. Then, by some unconscious process, control begins to develop. There is a cautious glow of satisfaction as we begin to scent success. Then, quite suddenly, the frustration is transformed into a feeling of power and control. It dawns upon us that when a wild horse ceases to be wild, it becomes an invaluable servant. The stabilizing force is not merely a defence system, a means of 'hanging on' over bumpy obstacles. It is a power for conquest, for changing our lives.

Once man has made this discovery, he looks around for new fields to conquer. This explains why we are the only creatures who seek out hardship for the fun of it: who climb mountains 'because they are there' and try to establish records for sailing around the world single-handed. We have discovered that an increase in Force C is a pleasure in itself. The late Ludwig Wittgenstein based his later philosophy upon a comparison of games and language, and upon the assertion that there is no element that is common to all games — say, to patience, and football, and sailing around the world single-handed. We can see that this is untrue. All games have a common purpose: to increase the stabilizing force at the expense of the destabilizing force. All games are designed to create stress, and then to give us the pleasure of controlling it. (Hence the saying that the Battle of Waterloo was won on the playing fields of Eton.) Man's chief evolutionary distinction is that he is the only creature who has learned to thrive on stress. He converts it into creativity, into productive satisfaction. The interesting result is that many people who are subject to a high level of stress are unusually healthy. A medical study at the Bell Telephone Company showed that three times as many ordinary workmen suffered from coronaries as men in higher executive positions. The reason, it was decided, is that higher executives have more 'status' than ordinary workmen, and this enables them to bear stress. An equally obvious explanation is that the executive has achieved his position by developing the ability to cope with problems and bear stress. A British study of people whose names are listed in *Who's Who* showed a similar result: the more distinguished the person, the greater seemed to be his life expectancy and the better his general level of health. And here we can see that it is not simply a negative matter of learning to 'bear stress'. The Nobel Prize winners and members of the Order of Merit had *reasons* for overcoming stress, a sense of purpose. The point is reinforced by a comment made by Dr Jeffrey Gray at a conference of the British Psychological Society in December 1981: that there is too much emphasis nowadays on lowering stress with the aid of pills. People should learn to soak up the worries of the job and build up their tolerance to pressure. Rats who were placed in stress situations and given Librium and Valium reacted less well than rats who were given no drugs. The latter were 'toughened up' and built up an immunity to stress. The lesson seems to be that all animals can develop resistance to stress; man is the only animal who has learned to use stress for his own satisfaction.

All this enables us to understand what it is that distinguishes the criminal from the rest of us. Like the rats fed on Valium, the criminal fails to develop 'stress resistance' because he habitually releases his tensions instead of learning to control them. Criminality is a short-cut, and this applies to non-violent criminals as much as to violent ones. Crime is essentially the search for 'the easy way'.

Considering our natural lack of fellow feeling, it is surprising that cities are not far more violent. This is because, strangely enough, man is not innately cruel. He is innately social; he responds to the social advances of other people with sympathy and understanding. Any two people sitting side by side on a bus can establish a bond of sympathy by merely looking in each other's eyes. It is far easier to write an angry letter than to go and say angry things to another person – because as soon as we look in one another's faces we can see the other point of view. The real paradox is that the Germans who tossed children back into the flames at Oradour were probably good husbands and affectionate fathers. The Japanese who used school-boys for bayonet practice and disembowelled a schoolgirl after raping her probably carried pictures of their own children in their knapsacks.

How is this possible? Are human beings really so much more wicked than tigers and scorpions? The answer was provided by a series of experiments at Harvard conducted by Professor Stanley Milgram. His aim was to see whether 'ordinary people' could be persuaded to inflict torture. They were told that the experiment was to find out whether punishment could increase someone's learning capacity. The method was to connect the victim to an electric shock machine, then ask the subject to administer shocks of increasing strength. The 'victim' was actually an actor who could scream convincingly. The subject was told that the shock would cause no permanent damage but was then give a 'sample' shock of 45 volts to prove that the whole thing was genuine. And the majority of these 'ordinary people' allowed themselves to be persuaded to keep on increasing the shocks up to 500 volts, in spite of horrifying screams, convulsions and pleas for mercy. Only a few refused to go on. In writing up his results in a book called *Obedience to Authority*, Milgram points the moral by quoting an American soldier who took part in the My Lai massacre in Vietnam and who described how, when ordered by Lieutenant Calley, he turned his sub-machine gun on men, women and children including babies. The news inter-viewer asked: 'How do you, a father, shoot babies?' and received the reply: 'I don't know – it's just one of those things.'

And these words suddenly enable us to see precisely why human beings are capable of this kind of behaviour. It is because we have *minds*, and these minds can overrule our instincts. An animal cannot disobey its instinct; human beings disobey theirs a hundred times a day. Living in a modern city, with its impersonality and overcrowding, is already a basic violation of natural instinct. So when Lieutenant Calley told the man to shoot women and children, he did what civilization had taught him to do since childhood – allowed his mind to overrule his instinct.

The rape of Nanking illustrates the same point. Rhodes Farmer wrote in *Shanghai Harvest, A Diary of Three Years in the China War* (published in 1945): 'To the Japanese soldiers at the end of four months of hard fighting, Nanking promised a last fling of debauchery before they returned to their highly disciplined lives back home in Japan.' But this shows a failure to understand the Japanese character. The *Japanese Yearbook* for 1946 comes closer when it says: 'By 7 December, the outer defences of Nanking were under attack, and a week later, Japanese anger at the stubborn Chinese defence of Shanghai burst upon Nanking in an appalling reign of terror.' In fact, the Chinese resistance – ever since their unexpected stand at Lukouchiao in July 1937 – had caused the Japanese to 'lose face', and they were in a hard and unforgiving mood when they entered Nanking. But then, we also need to understand why this loss of face mattered so much, and this involves understanding the deep religious traditionalism of the Japanese character. The historian Arnold Toynbee has pointed out, in *East to West* (pp. 69–71) that if the town of Bromsgrove had happened to be in Japan, the Japanese would know exactly why it was so named, because they would have maintained a sacred grove to the memory of the war-god Bron. And there would probably be a Buddhist temple next door to the pagan shrine, and the priest and the parson of the temple would be on excellent terms. When, in the nineteenth century, the Japanese decided to 'Westernize', they poured all this religious emotion into the cult of the emperor, who was worshipped as a god. The war that began in 1937, and ended in 1945 with the dropping of two atom bombs, was an upsurge of intense patriotic feeling similar to the Nazi upsurge in Germany. The outnumbered Japanese troops felt they were fighting for their emperor-god, and that their cause was just. *This* is why the stubborn Chinese resistance placed them in such an unforgiving frame of mind. Like Milgram's subjects, they felt they were administering a salutary shock-treatment; but in this case, anger turned insensitivity into cruelty.

Wells, oddly enough, failed to grasp this curiously impersonal element in human cruelty. Having seized upon the notion that slum conditions produce frustration, he continues with a lengthy analysis of human cruelty and sadism, citing as typical the case of Marshal Gilles de Rais, who killed over two hundred children in sexual orgies in the fifteenth century. In fact, de Rais's perversions throw very little light on the nature of ordinary human beings, whose sexual tastes are more straightforward. The Japanese who burnt Nanking, the Germans who destroyed Oradour, were not sexual perverts; they had probably never done anything of the sort before, and would never do anything of the sort again. They were simply releasing their aggression in obedience to authority.

Fromm is inclined to make the same mistake. He recognizes 'conformist aggression' – aggression under orders – but feels that human destructiveness is better explained by what he calls 'malignant aggression' – that is, by sadism. Sadism he defines as the desire to have absolute power over a living being, to have a god-like control. He cites both Himmler and Stalin as examples of sadism, pointing out that both could, at times, show great kindness and consideration. They became ruthless *only when their absolute authority was questioned*. But this hardly explains the human tendency to destroy their fellows in war. So Fromm is forced to postulate another kind of 'malignant aggression', which he calls 'necrophilia'. By this, he meant roughly what Freud meant by 'thanatos' or the death-urge – the human urge to self-destruction. Freud had invented the 'death wish' at the time of the First World War in an attempt to explain the slaughter. It was not one of his most convincing ideas, and many of his disciples received it with reservations – after all, anyone can see that most suicides are committed in a state of muddle and confusion, in which a person feels that life is not worth living; so the underlying instinct is for more life, not less. Even a romantic like Keats, who feels he is 'half in love with easeful death', is in truth confusing the idea of extinction with that of sleep and rest. If human beings really have an urge to self-destruction, they manage to conceal it very well.

Fromm nevertheless adopts the Freudian death-wish. He cites a Spanish Civil War general, one of whose favourite slogans was 'Long live death!' The same man once shouted at a liberal intellectual: 'Down with intelligence!' From this, Fromm argues that militarism has an anti-life element that might be termed necrophilia. But he demolishes his own case by citing two genuine examples of necrophilia from a medical textbook on sexual perversion: both morgue attendants who enjoyed violating female corpses. One of them described how, from the time of adolescence, he masturbated while caressing the bodies of attractive females, then graduated to having intercourse with them. Which raises the question: is this genuinely a case of necrophilia, which means sexual desire *directed towards death*? Many highly-sexed teenage boys might do the same, given the opportunity. It is not an interest in death as such, but in sex. A genuine necrophile would be one who preferred corpses *because* they were dead. One of the best known cases of necrophilia, Sergeant Bertrand (whom I discussed in Chapter 6 of my *Origins of the Sexual Impulse*) was not, in this sense, a true necrophile; for although he dug up and violated newly buried corpses, he also had mistresses who testified to his sexual potency. He is simply an example of a virile man who needed more sex than he could get.

So Fromm's whole argument about 'necrophilia', and his lengthy demonstration that Hitler was a necrophiliac, collapses under closer analysis. The Spanish general was certainly not a necrophile by any common definition: he was using death in a rather special sense, meaning idealistic self-sacrifice for the good of one's country. He certainly has nothing whatever in common with a morgue attendant violating female corpses. Hitler was undoubtedly destructive, but there is no evidence that he was self-destructive or had a secret death wish. On the contrary, he was a romantic dreamer who believed that his thousand-year Reich was an expression of health, vitality and sanity. Fromm's 'necrophilia', like Wells's notion of cruelty, fails to provide a satisfactory explanation of human cruelty; it is not universal enough.

The notion of 'losing face' suggests an interesting alternative line of thought. It is obviously connected, for example, with the cruelty of Himmler and Stalin when their absolute authority was questioned. They were both men with a touchy sense of self-esteem, so that their response to any suspected insult was vindictive rage. Another characteristic of both men was a conviction that they were always right, and a total inability to admit that they might ever be wrong.

Himmlers and Stalins are, fortunately, rare; but the type is surprisingly common. The credit for recognizing this goes to A. E. Van Vogt, a writer of science fiction who is also the author of a number of brilliant psychological studies. Van Vogt's concept of the

'Right Man' or 'violent man' is so important to the understanding of criminality that it deserves to be considered at length, and in this connection I am indebted to Van Vogt for providing me with a series of five talks broadcast on KPFK radio in 1965. Like his earlier pamphlet *A Report on the Violent Male*, these have never been printed in book form.

In 1954, Van Vogt began work on a war novel called *The Violent Man*, which was set in a Chinese prison camp. The commandant of the camp is one of those savagely authoritarian figures who would instantly, and without hesitation, order the execution of anyone who challenges his authority. Van Vogt was creating the type from observation of men like Hitler and Stalin. And, as he thought about the murderous behaviour of the commandant, he found himself wondering: 'What could motivate a man like that?' Why is it that some men believe that anyone who contradicts them is either dishonest or downright wicked? Do they really believe, in their heart of hearts, that they are gods who are incapable of being fallible? If so, are they in some sense insane, like a man who thinks he is Julius Caesar?

Looking around for examples, it struck Van Vogt that male authoritarian behaviour is far too commonplace to be regarded as insanity. Newspaper headlines tell their own story:

HUSBAND INVADES CHRISTMAS PARTY AND SHOOTS WIFE
Grief stricken when she refuses to return to him, he claims.

ENTERTAINER STABS WIFE TO DEATH – UNFAITHFUL HE SAYS
Amazed friends say he was unfaithful, not she.

WIFE RUN OVER IN STREET
Accident says divorced husband held on suspicion of murder.

WIFE BADLY BEATEN BY FORMER HUSBAND
'Unfit mother,' he accuses. Neighbours refute charge and call him a troublemaker.

HUSBAND FOILED IN ATTEMPT TO PUSH WIFE OVER CLIFF
Wife reconciles, convinced husband loves her.

Marriage seems to bring out the 'authoritarian' personality in many males, according to Van Vogt's observation. He brought up the question with a psychologist friend and asked him whether he could offer any examples. The psychologist told him of an interesting case of a husband who had brought his wife along for psychotherapy. He had set her up in a suburban home, and supported her on condition that she had no male friends. Her role, as he saw it, was simply to be a good mother to their son.

The story of their marriage was as follows. She had been a nurse, and when her future husband proposed to her she had felt she ought to admit to previous affairs with two doctors. The man went almost insane with jealousy, and she was convinced that was the end of it. But the next day he appeared with a legal document, which he insisted she should sign if the marriage was to go ahead. He would not allow her to read it. Van Vogt speculates that it contained a 'confession' that she was an immoral woman, and that as he was virtually raising her from the gutter by marrying her, she had no legal rights . . .

They married, and she soon became aware of her mistake. Her husband's business involved travelling, so she never knew where he was. He visited women employees in their apartments for hours and spent an unconscionable amount of time driving secretaries home. If she tried to question him about this he would fly into a rage and often knock her about. In fact, he was likely to respond to questions he regarded as 'impertinent' by knocking her down. The following day he might call her long distance and beg her forgiveness, promising never to do it again.

His wife became frigid. They divorced, yet he continued to do his best to treat her as his personal property, determined to restrict her freedom. When this caused anger and stress, he told her she ought to see a psychiatrist – which is how they came to Van Vogt's friend.

 The case is a good example of what Van Vogt came to call 'the violent man' or the 'Right Man'. He is a man driven by a manic need for self-esteem – to feel he is a 'somebody'. He is obsessed by the question of 'losing face', so will never, under any circumstances, admit that he might be in the wrong. This man's attempt to convince his wife that she was insane is typical.

Equally interesting is the wild, insane jealousy. Most of us are subject to jealousy, since the notion that someone we care about prefers someone else is an assault on our *amour propre*. But the Right Man, whose self-esteem is like a constantly festering sore spot, flies into a frenzy at the thought, and becomes capable of murder.

Van Vogt points out that the Right Man is an 'idealist' – that is, he lives in his own mental world and does his best to ignore aspects of reality that conflict with it. Like the Communists' rewriting of history, reality can always be 'adjusted' later to fit his glorified picture of himself. In his mental world, women are delightful, adoring, faithful creatures who wait patiently for the right man – in both senses of the word – before they surrender their virginity. He is living in a world of adolescent fantasy. No doubt there was something gentle and submissive about the nurse that made her seem the ideal person to bolster his self-esteem, the permanent wife and mother who is waiting in a clean apron when he gets back from a weekend with a mistress . . .

Perhaps Van Vogt's most intriguing insight into the Right Man was his discovery that he can be destroyed if 'the worm turns' – that is, if his wife or some dependant leaves *him*. Under such circumstances, he may beg and plead, promising to behave better in the future. If that fails, there may be alcoholism, drug addiction, even suicide. She has kicked away the foundations of his sandcastle. For when a Right Man finds a woman who seems submissive and admiring, it deepens his self-confidence, fills him with a sense of his own worth. (We can see the mechanism in operation with Ian Brady and Myra Hindley.) No matter how badly he treats her, he has to keep on believing that, in the last analysis, she recognizes him as the most remarkable man she will ever meet. She is the guarantee of his 'primacy', his uniqueness; now it doesn't matter what the rest of the world thinks. He may desert her and his children; that only proves how 'strong' he is, how indifferent to the usual sentimentality. But if she deserts him, he has been pushed back to square one: the helpless child in a hostile universe. 'Most violent men are failures', says Van Vogt; so to desert them is to hand them over to their own worst suspicions about themselves. It is this recognition that leads Van Vogt to write: 'Realize that most Right Men deserve some sympathy, for they are struggling with an almost unbelievable inner horror; however, if they give way to the impulse to hit or choke, they are losing the battle, and are on the way to the ultimate disaster . . . of their subjective universe of self-justification.'

And what happens when the Right Man is *not* a failure, when his 'uniqueness' is acknowledged by the world? Oddly enough, it makes little or no difference. His problem is lack of emotional control and a deep-seated sense of inferiority; so success cannot reach the parts of the mind that are the root of the problem. A recent (1981) biography of the actor Peter Sellers (*P.S. I Love You* by his son Michael) reveals that he was a typical Right Man. Totally spoiled by his mother as a child, he grew into a man who flew into tantrums if he could not have his own way. He had endless affairs with actresses, yet remained morbidly jealous of his wife, ringing her several times a day to check on her movements, and interrogating her if she left the house. She had been an actress; he forced her to give it up to devote herself to being a 'good wife and mother'. As his destructive fits of rage and affairs with actresses broke up the marriage, he convinced himself that he wanted to be rid of her, and persuaded her to go out with another man. But when she told him she wanted a divorce, he burst into tears and threatened to jump from the penthouse balcony. ('This was not the first time he had spoken of suicide. This was always his crutch in a crisis.')

The morbid sense of inferiority emerged in the company of anyone who had been to public school or university. When, at dinner with Princess Margaret, the conversation turned to Greek mythology, he excused himself as if to go to the bathroom but phoned his secretary and made her look in reference books and quickly brief him on the subject. Then he went back to the dinner table and casually dropped references to mythology into his conversation. His son adds: 'I saw him engage in this ploy on many occasions.'

Another typical anecdote shows the borderline between normal and 'Right Man' behaviour. The children's nanny was a strong-minded woman of definite opinions; one evening, Sellers had a violent disagreement with her and stormed out of the house; he went and booked himself into the RAC Club for the night. From there he rang his wife and said: 'What the bloody hell am I doing here? If anybody's going to leave, it's that bloody nanny.' He rushed back home, seized a carving knife and drove it into the panel of her bedroom door, shouting 'I'll kill you, you cow.' The nanny jumped out of the window and vanished from their lives.

Sellers's behaviour in storming out of the house could be regarded as normal; in leaving her on the battlefield he was acknowledging that she might be right. In the club, his emotions boil over as he broods on it; by the time he has reached home, he has convinced himself that he is right and she is wrong, and explodes into paranoid rage. Whether the threat to kill her was serious should be regarded as an open question. The Right Man hates losing face; if he suspects that his threats are not being taken seriously, he is capable of carrying them out, purely for the sake of appearances.

Van Vogt makes the basic observation that the central characteristic of the Right Man is the 'decision to be out of control, in some particular area'. We all have to learn self-control to deal with the real world and other people. But with some particular person – a mother, a wife, a child – we may decide that this effort is not necessary and allow ourselves to explode. But – and here we come to the very heart of the matter – this decision creates, so to speak, a permanent weakpoint in the boiler, the point at which it always bursts. The *Family Chronicle* by Sergei Aksakov provides an apt illustration: Aksakov is talking about his grandfather, an old Russian landowner.

And this noble, magnanimous, often-self-restrained man – whose character presented an image of the loftiest human nature – was subject to fits of rage in which he was capable of the most barbarous cruelty. I recollect having seen him in one of those mad fits in my earliest childhood. I see him now. He was angry with one of his daughters, who had lied to him and persisted in the lie. There he stood, supported by two servants (for his legs refused their office); I could hardly recognize him as my grandfather; he trembled in every limb, his features were distorted, and the frenzy of rage glared from his infuriated eyes. 'Give her to me,' he howled in a strangled voice . . . My grandmother threw herself at his feet, beseeching him to have pity and forbearance, but in the next instant, off flew her kerchief and cap, and Stephan Mikhailovich seized on his corpulent and already aged better half by the hair of her head. Meanwhile, the culprit as well as all her sisters – and even her brother with his young wife and little son [Aksakov himself] had fled into the woods behind the house; and there they remained all night; only the young daughter-in-law crept home with the child, fearing he might take cold, and slept with him in the servants' quarters. My grandfather raved and stormed about the empty house to his heart's content. At last he grew too tired to drag his poor old Arina Vasilievna about by her plaits, and fell exhausted upon his bed, where a deep sleep overpowered him, which lasted until the following morning. He awoke calm and in a good humour, and called to his Arishka in a cheery tone. My grandmother immediately ran in to him from an adjoining room, just as if nothing had happened the day before. 'Give me some tea! Where are the children? Where are Alexei and his wife? Bring little Sergei to me!' said the erstwhile lunatic, now that he had slept off his rage.

Aksakov sees his grandfather as a 'noble, magnanimous, often self-restrained man' – so he *is* capable of self-restraint. But in this one area of his life, his control over his family, he has made 'the decision to be out of control'. It is provoked by his daughter persisting in a lie. This infuriates him; he feels she is treating him with *lack of respect* in assuming he can be duped. So he explodes and drags his wife around by the hair. He feels no shame later about his behaviour; his merriness the next morning shows that his good opinion of himself is unaffected. He feels he was *justified* in exploding, like an angry god. Like the Japanese soldiers in Nanking, he feels he is inflicting just punishment.

What is so interesting here is the way the Right Man's violent emotion reinforces his sense of being justified, and his sense of justification increases his rage. He is locked into a kind of vicious spiral, and he cannot escape until he has spent his fury. Peter Sellers's son records that his father was capable of smashing every item in a room, including keepsakes that he had been collecting for years. The Right Man feels that his rage is a storm that has to be allowed to blow itself out, no matter what damage it causes. But this also means that he is the slave of an impulse he cannot control; his property, even the lives of those he loves, are at the mercy of his emotions. This is part of the 'unbelievable inner horror' that Van Vogt talks about.

This tendency to allow our emotions to reinforce our sense of being justified is a basic part of the psychology of violence, and therefore of crime. We cannot understand cruelty without understanding this particular mechanism. We find it incomprehensible, for example, that a mother could batter her own baby to death, simply because he is crying; yet it happens thousands of times every year. We fail to grasp that she is already close to her 'bursting point' and that, as the baby cries, she feels that it is wicked and malevolent, trying to drive her to distraction. Suddenly her rage has *transformed* it from a helpless baby into a screaming devil that deserves to be beaten. It is as if some wicked fairy had waved a magic wand and turned it into a demon. We would say that it is the mother who is turned into a demon; yet her rage acts as a kind of *magic* that 'transforms' the child.

The word 'magic' was first used in this sense – meaning a form of self-deception – by Jean-Paul Sartre in an early book, *A Sketch of a Theory of the Emotions*. In later work Sartre preferred to speak of '*mauvaise foi*' or self-deception; but there are some ways in which the notion of 'magical thinking' is more precise. Malcolm Muggeridge has an anecdote that illustrates the concept perfectly. He quotes a newspaper item about birth control in Asian countries, which said that the World Health Organization had issued strings containing twenty-eight beads to illiterate peasant women. There were seven amber beads, seven red ones, seven more amber beads, and seven green ones; the women were told to move a bead every day. 'Many women thought that merit resided in the beads, and moved them around to suit themselves,' said the newspaper.

This is 'magical thinking' – allowing a desire or emotion to convince you of something your reason tells you to be untrue. In 1960, a labourer named Patrick Byrne entered a women's hostel in Birmingham and attacked several women, decapitating one of them; he explained later that he wanted to 'get his revenge on women for causing him sexual tension'. This again is magical thinking. So was Charles Manson's assertion that he was not guilty because 'society' was guilty of bombing Vietnam. And Sartre offers the example of a girl who is about to be attacked by a man and who faints – a 'magical' attempt to make him go away. This is a good example because it reminds us that 'magic' can be a purely *physical* reaction. Magical thinking provides a key to the Right Man.

What causes 'right mannishness'? Van Vogt suggests that it is because the world has always been dominated by males. In Italy in 1961, two women were sentenced to prison for adultery. Their defence was that their husbands had mistresses, and that so do many Italian men. The court overruled their appeal. In China in 1950, laws were passed to give women more freedom; in 1954, there were ten thousand murders of wives in one district alone by husbands who objected to their attempts to take advantage of these laws.

But then, this explanation implies that there is no such thing as a Right Woman – in fact, Van Vogt says as much. This is untrue. There may be fewer Right Women than Right Men, but they still exist. The mother of the novelist Turgenev had many of her serfs flogged to death – a clear example of the 'magical transfer' of rage. Elizabeth Duncan, a Californian divorcee, was so outraged when her son married a nurse, Olga Kupczyk, against her wishes, that she hired two young thugs to kill her; moreover, when the killers tried to persuade her to hand over the promised fee, she went to the police and reported them for blackmail – the action that led to the death of all three in the San Quentin gas chamber. Again, this is a clear case of 'magical' – that is to say, totally unrealistic – thinking. And it shows that the central characteristic of the Right Woman is the same as that of the Right Man: that she is convinced that having her own way is a law of nature, and that anyone who opposes this deserves the harshest possible treatment. It is the god (or goddess) syndrome.

Van Vogt also believes that Adler's 'organ inferiority' theory may throw some light on right mannishness. Adler suggests that if some organ – the heart, liver, kidneys – is damaged early in life, it may send messages of inferiority to the brain, causing an inferiority complex. This in turn, says Van Vogt, could lead to the over-compensatory behaviour of the Right Man. He could well be right. Yet this explanation seems to imply that being a Right Man is rather like being colour blind or asthmatic – that it can be explained in purely medical terms. And the one thing that becomes obvious in all case histories of Right Men is that their attacks are *not* somehow 'inevitable'; some of their worst misdemeanours are carefully planned and calculated, and determinedly carried out. The Right Man does these things because he thinks they will help him to achieve his own way, which is what interests him.

And this in turn makes it plain that the Right Man problem is a problem of *highly dominant* people. Dominance is a subject of enormous interest to biologists and zoologists because the percentage of dominant animals – or human beings – seems to be amazingly constant. Bernard Shaw once asked the explorer H. M. Stanley how many other men could take over leadership of the expedition if Stanley himself fell ill; Stanley replied promptly: 'One in twenty.' 'Is that exact or approximate?' asked Shaw. 'Exact.' And biological studies have confirmed this as a fact. For some odd reason, precisely five per cent – one in twenty – of any animal group are dominant have leadership qualities. During the Korean war, the Chinese made the interesting discovery that if they separated out the dominant five per cent of American prisoners of war, and kept them in a separate compound, the remaining ninety-five per cent made no attempt to escape.

This is something that must obviously be taken into account in considering Becker's argument that all human beings have a craving for 'heroism', for 'primacy', which seems difficult to reconcile with our fairly stable society, in which most people seem to accept their lack of primacy. This could be, as Becker suggests, because we lose the feeling of primacy as we grow up; but anyone who has ever spent ten minutes waiting for his children in a nursery school will know that the majority of children also seem to accept their lack of 'primacy'. The 'dominant five per cent' applies to children as well as adults.

Now in terms of society, five per cent is an enormous number; for

not in present form (assembly)

example, in England in the 1980s it amounts to more than three million people. And society has no room for three million 'leaders'. This means, inevitably, that a huge proportion of the dominant five per cent are never going to achieve any kind of 'uniqueness'. They are going to spend their lives in positions that are indistinguishable from those of the non-dominant remainder.

In a society with a strong class-structure – peasants and aristocrats, rich and poor – this is not particularly important. The dominant farm-labourer will be content as the village blacksmith or leader of the church choir; he does not expect to become lord of the manor, and he doesn't resent it if the lord of the manor is far less dominant than he is. But in a society like ours, where working-class boys become pop-idols and where we see our leaders on television every day, the situation is altogether less stable. The 'average' member of the dominant five per cent sees no reason why he should not be rich and famous too. He experiences anger and frustration at his lack of 'primacy', and is willing to consider unorthodox methods of elbowing his way to the fore. This clearly explains a great deal about the rising levels of crime and violence in our society.

We can also see how large numbers of these dominant individuals develop into 'Right Men'. In every school with five hundred pupils, there are about twenty-five dominant ones struggling for primacy. Some of these have natural advantages: they are good athletes, good scholars, good debaters. (And there are, of course, plenty of non-dominant pupils who are gifted enough to carry away some of the prizes.) Inevitably, a percentage of the dominant pupils have no particular talent or gift; some may be downright stupid. How is such a person to satisfy his urge to primacy? He will, inevitably, choose to express his dominance in any ways that are possible. If he has good looks or charm, he may be satisfied with the admiration of female pupils. If he has some specific talent which is not regarded as important by his schoolmasters – a good ear for music, a natural gift of observation, a vivid imagination – he may become a lonely 'outsider', living in his own private world. (Such individuals may develop into Schuberts, Darwins, Balzacs.) But it is just as likely that he will try to take short-cuts to prominence and become a bully, a cheat or a delinquent.

The main problem of these ungifted 'outsiders' is that they are bound to feel that the world has treated them unfairly. And the normal human reaction to a sense of unfairness is an upsurge of self-pity. <u>Self-pity and the sense of injustice make them vulnerable and unstable</u>. And we have only to observe such people to see that they are usually their own worst enemies. Their moods alternate between aggressiveness and sulkiness, both of which alienate those who might otherwise be glad to help them. If they possess some degree of charm or intelligence, they may succeed in making themselves acceptable to other people; but sooner or later the resentment and self-pity break through, and lead to mistrust and rejection.

The very essence of their problem is the question of self-discipline. Dominant human beings are more impatient than others, because they have more vital energy. Impatience leads them to look for short-cuts. When Peter Sellers booked into the RAC Club, he could just as easily have phoned his wife, told her to give the nanny two months wages and sack her, and then got a good night's sleep. Instead, he behaved in a way that could have caused serious problems for everybody. It is easy to see that if Sellers's life, from the age of five, consisted of similar short-cuts, by the time he was an adult he would lack the basic equipment to become a normal member of society. Civilization, as Freud pointed out, demands self-discipline on the part of its members. No one can be licensed to threaten people with carving knives.

All this places us in a better position to answer Fromm's question: why is man the only creature who kills and tortures members of his own species without any reason? The answer does not lie in his genetic inheritance, nor in some hypothetical death-wish, but in the human need for self-assertion, the craving for 'primacy'.

The behaviour of the Right Man enables us to see how this comes about. His feeling that he 'counts' more than anyone else leads him to acts of violent self-assertion. But this violence, by its very nature, cannot achieve any long-term objective. Beethoven once flung a dish of lung soup in the face of a waiter who annoyed him – typical Right Man behaviour. But Beethoven did not rely upon violence to assert his 'primacy'; he realized that his long-term objective could only be achieved by patience and self-discipline: that is to say, by *canalizing* his energy (another name for impatience) and directing it in a jet, like a fireman's hose, into his music. Long discipline deepened the canal banks until, in the final works, not a drop of energy was wasted.

When the Right Man explodes into violence, *all* the energy is wasted. Worse still, it destroys the banks of the canal. So in permitting himself free expression of his negative emotions he is indulging in a process of slow but sure self-erosion – the emotional counterpart of physical incontinence. Without proper 'drainage', his inner being turns into a kind of swamp or sewage farm. This is why most of the violent men of history, from Alexander the Great to Stalin, have ended up as psychotics. Without the power to control their negative emotions, they become incapable of any state of sustained well-being.

If we are to achieve a true understanding of the nature of criminality, this is the problem that must be plumbed to its depths: the problem of the psychology of self-destruction.

Three

THE PSYCHOLOGY OF SELF-DESTRUCTION

In March 1981, Norman Mailer wrote an introduction to a volume of letters by a convicted killer, Jack Henry Abbott, *In the Belly of the Beast*. Abbott had written to Mailer from prison, and his letters convinced Mailer that this was a man with something important to say about violence. At thirty-seven, Abbott had spent a quarter of a century behind bars – for cheque offences, bank robbery, murder. In solitary confinement he had read history and literature, and become converted to Communism. Mailer convinced the prison authorities that Abbott had 'the makings of a powerful and important American writer' and that he could make a living from his pen. Abbott was paroled. The book was published and became a best seller. A few weeks later, in a New York restaurant, he became involved in an argument with a waiter – an out-of-work actor named Richard Adan – when Adan told him he was not allowed to use the staff toilet. Abbott quietly asked Adan if they could go outside to resolve the incident; there he produced a knife and stabbed him in the heart. After several months on the run, he was caught, and returned to prison – where, presumably, he will now spend the rest of his life.

The murder seems incomprehensible. If Abbott had become involved in a fight with Adan, and pulled a knife in the heat of the moment, it would be easy enough to understand – Abbott had become accustomed to violence and split-second reactions. But when he quietly asked his two female companions to wait, and walked outside, he must have known that he intended to kill Adan. He must also have known that he was throwing away all he had managed to achieve. Yet this was the man who wrote: 'I have been desperate to escape for so many years now, it is routine for me to try to escape. My eyes, my brain, seek out escape routes wherever I am sent.'

Abbott's book is a depressing document; it is easy to see why Mailer felt so much sympathy. After a childhood spent in foster

homes – presumably because his parents had deserted him – Abbott
was sent to a reformatory at the age of twelve for failure to adjust to
foster homes. At eighteen he was sent to jail for writing a dud
cheque; he escaped and robbed a bank, and received another
sentence. When he killed a fellow inmate in a fight he was sentenced
to another fourteen years. The rage and frustration are understandable. He describes how he would spend whole days kicking the walls
of his cell and screaming with rage. 'I was so choked with rage . . . I
could hardly talk, even when I was calm; I stuttered badly. I used to
throw my tray as casually as you would toss a balled-up scrap of
paper in a trash can – but would do it with a tray full of food at the
face of a guard.' When being sentenced for killing the other
prisoner, he threw a pitcher of water at the face of the judge. He
wrote of the warders: 'The pigs in the state and federal prisons . . .
treat me so violently, I cannot possibly imagine a time I could have
anything but the deepest, aching, searing hatred for them. I can't
begin to tell you what they do to me. If I were weaker by a hair, they
would destroy me.'

But the implication – that the violence was a response to intolerable pressures – is contradicted by his tendency to romanticize the
criminal. 'There is something else . . . it is the mantle of pride,
integrity, honour. It is the high esteem we naturally have for
violence, force. It is what makes us effective, men whose judgement
impinges on others, on the world. Dangerous killers who act alone
and without emotion, who act with calculation and principles with
acts of murder . . . that usually evade prosecution by law: this is a
state-raised convict's conception of manhood in the highest sense.'
But this is a schoolboy's conception of heroism. It makes us aware
that the talk about 'manhood in the highest sense' is romantic
verbiage. A dead waiter lying on the pavement is hardly a proof of
pride, integrity and honour; killing Richard Adan was about as
heroic as strangling a baby.

The killing only becomes understandable when we recall Van
Vogt's comment on the violent man: that he has made the *decision* to
be out of control in a particular area. Abbott made the decision to be
out of control in the area of wounds to his self-esteem (and no doubt
the presence of two women companions reinforced the decision). In
short, we are back in the realm of 'magical thinking' – that is,
thinking in which an emotion has been allowed to distort the sense of
reality. The result of magical thinking is some completely inappropri-

ate action that cannot possibly achieve the desired result – like the ostrich burying its head in the sand to make the enemy 'go away' (in fact, a gross libel on the ostrich, but an apt simile all the same). There is always an absurd, slightly comic element in magical thinking, like Bernard Shaw's description of his father 'with an imperfectly wrapped-up goose under one arm and a ham in the same condition under the other . . . butting at the garden wall in the belief that he was pushing open the gate, and transforming his tall hat into a concertina in the process . . .' But only for the onlooker. For the man beating his head against the brick wall, or the bee hurtling itself at the windowpane, the situation is grimly serious.

In a sense, the bee is behaving perfectly logically; it is only trying to escape towards the light, and can see no reason why it should not do so. We can see that one of its basic premises – that light cannot pass through solid objects – is mistaken, and that if it wants to achieve its objective it must change its direction. But the bee, conditioned by millions of years of evolution, is in no position to revise its instinct.

Human beings *can* change direction – which is why the behaviour of the violent man strikes us as so absurd. He seems determined to smash his way through the sheet of glass or destroy himself in the process. Yet to him this is not self-destruction so much as his own stubborn and quirky notion of courage. *The violent man's problem lies in his own logic* – that is, in his concept of what is a normal and rational response to the challenges of his existence. The premises of this logic contain a mistaken assumption – like the bee's assumption that the windowpane is unreal because it is invisible.

Abbott offers us a clue to his own premises in the list of men to whom he dedicates the book. Most of them are 'criminal rebels', and the first on the list is Carl Panzram, whose career exemplifies the logic of self-destruction.

Panzram, like Abbott, became a writer in prison; but in 1928 his autobiography was regarded as too horrifying to publish and had to wait more than forty years before it finally appeared in print. Panzram was awaiting trial for housebreaking; his confession revealed him as one of the worst mass murderers in American criminal history. The odd thing is that most of these murders were 'motiveless'. He killed out of resentment, a desire for revenge on society. Panzram's basic philosophy was that life is a bad joke and that most human beings are too stupid or corrupt to live.

His is a classic case of a man beating his head against a brick wall. His father, a Minnesota farmer, had deserted the family when Carl was a child. At eleven, Carl burgled the house of a well-to-do neighbour and was sent to reform school. He was a rebellious boy and was violently beaten. Because he was a 'dominant male', the beatings only deepened the desire to avenge the injustice. He would have agreed with the painter Gauguin who said: 'Life being what it is, one dreams of revenge.'

Travelling around the country on freight trains, the young Panzram was sexually violated by four hoboes. The experience suggested a new method of expressing his aggression. '. . . whenever I met [a hobo] who wasn't too rusty looking I would make him raise his hands and drop his pants. I wasn't very particular either. I rode them old and young, tall and short, white and black.' When a brakesman caught Panzram and two other hoboes in a railway truck Panzram drew his revolver and raped the man, then forced the other two hoboes to do the same at gunpoint. It was his way of telling 'authority' what he thought of it.

Panzram lived by burglary, mugging and robbing churches. He spent a great deal of time in prison, but became a skilled escapist. But he had his own peculiar sense of loyalty. After breaking jail in Salem, Oregon, he broke in again to try to rescue a safe blower named Cal Jordan; he was caught and got thirty days. 'The thanks I got from old Cal was that he thought I was in love with him and he tried to mount me, but I wasn't broke to ride and he was, so I rode him. At that time he was about fifty years old and I was twenty or twenty-one, but I was strong and he was weak.'

In various prisons, he became known as one of the toughest troublemakers ever encountered. What drove him to his most violent frenzies was a sense of injustice. In Oregon he was offered a minimal sentence if he would reveal the whereabouts of the stolen goods; Panzram kept his side of the bargain but was sentenced to seven years. He managed to escape from his cell and wreck the jail, burning furniture and mattresses. They beat him up and sent him to the toughest prison in the state. There he promptly threw the contents of a chamberpot in a guard's face; he was beaten unconscious and chained to the door of a dark cell for thirty days, where he screamed defiance. He aided another prisoner to escape, and in the hunt the warden was shot dead. The new warden was tougher than ever. Panzram burned down the prison workshop and later a flax mill. Given a job in the kitchen, he went berserk with an axe. He incited the other prisoners to revolt, and the atmosphere became so tense that guards would not venture into the yard. Finally, the warden was dismissed.

The new warden, a man named Murphy, was an idealist who believed that prisoners would respond to kindness. When Panzram was caught trying to escape, Murphy sent for him and told him that, according to reports, he was 'the meanest and most cowardly degenerate that they had ever seen.' When Panzram agreed, Murphy astonished him by telling him that he would let him walk out of the jail if he would swear to return in time for supper. Panzram agreed – with no intention of keeping his word; but when supper time came, something made him go back. Gradually, Murphy increased his freedom, and that of the other prisoners. But one night, Panzram got drunk with a pretty nurse and decided to abscond. Recaptured after a gun battle, he was thrown into the punishment cell, and Murphy's humanitarian regime came to an abrupt end.

This experience seems to have been something of a turning point. So far, Panzram had been against the world, but not against himself. His betrayal of Murphy's trust seems to have set up a reaction of self-hatred. He escaped from prison again, stole a yacht, and began his career of murder. He would offer sailors a job and take them to the stolen yacht; there he would rob them, commit sodomy, and throw their bodies into the sea. 'They are there yet, ten of 'em.' Then he went to West Africa to work for an oil company, where he soon lost his job for committing sodomy on the table waiter. The US Consul declined to help him and he sat down in a park 'to think things over'. 'While I was sitting there, a little nigger boy about eleven or twelve years came bumming around. He was looking for something. He found it too. I took him out to a gravel pit a quarter of a mile from the main camp . . . I left him there, but first I committed sodomy on him and then killed him. His brains were coming out of his ears when I left him and he will never be any deader . . .

'Then I went to town, bought a ticket on the Belgian steamer to Lobito Bay down the coast. There I hired a canoe and six niggers and went out hunting in the bay and backwaters. I was looking for crocodiles. I found them, plenty. They were all hungry. I fed them. I shot all six of those niggers and dumped 'em in. The crocks done the rest. I stole their canoe and went back to town, tied the canoe to a dock, and that night someone stole the canoe from me.'

Back in America he raped and killed three more boys, bringing his murders up to twenty. After five years of rape, robbery and arson, Panzram was caught as he robbed the express office in Larchmont, New York and sent to one of America's toughest prisons, Dannemora. 'I hated everybody I saw.' And again more defiance, more beatings. Like a stubborn child, he had decided to turn his life into a competition to see whether he could take more beatings than society could hand out. In Dannemora he leapt from a high gallery, fracturing a leg, and walked for the rest of his life with a limp. He spent his days brooding on schemes of revenge against the whole human race: how to blow up a railway tunnel with a train in it, how to poison a whole city by putting arsenic into the water supply, even how to cause a war between England and America by blowing up a British battleship in American waters.

It was during this period in jail that Panzram met a young Jewish guard named Henry Lesser. Lesser was a shy man who enjoyed prison work because it conferred automatic status, which eased his inferiority complex. Lesser was struck by Panzram's curious immobility, a quality of cold detachment. When he asked him: 'What's your racket?' Panzram replied with a curious smile: 'What I do is reform people.' After brooding on this, Lesser went back to ask him how he did it; Panzram replied that the only way to reform people is to kill them. He described himself as 'the man who goes around doing good'. He meant that life is so vile that to kill someone is to do him a favour.

When a loosened bar was discovered in his cell, Panzram received yet another brutal beating – perhaps the hundredth of his life. In the basement of the jail he was subjected to a torture that in medieval times was known as the strappado. His hands were tied behind his back; then a rope was passed over a beam and he was heaved up by the wrists so that his shoulder sockets bore the full weight of his body. Twelve hours later, when the doctor checked his heart, Panzram shrieked and blasphemed, cursing his mother for bringing him into the world and declaring that he would kill every human being. He was allowed to lie on the floor of his cell all day, but when he cursed a guard, four guards knocked him unconscious with a blackjack and again suspended him from a beam. Lesser was so shocked by this treatment that he sent Panzram a dollar by a 'trusty'. At first, Panzram thought it was a joke. When he realized that it was a gesture of sympathy, his eyes filled with tears. He told Lesser that if he could get him paper and a pencil, he would write him his life story. This is how Panzram's autobiography came to be written.

When Lesser read the opening pages, he was struck by the remarkable literacy and keen intelligence. Panzram made no excuses for himself:

If any man was a habitual criminal, I am one. In my life time I have broken every law that was ever made by both God and man. If either had made any more, I should very cheerfully have broken them also. The mere fact that I have done these things is quite sufficient for the average person. Very few people even consider it worthwhile to wonder why I am what I am and do what I do. All that they think is necessary to do is to catch me, try me, convict me and send me to prison for a few years, make life miserable for me while in prison and turn me loose again . . . If someone had a young tiger cub in a cage and then mistreated it until it got savage and bloodthirsty and then turned it loose to prey on the rest of the world . . . there would be a hell of a roar . . . But if some people do the same thing to other people, then the world is surprised, shocked and offended because they get robbed, raped and killed. They done it to me and then don't like it when I give them the same dose they gave me.
(From *Killer, a Journal of Murder*, edited by Thomas E. Gaddis and James O. Long, Macmillan, 1970.)

Panzram's confession is an attempt to justify himself to one other human being. Where others were concerned, he remained as savagely intractable as ever. At his trial he told the jury: 'While you were trying me here, I was trying all of you too. I've found you guilty. Some of you, I've already executed. If I live, I'll execute some more of you. I hate the whole human race.' The judge sentenced him to twenty-five years.

Transferred to Leavenworth penitentiary, Panzram murdered the foreman of the working party with an iron bar and was sentenced to death. Meanwhile, Lesser had been showing the autobiography to various literary men, including H. L. Mencken, who were impressed. But when Panzram heard there was a movement to get him reprieved, he protested violently: 'I would not reform if the front gate was opened right now and I was given a million dollars when I stepped out. I have no desire to do good or become good.' And in a letter to Henry Lesser he showed a wry self-knowledge: 'I could not reform if I wanted to. It has taken me all my life so far, thirty-eight years of it, to reach my present state of mind. In that time I have acquired some habits. It took me a lifetime to form these habits, and I believe it would take more than another lifetime to break myself of these same habits even if I wanted to . . .' '. . . what gets me is how in the heck any man of your intelligence and ability, knowing as much about me as you do, can still be friendly towards a thing like me when I even despise and detest my own self.' When he stepped onto the scaffold on the morning of 11 September 1930, the hangman asked him if he had anything to say. 'Yes, hurry it up, you hoosier bastard. I could hang a dozen men while you're fooling around.'

Here we can see clearly the peculiar nature of the logic that drove Panzram to a form of suicide. To begin with, he committed the usual error of the violent criminal, 'personalizing' society and swearing revenge on it. The address to the jury shows that he saw them as symbolic representatives of society. 'Some of you, I've already executed. If I live, I'll execute some more of you . . .' In his early days, his crimes were a 'magical' attempt to get his revenge on 'society' – magical because there is no such thing as society, only individuals. The seven-year sentence turned a petty crook into a man with a mission – to 'teach society a lesson'. But the Warden Murphy episode seems to have been a turning point. After his escape, Panzram fought a gun battle because he was too ashamed to return to the prison and look the warden in the face. The savage punishment that followed seems to have been something of a relief. At this point, Murphy might have completed the work of reformation by looking Panzram in the face and asking how he could have done it. But Murphy's patience was exhausted, and now Panzram despised and hated himself as well as society. The robbery and murder of sailors seems to have been an attempt to somehow convince himself that he was 'damned'.

What Murphy had done was to make Panzram realize that his logic – that 'society' was against him – was based on a fallacy. When Murphy treated him with sympathy, it must have begun to dawn on Panzram that his 'society' was an abstraction – that the world was made up of real individuals like himself. But when Murphy's regime collapsed because of Panzram's betrayal, Panzram went back to his false logic with redoubled persistence. 'They' – other people – were the enemy. However, no one can live out such a philosophy; everyone must have at least one close relationship with another person to remain human. The twenty murders Panzram committed after his escape could be regarded as a form of self-punishment. In 1912 he had broken back into jail to try and rescue Cal Jordan; by

1920, he had turned his back on personal feelings and committed murder as a kind of reflex.

By the time he was in jail again – this time for good – Panzram had achieved complete self-alienation. He had convinced himself that the world was vile, that human beings all deserve to be exterminated, and that therefore he had nothing to live for. Emotionally, he was in a vacuum. Yet this is clearly an unnatural state for any human being, particularly for one like Panzram. The autobiography reveals that he has the makings of a 'self-actualizer'. Lesser was surprised to find that he had read most of the major works on prison reform – no doubt stimulated by Warden Murphy; Panzram also read philosophy in jail, including Schopenhauer and Kant. (He seems to have borrowed his pessimism from Schopenhauer.) Yet this man, whose self-esteem was so high that he would allow himself to be tortured for days without giving way, had never achieved the most basic levels of Maslow's hierarchy of needs – for 'security' and for 'belongingness'.

In a sense, therefore, Lesser's present of the dollar was the cruellest thing he could have done. It testified that there *was* decency and kindness in the world. And this in turn meant that Panzram might, if he had made the effort, have achieved some kind of fulfilment in life. The mechanics of conversion demand that the sinner should make a full confession; and this is what Panzram immediately proceeded to do. Yet with twenty murders on his conscience, many of them children, he knew there could be no absolution. It was too late, far too late. He had thrown away his chances.

The implication of Abbott's book is that people like himself and Panzram never had a chance from the beginning. But is this true? Panzram had at least one chance, under Warden Murphy. Abbott had at least one chance, when his book was accepted. Both threw them away. The real problem seems to date from their original assumption that life had no intention of treating them fairly. According to Panzram, he was cuffed and kicked as a child and came to hate his mother. 'Before I left [home] I looked around and figured that one of our neighbours who was rich and had a nice home full of nice things, he had too much and I had too little.' So he burgled the house and landed in reform school. There again, he claims, 'everything I seemed to do was wrong', so he was punished and struck back viciously. 'Then I began to think that I would have my revenge

. . . If I couldn't injure those who had injured me, then I would injure someone else.' This weird logic of revenge was already fully formed by the age of thirteen. And it was clearly based on self-pity, on the notion that 'the world' had treated him badly. So instead of using his considerable intelligence and willpower to achieve success – and in that age he might have become anything from a circus stunt man to a movie star – he wasted himself in crimes of petty resentment.

Panzram also implies that he was in some way not to blame for his crimes – that if the tiger cub is badly treated it can be expected to turn savage. There is an obvious element of truth in this; but it manages to leave out of account the whole question of free choice: the *decision* 'to be out of control' that seems common to violent criminals.

Panzram's pattern of revolt is not unique; it can be seen in many criminals whose background and upbringing were completely unlike his. A case in point is the English 'acid bath murderer' John Haigh, executed in 1949 for six murders. A few years before this, Bernard Shaw and his secretary Blanche Patch were lunching at the Onslow Court Hotel, where Miss Patch lived, and Haigh was at the next table. A child sitting nearby dropped one of those toy bombs containing an explosive cap, and Haigh leaned over and snarled: 'If you do that again I'll kill you.' According to Miss Patch, who told me this story in 1956, Shaw then commented that Haigh would end on the gallows. It seems as if he had instinctively recognized the 'decision to be out of control' that is characteristic of the violent criminal.

Yet in every other respect, Haigh and Panzram were as unlike as possible. Haigh was the son of fond parents, of strong religious inclination; he was a brilliant musician who won a scholarship to a grammar school and became a choirboy. He loved good clothes and fast cars, and in due course a car-hire swindle landed him in court. At this point, he made the same decision as Panzram. His first period in jail faced him with a choice: either the game wasn't worth the candle and he had better make his peace with society; *or* society had declared war on him and he would teach it a lesson. He embarked on a career of swindling, punctuated by periods in jail, and ended by murdering several people who had entrusted him with their business affairs. The most obvious thing about his career of crime is that it was a miscalculation from beginning to end. From fifteen years of crime – many of these spent in jail – he earned about £15,000. He could have earned far more in any honest business. But he felt from the beginning that life 'owed' him a better start than he had been offered, and the 'logic of resentment' drove him to increasingly ambitious attempts at short-cuts to the things he felt he deserved.

This seems to be the basic pattern of the violent man who turns to crime. His starting point is the premise that 'life' has treated him unfairly. In an attempt to right the balance, he takes short-cuts to get what he wants. The result is usually the same: brushes with the law, clashes with authority, periods in jail, increasing resentment and a determination to look for even shorter short-cuts.

He may, if he is very lucky, escape the social consequences of his acts. But he cannot escape the personal consequences. This emerges clearly in a story Lesser tells of Panzram. One day, Lesser went into Panzram's cell to check the bars. Panzram seemed shocked. 'Don't ever do that again. Turning your back on me like that.' Lesser protested: 'I knew you wouldn't harm me.' 'You're the one man I don't want to kill,' said Panzram, 'but I'm so erratic I'm liable to do anything.' In effect, Panzram had become two persons – or rather, a man and a beast. Panzram was the man who wrote that extremely clear-sighted confession, and who felt the need to warn Lesser. But he had trained his instinct to become a killer as he might have trained an Alsatian dog. When Lesser turned his back, the Alsatian growled and tried to jump.

And now it becomes possible to see precisely what causes that element of self-destructiveness in the violent criminal. He believes that he is opposed to the values of 'society', and that he is setting up against these his own individual values. He ends by discovering that, in a completely real and practical sense, he has destroyed his own values and left himself in a kind of vacuum. Maxim Gorky tells the story of a Russian murderer named Vassili Merkhouloff, described to Gorky by the judge L. N. Sviatoukhin. Merkhouloff was an intelligent carter, and also a man of bull-like strength. One day he caught a man stealing sugar from his cart and hit him; the force of the blow killed the man. Sentenced for manslaughter, Merkhouloff was sent to a monastery to do penance. The thought of how easily he had snuffed out a life haunted Merkhouloff; as a priest talked to him about repentance, he could not rid himself of the thought that one violent blow could kill him too. One day after his release, he lost his temper with an idiot girl who was importuning him and struck her

a reality disturbance

with a piece of wood. The blow killed her. He served a term in prison and the obsession now became a torment. When he came out, his new employer was a kindly man, whom Merkhouloff liked. One day, in a kind of frenzy, Merkhouloff overpowered him, tortured and then strangled him. He committed suicide in prison, strangling himself with his chains.

Merkhouloff's confession to Judge Sviatoukhin makes it clear that he was not insane in any ordinary sense of the word: only obsessed by the thought that if life could be taken away so easily, then human existence *must be meaningless*. He had ceased to believe in the reality of the will, or of human values. 'I can kill any man I choose *and any man can kill me* . . .' That is to say, he had lost not only the sense of his own 'primacy' but all sense of his own *necessity*. When he killed his employer, he was driven by the same compulsion that made Panzram afraid of killing Lesser. The 'decision to lose control' had made him afraid of *something inside himself.*

The same motivation can be seen in the case of the twenty-two-year-old Steven Judy, executed in the electric chair in Indianapolis in March 1981. Judy had murdered and strangled a twenty-year-old mother and thrown her three children to their death in a nearby river. Child of a broken home, Judy had committed his first rape at the age of twelve, stabbing the woman repeatedly and severing her finger. He told the jury: 'You'd better put me to death. Because next time, it might be one of you, or your daughter.' And before his execution he told his stepmother that he had raped and killed more women than he could remember, leaving a trail of bodies from Texas to Indiana. Like Panzram, Judy opposed every effort to appeal against his death sentence.

It may seem that there is a world of difference between a Russian peasant suffering from 'obsessive neurosis' and a young American rapist. But it is important to try to go to the heart of the matter. Human happiness is based upon a feeling of the reality of the will, or the 'spirit'. When a man looks at something he has made with his own hands, or contemplates some catastrophe he has averted by courage and determination, he experiences a deep sense of satisfaction. Conversely, the feeling of helplessness, of losing control, is a good definition of misery. Physical strength is normally something that a man would be proud of; but when Merkhouloff feels that he can accidentally inflict death it becomes a source of misery. It destroys his relationships with other human beings; he cannot like someone without feeling that a single blow could terminate the relationship. Steven Judy is in the same position. Every time he sees an attractive girl he is tormented by desire; but after killing and raping a number of women, he knows that every twinge of desire is an invitation to risk his freedom and his life. Part of him remains normal, sociable, affectionate; like all human beings, he has the usual needs for security, 'belonging', self-esteem. But the killer-Alsatian guarantees that he will never be allowed to satisfy these in the normal way. It has placed him outside the human race.

What becomes clear is that the central problem of the criminal is the problem of self-division. And it is easy to see how this comes about. All human beings experience, to some extent, the need for 'primacy', the desire to be 'recognized'. This obviously means to be recognized *among* other human beings; the individual wishes to stand out as a member of a group. There *is* a great satisfaction in achievement for its own sake; but half the pleasure of achievement lies in the admiration of the other members of the group. Crime obviously demands secrecy. And this explains why so many clever criminals experience a compulsion to talk at length about their crimes once they have been caught. Haigh would probably never have been convicted if he had not boasted to the police about dissolving the bodies of his victims in acid and pouring the sludge out in the garden. Thurneman made his own conviction doubly certain by writing a detailed autobiography of his crimes.

Panzram's crimes were based upon a conviction that he would never achieve 'primacy' in the normal way – by winning the admiration of other people. After the Warden Murphy episode, he tried to live out this conviction with a ruthless and terrifying logic; his murders were a deliberate attempt to crush the 'human' part of himself out of existence. Yet it refused to die; maimed, bleeding, horribly mutilated, it still insisted on reminding him that he would like to be a man among other men. The declaration: 'I'd like to kill the whole human race' was a kind of suicide.

At this point, it is necessary to look more closely into this paradox of human self-destruction: the paradox of 'the divided self'.

The 'two selves' of the criminal are present in every human being. When a baby is born, it is little more than a bundle of desires and appetites; it screams for food, for warmth, for attention. These are all immediate needs, 'short-term' needs. The child ceases to be a baby from the moment his imagination is touched by some story. From that moment on, he has begun to develop another kind of need: for experience, for adventure, for distant horizons. These might be labelled 'long-term' needs, and most of us find ourselves involved in a continual tug of war between our short-term and long-term needs. The child experiences the conflict when he feels he ought to save his pocket money towards a bicycle – to satisfy that longing for distant horizons – while the 'short-term self' wants to spend it on a visit to the cinema and a box of chocolates.

The adult is, if anything, even worse off. With the need to worry about mortgages, television licences and the children's clothes, he almost forgets that distant horizons ever existed. In effect, we walk about with a microscope attached to one eye and a telescope to the other. But we hardly ever look through the telescope – that eye tends to remain permanently closed.

And now it becomes possible to see why criminality is related to hypnosis. The criminal is, of course, a man who is dominated by short-term needs; like a spoilt child, his motto is 'I want it now'. But it is one of the peculiarities of consciousness that short-term perception – as seen through the microscope – slips easily into sleep or hypnosis. This is why animals – who wear a microscope on both eyes – are so easy to hypnotize. We need the *sense of reality* – the telescope – to keep us alert. The chicken's sense of reality is restricted to scratching for food and sitting on eggs – which is why a mere chalk line can push its consciousness into total vacuity. And the criminal's sense of reality, limited to short-term objectives, also tends to drift into a state akin to hypnosis. To the rest of us, there is something rather insane about the conduct of a Haigh, putting people into baths of acid just for the sake of a few thousand pounds. The means seem out of all proportion to the end. He has lost all 'sense of reality'.

With their combination of 'microscope' and 'telescope', human beings were intended by evolution to be far harder to hypnotize than chickens and rabbits. And indeed, we would be, if we made proper use of the 'telescope' to maintain a sense of reality, of proportion. It is this absurd habit of keeping one eye almost permanently closed that makes us almost as vulnerable as chickens.

Then why do we do it? Again, we have to look closely at the peculiar workings of the human mind. When a child is born, he finds himself in a bewildering, frightening world of strange sights and sounds, none of which he understands. Little by little, he begins to recognize regular patterns, which he stores inside his head; and in the course of a few years he has collected enough patterns to create a whole world behind his eyes. So now, when he confronts some new situation, he does not have to study it in detail; the patterns inside his head enable him to master it in half the time.

But this useful mechanism – like all mechanisms – has a serious disadvantage. As the adult becomes more skilled at coping with new situations, he scarcely bothers to study them in detail, or to look for new points of interest. Sitting comfortably in the control room inside his head, he deals with them by *habit*. Gradually life and consciousness fall into a mechanical routine. *Human beings are the only creatures who spend ninety-nine per cent of their time inside their own heads.* Which means, of course, that we are only keeping our sense of reality alert for one per cent of the time. It is hardly surprising that we are so easy to hypnotize.

There is something very odd about the mechanism of hypnosis. It seems to be a method of utilizing the mind's powers *against itself*. Students of self-defence are taught how to immobilize an enemy by placing his legs around a lamp post in a certain position then forcing him to sit on his heels; it 'locks' him so that he cannot escape. The hypnotist seems to be able to 'lock' the mind in the same way. And the two 'legs' that obstruct each other to their mutual disadvantage are *habit* and *self-consciousness*. We have all had the experience of trying to do something under the gaze of another person and doing it badly because we have become self-conscious. This is because when some function – like driving a car – has been handed over to habit, then we do it best when we are not thinking about it. Asking someone to pay attention to a task he normally does mechanically is an infallible way of throwing a spanner in the works. This is exactly what the snake does when it fixes the rabbit with its gaze.

But people can become hypnotized without staring into the eyes of a hypnotist (or listening to his voice). If I go into a room to fetch something and then forget why I went there, I have slipped into one of the commonest forms of 'hypnosis'. The journey to the room has distracted my attention from my purpose, causing my mind to 'go blank'. There is a story of an absent-minded professor who went up to his bedroom to change his tie before guests arrived; when he failed to return, his wife went upstairs and found him fast asleep in bed. Removing his tie had made him automatically proceed to get undressed and into bed. We can see here how close absent-mindedness is to hypnosis: the professor behaved as if he had been given a hypnotic command to go to bed. And this came about because, as he went up to change his tie, he was living 'inside his own head', connected to reality by a mere thread. The unconscious suggestion that it was time to sleep snapped the thread, just as it might have been snapped by the command of a hypnotist.

It is important to recognize that most of us spend a large proportion of our lives in this state of near-hypnosis. And the chief disadvantage of this state is that it makes us highly susceptible to negative suggestion. Our moods change from minute to minute. The sun comes out; we feel cheerful. It goes behind a cloud; we experience depression. In a modern city, most of the sights and sounds are depressing: the screeching of brakes, the smell of exhaust fumes, the roar of engines, the people jostling for space, the newspaper placards announcing the latest disaster. To a man with a strong sense of purpose, these things would be a matter of indifference, for purpose connects us to reality. But the 'purposes' of the modern city dweller are almost entirely a matter of habit. So he spends most of his time bombarded by negative suggestions – often sinking into that state of permanent, undefined anxiety that Kierkegaard called *Angst* and that a modern doctor would simply call nervous depression.

The Hindu scripture says: 'The mind is the slayer of the real' – meaning that our mental attitudes cut us off from reality. Thomas Mann has a short story called 'Disillusionment' that might have been conceived as an illustration of that text. The central character explains that his whole life has been spoilt by boredom, by a 'great and general disappointment' with all his experience. Literature and art had led him to expect marvels and prodigies, and everything has been a let-down. 'Is that all?' Death, he believes, will be the final anti-climax, the greatest disappointment of all . . . We can see that his problem is not that life is a disappointment, but that he never *experiences* life. His 'life' is lived inside his own head. He is in a more or less permanent state of hypnosis. And, by its very nature, this state tends to be self-propagating. Lack of expectation – or negative expectation – induces 'hypnosis', and a man in a condition of hypnosis is susceptible to negative suggestion, which prolongs the hypnosis. It is a vicious circle.

As soon as we become aware of this mechanism, it becomes easy to observe it in ourselves. If, for example, I am feeling ill, trying not to be physically sick, I can observe how almost any thought can push me in one direction or another. The mere mention of food is enough to make me wonder what I ever saw in it. Yet it is equally easy for me to 'snap out' of it. I hear a pattering noise on the windowpane and think: 'Can it be raining?' And when my attention comes back to my stomach, I am no longer feeling sick. The rain has rescued me from my claustrophobic mental world, re-established my connection with reality.

And now it becomes possible to see how a Panzram or Mer-khouloff becomes locked into an attitude of self-destruction. His negative mental attitudes cut him off from reality like a leaden shutter. There would be no point in telling Merkhouloff that his fear of killing someone by accident is absurd; his anxiety has made him 'unreachable', like the girl Pauline, encountered in the first chapter, who was told to go and embrace the Abbé and could not be made to abandon the idea, even by the man who had implanted the sugges-tion. Panzram's tragedy was not that he was a social reject who was inevitably driven to violence and crime; it was that he was trapped in a state of 'negative suggestibility' so that he was totally unable to utilize his potential as a human being.

But is this necessarily so? For the criminologist, this is obviously the most important question of all. The answer, quite clearly, should be no. If the mind is the slayer of reality, it should also be the creator – or, at least, the amplifier – of reality. If the problem of criminality is due to negative attitudes, then it should be possible to solve it through positive attitudes. Panzram may have been resentful and vicious; but he was also highly intelligent. This in itself should have enabled him to break out of the vicious circle.

The revolutionary idea of 'curing' criminals by a change of attitude was not only suggested but demonstrated and proved by an American penologist named Dan MacDougald. His involvement in rehabilitation came about by accident. In the mid-1950s, Mac-Dougald, who is a lawyer, was approached by farmers who wanted to complain about the Federal authorities. The authorities were overloading the Buford dam in Georgia so that the overflow often ruined crops and drowned cattle. Their case seemed so reasonable and logical that MacDougald had no doubt it should be easily settled. To his surprise, it seemed practically impossible to persuade the authorities to listen. The engineers in charge of the dam told him you can't make an omelette without breaking eggs, and it took three years of arguing, and a cost of $46,000, to get things changed.

What baffled MacDougald was that it seemed so difficult to *get through* to the authorities; it was just as if they had put their hands over their ears. And he began to see the outline of an explanation when he heard about an experiment performed at Harvard by Dr Jerome Bruner. Bruner was trying to determine the way stimuli are conveyed to the brain. It was known that they travel along nerve fibres by means of electrical impulses, and the experimenters had put electrodes in the nervous system – they were using a cat for their experiments – so that they could see exactly what nervous impulses were passing at any given moment. They discovered that if a cat was placed in a quiet room and a sharp click was sounded in its ear, this click could be traced as it moved along the nerves all the way to the cortex.

They then tried placing a bell jar containing two lively white mice in front of the cat. The click was again sounded. And, oddly enough, their apparatus recorded no electrical impulse in the nerve. That seemed absurd. They could believe that the cat was ignoring the impulse as it gazed intently at the mice. But if the eardrum vibrated, then the impulse should have been carried along the nerve and registered on their oscilloscope. It looked as if the cat was somehow turning off the sound *at the eardrum*. What was actually happening, other experimenters discovered later, was that the cat sends counter-impulses to inhibit the sound – to block the nerve fibre, so to speak.

MacDougald also came across the astonishing piece of information that the five senses pick up about ten thousand 'units of information' per second and that all this information is forwarded to a processing system in the brain. But the mind can only use about *seven* out of the ten thousand. The other 9,993 units of information have to be ignored. *This* is why the mind has such an efficient 'filter' system. As I sit here, typing this page, my body is recording thousands of sensations. My feet are rather cold. I cut my thumb this morning and the end still hurts. My chin tingles faintly from the aftershave I put on it. I feel the pressure of the chair, the pressure of my clothes, the slight breeze from the open door and dozens of other minor sensations that I *can* focus on if I choose to. But when I am writing, I do not choose; I ignore them all. Or rather, my excellent inhibitory system does the work for me. If someone severed my inhibitory fibres, I would be unable to concentrate.

MacDougald's dazzling insight was that this explained not only the indifference of the Federal authorities but the anti-social behaviour of criminals. The criminal is essentially a man whose judgement on life is negative. He thinks he will only get what he wants by grabbing it. And he is literally blind to all the things that contradict his negative view of existence. Dickens's Scrooge is a good example of what MacDougald calls 'negative blocking'. A lonely childhood has convinced him that the world is an unpleasant place, so that his attitude to life is unyielding and defensive: 'Christmas, humbug!' The girl to whom he was once engaged puts her finger on his problem when she says: 'You fear the world too much.' He is thoroughly miserable in his cheerless room, yet is unaware of any other possibility. He is trapped in 'immediacy', the world of the microscope. All the ghost of Christmas Past has to do is to show him his own childhood; the ice around his heart melts and the 'faulty blocking vanishes'. 'He was conscious of a thousand odours floating in the air, each one connected with a thousand thoughts.' The sheer *multiplicity* of the world begins to break through.

We can also see that Scrooge's 'faulty blocking' would be reflected in his understanding of words. If a psychologist had presented him with an association test containing words such as 'Christmas', 'kindliness', 'charity', 'love', 'neighbourliness', his associations would have been words like 'humbug', 'gullibility', 'stupidity', 'feeble-mindedness' and 'nuisance'. The three ghosts alter and *broaden* his understanding of these words.

This was the basis of MacDougald's own solution to the problem of 'unblocking' criminals. He cites William James, who remarked: 'The greatest discovery of my generation is the fact that human beings can alter their lives by altering their attitudes of mind.' The key to a man's attitudes lies in his understanding of words, says MacDougald. And where crime is concerned, the key words are those associated with religion: love, sin, neighbour, punishment, responsibility, and so on. The anti-social personality's understanding of such words is often incomplete or contradictory. For example, most alcoholics agree that their situation is largely their own fault; yet they go on to deny that their failures are their own responsibility; they are inclined to lay the blame elsewhere. Clearly, their understanding of the notion of responsibility is vague and contradictory.

In effect, MacDougald set out to change the attitude of criminals by appealing to their intelligence, and by trying to instil into them a fuller understanding of these basic words. He was convinced that the New Testament contains the most comprehensive teaching for a harmonious society, and that in the original Aramaic, the meaning is even more precise than in the English translation. A single example will serve. The Aramaic word for 'self' is '*naphsha*'. This, according to MacDougald, means the 'true self', a man's essential being. We have been taught that love of 'self' is undesirable, another name for selfishness. Yet the New Testament tells us to love our neighbour as ourself. This seems to suggest that a man *should* love his 'self', and is, MacDougald believes, one of the key concepts of Christianity. In the case of Panzram, it is easy to see what he means. Panzram loathed himself, and said so repeatedly. Yet his autobiography reveals that he was a man of considerable intelligence and integrity, and that these were his 'essential' attributes. If Panzram had recognized this, he would never have become a criminal. Even *as* a criminal, his intelligence would almost certainly have responded to this recognition that he had good reason to love his 'naphsha' and should not be ashamed to do so.

MacDougald obtained permission to try out these ideas in the Georgia State Penitentiary at Reidsville. He started from the assumption that prisoners are intelligent enough to grasp the lesson of Bruner's experiment with the cat: that they are somehow *refusing* to see and hear certain things. It is a law of nature that each person seeks to achieve his own goals. The trouble with the criminal is that his faulty attitudes cause him to pursue these goals in such a muddled way that he never achieves them. As we have seen in the case of Haigh, the criminal's 'cleverness' is usually a form of stupidity. The criminal's chief problem is that, like the alcoholic, he feels helpless; nothing ever comes out right. He blames 'life'. MacDougald set out to show criminals that the real blame lay in their own muddle and confusion, their negative attitudes.

The results were spectacular. Initial tests at the Georgia Institute of Correction showed that sixty-three per cent of prisoners – many of them 'hard core psychopaths' (i.e., Panzram-types) – could be rehabilitated in a matter of weeks. Follow-up studies eighteen months later showed that there had been no backsliding. The instructors from MacDougald's institute (which at that stage was called the Yonan Codex Foundation, the name being that of the Aramaic version of the New Testament MacDougald preferred) began by instructing two prisoners in their methods for two weeks, and then the four of them instructed another twenty-two prisoners, four of whom were also chosen as instructors. Later the course was renamed Emotional Maturity Instruction.

MacDougald offers one remarkable illustration of the way it worked. One prisoner felt intense hostility towards another. Prison morality – as expounded by Jack Abbott – dictates that in a situation like this honour demands that the two of them fight it out, and that if one can kill the other, he does so. The man had concealed a piece of iron pipe in preparation for the showdown; but after a discussion and exploration of the meaning of the concept of forgiveness, this suddenly struck him as absurd. The man was his 'neighbour', and his own distorted concepts were urging him to an act that was basically *against his own interests*. So he bought the other man a sandwich and a coffee and talked the thing over. The two became friends.

At first sight, it looks as if MacDougald had simply found a way of importing old-fashioned evangelism into the prison, but closer examination shows that to presume this is to miss the point. His basic assumption was that most criminals are acting at a level far below their natural capacity and potential. All men have the same need to grow up, to evolve, to achieve their objectives. By treating them as intelligent human beings, by offering them the possibility of some kind of evolution, MacDougald had changed their basic attitudes. In fact, his discovery had been anticipated two decades before by a Hungarian named Alfred Reynolds, who had left Hungary in the 1930s and came to live in England. Reynolds was in Army Intelligence during the war, and in 1945 was given the almost impossible task of 'de-Nazifying' young Nazi officers who had been captured. Reynolds has described how, when he first entered the room, there was an atmosphere of cold hostility. They stared at him, prepared – like Bruner's cat – to 'cut out' anything he had to say at the level of the ear-drum. To their surprise, there was no homily on the evils of Nazism. Instead, he asked them to explain to him what they understood by National Socialism. Once they were convinced he really wanted to know, they began to talk. He listened quietly, asked questions, and pointed out contradictions. Within a matter of days, there was not a Nazi left among them.

All he had done, in effect, was to make them aware that all religions and ideologies prevent people from thinking for them-

a basic negative assumption

selves. He did not criticize Hitler. He simply let them expound Hitler's doctrines until it began to dawn on them that they had no need to swallow somone else's ideas – they were perfectly capable of formulating their own. And he did this by turning their de-Nazification session into a kind of debating society. The sheer pleasure of thinking for themselves did the rest.

Reynolds demonstrates that successful rehabilitation does not depend on the nature of the teaching – whether it is religious, moral, political or whatever. It depends solely upon making people use their minds, and thereby making them aware that they have minds. The criminal's violence springs out of a feeling that nothing less will enable him to achieve his goals. In fact, he is failing to achieve his goals because he proceeds on the negative assumption that they cannot be achieved. And negative assumptions, as we have seen, produce 'hypnosis'. The moment he substitutes a positive assumption, his 'controlling ego' wakes up and takes command. And the sense of a controlling ego is also the sense of self, of *naphsha*.

Maslow and other psychologists have demonstrated that alcoholics can be cured by inducing a similar recognition with the help of the psychedelic drug LSD. When the notion of using LSD as a cure for alcoholism first occurred to two doctors, Abram Hoffer and Humphry Osmond, their idea was to try and frighten the patient by an experience similar to DTs. It has been established that many alcoholics begin to recover after 'hitting rock bottom', often the experience of delirium tremens, and the doctors soon discovered that a positive LSD trip could be even more effective. LSD, like mescalin, causes a 'transformation of reality'; sights, sounds, smells, may become more intense. Hoffer and Osmond discovered that if their patients had religious or spiritual experiences under LSD, they were far more likely to be cured than if they had a bad trip, and Maslow made use of the same principle in some of his own experiments. He knew that alcoholics are often more sensitive and intelligent than the average person, and are consequently more likely to be depressed by difficulties and obstructions, and so take refuge in heavy drinking. At first, the drinking produces 'peak experiences' which relieve the tension; but very frequently it only produces depression, which leads to still heavier drinking. The whole negative cycle is further complicated by feelings of guilt and helplessness. Maslow questioned his patients about the kind of aesthetic experiences that had given them pleasure before they became alcoholics –

music, poetry, painting. Then, under mescalin or LSD, he induced 'peak experiences' – feelings of intense happiness and well-being – by means of music, poetry, colours blending on a screen. This method produced many startling cures. And the reason, apparently, was that when the patient experienced a sense of deep relaxation and happiness, it awakened all his hopes, his positive expectations of life. He would also see clearly that these could be best fulfilled if he stayed healthy and determined. He would recognize that to drink heavily to achieve the 'peak experience' is counter-productive. The 'self' would regain control, and the patient cease to be an alcoholic. In effect, Maslow was doing what MacDougald and Reynolds did: awakening the controlling ego.

But perhaps the most important point to emerge from these considerations is that they apply to *everybody*, not simply to criminals or alcoholics. All of us spend a large amount of our time in a state akin to hypnosis. All of us spend a large amount of our lives in a state of boredom or 'directionlessness'. And the insights of MacDougald, Reynolds and Maslow are just as applicable to company directors as to criminals. This has been recognized by Werner Erhard, the founder of the psychotherapeutic method known as *est*. As described in a biography of Erhard by W. W. Bartley, the essence of *est* is the recognition of 'true identity'. The key to Erhard's thought is the notion of the Self, and the recognition that this Self is able to take charge of the individual's life and personality. We are *not* 'creatures of circumstance'. We only believe we are when we are in a 'fallen' or untransformed state. And the essence of this state is the delusion that we are mere products of our mental and emotional activities, as heat is a product of a fire. An important American physician, Howard Miller – of whom we shall speak later – has made the same observation. The 'essential you' fails to grasp its own nature; it sits around passively in a corner of the brain, observing the body's physical and emotional states as if they were as uncontrollable as the weather. The moment any kind of crisis occurs, the ego awakens with a shock and hurls itself into its proper role as the *director* of consciousness. The situation could be compared to the captain of a ship who has suffered a bout of amnesia, and who sits gloomily in his cabin, staring out of the porthole and wondering why the ship seems to be going in circles. The reason, of course, is that there is nobody on the bridge.

* * *

Let us try to summarize these insights.

Crime is the outcome of negative attitudes. Negative attitudes are due to the selectivity of our perceptive mechanisms. A man who had just been reprieved from a firing squad would fling open his senses like windows; he would notice everything, and everything would strike him as beautiful and interesting. As the American gangster and multiple murderer Charlie Birger stood on the scaffold in 1927, he looked wistfully at the sky and said: 'It *is* a beautiful world, isn't it?' But he had noticed it too late. He should have noticed it earlier; then a number of people would have remained alive.

Once a man has deliberately closed his mind to all kinds of data – like the blueness of the sky – he has left himself connected to external reality by a dangerously thin thread – the thread of his immediate purposes. And, odd as it sounds, he is now living in a kind of cave inside his own head. That cave contains an enormous number of filing cabinets, full of photographs of the outside world, and the walls are covered with 'maps of reality' – *ideas* of how to deal with the problems of living. Religious people have religious maps; politicians have political maps; psychologists have psychological maps. Ordinary people have maps derived from their parents, from people they admire, and from their own experience – the latter usually being the least important. And when confronted by a new situation, each of them skims quickly through a drawerful of old photographs, glances hastily at his maps, and then responds 'appropriately'.

The photographs he chooses are those that *remind* him of the present situation. For example, if he is being introduced to a moon-faced stranger with a grey suit and a foreign accent, his memory will throw up photographs of various strangers, and various men with moon faces, grey suits and foreign accents. If he found most of these fairly likeable, then he will feel predisposed to like this new acquaintance – while firmly believing that he is forming a judgement solely on the basis of his present observations. Perhaps, as he is shaking the man's hand, the stranger smiles and shows a gold tooth which recalls a neighbour who once caught him stealing apples; immediately, he feels an inexplicable twinge of dislike.

All these complex mechanisms have been developed over millions of years of evolution. And it is easy to see that most of us are quite simply overweighted with habit mechanisms. We are like the dinosaurs, whose bodies were so gigantic that it cost them an immense effort to move. But with human beings, it is the 'robot', the 'habit-body', that has become so gigantic and complex that it does most of our living for us. The average human being lives in his habit-body like a mouse in a windmill. As we get older, the mechanism grows more rusty and cumbersome, and we experience less and less of those flashes of freedom – of sheer delight – that make life worth living. This is why, as Gurdjieff says, many people die long before their physical death. They continue to respond to external stimuli, immense, creaking windmills, tenanted only by a dead mouse.

In the light of this assessment, it may seem that the long-term future of the human race looks unpromising. But the comparison with the dinosaur may be misleading. This is not a problem of man's long-term evolution but of what happens during an individual's lifetime. As Wordsworth points out, children often see things 'apparelled in celestial light'; it is with the approach of adulthood that the 'shades of the prison house begin to close'. And we have seen that this is not as inevitable as Wordsworth thought. It is largely due to 'faulty blocking'. What is necessary, at this point in evolution, is for man to recognize that *he* is in charge of his consciousness, that if we can unconsciously close our minds to interesting data, then we can use conscious intelligence to open them again.

What prevents this recognition? The answer can be seen in the following paragraph, which is from a book called *Curious Facts*:

Mrs Marva Drew, a fifty-one-year-old housewife from Waterloo, Iowa, typed out every number from one to a million after her son's teacher told him it was impossible to count up to a million. It took her five years and 2,473 sheets of typing paper.

The sheer waste of time takes the breath away. Could anything more dreary, more pointless, more repetitious, be imagined? What could motivate any human being to do anything so futile? Yet the answer is plain enough. A schoolteacher – a figure of authority – told her son it was impossible. She decided that, in this single instance, she would prove she knew better than authority. So she wasted five years of her life. We can see that the attitude of mind is identical to Panzram's – the defiance of authority – and that the act has the baffling illogicality that is characteristic of crime. And, like the professor who went to bed instead of attending to his guests, there is also an element that savours of hypnosis. If the lady had had the common sense to say: 'But schoolteachers are not infallible', she would have saved herself five years – the equivalent of a prison sentence. But in order to *know* that, she would have had to change her whole attitude – not merely towards authority, but towards herself. Society had conditioned her to a certain view of authority and, therefore, of herself.

Man has achieved his present position as the 'lord of creation' because he is the most social animal on earth. But because he is a social animal, he keeps looking to other people for his cues to action. The key to crime, therefore, lies in man's history as a social being.

Four
HOW MAN EVOLVED

The following two extracts are examples of sadism, one real, one fictional:

We slept, having given the prize of the night to a tale of Enver Pasha, after the Turks re-took Sharkeui. He went to see it, in a penny steamer, with Prince Jamil and a gorgeous staff. The Bulgars, when they came, had massacred the Turks; as they retired, the Bulgar peasants went too. So the Turks found hardly anyone to kill. A greybeard was led on board for the Commander-in-Chief to bait. At last Enver tired of this. He signed to two of his bravo aides, and throwing open the furnace door, said, 'Push him in.' The old man screamed, but the officers were stronger and the door was slammed-to on his jerking body. We turned, feeling sick, to go away, but Enver, his head on one side, listening, halted us. So we listened till there came a crash within the furnace. He smiled and nodded, saying: 'Their heads always pop like that.'

That night, after a quick round of buggery with Saint-Fond, I withdrew to my apartment. But I couldn't sleep: so stirred up was I by Clairwil's violent words and actions, I had to commit a crime of my own.

My heart beating wildly at the evil thoughts racing through my brain, I leapt out of bed and dashed to the servants' quarters. There I stole a butler's clothes and a guard's pistol. Then, looking very much like a gentleman of fashion [the narrator is a woman], I slipped into the night.

At the first street corner to which I came, I stationed myself inside a doorway and waited for someone to pass. The prospect of the crime which I was about to commit thrilled me like nothing I had ever experienced. My body glistened with sweat. My insides churned with the turmoil which precedes sexual congress – a fundamental excitement which honed all my senses to a fine cutting edge. I was aflame, ablaze now, for a victim.

Suddenly, in response to my devil's prayer, I heard groans – a woman's voice, soft, low-pitched and mournful. Racing in the direction from which the sounds came, I found a tattered, feeble-looking creature huddled upon a doorstep.

'Who are you?' I demanded, drawing closer.

'One cursed by fate,' she replied; 'if you are the harbinger of death, I will embrace you gladly.'

'What are your difficulties?' I asked, noticing that, in spite of her grief, she was rather a comely creature.

'My husband has been put in jail, my babies are starving; now this house on whose steps I sit, this house which once was mine, has been taken away from me.'

'By fuck!' I cheered. The sexual heat welling up inside my body had become almost unbearable. 'Come now, let me put your talents to the test.'

So saying, I seized her by the hair and jerked her to her feet. Wrapping one arm around her waist and urging her hips forward, I jammed the pistol barrel into her vagina. 'Goodbye, bitch,' I said softly. 'Here's a fucking you'll never forget.' Whereupon, pulling the trigger, I sent her spinning off into eternity.

The first excerpt is from T. E. Lawrence's *Seven Pillars of Wisdom*, the second from de Sade's novel *Juliette* (here slightly abbreviated, since de Sade enjoys spinning out the woman's pleas for mercy). It is one of de Sade's milder inventions. The difference in the quality of the cruelty is immediately apparent. De Sade makes it clear that his Juliette is experiencing intense sexual excitement at the thought of committing murder. It is doubtful whether Enver Pasha experienced anything at all except a kind of savage amusement. Enver's cruelty is a form of stupidity, springing out of complete lack of imagination. De Sade's cruelty is totally conscious; in fact, it was the result of too much imagination, of years spent in prison with nothing to do but indulge in erotic daydreams. Yet the essence of the sadism, in both cases, is *an inflated ego*. The sadist derives from his act the same feeling of power that the Right Man experiences when he gets his own way by shouting and bullying.

This, clearly, is the very essence of crime: the self-absorption and lack of imagination. A delinquent who mugs an old lady or wrecks a telephone kiosk is as absorbed in his own needs as a baby crying to be fed. Freud revealed his own insight into crime when he remarked that a baby would destroy the world if it had the power.

In 1961, two psychiatrists, Samuel Yochelson and Stanton Samenow, began to study the mentality of criminals at St Elizabeth's Hospital in New York. Their initial premise was that men become criminals because of 'deep-seated psychologic problems'. They became popular with their patients because their attitude was permissive and compassionate. They believed that most criminals are the product of poor social conditions or problems in early childhood, and that with enough insight and understanding they could be 'cured'. Gradually, they became disillusioned. They noticed that no matter how much 'insight' they achieved into the behaviour of a murderer, rapist or child-molester, it made no difference to his actual conduct; as soon as he left the doctor's office, he went straight back to his previous criminal pattern. He didn't *want* to change. Yochelson and Samenow also became increasingly sceptical about the stories told by criminals to justify themselves. They found them amazingly skilful in self-justification – suppressing any material that might lose them sympathy – but the real problem lay in the criminal character. They lied as automatically as breathing. They had a strong desire to make an impression on other people – they were what David Reisman calls 'other directed' – and a great deal of their criminal activity sprang from this desire to show off, to 'look big'. They were also skilful in lying to themselves. Particularly striking is Yochelson's observation that most criminals – like Bruner's cat – have developed a psychological 'shut-off mechanism', an ability to push inconvenient thoughts out of consciousness – even to forget that they had made certain damaging admissions about themselves at a previous meeting. 'This,' as Yochelson observes, 'meant that responsibility, too, could be shut off.' In short, the central traits of the criminal personality were weakness, immaturity and self-deception. In the case of the child-molester who was finally 'cured', they observed that psychological insight 'was not responsible for the success, but rather the fact that he applied choice, will and deterrence to a pattern that offended him' (i.e., got him into trouble). He stopped because he wanted to stop; and most criminals went on being criminals because they could see no reason not to.

Another striking insight relates to sexuality. 'Almost without exception, the participants in our study were either involved in sexual activity very early or [indulged in] a great deal of sexual thinking . . .' The criminal 'peeks through cracks in doors and peers through keyholes to catch glimpses of mother, sister or a friend's mother or sister as she dresses, bathes or uses the toilet'. One habitual criminal began engaging in sex games at the age of four, with the daughter of a neighbour who took him to school. Later, he was part of a gang who used to grab girls in alleyways and commit rape – although if the girls showed no objection, they were allowed to go; it was essential that they should cry and struggle.

Most children experience curiosity about sex; in the criminal, it seems to be an obsession that narrows down the focus of his consciousness to the idea of exploring the forbidden, of committing stealthy violations of privacy. His sexuality becomes tinged with violence, and his criminality with sex. One of the most puzzling things about many cases of rape is the damage inflicted on the victim, even when she makes no resistance. This is because, in the criminal mind, sex *is* a form of crime, and crime a form of sex. The passage from de Sade is a remarkable illustration of this connection – Juliette's intense sexual excitement as she waits to commit a crime. What Yochelson's observation shows is that there is a sexual component in all crime; the criminal is committing indecent assault on society.

This, then, brings us close to the essence of criminality. It is a combination of egoism, infantilism and sex. No animal is capable of 'crime' because for animals sex is as natural as eating and defecating. Moreover, animals become mature as soon as they are fully grown. And, as far as human beings can judge, they seem to lack all sense of ego. With the possible exception of greed, animals lack all the basic qualifications for crime.

But it is important to get all this into perspective. We are speaking as if criminality had always been the same at all times, and this is untrue. Yochelson and Samenow conducted their research in the second half of the twentieth century, and we must bear in mind – as H. G. Wells once pointed out – that the world has changed more in the past century than in the previous five thousand years. Until fairly recently, life was incredibly hard for all but about one per cent of the population. It was an endless battle against starvation, cold and ill-health. As Henry Hazlitt put it in *The Conquest of Poverty* (New York, 1973):

The ancient world of Greece and Rome . . . was a world where houses had no chimneys, and rooms, heated in cold weather by a fire on a hearth or a fire-pan in the centre of the room, were filled with smoke whenever a fire was started, and consequently walls, ceiling and furniture were blackened and more or less covered by soot at all times; where light was supplied by smoky oil lamps which, like the houses in which they were used, had no chimneys; and where eye trouble, as a result of all this smoke, was general. Greek dwellings had no heat in winter, no adequate sanitary arrangements, and no washing facilities.

And two thousand years later, things were just as bad:

The dwellings of medieval labourers were hovels – the walls were made of a few boards cemented with wood and leaves. Rushes and leaves or heather made the thatch for the roof. Inside the house there was a single room, or in some cases two rooms, not plastered and without floor, ceiling, chimney, fireplace or bed, and here the owner, his family and his animals lived and died. There was no sewage for the houses, no drainage, except surface drainage for the streets, no water supply beyond that provided by the town pump, and no knowledge of the simplest forms of sanitation . . .

From I. E. Parmalee Prentice: *Hunger and History*, quoted by Hazlitt.

And again and again there were appalling famines. In Rome in 436 B.C. it was so bad that thousands of starving people threw themselves into the Tiber; in England in the eleventh and twelfth centuries there was a famine approximately every fourteen years, in one of which 20,000 people died in London alone.

In our comfortable twentieth century, we have forgotten the way our ancestors lived for thousands upon thousands of years. Of course there must have been crime in these ages of hardship and poverty; but it was nearly all crime of want. The kind of crime discussed by Yochelson and Samenow is essentially that of a luxury society. The peasant of the Middle Ages had almost no *choice*; he could not even leave his village without the permission of the local lord. By comparison, modern man – even the poorest tramp – has a thousand choices. And the essence of criminality is that it is the choice of the 'soft option'. Yochelson and Samenow observed that one of the central characteristics of the criminal is 'the quest to be an overnight success'. They cite the case of a soldier who had won medals in Korea and who was arrested for robbing a petrol station when he came out of the army. The newspapers treated this as the story of a war hero who found civilian life too harsh and difficult. The truth is that the man had become accustomed to admiration and success and found civilian life an anti-climax; he decided he might as well use his army training in a career of robbery. It seemed to be 'the soft option'. The decision was typical of the criminal's short-sightedness, and consequent poor judgement.

Yochelson and Samenow make us aware that the patterns of criminality change from age to age, and that it is rash to make generalizations about 'human nature' without specifying which period of history we are talking about. The statement 'You can't change human nature' is based on a fallacy. Human nature began to change about half a million years ago, when man's brain – for some unknown reason – began to expand far beyond his needs. It has been changing ever since.

Even the statement 'War is as old as humanity' has been challenged by the historian Louis Mumford. In *The City in History*, he argued that it was when men came to live together in cities – in about 5000 B.C. – that they began to make war. When primitive man formed a raiding party, it was not to kill people and burn villages but to take a few captives for sacrifice to the gods and for ritual cannibalism.

Mumford's own view of the fall of man into warfare and crime runs like this. When ancient man became a farmer – about 12,000 years ago – he recognized more than ever before his dependence on the earth and its bounty. Even as a stone age hunter, he had his gods and nature spirits, and his shamans worked their magic rituals before the hunting party set out. Now that he harvested crops, he became aware of the earth as a living being, a great mother. The shamans became a priestly caste; primitive temples and sacred groves became the focus of village life. The king was chosen, not as a leader, but as an intermediary between man and the gods – rather as the pope is chosen nowadays. And if the harvest failed, the king would be sacrificed to propitiate the gods. (This part of Mumford's argument is based on Frazer's *Golden Bough*.)

Now, a mud village with its domestic shrines and its witch doctor is one thing; an enlarged village with its temple and god-king quite another. It is already, in fact, a small city. And this, Mumford believes, is how cities first came about. It was also the beginning of the 'fall'. 'Once the city came into existence with its collective increase in power in every department, this whole situation underwent a change. Instead of raids and sallies for single victims, mass extermination and mass destruction came to prevail. What had once been a magic sacrifice to ensure fertility and abundant crops, an irrational act to promote a rational purpose, was turned into the exhibition of the power of one community, under its wrathful god and priest-king, to control, subdue or totally wipe out another community . . .'

What Mumford has omitted to mention is that these early wars were not fought to collect victims for sacrifice, but for territory. When Mumford was writing *The City in History* (which was published in 1961), the importance of 'territory' was not understood. It was Konrad Lorenz and Robert Ardrey who first made the general public aware that one of the most basic impulses in all animals is the urge to establish an area that belongs to the family or the tribe, and from which all invaders are repelled. The first written records at

Sumer – in Mesopotamia – show that the earliest wars were boundary disputes. A city needed farmland to supply it with food; when another city crossed the boundaries, there was war. Birds and animals seldom actually fight for territory; if a bird tries to invade a tree held by another bird, the incumbent will advance with a great show of rage, and this is usually enough to drive off the invader. The same kind of thing probably happened among the earliest farmers. But once a city's 'territory' became hundreds of square miles, invaders could slip over the borders, and there was nothing for it but to try to hurl them back by force of arms. The birth of the city made warfare inevitable because boundary disputes could no longer be solved by sabre-rattling.

But it would be a mistake to imagine that, because he marched against his neighbour, man suddenly became ruthless and cruel. In fact, there is a certain amount of evidence that cruelty was a fairly late development. We have a comprehensive record of the everyday life of these early civilizations – in Egypt and Mesopotamia: first in wall paintings, later in writing (which was invented in Sumer about 3500 B.C.). There are no scenes of brutality and harshness in Egyptian wall paintings, and the ancient Egyptians are known to have treated their defeated enemies with gallantry and consideration. The Hittites were among the most formidable warriors in the Middle East; yet the archaeological record shows that they were singularly humane. Sargon of Akkad, the first great empire builder – who lived about 2300 B.C. – has left the usual boastful records of his conquests and achievements; but they are free of the sadistic brutality of later conquerors. As Samuel Noah Kramer demonstrates in *History Begins at Sumer* (New York, 1959) the early Sumerian writings show that they were a people of high moral ideals. The first recorded murder trial took place in Sumer about 1850 B.C. – when three men were sentenced for killing a temple servant named Lu-Inanna – and the text states: 'They who have killed a man are not worthy of life.'

For what we must understand about the men of these early civilizations is that they regarded themselves as the servants of the gods. And the king himself was still nothing more than a servant. In the first chapter of *The Martyrdom of Man* Winwood Reade says about the early pharaohs:

He was forbidden to commit any kind of excess: he was restricted to a plain diet of veal and goose, and to a measured quantity of wine. The laws hung over him day and night; they governed his public and private actions: they followed him even to the recesses of his chamber, and appointed a set time for the embraces of his queen.

This is why those early civilizations were merciful to their vanquished enemies: they were ruled by the gods, and the gods taught the sanctity of human life. Besides, cruelty requires a certain degree of egoism, and a man who believes he is a servant of the gods keeps his individuality suppressed like the medieval craftsmen who built the cathedrals.

In the second millennium B.C., things began to change. The king ceased to be a mere figurehead and began to exercise real power. As other cities were conquered, a degree of ruthlessness became necessary. Sargon of Akkad was not particularly ruthless, and this may be why his empire lasted such a short time; in his last years, many cities rose up against him. Later kings recognized the importance of sternness and terror. The legal code of Hammurabi – who lived about 1800 B.C. – is famous for its balanced sense of justice; but it is far harsher than the earlier fragments of legal codes that have come down to us. An official of king Zimri-lin of Mari – a friend of Hammurabi – wrote to the king protesting about nomads who refused to be conscripted into the army, and suggesting that they should behead a criminal and send his head around to various encampments 'that the troops may fear and quickly assemble'. Later still, the kings would have sent their soldiers to behead dissenters in public squares.

According to this theory, then, man's development into criminality was inevitable. First he became a social animal, then a religious animal; then he became a villager, then a city dweller; then his territorial instinct pushed him into slaughtering his own kind in war . . . But this account still leaves unanswered the question raised by Erich Fromm: *Why* is man the only creature who kills and tortures his own kind without reason? Most animals feel a specific prohibition about killing their own kind. If two animals are fighting, and one of them wishes to surrender, it only has to roll on its back and show its stomach; the other animal then becomes incapable of continuing to attack. Man is the only creature who lacks this built-in mechanism.

One of the odder attempts to explain this anomaly was made by a Hungarian anthropologist Oscar Kiss Maerth, in a book called *The*

Beginning Was the End (1971). Maerth's theory takes as its starting point the evidence for widespread cannibalism among our ancestors – which is again something rarely found among animals. Basing his theory on his study of modern head-hunters in Borneo, Sumatra and New Guinea, Maerth argues that the eating of human brains stimulates intelligence and increases sexual excitability. He points out that in parts of Asia, fresh ape brain is still regarded as a delicacy, and can be bought in restaurants. The animal is killed immediately before the meal, and its brains are eaten raw. 'According to my own experience, about twenty hours after such a repast there is a feeling of warmth in the brain, like a gentle pressure. After about twenty-eight hours the body is flooded by vitality, with increased sexual impulses.' Early man ate the brains of his enemies – perhaps believing he could absorb his courage and other virtues – and discovered that it made him more intelligent. It also caused him to become obsessed by sex, and removed the animal inhibition against having sex when the female was not in season.

At the moment, Maerth's theory can be neither proved nor disproved, since there is no evidence that the eating of brains produces the effects he alleges. But it is worth mentioning here because it is at least an attempt to explain how man developed into a killer of his own kind. Konrad Lorenz's theory is far less heterodox, but it is open to equally strong objections. He suggests that harmless species, such as doves, hares and roebucks, have no appeasement signals to stop aggression, because in normal circumstances they cannot do one another a great deal of damage. To support this assertion, Lorenz describes how he placed two doves together in a cage and one of them almost pecked the other to death. Man, he says, being basically a harmless creature, without tusks or claws, also lacks appeasement signals. This explanation has been challenged by Elaine Morgan in a book called *The Descent of Woman*; she points out that man still has strong canine teeth, which must at one time have been far bigger. Baboons have similar teeth, and they have appeasement signals. She goes on to propound her own theory of how man came to lose his inhibition about killing defeated enemies. At one time, she suggests, our remote ancestors returned to the water when droughts reduced the food on land. (This theory was first put forward by the zoologist Sir Alister Hardy.) This is how man came to walk upright on his hind legs – because it is easier to walk upright in water; it also explains how he came to lose his body hair, since hair would impede his swimming. (Water animals, like otters, have short hair.) A point came when the upright, hairless male tried having sex in the frontal position, instead of from the rear. The reaction of most females to this, Elaine Morgan argues, would be to fight for their lives. But the females who succumbed to frontal 'attack' would have babies; the others wouldn't. Moreover, the ruthless males who ignored the females' cries for mercy would become fathers; the more scrupulous or timid males would die without issue. And so, eventually, the ruthless male who could ignore pleas for mercy would replace those who responded to appeasement signals.

There is one obvious objection to this interesting theory. The more scrupulous males would continue to mate from the rear when the female was on heat, and so there would be no reason for the more old-fashioned humans to die out. In addition, any sensible female, lying in a cave beside her mate, would quickly recognize that he was not trying to kill her when he mounted from the front. So she would have no need to make appeasement signals, and he would have no reason to overrule them. One more stimulating theory of human violence has to be abandoned.

In *African Genesis*, Robert Ardrey put forward the hypothesis that when man learned to kill with weapons his life became more violent and dangerous, so that it was the most skilful killers who survived. He later had to admit that this failed to explain why early man – like the men who lived in the Chou-kou-tien caves – made war on other tribes. (Mumford, of course, would reply that they were simply small expeditions to seize a few captives for sacrifice.) In a later book, *The Social Contract*, Ardrey had another suggestion: that man became dangerous when he ceased to be a hunter and became a farmer. The habit of hunting was still in his blood, and he turned from hunting animals to making war on men. This view had to be abandoned when Ardrey discovered that in the earliest of all cities, Jericho – dating back to 6500 B.C. – the citizens had built three sets of walls, as well as an enormous defensive moat. That argued that they were afraid of attack from nomadic farmers, even at this early date. (In fact, farming had been in existence for about three thousand years by this time.) But this evidence of Jericho certainly undermines Mumford's theory that warfare appeared in history only when there were rival cities. And Ardrey's hypothesis about out-of-work hunters is contradicted by the skulls in the Chou-kou-tien caves; man was dangerous even half a million years ago.

In 1972, Ardrey debated with Louis Leakey about the origin of war. Leakey agreed that the likeliest date was about 40,000 years ago; but his reasons were quite different from Ardrey's. He noted that Cro-Magnon man learned to make fire about 40,000 years ago. So man could sit around after dark, instead of being forced to go to his bed. And so for the first time, they could indulge themselves in conversation, and the children could sit and listen. Story telling became an art, and most of the stories were about hunting and clashes with other hunters. For the first time, man began to think in terms of 'them' and 'us'. This was Leakey's own imaginative theory of how man's imagination became possessed by war.

Like most theories of ancient man, this has the disadvantage that it can neither be proved nor disproved. But from our point of view, it is important because it firmly puts a finger on that central problem of criminality: xenophobia, the feeling of *non-fellowship* towards fellow human beings. And this is just as likely to be found among primitive people as among the 'underprivileged' in a modern city. In *Crowds and Power*, Elias Canetti cites an example of inter-tribal warfare in South America in the early twentieth century. A warrior of the Taulipang tribe described in detail how they annihilated the neighbouring tribe called the Pishauko. The quarrel seems to have started about women, and some Taulipang men were killed. The Taulipang decided that the Pishauko intended to destroy them, and that the only solution lay in striking first. Canetti describes how they crept up on the Pishauko village at night, when everyone was in the communal hut. Apparently a witch-doctor of the Pishauko warned them that their enemies were approaching. He was ignored. The Taulipang warriors cut their way through the lianas of the stockade, then rushed into the hut and began laying about them with their clubs; after this they set the hut on fire. 'The children wept. All the children were thrown into the fire . . . The Taulipang seized the fallen Pishauko one after the other and cut them right in two with a forest knife . . . Then they seized a dead woman. Manikuza pulled her genitals apart with his fingers and said to Ewana: "Look, here is something good for you to enter."' Here we see the close juxtaposition of the elements of cruelty (throwing the children into the flames), vindictiveness (cutting the bodies in two) and sexuality.

At first sight, this story offers support to the view that this kind of violence was a latecomer on the stage of history. This quarrel was about women. But if the Taulipang and the Pishauko had been two neighbouring groups of apes, such a quarrel would have been unlikely, for the apes would have mated within their own group. Neither would apes quarrel about territory; they would settle territorial disputes by the usual aggressive displays on the boundaries, followed by appeasement signals if things went too far. Presumably there must have been a time when our ancestors behaved more like the peaceable apes than warlike human beings. Then we recollect the skulls in the Chou-kou-tien caves, and doubts begin to arise. *That* happened half a million years ago; and one group still went on to annihilate another – or, at least, take a large number of them prisoners and kill them.

Until the end of his life, Robert Ardrey remained impenitently convinced that man became man because he lived by killing. This is what he calls 'the hunting hypothesis'. That is to say, man developed his human qualities because, from a very early stage, he learned to co-operate with other men in hunting wild animals. As a result, his social instinct developed side by side with his killer instinct. Just how long ago was not recognized until after 1960, which was the year Louis Leakey made an important discovery at Fort Ternan in Kenya. There were the bones of one of man's remotest ancestors, dating back fourteen and a half million years; he was called Ramapithecus, and he seems to have walked upright most of the time. And on the same site were hundreds of antelope bones. So this early ape was a hunter – which means, presumably, that he hunted in packs, and therefore had some kind of social co-operation. A battered chunk of lava suggested that it could have been used for extracting the marrow from the bones, and that therefore Ramapithecus was already a tool user. It was the Fort Ternan evidence that exploded a theory put forward by Ardrey in *African Genesis*, to the effect that Australopithecus became a meat-eater (and therefore a killer) during the droughts of the Pliocene period (more than three million years ago) when vegetation became scarce. But it also strengthened Ardrey's theory that man became human because he is a hunter.

Ten million or so years later came Australopithecus; he looked like an ape, was about four feet tall, and had a brain weighing about a pound (500 grams or 600 cc), one-third of that of modern man. This was not a very notable advance on the Ramapithecus's 400 cc. (Even a chimpanzee has a brain about 400 cc.) But this was the creature who first discovered the use of deadly weapons. Not long after this, there emerged another form of man with a still larger brain – about 700 cc – and who used primitive flint tools. He has been labelled *homo habilis*. And he, like Australopithecus, was active during an epoch of unprecedentedly bad weather – droughts, floods, ice ages – called the Pleistocene, which began about two million years ago. No one knows quite what caused the Pleistocene. The most popular theory is that polar ice reached such proportions that it began to split apart under its own pressure and giant icebergs floated towards the equator. But from man's point of view, the ice and floods of the Pleistocene were infinitely preferable to the long drought – in Africa, almost twelve million years long – of the Pliocene. This was the period when man suddenly put on an evolutionary spurt and began to outdistance every other animal on the face of the earth, including his cousin the ape. And during the next million years there emerged the creature who murdered his prisoners in the caves at Chou-kou-tien: *homo erectus*. His brain was about twice as big as that of Australopithecus – which makes it about two-thirds the size of that of modern man. We know that he used fire, although he did not know how to make it; and this itself argues a highly evolved social life. It implies that when hunters came upon a tree that had been set on fire by lightning, they carefully carried away burning branches and then appointed guardians to keep it permanently alight. Man was learning to think ahead, and had therefore outpaced every other living animal. From the fact that only skulls were found in the Chou-kou-tien caves, we may speculate that *homo erectus* was a head hunter, and that therefore his capacity for violence was already well developed.

And still the human brain went on expanding. In the half million years between Peking man and ourselves, it grew by another third, and most of that growth was in its top layer, the cerebrum – the part with which we think. No one knows quite why it expanded so fast. Ardrey even suggests the fascinating notion that it may have been connected with a huge meteor – or perhaps a small asteroid – that exploded over the Indian Ocean about 700,000 years ago. Its fragments – known as tektites – can still be found scattered over more than twenty million square miles. At the same time, the earth's poles reversed, so that south became north and vice versa. No geologist can yet explain why this happened – or why it has happened on a number of previous occasions in the earth's history. At all events, Ardrey suggests that the explosion, or the reversal of the earth's polarity, or both, somehow triggered the 'brain explosion'. During the reversal period, the planet would be temporarily without a magnetic field, and the result could be that earth experienced a sudden heavy bombardment of cosmic rays and other high-speed particles of the kind that are at present diverted by the Van Allen belts around us. There would also be a sudden rise in the temperature of the earth's atmosphere. Both these factors could cause genetic mutations which might be responsible for the 'brain explosion'. On the other hand, this 'catastrophe theory' may be unnecessary. If man's brain had already doubled in size between Australopithecus and the first *homo erectus* about a million years later, then there is nothing very startling in a further increase of about a third in another half million years.

There is, however, one outstanding mystery. Peking man already had a brain that was far bigger than that of Australopithecus; in fact, some of the larger-brained Peking men had brains as big as some smaller-brained modern men. What did he *do* with it? He certainly learned to build himself crude shelters made of branches, and developed more elaborate hunting techniques – he had even learned to kill elephants. Yet his tools made practically no advance. A mere 300,000 years ago, *homo erectus* was still using the crude flint choppers that *homo habilis* had been using two million years ago. And so things continued down to the time of Neanderthal man, who appeared on the scene only about a hundred thousand years ago. He was still a thoroughly ape-like creature with a receding chin and receding forehead, and his cave-dwellings indicate that he was also a cannibal. And he vanished from the face of the earth between thirty and twenty-five thousand years ago, when Cro-Magnon man – direct ancestor of modern man – appeared on the scene. Ardrey has no doubt whatever that Neanderthal was exterminated by Cro-Magnon man, and it seems a reasonable hypothesis even though most experts prefer to leave the question open. And Cro-Magnon man was the first creature to make obvious use of the enlarged brain. He made paintings on the walls of his caves; he even invented some crude form of notation on reindeer bones, probably to indicate the phases of the moon. In due course, he invented agriculture and built cities. He advanced more in twenty-five thousand years than his ancestors had in two million.

As usual, Ardrey has a striking theory to explain what happened. He points out that the 'tanged' arrowhead – a head that could be fastened to a shaft – was invented by a species of Neanderthal man – Aterian – who lived in the Sahara (in the days when it was a green paradise) about forty thousand years ago. That argues that they also invented the bow. And the bow and arrow, Ardrey believes, were as crucial to the ancient world as the atomic bomb is to the modern. It was the first 'long distance' weapon. It meant that a hunter was no longer tied to his tribe; he could go off on his own and stalk small game. And once man had become used to hunting alone – to being an *individual* – he probably began to develop the habit of thinking for himself. It is an exciting theory, and open to the single objection that, for some odd reason, the bow and arrow failed to spread beyond the Sahara culture that invented it. But then, as Ardrey points out, Cro-Magnon man knew about the sling, another long-distance weapon . . .

This hypothesis may prove to be as unnecessary as the 'big bang' theory of the brain. To begin with, Neanderthal man seems to have been far less ape-like than we used to assume. He buried his dead with some form of ritual. The seeds of brightly coloured flowers have been discovered in Neanderthal graves – they were probably woven into some sort of screen to cover the body. Chunks of manganese dioxide – a colouring material later used by Cro-Magnon man – have been found in his caves, some of them worn down on one side as if used as crayons. Smaller quantities of other colouring materials – like red ochre – have also been found. So it seems conceivable that he used them for colouring animal skins. Neanderthal woman may have been a slut – the caves seem to be knee deep in animal bones – but that is no reason why she may not have enjoyed wearing brightly coloured clothes. Another puzzling feature of Neanderthal man is that he manufactured stone spheres, as did his ancestors a million years earlier. A large white disc of flint, twenty centimetres wide, was discovered in a cave at La Quina, in France. Every student of mythology knows that such discs usually represent the sun; these stone spheres may also be sun or moon images. All this strongly suggests that Neanderthal man, in spite of his bestial appearance, had some form of religion. And religion is undoubtedly the outcome of man's thinking – and feeling – about the universe. It sounds very much as if Neanderthal man was already an individual before he invented the bow and arrow.

The real objection to most of these theories – from Maerth's brain-eating to Ardrey's bow and arrow – is that they all seem to assume that man is a basically passive creature who needed to stumble upon the discoveries that accidentally triggered his evolution. Ardrey and Lorenz suggest that man's discovery of weapons led to a better co-ordination of hand and eye, and so developed the brain. Ardrey suggests that long-distance weapons created 'individuality'. Speaking about the mystery of the enlarged brain, he says that it is rather as if someone had invented the Rolls-Royce before the discovery of petrol. And that in itself suggests that he may simply be holding his facts upside down. Suppose it happened the other way round, and man made his discoveries as a result of seeking the answers to problems?

Let us look carefully at this alternative view. We can begin with the known fact that at some remote point in prehistory, between twenty-five and fifteen million years ago, our remote simian ancestors descended from the trees because they found it more profitable to live on the ground. They dug for roots (as modern apes do), and ate small animals (again, as modern apes do). At times, they came upon larger animals – like deer – that had been trapped in thickets or swamps, and a point came when it struck them that big-game hunting made more sense than catching rodents and monkeys.

The upright posture may have developed because these hunters had to carry their game back to their living sites. An animal drags its prey in its teeth; these three-foot man-apes were too small for that. They learned the trick of carrying their prey on their shoulders as they tottered forwards on their unsteady legs.

The upright posture brought another advantage: they could see farther, an immense advantage for a hunter. Besides, there is something rather satisfying about seeing into the distance. Why do we all enjoy panoramic views, and feel stifled if we have to spend too long in a small room? Distant prospects are what animal ethologists call a 'releaser'; they arouse in us a definite response, like food or sex. The reason may be that for millions of years our ancestors experienced a surge of interest and anticipation when they climbed a tree and looked over a distant plain; now we still feel the same when we look down from a mountain top, even though we are no longer looking for game. We call it the sense of beauty but its origin may lie in the stomach.

And now we come to the heart of the mystery. The first men hunted in packs, like wolves – Ardrey even refers to Australo-pithecus as a 'wolf-ape'. Then why has man evolved to become the 'lord of the earth' when the wolf has remained more-or-less unchanged? (The ancestor of wolves and dogs, tomarchus, was on earth at the same time as Ramapithecus.) Moreover, both men and apes descended from the same tiny creature, a kind of tree shrew. So why have our cousins remained much as they were fifteen million years ago? In fact, precisely *why* did we evolve? For evolution is *not* 'normal'. The shark has not changed in a hundred and fifty million years; it is such an efficient predator that it has never needed to change its methods. Evolution takes place only when creatures have to adapt, and therefore to strive. The Pliocene and the Pleistocene were certainly difficult periods, but they were equally difficult for all creatures. So why did man outstrip all the others?

Oddly enough, most evolutionists seem to have overlooked the most obvious possibility: sex. Desmond Morris devotes some interesting pages to the development of female anatomy, and Elaine Morgan suggests that woman's breasts may have enlarged to make them more accessible to the baby (which no longer had hair to cling to during the feeding periods). But neither seems to have recognized that woman's sexual transformation could have been the single most important factor in human evolution.

The female ape is receptive to the male for only one week in the month. At some point in her history, the human female ceased to be seasonal and became receptive to the male at all times. The likeliest explanation is surely that when the males of the tribe were away hunting for days or weeks at a time, they expected to receive their sexual reward whether the female was in season or not. So in due course, the women who had no strong objection to all-the-year-round lovemaking bred more of their kind, while the others were gradually eliminated by natural selection. Since Leakey's discovery that Ramapithecus was already a hunter, it is conceivable that the change took place at a very early point in the history of our species.

In the lives of most animals, sex is an occasional indulgence; what really interests them is food. But once woman became permanently receptive, and began to develop characteristics that males found exciting – large breasts, full lips, rounded buttocks – then the males in turn had a strong motive for trying to show off their bravery and skill. The presence of unattached females in the group must have introduced an element of competition and excitement found in no other animal pack. Suddenly there was a reason for trying to become a mighty hunter. The psychology of the *Morte d'Arthur* and the

Chanson de Roland may have emerged in our ancestors long before
they developed other human characteristics. In which case, Goethe
put his finger on the central truth about human evolution when he
wrote that 'the eternal womanly draws us upward and on'.

And why should this kind of 'romantic' sexual selection have
produced a larger brain? Because the great hunter requires intelligence as well as bravery. This is why the brain increased in size – at
first very slowly, so that it took ten million years for the brain of
Ramapithecus to enlarge from 400 cc to the 600 cc of Australopithecus; then with increasing tempo, so that the brain of *homo
erectus* had increased to 1,000 cc in less than two million years.
(Robert Ardrey mentions that the brain of Anatole France was only
1,000 cc, demonstrating that Peking Man was already potentially the
intellectual equal of a college professor.) Then came the 'brain
explosion', when the average human brain enlarged by another third
in a mere half million years.

Now if the 'romantic' theory of evolution is correct, we no longer
need to ask why the human brain developed at such a speed. It
developed because sex had provided man with a motivation for using
his intelligence. It is true that this theory arouses immediate
misgivings in anyone who thinks in terms of twentieth-century
sexuality; when the male sex symbol is the pop singer wearing a
leather jacket and thrusting out his pelvis in time to the music,
intelligence seems superfluous. But the pop singer can survive
without intelligence, and the hunter cannot. We acknowledge this
when we say that someone's hand 'has not lost its cunning',
recognizing cunning as one of the basic attributes of the man who
pits his intelligence against the animal's instinct for survival: the
trapper, the patient watcher, the stalker of game.

And what, asks Robert Ardrey, did man *do* with his increased
brain? It may or may not be a coincidence, but the 'brain explosion'
began at about the same time as the last great ice age, half a million
years ago. From then until about ten thousand years ago, the ice
periodically advanced and retreated. In an ice age, hunting becomes
more difficult, and the need for intelligence and skill therefore
increases. On the other hand, such increased skill would not be
obviously reflected in man's artifacts; his chief weapon, the spear,
would remain unchanged. As far as *homo erectus* was concerned, the
greatest of his discoveries was the hand axe, which first appears
about a million and a half years ago. And there are no remarkable

changes in this simple tool for well over a million years. Why should there be? Its purpose was the skinning of animals and the trimming of branches – and possibly the opening of skulls to extract the brain – and these also remained unchanged.

There is, though, one curious piece of evidence that man had learned a new skill. It dates from about 200,000 years ago and was found at Pech de l'Azé, in the Dordogne in France; it is the rib bone of an ox, and it contains the world's earliest engraving. It is not particularly exciting: three arc-like patterns that overlap, and a few lines and V-shaped marks that could be natural damage. What is exciting about this bone is that it must have been engraved by *homo erectus*. And the next engraved bones date from a period about 175,000 years later; they were manufactured by our direct ancestor, Cro-Magnon man, the world's 'first artist'.

The discovery of Cro-Magnon art dates from 1865, when Edouard Lartet, a French lawyer, discovered bones engraved with reindeer and other animals near the town of Les Eyzies in the Dordogne. These went on show at the Paris exhibition of 1878, and were seen by a Spanish nobleman named Don Marcelino de Sautola. On his estate near Torrelavega, at a place now called Altamira, there was an underground cave that had been found accidentally when a hunting dog fell down a crack in the ground. Don Marcelino had already discovered the bones of bison and wild horses there; now he explored it thoroughly and found that the walls and ceilings were covered with vivid paintings of bison, deer, wild boar and wild horses. The discovery brought him little but bitterness, for a congress of scholars declared the paintings to be faked; when he died in 1888, Altamira was already forgotten. Then more paintings were found in caves in France. Belatedly, the importance of Altamira was recognized. When paintings in a Dordogne cave were found to be partly covered by layers of chalk and stalagmites, the last doubts about their antiquity vanished.

It was natural that the late Victorians should assume that the paintings were simply primitive works of art – representing the leisure hours of Cro-Magnon man. The first to cast doubt on this view was Salomon Reinach, a member of the French Institute, who suggested as early as 1903 that the paintings were part of a magic ritual to lure the bison and boar into the traps of the hunters. One of the best known palaeolithic drawings – from the Caverne de Trois Frères in the Dordogne – looks like a bison with human legs performing a kind of dance. It is obviously supposed to be a man wearing the skin of a bison; another one shows a man wearing a deer's antlers. We know that modern primitives perform 'magic' rituals that involve images of animals: Congo Pygmies draw the hunted animal in the sand and fire an arrow into its throat: Tungus carve the animal they intend to hunt; Yeniseis make a wooden fish. Books such as Carleton S. Coon's *The Hunting Peoples* and Joseph Campbell's *Masks of God* contain literally dozens of similar examples. So, in spite of the scepticism of some modern scholars, there seems no reasonable doubt that the animal paintings of Cro-Magnon man were intended purely for ritual purposes, as part of a ceremony to ensure successful hunting. Some of the animals are drawn several times, one on top of the other, which clearly suggests that they had to be sketched as part of some ritual. (A puzzling drawing from La Marche seems to show a praying female figure intertwined with the dancing shaman, suggesting that a 'sorcerer' may have used his arts to try and lure a desirable female.)

In the early 1960s, a scientific journalist named Alexander Marshack was studying some of the more puzzling finds from the Dordogne caves. These consisted of pieces of reindeer antler or bone incised with small marks – in some cases dots, in others, parallel lines. Marshack was writing a book on space exploration and wanted to write a section on the beginnings of science and mathematics. He was worried by what he calls 'a series of suddenlies' – Greek science started 'suddenly', astronomy started 'suddenly' in Mesopotamia, writing appeared 'suddenly', agriculture began 'suddenly', and so on. It all seemed absurdly unlikely. After all, Cro-Magnon man had a brain as large as that of modern man, and he was on earth forty thousand years ago. So was it not more likely that these discoveries actually had a long history extending back into the last ice age? Examining one of the 'dotted' bones through a microscope, Marshack observed that the dots had been made at different times by different instruments. This implied that they contained some kind of message. The dots were in a 'snakey' path, and Marshack concluded that their purpose was to make a note of the times of the rising of the moon over a period of months. Marshack studied dozens of bones, some dating back to 34,000 B.C., and concluded that all the marks could be interpreted as references to the moon and the seasons. In other words, they were primitive calendars. And why should stone age man be concerned with the times of the rising moon? Presum-

animals ask no questions

ably because he wanted to know when to anticipate the seasonal movements of animals – the migration of bison and reindeer, the spawning season of salmon. These conclusions were set out in a remarkable book, *The Roots of Civilization*, whose central thesis is that our Cro-Magnon ancestors were far less 'primitive' than anyone had ever realized. They had, in effect, invented a simple form of writing.

Now it becomes possible to see the significance of the engraved bone from Pech de l'Azé. Its overlapping lines seem to make no sense, and strike the casual observer as a form of doodling. But if Marshack is correct, ancient man did not indulge in doodling. His art was strictly purposeful. And if Cro-Magnon art was basically concerned with religious or magical ritual, then it is a safe assumption that the same would be true of the 'art' of *homo erectus*. In fact, if Marshack's argument – about 'suddenlies' – is valid, then we would expect to find that the origins of religious 'art' extend back far beyond the highly developed art of Cro-Magnon man.

All this offers us one of the most interesting clues so far to the mysteries of human evolution. It offers, to begin with, an answer to Ardrey's question about what *homo erectus* did with his enlarged brain. He used it to create the earliest form of science. Science is, after all, an attempt to understand and control nature by the use of reason. And a shaman performing elaborate ceremonies to ensure good hunting is as much a scientist as an atomic physicist searching for quarks.

Why do we find this idea so difficult to accept? It is not simply because we find it hard to believe that the ape-like *homo erectus* had fairly complex ideas: modern anthropology has revealed that many primitive people have highly complex belief systems. It is because we feel that religion is a specifically 'human' characteristic. It is quite impossible to imagine a horse or a gorilla having religious ideas, because they seem to have no capacity to *ask questions*. They take life 'as it comes'. And reconstructions of *homo erectus* make him look more like a gorilla than a man.

Our mistake could lie in the notion that religion is a matter of 'asking questions'. Auguste Comte said that religion is the attempt to account for the world in terms of supernatural beings. But that is typical of nineteenth-century rationalism. He imagines primitive man saying 'What causes thunder?' and answering 'An angry god.' But primitive people do not ask 'What causes thunder?' They simply respond to it with feelings, with intuitions.

The Taulipang's description of the massacre of the Pishauko tribe offers an important hint: 'A sorcerer was in the house who was just blowing on a sick man. He said: "There are people coming!" and thus warned the inhabitants of the house . . .' A few minutes later: 'The sorcerer went on warning them and said: "The people have arrived . . ."' How did the sorcerer know? It is quite impossible that he could have heard the approach of the hostile Taulipang. But primitive people take this kind of power for granted. Their shamans become shamans because they possess the gift of 'second sight' – or what the Highland Scots call simply 'the sight'. In *The Occult* I have mentioned a case described by the novelist Norman Lewis: of how the Huichol shaman, Ramon Medina, sensed as soon as he came into a village that there was a dead man concealed in a certain house, and was able to locate the corpse of a murdered man hidden in a roof space. Lewis remarks that the discovery was made 'through what is completely accepted in this part of the world – even by Franciscan missionary fathers – as extra-sensory perception.'

Even if we are inclined to discount the possibility of this kind of extra-sensory perception, it is difficult to deny the evidence for the ability of primitive people to locate water by some form of instinctive perception. The ability to 'dowse' with a forked twig is widely accepted today in most country areas; but the aborigines of Australia seem to be able to locate underground water even without the aid of a twig. Scientists who have investigated dowsing – such as Professor Y. Rocard of the Sorbonne – have concluded that underground water causes slight changes in the earth's magnetic field, and that these changes can be detected by the dowser. This explanation seems logical enough, since it now seems well established that birds migrate with the aid of the earth's magnetic field. Experiments conducted at Manchester University by Dr Robin Baker showed that human beings are also sensitive to earth magnetism; blindfolded students were driven long distances – as much as forty miles – by a circuitous route, and then asked to point in the direction of 'home'; sixty-nine per cent were accurate within an arc of 45 degrees, almost a third of them within 10 degrees.

It is easy enough to see that the ability to find water and to 'point' in the direction of home must have been essential for our ancestors for millions of years, and that this explains why their descendants still possess these abilities. This, in turn, suggests answers to certain questions raised by Marshack's analyses. He argues convincingly that the series of snakey dots on a piece of bone are a code indicating the times of the rising of the moon. But why should our ancestors have been interested in what time it rose? They did their hunting by day, not by night. And if their aim was simply to work out when herds of reindeer or bison would begin their annual migration, then small vertical notches – such as are found on other pieces of bone – would serve just as well for a 'tally'.

We know that the moon has a powerful influence on the earth's magnetic field – just as on the tides; it is probably this magnetic influence that causes disturbances in mental patients at the time of the full moon (and which leads us to speak of 'lunacy'). Researches carried out by Dr Leonard Ravitz of the Virginia Department of Health showed that there is a difference in electrical potential between the head and chest, and that in mental patients there are far greater fluctuations in this difference than in normal people; the greatest fluctuations occur at the times of the new and full moon. A Japanese doctor, Maki Takata, showed in the 1940s that the rate at which blood curdles – the 'flocculation index' – is affected by sunspot activity. Experiments on the electrical field of trees – carried out by Harold Saxton Burr and F. S. C. Northrop in the 1930s – showed that this was also affected by sunspots. But the most significant deduction from their experiments was that living matter is somehow held together, shaped, by electrical fields just as iron filings are held together and shaped by a magnet. This is the reason why if half a sea urchin's egg is killed with a hot needle, the remaining half develops into a perfect but half-sized embryo (an experiment performed early in this century by Hans Driesch); each half contains a complete electrical 'blueprint' of the whole. But the astonishing thing is that the electric field should have a shape, like the jelly-mould that turns a blancmange into a miniature castle. (It is this same mould that allows certain creatures to re-grow lost limbs.) It is as if the force of life controlled matter by means of electric fields.

So there is nothing surprising in the discovery that animals are sensitive to the earth's magnetic field; it would be astonishing if they were not. And since this field is altered by the movements of our neighbours in space – the planets as well as the sun and moon – it would also be surprising if our remote ancestors did not feel instinctively the connection between the earth beneath his feet and the heavens above his head. The sensitivity to underground water

– and its electrical fields – must have been developed by our ancestors millions of years ago, perhaps in the great droughts of the Pliocene.

All of which suggests that there was no need for ancient man to 'ask questions' about the forces of nature; he felt them around him, as a fish can feel every change in the pressure of the water through nerves in its sides. The result must have been a curious sense of unity with the earth and heavens that *homo sapiens* lost a long time ago. Ancient man's religion was not an attempt to 'explain' the universe; it was a natural response to its forces, like the response of the skin to sunlight.

This still leaves unexplained how the Pishauko witch-doctor was able to sense the approach of enemies. Modern psychical research would probably explain it in terms of telepathy. But it is important to bear in mind that the witch-doctor himself would not accept such an explanation for a moment. Throughout history, *all* shamans, witch-doctors, 'magicians' and witches have claimed that they derived their powers from 'spirits', usually those of the dead. The power to respond to earth forces – to find water or ensure an abundant harvest – is regarded as part and parcel of the shaman's ability to establish contact with the world of spirits. We may dismiss this as primitive superstition; but again, we shall be missing the point if we think of it as an attempt to 'explain' the problem of what happens after death. Shamans do not 'believe' in spirits; they experience them – or at least, experience something that they accept as the spirit world. So it is unlikely that Neanderthal man performed burial rituals because he had decided there must be life after death. He performed them because he took it totally for granted that he was surrounded by spirits, and that these included the spirits of the dead and the spirits of nature – 'elementals'. The same argument applies to *homo erectus*. If he made bone carvings (and possibly rock paintings, since the two seem to go together) it was because they were part of his religious rituals. And if he possessed religious ideas, then they were certainly connected with the spirits of the dead and the spirits of nature. Moreover, there is no need to assume that such ideas were a late development. If religion is a sensitivity to natural forces, then its origins probably lie in the dawn of prehistory; Ramapithecus probably had his own equivalent of 'hunting magic'.

And what of the human – or animal – sacrifice that always seems to be a part of primitive religion? Why did primitive man feel the need to make offerings to the spirits? Here we can only point to a well-established fact: that throughout the history of magic, at all times and in all cultures, man has believed that magic is carried out with the aid of spirits. And from ancient Babylonia to modern Brazil, he has also believed that the spirits must be paid with certain 'offerings', which must be accompanied by an extremely strict ritual. As I have described in my book *Poltergeist*, the modern Brazilian 'spiritist' believes that the spirits wish to continue tasting the pleasures of this world: food, alcohol, sex, a good cigar, and will perform certain services – such as poltergeist hauntings – in return. The western mentality finds such beliefs absurd; but if we are to understand primitive religion, we must recognize that they can be found in every culture at all periods of history. If *homo erectus* performed human sacrifice in the Chou-kou-tien caves, then we should at least give consideration to the notion that magic is far older than *homo sapiens*.

All this, then, would explain why Cro-Magnon man was preoccupied with the phases of the moon, and why the earliest science in Sumeria was astronomy. It was not the result of intellectual curiosity about the stars, or an attempt to create a seasonal calendar for agricultural purposes. (In Egypt the Nile itself was the best of all calendars.) It was a development of religion – of man's sense of involvement with the forces of the earth and the powers of the heavens.

Cro-Magnon man also seems to have continued the practice of human sacrifice – at least, signs of cannibalism have been found at Cro-Magnon sites near Chou-kou-tien. This should not be regarded as evidence that our immediate ancestors were prone to cruelty or aggressive violence – any more than Jewish ritual slaughter is evidence of sadism, or the Christian eucharist of cannibalism. Religious sacrifice is performed in a spirit of self-effacement, in the service of the gods. It stands at the opposite extreme from criminality, which is an expression of individual self-assertion.

At a certain point in history, man began to lose this sense of involvement with the gods. According to Wells, this was when he first became a city dweller; but we have seen that this is not entirely accurate. Three thousand years after the foundation of the first cities, the king of Sumer still regarded himself as no more than a servant of the gods. So did his people. In *History Begins at Sumer*, Samuel Noah Kramer writes: 'Sumerian thinkers . . . were firmly convinced that man was fashioned of clay and created for one purpose only: to serve the gods by supplying them with food, drink and shelter.' It was a long time before the inhabitants of these temple-cities turned into Wells's 'jostling crowds', and crime ceased to be the exception and became the rule.

How this came about deserves to be considered in a separate chapter.

early notions of service to God
— materialistic / non-individualistic
levels

crime as a destruction
or lack of empathy
at the individual &
communal level;
cause of this lack
is need to bolster
self esteem in an
anonymous world

Five
THE DISADVANTAGES OF CONSCIOUSNESS

One day in 1960, at precisely ninety seconds before midday, a young student named Klaus Gosmann walked into a block of flats on the Tuchergarten Strasse in Hersbruch, near Nuremberg. He was a quiet, serious young man, known to his few acquaintances for his deep interest in mystical theology: his daydream was to find a job as pastor at some quiet little country village, where he could lead a life of dedicated service.

He chose a flat at random and knocked on the door. A young man opened it. It was thirty seconds to midday. Gosmann said: 'Sir, I wish to ask you a question and I shall not repeat it.' 'What?' 'Your money or your lives?' At that moment, the bells of the local churches began to chime midday, making a deafening noise. Gosmann drew a revolver from his pocket and carefully shot the young man in the heart. The man's fiancée, who was looking curiously over his shoulder, began to scream. Gosmann shot her through the head. Then, before the bells had finished chiming, he turned and walked home. There he wrote up the story of the murder in his diary. He was pleased that he had timed it to a second – so that the bells would drown the shots – and that he had remained perfectly calm and controlled.

Gosmann committed four more murders during the next seven years. One was of a bank director – again at precisely midday – from whose desk Gosmann snatched a few thousand marks. Another was of a doorman in a bank he had just robbed – the man was reaching to his pocket for his glasses when Gosmann fired. And to obtain more weapons, Gosmann shot the widow who ran a gun-shop in Nuremberg and her twenty-nine-year-old son. His next crime was his undoing. In July 1967, he snatched the handbag of a woman in a department store; when she screamed he fired at her but missed. He also fired at a store official who chased him and hit his briefcase. Beaten to the ground, he was thinking; 'How ridiculous – it can't be happening.' He fired one more shot, killing the man who had chased him. Then he was arrested.

Why did Gosmann kill? No doubt a psychiatrist would be able to uncover the roots of the obsessions and emotional disorders that turned his thoughts towards crime. (He revered the memory of his father, an army captain, who had been shot by the Americans at the end of the war.) But the central motivation was undoubtedly the need to bolster his self-esteem. Gosmann felt himself to be weak and inadequate – a thinker who was incapable of action. His crimes were a deliberate attempt to strengthen his identity. And just as some couples enjoy sex more if they can see themselves in a mirror, so Gosmann tried to add a dimension of reality to his crimes by describing them in his diary. In prison he wrote in his journal: 'I would say there is a great difference between me and Raskolnikov [in *Crime and Punishment*]. Just as long as I don't get it in the neck from the judge, I don't have to consider myself as the perpetrator. Raskolnikov always thought of himself as the perpetrator . . .' It is an interesting comment that reveals that even his present situation had not succeeded in rescuing him from his sense of unreality: 'How ridiculous – it can't be happening.' Gosmann *did* 'get it in the neck' from the judge; he was sentenced to life imprisonment with no possibility of release.

In the case of Klaus Gosmann we can see clearly the connection between crime and the sense of identity. If Gosmann had possessed the simple consciousness of an animal, he would have been incapable of crime. Most young people understand that need to deepen the sense of identity, and the feeling of envy and admiration for people of strong personality who seem to 'know who they are'. (No doubt this was the basis of Gosmann's admiration of his own father.) A great many of the activities of the young – from wearing strange garments to driving at ninety miles an hour – are attempts to establish the sense of identity. A dog has no such problems. It is entirely lacking in reflective self-consciousness. Consequently, it would be incapable of 'crime' in our human sense of the word. Crime is basically the assertion of the 'I'. 'I' strike someone in the face; 'I' order the bank clerk to hand over the money; 'I' pull the trigger.

Now it should be quite obvious that without this sense of 'I', there can be no crime. If your dog chases sheep and you give it a beating, it will in future feel an inhibition about chasing sheep. Even when it is out for a walk on its own, it will remember that chasing sheep is a forbidden activity. Yet a burglar who has spent five years in prison – a far more savage punishment than a good beating – may ignore the inhibition next time he sees an open window. And this is because it is no longer a simple matter of response (crime) and inhibition (punishment). A third element has entered the situation: the burglar's sense of his own personality, his ego. A sudden opportunity presents him with a challenge – 'I can probably get away with it' – and if he gets away with it, there is a feeling of self-congratulation: 'I did it!' – the feeling Klaus Gosmann recorded in his diary after his first murder. When man first became capable of that kind of self-congratulation – a fairly common form of self-awareness – he also became capable of crime.

The question of precisely when this happened may seem un-answerable. But a startling and controversial theory has been advanced in a book called *The Origin of Consciousness in the Breakdown of the Bicameral Mind* by Dr Julian Jaynes, of Princeton University (published by Houghton Mifflin in Boston in 1976). When it appeared reviews were almost uniformly hostile, and it is easy to understand why. According to Jaynes, the authors of the Old Testament and the *Epic of Gilgamesh*, of the *Iliad* and *Odyssey*, were entirely lacking in what we would call 'self-consciousness'. Their consciousness looked outward, towards the external world, and they had no power of looking inside themselves. He says of the characters in Homer: 'We cannot approach these heroes by inventing mind-spaces behind their fierce eyes . . . Iliadic man did not have subjectivity as we do; he had no awareness of his awareness of the world, no internal mind space to introspect upon.'

This is a baffling statement, because we are so accustomed to 'looking inside ourselves' when we have to make a decision. 'Shall I go by train or bus?' We *talk to ourselves*, just as we would to another person. And it is hard to imagine how we could make any decision without this kind of introspection. It is true that if I step off the pavement as a bus comes round the corner, I jump back without a moment's hesitation; but that is a very simple 'decision'. To decide whether to take a bus or a train, I must form a mental picture of the two alternatives and compare them; I *must* look inside myself. And it is quite impossible to imagine how King Solomon or Ulysses made up their minds without going through a similar process.

According to Jaynes, the answer is that they heard voices that told them what to do: voices inside their heads. Jaynes first became convinced of this possibility when he had a similar experience. 'One afternoon I lay down in intellectual despair on a couch. Suddenly, out of an absolute quiet, there came a firm, distinct loud voice from my upper right which said, "Include the knower in the known!" It lugged me to my feet, exclaiming, "Hello?" looking for whoever was in the room. The voice had an exact location. No one was there!' It was an auditory hallucination, and the experience led Jaynes to study the subject. He discovered that a surprisingly large number of ordinary people have had auditory hallucinations. And in ancient texts – such as the Bible and the *Iliad* – Jaynes found a total lack of evidence for any kind of introspection but an enormous amount for auditory hallucinations – which were interpreted as the voice of God, or one of the gods.

In support of this part of his argument, Jaynes draws upon the relatively new discipline of split-brain research, based upon discoveries made by Roger Sperry in the 1950s (and for which he has since received the Nobel Prize). The brain is divided into two halves, which appear to be mirror-images of each other. The specifically human part of the brain, as we saw in the last chapter, is the part that presses against the top of the skull – the cerebrum. This looks rather like the two halves of a walnut, joined in the middle by a thick bridge of nerves called the corpus callosum.

In the 1930s, it was discovered that attacks of epilepsy could be controlled by severing this bridge, and so preventing the 'electrical storm' from spreading from one side to the other. And, oddly enough, it seemed to make no difference whatever to the patient, who went about his business exactly as before. It was Sperry who made the remarkable discovery that the split-brain patient actually turns into two people; but they continue to work in such close co-operation that no one notices. It is only when they are subjected to experiments that prevent them from co-operating that the difference can be observed.

It has been known since the mid-nineteenth century that the left cerebral hemisphere controls our powers of speech and reason, while the right seems to be concerned with intuition and with recognizing shapes and patterns. A patient whose left hemisphere has been damaged suffers from impaired speech but can still appreciate art or enjoy music. A patient whose right hemisphere has been damaged can speak perfectly clearly and logically, yet cannot draw the simplest pattern. Oddly enough, the left side of the brain controls the right side of the body and vice versa. If someone puts an object – say a key – into the left hand of a split-brain patient (without allowing him to look at it), he knows perfectly well what it is, yet he cannot 'put a name' to it. If he is asked: 'What are you holding in your left hand?' he has no idea of the answer. For the person called 'you' seems to live in the left brain, and has no idea of what is concealed in his left hand.

With the eyes it is slightly more complicated, since half of each eye is connected to the left brain and half to the right. But if the patient is asked to stare rigidly in one direction, an object can be shown only to the left or right visual field. If a split-brain patient is shown an orange with the right brain and an apple with the left, and is asked to write with the left hand what he has just seen, he will write: 'Orange'. If he is asked to state what he has just written, he will reply: 'Apple'. When one split-brain patient was shown an indecent drawing with the right half of the brain, she blushed; asked why she was blushing, she replied: 'I don't know.'

There is therefore strong evidence that 'you' inhabit the left cerebral hemisphere, and that the person in the right is a stranger. And although it could be argued that this does not apply to most of us, since we are not split-brain patients, this inference would be incorrect. Otherwise, split-brain patients would know that their corpus callosum had been severed – they would be aware that they have been cut off from their 'other half'. In fact, they notice no difference – which suggests that, for practical purposes, they were already split-brain before the operation. In fact, a little thought will show that we are all split-brain patients. When I experience an intuition, a 'hunch', it walks into my left brain – my conscious, wide-awake self – from the domain of that other 'self' (which appears to be the gateway to the unconscious).

Jaynes believes that auditory hallucinations originate in the right brain. And he suggests that when one of the ancient heroes of Homer heard the voice of a god advising them what to do, this voice originated in the right brain, and sounded in the left brain as if through a loudspeaker. We have already seen that the ancient kings of Egypt and Mesopotamia regarded themselves as mouthpieces of the gods, which seems to lend support to Jaynes's theory.

Jaynes believes that man began to develop language – simple cries like 'Danger!' and 'Food!' – as recently as seventy thousand years ago. He did not learn to speak simple sentences until much more recently – between twenty-five and fifteen thousand years ago. But although he had language, he had no self-consciousness. So a man who had been ordered to go and build a dam upstream had no way of reminding himself what he was supposed to do; 'reminding myself' demands self-awareness. He might, of course, repeat his instructions – the simple word for 'dam' – non-stop all the way up the river. But then, his right brain could help him not to forget. Most people can tell themselves that they must wake up at six in the morning, and wake at precisely six o'clock. The right brain has acted as an alarm clock. So the primitive hunter's right brain would repeat the word for 'dam' when he reached the correct place, and he would hear it as a voice – probably speaking from the air above the left side of his head.

Jaynes suggests that this happened some time after the advent of the earliest agriculture, about 10,000 B.C. This was the time when men began living in larger groups – no longer a small band of hunters living in a cave, but anything up to two hundred people living in a settlement of fifty or so houses. A group that large would need a leader – a king. But when the king died, his subjects would continue to hear his voice; hence they would assume that he was still alive – a god. This, says Jaynes, is how man came to believe in the gods. The gods were an inevitable consequence of the development of the 'bicameral mind'.

So, according to Jaynes, those early civilizations were 'bicameral'. Men were not responsible for their actions; they obeyed the voice of the gods. And then, very slowly, consciousness (i.e. self-awareness) began to develop. This was due to a number of causes, but the main one was the invention of writing, some time before 3000 B.C. Writing – whose purpose is the storage of information – drove man into a new kind of complexity. For as soon as I begin to store information, I am forced to become more complex, whether I like it or not. An obvious example of the process is a library. I may collect books because I enjoy escaping from the real world. But as my collection expands, I must keep it in some sort of order. I must make bookshelves and adopt some kind of system of classification. This may strike me as tiresome; but unless I want to keep falling over books on the floor, or unless I keep giving them away, then I must teach myself the elementary principles of librarianship. Whether I like it or not, I have to 'get organized'.

So the development of writing created a new kind of complexity

Velikov

that undermined the bicameral mind. (In the first chapter of my book *Starseekers* I reviewed the evidence that the Great Pyramid – dating from about 2500 B.C. – and megalithic monuments like Stonehenge were built as 'computers' whose purpose was to enable the priests to create astronomical tables.) Moreover, the second millennium B.C. was a time of unprecedented catastrophes and stresses. 'Civilizations perished. Half the world's population became refugees. And wars, previously sporadic, came with hastening and ferocious frequency as this important millennium hunches itself into its dark and bloody close.' The tremendous volcanic explosion of the island of Santorini – about 1500 B.C. – devastated the whole Mediterranean area. Then, between 1250 and 1150, the same area became a prey to hordes of invaders known as 'the Sea Peoples', who attacked the bleeding civilization like sharks. Under all this stress, the old, child-like mentality could no longer cope. The men who rebuilt civilization needed new qualities of ruthlessness and efficiency. Besides, all this violence demanded a more subtle response. 'Overrun by some invader, and seeing his wife raped, a man who obeyed his voices would, of course, immediately strike out, and thus probably be killed. But if a man could be one thing on the inside and another thing on the outside, could harbour his hatred and revenge behind a mask of acceptance of the inevitable, such a man would survive.'

The first sign of this 'change of mind', says Jaynes, can be found in Mesopotamia. Around 1230 B.C. the Assyrian tyrant Tukulti-Ninurta I had a stone altar built, and it shows the king kneeling before the *empty* throne of the god. In earlier carvings, the king is shown standing and talking to the god. Now the king is alone; the god has vanished. A cuneiform text of the same period contains the lines:

> One who has no god, as he walks along the street
> Headache envelops him like a garment.

Headache is the result of nervous tension, of losing contact with the intuitive self. And when man suffers from stress, he reacts to problems by losing his temper. And it is at this point, according to Jaynes, that cruelty first becomes a commonplace of history. It is in the Assyrian carvings of about this period that we first see illustrations of men and women impaled, children beheaded.

This, then, is Jaynes's fascinating if highly controversial account of the coming of self-awareness and of crime. And it is open to one very obvious objection; that it is practically impossible to imagine complex human beings – such as Sargon of Akkad or Hammurabi – without self-awareness. Jaynes points out that consciousness is not nearly so important – or so necessary – as we seem to think; a man playing the piano performs an extremely complex set of operations while his mind is elsewhere, enjoying the music. If he becomes conscious of his fingers, he plays badly. But this example is deceptive. The man had to learn to play the piano slowly and consciously; only then could he do it 'automatically'. If he had never possessed self-consciousness, he would have been incapable of learning to play, since playing – like any other complex operation – demands self-criticism.

There are other strong objections to this aspect of Jaynes's theory. Professor Gordon Gallup of New York State University, has conducted a series of experiments in an attempt to determine whether animals possess self-awareness. Various animals – seventeen species in all – were placed in a cage with mirrors. Then the animal was anaesthetized and its face painted with a red, odourless dye. When the animal woke up, it was easy to see whether it recognized – through its mirror-image – that its face had been dyed. Two species – chimpanzees and orang-outangs – inspected their faces in exactly the same way that a human being would under similar circumstances; none of the others showed the least interest in their reflections. Most other species behaved in various ways that showed they regarded their mirror-images as other members of the same species – making friendly overtures or even attacking the image. Some of them continued to behave in this way even after years of acquaintance with mirrors, revealing total inability to recognize themselves.

Significantly, gorillas were among those unable to recognize themselves – significantly because gorillas are closely related to chimpanzees and orang-outangs. There is one basic difference: the gorilla brain is far less 'lateralized' than those of the chimpanzee and orang-outang; it has not yet split into 'identical twins' – which in turn may explain why the gorilla lacks self-awareness.

Gallup goes on to argue that, once an animal can become the subject of its own attention, it can contemplate its own existence; and if you can contemplate your existence, you can also contemplate your non-existence. We have seen in the last chapter that Neanderthal man buried his dead with elaborate ceremonies, which certainly indicate that he was aware of his mortality. Ergo, Neanderthal man possessed self-awareness. Again, Jaynes argues that man invented the gods some time after 10,000 B.C. when he began to 'hear voices'. But the discs and spheres carved by Neanderthal man suggest that he worshipped the sun and moon. In fact, if the skulls in the Chou-kou-tien caves are evidence of ritual sacrifice, then man's religious sense probably dates back half a million years.

All this might seem to leave very little of Jaynes's theory still standing. But on closer examination, this proves to be untrue. From Jaynes's point of view, it is a pity that he regards 'the origin of consciousness in the breakdown of the bicameral mind' as the essence of his theory. For this may, in fact, be its most dispensable aspect. Jaynes's real achievement lies in pointing out that man probably developed his present form of 'alienated' consciousness at a fairly late stage in his history. And once this has been pointed out, we can see that it is not only consistent with the findings of split-brain research but that it has many other interesting implications. If a man is concentrating on a practical task – like driving in the rush-hour – an electro-encephalograph machine shows that his brain is 'desynchronized' – that most of the activity is going on in the left. When a yogi goes into meditation, the pattern becomes synchronized as the two sides work in harmony. And we can recognize this in ourselves. When we are deeply relaxed, we have a clearer sense of reality; we feel more 'in touch' with the world around us. The more we experience stress, the more we lose that sense of reality; in some odd sense, we no longer *believe* in the existence of external reality – it has become a kind of dream.

In spite of this unpleasant side-effect, 'desynchronization' is a considerable evolutionary achievement. A gorilla cannot (presumably) become desynchronized; it has no ability to detach a part of its attention from the total act of living. Human beings have a similar problem when under the influence of alcohol; they have difficulty in reading a piece of abstract prose, or following a mathematical argument. Our ability to desynchronize consciousness brings an enormous gain in intellectual power. Wagner once remarked that art 'makes life appear like a game, and withdraws us from the common fate'. In fact, all intellectual activity has this power to withdraw us from life, to enable the mind to hover like an eagle above the world of matter. There must have been a time in human history when we

had no power to desynchronize – when, in effect, we were permanently drunk. This must have had the same advantage as being
intoxicated – that feeling of relaxation, of 'belonging', of feeling at
home in the world. But it also meant that we had no power to detach
ourselves from the present moment, or to disobey the immediate
promptings of instinct.

It might seem common sense to assume that the human brain
began to 'desynchronize' as we developed the power to use language.
But then, we know that children with left-brain damage can use the
right brain for learning language – but only up to the age of about
seven, when the two halves of the brain begin to specialize. If our
remote ancestors were like children under seven, then the emergence
of speech need not necessarily lead to desynchronization. It is easy
enough to imagine the first agriculturalists, even the first city-
builders, as simple, 'unicameral' beings – after all, a city is not so
different from an ant hill or a wasps' nest. But the city seems to have
made war inevitable. Robert Ardrey tells the story of the zoologist
C. R. Carpenter, who transported a colony of 350 rhesus monkeys
from India to an island off Puerto Rico, to study them in a restricted
environment. On land, monkeys choose 'territory' – a tree or groups
of trees – and live in peace with one another. On board ship, this was
impossible. The monkeys also had to be kept hungry, to accustom
them to new types of food. And the result was that mother monkeys
tore food from their babies, and male monkeys ceased to defend
their mates from attacks by other males. The infant mortality rate
soared. Once on the island, the monkeys established themselves in
various 'territories', and once again the males defended their mates
and the mothers defended their babies. The lesson seems to be that
without proper territory, the monkey instinct for preservation of the
species becomes eroded. A similar discovery was made about human
beings when city planners began to build high-rise flats with
communal corridors. The rate of vandalism and mugging soared and
some showpiece developments had to be demolished. Some planners
tried applying what we have learned about territory, replacing the
high-rise flats with small houses with individual front gardens;
instantly, the crime rate fell dramatically.

In the first towns and cities, men still had their individual
territory. But when cities built walls, and the population grew,
overcrowding was inevitable. The result was the same as among
Carpenter's monkeys and among high-rise flat dwellers: crime,

vandalism, unchannelled aggression. At first, this would be held in check by strong religious prohibitions. We know these began to break down after about 3000 B.C. – which, by coincidence, is also the date of the development of writing. Man became the kind of creature we know today – warlike, and inclined to individual violence against his own kind.

Now according to the Jaynes argument, there was a difference between the purely territorial disputes of the early city dwellers and the murderous savagery that began to develop towards the end of the second millennium B.C. The well-known palette of King Narmer – an early king of Egypt, possibly identical with the legendary Menes – dates from some time before 3000 B.C. and shows the king strutting towards a double row of decapitated enemy corpses; the inscription seems to mention a total of 120,000 prisoners. Another picture shows Narmer holding a prisoner by the hair, while he holds some kind of club aloft, apparently about to dash the man's brains out. Closer examination suggests that he is brandishing his sceptre above his head in symbol of triumph – like a boxer shaking his hands above his head – and merely holding the prisoner in a position of ritual abasement. The beheaded enemies have not necessarily been executed. They may be merely symbols of enemies killed in battle and beheaded – like the skulls in the Chou-kou-tien caves – as part of some ritual. There is no evidence here of deliberate cruelty.

By the time of Hammurabi, more than twelve hundred years later, the empire of Sargon of Akkad had risen and fallen, and the age of the gods was drawing to a close. Jaynes speaks of the stele that bears the famous code of Hammurabi, and remarks on its boastful introduction and epilogue, in which Hammurabi describes his conquests; he points out that the code of laws sandwiched between these two has a completely different tone, serene and rational. Jaynes believes this to be evidence that Hammurabi was 'bicameral', and took down the laws from the dictation of his right brain, which he assumed to be the voice of the god Marduk. The likelier explanation is that the code of Hammurabi is a digest of several earlier codes and adopts their tone and phrasing. But the boastful tone of the introduction and epilogue certainly indicates that this king regards himself as a great deal more than a mouthpiece of Marduk.

The stele of Hammurabi dates from about 1750 B.C. After that period came the 'dark ages', when half the population of the Mediterranean world became refugees. In Egyptian art, scenes of warfare become more frequent. In *The First Great Civilizations* Jacquetta Hawkes mentions (p. 386) reliefs of prisoners 'trussed in a variety of painful and humiliating ways'. And a scene from the time of Rameses III – who reigned shortly before 1100 B.C. – shows piles of chopped-off hands. By this time, according to Jaynes, the bicameral period was at an end. The human brain had become desynchronized. At about the same time, Tiglath-Pileser I, king of Assyria, formulated another code of laws that makes a grim contrast to the code of Hammurabi. (And we may recollect that even the code of Hammurabi is harsher than earlier codes of laws.) Jaynes writes: 'His exploits are well known from a large clay prism of monstrous boasts. His laws have come down to us in a collection of cruel tablets. Scholars have called his policy "a policy of frightfulness". And so it was. The Assyrians fell like butchers upon harmless villagers, enslaved what refugees they could and slaughtered others in thousands. Bas-reliefs show what appear to be whole cities whose populace have been stuck alive on stakes running up through the groin and out of the shoulders. His laws meted out the bloodiest penalties yet known in world history . . .' The cruelty is partly the result of the desynchronization – like the driver losing his temper in a traffic jam – and partly the result of natural selection, a thousand years of violence and hardship.

And this murderous violence also brings about a change in the pattern of history. The pendulum now swings between savage oppression and the equally savage destruction of the oppressors. The twentieth century has seen this pattern in the rise and fall of the Nazis. And it emerged for the first time in the first millennium B.C. in the story of the rise and fall of the Assyrian empire. The Assyrians had played an important part in the history of Mesopotamia for more than a thousand years. The murder of Tiglath-Pileser in 1077 B.C. brought its first great epoch to an end. For more than a century, during what George Roux calls (in chapter 17 of *Ancient Iraq*)'the dark age in Mesopotamia', Assyria was in eclipse. In 911 B.C. it began to hack its way back to greatness; Jaynes writes: '. . . the Assyrians [began] their reconquest of the world with unprecedented sadistic ferocity, butchering and terroring their way back to their former empire and then beyond and all the way to Egypt and up the fertile Nile to the holy sun-god himself, even as Pizarro was to take the divine Inca captive two and a half millennia later on the opposite side of the earth. And by this time, the great transilience in mentality

had occurred. Man had become conscious of himself and his world.'
And from then until their final downfall in 610 B.C., they ruled and
conquered with a ferocity that makes the Nazis seem almost
benevolent by comparison. In the British Museum can be seen the
tablets of Assurakbal III, depicting the torture of captives who are
stretched naked on the ground and tied to pegs; some are being
skinned alive, others are having their tongues and ears ripped off
with pincers. (Some of the more hair-raising tablets are hidden away
in the basement of the Museum.) When Sennacherib invaded
Babylon in 689 B.C. he carried out the systematic slaughter of all its
inhabitants until the street was piled high with corpses; then he
razed the city to the ground and diverted a canal through it to wash
away the ruins. (Eight years later, he was assassinated by his sons as
he was praying in the temple at Nineveh.) By the middle of the
seventh century B.C., the Assyrian war machine was the most
efficient and brutal the world had ever known. Tiglath-Pileser III
(744–727 B.C.) invented a new method of crushing revolt – mass
deportation to distant places; he was indifferent to the number who
died of starvation and exhaustion en route. In one year (744), sixty-
five thousand people were deported.

Many powerful nations have collapsed because they became lazy
and effete – like the Romans and Persians of later times. The
Assyrians never made that mistake. They were prepared to smite
hard and brutally to maintain their grip on their subjects. And it was
this very efficiency that brought about their downfall. The Semitic
peoples have never been notable for co-operation; they are too much
inclined to squabble amongst themselves. But the brutality of the
Assyrians finally drove their enemies to unite. Around 654 B.C.,
Assurbanipal was faced by a hostile coalition of Babylonians,
Elamites, Chaldeans and half a dozen other peoples, led by his own
brother, the king of Babylon. The Assyrian war machine ground
into action; Babylon, now rebuilt, was starved into submission; the
king escaped being tortured to death by burning himself alive in his
own palace. Then Assurbanipal went about 'pacifying' the various
rebels with his usual sadistic brutality. By 639 B.C. all his enemies
had been smashed into submission and the land of Elam had been
erased from the map. From his magnificent palace in Nineveh,
Assurbanipal contemplated the whole world prostrate at his feet, and
savoured his victory. But it was at the cost of inflaming the whole
Mediterranean world with a frenzied and impotent hatred. And

when Assurbanipal died, they rose up again; and this time they succeeded. The Assyrians received no more mercy than they had given. Their enemies – led by king Nabopolassar of Babylon – set out to exterminate them as if they were plague rats. They were so thorough that they left no Assyrians to recall the story of their greatness. Two centuries later, the Greek mercenaries of Cyrus were retreating up the Tigris valley – the famous story is told by Xenophon – when they passed the gigantic ruins of Nineveh and Kalah. They were baffled by the mystery of these great empty cities, whose immense fortifications made them look impregnable. All Xenophon could find out – from local peasants – was that the cities had been miraculously depopulated by direct intervention of the gods. The conquerors who had terrorized the Middle East for so many years were no longer even a legend.

There is a baffling paradox involved in all this. The Assyrians responded to the challenge of disaster and chaos by becoming the most ruthlessly efficient conquerors the world had ever seen. They were undoubtedly the 'fittest', and according to the Darwinian principle, they should have survived. Yet, for some reason, human history contradicts the Darwinian principle – not once, but again and again.

From the time of the Assyrians to the time of the Nazis, history has been full of ruthlessly efficient men who ended in failure. And it is of central importance to understand why this is so; for we are now dealing with the essence of crime. The criminal is basically a person who sees no reason why he should not get what he wants by stealth, or by force, or both. Confronted by a difficult knot, his first impulse is to take a knife and cut it. In the short run, this is usually successful; but even in the moderately short run, things usually begin to go wrong. In the case of the individual criminal – like Carl Panzram – the reason is obvious enough. In the case of nations – like the Assyrians, the Huns or the Vandals – it may be rather more complicated, but it amounts finally to the same thing. The real objection to criminal violence is not the harm it inflicts on society – although this can be horrific enough – but the fact that, in the long run, it invariably fails to achieve the criminal's objective. It is basically a miscalculation. For crime is essentially a *left-brain* way of achieving objectives. It refuses to recognize any value but the achievement of the objective. And somehow, the objective gets lost in the process.

It was this paradox that fascinated the historian Arnold Toynbee, who has described how he became aware of it on a May evening in 1912. Toynbee had spent the day in the deserted citadel of Mistra, which looks out over the plain of Sparta. For six hundred years, Mistra had been a flourishing town, until one morning in 1821 a horde of wild invaders had massacred its inhabitants and left it a ruin. Pondering on this completely pointless slaughter and destruction, Toynbee was overwhelmed by 'a horrifying sense of the sin manifest in human affairs', and of 'the cruel riddle of mankind's crimes and follies'. Why is man the only animal who takes pleasure in destruction for its own sake? This is the question that runs through the eight thousand or so pages of Toynbee's *Study of History*.

It is appropriate that the scene of the realization should have been above the plain of Sparta. For the Spartans, like the Assyrians, are an example of the futility of sheer ruthlessness. In the eighth century B.C., the Lacedemonians (Sparta is the capital of Lacedemon) found their own land too small for the growing population, so they invaded the territory of their neighbours, the Messenians. For sixteen years the Messenians fought like tigers, but the Spartans finally conquered. However the Messenians detested the invaders, and a century later they made a desperate and tremendous attempt to throw off the foreign yoke. This war was even bloodier, and it lasted twenty years. At the end of it, both sides were exhausted; but the Spartans were the winners, and they took murderous reprisals. And now they took the step that would eventually turn Sparta into a living fossil. The sheer agony of that long battle made the Spartans determined never to allow it to happen again. So they turned Lacedemon into one vast army camp. They thought and ate and drank nothing but military discipline. Messenia had to be held in an iron grip, so they set out to transform themselves into iron men.

The land of Messenia was divided into equal allotments, each of which was handed over to a Spartan 'peer'; the natives became slaves – helots – whose business was to support him. If any child of a helot showed the least sign of talent or brilliance, he was promptly murdered; the Spartans were determined to save themselves trouble in the next generation. All their own children – girls as well as boys – were destined for military training from birth. (Weak children were condemned to die of exposure.) At the age of seven, Spartan children left their homes and went into training camps. Girls received the same military training as boys; in athletics, they competed with them on equal terms, even wrestling naked with them in front of a male audience. The highest virtue in Spartan life was sheer toughness, ability to endure pain and hardship. In due course, the males entered the army. There was no family life for them; they lived in a barracks and ate in the mess. On a girl's wedding night, she surrendered her virginity, then her husband left her and went back to barracks. To show she was a soldier's wife she cut her hair short and wore male clothes. If her husband seemed unable to produce healthy children, he was expected to find a better man to occupy his bed; if he was unwilling, then his wife had to arrange it. A man who ate poorly at mess was likely to be penalized; it was evidence that he had been indulging himself in the debilitating pleasantness of family life.

It all sounds rather like *Nineteen Eighty-Four* – and even more like that giant in Wagner's *Ring* who killed his brother to get the Nibelung's treasure, then turned himself into a dragon and spent the rest of his life guarding it. The Spartans became the dragons of the Hellenic world. When their neighbours, the Athenians, looked like becoming too powerful, the Spartans felt they had to conquer Athens to maintain their own position. And after a war that dragged on for twenty-seven years, they were again victorious. Yet the one thing they were *not* ready for was the leadership of the Hellenic world. They had trained themselves for hardship and struggle; success demoralized them. Some of the soldiers they sent abroad to govern colonies became notorious for debauchery. And the Spartans who stayed at home remained rigid, completely fixed in their conservatism; Toynbee compares them to soldiers standing permanently on parade with arms presented. And while they stood there, the cobwebs grew all over them. The Spartans did not vanish in a spectacular holocaust, like the Assyrians; they merely became the victims of a kind of spiritual arthritis and quietly faded out of history.

Here we can see very clearly the importance of Jaynes's insight. The Spartans were the ultimate 'left brainers'. They fixed their minds on one thing and one thing only, and pretended that nothing else existed. Before the Messenian war, Sparta was creating its own tradition of art and music; this came to a complete halt in the middle of the sixth century B.C. It was not revived until more than five hundred years later, when the militarist system in Sparta was finally smashed in the second Macedonian war. A symbol of the sheer futility of the Spartan ideal can be seen in their later custom of inducing boys to display their toughness by allowing themselves to be flogged to death at the altar of the moon goddess.

The left cerebral hemisphere is the critical part of the brain, the part that can overrule our impulses. (This explains why even cats and dogs have two hemispheres; all creatures need the power to change their minds.) It would not be too inaccurate to say that the Spartans outlawed creativity and turned themselves into a nation of critics. The left brain directs our energies into a narrow, fast current like a mountain stream; the right allows them to spread into a broad, slow-moving river. But the right also enables us to see where we are going, to survey the surrounding landscape and decide where we want to go next. The left becomes easily trapped in its own obsessive forward movement and loses all ability to change direction. When this happens, there are two possibilities: self-destruction or slow exhaustion. The Assyrians are an example of the first alternative, the Spartans of the second.

Two thousand years or so later, Sherlock Holmes found himself confronting the same dilemma. In his earlier days, Holmes was much given to relieving his boredom with morphine or cocaine. When, in *The Sign of Four*, Watson asks him whether he has any work on hand at the moment, Holmes replies: 'None. Hence the cocaine. I cannot live without brainwork. What else is there to live for? Stand at the window here. Was ever such a dreary, dismal, unprofitable world? See how the yellow fog swirls down the street and drifts across the dun-coloured houses. What could be more hopelessly prosaic and material? What is the use of having powers, doctor, when one has no field upon which to exert them?' When Doyle wrote *The Sign of Four*, it was not recognized that cocaine was addictive (Freud made his original reputation by administering it to cure morphine addiction); and in any case Holmes was saved from addiction by his own increasing success. But the example serves to show us that the nature of the problem has not changed in the three thousand years since Rameses III. Man has achieved his pre-eminence by showing himself to be the greatest of all survivors; he has survived droughts, ice-ages, famines and earthquakes. And at a certain point in his history, evolution subjected him to the strangest of all experiments: confining his sense of identity to his left brain. (It makes no difference whether or not we accept Jaynes's estimate of *when* this happened; the important thing is that it happened.) It paid off spectacularly. With this new detachment from nature, man began to study it with a critical eye and observe its habits. In the third century B.C., a Greek philosopher named Eratosthenes, who lived in Alexandria, heard that there was a well in a town called Syene – modern Aswan – where the sun was reflected at midday on midsummer day. This meant that it was precisely overhead, and that a tower in Syene would cast no shadow. But towers in Alexandria *did* cast shadows at midday on midsummer day. Eratosthenes measured such a shadow, and calculated that the sun's rays struck the tower at an angle of 7½°. And if the earth is a globe (a traditional piece of knowledge that seems to date back to ancient Egypt), then the distance from Syene to Alexandria must be 7½° of the earth's circumference. Since this distance is five hundred miles, Eratosthenes was able to work out that the circumference of the earth must be 24,000 miles. The modern measurement is 24,860 miles at the equator, so Eratosthenes was incredibly accurate. Another Alexandrian Greek, Aristarchus, measured the angle from the earth to the sun when the moon was directly overhead and half-full, then used simple trigonometry to work out the size of the sun and moon and their distances from earth. His calculations were not quite as accurate as Eratosthenes', because of the difficulty of judging exactly when the moon was half-full; but he worked out that the moon is fifty-six thousand miles away and the sun well over a million. The impact upon his fellow Alexandrians must have been stunning. The story of Icarus told them that if a man flew too high he would get close to the sun and melt his wings; now Aristarchus was telling them that a man could fly a thousand miles high and hardly be any closer to the sun. He added that, since the sun was far larger than the earth, it was quite possible that the earth travelled round the sun and not vice versa.

These remarkable discoveries reveal the impact of man's newly-acquired 'bicameralism'. The earliest farmers were undoubtedly interested in the sun and moon; but they would not have dreamed of doing anything so boring as measuring angles and calculating distances. Yet this was one of the most important consequences of bicameralism; it meant that people often did 'boring' things merely to escape from boredom – a paradox with which we are all familiar. The result was the discovery that calculation and measurement give us a new power over the physical world.

But it was another 'change of mind' that had – and continues to have – the greatest consequences for the human race. When a man is trapped in this thin and unsatisfactory left-brain awareness, he hungers for the richer consciousness of an animal as a starving man dreams of food. He craves the sense of oneness with nature, that immediate, comfortable feeling of contact with reality. The result is the attitude we now call 'romanticism' – the obscure longing for distant horizons, for 'unknown modes of being'. As W. B. Yeats put it:

> What the world's million lips are searching for
> Must be substantial somewhere. . .

In short, being stranded in left-brain consciousness turned man into a dreamer.

When a dreamer has an army at his disposal, the result can be frightening and spectacular. In about 367 B.C., a fifteen-year-old prince named Philip of Macedon was seized by the Greek general Pelopidas and sent to Thebes as a hostage to guarantee the good behaviour of his elder brother, King Alexander. In comparison with Thebes, Macedon was a provincial backwater. Philip was dazzled by the culture and sophistication of the Greeks. He was a naturally intelligent youth – his elder brother Perdikkas was in correspondence with Plato – and he threw himself into the study of literature, philosophy and the art of public speaking. When Alexander was assassinated, Philip returned to Macedon and no doubt found the place unbearably provincial. So when Perdikkas – who had succeeded Alexander – was also murdered, Philip seized the throne and set about the task of turning Macedonia into another Greece. He was a born soldier and soon converted the army from a disorganized rabble into a fighting machine comparable to the Spartans or Assyrians. He subdued the hill tribes in his own country and then, full of euphoria, went on to conquer the lands from the Danube to the Hellespont. This was not – like the empire-building of Sargon of Akkad – an attempt to win security for his own people and extinguish petty rivalries; it was fighting for purely romantic reasons, fighting for the joy of fighting, fighting for glory and renown. Above all, it was fighting to become worthy of the admiration of the Greeks. Like some medieval knight, Philip was doing battle for the honour of his lady. And when he had subdued the lands to the north and east, he marched south into Greece and conquered the lady herself. Thebes was occupied by a Macedonian army – a conquest that was to have terrible consequences for the Thebans. Athens, which had led the resistance to Philip, expected a fight to the death; but Philip behaved like a perfect gentleman. He was not out for revenge: he only wanted to be regarded as a Greek.

Two years later, at the age of forty-six, Philip was murdered and his twenty-year-old son Alexander became king. Greece heaved a sigh of relief, convinced they had nothing to fear from this boy. In the following year, rumours of Alexander's death led to a revolt in Thebes. Alexander descended like a thunderbolt; when the Thebans shouted defiance from their walls, he took the town by storm and massacred all the inhabitants. Unlike his father, Alexander had no sentimental attachment to Thebes.

But he resembled his father in one important respect: he was a romantic who dreamed of far horizons. He crossed the Hellespont and defeated a Persian army – by attacking them without delay, instead of spending two days preparing for the battle as they expected. King Darius of Persia raised another army; Alexander defeated that as easily. The chronicle tells how, after this victory at Issus, Alexander moved into the king's tent, bathed himself in the royal bath, then stretched out on a silken couch and raised his goblet of wine. 'So this is what it's like to be royalty . . .' He pressed on into Syria, then into Egypt, where he founded the city of Alexandria. Then he went back and defeated Darius yet again and moved into Babylon. Typically, he treated Darius's womenfolk with the greatest courtesy, and married one of them. After this, he spent five years wandering around his newly won empire. His men finally begged him to take them home and Alexander marched reluctantly back to Babylon. He was still searching for the city of his dreams. He was planning the invasion of Africa when, at the age of thirty-two, he caught a fever and died.

Modern research has added a valuable piece of information to the history: that Alexander probably died of alcoholism. This provides an important missing piece of the jigsaw. We know that Alexander was a man of extremes; on several occasions he ordered whole towns to be massacred, down to the last woman and child; yet he was also capable of gallantry and generosity. When his friend Hephaestion died, Alexander's grief was deep and genuine; but he also ordered the crucifixion of the doctor who had attended Hephaestion's deathbed. After an argument with his foster brother Kleitus, Alexander seized a spear from a guard and ran him through; then, when he realized what he had done, he tried to run it into his own throat. These are the typical extremes of an alcoholic, with his drunken furies and fits of sentimentality and generosity. Above all, the alcoholism confirms the diagnosis of Alexander as a self-divided man, desperately trying to escape the narrowness of left-brain consciousness. He would have been happier if he had been stupider, but he came of a family of intellectual romantics. We have seen that his father studied philosophy at Thebes; and when it came to choosing a tutor for his son, Philip chose Plato's pupil Aristotle. But Alexander, like Philip, was too emotional, too undisciplined, to enjoy the consolations of philosophy. Wine was for Alexander what cocaine was for Sherlock Holmes: an escape from the boredom of a dismal, dreary, unprofitable world. The story of Alexander crying for fresh worlds to conquer is probably apocryphal; but it catches the essence of his craving for unexplored horizons.

It is important to grasp that boredom is one of the most common – and undesirable – consequences of 'unicameralism'. Boredom is a feeling of being 'dead inside'; that is to say, loss of contact with our instincts and feelings. Experiments with EEG machines have shown that when we become bored the right cerebral hemisphere begins to display alpha rhythms – the rhythms that appear when the brain is 'idling'. Robert Ornstein, one of the pioneers of split-brain research, discovered that this happens when someone is doing mental arithmetic. It happens, in fact, during any activity in which we are not really interested. But if the right brain 'idles' too much, it goes to sleep. The psychologist Abraham Maslow described a case of a girl who suffered from depression and a sense of meaninglessness; she had even ceased to menstruate. He discovered that she wanted to study sociology and was being forced – by financial necessity – to do a boring, repetitive job. When Maslow suggested that she should go to night school and continue her studies of sociology, her problems promptly vanished. The boredom had caused her right brain to spend most of its time 'idling'; as soon as she began to think in terms of purpose and motivation, she also began to feel again.

The business of that 'other self' is to add a third dimension – of reality – to human existence. If the brain becomes too obsessed by analysis – grappling with complicated problems or simply impatient over futile tasks, the right yawns and stares gloomily out of the window, and reality becomes oddly unreal. When this happens, we experience an immediate impulse to 'find something interesting' to do. A child switches on the television; a woman goes and buys herself a new hat; a man decides to forget the lawnmowing and go fishing. Alexander looked at the map and planned new conquests. But even conquest has its moment of tedium: long marches, rainy days when nothing happens. As soon as he began to feel bored, Alexander reached for the bottle.

So it seems that, in the case of Alexander at least, we have answered Fromm's question of why man is the only creature who kills and tortures his own kind. Aggression, like alcohol, readjusts the balance between right and left; it 'rescues us from our cold reason', restores that feeling of instinctive purpose. And in recognizing this we have also identified one of the basic motivations of all criminality. A bored child can just as easily look around for some mischief to get into; the bored teenager may go and vandalize a telephone box or pull up all the shrubs in a public garden . . . Even adults may be driven by 'left-brain isolation' to curious acts of protest or rebellion. The bored business man seduces his secretary when he doesn't really find her attractive; the bored housewife goes out shoplifting when her income is more than adequate. Dostoevsky devoted a whole novel, *The Possessed*, to a study of a man who does scandalous things without any apparent motive, and who admits in his 'Confession' that it all sprang out of a sense of having nothing to do with his strength. Gide's Lafcadio pushes a stranger from a train for much the same reason. In Sartre's *Age of Reason*, a student named Boris steals from shops merely for the sake of the excitement.

But when we turn from literature to the real world, it is obvious that no one is going to commit a serious crime merely because he is bored; it fails to provide an adequate explanation for crimes like those of Klaus Gosmann, Ian Brady, Sigvard Thurneman – or even, for that matter, of a fairly straightforward swindler like John Haigh. The essence of crime, as we have seen, is a certain self-consciousness, an awareness of doing 'wrong'. Strictly speaking, the massacres of Alexander the Great cannot be regarded as crimes. When Alexander ordered the massacre of every inhabitant of an unnamed town in India, it was because they were the descendants of the Greeks who had, a hundred and fifty years earlier, handed over the treasures from the temple of Apollo to the Persian king Xerxes;

Alexander felt he was an instrument of divine justice. Even if the massacre had been performed in a spirit of sadistic pleasure, it would still not be semantically accurate to describe it as a crime. The ancient world was full of tyrants who killed for pleasure; Plutarch writes about one Alexander of Pherae, in Thessaly, who buried men alive, 'and sometimes dressed them in bears' and boars' skins, and then baited them with dogs.' The same tyrant called together the inhabitants of two friendly cities for an assembly, and had them surrounded and cut to pieces. But again, he regarded it as his *right* to do this kind of thing; so there was no consciousness of crime or guilt. (It is pleasant to record that he was assassinated, with his wife's connivance.)

By contrast, Klaus Gosmann and Ian Brady committed their crimes with a backward glance of guilt towards society. For all their bravado and defiance, they felt they were doing 'wrong'. Their mental attitude differed from that of tyrants in the way that the attitude of a schoolboy differs from that of a schoolmaster. Which leads us to the interesting recognition that crime becomes possible only when there is an authority against whom it can be directed. In these early cities, in which the king regarded himself merely as a servant of the gods, crime was probably virtually non-existent. To commit a crime – say theft or murder – a man would have to set himself up against the will of the gods; and under the psychological conditions of a theocracy, this would be tantamount to suicide. It was not until kings became tyrants – that is, men who had seized power in their own name – that the basic psychological condition for crime came into existence. To commit a crime, a man must both recognize authority and regard it with resentment. Crime is, by its essential nature, anti-authoritarian. We can see the way in which this resentment comes to be formed in the following story (quoted by Ludovic Kennedy in *A Book of Railway Journeys*):

Another Englishman travelling on the continent, Lord Russell, was acclaimed for putting a native with whom he was sharing a compartment in his place. As the train drew out of the station the foreigner proceeded to open his carpet bag, take out a pair of slippers and untie the laces of his shoes.

'If you do that, sir,' proclaimed the great Victorian jurist, 'I shall throw your shoes out of the window.'

The foreigner remarked that he had a right to do as he wished in his own country, so long as he did not inconvenience others. Lord Russell demurred. The man took off his shoes, and Lord Russell threw them out of the window.

What is interesting about this anecdote is the phrase 'was acclaimed for putting a native . . . in his place'. There seems to be no awareness that Lord Russell was behaving with the utmost unreasonableness. As a leading citizen of the great British empire, he felt he had every right to order a foreigner not to take off his shoes; the British had been doing the same kind of thing all over the world for centuries. We feel, as we read it, that the foreigner would have been justified in taking Lord Russell by the throat and throwing *him* out of the window. Such self-confident stupidity arouses murderous rage. And it is this feeling that authority deserves to be treated with violence that constitutes the essence of crime. It was the same feeling that made Cromwell decide to cut off King Charles's head. Every crime is, in a sense, a one-man revolt against authority.

This kind of sentiment makes an appeal to the anti-authoritarian in all of us. It is the basis of all left-wing political philosophies, from Rousseau to Marcuse. But before we allow ourselves to be seduced into sympathy by the notion that crime is a healthy protest against authority, it is important to bear in mind that anti-authoritarianism is a legacy of childhood. This emerges clearly in a collection of children's jokes made by an American sociologist, *Children's Humour* by Sandra McCosh.

There's this little lass, and her mother's in bed poorly and she don't want to be disturbed, and so she says to her father, Daddy, can I come to bed with you? So he says no and she says I'll scream, so he says ok then. So they go to bed. And the daughter says, Daddy, what's that long thing? And he says it's a teddy bear, so she says can I play with your teddy bear? So he says no, so she says, I'll scream, so he says ok then, but let me get to sleep, I've got to get to work early tomorrow. So in the morning he wakes up and there's blood all over the covers, and he says, what you done? so she says your teddy bear spit at me so I bit its head off.

Johnnie Fuckerfaster, named that by his mom, was under the house with a girl, and his mom didn't know he was there with a girl. And she calls, Johnnie, come here. And Johnnie says, I guess I'll have to go, even though they were in the middle of it, and she yells again, Johnnie Fuckerfaster, and so he yells back: I'm fucking her as fast as I can.

In another typical joke, the mother orders her daughter not to climb lamp posts, because the boys only want to see the colour of her knickers. Next time the girl admits to climbing a lamp post, her mother says: 'I thought I told you not to do that.' 'It's all right – I took my knickers off first.'

After a few pages, these jokes begin to produce an oddly claustrophobic effect; their outlook is so uniformly negative. The adult is bothered by their illogicality; the father has an orgasm in his sleep – which is just possible – but he then sleeps on when his daughter bites off the end of his penis. The mother has named her son Johnnie Fuckerfaster, but he does not recognize his own name when she calls him, and thinks she is giving him an order. It requires a major suspension of disbelief – and all for the sake of a mildly 'naughty' conclusion:

A mother's boy got married, and when he got in bed with his wife he didn't know what to do. So she said: Get on with it, and he said: Get on with what? So she said: Well, do something dirty. So he shit the bed.

It is 'naughty' for a girl to let a boy see her knickers. Sex is dirty, like shitting the bed; conversely, shitting the bed is funny because it is also forbidden. There are long, elaborate stories in which children are misinformed about the meaning of words: father's penis is a train, mother's vagina is a tunnel: (Hey Sis, come and look; Dad's train's got stuck in Mom's tunnel . . .) Fuck means to go and get washed, shit means food, bastard means vicar: (Hello bastard, mom's just getting fucked before she serves the shit.) Again, the whole point of the rigmarole is that the child should innocently undermine the authority of his parents or the vicar or his schoolteacher. Other jokes make their effect simply by being nauseating; a tramp eats a dead cat, or drinks the contents of a spittoon. This, like shitting the bed, is 'dirty' and must therefore be funny. And the 'dirty' is forbidden, and must be funny too.

These jokes enable us to reconstruct the peculiar mental world of the child, which most of us have so conveniently forgotten: the world seen from a worm's eye view. Adults have their own strange ideas about what is 'fun' – religion, politics and sport. But every child knows better. They know that 'fun' is doing those exciting things you are not supposed to do, all those things that adults call 'naughty'. This is why most children have a streak of cruelty that makes them enjoy pulling wings off flies or throwing lighted matches at the cat; here, on a small scale, they can become an Alexander the Great, free to give way to the normally forbidden desire to cause pain. The child's world is almost entirely defined by the authority of adults, and by their secret desire to flout that authority.

But have adults really outgrown these attitudes? A comedian only has to make a disparaging remark about a well-known politician to bring loud laughter, even applause. It need not be a particularly funny remark, provided it has a touch of malice – a sense of giving the two-finger salute to authority. Humorists who make a virtue of anarchism – the Marx Brothers, Lennie Bruce, Mort Sahl, Spike Milligan – are generally regarded as the comedians of the intellectual, for the man with a sophisticated sense of humour, more 'daring' and therefore funnier than the straightforward clown. (Even T. S. Eliot admired Groucho Marx.) Yet anyone who is slightly over-exposed to this type of humour – say, watching a season of Marx Brothers films on TV – soon becomes aware that its premises will not bear close scrutiny. Defiance of authority, deflation of dignity and pomposity, are really rather thin stuff after the first five minutes. Refusal to take anything seriously is only funny up to a point; then an odd taste of futility begins to creep in. When Groucho sings 'Whatever it is, I'm against it', we only find the sentiment amusing for as long as we fail to think about it. Chaos is refreshing only so long as we can feel that pleasant sense of law and order hovering in the background.

We have here the same fallacy that vitiates the work of de Sade. The heroes of *The 120 Days of Sodom* are really schoolboys who believe that something must be pleasant because it is forbidden. There is one passage in which a prostitute describes how one of her clients made her leave her feet unwashed for weeks, then ate the dirt from between her toes. While most of the libertines grimace with disgust, Curval takes the prostitute's foot and sucks between her toes. (Significantly, Curval is a Lord Chief Justice – de Sade's equivalent of the anti-politician joke.) But another of the libertines goes on to make the significant remark: 'One need but be mildly jaded, and all these infamies assume a richer meaning: satiety inspires them . . . One grows tired of the commonplace, the imagination becomes vexed, and the slenderness of our means, the weakness of our faculties, the corruption of our souls lead us to these abominations.' And, apparently unaware that he has just levelled the most devastating criticism at his own philosophy, de Sade proceeds to his description of the next perversion – an elderly general who likes to masturbate himself against the scars of an old woman who has often been flogged in public for theft.

This, then, is the essence of crime: unreasoning resentment of authority. The child is, in a sense, a natural criminal, since he lives in a world of authority: authority stretching as far as the eye can see, from parents and schoolteachers to policemen and prime ministers. As he grows up, he learns to share the burden of authority – perhaps over younger brothers or sisters, or over younger children at school. Eventually, he has children of his own, so that he now slips naturally into his place in the adult power structure. Yet although his reason is now convinced of the need for authority and law, his emotions continue to resent it – hence the laughter when a comedian makes a joke against authority. In most of us, the two never come into open conflict. The head remains a supporter of law and order, the heart of anti-authoritarianism. The case of de Sade is of symbolic importance because he not only tried to reconcile the two: he attempted to justify his heart with the use of his head. De Sade is anarchy incarnate; he performed the service of carrying its arguments to the point of absurdity.

Yet it is de Sade who can provide us with the deepest insight into the question: why is man the only creature who kills and tortures his own kind? This is because de Sade is, in himself, a kind of one-man textbook of criminology. His view of human beings is determinedly materialistic and pessimistic. If he were alive to see the rising crime figures of the late twentieth century, he would laugh sarcastically and say: I told you so. For, according to de Sade, man is a being who was created accidentally by Nature, and who has only two basic urges: survival and satisfaction of his desires. This situation is bound to produce a conflict of interests. The hungry tiger needs food; the antelope often has no choice about becoming its dinner. Human society has its own equivalent of tigers and antelopes: the 'haves' and 'have nots'. The haves not only use their superior strength (or wealth) to satisfy their desires; they also use their cunning to convince the have-nots that there are moral laws that forbid robbery and murder. Sooner or later, says de Sade, the have-nots are bound to discover that moral laws are an invention of the rich; then they will try and take what they want, and the crime rate will soar . . .

According to de Sade, man's basic desire is to become a god. And if any man could become a god, he would experiment with every kind of pleasure: eat things he had always wanted to eat, do things he had always wanted to do, take revenge on old enemies, torment

to call this desire "criminal" is an ideological, augural [an interp 'n] others are possible

people he loathed. Above all, he would satisfy his sexual desires with everyone who aroused them, probably a hundred times a day. Can any human being honestly declare that he would behave differently? If not, then the point is proved. Man is naturally a criminal, but fear of punishment forces him to restrain his desires . . .

If we accept de Sade's materialistic premises – which, after all, are the same as those of many modern scientists and philosophers – then his arguments are difficult to refute. Yet there *is* one obvious point at which they are open to objection. The satisfaction of every casual desire does not seem to guarantee happiness. Desires seem to be subject to the 'law of diminishing returns'. A man who could satisfy every desire the moment it arose would probably end by committing suicide out of boredom. This was de Sade's own problem. As a wealthy and reasonably good-looking young man, he had tried all the 'normal' sexual pleasures before he was in his mid-teens. He spent the rest of his life in pursuit of 'the forbidden', the ultimate sexual pleasure. And the harder he tried, the more it seemed to recede from him. The perversions became so extreme that they became wild and grotesque – almost funny.

When we examine this 'infinite regress', we can pin it down to what might be called 'the fallacy of simple experience' – de Sade's conviction that experience satisfies the senses in the same straightforward way that food satisfies the stomach. When I am empty, food is bound to have the effect of filling my stomach – this is a physical law. Yet even so, I might find it appetizing, or boring, or even nauseating, depending on my state of mind. We all know that good digestion is fifty per cent 'mental'. And sex is a great deal more than fifty per cent. In the wrong mood, sexual fulfilment is a will o' the wisp, flickering in the distance and then vanishing. De Sade's conviction that there is an 'ultimately satisfying' sexual experience – if only we had the moral courage to try and find it – is an illusion.

The answer to de Sade is contained in a passage in Kierkegaard's *Either/Or*:

The history of [boredom] can be traced to the very beginning of the world. The gods were bored, so they created man. Adam was bored alone, and so Eve was created. Thus boredom entered the world, and increased in proportion to the increase in population. Adam was bored alone; then Adam and Eve were bored together; then Adam and Eve and Cain and Abel were bored *en famille*; then the population of the world increased and the people were bored *en masse*. To divert themselves they conceived the idea of constructing a tower high enough to reach the heavens. This idea is itself as boring as the tower was high, and constitutes a terrible proof of how boredom had gained the upper hand . . .

The fallacy here lies in the notion that the answer to boredom lies in distraction, in looking for something 'interesting' to do. De Sade's work is a kind of sexual tower of Babel. The true answer to boredom, says Kierkegaard, lies in the 'rotation method', the method by which a farmer changes his crops from year to year so that the *ground itself* never becomes exhausted. 'Here we have . . . the principle of limitation, the only saving principle in the world. The more you limit yourself, the more fertile you become in invention. A prisoner in solitary confinement for life becomes very inventive, and a spider may furnish him with much amusement. One need only hark back to one's schooldays . . . how entertaining to catch a fly and hold it imprisoned under a nutshell . . . How entertaining sometimes to listen to the monotonous drip of water from the roof . . .'

What does the prisoner in solitary confinement actually *do*? What does the schoolboy do as he listens to the rain? The answer is that lack of expectation makes him slow down his senses, which has the effect of amplifying his perceptions. And he produces this 'slowing down' by *increasing his attention*. It could be compared to a scientist focusing a slide under a microscope, or a man pouring wine through a funnel so that not a drop shall be lost. The schoolboy 'funnels' his attention on to the beetle under the nutshell. De Sade has the temperament of a spoilt brat; he is too impatient to 'funnel' his attention, and then wonders why the experience is so unsatisfying.

This effect is explained by an observation made by Roger Sperry. He noted that the right brain – the intuitive hemisphere – works at a slower pace than the left. The left brain – the 'you' – is the part that copes with the world, and it always seem to be in a hurry. The right ambles along casually at its own pace. The result is that the two halves are always losing contact. Every time 'you' become tense or anxious or over-tired, the gap between them increases and life begins to take on an air of unreality. This is because it is the business of the right brain to provide experience with a third dimension of reality. And it can only do this when the two halves are, so to speak, strolling side by side.

So when the prisoner focuses on the spider, when the schoolboy focuses on the beetle, he is slowing down the left until it is moving at the same pace as the right. And when this happens, the experience becomes 'interesting'. He has, in effect, pressed a switch that alters consciousness from the left brain 'thinking mode' to the right-brain 'feeling mode'. This also explains why alcohol can sometimes produce those delightful states of relaxation in which we feel totally contented to rest in the sensory reality of the present. It halts the impatient forward rush of the left brain and persuades it to relax. De Sade had discovered that sex can produce the same effect. But neither alcohol nor sex works all the time; the left brain may simply refuse to slow down.

All this makes it clear that crime is an unfortunate waste-product of human evolution. Human intelligence involves the power of *foresight*, and foresight enables a man to calculate how to achieve comfort, security and pleasure. It also makes him a potential criminal, for the simplest way to achieve what he wants is to go out and grab it – the method advocated by de Sade.

If Jaynes is correct, this presumably did not apply to our cave-man forebears, for their right and left brains had not yet lost contact. It was only the complexities of civilization that led man to develop the independent left brain so that criminality became possible.

We have already seen why de Sade's approach – the criminal approach – fails to achieve its object. Its sheer obsessiveness defeats its aims. The manic egoist, driven by resentment, gradually destroys his own sense of reality. (Panzram is an obvious example.) The result may be self-destruction; but, if he is lucky, he recognizes his mistake in time and reverses his direction. (Many of the saints were men who began life as 'sinners' and egoists; they discovered their mistakes in time.)

All human beings contain an element of the criminal; as Becker points out, every child is a manic egoist. Fortunately, few of us go as far as Panzram or de Sade. And this is not, as de Sade believes, because we are intimidated by society and its laws. It is because we are intelligent enough to recognize Kierkegaard's 'principle of limitation'. This is not a recent development; it seems to be as old as man's recorded history. The 'principle of limitation' – the recognition that human happiness depends upon self-discipline – can be found in Hindu scriptures dating from 1000 B.C., and is present in pyramid texts and early writings from Mesopotamia.

Man may be a criminal animal; but he is also a religious animal. And the religion seems to be far older than the criminality.

Crime can be understood only as a part of the total evolutionary pattern. Man developed his 'divided consciousness' as a means of survival. In a sense, he was better off as an animal, for the animal's consciousness is simpler and richer. (We can gain some inkling of it from the effects of alcohol – that sudden feeling of warmth and reality.) But this instinctive consciousness has one major disadvantage; it is too narrow. It restricts us to the present moment. So man developed the left brain to escape this narrowness. It has the power of reaching beyond the present moment: the power of abstraction. And it does this by turning reality into symbols and ideas. *The left brain is fundamentally a map-maker.*

Imagine a stranger who comes to a large but primitive city. His business involves travelling all over it. He can ask his way around, or hire a local man as a guide; but neither of these methods is very satisfactory. If he wishes to be independent, his best way is to acquire a map. And if maps do not exist, he will have to make one. Once he has done this, he can find his way around the city as confidently as the oldest inhabitant. Moreover, he will know it a great deal better than many inhabitants, who are familiar only with their own quarter.

Yet in another sense, he does not 'know' it at all; he knows only an abstraction, a map, reinforced by a few selected areas of 'reality'.

This is man's present position. In fact, he spends a large part of his early life at school, acquiring a 'map' of the world he lives in. Yet when he leaves school, his knowledge of the *reality* of that world is very patchy. And modern life is so complex and confusing that huge areas of the map are bound to remain unexplored and 'unrealized'. A savage who has spent the same number of years hunting and fishing will admittedly have a narrower view of the world; but what he *does* know will have the genuine flavour of reality. In a sense, modern man seems to have made a very poor bargain. He has acquired a map, and not much else.

The 'map' concept explains the problem of crime. A man whose actual acquaintance with the real world is fairly limited looks at his map and imagines he can see a number of short-cuts. Robbery is a short-cut to wealth. Rape is a short-cut to sexual fulfilment. Violence is a short-cut to getting his own way. Of course, each of these short-cuts has major disadvantages; but he is unaware of these until he tries them out in the real world.

Maps & crime

So crime is the outcome of man's greatest evolutionary achievement; his ability to make 'maps'. Fortunately, it is not a permanent drawback. For it is not really a choice between a real world and an unreal map. It is true that the oldest inhabitant knows the city a great deal better than the map-maker. But then, if the map-maker really wants to get to know the city, he can do it in far less time than it took the oldest inhabitant. Making use of his map, he can get to know it in weeks instead of years. Man's map-making ability, his ability to use his mind, gives him a potential for mastering reality that makes the drawbacks seem unimportant.

Before we embark on the main part of this history of crime, creativity and civilization, let us try to summarize what we have learned so far.

Since his advent so many millions of years ago, man has shown himself to be the most remarkable creature who has ever walked the earth. With none of the advantages of the big predators, he taught himself to survive by the use of intelligence. But even so, the stream of evolution from Ramapithecus, through Australopithecus and *homo habilis* was like a broad, meandering river. Man developed because he learned the use of weapons and tools; but his development was slow because he had not yet learned to use that most valuable of all tools, his mind.

With *homo erectus*, the river entered a valley and became a fast-flowing stream. A million and a half years later – which, in geological time, brings us almost to the twentieth century – came Neanderthal and Cro-Magnon man, and it is as if the river entered a gorge and suddenly turned into a torrent. The pace quickened again with the beginning of agriculture. With the building of the cities, the gorge narrowed and the rapids became dangerous.

It would hardly seem possible that evolution could flow faster still, but that is what happened at some time between the founding of the cities and the civilizations of ancient Crete and Mycenae. The sheer danger of the rapids created a new level of alertness and determination. Roaring along at top speed between narrow walls, man was forced to concentrate as he had never concentrated before. Bodies struggled in the water; wrecks drifted past him; but the noise and exhilaration swallowed up the screams of the drowning. A man who steers his raft with his jaw set and all his senses strained to the utmost has no time for compassion.

As he developed determination, man also developed ruthlessness. The narrowing of the senses became a habit – so that whenever he found himself in a quieter patch of water, protected by some buttress from the torrent, he no longer knew how to relax and enjoy the relative calm.

This explains why man has ceased to be the gentle vegetarian described by Leakey and Fromm. But he has no reason to envy those other animals who are still drifting placidly down broad rivers. For he has developed a faculty that outweighs all the danger, all the misery and violence. He has learned to steer.

When he learned to use his mind, this ability to steer made him also the first truly creative and inventive creature. He has poured that narrow jet of energy into discovery and exploration. But the sheer force of the jet has meant that whenever it has been obstructed – or whenever men have lacked the self-discipline to control it – the result has been chaos and destruction. Crime is the negative aspect of creativity.

Throughout history, the ruthless – from Sennacherib to Hitler – have ended by destroying themselves, for their tendency to violence makes them bad steersmen. It is true that their crimes seem to dominate human history. But, as we shall see, it is the good steersmen who play the major part in the story of mankind.

Crime = negative creativity

Part Two

A CRIMINAL OUTLINE
OF HISTORY

One

PIRATES AND ADVENTURERS

"Crime" as norm in earlier ages

When we complain about the rising crime rate, we speak as citizens who take the protection of the law for granted. Police patrol our streets and country lanes. Burglary and mugging may be on the increase; but at least the robbers take their freedom into their hands every time they set out to commit a crime.

If we are to understand the history of the past three thousand years we have to make an effort of imagination, and try to forget this notion of being protected by the law. In ancient Greece, the problem was not simply the brigands who haunted the roads and the pirates who infested the seas; it was the fact that the ordinary citizen became a brigand or pirate when he felt like it, and no one regarded this as abnormal. In the *Odyssey*, Ulysses describes with pride how, on the way home from Troy, his ship was driven near to the coast of Thrace; so they landed near an unprotected town, murdered all the men, and carried off the women and goods. Greece was not at war with Thrace; it was just that an unprotected town was fair game for anyone, and the war-weary Greeks felt like a little rape and plunder. This state of affairs persisted for most of the next three thousand years, and explains why so many Mediterranean towns and villages are built inland.

What is far more difficult to grasp is that 'law abiding' countries like England were in exactly the same situation. Just before the time of the Black Death (as Luke Owen Pike describes in his *History of Crime in England*, 1873), 'houses were set on fire day after day; men and women were captured, ransom was exacted on pain of death . . . even those who paid it might think themselves fortunate if they escaped some horrible mutilation.' And this does not relate to times of war or social upheaval; according to J. F. Nicholls and John Taylor's *Bristol Past and Present* (1881) England was 'prosperous in the highest degree; populous, wealthy and luxurious . . .' (p. 174). Yet the robber bands were like small armies. They would often descend on a town when a fair was taking place and everyone felt secure; they would take over the town, plunder the houses and set them on fire (for citizens who were trying to save their houses would not organize a pursuit) and then withdraw. In 1347 and '48, Bristol was taken over by a brigand who robbed the ships in the harbour – including some commissioned by the king – and issued his own proclamations like a conqueror. His men roamed the streets, robbing and killing as they felt inclined – the king had to send Thomas, Lord Berkeley, to restore order. When a trader was known to have jewels belonging to Queen Philippa in his house, he was besieged by a gang led by one Adam the Leper and had to hand over the jewels when his house was set on fire. The law courts were almost powerless; when a notorious robber was tried near Winchester, the gang waited outside the court and attacked everyone who came out; so the case was dropped.

Things were still almost as bad four centuries later, in the time of Dr Johnson; gangs of robbers attacked houses in the country at night and sometimes burned them down. Bands of footpads armed with knives attacked parties of prosperous-looking people in London's Covent Garden, and Horace Walpole was shot by a highwayman in Hyde Park. 'The farmers' fields were constantly plundered of their crops, fruit and vegetables were carried off, even the ears of wheat were cut from their stalks in the open day. The thieves boldly took their plunder to the millers to be ground, and the millers, although aware that fields and barns had been recently robbed, did not dare to object, lest their mills should be burnt down over their heads.' This is described by Major Arthur Griffiths in his *Mysteries of the Police and Crime* (Vol. 1, p. 66). In Queen Victoria's London, according to works such as Mayhew's *London Labour and the London Poor* and *The Victorian Underworld* by Kellow Chesney, footpads could operate by day, sometimes in upper-class residential districts. Even children were not safe; 'child strippers', mostly women, would lure children into doorways and steal their clothes.

What is so hard for us to grasp is that the whole of society, from top to bottom, operated upon principles that would seem ferociously cruel to a modern citizen of the western world. Our present concern for children and animals would have struck an early Victorian as ludicrous, while Dr Johnson would simply have condemned it as dangerous sentimentality. Boswell tells in his *Life of Johnson* (Everyman edition, Vol. 2, p. 447) that when, in the 1780s, there was talk

discovery of pity as a social emotion

of doing away with Tyburn, where executions were turned into public holidays and children were often hanged for stealing, Johnson said indignantly that 'executions are intended to draw spectators. If they do not draw spectators, they don't answer their purpose . . .' Writing about this period, an English historian of crime and punishment says:

Children were starved by drunken parents and parish nurses, they were sent out to pick pockets, they were forced to become prostitutes and many not more than twelve years old were 'half eaten up with the foul distemper' of venereal disease, they were made to beg and sometimes scarred or crippled so they might be more successful in exciting pity. They seldom did excite it. Pity was still a strange and valuable emotion. Unwanted babies were left in the streets to die or were thrown into dung heaps or open drains; the torture of animals was a popular sport. Cat-dropping, bear-baiting and bull-baiting were . . . universally enjoyed.

Christopher Hibbert: *The Roots of Evil*, p. 44.

And it was not only animals who were at risk. England had no love of foreigners, and they were likely to be jeered at and pelted with mud as they walked through the streets of London. One Portuguese visitor who got into a fight with an English sailor had his ear nailed to the wall, and when he broke away he was battered and stabbed by the mob until he died. Offenders who were sentenced to be exposed in the stocks were often stoned to death. But such brutality was not confined to the lower classes.

The Mohocks, a society whose members were dedicated to the ambition of 'doing all possible hurt to their fellow creatures' were mostly gentlemen. They employed their ample leisure in forcing prostitutes and old women to stand on their heads in tar barrels so that they could prick their legs with their swords; or in making them jump up and down to avoid the swinging blades; in disfiguring their victims by boring out their eyes or flattening their noses; in waylaying servants and, as in the case of Lady Winchelsea's maid, beating them and slashing their faces. To work themselves up to the necessary pitch of enthusiasm for their ferocious games, they first drank so much that they were quite 'beyond the possibility of attending to any notions of reason or humanity'. Some of the Mohocks also seem to have been members of the Bold Bucks who, apparently, had formally to deny the existence of God and eat every Sunday a dish known as Holy Ghost Pie. The ravages of the Bold Bucks were more specifically sexual than those of the Mohocks and consequently, as it was practically impossible to obtain a conviction for rape and as the age of consent was twelve, they were more openly conducted.

The Roots of Evil, p. 45

[handwritten: invention of public conscience]

[handwritten: (workhouses saw people as resources not people]

In the anonymous Victorian autobiography *My Secret Life*, the writer describes how he picked up a middle-aged bawd and a ten-year-old-girl at Vauxhall Gardens and possessed the girl several times. 'Oh, he ain't going to do it like that other man – you said no one should again.' 'Be quiet you little fool, it won't hurt you. Open your legs.' And the writer admits cheerfully (Vol. 2, chapter 9): 'I longed to hurt her, to make her cry out with the pain my tool caused her, to make her bleed if I could.'

In judging the author of *My Secret Life* we should bear in mind that, had the girl been two years older, she could have legally consented to her own seduction; it was not until 1875 that the age of consent was raised to thirteen. Fifty years earlier, as Arthur Koestler and C. H. Rolph relate in *Hanged by the Neck* (1961), children were still being hanged or transported to the colonies in 'hulks'. (There was even a special prison ship for children, which was in use until 1844.) In 1801 a boy had been hanged for stealing a spoon; in 1808, two sisters, aged eight and twelve, were hanged at Lynn; in 1831, a boy of thirteen was hanged at Chelmsford for setting fire to a house; in 1833, a boy of nine was sentenced to death – but reprieved – for pushing a stick through a cracked shop window and stealing two pennyworth of printer's colours. Homeless children walked the streets and could be charged with vagrancy and sent to prisons which had a part set aside for their accommodation. In *Nineteenth Century Crime* J. J. Tobias mentions a Report by the Inspector of Prisons for 1836 which describes the children's section of Newgate and mentions that, out of twenty-four, 'seven had been committed for robbing their masters, one for purloining from his father, and another from his aunt' (p. 152).

By the mid-nineteenth century, the public conscience had begun to wake up, largely as the result of the work of humanitarian novelists such as Dickens and Victor Hugo. It is interesting that all that was needed to bring about the change was to touch people's imagination. On the page before he quotes Dr Johnson on the abolition of public executions, Boswell says 'Such was his sensibility, and so much was he affected by pathetick poetry, that when he was reading Dr Beattie's "Hermit" in my presence, it brought tears into his eyes.' A 'pathetick poem' about public executions would probably have changed Johnson's mind about Tyburn.

By the 1850s, people all over the civilized world were shedding tears over the fate of little Nell and the hunchback Quasimodo who died for love. When, in 1862, Sioux Indians went on the rampage in Minnesota – because they felt they had been cheated out of their land – accounts of the rising emphasized the suffering of children.

The hero of the day was an eleven-year-old boy named Mertin Eastlick, who carried his fifteen-month-old brother Johny on his back for fifty miles, but died shortly afterwards from exposure, over-exertion and lack of nourishment. Mr Eastlick had been killed, and Mrs Eastlick was lying helpless on the ground from a bullet wound. Her two little boys, named Freddie and Frank, were with her. Two squaws saw them, and catching the children they beat them to death before the helpless mother's eyes. Many other children were only beaten, until they became helpless, and then left to die from hunger and exposure to the storm.
History of the Indian Outbreaks by Judge Buck, quoted in Thomas Duke's
Celebrated Criminal Cases of America, p. 388.

The resulting storm of outrage convinced Americans that the Indians deserved to be deprived of their land and herded into reservations. The feeling is understandable; but we can now see that it was the Indians who were being victimized by history. They were simply behaving as they had for centuries; their cruelty was part of the warrior tradition, as the historian Francis Parkman recognized:

An inexorable severity towards enemies was a very essential element in their conception of the character of the warrior. Pity was a cowardly weakness, at which their pride revolted. This, joined to their thirst for applause and their dread of ridicule, made them smother every movement of compassion, and conspired with their native fierceness to give a character of unrelenting cruelty rarely equalled.
From *Half a Century of Conflict*, quoted by John Andrew Doyle in *Essays on Various Subjects*, 1911, p. 75.

As with the 'rape of Nanking', we are dealing with the traditional warrior mentality and the need to 'save face'. The essential point is made in an essay on Parkman by John Andrew Doyle: 'The cruelties of the Indians were not so remote from the ideas and practices of civilized men in that age as they are now.' Doyle is speaking of the Indians of an earlier age, whose ruthlessness was not very different from that of their white conquerors. Parkman describes the massacre of English settlers by Indians who were in the pay of the French: 'A hundred and four persons, chiefly women and children half-naked from their beds, were tomahawked, shot or killed by slower and more painful methods.' And at the conclusion of the massacre, a Jesuit priest who accompanied the Indians said a mass. The French employed the Indians because they were cheaper than white soldiers, and had no objection to their methods; a French priest told a correspondent: 'They kill all they meet; and, after having abused the women and maidens, they slaughter or burn them.' Parkman also mentions that the French handed over prisoners to the Indians, knowing they would be tortured and burned alive.

But then, this was in the century before the Sioux revolt in Minnesota, and the English were capable of showing the same ruthlessness towards their enemies. England had been at war with Spain, on and off, since the time of Elizabeth I, and the government actively encouraged pirates – called 'privateers' – to prey on Spanish ships; it was not unusual for everyone on board such a ship to be murdered. In England itself, coastal villages were encouraged to engage in 'wrecking' foreign ships, luring them on to the rocks with false lights. In *Roots of Evil* (page 40) there is the story of the captain of a wrecked ship who struggled to shore in Cheshire only to be stripped naked by villagers, who cut off his fingers to get his rings; the earlobes of a sailor were bitten off to get his ear-rings. It was only because the wreckers made no distinction between British and foreign ships that wrecking was finally made a capital offence in 1753.

We have no way of knowing when piracy and banditry became common in Europe; but it was probably towards the end of the third millenium B.C., around the time of that early Napoleon, Sargon of Akkad (2350 B.C.). The first walled cities date from about six hundred years before Sargon, suggesting that war was becoming the rule rather than the exception. Gordon Childe points out in *What Happened in History* (p. 154) that graves of this period in the small Aegean islands (the Cyclades) contained many metal weapons, 'so it may be suspected that these insular communities combined piracy with peaceful trade, adding loot to profits, a practice normal in the Mediterranean at many subsequent periods.' Great wars like those conducted by Sargon must have unsettled the whole region and left behind the usual aftermath of robbery and violence. When small cities and tribes are welded together into a great empire, one of the consequences is a feeling of loss of identity, which – as in the case of the Ik – leads to an increase in selfishness and ruthlessness. Dispossessed rural populations have to survive as best they can. And when kings destroy cities and their soldiers are allowed to loot and rape, some men are bound to acquire a taste for more exciting and violent ways of making a living. In his essay 'Civilized Life Begins', M. E. L. Mallowen says:

> The widespread contact between distant parts of the civilized world at that time implied a desire to share in the wealth available to man, and a determination to compete for it if it were withheld.
> From *The Dawn of Civilization* ed. by Stuart Piggott, Thames and Hudson, 1961.

The Mediterranean area was turning into a melting pot, and the age of violence was beginning.

Unfortunately, we know next to nothing about the rise of piracy and banditry in the Mediterranean. The Greek historian Thucydides, writing towards the end of the fifth century B.C., gives the best picture of what it must have been like more than a thousand years earlier.

In ancient times, both Greeks and barbarians, the inhabitants of the coast as well as of the islands, when they began to find their way to one another by sea, had recourse to piracy. They were commanded by powerful chiefs, who took this means of increasing their wealth and providing for their poorer followers. They would fall upon the unwalled or straggling towns, or rather villages, which they plundered, and maintained themselves by plundering them; for as yet such an occupation was held to be honourable and not disgraceful. This is proved by the practice of certain tribes on the mainland who, to the present day, glory in piratical exploits, and by the witness of the ancient poets, in whose verses the question is invariably asked of newly arrived voyagers, whether they are pirates; which implies that neither those who are questioned disclaim, nor those who are interested in knowing censure the occupation. The land too was infested by robbers; and there are parts of Hellas in which the old practices still continue . . . the fashion of wearing arms among these continental tribes is a relic of their old predatory habits. For in ancient times, all Greeks carried weapons because their homes were undefended and intercourse was unsafe . . .

He shows us a time when local chieftains sailed the seas and plundered undefended villages, probably carrying off some of their inhabitants as slaves. Piracy was honourable because it was still regarded as a form of war, and there was almost certainly no question of indiscriminate slaughter or cruelty – otherwise piracy would not have been tolerated, even considered honourable. These people were simple, direct, violent, but not sadistic. Thucydides, regarding the 'barbarians' from the safety of Athens, sounds rather like a New Yorker of the nineteenth century commenting on the Wild West. He also tells us that the legendary King Minos of Crete conquered most of the Mediterranean and cleared the seas of pirates. This Minos is, of course, the king who is supposed to have built the labyrinth, and whose wife fell in love with a bull and produced the minotaur. Since Minos is supposed to be the son of the god Zeus and the maiden Europa – another lady who admired the bull's sexual equipment – historians of the nineteenth century assumed him to be purely mythical. But in 1900 an Englishman named Arthur Evans began digging at Knossos, in Crete, and soon started to uncover the walls of an enormous palace. The size of its walls and the richness of its decorations made it clear that it was a remnant of a mighty civilization, but the astonishing thing was that, although it was fairly close to the sea, it appeared to have no defending walls; clearly its inhabitants were not afraid of pirates. The remains of a mighty fleet solved this puzzle: Crete had no need to fear pirates. The palace's rooms and corridors were so confusing that Evans suspected he had found the origin of the legend of the labyrinth. The Cretans – or Minoans, as Evans called them – certainly seemed to be obsessed by bulls. Wall paintings showed youths and maidens vaulting over the backs of bulls, and on the roof of the palace there are two carved stones that look like horns. In short, there is much evidence that King Minos really existed and that the legends are based on fact.

A later Greek historian, Plutarch, has more to tell us about King Minos – how Minos's son was murdered by the Greeks, and how, after a bitter war, Minos agreed to receive a tribute of seven youths and seven virgins every nine years. These were sacrificed to the Minotaur, who lived in the labyrinth. The hero Theseus, son of the king of Athens, went to Crete and slew the Minotaur. Evans argues that the Greek hostages probably *were* sacrificed to the bull-god, or made to take part in gladiatorial contests with bulls. This same hero Theseus, according to Plutarch, had spent his early years clearing the roads around Athens of criminals. 'For it was at that time very dangerous to go by land on the road to Athens, no part being free of robbers and murderers.' One of these robbers was a woman named Phaea, 'full of cruelty and lust . . . and had the name of the Sow given her from the foulness of her life and manners' – the first female criminal in history. Theseus also killed a bandit named Sciron who used to order strangers to wash his feet and then, as they bent over, kick them from the rock – named after him – into the sea. Plutarch mentions that Jason, another legendary hero who lived at the time of Minos, was given the task of clearing the seas of pirates. So although we have no way of drawing the line between fact and fiction, it seems clear that a king called Minos really existed around 1600 B.C. and that by that time piracy and brigandage were common in the Mediterranean. Knossos itself was finally destroyed around 1380 B.C., by pirates and other raiders. These were dangerous times to live in. The people who survived had to be fierce and brutal.

It is important to remember that these early pirates were not the 'criminal rats' who came to overrun the Mediterranean in later years. They regarded themselves as warriors. What they were after was easy pickings. Civilization was expanding; the Mediterranean was becoming more and more prosperous, and the pirates could see no reason why they should not help themselves to other people's riches. The fifteenth and fourteenth centuries B.C. were a 'boom time' in the Mediterranean.

After the fall of Knossos, a people called the Achaeans began to build themselves a stronghold at Mycenae; they had come from somewhere in the north and hacked their way into Greece. Mycenae's defensive walls were built of blocks of stone so immense that later Greeks believed they could only have been moved by giants and so called them 'cyclopean'. Mycenae became as prosperous as Knossos had been. Agamemnon, the king who led the Greeks to Troy, was king of Mycenae. Troy fell about 1184 B.C. and Agamemnon returned home to be murdered by his wife Clytemnestra and her lover, according to legend. In any case, the kingdom of Agamemnon did not long survive its greatest king; invaders called the Dorians poured down from the Danube basin and another great civilization collapsed. The next three hundred years were the period known as the Dark Ages – not because it was a time of new barbarian invasions, as in the Dark Ages of Europe after the collapse of Rome, but because there is so little written evidence from the period. There were no more vast kingdoms such as the Minoans and Achaeans – only dozens of small countries with dozens of small towns surrounded by walls. Even the farmers moved close to the towns. The seas were still full of pirates – even though the pickings had long ago ceased to be rich – and these were not warrior chieftains like Achilles and Ulysses, but small-time operators who probably had long periods with empty bellies. Small towns and villages do not have much opportunity to get rich. Most people were half starved; there was meat only on holidays, and for the rest of the year it was fruit, olives and barley porridge. But then, for the pirates, there was always the possibility of a good haul – if only the food that had been stored up for the winter by poor villagers. Another important motive was rape. As N. K. Sandars remarks of an earlier period: 'The whole purpose of the hero's activity is spoil.' 'Silver, gold, bronze, horses, cattle and sheep, women, above all, treasure and women.' (*The Sea Peoples* p. 186.) And when treasure became scarce, there was still rape. People who live in small communities usually have strong views on immorality; they want their daughters to remain virgins until after marriage. The male, on the other hand, is naturally promiscuous. So rape no doubt continued to be one of the pleasanter rewards of piracy. When the women had been possessed, they could be sold as slaves – for at this period, and for many centuries to come, all civilized life was based on the institution of slavery.

The post-Homeric age is, of course, the age of Jaynes's 'breakdown of the bicameral mind'. And whether or not we accept his theory about the 'coming of consciousness' there can be no doubt that this was an age of increasing individualism. The usual explanation is that people living in small towns and villages grew tired of kings (or chieftains), preferring to be ruled by councils of leading citizens – the oligarchies. But a council still amounted to a 'privileged few', and the citizens found these irritating, which provided an ideal opportunity for rabble-rousers to preach against the aristocracy, gather a few followers with knives and cudgels and set themselves up as tyrants or despots. But the Greeks, having acquired a taste for individualism, finally got rid of these tyrants, and the result was, eventually, the world's first democracy.

According to this view, individualism was the outcome of the disappearance of big cities – like Knossos and Mycenae – and their replacement by small towns and villages. But there had been towns and villages since 6000 B.C. and they had peacefully accepted the rule of kings and priests. The new individualism in Greece was the rise of a new kind of consciousness – the same consciousness that soon created science and philosophy. Endless hardships and dangers had created a race of survivors, of claustrophobic little communities who regarded the rest of the world with a certain mistrust. Vigilance and determination had turned them into 'left brainers'.

What is certainly true is that the rule of tyrants gave the Greeks a taste for freedom. 'Tyrant' meant simply a ruler or king, with no implication of cruelty; but, as Herodotus remarks:

Even the best of men, were he granted such power, would alter the train of his thoughts. Insolence will be engendered in him by the advantages of his position, and envy . . . With these two in his soul he is filled with every wickedness, for insolence will cause him to break into many acts of wantonness, and envy into many more.   Book 3, para 80.

We have already encountered the tyrant Alexander of Pherae, who buried men alive and hunted them with his dogs. The tyrant Phalaris of Acragas in Sicily is famous for his unpleasant habit of roasting people he disliked in a bronze bull, his first victim being the craftsman who made it; he was overthrown and met the same fate himself.

Herodotus's mistrust of tyrants emerges in a gruesome story he tells about the Median ruler Astyages (about 600 B.C.). Convinced by a dream that his grandson would supplant him on the throne, Astyages handed him over to a servant named Harpagus with orders to kill the baby (whose name was Cyrus). Shocked at the idea, Harpagus handed over the child to a herdsman whose own baby had just died – the corpse of the baby was shown to the guards of Astyages to convince him that his orders had been carried out.

When the child was ten, his identity was discovered. His play-mates had made him king in one of their games, and he beat the son of a nobleman who refused to obey him. The affair came to the ears of Astyages, who sent for Cyrus and observed his resemblance to himself. The herdsman was questioned, and the truth came out. Harpagus was then invited to supper and asked to send his only son – a boy of thirteen – to the palace. The boy was killed, then cut up and roasted. When Harpagus sat down to supper, he ate his own son. After the meal, he was handed a basket containing the boy's hands, feet and head.

The point is further underlined by Harpagus's reaction; he bows his head and says that whatever the king does must be right. Harpagus is so accustomed to absolute submission that he has no difficulty in concealing his feelings on learning that he has eaten his son. And Astyages is so used to absolute obedience that he assumes Harpagus bears him no ill-will. Suddenly, we become aware of the immense distance that separates this Persian monarch from the Egyptian and Sumerian kings of two thousand years earlier – kings who regarded themselves as servants of the gods and who were as much subject to the rule of law as any of their people. Astyages is not even necessarily a cruel man. It is his ego that is offended by disobedience, and he coldly calculates a 'suitable' punishment.

And once again, we must bear in mind that this kind of cruelty is the outcome of 'divided consciousness', of the man who stands alone and no longer hears the voice of the gods. But this same divided consciousness soon led to the achievements of Pythagoras, Socrates, Plato, Aristotle, Eratosthenes. Divided consciousness produced democracy – the political system of men who stand alone, no longer united by the will of the god. But this same democracy revealed its shortcomings in the execution of Socrates for impiety against the gods – emphasizing that the sum of a thousand small egos is one small ego. Left-brain consciousness makes men obsessive. Obsession gives birth to blindness and narrowness, to cruelty and stupidity – but also to science and philosophy. And so the pendulum of history continues to swing between these extremes, and the story of civilization is the story of creativity and of crime.

This book is centrally concerned with crime; but if we ignore the creativity, we shall not only fail to understand the crime: we shall miss the whole point of human history. Those Greeks who invaded Crete and built Mycenae were driven by this unique human craving for adventure, by the feeling that life without conquest is a bore. In this spirit they cheerfully killed their enemies, raped their female captives and plundered undefended cities. It was not innate wickedness so much as the spirit that makes boys play at pirates. But four centuries later, when a blind singer named Homer recited these episodes, his audience was able to enjoy the excitement of the adventure without stirring from their firesides. In a sense, they were enjoying the adventure more than those ancient heroes did, for it is always easier to appreciate life in retrospect than when coping with its everyday details. This love of song and recitation developed to such a point that by the reign of Pisistratus, the first great tyrant of Athens (561–528 B.C.), the festival of the god Dionysus had turned into a kind of song contest. One day, the audience was startled and puzzled when the chorus leader began to declaim his lines as if he himself were the legendary hero he was singing about; but they soon found this new method of presentation more dramatic and absorbing than a mere narration. It made them participants in the fall of Troy, the murder of Agamemnon, and the tragedy of Oedipus or Philoctetes. The author of this new method, Thespis, had invented the drama. And a century later an enormous theatre, capable of holding twelve thousand people, was built at the foot of the Acropolis. The actors, walking on shoes that made them artificially tall, and speaking through wooden masks that amplified their voices, brought to life again these great dramas of the past, and the silence was so total that no one missed a word. No wonder this golden age saw the sudden flowering of science and philosophy, as well as of poetry. Man had at last stumbled upon his most unique and incredible accomplishment: living in two worlds at once: the real world and the world of imagination. It was a trick the Spartans never mastered, for they chose the way of obsession. But Alexander the Great was driven to conquer the world by his imagination, rather than by the political realism that had driven Sargon the Great and King Minos. He was the first hero who was conscious of his role as hero; he played the conqueror like an actor on the stage.

Now in a sense, the criminals of this time, the pirates and bandits, continued to belong to that earlier age of the Trojan war. As far as we can tell, crime had still not entered its sadistic stage – for we can be sure that, if any pirate or brigand was noted for his cruelty, like the legendary Procrustes who cut down travellers to fit his bed, his deeds would have been recorded and exaggerated. Our ancestors loved hair-raising tales as much as we do, and had not yet become sated with horrors. After the defeat of Athens by Sparta in 400 B.C., piracy returned to the seas and banditry to the roads, for after so many years of war, the roads were full of wandering soldiers who knew no other trade. (Ten thousand of them were enlisted by the Persian Cyrus – a descendant of Cyrus the Great, whom we have already met as a child – and they won many spectacular victories in Persia before Cyrus was killed in battle and the army had to fight its way back to the sea – passing, en route, those vast ruined cities of the Assyrians whose names had been forgotten.) In his novel *The Golden Ass*, Lucius Apuleius, writing three centuries later, describes the brigands who capture the hero (who has been transformed into an ass). They burst into the courtyard of the house, armed with swords and axes, and into the strong room that contains the valuables. They kill nobody, and make off as quickly as they can, loading some of the valuables on to the hero. In their robbers' cave, they wash in hot water, then settle down to a huge meal – cooked by an old woman – washed down with wine. 'They bawled songs, yelled obscenities at each other, and played practical jokes on one another.' In fact, they sound like the Greek army in front of Troy.

The robber chief makes a long speech after their meal, in which he describes some of their exploits. These are designed to emphasize the bravery and toughness of their band. Their former leader had carved a hole in a door, and was groping around inside to find the handle, when the owner of the house took a hammer and nailed the robber's hand to the door. To escape, they were forced to hack off his arm at the elbow. In the chase, he began to lag behind; and since being caught would mean crucifixion, he committed suicide with his sword. His companions, deeply moved, wrapped his body in a cloak and consigned it to the river.

Another bandit had got into the bedroom of an old woman and, instead of strangling her, threw all her belongings out of the window to his companions below. Then he tried to throw out her bedding, and the old woman tricked him into thinking he had been throwing the goods into her neighbour's back yard. The bandit leaned out of the window, and the old woman pushed him out; he broke his ribs on a block of stone, and coughed up his life. But there is no mention of the other bandits rushing upstairs to avenge their comrade; they only consign him to the river, like the robber chief.

Later, the bandits go out marauding and capture a beautiful girl. There is no suggestion of rape. They tell her: 'You are perfectly safe, madam. We have no intention of hurting you or showing you any discourtesy . . .' It is true that Apuleius's bandit troup has a distinctly operatic air; but Apuleius takes so much delight in a kind of brutal realism that it seems unlikely that he has deliberately toned down the picture.

What emerges from Apuleius is that the bandits regarded themselves as adventurers, making a living as best they could. They strangle old ladies, cut throats, and even make use of torture – to extort information; but then, they are crucified when caught, much as rustlers were lynched in a later century. In fact, accounts of robbery and piracy in this period remind us constantly of the Wild West. They are no longer more-or-less respectable, as they had been in the good old days. One historian tells us:

. . . as the growing City State became more powerful, it learnt how to extend its strong arm over the haunts of the robber folk. It explored and cleared their mountain fastnesses – those great limestone caves so common in Greece, sometimes mere indistinguishable slits in the hillside, but leading down through difficult ways into high and spacious halls. Here, where the robbers of old had lived and caroused and carved altars to their gods, quiet citizens from below, shepherds with their flocks in the summer pastures, now met to talk and pipe and sleep . . . And the sea robbers, too, had to leave their old established hiding places. The rocky island across the bay, with its one little cove, so convenient for small boats, and its famous spring of clear water, became just an extra piece of the city's pasture ground, very useful in winter when there was snow on the heights . . . Only some bold spirits resisted and moved farther afield, where as yet law could not follow. Thus the gap slowly widened between the adventurer and the honest citizen . . .

Alfred Zimmern: *The Greek Commonwealth*, Part 3, chapter 4.

For now, in the centuries that followed the golden age of Athens, the slow spread of civilization in the Mediterranean was making the profession of 'adventurer' almost impossible. The Greeks were carrying their arts of civilization everywhere. They carried them, for example, to some barbarous tribes who lived on the green plains of a peninsula called Vitelliu – 'calf-land' – a word that later dropped its first and last letters and became Italy. The tribes were called Latins – after their country, Latium – and they had founded their city upon low hills as long ago as 900 B.C. They had learned much from a mysterious Asiatic people called the Etruscans, northern neighbours who once conquered their seven-hilled city and later vanished from history as mysteriously as they came into it. *China?*

This city would be the chief instrument of human progress for the next thousand years. But whether it could really be called progress is another matter. If a god could have watched the course of human history, from the building of the cities and the foundations of the great empires – Egyptian, Akkadian, Minoan, Assyrian, Macedonian – he might have felt that the evolution of humanity was proceeding in a tortuous but, on the whole, satisfactory manner. The gamble of 'double consciousness' was paying off.

With the coming of the Romans, history seemed to take a wrong turn. Everything that *could* go wrong with double consciousness went wrong. And when they vacated the scene, around 500 A.D., they left behind a strange double legacy of civilization and criminality.

Two

NO MEAN CITY

outlaw origins

These citizens of Rome – as they called their town – were tempera-
mentally similar to the Spartans: hard-headed, practical, disciplined.
But they were overawed by Greek culture and Greek subtlety, and
set out to learn all they could from them. They adopted the Greek
gods, changing Zeus to Jupiter, Eros to Cupid. They even paid them
the compliment of adopting a little of their history, claiming that
Rome was founded by Aeneas, the Trojan prince who fled from the
Greeks after the fall of Troy. Another version of early Roman
history, as recounted by Winwood Reade, declares that 'a rabble of
outlaws and runaway slaves banded together, built a town, fortified
it strongly, and offered it as an asylum to all fugitives. To Rome fled
the over-beaten slave, the thief with his booty, the murderer with
blood red hands. This city of refuge became a war town . . . its
citizens alternately fought and farmed; it became the dread and
torment of the neighbourhood.' And because their city had no
females, they kidnapped the women of the nearby Sabine tribe. It is
an interesting story; for this tale of the founding of Rome by slaves
and murderers helps to explain a certain fatal deficiency in the
Roman soul – a curious insensitivity and literal-mindedness. The
Romans never learned to inhabit the world of imagination.

It is as a result of their materialistic outlook that the history of
Rome contains more crime and violence than that of any other city in
world history; to read the story of Rome from the early struggles
between the plebs and patricians (common people and aristocracy) to
its downfall under Romulus Augustulus is to feel that this is a
magnified version of Calhoun's 'behavioural sink'. The poet Robert
Graves was one of the first to recognize its possibilities for sensational fiction, and his novels *I, Claudius* and *Claudius the God* give an
impression of non-stop murder, assassination, intrigue, promiscuity
and sexual perversion. One is left with the feeling that life under
Augustus, Tiberius and Caligula must have been far more dangerous

than in Chicago in the days of Al Capone; and, allowing for the exaggeration which springs from the novelist's selectivity and compression, this impression is not inaccurate. Rome typifies what can go wrong when human evolution is restricted to the purely material level.

It is true that, on this level, the achievement of Rome was very remarkable indeed. Roman engineering created roads and aqueducts from Scotland to Africa, and the Roman armies carried the ideals of Greek civilization over millions of square miles. But in Rome itself there was a continual bitter power struggle. The Greeks invented the democratic system of election. The Romans have the dubious distinction of having invented the homicidal system of election – the deliberate development of murder as a political engine. Most historians date this from the murder of the tribune (or people's representative) Tiberius Gracchus in 133 B.C. and state that the Emperor Augustus put a stop to it about a century later; in fact, it started in the early days of republican Rome and continued until its downfall in the fifth century A.D. By then it had become such a tradition that it continued intermittently down the ages, so that the history of the popes often reads like pages of *I, Claudius*.

The real history of Rome begins from the period when the last of the Etruscan conquerors was expelled, about 509 B.C.; then Rome, like Athens, became a republic. At the time when Athens was fighting for its life against Persian invaders, Rome was demonstrating its own peculiar originality by staging the first strike in history; in 494 B.C., the plebeians, angry at class-injustice, all marched out of Rome up the Tiber and declared that they would simply found another city unless they were given their rights. This mass withdrawal of organized labour had the desired effect, and the patricians were forced to grant the people their own representatives. But when in 486 B.C. a patrician named Spurius Cassius proposed to grant the plebs the right to public land, the patricians rose as one man; Cassius was accused of wanting to become tyrant and executed. And when, in 440, a rich plebeian named Spurius Maelius tried to become a popular leader during a famine and lowered the price of his corn, he was summoned before a hastily appointed dictator and murdered. To pacify the people, his corn was distributed free; those who talked of avenging his death were quietly disposed of. Rome was learning the arts of gangster rule. But at least it was administered with an air of public concern worthy of Orwell's Big Brother. Marcus Manlius

✓ like modern Russia

Gaulish occupation 370 BC

was a national hero who had been responsible for saving the Capitol during the occupation of Rome by the Gauls in 390 B.C. (every schoolboy used to know the story of how the geese sounded the alarm). Saddened by the spectacle of brave ex-soldiers being thrown in jail for debt, Manlius began freeing debtors with his own private fortune. Aghast at this spectacle of demoralizing altruism, the patricians accused him of wanting to become tyrant and incited the plebs to sentence him to death. Manlius was thrown from the Tarpeian rock.

Perhaps it was the occupation by the Gauls that shocked the Romans into a new kind of unity. At all events, Roman expansion now continued steadily for century after century; little more than a hundred years after the execution of Manlius Rome ruled all Italy. Conquered citizens were not regarded as mere subjects but were made citizens of Rome, with full voting privileges. Understandably, most of them preferred this new status to that of enemy.

At this point, Mediterranean piracy played a decisive part in history and started the Romans on their conquest of the world. The only city in the Mediterranean whose power compared with that of Rome was Carthage in North Africa (what is now Tunisia). It had started as a Phoenician trading post, which had swiftly expanded – rather like modern Hong Kong – until it became a melting pot of nationalities. And since the Mediterranean was not only full of pirates but also of predatory Greeks, Macedonians, Lydians, Syrians, Etruscans and Romans, Carthage had also become a maritime power. For a while, Carthage united with Rome against the Greek general Pyrrhus, king of Epirus (282–272), but when Pyrrhus withdrew he left the allies facing each other across the straits of Sicily – too close for comfort.

Carthage fought its wars with mercenaries, and in 289 B.C. these included an Italian tribe who called themselves Mamertines. Out-of-work mercenaries are always a public danger, and on their way home from a war against Syracuse (in Sicily), these mercenaries took a great liking to a pleasant little Greek town called Messana (modern Messina) which had offered them hospitality. In the middle of the night they rose from their beds, slit the throats of the men and seized the women. And, being adventurers, they decided that they preferred piracy to farming and trade. For the next twenty-five years they were the scourge of the area, preying largely on ships from Syracuse and Carthage.

At Rhegium, in the toe of Italy, another Mamertine regiment heard about this exploit and decided to imitate it; they slaughtered their hosts and seized the town. But since they were supposed to be a Roman garrison, the Romans sent an army against them. They took the town by siege and proceeded to a mass execution of the rebels, four hundred of them. They were aided by a Greek ruler named Hiero of Syracuse, who then decided to go and smoke out the nest of pirates in Messana. The Carthagians agreed this was an excellent idea and sent help. And the Messanian pirates had the remarkable impudence to send to Rome for aid. They were in luck. Although the Roman senate said it would be absurd to help pirates – especially after punishing the rebels at Rhegium – the plebs scented plunder and conquest and overruled the senate. It was, as the German historian Mommsen called it, 'a moment of the deepest significance in the history of the world', for it was the first step towards the Roman empire. H. G. Wells says indignantly in his *Outline of History* (Book 5): 'So began the first of the most wasteful and disastrous series of wars that has ever darkened the history of mankind.' He is convinced that this decision was the moral turning point in Roman history – that it was the beginning of that epoch of slaughter, cruelty, vice and betrayal that has made the name of Rome a synonym for decadence.

There is an element of simplification in this view – as if Rome were a character in a Victorian melodrama who takes the 'wrong turning' and slips into vice and ruin. The tragedy of Rome was more complex. The Romans were an eminently practical and sensible people – the compromises between plebs and patricians show that. They lacked Greek subtlety and Greek intellectuality and, unlike Alexander, were not even worried about the lack. Like some simple and good-tempered country lad, they had the temperament to be happy and uncomplicated. The first Punic war (*punic* meaning Phoenician), which dragged on for a quarter of a century and which almost brought Rome to its knees, forced them to develop a new set of qualities: ruthless determination, intense patriotism; above all, aggressiveness. And nations are like individuals: once they have developed such qualities, they are stuck with them.

In 1935 a remarkable novel called *No Mean City*, by A. MacArthur and A. Kingsley Long was published. It was about the Glasgow slums, of which the authors obviously had first-hand knowledge. The title refers to St Paul's 'I am a citizen of no mean city', and the novel is the story of a simple and ordinary youth, Johnnie Stark, who is forced to learn the arts of self-defence, and who is so successful that he becomes known as the 'Razor king'. But this kind of success is in itself a trap; like an actor who cannot escape a certain type of role, he is forced by the nature of his self-image to go on radiating aggression and violence. There is no way in which he can relax into a more productive frame of mind. Inevitably, he dies in a street fight. Johnnie Stark is a symbol of the Roman Empire.

Rome's progress towards becoming the razor king of the Mediterranean began with setbacks. Rome and Carthage were evenly matched; the war dragged on, and after twenty-four years both sides were exhausted. It was Carthage that sued for peace; but Rome had lost two hundred thousand men and five hundred ships. When the Carthaginian general Hamilcar conquered Spain, Rome was piqued and alarmed to see its old rival back in business, and the two antagonists were soon squaring up again.

This time, Hamilcar's son Hannibal seized the initiative and invaded Italy across the Alps. For years his successes were brilliant; he beat Roman army after Roman army. Most of southern Italy came over to his side. But the Romans had a bulldog stubbornness. Their general, Fabius – the one after whom the Fabian Society was named – took care to avoid battle, but concentrated on harassing the invaders. Finally, the Roman Scipio carried the war back into North Africa, and Carthage was once again obliged to sue for peace. Rome acquired Spain and settled down to enjoy its new position as master of the Mediterranean.

The last act of the tragedy took place half a century later. Carthage was now a harmless municipality, a city without an empire; the peace treaty with Rome did not even allow her to possess an army. But like many conquered nations, she showed astonishing resilience, and was soon as prosperous as ever. Rome now longed to see her enemy trampled into the dust; one old statesman, Cato, used to conclude all his speeches in the senate – on whatever subject: 'Carthage must be destroyed.' The trouble was to find a pretext; Carthage was now so obviously harmless. And finally, for lack of anything better, the flimsiest of pretexts had to serve. Carthage's neighbour, Numidia – an ally of Rome – began making raids, and Carthage had to arm herself. Rome declared that she had broken their treaty and made threatening noises. Like a dog rolling on its back, Carthage offered instant and total obedience, and for a while the Romans thought they were going to be deprived of their war and the rich booty it would bring. So they ordered the Carthaginians to abandon their city and to move ten miles inland – a course that would inevitably destroy a city that depended on the sea for its trade. This had the desired effect of making the Carthaginians angry. Rome was able to declare war.

For an earlier generation of Romans, the conquest of Carthage would have been an easy matter. But things had changed since the last Punic war. Riches had flooded into Rome, permitting unheard-of luxuries – such as taking baths in milk. Political corruption had become commonplace; but the politicians also set out to corrupt the plebs with flattery and amusements. A man who wanted to become a consul had to put on a gladiatorial show costing thousands of pounds; the richer the show, the more likely he was to be elected. The old Romans had had only one festival a year; now there were dozens. The intellectuals read the Greeks, quoted Plato, and cultivated a taste for boy-love. Rich young dandies wore semi-transparent robes and took a pride in their hair-dos. In a mere half-century, Rome had turned into a kind of Sodom.

The result was that the first attack on Carthage was a failure, almost a disaster. The defenders hurled back the attacks, and disease reduced the morale of the Roman besiegers. The second year of war was just as bad, the Romans wasting themselves in attacks on outlying towns. Finally, the Romans appointed a young general named Scipio – grandson of the man who had won the previous war with Carthage – and the fortunes of the Carthaginians took a turn for the worse. Scipio built a mole across the harbour to prevent supplies getting in. Carthage began to starve to death. They took Roman captives on to the walls, tortured them, and hurled them down at the besiegers. The Carthaginians – always given to internal intrigues – began to quarrel among themselves, and men were crucified in the streets. Children were sacrificed to the God Moloch, rolled down into a furnace, to try to avert disaster.

When the Romans assaulted again, the city fell. They hacked their way in, burning houses as they went. The defenders now fought grimly, retreating street by street. They were too weak to resist for long. Even so, it took the Romans six days to reach the citadel, the steep rock in the centre of the town with a temple on its summit. The last of the Carthaginians surrendered. In the temple, nine hundred Roman deserters who knew they could expect no mercy set the temple on fire and died in the flames. The prisoners were sold into slavery, and Carthage was burned to the ground. The senate issued orders that not a stone was to be left standing. When the city was reduced to ashes, the ground was ploughed. Julius Caesar later built another Carthage, but not upon the same spot. The ground that had seen so much agony was accursed. (And the phrase is here meant literally – the Roman priests performed an elaborate ceremony to curse the ground.)

In the same year, 146 B.C., the Romans intervened in a quarrel between Greeks – who regarded themselves as Rome's allies – and treated the city of Corinth as they had treated Carthage, levelling it to the ground, cursing the site and selling all its citizens into slavery. A few years later, when the province of Lusitania, in western Spain, rebelled against Roman occupation, its city of Numantia was wiped off the face of the map and its citizens massacred or sold into slavery. None of these acts of terrorism was necessary. But Rome was trying to make up in violence what it lacked in strength and discipline.

The trouble was that Rome was becoming fat, lazy and vicious. A few Romans of the old school warned against the danger; but the majority of their fellow citizens simply could not see what they were talking about. Rome had overrun the Mediterranean; it had even added Macedonia, the country of Alexander the Great, to its conquests. Wealth was flooding in from all sides. Everyone benefited; the plebs were always being given free hand-outs and treated to public spectacles in which captives had to fight for their lives against lions and tigers. They were not going to complain about the increasing power of the rich so long as the rich kept them so well entertained. In a city as wealthy as Rome, there was plenty for everyone.

What worried men like Tiberius Gracchus – another grandson of the great Scipio Africanus – and his brother Gaius, was that most of the wealth and land was passing into the hands of a few people, and that these were mostly corrupt. Rome's greatness had been founded on small farmers who owned their own land; such men might have a few slaves, but these were treated almost as members of the family. And now, just as in the time of Marcus Manlius, soldiers returning from the war were being jailed for debt and the small farms were being gobbled up by the wealthy landowners. These new super-farms were being stocked with slaves by Mediterranean pirates, and the cheap grain was putting the remaining small farmers out of business. The fields were full of chained slaves who were branded like cattle. Naturally, these escaped whenever they could, and went around committing robbery and murder until they were caught and tortured to death. When the Sicilian slaves revolted, in 134 B.C., seventy thousand of them took over the island. The Romans finally had to kill the lot. A happy and contented land was turning into a land of suffering and crime.

In the year of the slave revolt in Sicily, Tiberius Gracchus was elected tribune of the people. And his first act was to propose a law to limit the amount of land that could be held by a single family. He suggested too that land should be given to homeless soldiers. This was too much. His fellow senators rose up against him, chased him into the street, and beat him to death with table legs. Ten years later, his brother Gaius – another 'troublemaker' – was murdered under almost identical circumstances.

The Romans were slipping into violence by a process of self-justification. And once a nation – or an individual – has started down this particular slope, it is almost impossible to apply the brakes. The Roman people were too unimaginative and short-sighted to realize that, once murder has been justified on grounds of expediency, it can become a habit, then a disease.

The man who was most responsible for bringing the disease to Rome was not a criminal or degenerate; in fact, he possessed all the Roman virtues. Gaius Marius was the son of a farm labourer; he rose to eminence in the army, married a patrician girl, and succeeded in getting himself elected tribune – a spokesman of the people. He was in his mid-forties when an African general named Jugurtha rose up in revolt. Jugurtha's skill in guerrilla warfare enabled him to defy the might of Rome for four years. Finally, Marius marched off to try his luck. He soon decided to abandon force in favour of treachery. Jugurtha's father-in-law was bribed to betray him, and lure him into a trap laid by a brilliant young officer known as 'Lucky Sulla'. Marius was able to keep his promise to drag Jugurtha back to Rome in chains. The angry populace tore off the captive's jewels and clothes, yanking the ear-rings so violently that they ripped off the flesh. Jugurtha was thrown into an icy dungeon and executed a few days later. Marius became the most popular man in Rome, and was awarded a triumph.

Rome undoubtedly needed Marius. Barbarian invaders, including Germans (making their first appearance in history), poured in from the north. A Roman army had been virtually wiped out at Arausio, on the Rhone – the most shattering defeat since Hannibal. Marius was hastily despatched to meet them as they poured into Italy. Fortunately, the barbarians had divided their forces. Marius drove the Teutons back into Aix en Provence, where he annihilated them; then he caught up with the other half, the Cimbri, and routed them at Vercellae, near Milan.

Once again, he was the hero of Rome. He was elected consul for the sixth time in succession – a glorious but illegal achievement, since each of the two consuls – who were together virtually governors of Rome – was only supposed to serve for a year at a time. He joined forces with two popular demagogues, Saturninus and Glaucia, and set out to topple the conservatives and make himself master of Rome. Unfortunately, his talents as a politician were mediocre – his manners were too blunt and harsh. He tried intriguing with both sides at once and lost his friends and allies in the process. The planned 'revolution' was a total failure; riots broke out and, as consul, Marius was forced to call out the army against his former allies. They took refuge in the Capitol and were murdered by a mob. Suddenly, the 'saviour of Rome' found himself a political has-been. It had all happened so quickly – within a month or two of his victorious return – that he found it difficult to grasp. He had always had an imperious temper; now he became suspicious and paranoid.

But the conservatives had also overreached themselves. There really *was* an urgent need for reform – not just in Rome but in the whole of Italy. The people needed champions to defend them against the wealthy; but as soon as a champion appeared, he was murdered. When this happened to a reformer named Drusus – another 'leftist' – Italy flared into civil war. Once again, Marius was needed. He and his old subordinate 'Lucky Sulla' – now his bitter rival – were placed in command of the armies and marched off to slaughter men who had once fought under them – mostly dissatisfied Italians who felt they had a right to become Roman citizens. At this point, a king named Mithridates of Pontus – on the Black Sea – decided to seize this opportunity to acquire himself an empire. He invaded Syria and Asia Minor and sent out secret orders that all Romans living in conquered cities should be put to death. When the day came, more than a hundred thousand men, women and children were dragged out into the streets and massacred.

The people of Rome were shattered by the news – it seemed

incredible that Romans could be treated like the inhabitants of Carthage and Corinth – mere cattle. The rich were even more shaken by loss of revenues. The treasury was suddenly empty. The senate decided that, instead of slaughtering the Italians, it might be a better idea to give them what they wanted and then send them to fight Mithridates. So the Italians finally achieved their Roman citizenship.

It might be assumed that, in the face of the Asian threat, Rome would cease its internal squabbles. But the Romans had become too accustomed to quarrelling amongst themselves. To begin with, Marius and Sulla both thought they ought to have the honour of destroying Mithridates. The senate preferred the patrician Sulla. Marius threw in his lot with a popular demagogue named Sulpicius, who appealed directly to the people. They not only voted him command of the army; they also went off looking for Sulla to tear him to pieces. Sulla had to flee from Rome. But he fled to his soldiers – the ones who had helped him to put down the rebellion – and marched on Rome. After some bitter fighting, it was Marius's turn to flee, together with his friend Sulpicius, who was caught and executed while Marius escaped to Africa. Having settled this little quarrel, Sulla made himself master of Rome, murdered a few hundred of Marius's supporters, passed some laws, and finally marched off to fight Mithridates.

The moment his back was turned, Marius hurried back to Rome. Paranoid, vengeful, eaten up with jealousy and hatred, he behaved like a maniac. Like Sulla, he had his faithful army – his soldiers liked to call themselves 'Marius's mules' – and he now began a reign of terror such as no great city had ever seen. He had the gates of Rome closed, then ordered his men to kill all his 'enemies' – that is, anyone against whom he nursed a grudge. And since a paranoid has a grudge against half the world, thousands of Rome's most distinguished men died in those few days. When Marius walked through the streets, men hastened to salute him. If Marius looked the other way, it was a sign that the man was one of his enemies, and his soldiers cut him down on the spot.

Marius had become insane, a victim of his own obsessions. Soon he began to find it impossible to sleep, even though he drank himself into a stupor every night. And after being elected consul for the seventh time he fell into a fever and died. All Italy heaved a sigh of relief.

But his death brought no deliverance. When Sulla arrived back in

Rome – after forcing Mithridates to make peace – he murdered as many of Marius's supporters as he could find. Another reign of terror began. Senators and officials were killed by the thousand. And very shortly, the murders ceased to be purely political. For, as all dictators have discovered, it is hard to see the difference between a man you dislike for political reasons and a man you just happen to find dislikeable. After a while, it is not even necessary to dislike a man in order to kill him. If he has a desirable estate, and you want it for one of your friends, it seems natural to regard its owner as a tiresome obstacle. Beginning as the 'liberator' of Rome, Sulla ended as its first dictator in the modern sense.

At the end, he lived up to his nickname of Lucky Sulla. Instead of suffering the fate of men who are universally hated and feared, he laid aside the responsibilities of office, retired to his estate and died peacefully in his bed. As an old soldier, he found politics boring. We may also suspect that he felt that these degenerate Romans were not worth the waste of his time. Sulla had been born in the days of the third Punic war, when Rome was still proud, independent and democratic. Now most of the old breed were dead – many of them executed by Marius – and the rest were like sheep. The true 'decline' of Rome had begun.

What had happened? We have seen that Rome's lasting problems began when she set out to conquer the Mediterranean, and became the richest city in the world. But the problem went deeper than that. In the year that the first war with Carthage began – 264 B.C. – a king named Asoka came to the throne in India; and, like most empire builders, he went to war to establish his position. The war was entirely successful, but Asoka was revolted by the slaughter. He decided that he would establish a different kind of empire – a religious empire. It was the faith of Gautama, the Buddha, that made the deepest appeal to Asoka, with its teaching that men's desires only bring them suffering and that the escape is to lead a life of moderation with the mind directed towards Enlightenment. Asoka's empire spread like that of Alexander the Great, but by entirely peaceful means.

It is an interesting historical fact that the craving for enlightenment, for salvation or inner wisdom, spread across the civilized world from a number of completely independent points at roughly the same time – the fifth century B.C. In Greece there was Socrates,

in Persia, Zoroaster, in Israel, Jeremiah, in China, Confucius, Lao
Tzu and Mo Tzu, in India, the Buddha, Mahavira – founder of
Jainism – and Vyasa, legendary author of the *Mahabharata*. It
arouses the vague suspicion that great ideas are diffused by a kind of
telepathy when the human race is ready for them. All these teachers
have in common a certain basic recognition: that although our
desires grope instinctively towards physical fulfilment – food, sex,
pleasure, security – they can never be fully satisfied by the physical
world. They always leave behind a curious craving for something
more, something deeper. Like an alcoholic, man seems to be driven
by a perpetual thirst; but there is no wine that can slake it. Socrates
believed it was a craving for knowledge; the Buddha, a craving for
eternity; the Jewish prophets, a craving for God. Yet all have in
common the insight that it is a desire for *inner* peace, a certain access
to some inner world, and that our preoccupation with the material
world is the result of some kind of confusion.

The Romans seem to have been completely devoid of this insight.
Their immense vitality found its highest expression in self-control,
self-discipline. They lacked the evolutionary appetite for wisdom or
the mystical craving for eternity. Like all ancient peoples, they
possessed strong religious beliefs; but these expressed themselves in
the form of superstitions: sacrifices to the gods, belief in oracles and
omens. To us, these seem to have as little to do with religion as
crossing yourself to avert the evil eye has to do with Christianity.

In its mystical or evolutionary form, the religious impulse may be
seen as man's attempt to escape the limitations of left-brain consciousness. Human beings, alone of all animals, developed this
divided form of consciousness in order to be able to *concentrate on the
particular*. We needed to learn to cope with problems and intricacies
that would have given any other creature a nervous breakdown. This
ability carries heavy penalties: tension, headache, exasperation, a
sense of entrapment.

For various reasons, the people of Europe developed left-brain
consciousness a great deal faster than the people of the east – of India
and China, for example. This could simply be due to later development in the east; rice was not introduced into China until 2000 B.C.,
bringing about an agricultural revolution that made large communities possible. Even under the Shang dynasty, which began around
1500 B.C. – the time of the destruction of the Minoan empire – China
remained a country of small villages and farms. The sheer vastness of

the country meant that the majority of its people lived in peace, far from the incursions of border raiders – it was not until the third century B.C. that Shih Huang ordered the building of the Great Wall. Similar reasons probably explain why India remained an essentially 'right-brain' culture, even after the incursion of the Aryans – who became an aristocratic warrior class – around 1500 B.C. (Again, we observe this odd coincidence of dates.) India's first contact with the megalomaniac left-brain mentality occurred when Alexander the Great invaded in 327 B.C. (although the Persians had made north-western India a province two centuries earlier). And Alexander's conquests hardly took him beyond the Indus. Significantly, the unrest that followed his death led to the founding of the first Indian empire under Chandragupta. Asoka was his grandson; and we have seen that he gave a completely new meaning to the notion of empire.

It was probably the earlier rise of agriculture in the Mediterranean – the ability of its farmers to feed large conglomerations of people – that led to its accelerated development; so did the fact that it was so much more vulnerable to invasion. The Romans developed from simple agriculturalists to empire builders in a few centuries, while the same development in China and India took millennia. The Mediterranean was a Darwinian forcing house, where success was achieved at the cost of ruthlessness. The Greeks had been concerned with questions about the universe and the nature and destiny of man; but the miseries of the Peloponnesian war made the Athenians as cruel and ruthless as the Romans who later destroyed Carthage. When Melos expressed a desire for independence in 428 B.C. the Athenians killed all the males and sold the women and children into slavery. Thucydides said that the trouble with Athens was that it was unable to make up its mind; new leaders would be elected one day and executed the next. The philosophical temperament was unfitted for survival in the Mediterranean.

No one could accuse the Romans of being unable to make up their minds. When they made a decision, they stuck to it. And while Rome was fighting for its life against Etruscans and Gauls, this quality gave them greatness. The Etruscans were also philosophers; they had a touch of the eastern temperament; they vanished from history. Rome, with the magnificent simplicity of a healthy peasant, went on cutting down its enemies with the short sword. The riches of Carthage made the Romans greedy; and, like the Persians before them, they began to pay too much attention to the pleasures of the bed and the table. In this new situation of 'conspicuous consumption', the lack of imagination that had made them great now made them brutish and short sighted – neither of them qualities that conduce to survival. At the point when the Romans could afford to be influenced by the Greeks and think about larger questions, they were incapable of thinking beyond the needs of the present moment. So in spite of emperors like Augustus, Claudius, Hadrian and Marcus Aurelius, the decline of Rome was irreversible.

The rest of the story of Rome is mainly one of criminal violence. It began immediately after the death of Sulla in 78 B.C. The roads of Italy, and even of Rome itself, were overrun with robbers and murder became commonplace. The sea was suddenly full of pirates – Mommsen calls it 'the golden age of buccaneers'. It became so bad that only about a third of the corn Rome imported from Africa and Egypt actually reached Roman ports. Pirate vessels were usually light craft with shallow draught and a formidable turn of speed. They could follow a merchantman at a distance, too low in the water to be seen, and attack by night – sometimes even following the merchantman into port, killing the man on watch and slipping out again before dawn loaded with plunder. Men and women were prized as much as other booty, for they could be sold as slaves. The Greek island of Delos became virtually a slave market, with tens of thousands changing hands every day. The pirates were soon strong enough and rich enough to demand 'protection' money from ports and to use them when they needed repairs. The province of Cilicia, in what is now southern Turkey, became a pirate stronghold. Rome was largely responsible for all these outlaws, for the destruction of cities like Corinth and Carthage had left large numbers of people with no other means of livelihood.

Five years after the death of Sulla, a gladiator named Spartacus – a deserter from the Roman army who had been caught and enslaved – escaped from the gladiator school at Capua and hid on Mount Vesuvius, together with a small band of slaves. As other slaves heard about the group, they came and joined them. Then, because they knew they would be tortured to death if they were recaptured, they fought like demons against the armies sent out against them and achieved a remarkable series of victories. The Romans were stunned – they had come to believe that their armies were invincible. Worse still, they had no competent general to send against the rebels – their best man, Pompey, was away in Spain fighting another rebel. Eventually, the Romans decided to appoint a millionaire called Crassus – an opportunist who had made his fortune buying up the land of proscribed senators and by setting up Rome's first fire brigade. *The delibrations of victory*

Crassus was lucky. Their string of victories had turned the slaves into a murderous rabble whose only interests were murder and rape. On a small scale, Spartacus's slaves were repeating the history of Rome: effort and determination leading to success, and success leading to degeneration and viciousness. Drunk with revenge and plunder, the slaves refused Spartacus's pleas to leave Italy; they were enjoying themselves too much. Against Spartacus's better judgement, they charged into battle against the well-trained Roman army, which hacked them to pieces. Spartacus was killed in battle and six thousand of his followers were crucified along the road to Rome.

Pompey came rushing back from Spain in time to cut down the fugitives. He then managed to arrive in Rome before Crassus and was awarded a full-scale triumph; Crassus had to be content with a more modest victory parade.

This Pompey – known as 'the Great' after an early triumph in Africa – was another soldier cast in the same mould as Marius and Sulla: a formidable general (with more than a touch of vainglory), an honest man, but a less than brilliant politician. Two years after his 'victory' over Spartacus, he stood for consul; when the patricians rejected him as too young (he was thirty-six) he changed sides and joined the people's party, of which Crassus was a leading light. So was a younger man named Julius Caesar, a nephew of Marius, whose talents had been so obvious when he was in his early twenties that it was only with difficulty that the dictator Sulla was dissuaded from having him killed. Like his uncle Marius, Caesar dreamed of glory and triumph. This oddly assorted trio – the egotistical general, the good natured millionaire and the rather foppish young intellectual – entered into a partnership that would eventually make them masters of Rome.

During the war with Spartacus, the pirates had become bolder than ever and the Romans were desperate. Half their corn was being intercepted. Coastal towns had been raided and sacked so many times that the survivors had simply moved inland. The pirates landed where they pleased, and often roamed around until they found someone who was worth kidnapping for ransom. When they had raided a town or village, they relaxed on the sea shore to enjoy themselves; but – unlike Ulysses – they were seldom surprised by an avenging army. The Romans felt a terrible sense of helplessness: there were so many pirate vessels all over the Mediterranean, and the strongest army could do nothing against them.

In 68 B.C., Pompey and his supporters persuaded the people of Rome that something had to be done, even if it cost thousands of talents. The following year, Pompey raised 120,000 men, 270 ships, and 6,000 talents (about six million pounds). He knew which towns were pirate strongholds. It was a matter of attacking them all at once so that the pirates could not co-operate or reinforce one another. He had been given three years to complete his task. He struck so suddenly and violently that he completed half of it in the first forty days. The Romans were poor seamen, but it turned out that this made no difference. The pirates fled into their strongholds as soon as the Romans appeared on the horizon, and then Roman soldiers poured on shore and drove them out. These murderers and robbers were no match for trained Roman legions; and when the word got around that Pompey would be merciful to all who surrendered, they gave up by the thousand. Mithridates of Pontus, who had supported the pirates of Cilicia, watched in dismay as the strongholds crumbled. Twenty thousand pirates were captured, ten thousand killed, and all their strongholds and shipyards destroyed. Then, instead of crucifying his captives, Pompey resettled them in some of the abandoned towns, knowing that most of them would settle down to earning a respectable living when given the chance. He proved to be correct. In three months, Pompey put an end to Mediterranean piracy.

After this triumph the Roman people were convinced that Pompey was irresistible, so they sent him with an army to Asia Minor to finish off Mithridates, who was now being more troublesome than ever – encouraging his son-in-law Tigranes to annex Syria and Cappadocia. Pompey captured Tigranes, and pursued Mithridates to the Crimea, where the latter committed suicide on hearing that his son had rebelled. Pompey, apparently unstoppable, went on and conquered Jerusalem, and marched as far as the Caspian Sea. His achievement was as remarkable, in its way, as that of Alexander the Great.

Meanwhile Pompey's ally Julius Caesar was making a name for

himself in Spain. This Caesar was a remarkable young man, but no one expected him to become a great national leader. As a youth he had been fashionably 'precious', writing poetry, perfuming and curling his hair and having love affairs – apparently with men as well as women. He was regarded much as Oscar Wilde was in the 1890s. Mommsen describes him as Rome's sole creative genius; but, like most Romans, Caesar lacked the imagination to be genuinely creative. He also possessed a good measure of the Roman ruthlessness. As a young man, he had been captured by pirates, who had told him they wanted twenty talents ransom; Caesar said haughtily that they were insulting him and he would give them fifty. Waiting for the ransom to arrive, he lived among them as if they were his servants, telling them to be quiet when he wanted to sleep. He joined in their games and made them sit and listen while he read them his poetry; when they proved less than appreciative, he called them barbarians and told them he would have them crucified when he was freed. They laughed indulgently at the spoilt and imperious young man. As soon as the ransom arrived, Caesar hurried to the nearest port – Miletus in Asia Minor – commandeered several ships and returned to surprise the pirates. He then had them crucified but, as a humane concession, cut their throats before nailing them to the cross.

Back from Spain, Caesar was appointed aedile, the master of ceremonies in public celebrations. He borrowed large sums from Crassus and staged some spectacular shows, one of them with 320 pairs of gladiators. This made him immensely popular with the people – which is why Crassus wanted his friendship. When Pompey came back from his conquests in 62 B.C., Julius Caesar was becoming a power to be reckoned with, while the senate showed its jealousy of Pompey by snubbing him (after all, he had gone over to the people's party). Caesar suggested an alliance: he was the most popular man in Rome, Crassus was the richest, Pompey was its greatest hero; together they could do what they liked. The senate could be overruled by the people. Ever since that unfortunate affair of the triumph over Spartacus, Pompey and Crassus had been rivals. Now they both saw the virtue of the alliance. They became known to their friends as the triumvirate, to their enemies as the three-headed monster.

In the following year, 59 B.C., the three-headed monster achieved the first of its aims: Caesar was elected consul, in the teeth of bitter opposition from the patricians. He then used his power to get Pompey what he wanted: land for his soldiers. Pompey and Crassus were appointed head of a commission to administer new laws. The three men were virtually the rulers of Rome.

It could have been the beginning of a new era. All three men were intelligent. None of them had the temperament of a dictator. Together they could have steered the whole country into a new age of prosperity and enlightenment. But somehow Rome was not destined to become another Athens. It had gone too far along the road into power politics. Caesar soon became tired of the endless back-biting and in-fighting, and marched off to Gaul, looking for adventure and glory. He found both over the next five years, as his armies subdued the Gauls from the Rhine to the North Sea, then crossed the Channel and conquered half of Britain. Back in Rome, Pompey and Crassus viewed these triumphs with mixed feelings. Crassus got himself appointed to the command of the army in Syria and went off to try and outdo Caesar. It proved to be a disaster. He was an incompetent, and ended by getting his troops massacred and himself beheaded. When the patricians offered to make Pompey sole consul of Rome, he decided to betray Caesar and change sides.

When Caesar was ordered to leave his army and return to Rome, he realized that things had taken a dangerous turn. To us, it sounds preposterous that the man who had conquered half Europe should have anything to fear. But Caesar knew that his conquests had only aroused envy. Like all trivial people, the Romans hated greatness. So he decided to disobey orders and marched his army to the banks of the river that divided France from Italy – the Rubicon. And when the senate ordered him to disband his army or be considered a public enemy, he gave the order to cross.

Pompey fled to Greece, and Caesar entered Rome in triumph and had himself appointed consul instead. Then he went to Greece and defeated Pompey's vastly superior forces at the battle of Pharsalus. Pompey sailed for Egypt and, as he stepped ashore, was stabbed in the back by his Egyptian hosts. Egypt was not interested in defeated generals.

Unaware that Pompey was dead, Caesar followed him to Egypt and found himself embroiled in a squabble between the boy king Ptolemy and his sister Cleopatra. Caesar took Cleopatra's part – fathering a son on her, according to Plutarch – and defeated Ptolemy's army, with some help from the son of Rome's old enemy

Mithridates. Cleopatra was installed on the throne of Egypt and Caesar sailed back to Rome and to a magnificent public triumph – the leading chariot bore the words 'I came, I saw, I conquered.' Unlike Marius and Sulla, Caesar pardoned all his former enemies. This proved to be a mistake; they stabbed him to death in the senate on the morning of 15 March 44 B.C.

It seems typical that the Romans should murder the greatest man that they had yet produced – the man who had restored to them something of the greatness of earlier centuries. But then, Rome had become a sewer. Although Caesar had given them back empire and riches, nothing could save them from the consequences of their own triviality and viciousness.

The next part of the story is known to everyone who has read Shakespeare – Mark Antony's oration, which turned the Roman mob against the assassins, the squabble between Antony and Caesar's nephew and heir, Octavius, and their subsequent uneasy partnership, Antony's famous affair with Cleopatra in Egypt and his abandonment of his wife Octavia (who was Octavius's sister); and, finally, the sad ending of it all with the suicide of Antony and Cleopatra after the battle of Actium. But at least Octavius became the master of Rome and, as the emperor Augustus, ruled wisely and well for more than forty years.

The Roman historian Suetonius, the author of a gossipy and often thoroughly scandalous book on the Caesars, tells us that Augustus's personal life was unexceptionable – after mentioning a dozen or so tales that suggest that Roman standards of respectability must have been unusually low. These include the suggestions that Julius Caesar had adopted Octavius as his heir in exchange for being allowed to sodomize him, that Octavius was fond of committing adultery (on one occasion dragging the lady from table to bedroom in front of her husband and bringing her back with blushing cheeks and disordered hair) and that even as an old man he was fond of deflowering very young girls, who were procured for him by his wife Livia. Yet in theory he believed strongly in the old Roman virtues and did his best to bring them back into favour; when he discovered that his daughter Julia – married to the future emperor Tiberius – was a nymphomaniac who continually seduced her husband's soldiers, and even slaves, he was so shocked that he had her banished for life.

If Augustus himself – not to mention his daughter – could set such a bad example, what could he expect of the rest of Rome? Augustus could use the empire's wealth to rebuild Rome in marble, to clear the roads of robbers, to set up the city's first police force and a fire-fighting service that would extinguish blazes without preliminary bargaining; he could banish Ovid, who wrote *The Art of Love*, and shower favours on Virgil, who wrote about the fields and wanted to see a return of the old ways; but the mob wanted their entertainments and free hand-outs, and Augustus had to keep them happy with an increasing number of public holidays and spectacular shows until in the end there were holidays on 117 days of the year. And with so much money in circulation, upper-class Romans devoted themselves to entertainment, overeating and sex. Augustus tried to remedy the situation with laws – he even passed a law that regulated how much wine a man could drink with his meals – but they were unenforceable. When he finally died, in 14 A.D., Augustus had brought Rome peace and prosperity, but there was nothing he could do about its now incorrigible criminality.

His successor, Tiberius, Livia's son by her first husband, was a sour, withdrawn, introverted man who was fifty-six when he became emperor. In his early manhood he showed himself to be a brave soldier. He was married to Vipsania, with whom he was deeply in love, when his step-sister Julia (Augustus's daughter) fell in love with him; Augustus ordered him to divorce his wife and marry Julia – such marital rearrangements being common among the Roman aristocracy, where marriage was made to seal political bonds. Tiberius did as he was told – he had no choice – but he never reconciled himself to Julia, whose sexual demands exhausted him. In his mid-thirties, he voluntarily exiled himself to the island of Rhodes – or, more probably, was exiled by Augustus at Julia's instigation – and spent seven years there. Restored to favour, he again performed excellently as a soldier, suppressing a revolt in Illyria; his obsessive strictness made him disliked by his soldiers, but he is quoted as saying: 'Let them hate me so long as they obey me.' Julia had presented Augustus with three grandsons, who might have been regarded as having greater claims to the imperial crown than Tiberius; but two of them died under mysterious circumstances – probably murdered by Livia – and the third was murdered immediately after Augustus's death. So in 14 A.D. Tiberius became 'princeps', the first man in Rome.

As emperor he proved to be as strict a disciplinarian as he had been when a general; and made a determined attempt to improve the morals of Rome by making laws against adultery. Suetonius offers us a glimpse of the morality of the period when he says: 'When one Roman knight had sworn that he would never divorce his wife whatever she did, but found her in bed with his son, Tiberius absolved him from his oath. Married women of good family were beginning to ply openly as prostitutes . . . All such offenders were now exiled . . .' He made himself unpopular with the mob by cutting down on their 'bread and circuses'. Suetonius is convinced that Tiberius's strictness was disguised sadism – as, for example, when he ordered all the witnesses in some obscure law case to be tortured to try to clarify the evidence.

For the first dozen years of his reign, Tiberius followed conscientiously in the footsteps of Augustus, and his occasional savageries were excused as military severity. Then his most trusted adviser, Sejanus – prefect of the guard – persuaded him to move away from Rome to Capri, pointing out that Tiberius was so much disliked in Rome that his presence there did no good. (In fact, Sejanus was hoping to succeed Tiberius as emperor.) There, Tiberius seems to have thrown off all restraint and to have devoted himself to various sexual perversions he had developed in his younger days. Suetonius describes with relish the rooms furnished with indecent paintings and statues, in which Tiberius took his pleasure both with boys and girls. He alleges that Tiberius trained little boys to chase him when he went swimming and to nibble his penis, and that he had bands of young men and women trained in 'unnatural practices'. 'The story goes that once, while sacrificing, he took an erotic fancy to the acolyte who was carrying the incense casket and could hardly wait for the ceremony to end before hurrying him and his brother, the sacred trumpeter, out of the temple and indecently assaulting them both. When they protested at this dastardly crime he had their legs broken.'

Sejanus was now in almost sole control in Rome and seems to have spent his time making accusations against knights and ensuring that they were executed or committed suicide. In 23 A.D. he poisoned Tiberius's son Drusus, making it look like a disease. But with a master as pathologically suspicious as Tiberius, Sejanus was bound to make a mistake. He was arrested and accused of conspiracy; after execution, his body was thrown to the rabble, who abused it for three days. Sejanus's three children were also executed; the girl of fourteen was a virgin, and protected by Roman law, so the executioner raped her before killing her. On hearing rumours that his son Drusus had been murdered, Tiberius instituted another reign of terror, that continued more or less unchecked until his death six years later. Citizens were tried and executed on the slightest of pretexts. When he finally died, at the age of seventy-eight – probably smothered by his chief henchman – the people of Rome went wild with joy.

It is only fair to add that some historians regard the accusations of sexual perversion contained in Suetonius and Tacitus as mere gossip, and believe that Tiberius withdrew to Capri because he could not tolerate the corruption and vice of his capital. This could be true; but the record of men tried and executed on absurd pretexts could hardly be faked. In fact, what happened to Tiberius begins to seem monotonously inevitable when we study the history of Rome. Faced with adversity or interesting challenges, he was admirable; when allowed to do whatever he liked, he became the victim of his emotions and of boredom. It was a lack of what we have called the stabilizing force, 'force C', that turned him into a criminal. Lacking imagination, lacking any deeper religious or philosophical interest, the Romans needed practical problems to bring out the best in them; success left them at the mercy of their own worst qualities.

This is even more appallingly obvious in the case of the man Tiberius appointed as his successor, Gaius Caligula. He was twenty-five when he took over, and he immediately increased his already considerable popularity by showering gifts of money on the people and holding magnificent gladiatorial contests. His pleasure in spending money amounted to a mania. He had ships anchored in a double line three miles long and covered with earth and planks so that he could ride back and forth; for a soothsayer had once remarked that Caligula had no more chance of becoming emperor than he had of riding dryshod over the Bay of Baiae.

It soon became clear that absolute power had driven him insane. He announced that he was a god and that Jupiter had asked him to share his home. He committed incest with his three sisters, on the grounds that it was the correct thing for a god to do – Jupiter having slept with his sister Juno. And he began to kill with total abandon, without any of Tiberius's pretence of legality. One day, when he was fencing with a gladiator with a wooden sword, the man fell down deliberately; Caligula pulled out a dagger, stabbed him to death, then ran around flourishing the bloodstained weapon as evidence that he had won. One day when he was presiding at a sacrifice in the temple – at which he was supposed to stun a beast with a mallet – he swung the mallet at the priest who was supposed to cut its throat and knocked him unconscious; it was his idea of a joke. At one of his banquets he began to laugh, and when politely asked the cause of his mirth, answered: 'It just occurred to me that I only have to give one nod and your throats will be cut.' When he was told the price of raw meat for the wild animals in the circus, he decided that it would be cheaper to feed them on criminals; he had a row of malefactors lined up and told the soldiers: 'Kill every man between that bald head and the one over there.' He called Rome: 'The city of necks waiting for me to chop them.' And when he ran out of money, he adopted the now time-honoured system of accusing rich men of various crimes and seizing their property. His favourite method of execution was what might be called 'the death of a thousand cuts', in which hundreds of small wounds were inflicted.

It seems surprising that Caligula survived as emperor for as long as he did – it was partly because he surrounded himself with a specially picked bodyguard of German troops. One day at the arena he took a brief stroll to a hallway under the grandstand, and one of the officers of the royal guard cut him down, then stabbed him – appropriately – in his genitals. Other guards went to the palace, killed Caligula's wife and dashed out the brains of his baby daughter against the wall.

Behind a curtain the palace guards found Caligula's uncle Claudius in a state of abject terror. Claudius, who was lame and stammered, had survived this long (he was fifty) because he was generally regarded as a harmless idiot. The guards liked him and proclaimed him emperor. And in fact Claudius proved to be an excellent emperor, ruling for the next thirteen years – until his murder – as soberly and fairly as Augustus.

Through the two novels by Robert Graves, Claudius has become one of the best-known of the twelve Caesars. Graves represents him as a kindly and decent man, somewhat the dupe of his servants and his wives, but shrewd and well-intentioned. Most of this is true; but to balance the picture we have to take into account Suetonius's less partial portrait. Suetonius mentions that his 'cruel and sanguinary' disposition was much in evidence – that he made a point of watching criminals being put to the torture, and witnessing 'ancient style' executions in which a man was flogged to death; clearly, he inherited some of the sadistic disposition that characterized other members of his family, including his uncle Tiberius. Like Tiberius and Caligula, he seems to have been something of a sex maniac, 'setting no bounds to his libidinous intercourse with women'. When annoyed by the failure of mechanical devices at the arena, he was likely to order the carpenter responsible to go and fight the lions. Suetonius lists some of the executions ordered by Claudius: Appius Silanus, father of his son-in-law, Cneius Pompey, husband of his eldest daughter, two nieces, thirty-five senators and three hundred knights. Graves represents Claudius as the dupe of his nymphomaniac wife Messalina and of various scheming freedmen; but since Suetonius mentions that his two nieces were executed 'without any positive proof of their crimes . . . or so much as allowing them to make a defence', it is difficult to regard Claudius entirely as an innocent dupe. When, eventually, Claudius found out about Messalina's sexual misdemeanours – including a contest with a famous prostitute to see who could satisfy most men in a single night – he ordered her execution, then that of more than three hundred men and women who had been involved with her in sexual orgies. Claudius then decided to marry his niece Agrippina, daughter of his brother Germanicus and Caligula's sister, and had the law against incest changed especially for this purpose. Agrippina was another schemer, like the empress Livia, and persuaded Claudius to adopt her son by a previous marriage, Nero, as his heir. When she suspected that Claudius was about to change his mind, she fed him poisoned mushrooms, and the brief but, on the whole, prosperous reign of Claudius came to an end.

So although Claudius was undoubtedly one of the 'better' Caesars, it is hard not to feel that by any objective standard he was something of a monster. The humiliations and difficulties of his early life, and the problems of preserving his neck under Tiberius and Caligula, seem to have acted as a discipline that preserved an element of moderation in his character. But the position of absolute power brought out his worst qualities, just as with Marius and Sulla, Tiberius and Caligula.

One act of Claudius's reign should be noted in passing, since it had far-reaching consequences. In 43 A.D. he invaded Britain, which had – since the time of Julius Caesar – been friendly to Rome but was not a Roman province. Claudius conquered, and Britain became Romanized. And he paid various British chiefs large sums of money to aid the process. But seven years after Claudius's death, in 61 A.D.,

Roman stupidity and Roman brutality produced effects that had become grimly familiar over the past three centuries, since Rome extended its boundaries beyond Italy. The Roman occupiers were callous and tactless, behaving as if everything in Britain was theirs for the taking. The British were regarded as barbarians and treated with patronizing contempt.

One of the subject kings, Prasutagus, ruled a tribe called the Iceni in what is now East Anglia. He regarded himself as friendly to Rome and had, in fact, borrowed heavily from Roman moneylenders. When he felt his end approaching, in 59 A.D., he decided that it might benefit his wife and two daughters if he left half his fortune to the new Roman emperor, Nero. But after his death, the procurator of Britain – a treasury official named Catus Decianus – took a different view; it was his understanding of Roman law that all Prasutagus's estate belonged to Rome. In 61 A.D. he presented himself at the palace of Prasutagus's queen Boudica (sometimes spelt Boadicea) and made some completely impossible demand. (He regarded these Britons in much the same way that later imperialists – including the Britons themselves – would regard savage tribes in Africa). When Boudica protested he ordered his soldiers to strip and flog her. The men seized the opportunity to grab her daughters and commit multiple rape. Then they proceeded to seize what they could for the Roman treasury (and their own pockets – Roman officials were expected to be corrupt).

But the Roman had underestimated Boudica. She began to plan a rebellion. A few months later, in June, she heard that a Roman army had invaded the island of Anglesey in Wales, and massacred the Druids – priests of the suppressed British religion – and their followers. This was the signal for revolt. Boudica and her troops marched against the Roman fortress town of Camulodunum – Colchester, which had a population of about twenty thousand. Colchester sent to London for reinforcements; but the incompetent Catus Decianus sent only two hundred men. The Britons attacked savagely; after two days they burst into the town, and the survivors all retreated into the half-completed temple of Claudius (who had been voted a god). The Iceni heaped brushwood round the walls and set fire to it. All the defenders – including women and children – died in the flames.

A relief force of five thousand legionaries marched from Lincoln; Boudica ambushed them and cut most of them down – only some cavalry escaped. She marched on the new Roman town of Londinium (London). The Romans fled, and half the population fled with them. Then the Britons arrived – 120,000 of them – and treated London with the same brutal thoroughness as Colchester. The cruelties are described by the historian Dio Cassius: '. . . they hung up naked the most noble and distinguished women and they cut off their breasts and sewed them into their mouths in order to make the victims appear to be eating them; afterwards they impaled the women on sharp skewers run lengthwise through their bodies.' These atrocities probably had a ritual element – not unlike the Mau Mau in modern times. The men were treated with similar ferocity. The Britons were taking revenge for more than a decade of swaggering Roman brutality. London was burnt to the ground.

Boudica now found herself confronting the same problem that had destroyed Spartacus in the previous century – how to discipline an unruly mob of looters. The governor of Britain, Suetonius Paulinus, had an army only a tenth as large as that of Boudica; but her troops were now overconfident and careless. Instead of waiting for the Romans to attack, they made the mistake of hurling themselves on the packed ranks of shields. When attack after attack broke like the sea against these highly-trained veterans, the Britons became discouraged and began to weaken; then a Roman advance scattered them. The Britons fled towards the carts in which their families were waiting; the Romans followed and began a massacre. Even the horses in the shafts were killed. Everything was set on fire. Boudica escaped from the battlefield, but committed suicide by poison, together with her daughters. Paulinus then sent for more legions from Gaul and Germany and settled down to dispensing revenge. The Roman historians, understandably, offer no details, but we are told that Paulinus punished tribes who had remained neutral as well as rebels. He seems to have seized stores and standing crops, creating a famine just as winter was coming on. And there can be no doubt that Paulinus crucified and tortured on a massive scale – so much so that even the emperor Nero was shocked; he replaced Paulinus with another governor and ordered that there should be a new principle of reconciliation. It is not clear what became of Catus Decianus, the man who caused the whole thing by ordering the flogging and rapes; no doubt he continued to rise in the Roman civil service.

The story does no credit to anyone. But it is worth telling to show what Roman occupation actually meant to hundreds of subject tribes from Syria to northern Britain. The school history books assure us that, whatever their faults, the Romans carried civilization over the world. But the story of Boudica reminds us that millions of their subjects regarded the Romans as we now regard the Nazis who burned the Warsaw ghetto and destroyed Lidice and Oradour-sur-Glane – with a hatred that could only be satisfied with their total annihilation. Whatever the 'benefits' they conferred, there can be no doubt that, from the point of view of human evolution, the Romans were a step in the direction of the ape.

history needs to be rewritten from the pt of view

Three

FROM NERO TO CONSTANTINE

In the emperor Nero we encounter the essence of the problem of human criminality. Marius was pananoid; Tiberius an embittered sadist; Caligula insane. Nero was none of these things. When he became emperor at the age of seventeen, in 54 A.D., he seems to have been a fairly ordinary young man with artistic tastes and a strong desire to be liked and admired. He had spindly legs, a podgy stomach and a rather self-indulgent face. (Since he was the son of Agrippina, one of Caligula's three sisters, it is just conceivable that he was actually Caligula's son.) The only doubtful element in the character of the new emperor was the sheer intensity of his naive egoism. He found himself inexhaustibly interesting.

His taste for applause dated from childhood, when he had performed a part in a play about Troy in the circus. And the rabble found that, as an emperor, he was just as anxious to be liked and applauded. He began his reign by announcing that he intended to follow in the footsteps of his great-great-grandfather Augustus and distributed largesse to the people; he followed this with some of the most spectacular games they had ever seen. But since he hated the sight of blood, no one was allowed to be killed in the contests – even criminals were spared. The emphasis was on drama, athletics and horsemanship – Nero adored horses. He was also a passionate lover of music, and he had no military ambitions whatever. Altogether, he seemed to have the makings of a very tolerable emperor.

His vanity, while rather absurd, seemed quite harmless. He had taken lessons in singing and playing the lyre. His voice was light, and he was told that if he wanted to make it stronger he would have to lie on his back with heavy weights on his chest to strengthen the breathing muscles; he did this conscientiously. Then he began singing to his dinner guests, and was so encouraged by their enthusiasm that he decided to make a stage appearance. Perhaps out of caution he chose Naples rather than Rome, and the theatre was shaken by an earthquake during his performance; but he sang on to the end, obviously feeling that the show must go on. When the Roman crowds learned about his performances, they clamoured to hear him; Nero announced that he would sing later in the palace gardens; but when his guards begged him to sing immediately, he graciously complied. The applause made him decide to enter a public competition for lyre-playing; when it came to Nero's turn, he proceeded to sing an immensely long opera that went on for hours. Soon Nero was appearing regularly on the stage in various tragedies. Since, like most cultured Romans, he regarded Greece as the home of music and drama, he began making regular excursions there to take part in lyre contests – which, of course, he invariably won. Because they always asked him to sing after dinner, Nero announced: 'The Greeks alone are worthy of my genius . . .'

His first murder took place about a year after he became emperor: it was his half-brother Britannicus, the son of Claudius and Messalina, who might have been regarded as having a better claim to the throne than Nero himself. Nero hired a poisoner called Locusta – who is reputed to have supplied the poison that killed Claudius – to rid him of Britannicus. The boy was understandably cautious and had his food sampled by a taster. One day, at a banquet, Britannicus tried a drink after his taster had tried it, found it too hot, and asked for water to be added. The water had been poisoned, and Britannicus promptly went into convulsions and died. Nero looked on unconcernedly and commented that such attacks often happened to epileptics.

Another problem was Nero's mother Agrippina. She was only twenty-two years his senior and he seems to have had a Freudian fixation on her. When Nero became emperor, Agrippina – who had been the real emperor in Claudius's last years – naturally expected to continue to play a leading part. At first, Nero let her do as she liked; but he was finding his feet and soon began to resent the way she seemed to want to run the empire. Early coins of his reign show Nero and his mother facing each other; within a year, they were facing in the same direction, with his head almost eclipsing hers. Agrippina was inclined to lose her temper at snubs like this, then would obviously reflect that it was now Nero who held the reins and go to the opposite extreme, trying to win him over with flattery and affection. When Nero began a love affair with a freedwoman named Acte, Agrippina at first opposed it violently; then, as Nero's smart young friends urged him on, decided to support the intrigue and since Nero felt it had to be kept secret from the people as he was already married, offered her son the use of her bedroom and bed. Finally, she seems to have decided on an even more drastic measure – to allow Nero to commit incest with her. Details are lacking, but Suetonius records that it occurred whenever he rode with her in an enclosed litter and that the disarranged state of his clothes when he emerged proved it. (The Roman toga was a rather complicated device compared to modern garments.) But the forbidden seems to have lost its charm the moment it ceased to be forbidden, and Nero turned to other sexual outlets, both male and female. Relations between mother and son once again soured. Since he undoubtedly knew that she was behind the poisoning of the emperor Claudius, Nero may have begun to worry that he might be next on the list (as Suetonius suggests). At all events, he decided that she had to be removed.

At this point, Nero's former tutor produced an ingenious suggestion. He had been appointed commander of the fleet and told Nero that it should not be too difficult to construct a boat that would fall to pieces when at sea. Accordingly, Nero invited his mother to join him at the festival of Minerva at Baiae, on the Bay of Naples. The evening before, they dined at Bauli, not far from Baiae; the party was arranged by Nero's millionaire friend Otho, who was also his go-between with Acte. Nero seems to have paid special attention to his mother and treated her with a kindness that suggested remorse; the aim was to lull any suspicion she might feel when he told her she was to travel by sea, he by land. Then the ship with Agrippina sailed for Baiae. It seems to have been fairly large – perhaps twenty or thirty feet long – and covered with a wooden roof. It was a still, starlit night, and Agrippina was in a good mood as she sat on a settee, with her feet in the lap of her friend Acerronia, and discussed the change in Nero's attitude towards her. At a signal, the roof suddenly caved in, under pressure of heavy lead weights. One of Agrippina's friends, Crepereius Gallus, was standing, and caught the full force, which killed her immediately. But the back of the settee took the weight and, since Agrippina and Acerronia were reclining, they were untouched. The ship should then have fallen apart; but apparently it failed to do so. Oarsmen who were in the assassination plot tried to capsize the ship by throwing their weight on one side. Acerronia, in an attempt to save Agrippina – for by now it must have been obvious that this was a murder attempt – began to call out: 'Help, I'm the emperor's mother.' At this, the crew beat her to death with oars. The real Agrippina slipped over the side in the confusion; in spite of an injured shoulder, she managed to swim to some sailing boats, one of which took her back to Bauli.

There she sent a message to Nero saying that by the grace of the gods she had escaped a serious accident. This was undoubtedly a mistake; she should have hurried back to Rome and allowed rumour of the murder attempt to circulate so that, if Nero tried again, no one would have any doubt about the instigator.

When Agrippina's freedman arrived with the message, Nero did some quick thinking. He had to make it appear that it was *his* life that was in danger, and that his mother was responsible. He dropped a sword on the ground, and then cried out that the man had been sent to kill him.

News of the attempted drowning had spread in Bauli. Crowds gathered on the seashore but were dispersed by troops. Meanwhile, Nero sent his ex-tutor – inventor of the collapsing ship – with two henchmen to kill his mother. As they forced their way into her bedchamber, she seems to have assumed that they had come to find out if she was well; then, when one of them struck her on the head with a club, she grasped the truth. Tacitus says that, as one of the men drew his sword, she presented her belly and told him to strike her there – in the womb that had borne Nero. She was hacked to pieces.

Nero, typically, was now in a state of funk, probably expecting a general revolt when the news became public. He began to feel better when two of his praetorian guards came to congratulate him on his 'narrow escape'; it no doubt dawned on him for the first time that the emperor could do exactly as he liked. So he wrote a letter to the senate, accusing his mother of an attempt on his life; he added that, conscious of her guilt, she had paid the penalty – implying that she had committed suicide. Then he hurried to Bauli – no doubt to make sure that his mother was dead and to remove the evidence that would prove she had not died by her own hand. He is reported to have viewed the body and admired its beauty – although, in view of his dislike of blood, this is probably an invention. What is certain is that Agrippina was promptly cremated. Even so, Nero was unable to summon the courage to return to Rome and face the senate and the populace; he stayed away from March 59 A.D. – when the murder took place – until September. When he finally arrived in Rome, he was relieved to find that his popularity with the mob was unimpaired. Rome was far too accustomed to murder to be shocked at a little matricide, and an emperor who gave them such magnificent public spectacles was not to be upset.

Without the frowns of his mother to restrain him, Nero was able to fling himself into his amusements with total abandon. He began to spend his evenings in taverns with selected companions – such as Otho – break into shops, and attack late night travellers. He seems to have lost his distaste for blood to the extent of stabbing them if they struggled. His banquets lasted from midday until midnight, and, according to the *Satyricon*, a vast novel by his friend Petronius, aphrodisiacs played an important part in the menu.

Not long after his mother's death, Nero fell in love again; the new mistress was Poppaea, the wife of his friend Otho. At first they seemed to have shared her favours; then Nero grew jealous at the thought of her sleeping with her own husband. Otho would probably have died of poison; but Nero's tutor Seneca – a distinguished dramatist and philosopher – managed to persuade Nero to send his former friend to Portugal as a governor. Soon afterwards, to Nero's delight, Poppaea became pregnant; he had always wanted an heir. There was only one obstacle in the way of marrying Poppaea, Nero's wife Octavia. They had been betrothed as children – she was the daughter of Claudius and Messalina – and she was now only just out of her teens. Her conduct was irreproachable, so she had to be 'framed'. The commander of the guard, Tigellinus, was given the job of torturing her slaves until he had enough confessions to ensure a divorce. At this point, the unpredictable Roman populace suddenly decided to take the part of Octavia and demonstrated in front of the palace. More evidence was needed, so Nero's friend Anicetus – the one who had designed the collapsing ship – made a public confession that he had committed adultery with Octavia and that she had aborted a child. The divorce went through. Octavia was exiled to an island and then ordered to kill herself. When she protested, Nero's henchmen bound her and opened up her arteries. To hasten the process, she was placed in a steam bath. Tacitus states that her head was sent to Poppaea to convince her that her former rival was dead. It was something of an anticlimax when Poppaea presented Nero with a daughter.

In the following year, 64 A.D., Rome was devastated by a fire that lasted a week. The later rumour that Nero started this fire is undoubtedly false; on the other hand, there seems to be some evidence that he 'fiddled' while Rome burned – in fact, he took his lyre and sang a tragic song of his own composition called 'The Fall of Troy'. Since the fire lasted so long, Nero can hardly be accused of callousness for singing during that period; but when the story became current, it caused a steep decline in his already plummeting popularity. When the fire was finally halted – by demolishing public buildings – Nero seems to have behaved rather well. He organized relief, had large quantities of corn brought in from Ostia, and cut its price to one sixteenth of normal.

Why should Nero have wanted to start a fire? According to the historians, because he wanted to clear a large area in the centre of the city to build himself a new palace. In fact, Nero did build himself an immense and magnificent palace called the Golden House. He also rebuilt a great deal of the rest of Rome. But the rumours of his responsibility for the fire persisted, and Nero looked for scapegoats. This was no problem, since Rome was now full of members of a 'deadly superstition' called Christianity. (Tacitus mentions that its prophet, Jesus, had been executed in Tiberius's reign by Pontius Pilate.) Rumours of the 'notoriously depraved Christians' spread. The Romans disliked Christians partly because they were associated with the Jews, and the Jews were regarded as religious fanatics who caused endless trouble. Tacitus also remarks that the Christians hated the human race. To the Romans, this foreign religious sect, with its belief in the imminent end of the world, must have seemed almost insane. If the Christians hated 'earthly things', then it seemed quite possible that they might have started the great fire. What struck the Romans as even more incredible and disgusting was that many of these Christians seemed to have no fear of dying for their religion and confessed to it willingly. So the Christians were killed with exceptional ferocity. They were smeared with tar and tied to posts, to be ignited as living torches after dark. They were dressed in animal skins and then set upon by wild dogs who tore them to pieces. They were thrown to wild beasts in the arena, and crucified in enormous numbers. And yet, paradoxically, Nero's good intentions backfired. He had overestimated the bloodthirstiness of the Roman populace. People were sickened by so much torture, and his popularity declined yet again.

Nero's problem was that he was too self-absorbed to react to the state of public opinion. It seemed to him that he was an excellent emperor who was always giving the public what it wanted. As to being bloodthirsty, he felt it was shockingly untrue. In 61 A.D., the prefect of the city had been murdered by one of his slaves – probably in a homosexual quarrel – and law decreed that every slave under the same roof be executed, including women and children. The populace rioted on behalf of the unfortunate slaves – four hundred of them – and Nero, who was a liberal in theory, agreed entirely with the people. The senate felt otherwise – they were afraid that, if murder by slaves was tolerated, they might all be murdered in their beds. So soldiers had to line the route when the four hundred men, women and children were taken to execution, and the populace had put the blame on Nero. He felt that he was a misunderstood saint. His reaction to this latest misunderstanding was to spend more money, organize more games and entertainments, and to spend more time in the company of selected sycophants such as the elegant aesthete Petronius. (But Petronius eventually fell from favour; accused by Tigellinus of plotting against Nero's life, he committed suicide by severing his veins in his bath.)

In 65 A.D., Poppaea died; Nero had lost his temper and kicked her when she was pregnant. Her death shattered him; the funeral was of unparalleled lavishness, and the spices that were burned were the equivalent of a full year's supply from Arabia. Poppaea was pronounced a goddess; Nero's fancy fell upon a eunuch named Sporus, whose looks reminded him of Poppaea. Suetonius alleges that it was Nero who made Sporus into a eunuch by castrating him, attempting to turn him into a girl. He then went through a wedding ceremony with Sporus, dressed him in female clothes and treated him like a wife. The orgies became wilder, Nero seems to have discovered the pleasures of binding, and invented a new game. Men and women were tied to stakes, and Nero, dressed as a wild beast, came bounding at them and pretended to eat their genitals. The game ended with Nero being sodomized by his freedman Doryphorus. Apparently anxious to try every sexual experience, Nero had another 'wedding ceremony' performed – according to the scandal-loving Suetonius – with himself as the bride and Doryphorus as the groom; while being deflowered he imitated the screams and moans of a girl.

Nero found it easy to slip into the Roman habit of ordering executions whenever he felt like it. A half-hearted conspiracy to murder him, led by an aristocrat named Piso, provided him with an admirable excuse in 65 A.D.; Petronius was one of the victims on this occasion; so was Nero's old tutor Seneca. Unlike Claudius, Nero derived no pleasure from watching men die; instead, he preferred to order them to commit suicide. Soon he was adding disapproving senators to the list, in the best tradition of Tiberius and Caligula. It began to dawn on the senate that getting rid of Nero was a matter of self-preservation.

Meanwhile, Nero was preoccupied with grandiose schemes. He was rebuilding Rome, with wide streets and buildings of stone and marble. His own Golden House had an arcade a mile long, and his apartments were plated in gold set with jewels. The ceilings slid back so that showers of perfume could be sprinkled down, or a rain of flowers. (Flowers were a kind of status symbol in Rome – one rich man spent a hundred thousand pounds – four million sesterces – on roses for one banquet.) At the entrance stood an immense statue of Nero, twelve storeys high.

In 67 A.D. – the twelfth year of his reign – Nero set off on a tour of Greece, taking part in various games and contests. He continued to be obsessed by the thought of plots against him and, while he was in Greece, sent for his greatest general, Corbulo, and ordered him to commit suicide; as he died, Corbulo murmured the ambiguous phrase 'Serves me right'. Nero also suspected the loyalty of his Rhine armies – completely without reason – and sent for the two brothers who commanded the provinces on the Rhine. Without being allowed to defend themselves or see Nero, these were also ordered to commit suicide.

But things were already drifting towards the point of no return. In Judea, the Roman prefect was causing deep offence by trying to force the temple treasury to pay enormous tax arrears, and when he allowed his men to plunder parts of Jerusalem, Jewish terrorists organized a revolt; the Roman population of Jerusalem was massacred. The governor of Syria tried to recapture Jerusalem and was driven back with heavy losses. Nero appointed a middle-aged general named Vespasian to suppress the revolt. Then, in March 68, he heard that the governor of Gaul, Gaius Vindex, had also rebelled, after issuing a proclamation denouncing Nero's extravagances. He was supported by Galba, the governor of Nearer Spain, and by Nero's one-time friend Otho, governor of Portugal. The neurotic emperor was thrown into a panic by the news, and it was obvious to his guards that he was totally incapable of dealing with the situation – he left the dining-room one day with his arms around the shoulders of two friends, explaining that he intended to go to Gaul, stand in front of the rebel army and weep and weep until they felt sorry for him; then, he said, he would stroll among his troops singing paeans of victory – which, come to think of it, he ought to be composing at this very moment. What really seems to have cut him to the quick was a comment by Vindex that Nero played the lyre very badly.

On 8 June a report arrived stating that an army in northern Italy had decided to join the rebels. For Nero, this was the last straw; he decided to flee to Egypt. It was a scheme he had been considering for some time – he had remarked that, if he lost the throne, he could always live by his art. He left the Golden House and moved to his mansion in the Servilian gardens, en route for the port of Ostia, where ships had been ordered to get ready. When he woke from a short sleep to find that the Praetorian guard was no longer on duty, he seems to have realized that this was the end. In fact, the commander of the Praetorian guard had decided to go over to Galba and had bribed the men with an offer of 30,000 sesterces each (about £750) to proclaim Galba emperor. Nero hurried to the houses of various friends but could get no reply. Returning to his house, he found that his bodyguard had fled and had taken his bedclothes and his box of poison. Sounds of shouting and cheering from a nearby army camp convinced him that the revolt was spreading. With only four companions – including his 'wife' Sporus – he set out for the house of his freedman Phaon nearby. There he crawled into a cellar, ordered his grave to be dug, and had hysterics, repeating over and over again: 'What a loss I shall be to the arts.' A runner arrived with a message; it declared that the senate had branded him a public enemy and decreed that he should be executed in the 'ancient style' – which meant being flogged to death. He asked one of his companions to commit suicide first, and then, when he showed reluctance, muttered: 'How ugly and vulgar my life has become.' When he heard the sound of approaching hooves, he placed the sword point to his throat; one of the others also placed his hand on it, and pushed it in. He was already dying when a centurion entered to arrest him; as the man tried to stanch the blood with his cloak, he murmured 'How loyal you are,' and expired.

The lesson of Nero is very simple. He makes it possible to see that criminality is basically childishness. He was not a particularly 'evil'

need for necessity

man — he completely lacked the kind of misdirected resentment that characterizes most real criminals, from Alexander of Pherae to Carl Panzram. But because he became Caesar before he had time to grow up, he was totally subjective, completely self-absorbed. He saw other people as slightly unreal; to him, in fact, the whole world was slightly unreal. So when he wanted something, he simply grabbed it. When someone stood in his way, he 'removed' him. Because of his childishness, this came as naturally to him as killing mice to a cat.

In Nero, we can see the basic problem of human development: the moment human beings are released from the pressure of necessity they seem to go rotten. And if that is so, then there is something self-defeating about the very idea of civilization, since its aim is to release us from necessity. It seems to be a vicious circle. Man is brilliant at solving problems; but solving them only makes him the victim of his own childishness and laziness. It is this recognition that has made almost every major philosopher in history a pessimist.

Yet although this is the truth, it is not the whole truth. As we examine human history, we realize that man also seems to possess an instinctive counterbalance to this natural drift towards criminality. In its most basic form, this seems to consist of an intuitive certainty that this narrow world of the personal ego is *not* the whole world — that something far greater and more interesting lies beyond it. This excited feeling of the sheer *interestingness* of the universe is inherent in all poetry, music, science, philosophy and religion. When we read of great men — an Alexander or a Frederick II — dying in a state of world-weary pessimism, we feel that they have somehow allowed themselves to become blinded by fatigue and allowed their senses to close. Somewhere along the way, they have missed the point. And when the conquerors and criminals have wreaked their havoc and left the scene, the sense of magic and mystery flows back like a tide and sweeps away the wreckage, leaving the beach smooth and clean again.

It is necessary to grasp this if we are to understand the remarkable spread of Christianity across the civilized world. There had been dozens — probably hundreds — of religions before Christianity; we have seen that there was a kind of worldwide religious explosion in the fifth century B.C. None had achieved the same impact or spread with the same speed as Christianity. And this is basically because Christianity was a reaction against Roman materialism. Just as a pessimist is a man who has to live with an optimist, so an idealist is a man who has to live with a materialist. Roman religion was almost comically literal-minded; they believed, for example, that a vote in the senate could send their late emperor to the abode of the gods. (It is true that this is not so different from the Catholic Church's procedure for canonization.) Roman religion was not even original; it was simply taken over wholesale from ancient Greece. Roman literature, Roman art, Roman philosophy, were all superficial. There was nothing in Roman culture that could appeal to a man of imagination. Christianity was an expression of a craving for a deeper meaning in human existence.

The agitator known as Jeshua – or Jesus – of Nazareth was born in about the twentieth year of the reign of Augustus – around 10 B.C. Pompey the Great had placed the Jews under Roman rule in 63 B.C., and the Jews loathed it. Crassus had plundered the temple. Herod the Great, appointed by the Romans to rule Judea, was as violent and murderous as any of the later Roman emperors, and was hated by all the religion factions with the exception of the Hellenized Sadducees. So the expectation of the long-awaited Messiah, a warrior- king who would free the Jews from foreign rule, increased year by year.

The early records of Jesus of Nazareth were so tampered with by later Christians that it is difficult to form a clear picture of his few brief years as a teacher and prophet. Even his physical description was altered; it was reconstructed in the 1920s by the historian Robert Eisler in *The Messiah Jesus and John the Baptist*. Among the documents Eisler used was a 'wanted notice' probably signed by Pontius Pilate, and later quoted by the Jewish historian Josephus, whose reconstructed text runs as follows:

At this time, too, there appeared a certain man of magical power, if it is permissible to call him man, whom certain Greeks call a son of God, but his disciples the true prophet, said to raise the dead and heal all diseases.

His nature and form were human; a man of simple appearance, mature age, dark skin, small stature, three cubits high (about five feet), hunch-backed, with a long face, long nose and meeting eyebrows, so that they who see him might be affrighted, with scanty hair with a parting in the middle of the head, after the manner of the Nairites, and an undeveloped beard.

This original portrait of Jesus – with a humped back, long nose, half-bald head and scanty beard – was altered by later Christians to read:

ruddy skin, medium stature, six feet high, well grown, with a venerable face, handsome nose, goodly black eyebrows with good eyes so that spectators could love him, with curly hair the colour of unripe hazel nuts, with a smooth and unruffled, unmarked and unwrinkled forehead, a lovely red, blue eyes, beautiful mouth, with a copious beard the same colour as the hair, not long, parted in the middle, arms and hands full of grace . . .

And so it went on, turning the unprepossessing little man into an early Christian equivalent of a film star. It is easy to see why it is difficult to take most of the Christian texts about Jesus at their face value.

If the Romans had been coarsened by success and victory, it could be said that the Jews had been refined by failure and defeat. At about the time the Mediterranean was undergoing its ordeal by fire at the hands of the 'sea peoples', the Hebrews, who lived in the land of Goshen near the Nile delta, had been enslaved by the Egyptians. At about the time of the Trojan war, they were led out of Egypt by Moses and spent hard years wandering in the wilderness of the Sinai peninsula. Hardship deepened their religious sense; they became a people of one God, whose laws were based on religious ideals. (The story of the dance around the golden calf suggests that at an earlier period they were polytheistic, like most Semitic peoples.) Under Joshua, they achieved victories in the land of Canaan and adopted many of the ways of the Canaanites. Then there was a long and desperate struggle against the Philistines, who were finally conquered by King David around 1000 B.C. But after the death of Solomon (about 930 B.C.) there were unsettled times, and two centuries of strife and civil war. In the eighth century B.C., the Israelites came under the brutal Assyrian yoke, and in 705 B.C. the kingdom of Israel ceased to exist. After the destruction of Nineveh (612 B.C.), the Babylonians became the dominant power in the Middle East, and the Jews were again dragged into captivity. They were allowed to return to the ruined city of Jerusalem when Cyrus of Persia conquered the Babylonians (538 B.C.), but remained under Persian rule for two centuries. Under the leadership of the Persian Jew Nehemiah they rebuilt the walls of Jerusalem and returned to the old religious ways taught by Moses. In 332 B.C. Persian rule was overthrown by Alexander the Great, and for nine years the Jews were his subjects. After his death, they again fell under the rule of Egypt. One of Alexander's generals, Seleucas, had conquered an empire and founded a dynasty, so from 198 to 168 B.C. the Jews were ruled by the Seleucids. It was the attempt of the Seleucid king Antiochus IV to Hellenize Judea and ban the Jewish religion that led to the revolt of Judas Maccabeus and a brief period of political freedom. But less than a century later, Pompey conquered Jerusalem, and the Jews become Roman vassals.

So, over the course of many centuries, the Jews had become accustomed to war, persecution and a foreign yoke. The Jewish religious impulse was deepened by adversity. Understandably, it laid emphasis on pacifism, on gentleness and mercy, on the blessedness of the meek and humble and the rewards of the next world. Rabbi Akiba said that the essence of the Mosaic message is to love one's neighbour, while Rabbi Hillel stated that the central message of Judaism is to do unto others as you would have them do unto you.

In the time of Jesus, there were three main religious sects in Judea: the Sadducees, who were conservatives, the Zealots, who were revolutionaries, and the Pharisees, who occupied the middle ground. There was also a powerful group known as the Essenes, who might be called 'withdrawalists'. Like modern Quakers, they founded their own communities, where they lived pious and abstemious lives. Their teachings had come down to them, they asserted, from a certain Teacher of Righteousness who had been killed by the forces of darkness. In 1947, some of the scriptures of the Essenes came to light in caves on the shores of the Dead Sea – where the Essenes had once lived. These Dead Sea scrolls revealed that the Essenes called themselves the Elect of God, that they initiated new members through baptism, and that they had a protocol for seating that resembles that of the Last Supper described in the New Testament. John the Baptist was almost certainly an Essene. And the Dead Sea scrolls make it clear that Jesus was heavily influenced by them.

So the doctrines we now associate with Jesus were familiar in the Jewish world for centuries before his arrival. Judaism already forbade men to hate their enemies. This carpenter's son from Nazareth, who began to preach in the twenty-eighth year of his life, went a step further and declared that we should also love our enemies, and that if someone strikes us on one cheek, we should turn the other. In the time of Roman occupation, this must have seemed to most people sheer stupidity – rather as if some English religious teacher had declared in 1939 that there should be no resistance to Hitler. Clearly, this pacifistic doctrine can have had no wide appeal in 20 A.D., the sixth year of the reign of Tiberius, even though

Jesus's personal magnetism seems to have been remarkable. How, then, did he make an appeal to the intensely patriotic Jews of his time? The answer which emerges from contemporary documents is that Jesus taught that some immense, catastrophic change was about to take place: in fact, the end of the world. The kingdom of God was at hand. There would be wars and rumours of wars, famine and earthquakes. The dead would be brought back to life. The sun would be turned into darkness and the moon to blood, and stars would fall from heaven. All this would not be at some vague date in future centuries, but within the lifetime of people then alive. Accordingly, it would be better for the faithful to take no thought for the morrow – God would provide.

The teachings of this apocalyptic preacher offended Pharisees, Sadducees and Zealots alike. The Zealots – who wanted to see Rome destroyed – had no patience with this preaching about 'kingdom come'. It could only distract attention from the real struggle. The Sadducees were inclined to Hellenism and disbelieved in life after death; for them Jesus was an uncultivated fanatic. The Pharisees were the Temple party and stood for strict observance of every minor religious ritual. Jesus felt about them as Martin Luther was later to feel about the Catholic Church, and he went out of his way to attack them. The result is that Jesus had few real supporters during his lifetime. He was a minor and rather unpopular prophet; if he had lived to be seventy and died in his bed, he would probably now be totally forgotten.

But after four years of preaching, Jesus rode into Jerusalem on a donkey and proclaimed himself the Messiah, the saviour who had been awaited for centuries. This made him suddenly dangerous to the Jewish establishment. Accordingly, he was arrested and taken before the high priest. Caiaphas has come off rather badly in the history books, but he cannot really be blamed for what followed. When asked if he was the Messiah, Jesus replied in the affirmative. Caiaphas was understandably outraged, for it must have seemed obvious to him that nothing was less likely than that this unprepossessing little man with his hump-back and straggly beard could be the man destined to lead the Jews to freedom. He called Jesus a blasphemer – which, technically speaking, he was – and sent him off to Pilate to be judged, confident that the Roman would recognize the danger. But Pilate was a cultured Roman, and when he asked Jesus the same question, Jesus was cautious enough to reply only 'You have said so.' Pilate had been a weary spectator of the endless religious squabbles of the Jews for years – he probably thought they were all mad, or at least deluded – and he no doubt resented the attempt of Caiaphas to make *him* the executioner of this gentle-looking little man. He tried to get Jesus released – mercy was shown to a condemned man every Passover – but the people, who were as clamorous as a Roman mob, said they would prefer another rebel called Barabbas, who at least had tried to kill a Roman guard. Pilate gave way – he had sentenced so many rebels to death that it made little difference; in fact, this Jesus was to be crucified between two of them. And so, like thousands of other victims of Rome, Jesus of Nazareth died on the cross.

And how did he go on to conquer the world? Again, the reasons are complex. The most important is undoubtedly that soon after his death his disciples claimed to have seen him again, and actually touched him. One historian, Hugh Schonfield, argued in *The Passover Plot* (1966) that Jesus was probably given a drug that made him appear to be dead and that he revived in a perfectly normal way. It is just conceivable. It is just as conceivable that Jesus was not completely dead when taken from the cross – a good bribe to a Roman centurion could work wonders. In another controversial book, published in 1982 (*The Holy Blood and the Holy Grail* by Henry Lincoln, Michael Baigent and Richard Leigh), Henry Lincoln also suggested the drug hypothesis; and he went further to cite a secret Rosicrucian tradition that Jesus was married, and left Judea with Mary Magdalene to live out the remainder of his life in Gaul, where his descendants became the Merovingian kings. (He argues that the discovery of this secret explains the mystery of Rennes-le-Château and how a poor Catholic priest became rich overnight.) Sceptics may feel that the explanation could be altogether simpler, and that the whole story of the Resurrection was invented by the followers of Jesus. Whatever the explanation, it is certain that stories of Jesus's miraculous revival after death were circulating soon after the crucifixion.

One thing about Jesus that seems very clear is that he possessed remarkable healing powers. Josephus, as we have seen, describes him as a magician. It makes no difference whether we attribute such powers to suggestion or to some genuine ability to release a healing force; what seems quite clear is that they work, and can be developed. Jesus had developed them to a high degree, and this seems to explain why he was regarded as a magician.

Nothing spreads faster than tales of the marvellous; and this undoubtedly explains why Jesus's death on the cross only made his name more potent than ever. At this early stage there were two distinct groups of disciples. The Nasoraeans, or Messianists, were the original followers, who believed that Jesus was a political Messiah who would lead the Jews to freedom. He was still alive, and would in due course reappear to fulfil his promises. (King Arthur later inspired identical beliefs in Britain, and many people were still expecting him six centuries after his death.) They most emphatically did not believe that Jesus was a god in any sense of the word – this would have been contrary to all Jewish religious teaching. The other group, who came to be called Christians, were followers of Paul as much as of Jesus. Within a few years of the crucifixion, this Paul, who loathed the Messianists, had undergone a sudden conversion, which suggests that his original hatred of Jesus was based upon some deep fascination that he found unacceptable. Paul created a new version of Messianism that was far more strange and mystical than that of the Nasoraeans. Paul's Jesus was the son of God, who had been sent to earth to save men from the consequences of Adam's sin. All men had to do was to believe in Jesus and they were 'saved'. And when the end of the world occurred – as it was bound to do within the next few years, according to Jesus – these 'Christians' would live on an earth transformed into paradise.

The Messianists and the Christians detested one another with the peculiarly virulent loathing that seemed to characterize Jewish religious controversies. Paul's version won through a historical accident. As we have seen, the Jews broke into open rebellion just before the end of the reign of Nero, and he was forced to send his general Vespasian to try and subdue them. But in the year after Nero's suicide, Rome had four emperors. The first was Galba, the Spanish governor who had joined Vindex in the rebellion. Within a short time the Praetorian guard found him too strict and closefisted, and murdered him. They appointed Nero's friend Otho, from Portugal. Meanwhile, the German troops had proclaimed their general Vitellius emperor, and he marched on Rome and defeated Otho. Otho committed suicide. Then Vespasian, still on the other side of the Mediterranean, was proclaimed emperor by his troops. He seized Egypt and cut off Rome's grain. When legions from the Danube marched on Rome and killed Vitellius, Vespasian was next in line for the post of emperor, and was appointed by the senate in 70

A.D. He sent his son Titus to subdue the Jewish rebels, and Titus did it with Roman brutality and ruthlessness. After a six-month siege, the temple was burned, the Zealots massacred (more than a million of them), and the treasures of the Temple were carried back to Rome. The Messianists were among those who were slaughtered. So Paul's Christians (who were scattered all over the place) were the only followers of Jesus left.

Any Messianists who remained must certainly have felt that this Christianity of Paul was a blasphemous travesty of the teachings of their Messiah; and, in a literal sense, they were correct. Whether Jesus was Jewish by nationality or not (and Galilee contained more Arabs than Jews), he was undoubtedly a Jew by religion, and as such would have been horrified at the notion that he was a god. That was the kind of blasphemy that was typical of the Romans – Pontius Pilate had mortally offended the Jews by allowing his legionnaires to march through Jerusalem with a picture of the deified Augustus on their standards. Yet in another sense, Paul's Christianity was an accurate reflection of the basic spirit of the ideas of Jesus. Bernard Shaw once suggested that Jesus went insane at some later point in his career – when he became convinced he was the Messiah – for Shaw felt that the earlier Jesus regarded himself as an ethical teacher and no more. But there is no evidence that Jesus ever took such a rationalistic view of his mission. His statement that he could forgive sins suggests that he believed he was in some kind of direct communication with God. Christians believe, of course, that this was true; but it seems clear that Jesus also believed that the end of the world was about to occur, and if he believed that this was also a message from God, he was mistaken. By modern standards, Jesus was suffering from delusions.

Paul seems to have been fascinated by the parallel between Jesus and various other Middle Eastern gods who died and were resurrected – Attis and Adonis, the Egyptian Osiris, the Babylonian Tammuz – such stories were common at the time. Paul was also a Jew, and the Jews in the time of Jesus were much preoccupied with the question of how, if God is good, He could have made so much misery and suffering. The answer of the rabbis, of course, was that Adam had sinned, and so been expelled from Eden. Now, in one stroke, Paul had added an amazing new dimension to Judaism: not only a traditional saviour-god, but one who had come to solve that ancient problem of misery and sin. Jesus had vicariously atoned for the sins of mankind; after Armageddon, his followers would live for ever.

This new version of Christianity appealed to gentiles as much as Jews. Anyone of any sensitivity only had to look at the Rome of Tiberius, Caligula and Nero to understand just what Paul meant about the fall of man. These sex-mad drunkards were a living proof that something had gone wrong. And the Roman matrons who took up prostitution for pleasure revealed that Eve had fallen just as far as Adam. The world was nauseated by Roman brutality, Roman materialism, Roman licentiousness. Christianity sounded a deeper note; it offered a vision of meaning and purpose, a vision of seriousness. For the strong, it was a promise of new heights of awareness. For the weak, it was a message of peace and reconciliation, of rest for the weary, of reward for the humble. And for everyone, it promised an end to the kingdom of Caesar, with its crucifixions, floggings and arbitrary executions. The Christians hoped it was a promise of the end of the world.

For a while, it looked as if that promise was about to be fulfilled, just as the god-man had foretold. Nero was indeed the last of the hereditary Caesars. And in the reign of his successor Titus – the man who besieged Jerusalem – there was a plague in Rome, followed by another great fire. In 79 A.D., Mount Vesuvius erupted, causing a darkness that lasted for days, and burying Pompeii and its sister town Herculaneum under many feet of muddy ash. Fortunately, most of the inhabitants escaped; but the curiosity of the naturalist Pliny cost him his life – he sailed across the bay to see what was happening and was asphyxiated.

Incredibly, Rome had still not learnt its lesson: that allowing a man to become Caesar merely because he is the 'next in line' is a sure formula for creating mad dictators. It happened again when the good-natured Titus died (after only two years in power). He was succeeded by his surly brother Domitian – who had been jealous of Titus – a man whose temperament resembled that of Tiberius. But he was soon behaving rather worse. After an attempted rebellion of the Rhine troops, he extracted confessions by a new form of torture – holding a blazing torch under the prisoners' genitals (he seems to have been a homosexual sadist); after which he held mass executions. There followed the usual vicious circle of tyranny; as he became more suspicious of plots, he became a madman, having senators executed on trivial charges and courtiers crucified upside down for chance remarks. (One member of the audience in the newly-built Colosseum was dragged into the arena, tied up and torn to pieces by wild dogs for a mildly offensive joke.) The more violent he became, the more his subjects plotted against him. We know rather less about his crimes than about those of earlier Caesars, for by the time Suetonius reached Domitian (the last of his *Twelve Caesars*) he had grown tired of cataloguing horrors; but it seems clear that Domitian was as bad as the worst of the emperors. As with Caligula, his madness took the form of self-aggrandizement; he insisted on being addressed as 'Lord God' and had endless gold statues and triumphal arches erected to himself all over the empire. (To do him justice, he *had* remarkable successes as a general against Germans and Dacians.) And because he regarded himself as a god, he ordered violent persecution of the Christians, who had the temerity to refuse to pay homage to his divinity. (The followers of the religion of Mithras, which came from Persia and was equally popular at the time, had no such problem and so escaped persecution.)

The non-stop slaughter made Domitian's assassination inevitable, and it finally happened in 96 A.D., the fifteenth year of his reign. Suetonius, who lived through Domitian's reign, was able to procure a remarkable first-hand account of the killing. Soothsayers had prophesied the death, and Domitian was even told when to expect it – in the fifth hour of the day. At dawn, he condemned to death a German soothsayer who had prophesied bloodshed. Domitian scratched a pimple on his forehead and made it bleed, commenting: 'I hope this is all the blood that needs to be shed.' He asked his servant the time, and the man – who was in the plot – answered 'Six o'clock.' Domitian heaved a sigh of relief and went off to his bath. On the way there, he was told that a man had arrived with news of another plot and was now waiting in his bedroom; so Domitian hurried back. The assassin was waiting for him, holding a list of names of people supposed to be in the plot; as Domitian read it, the man stabbed him in the groin. Domitian grappled with him and fought like an animal. He shouted to his boy to hand him the dagger from under his pillow, then run for help. But the conspirators had removed the blade of the dagger and locked the door. Domitian tried to wrest the knife away from the assassin, and cut his fingers to the bone; then he tried to claw out the man's eyes. The assassin managed to go on stabbing until Domitian collapsed and died. The news of his death brought universal rejoicing. His name was removed from all public monuments.

And at last, even Rome had learnt the lesson: that power can turn a despot into a homicidal maniac, and that the solution was not to leave the choice of emperor to chance or heredity but to select him with some care. The result was five excellent rulers – Nerva, Trajan, Hadrian, Antoninus and Marcus Aurelius – and almost a century of peace and prosperity. Nerva, selected by the senate, was seventy at the time and died two years later. But he had chosen as his successor a brilliant general, Trajan, who proved to be a second Julius Caesar. In his nineteen-year reign he conquered the Dacians to the north of the Danube and the Parthians to the east of the Euphrates, and pushed the bounds of the Roman empire to its farthest limits. What he failed to see was that, in over-extending Rome's manpower, he was leaving a considerable prob-lem to most of his successors – a problem that would be solved only with the final collapse of the empire nearly four centuries later.

However, his successor – his cousin Hadrian – recognized the problem, and began his reign by contracting his eastern bound-aries. This had the desired effect, and enabled Hadrian to spend most of his long reign making a leisurely tour of his empire. The roads were now safe, the seas free from pirates. As he wandered at large from Egypt to Scotland, Hadrian built roads, aqueducts, theatres, bridges, temples, even cities – the discovery of concrete enabled his engineers to build faster and more magnificently than ever before.

Hadrian had the interesting idea of choosing two emperors to reign jointly, like the consuls of old; they were called Marcus Aurelius and Lucius Verus; and since both were little more than children when Hadrian's health began to fail, he appointed a caretaker emperor, Antoninus Pius. In the old days this would have been a certain formula for murder and despotism; but Hadrian had chosen well. Antoninus ruled peacefully for twenty-three years, and had Hadrian declared a god.

When the two consul-emperors came to the throne – in 161 A.D. – the age of peace had come to an end. For almost half a century, Rome had basked in a golden age; now the barbarians were again at the frontiers. The result was that Rome's only philo-sopher-emperor, Marcus Aurelius (his fellow emperor died after eight years), had to spend most of his reign raising armies and marching to remote parts of his empire.

Marcus Aurelius was a stoic, and the stoics regarded life as a difficult voyage in which most men are shipwrecked; they felt that man's only chance of escaping shipwreck was through reason and self-discipline. The emperor had good reason to take a stoical view of existence; he had to jot down his famous *Meditations* in his tent between battles. His wife Faustina was constantly unfaithful, and his son Commodus was a spoilt young man who became one of the worst emperors Rome had ever known. At one point, Marcus Aurelius even had to sell all the treasures in his palace to replenish the treasury. When he died at the age of fifty-nine, the task of shoring up the Roman empire was still uncompleted. Yet the *Meditations* reveal that he had achieved the serenity of a man who knows that the key to the mystery of existence lies in the mind itself. In the murderous history of the Roman emperors, Marcus Aurelius stands out like a beacon.

If he noticed that his son was a vicious ruffian, it was too late to prevent his becoming emperor. The moment his father died, Commodus abandoned the war against the northern tribesmen and rushed back to Rome to enjoy himself. He changed the name of Rome to Commodiana, voted himself the name 'Hercules' and behaved exactly like every bad emperor in Rome's violent history. Nero had been an aesthete; Commodus liked to think of himself as an athlete. His greatest pleasure was to fight in the arena against carefully chosen opponents – whom he despatched with his sword – and to take part in the chariot races. He boasted that he had killed thousands of opponents with his left hand only. This homicidal maniac was probably insane. He would dress up as Hercules and then walk about hitting people with his club. An attempt on his life made him paranoid, and he proceeded to execute senators by the dozen. Finally, when it became clear that no one's life was safe, his own mistress poisoned him, then a wrestler throttled him. In a mere twelve years, he undid all the good work of the previous four emperors and left Rome bankrupt.

Commodus was probably the worst thing that had ever happened to Rome. It was not that he was worse than Caligula or Nero; only that the empire was bleeding to death and could not afford another madman. It had once been a privilege to be a citizen of Rome; now it only meant paying heavy taxes to a series of generals who managed to fight their way into power. When Commodus died, four would-be emperors scrambled for power. The winner was, ironically, a Carthaginian named Septimius Severus, a coarse, brutal but efficient soldier who re-established Rome's military supremacy, murdered the regulation number of senators, and died a natural death after ruling for eighteen years. He advised his two sons to stick together, pay the soldiers, and forget the rest. They ignored his advice and set about trying to murder each other; Caracalla, the elder, proved to have a better grasp of the science of treachery; he invited his brother to a conference in their mother's boudoir and had him hacked to death in his mother's arms. Caracalla then murdered twenty thousand men he suspected of supporting his brother and instituted a reign of terror reminiscent of Marius. He surpassed most previous emperors in sheer malignancy when he went to Alexandria – against whose citizens he held a grudge – and invited most of its youths to some celebration on the parade grounds; then his soldiers surrounded them and cut them down. The one act for which he deserves credit was granting Roman citizenship to all the freedmen of the empire; but even this was probably a measure to increase the number of taxpayers. When Caracalla was murdered by his own officers, the senate was bullied into proclaiming him a god.

After that, 'barrack emperors' came and went with vertiginous speed, most of them assassinated. One of the few whose name is recalled by posterity was Heliogabalus (218–22 A.D.), whose name has become a synonym for peculiar vices. In fact, he was merely what we would now call a transsexual – a woman born in a man's body. Soon after he became emperor – at the age of fifteen – he advertised for a doctor who could perform the sex-change operation, but finally settled for castration. He then married a beefy slave called Zoticus, and the ceremony was followed by a ritual defloration and honeymoon. The 'empress' (as he insisted on being called) then decided to become the patroness of the city's prostitutes; he called them all together and made a speech in which he showed an exhaustive knowledge of every perversion that they might be called upon to satisfy. This interest in prostitutes soon revealed itself as a desire to take up their calling; he began to tour the city at night, offering sodomy or fellatio to the males he accosted. On one occasion he even went into a brothel, threw out all the prostitutes and settled down to satisfying all the customers himself.

After four years of this, his soldiers decided they would prefer a real emperor; Heliogabalus was murdered in the lavatory in 222 A.D. and his body tossed into the Tiber.

After this light relief, Rome returned to the serious business of conspiracy and assassination. In seventy years there were more than seventy emperors or would-be emperors. This high turnover was due to the fact that the army was now the only real power, and if the soldiers took a dislike to an emperor, they killed him. Meanwhile, the threat from the barbarians was growing. A great Persian king, Artaxerxes, overthrew the reigning Parthian dynasty and founded a new line of kings, the Sassanids. While Artaxerxes threatened Rome's eastern frontier, the Germans and Goths poured in from the north. The beautiful queen Zenobia of Palmyra in Syria led a revolt that took three years to suppress – she was finally led off to Rome in golden chains, where she married a senator and died a Roman citizen. In Britain, invaders demolished huge sections of Hadrian's wall. The roads of the empire became infested with bandits again. Fields lay uncultivated. Plagues swept across the empire for fifteen years. Rome was unable to feed her peoples, for – unlike the Chinese, who had made their land fertile with canals – Italy's food production was always low; she depended heavily on imports. Finally, from a welter of would-be emperors there emerged one remarkable man, Diocletian, who seized the throne in 284 A.D. and held on to it for twenty-one years. He set out ruthlessly to patch up the leaks in the sinking empire. He did it by sheer brute force, and most Romans would undoubtedly have preferred it to disintegrate, for Diocletian squeezed them as they had never been squeezed before. His armies flung bands of steel around the empire; but the towns and villages in which they were garrisoned had to feed them for nothing. Shipowners had to provide free passage for the army. Taxes were so high that businessmen gave up their businesses and farmers left their land untilled – until Diocletian passed laws forbidding them to retire.

Recognizing that the empire was now too big and too chaotic for one man to govern, Diocletian appointed three other 'Caesars' to help him. The main partner was his most trusted officer Maximian, who governed the west from Milan. Diocletian governed the east from Nicomedia, in Asia Minor, which he turned into a miniature Rome. His son-in-law Galerius ruled what are now called the Balkans, while Maximian's son-in-law, Constantius Chlorus, ruled Gaul. And finally, when he was convinced that the empire had been stuck together again, Diocletian retired and persuaded Maximian to do the same. The empire promptly began to fall apart.

The complicated struggle for succession went on for the next seven years, the main contenders being Galerius, Maxentius (who was the son of Maximian) and Constantine, the son of Constantius Chlorus (apparently so-called because his face was a bilious green). When Chlorus died in Britain, Constantine was hailed as emperor by his father's troops. Finally, Constantine invaded Italy, fought a battle against Maxentius at the Milvian Bridge, and threw his rival's body into the Tiber. After another dozen years of civil war, he became Constantine the Great, sole ruler of the Roman empire.

And here we come to one of the major unsolved puzzles of history. Constantine was as unpleasant a character as we have encountered so far in the story of Rome, not merely ruthless but gratuitously cruel. One example will suffice. When he decided to get rid of his wife Fausta – daughter of Maximian and sister of Maxentius, both of whom Constantine had killed – he had her locked in her bathroom and the heating turned up until she literally steamed to death. Yet this is the man who claimed he had been converted to Christianity in rather the same manner as St Paul. He alleged that, on the eve of the battle of the Milvian Bridge, he had seen a cross in the sky and the words 'By this sign shall ye conquer.' Constantine went into battle with a spear turned into a cross as his standard, and conquered. From then on, Christianity became the religion of the Roman empire. Christianity has naturally been grateful to Constantine ever since, and his biographer Eusebius explains how Constantine had prayed earnestly for a sign from God, which was given in the form of the cross. The fact remains that Constantine did not become a Christian until he was on his death bed. And a life of betrayals, perjuries and murders – including his own son – indicate that he remained untouched by the spirit of Christianity.

So why did Constantine decide to make Christianity the official religion of the empire? There are several possible explanations. One is that he did indeed see a cross in some natural cloud formation which he superstitiously took to be a 'sign' – we have seen that the Romans were obsessed by omens. Another possibility is that he was influenced by his mother Helena, a British princess (or, according to Gibbon, an innkeeper's daughter), who at some point became a Christian and later made a famous pilgrimage to the Holy Land and located the cross on which Jesus was crucified. This is just possible, except that Constantine saw very little of his mother during his early manhood – he was too busy struggling for power – and in any case, does not seem to have been the sort of person who would be influenced by his mother's ideas. Another possible explanation is that he was influenced by the death – by disease – of the 'Caesar' Galerius, who had persuaded Diocletian to persecute the Christians and who died believing that his illness was sent by God to punish him. Finally – and most likely – seems the explanation that Constantine thought it would be appropriately dramatic for the all-powerful conqueror to raise up the minority religion (only about one-tenth of his subjects were Christians) to a position of supreme importance.

Whatever the answer, it seems unlikely that Christianity finally conquered because Constantine became convinced of its truth. The historian Eusebius was being either naive or dishonest when he wrote: 'When I gaze in spirit upon this thrice-blessed soul, united with God, free of all mortal dross, in robes gleaming like lightning and in ever-radiant diadem, speech and reason stand mute.' For it seems likely that the empress Helena made her pilgrimage to the Holy Land in an attempt to atone for the crimes committed by her son, while Constantine himself felt no such misgivings.

When, in 326 A.D., Constantine decided to move his capital from Rome to Byzantium, on the Hellespont, he was, in effect, handing over Rome to the Christians. The city whose name had become identified with materialism and violence became the city of love and salvation; Caesar surrendered his crown to the pope. Subsequent history, as we shall see, raised the intriguing question of which actually conquered the other.

Four
THE END OF THE ROMAN EMPIRE

Within a year of achieving respectability, in 313 A.D., the Christians were squabbling like children. The cause of the quarrel was that one party found it impossible to forgive the other for compromising with the Roman authorities during Diocletian's persecutions. The Christians had been ordered to hand over their sacred books. Some had refused and been martyred. Some had handed over books that they claimed to be scriptures, secure in the knowledge that the police were illiterate – one bishop handed over medical textbooks. A few had actually handed over their sacred books for the duration of the persecution. Now these compromises became the object of rage and contempt, and the non-compromisers wanted to see them punished and ejected from the church. The non-compromisers called themselves Donatists (after a Bishop Donatus who held their views). To Constantine's mild astonishment, these advocates of love and forgiveness began to assail one another in public. He was dragged into the quarrel himself when he ordered that confiscated church buildings should be handed back to the Christians; now he had two lots of Christians each claiming they were the rightful owners. The Bishop of Rome sided against the non-compromisers; so did a council of bishops who met in Arles in 314 A.D. The indignant Donatists rejected their decision and proceeded to kill their opponents. Belatedly, it must have dawned on Constantine that these Christians were just as quarrelsome and difficult as the Jews, and that he had made a grave mistake in substituting their religion for the easygoing paganism of the Romans. It may well have been the sight of his Christian subjects snarling at one another that decided him to flee to Byzantium. But his hope of peace was again disappointed. The Greek church was just as bitterly divided. And the cause, it seemed, was that a priest named Arius was unable to swallow the notion that Jesus was actually the God who had created the universe, and that this commonsense notion scandalized the

Bishop of Alexandria. Arius appealed to the historian Eusebius – the one who thought Constantine was free of all mortal dross – and Eusebius agreed with him. The struggle soon became so fierce that Constantine was forced to call a special council of bishops at Nicaea, near Nicomedia (just across the Hellespont from Byzantium). This council came down against Arius and in favour of the proposition that Jesus *was* God the Father – a notion that would have shocked the founder of Christianity, or possibly, since he seems to have had a sense of humour, made him smile. The decision made, of course, no difference whatever to Arius and his supporters, who remained convinced – rightly – that commonsense was on their side, whatever the Nicene Creed said to the contrary. Arius's opponents declared him a heretic – taken from a Greek word meaning to think for oneself (which Christians found increasingly reprehensible), and he was refused communion. When Arius died, his chief opponent, Athanasius, circulated a story that he had been struck down by direct heavenly intervention, presumably by a thunderbolt.

And while the Christians squabbled and killed one another, the Roman emperors continued to do the same. Constantine died in 337 A.D., just after being baptized. The fact that his heirs were Christians did not prevent them from adopting traditional Roman methods of settling the succession; two nephews whom Constantine had included among his heirs were executed, and his three sons then ruled the empire jointly, the one called Constantius taking over the throne in Byzantium (now called Constantinople). His first act was to allay the fears of various uncles and aunts by personally guaranteeing their safety. His next was to plot against them. The bishop of Nicomedia entered into the plot and provided a forged document, supposed to be written by the emperor Constantine, declaring that he had been poisoned by his brothers. The soldiers were shown this document, and they went off and massacred two uncles, seven cousins and numerous other kinsmen. The only members of the family who were spared were two children named Gallus and Julian. Meanwhile, the other two brothers of Constantius quarrelled and went to war; one killed the other; then the killer was in turn killed by a rebel officer who wanted to seize the throne. Constantius killed the rebel and so became sole emperor. In due course, perhaps out of guilt, he appointed Gallus as joint Caesar, but soon regretted the decision and had him arrested and beheaded like a criminal.

Meanwhile, Constantius's cousin Julian showed no desire to

become emperor. He was a bookworm by temperament. This did not save him from being arrested and kept at the court of Milan for seven months, where his life was in continual danger. But he was so obviously harmless that Constantius finally allowed him to go to Athens to study. There he became absorbed in philosophy and lived as an ordinary student. And eventually Constantius appointed Julian to be Caesar of Gaul and the northern countries. There Julian showed himself to be a natural soldier and won some important victories over French and German tribes. But when he began to suspect that Constantius was changing his mind, and that he would be next on the list for assassinations, he decided to put up a fight and marched south with his army. The fight proved to be unnecessary; Constantius died before they clashed, and the book-worm Julian – like Claudius before him – became emperor of Rome.

Understandably, Julian did not feel particularly friendly towards the Christians, recalling the role of the Bishop of Nicomedia in the murder of his family. Being a philosopher rather than a statesman, he saw that Constantine had made a mistake in raising Christianity to the position of official religion of the empire. The proof was that the Christians were still denouncing one another as heretics and assassinating one another when the opportunity arose. Power had proved as dangerous to the Christians as it had to the Caesars. The gentle, neighbour-loving apostles of the man-god were becoming rather worse than the Jewish zealots who had caused so much trouble to the Caesars. During one squabble about rival popes in 366 A.D., their supporters fought in church and left behind a hundred and thirty-seven corpses. The historian Ammianus remarks mildly that 'wild beasts are not such enemies to mankind as are most Christians in their deadly hatred to one another'. So Julian decided to do what he could to restore the balance. It was not his intention to persecute, or even suppress, the Christians. He only wanted to make them stop squabbling and behave like Christians. So he summoned the various bishops who were denouncing one another and asked them to desist. He restored the rights of 'heretics' who had been banished and allowed them to return. He withdrew the special privileges enjoyed by Christians – such as tax concessions. He opened pagan temples and tried to bolster the morale of pagan priests, who were in a state resembling shellshock after half a century of Christian persecution. Julian was attempting

vis a vis pagans

to restore some of the old religious tolerance that had existed before Constantine had given the Christians the whip hand.

There was a yell of outraged indignation from the Christians, who immediately labelled him Julian the Apostate. Christian writers poured out blistering denunciations. One of these was the emperor's old schoolfriend Gregory of Nazianz, to whom Julian had been helpful; in his epistles against Julian, Gregory had to find discreditable reasons for Julian's kindness; he even accuses him of failing to persecute the Christians in order to deny them the glory of martyrdom.

It was unfortunate that, like Marcus Aurelius, this mild philosopher-emperor was unable to remain at home and devote himself to his literary works. The barbarians were still knocking at the door; he had only been emperor for two years when, on his way back from a successful campaign in Persia, he died from an infected lance wound. The Christians breathed a sigh of relief and went back to denouncing and killing one another, and to persecuting the pagans.

And, with the irony of history, Julian's tolerance made the situation worse. In allowing 'heretics' to return home, he restored the anti-Arians to power (Constantius had supported Arius), and the Nicene view that Jesus was God the Creator eventually triumphed as a consequence. And so the quarrels and schisms went on. Winwood Reade says, with superb sarcasm in his book *The Martyrdom of Man*: 'The bishops were all of them ignorant and superstitious men, but they could not all of them think alike. And as if to ensure dissent they proceeded to define that which had never existed, and which if it had existed could never be defined. They described the topography of heaven. They dissected the godhead and expounded the miraculous conception, giving lectures on celestial impregnations and miraculous obstetrics. They not only said that 3 was 1, and that 1 was 3; they professed to explain how that curious arithmetical combination had been brought about.' But amidst all their own quarrels, they had no hesitation about persecuting pagans. The emperor Theodosius, a Spaniard who came to the throne in 379 after a quick succession of 'barrack emperors', issued an edict saying that all his subjects should be called Catholic Christians, and that the rest 'whom We judge demented and insane, shall sustain the infamy of heretical dogmas . . . shall be smitten first by divine vengeance and secondly by the retribution of Our own initiative . . .' The pagan writer Symmachus pleaded eloquently: 'Everything is full of God.

We look up to the same stars . . . What does it matter by what system of knowledge we seek the truth? It is not by one single path that we arrive at so great a secret.' But the Christians emphatically disagreed.

It would, of course, be a crude oversimplification to say that the triumph of Christianity was a triumph for some of the worst elements in human nature. After all, the worst elements had already had it mostly their own way for over two thousand years, since the great wars that tore the Mediterranean apart. And they continued to have it their own way in spite of, rather than because of, Christianity. The Christian emperor Theodosius, for example, behaved exactly like all other 'Right Men' who have managed to acquire power; any kind of slight to his authority aroused him to a frenzy. The people of Antioch became increasingly restless at their burden of taxes, and their complaints were treated as rebellion by the governor. Finally, there was an explosion of popular fury, and statues of the emperor and members of his family were overthrown. A company of soldiers quickly restored order, but Theodosius was infuriated. He declared that Antioch was no longer a city but a village, suspended the distribution of corn, and ordered the examination of large numbers of citizens by means of torture. Most of them were sentenced to death. But one of the appointed judges went back to Constantinople to beg for leniency and found that Theodosius had already half-forgotten the affair. So, congratulating himself on his generosity, Theodosius bestowed his pardon, and basked in the praise of the grateful people of Antioch, who set up statues by the hundred.

The citizens of Thessalonica, in Greece, were less fortunate. One of their favourite charioteers had a homosexual affair with a pretty slave boy and landed in gaol. At the time the people were already angry about various repressions, and when their favourite charioteer failed to appear at the circus they revolted and murdered the garrison commander and some of his officers. This time, Theodosius's rage had no time to subside; besides, he could not have the whole populace put to the torture. So the inhabitants of Thessalonica were invited to games in the circus – seven thousand of them – and then the doors were closed and the soldiers given the signal for a massacre. It took three hours, and at the end of that time all the citizens were dead.

Bishop Ambrose of Milan was horrified by news of the massacre. Theodosius was in Milan – which had been one of the empire's capitals since the time of Diocletian – and Ambrose wrote him a letter declaring that he had seen a vision ordering him to excommunicate Theodosius until he did penance. Theodosius went to church to obey, but was met by Ambrose, who told him that he had to do penance in public. This was too much for a man of the emperor's violent temperament, and he stayed away from church for some time. But Ambrose won in the end; Theodosius was obliged to remove his imperial robes in front of a crowded congregation and ask forgiveness for his sins.

The episode is certainly a dramatic illustration of the power for good that Christianity could bring to bear on a tyrant. But when we look into it a little more closely, it ceases to be a simple parable of good versus evil. Shortly before the massacre, the emperor had heard that Christian zealots in a town on the Persian frontier had burned a Jewish synagogue. The local bishop, who had allowed them to do it, was ordered to make restitution out of the church funds. Ambrose wrote an extraordinary letter to the emperor, declaring that to tolerate Jews was tantamount to persecuting Christians, and that if he refused to change his mind he was probably damned. And when Theodosius came to church, Ambrose halted the eucharistic liturgy and directly addressed the emperor from his pulpit. Reluctantly, against his better judgement, Theodosius gave way.

At this point we become aware that the excommunication episode was not simply a matter of saintly virtue (Ambrose was later canonized) versus criminal egoism. In the matter of the restitution to the Jews, Ambrose was in the wrong, and Theodosius was behaving like a just and responsible emperor. All of which suggests that Ambrose was another Right Man, and that what happened is what usually happens when two Right Men meet head on: the weaker of the two concedes the point.

It would be easy to draw the moral from this, and other episodes of Christian intolerance, and conclude that the criminal streak in man found it as easy to express itself under Christian emperors and bishops as under Greek tyrants and Roman Caesars – in fact, in some ways rather easier. This would be inaccurate and unfair; for the great virtue of Christianity was that it remained actively self-critical. In fact, Christianity, like Hinduism and Buddhism, recognized that one of man's chief problems is his egoism, and that the ego stands in the way of 'enlightenment'. The moment the church became 'established', deeply religious men began to ask whether this was really what Christ wanted. That magnificent fervour of the early Christians, their ecstatic certainty of salvation through suffering, evaporated like morning dew. So the deeply religious did what they had done in Palestine long before Jesus: they withdrew into the solitude of the desert. The great ascetic movement began. It had first started as early as 285 A.D., in the reign of Diocletian, when St Anthony withdrew into the desert – for waterless places were regarded as the abode of demons, and therefore the best place for a saint to engage in the 'unseen warfare' of the spirit. And a century later, when the church could now offer an established position to the careerist, the ascetics fled to the wilderness in droves. They slept on sharp stones; they flogged themselves with knotted leather thongs; they took care not to scratch themselves when lice crawled through their matted beards. Some – like St Simeon – sat on top of high pillars for years; others chained themselves to rocks; others stood on one leg like an ostrich, or remained in strange acrobatic positions for so long that the nails became curved like claws and grew back into the flesh. Some were fortunate enough to have suffered for their faith – St Paphnutius the Great, who lived in the desert with St Anthony, had one eye plucked out and one leg hamstrung under the emperor Maximus; others inflicted the suffering upon themselves. It was St Paphnutius who converted the famous courtesan Thais of Alexandria and ordered her to do penance by being walled up for three years in a cell. In his delightful novel *Thais*, Anatole France was later to make fun of this episode, showing the ascetics as ignorant bigots who made the supreme error of directing their loathing at the human body and its sexual functions – in France's version, Paphnutius himself is 'de-converted' and tries to lure Thais back into sin. But France's view is superficial; he fails to grasp the underlying reasons why the Christians were suspicious of sexuality. And these are of immense importance for the understanding of human criminality.

We must note, to begin with, that in most of the early civilizations we have been considering – Greek, Assyrian, Persian, Roman, and so on – woman was taken for granted as a kind of domestic animal, often rather less valuable than a cow or pig. As Shaw comments, man built civilization without her permission, taking her domestic labour for granted as its foundation. Earlier cultures seem to have taken a more idealistic view of woman, if statues like the Venus of Willendorf can be regarded as evidence; they saw her as the incarnation of the earth-mother goddess. The priestesses of Greece and Rome are a remnant of this earlier attitude. But as man became domesticated, woman became a beast of burden: the water carrier, the maize-thresher, the bearer of children. As civilization developed, it was the males who enjoyed its benefits: the baths, the gymnasia, the clubs, the philosopher's classrooms. The women stayed at home and looked after the children. This explains the high incidence of homosexuality in Greek, Roman and oriental civilization; the men spent their leisure in one another's company; they ate together and bathed together, and when spring made a young man's fancy turn to thoughts of love, they were more likely to settle on some good-looking youth than on a pretty girl; he had little opportunity to meet a pretty girl socially. In our unsegregated society, men and women have daily opportunity to size one another up. Ian Brady was in the same office with Myra Hindley for six months before he deigned to notice her; but because they were in each other's company every day, they ended as lovers. In ancient Rome, the stock clerk and the stenographer would both have been male.

But as civilization affords more opportunity for leisure, it is inevitable that woman ceases to be merely the household slave. She becomes, for example, the hostess – and we have seen the god Augustus hurrying his hostess off to the bedroom under the eyes of her husband. As soon as women are 'on show', men can watch them moving around, wait for the charming glimpse of thigh or naked breast, and lick their lips. 'Women's lib' began in imperial Rome; Tiberius had to pass edicts against patrician women who expressed their boredom with domestic life by going 'on the game'. A series of empresses wound the emperor around their little fingers – from Augustus's Livia, Claudius's Messalina, Nero's Poppaea, Marcus Aurelius's Fausta, to the empress Theodora, a nymphomaniac prostitute who dominated the later emperor Justinian.

So in the Roman empire in the fourth century A.D., the image of woman had become exciting, disturbing, voluptuous. She had still not become the ideal creature of Dante and Petrarch and the troubadours; but she had reached the halfway stage. Courtesans such as Thais of Alexandria could become wealthy because men had learned to dream about women instead of about pretty slave boys or handsome youths.

So the Christian rejection of sexual pleasure was more than a reaction against Roman sensuality. It was a recognition that when man idealizes woman, he also creates a false image of her. This masculine distortion can be seen in any piece of cheap pornography; the seduction is described in minute physical detail, and the final coupling made to sound like the climax of a symphony. But missing from all this is the interaction of two *personalities*. It is two persons who find themselves in bed together when the excitement has died down, and their future relationship will depend on whether they *like* each other.

In woman, the sexual delusion usually takes a less impersonal form. Her instinct is directed at finding a husband and protector; so while the male sexual delusion tends towards promiscuity, the female tends towards monogamy. Her problem is that she may fall in love with a completely unsuitable male because she finds him 'dashing' and exciting, and find herself in conflict with his male instinct for promiscuity. In the sense that it is more personal, the female sexual delusion is more realistic than the male version.

The Christian attitude to sex was based upon a recognition of this element of unreality in the sexual relation, the 'baited hook'. So the Christian view of sex is that it is primarily a personal relationship whose aim is monogamy and the raising of a family.

When we consider the mechanism of the sexual delusion, we can see that it depends on the tendency of the human imagination to exaggerate the importance of the 'forbidden'. And this same obsession with the forbidden is – as we have seen – the basis of criminality. Which means that the ideals of these early Christians were basically an attempt to combat the sexual delusion and the criminal delusion. They saw man as a spirit who has become entangled in a prison of matter – light entangled in darkness. (Some even went so far as to accept the teaching of the Persian prophet Mani, who said that all matter is evil.) The great theologian Origen asserted that God originally created a realm of pure spirit inhabited by angels, but that because there was nothing to struggle against, the angels became bored and turned away from God. So God created matter to provide the fallen angels with something to struggle against – a kind of gymnasium in which man can be trained and educated. The ascetic is not really dedicated to self-torment, but to learning to use the gymnasium to struggle back towards the realm of pure spirit. And this is why, for all its drawbacks, Christianity was one of the most important milestones in human history. Paganism was a kind of lowest common multiple. If you were a citizen of Rome around 100 A.D., it made no real difference whether you worshipped Osiris or Tammuz, Mithras or the emperor; in fact, many pagan gods had conveniently amalgamated so that a Celt, an Egyptian or a Babylonian could go and make his sacrifice in a Roman temple. There were no great pagan scriptures to rival the dialogues of Plato or the New Testament. We have seen that, at its popular level, Christianity was no better than paganism. But it had its saints, its ascetics, its great thinkers; and these poured their insights into the repository of the Church. Plato said that the perfect state would be governed by a philosopher-king. Christianity *was* a state within a state, and if it was not governed by philosophers and saints at least the philosophers and saints played a vital role in its development. After the murderous chaos of the Roman empire, it was one of the greatest steps mankind had so far taken.

Before we can complete the story of the downfall of Rome, it is necessary to look at the rest of the vast landmass that surrounded the Roman empire. Most of the earth was still covered with forest, jungle and desert. The Mediterranean itself had once been an immense desert with a few lakes and pools until, around five and a half million years ago, the Atlantic ocean managed to burst through the wall of mountains that ran from present-day Spain to north Africa; the giant waterfall turned the area into the tideless sea that later nurtured the Greeks and Romans. At the time the Sumerians invented writing, the Sahara was covered with forests and grass; elephants and hippopotamuses cooled themselves in its lakes. But the climate had been slowly changing for the past seven thousand years, and by the time of Sargon the Great it was turning into a desert – aided by nomads whose flocks trampled and chewed the last of the grassland.

To the south there was the unknown land of Africa, still peopled by men of the stone age. To the north there was Germany, with its great dark forests, which continued on into Russia. To the south-east lay the unknown continent of India, with its religion of peace and contemplation. The Indians also civilized their neighbours in Burma, Malaya, Siam, as far as Indochina, but with missionaries and merchants, not armies and tax collectors.

To the east lay the vast and totally unknown continent of China. Although it had also had its share of local wars, that immense land had turned into an empire rather more peacefully than its western neighbour. The Chou dynasty had conquered around 1000 B.C.; they were barbarian warriors who absorbed the best of what their predecessors – the Shang dynasty – had to offer. After 500 B.C. great canals brought prosperity to the land; small farms were replaced by huge fields like the prairies of Canada and America. After seven hundred years, the Chou empire was fragmented in a power struggle, and Shih Huang-ti, the 'Great Lord of Ch'in', finally became master.

Unlike the Roman empire, this immense continent was not under constant stress from internal revolts and enemy nations. There *were* enemies along the northern boundaries – horse nomads of the steppes – but China itself (named after the province of Ch'in) was too vast for nomads to penetrate very far; besides, the men of these northern borders – like the Ch'in – were as tough and hardy as the nomads. So while the Roman empire was convulsed with warfare, most of China – like its neighbour Japan – lay in a kind of sleep. With its canals and rice fields, the landowners grew rich. Of course, they squabbled among themselves, like medieval barons – in fact, before the coming of the Great Lord of Ch'in, China was very like England or France in the Middle Ages.

Shih Huang set out to forge a Chinese empire; and he ordered the building of the Great Wall to keep out the nomads; it extended for nearly two thousand miles. He built roads and started a postal system. He decreed a standardized writing. He persuaded feudal barons to move to the capital. He was, in fact, a kind of Chinese Augustus or Constantine. And because he believed that the emperor's will should prevail over all others, he objected to the Confucian classics, which insisted that the king rules by the will of heaven, and ordered the books to be burned. When he died in 207 B.C. there was a revolt, and the ruthless Ch'in were replaced by the milder and gentler Han dynasty. But for all their moderation as rulers, the Han emperors proved to be formidable conquerors. Instead of merely trying to keep out the wild horsemen of the northern steppes, Wu, the 'Martial Emperor' (140–87 A.D.) went out and attacked them. These barbarians were known to the Chinese as the Hsiung-nu. In the west, they became known as the Huns.

In earlier centuries, when these wild horsemen had been driven west by war or starvation, they had encountered the west's own equivalent of Huns – the Scythians. These savages lived to the north of the Black Sea, between the Danube and the Don (in what is now the Ukraine), and Herodotus was so fascinated by tales of their cruelty and brutality that he made a special trip to find out all he could about them. He described a people who skinned their enemies and made coats of the skins; who sawed off the tops of their skulls and used them as drinking vessels, and who sometimes drank the blood of their enemies from these gruesome relics; who put out the eyes of their slaves to prevent their running away, and who regarded it as manly to take at least one human life every year. They terrorized the Persians, and an expedition against them by King Darius had no success whatever. In due course, the Scythians were driven south by an enemy from over the Danube, the Sarmatians, defeated by Philip of Macedon and finally crushed by Rome's old enemy Mithridates. (But a closely related people, the Parthians, continued to give as much trouble as ever.) And with this race of fierce warriors finally out of the way, the slit-eyed Huns from Mongolia could move westward. So it was the more-or-less peaceful expansion of China that finally caused the break-up of the Roman empire.

But it was not only from the east that Rome was threatened. All kinds of barbarian hordes were pouring across the west. Wild men from Gothland – in Sweden – had moved south to the Black Sea and become pirates; in 251 they had fought a battle against the 'barrack emperor' Decius and killed him. At about the same time, a German tribe called the Franks (who would later give their name to France) crossed the Rhine into Gaul, while another tribe, the Alemanni, invaded Alsace. In 376 the Visigoths, or West Goths, crossed the Danube, defeated the Roman army and killed the emperor Valens. But their aim was not conquest; they were fleeing from the Huns and only wanted to be allowed to settle in the relative security of the Roman empire; they won their point, and many of them became defenders of the empire. So did many other barbarians, including members of a tribe called the Vandals. But in 406, the German branch of the Vandals also crossed into Gaul, then went down into Spain across the Pyrenees and set up a kingdom there. Twenty years later they had crossed the sea and taken Carthage. In 407, the Romans had been forced to summon their legions from Britain to try to stem the tide of invaders.

One of the most remarkable of these was a Goth named Alaric, who had applied to become a Roman commander and been turned down. The Roman empire now had two emperors, the two sons of Theodosius the Great – Honorius (in Rome) and Arcadius (in Constantinople) – neither of them men of much force of character. Honorius was supported and defended by a Vandal general named Stilicho – he had even married Stilicho's daughter. For a while, Alaric supported Arcadius. Then Alaric grew tired of the general untrustworthiness of these effete Romans and went raiding on his own account. He plundered Thrace and Dacia, then crossed to Greece. He left a terrible trail of destruction behind him – one ancient historian compares the devastated Athens to the bleeding and empty skin of a slaughtered victim. Gibbon mentions that his men killed the males, burnt the villages, and made off with cattle and all the attractive females. Stilicho hurried to Greece, and finally trapped the Goths at the foot of a mountain. Their water supply was diverted and, as they began to suffer from thirst, Stilicho decided that he could afford to relax and went off to attend a public festival with games ('and lascivious dances' adds Gibbon – this bachelor historian seems to dwell on rapes and orgies with a certain morbid satisfaction). Stilicho's soldiers wandered off to look for plunder, and the wily Alaric led his men through the Roman lines, across thirty miles of rough country and over the Gulf of Corinth. He had vanished before Stilicho had time to grasp what was happening.

Five years later, in 402, Stilicho frustrated an attempt of the Goths to land in Italy, and in 406 he defeated an invading army of barbarians at Florence. With a record like this, he should have been regarded as above suspicion. But Honorius's court was the usual Roman hotbed of intrigue, and rumours went around that Stilicho was in league with the Goths. Honorius, who was a fool and a weakling, was willing to listen. He disliked his barbarian soldiers; and, being a religious bigot, objected to the fact that many of them were still pagans. Removing Stilicho and his barbarians would obviously be a complicated undertaking, but not beyond the enterprise – and treachery – of a Roman emperor. One day, at a signal from Honorius, Roman troops at Pavia grabbed many of Stilicho's friends and murdered them. Stilicho, still failing to grasp the enormity of the betrayal, took refuge in a church in Ravenna. He was lured out on a promise of safety, and promptly executed. Like Nero's general Corbulo, he probably muttered 'Serves me right.'

At another signal, there was a massacre of barbarian families in cities all over Italy. The decision was stupid as well as criminal, for these barbarians had proved themselves loyal to Rome. Now there was nothing to stop Alaric, and he marched his Goths straight to the walls of Rome.

The Romans found it hard to believe they were not dreaming. It seemed incredible that this unwashed barbarian was threatening the imperial capital. But as Alaric prevented food and water from getting into the city, they began to realize that their situation was perilous. The Romans were furious, and their sense of outrage was directed at Stilicho's widow, who was accused of corresponding with Alaric and strangled on the orders of the senate. Then outrage turned to depression as they began to starve. Five and a half centuries after the siege of Carthage, the Romans were tasting their own medicine. The rich managed to stay alive; the poor died by the thousand. They began to practise cannibalism. Inevitably, the rotting corpses caused disease, and as the plague swept the city, ambassadors went to ask Alaric what he would take to go away. Alaric finally agreed to a vast sum in gold and silver (and, oddly enough, pepper, used for preserving meat).

But there was no money in the treasury. Honorius and his court had moved to Ravenna – the emperor had decided it made a safer capital than Rome since it was surrounded by marshes. Negotiations dragged on; Alaric besieged Rome again, then marched on Ravenna. Honorius allowed some of his allies to slip out, make a surprise attack, and slip back before Alaric had time to recover his wits. This was the last straw. In a violent rage, Alaric marched again on Rome, once again besieged it, and this time succeeded in breaking in. It was mid-August, 410 A.D., and the first time invaders had been inside the city for more than six hundred years. Still smarting from the surprise attack, Alaric's men raped and slaughtered with the abandonment of soldiers who had become bored, resentful and sex-starved. 'The brutal soldiers,' says Gibbon with a sigh of regret, 'satisfied their sensual appetites without consulting either the inclination or the duties of their female captives,' and he goes on to discuss the interesting question of whether a virgin who had been violated can still be regarded as 'chaste' and therefore still a virgin.

In Ravenna, one of Honorius's eunuchs brought him the news. Honorius apparently kept chickens and was particularly fond of a cock named Roma. When the eunuch said 'Rome is lost,' Honorius gave a yelp of agony. 'That's impossible. He was just eating out of my hand.' When told that the eunuch meant the city, not the bird, he gave a sigh of relief.

After six days the Goths left Rome, which now had nothing more to offer them, and marched south, taking Nola and Capua on the way. Alaric's fleet sailed for north Africa; but his luck had run out. They were scattered by winter storms, and Alaric died shortly afterwards.

It was the beginning, not the end, of Rome's troubles; but the story of its remaining sixty-five years as the capital of an empire has a curiously repetitive air. Honorius's successor, the emperor Valentinian III, was also lazy, foppish and vicious. During his unfortunately long reign, the Vandals crossed from Spain to north Africa and devastated the Roman province there with a thoroughness that has made their name a byword for mindless destruction. Valentinian's sister was a nymphomaniac named Honoria, who got herself pregnant by the court chamberlain and was packed off to the care of some religious aunts in Constantinople. Bored and sex-starved, she wrote a letter to a sinister barbarian named Attila the Hun, begging him to come and rescue her. Attila was a descendant of the Mongols who had been driven out of northern China, and Honoria was undoubtedly unaware that he was short and squat, with a face like an ape. Attila probably had no sexual interest in Honoria; he already had several dozen wives and, to a puritanical savage, the knowledge that she had already got herself pregnant would seem disgusting. But the opportunity for blackmail was too good to miss; so Attila sent Valentinian a message asking for his sister's hand, and demanding half the empire as dowry. Valentinian refused indignantly, and Attila declared war. Fortunately for Italy, he decided that Gaul would be an easier target, and swept across Europe, capturing city after city. If he had captured France, present day Englishmen and Frenchmen would probably have slit eyes and yellow features. But a Roman general defeated him at Chalons, and Attila led his army back into Italy, where Valentinian was forced to bribe him to go away. Soon after this, Attila died in a manner worthy of a conqueror, bursting an artery in the act of taking the maidenhead of a beautiful virgin.

Valentinian himself was eventually murdered by a general named Maximus, whose wife he had raped. Maximus made the mistake of marrying Valentinian's empress Eudoxia, who disliked him so much that she sent a message to the Vandals in north Africa asking them to come and save her. Honoria's example should have taught her better. The Vandals came and sacked Rome, and when Eudoxia rushed with outstretched hands to meet them, stripped her of her jewellery and carried her and her two daughters off to Africa as slaves.

This was virtually the end of Rome. It staggered on for another twenty years under various emperors and pretenders, the last of whom was a mere boy, Romulus Augustulus. By this time the Roman empire was really in the hands of several barbarians who had enlisted as Roman soldiers; when they asked the emperor's father to share out the empire, he refused, and they murdered him. The boy-Caesar resigned after only eleven months. After that, there were no more Roman emperors, either in Rome or Ravenna. The Christian pope remained the real master of Rome, as he has to this day.

The story of Constantinople must be continued for a few more years – the throne endured for another thousand – because it is the necessary prelude to the next stage in the history of Europe.

The emperor Justinian, who came to the throne in 527 A.D., was possibly the worst ruler since Caligula and killed more people than all the other Roman emperors put together. This was not out of sadism, but because he fancied himself another Constantine and tried to force all the pagans in his empire to accept Christianity; those who refused were killed, and vast numbers refused. He left behind a legacy of bitterness that paved the way for the success of Mohammedanism a century later. It is one of the tragedies of European history that this weak, vicious and disagreeable man held the throne for so long – thirty-eight years. It is not, however, a mystery; he owed most of his success to his empress, the ex-prostitute Theodora.

Justinian met Theodora four years before he became emperor. She was the daughter of a man who looked after the circus animals, and she and her two sisters went on the stage as members of the Roman equivalent of a song and dance act. They became high-class tarts; even as a child, Theodora knew how to satisfy lovers – the historian Procopius said that she was so expert at fellatio that people said she had a second vagina in her face.

Justinian quickly became her slave and, when he became emperor, had the law changed so he could marry her. She proved to be an excellent choice; she had a stronger character than Justinian, and a good head for business.

Trouble almost ended his reign before it had properly started. Constantinople was obsessed by sport, and its two leading factions – equivalents of modern football hooligans – were called the Greens and the Blues. These also took opposite sides in one of the sillier Christian controversies, the question of whether the divine and human natures in Christ were joined together or separated; in the true Christian tradition, they reinforced their arguments by murdering one another. In 532, the prefect of police ordered them to stop the killing, and in the resulting riots, half Constantinople was set on fire. Justinian was terrified and wanted to flee; Theodora called him a coward and refused to budge. Justinian's greatest general, Belisarius, settled the matter by taking his army into the streets and killing thirty thousand people, which convinced the Blues and Greens that they had better return to a less ambitious scale of homicide.

Unfortunately, Justinian was deeply impressed by this beautifully simple way of settling political questions, and decided to apply it to the rest of his empire. He sent Belisarius off to north Africa to convert the Vandals; these were, it is true, already Christians, but of the Arian persuasion. Since Belisarius happened to be the greatest military genius of his age, he was able to carry out this order with magnificent efficiency, exterminating all who declined to believe that Jesus had no beginning. Next, Belisarius was sent off to convert the Goths, who were also Arians; this took him five years and drastically reduced the Goth population. Justinian was by this time in the grip of a curious dilemma. He was convinced that Belisarius wanted to usurp the throne – a suspicion that was entirely without foundation, Belisarius being almost moronically loyal. So when he had to send Belisarius off to Syria to fight the Persian king Chosroes, he reduced his armies to a minimum, half-hoping to see him defeated. In spite of this, Belisarius performed miracles and came back victorious; at which point, Justinian allowed him to vanish into more-or-less dishonourable retirement. Since Belisarius also had a nymphomaniac wife, who had seduced his adopted son, he had more than enough to occupy his mind until Justinian was forced to call him from retirement to drive the Huns away. After that victory, Justinian had him arrested on a trumped-up charge and thrown into jail. The death of both men put an end to a story that would no doubt have gone on repeating itself indefinitely, since Belisarius seems to have been incapable of learning from experience. As soon as Justinian was in the tomb, his empire collapsed like a pack of cards.

We have been witnessing once again the sheer inadequacy of human beings to deal with affairs that extend more than a short distance beyond their personal horizons. Justinian was not actually a bad man, and his achievement in rebuilding the empire, in creating vast public works, in reforming the law and improving administration, has led historians to label him 'the Great'. But the moment we look at Justinian the man, we can see why human history is basically a record of 'crimes and follies'. To place him in charge of an empire was like placing a ten-year-old boy in charge of a transatlantic jet. He was simply too childish for the job.

This, we can see, was also the trouble with the Roman empire. It grew of its own accord, like a snowball rolling downhill, because the challenge of invaders turned the Romans into soldiers. But from the founding of the Republic, it was built on selfishness and injustice, and its expansion beyond the shores of Italy was an act of criminal aggression. Yet Rome flourished because it had its own peculiar genius: a genius for imposing order. It was this genius that was lacked by the barbarians – the Goths, the Vandals, the Huns: this is why they vanished from history so quickly.

In retrospect, it is obvious that the failure of the Roman emperors was the failure of Rome itself. With a few rare exceptions, they were egomaniacs who loved the sensation of power; and Rome developed the same taste for giving orders. In its early days, Rome was secure because men were proud to be called Roman citizens. In the Christian era, this came to mean less and less. The citizens had no say in the running of the empire, or even of their own city. In order to have influence, you had to fight your way into a position of power. This explains why the citizens of Thessalonica and the Blues and Greens of Constantinople were so obsessed by their chariot races; they were the only outlet for surplus energies. The citizens were treated like children and they behaved like children. Meanwhile, Justinian and Theodora ruled like juvenile delinquents. And Europe's greatest attempt at civilization collapsed into the chaos of the Dark Ages.

? I like modern sports

✓ important phrase

Five

EUROPE IN CHAOS

a good perspective

To grasp what has happened to our earth in this thousand-year period of the Roman empire, let us imagine that we are visitors from another star system, hovering over the surface of the earth in the year 500 B.C. From a thousand miles out in space, it looks hospitable enough, with its blue-green haze and its misty seas. But the polar ice caps are considerably larger than in our own time. In fact, this has only happened in the past few centuries, for the climate of our planet swings through its variations every thousand years or so. In the time of King Minos it had been as warm as today; a thousand years later, it had become cold and wet. Our space travellers would see no sign of human habitation, even from a mere fifty miles or so. The cold has driven civilization into the valleys; the higher passes are closed, and glaciers like those of the last ice age have appeared once more.

Much of this earth is covered with forest – Russia is one vast carpet of forest, which still conceals the gigantic prehistoric ox called the auroch. But the forests are shrinking, replaced by peat bogs – damp, marshy ground covered with plants like sphagnum moss. The space ship can float over whole continents – such as Australia – without seeing a sign of life except for ostriches.

Over the Americas, the travellers would have to fly low and search hard for signs of human existence. In fact, a mongoloid race – of the same stock as the Huns – had moved on to the American continent two or three thousand years earlier, when there was a land bridge across what is now the Bering Strait joining eastern Russia to Alaska. These Mongols had slowly penetrated south. On the prairies of Arizona, which are green and rich, they hunt the bison and the reindeer; farther south, in the forests of Yucatan, they have begun to create the civilization of the Mayas.

If the space travellers moved west, they would pass over the islands of Japan, inhabited by a race who moved down from Siberia;

5th Century — century of teachers

Europe in Chaos 249

the Japanese are as primitive as the American Indians; they wear clothes of bark and skins and live by fishing and hunting, with a little agriculture. China at first seems another empty continent, for it contains very few human beings in comparison to its size; its largest pocket of civilization is to be found in the extreme east, in the Shantung peninsula, and the capital, Anyang, is located on a bend of the Yellow River. Here the upper classes live in wooden houses built on platforms of earth, and they wear linen, wool and even silk. But most of the people of China are peasants who live in clay huts, just above the flood level, in extreme misery and poverty. Canals have not yet revolutionized the agriculture of China, so the areas of cultivated land are hard to see from the air. A middle-aged philosopher named K'ung, later latinized as Confucius, has just set out on his travels, looking for a wise ruler who will put his precepts into practice; but he will die without finding him.

The sub-continent of India is in much the same stage of civilization. There are parts where life has not advanced beyond the Stone Age. In the north, the Aryans have brought their culture and their religion, and the number of temples points to a highly developed religious life. In fact, Gautama, the Buddha, is now alive, and has achieved a far wider acceptance than his contemporary Confucius in China. But then, his philosophy of renunciation is appropriate in this poverty-stricken land. Another great teacher, Mahavira, is also wandering around and preaching; his doctrine is closer to the ideas that Jesus will preach five centuries later: reverence for all life. As the travellers move westward, along the Indus valley, they observe that these human beings are more interested in conquest than in high moral doctrines; the Persian king Darius is in the process of adding this part of India to his empire. And as they move west towards the Caspian sea, the travellers will observe the first signs of a great civilization: the mighty cities with their walls and temples and palaces. This Persian empire has no less than four capitals: Persepolis, Babylon, Susa and Ecbatana, and its towns and provinces are joined by long, straight roads with post stations every few miles. Yet in a mere ten years from now, in 490 B.C., the Greeks will call an abrupt halt to the spread of this great empire at the battle of Marathon.

And so the travellers come to the true centre of civilization on this blue-green planet: the Mediterranean. They can observe Athens in its finest period, and Sparta at the height of its power. The Roman republic has only just come into existence, and is being threatened again by her old enemy – and neighbour – the Etruscans. This new republic is healthy, vigorous, and full of high ideals – many of them derived from the Greeks; the centuries of warfare, murder and betrayal lie ahead. Across the Mediterranean, Carthage is already a sea power and has waged several successful wars – at this stage it looks like the chief contender for the position of master of the Mediterranean. Darius the Persian has not penetrated that far to the west, and he never will; but he has conquered Egypt. And the Jews, only just back in Jerusalem from their Babylonian exile, are also subjects of the Persian monarch.

As to the lands of northern Europe, these are now dominated by a mysterious warrior-race called the Celts – a race quite as remarkable in their way as the Greeks and Romans. They are artists, mystics and nature worshippers; they believe that woodlands are full of tiny nature spirits called fairies. Unlike the Romans, these mighty warriors are dreamers, with a strong tinge of pessimism. They are now masters of Germany, France and England. The one civilized art they have not yet acquired is writing, and this explains why we now know so little about them.

This, then, is the world as seen from a space ship in the year 500 B.C., and the visiting scientists would find it an exciting and intriguing place. We can imagine them compiling a report which runs something like this:

For reasons not yet determined, the upright creatures on this planet have entered a sudden phase of accelerated evolution. We can state this with authority since the simpler and less evolved type still exists in large numbers, and their mode of existence is primitive. Yet we have also observed among them thinkers and philosophers who have achieved an astonishingly high level of abstract thought. This is all the more remarkable since their technical achievements are unimpressive, except in mere size, and their scientific insight is almost non-existent.

We theorize that their evolution has been accelerated by acute survival problems, and that it has proceeded in two directions at once: aggression and intellectual insight. The aggressiveness means that their more highly civilized types are almost permanently involved in warfare. Yet their finest thinkers show a truly remarkable degree of insight and self-knowledge. It seems to us an interesting question which of the two will cancel out the other.

Our neuro-physiologist believes he knows why they are so aggressive. All brains on this planet are bi-compartmented, to permit the creature to monitor and regulate its conduct through self-criticism. Survival problems have apparently driven the human creature to go farther than this, and to devote one half of its brain to scanning the material world for dangers. The absurd result is that when they have achieved conditions of peace, in which they can afford to relax, they are unable to switch off this danger-scanning device, and can only release the tensions thus created by going out and looking for challenge – i.e. war.

The problem is increased by a robotic learning device, through which these creatures can store a remarkable amount of information derived from past experience. Unfortunately, this has become so efficient in the case of their 'civilized' beings that they are at the mercy of their mechanical reactions, and their intuitive awareness of this makes them inclined to regard themselves as machines. As we see it, this low level of self-esteem, combined with an obsessive need to seek excitement in order to feel fully alive, constitutes the greatest danger faced by this interesting species.

Now let us imagine that the same expedition has returned to earth one thousand years later. It can see from a considerable distance that the planet is passing through another of its fluctuations in climate and is far more dry than on the previous occasion. Large areas that were formerly green are now brown; some have even become deserts. The Caspian sea, for example, has dropped by several feet in the past five hundred years and is consequently a great deal smaller.

The travellers begin their survey over Australia and New Zealand, which they find almost unchanged from the earlier visit. In South America, civilization has expanded dramatically; the Mayans have now created something like an empire in the northern part of South America; in Peru there are no less than three major cultures, including the Incas. But their level is roughly that of the ancient Egyptians or Sumerians more than three thousand years earlier. The Indians of North America are still virtually Stone Age hunters.

In the islands of Japan, civilization is seen to be evolving at an unhurried but steady pace. They are a peaceable nation, these 'dwarfs' (as a Chinese traveller of 400 A.D. called them). Their farming methods have steadily improved, and they have learned the art of weaving, so they are no longer dressed in skins. They have already a rigid sense of social order and bury their noblemen in great earthen mounds. Chinese influence is strong – and the Japanese are eager to learn from their Chinese neighbours. There are, of course, local wars, and one great prince from the southern island of Kyushu has set up his capital on the Nara plain on the central island. But it seems clear that this race will not be torn apart by violent convulsions. They love nature, and their simple religion – Shinto – is basically a form of nature worship. Everyone seems to 'know his place', and they have deep respect for their aristocrats and rulers. The neurophysiologists of the team might speculate that the peaceable development of their civilization is due to the fact that the Japanese brain seems to be less 'divided' than that of Europeans; its left half seems to process intuitions and patterns as well as words and ideas so that the Japanese still possess some of that unity of the earliest human beings. Yet this may also explain why the Japanese are less inventive than the Chinese, and are so fascinated by their more turbulent neighbours.

In China, the changes of the past thousand years are dramatic. The Great Wall reveals that this land is afraid of its northern neighbours, and the walled cities show that the Chinese are also afraid of one another. In spite of the wall, Mongol raiders have swept down from the north, armed with crossbows and riding fast ponies, and have driven immense numbers of people to the south. So this continent is at present in chaos with many refugees. Yet the Chinese, like the Japanese, are a people who love tradition, and who like to think carefully before they act. Buddism has spread from India and is now as influential as Confucianism or Taoism. This is not because the Chinese are deeply pessimistic about life – they take it calmly and philosophically, neither expecting too much nor assuming the worst – but because Buddhism is a meditative religion and the Chinese feel instinctively that meditation is as important as action. They are also a practical people: they have already invented paper and porcelain, and in a few centuries will invent printing and gunpowder.

Their neighbours in northern India are enjoying a period of relative stability, although they too have suffered greatly from the Mongol invaders. Half a century earlier, their King Skandagupta defeated the Huns and drove them out of India. Under the Gupta dynasty – which began in 320 A.D. – art and literature have flourished. These Hindus are the most profoundly spiritual people on the earth. Like the Chinese, they realize intuitively that the right brain must be allowed to express itself as fully as the left; so meditation is a part of the Hindu way of life. But this unworldliness means that life for the poor is harsh and brutal. There are times when spirituality comes dangerously close to stagnation.

Arthur

As the travellers move west over Persia, it is obvious that this great country is still as powerful as it was under Darius a thousand years before. Under the Sassanid dynasty – founded by Artaxerxes (Ardashir) in 226 A.D. – the empire has remained warlike and prosperous. There have been no less than seven wars with Rome since Artaxerxes came to the throne, and there will be three more. The Persians have shown themselves a great deal more tolerant than the Christians, and allow Christians to worship within their empire. But at the moment the country is torn by religious dissension, due to a high priest named Mazdak, who has gained many converts with his puritanical and communistic doctrines, and whose followers have caused a civil war with their intolerance.

And so on once more to the Mediterranean, over the mighty city of Constantinople, with its walls and towers and its superb position looking out over the Bosphorus. In this year 500 A.D., Constantinople is being governed peacefully and well by the servant-emperor Anastasius. All these Mediterranean countries are crossed by Roman roads; the sea is still full of Roman and Byzantine ships. Yet Rome itself is ruled by a barbarian, Theodoric the Goth, who is much resented by the Italians. The last Roman emperor – the boy king Romulus – was deposed by Germans nearly a quarter of a century ago. Theodoric killed the leader of the Germans – Ordovacar – with his own hands, and ordered a massacre of his troops.

Nothing is more obvious than that this whole area has been under the sway of a mighty empire, men whose engineering works will last for more than a thousand years. (Of how many modern constructions can we say the same?) In Spain, in Greece, in north Africa, everything reveals their presence. Then where are they? They are already in the process of disappearing, like the Vandals, Huns and the Goths. Like a balloon that has exploded, their fragments now litter the Mediterranean.

The Celts have also virtually disappeared – driven into remote places such as Scotland and Wales by the barbarians – although one of their last great generals, the British Artorius (later known as king Arthur) will hold the barbarians at bay in England for another half century. In the rest of Europe, the barbarians find themselves in possession of the remains of the Roman empire, and its sheer size and magnificence makes them feel awkward and uncomfortable.

The scientists would conclude their report:

Our earlier speculations about evolution have undoubtedly been confirmed. These highly civilized people have become so obsessed with the external world that they are unable to make proper use of their inner resources. And yet they are intuitively aware that they *ought* to be exploring them, and so find themselves in a permanent state of dissatisfaction and discomfort. Our investigation has shown that these Romans succumbed to the problem of the *nouveau riche* – that is to say that the moment they became wealthy and comfortable, the moment external challenges ceased to keep them up to the mark, they became lazy and corrupt.

Fortunately, Roman materialism has caused a powerful reaction, and the empire is now dominated by a sect called Christians who are far more aware of their wasted potentialities. We predict, however, that their rather simple-minded religion, directed towards a God outside themselves and a crude system of reward and punishment after death, will eventually provoke another powerful counter-reaction that will once again direct attention towards the inner resources.

sense of destiny

For *this* was the central problem at this stage of human evolution. Man found himself stranded in the material world, like a passenger left standing on the platform when the last train has gone. Instinctively, he knew he ought to be *going somewhere*, for this internal compulsion to go somewhere has made man the most highly evolved creature on earth. And this has led to one of the major paradoxes of human history – a paradox explored by Arnold Toynbee in *A Study of History*: that men are at their very best when they are 'up against it' and at their worst when success has allowed them to relax. Herodotus has a story of how some Persians came to their King Cyrus and suggested that, now they had become conquerors, they should move to a more comfortable and pleasant land. Cyrus's reply was: 'Soft countries breed soft men.' Toynbee devotes a whole chapter (pp. 31–73 of Vol. 1) to examining the difference between hard and soft environments, and shows that the hard environments produce greatness and the soft ones weakness. In China, conditions for civilization were far easier on the Yangtse River than on the Yellow River, which was usually frozen or flooded or choked with swamps. Yet Chinese civilization came to birth on the Yellow River, not the Yangtse. In South America, the civilization of the Andes came to birth in the harsh northern desert, not in the far more pleasant part which the Spaniards called Valparaiso ('paradise valley'). And so he goes on, with example after example, showing that 'tough' countries make creative human beings: Attica and

Boeotia, Rome and Capua, Byzantium and Calchedon, Brandenburg and the Rhineland, even the Black Country and the Home Counties of England.

Now this is not, of course, a specifically human phenomenon. All wine lovers know that the best wines in the world come from areas where the grapes have to put up a struggle: in Bordeaux, they have to burrow through deep gravel, in Champagne they have to fight the cold. Good soil and good weather – as in the Rhone valley or in Italy or north Africa – produces a wine that is strong but lacking in character. Plants, like animals, are largely 'mechanical', a mass of ingrained habits that ensure their survival, but also their stagnation. Habit causes them to make no more effort than they have to. Man is the only animal on the earth who experiences an urge to 'go somewhere', to move forward. But whereas most animals are limited by habit, man is limited by habit *and* his brain. He has developed too much of an 'eye to business', coping with external problems. So that whenever these problems vanish, he finds himself becalmed and bewildered. *need for an internal life*

Clearly, what he needs to develop is an *inward eye* – an eye not merely to business but to *purpose*. It is self-evident that man is at his best when he is driven by some sense of long-term purpose, and that, conversely, he 'goes to pieces' when he lacks all sense of purpose – this explains why so many men die shortly after retiring. Our everyday purposes – keeping ourselves physically and emotionally satisfied – are too small, too fragmentary and piecemeal, to summon the best that is in us. 'They lived happily ever after' is actually a formula for mediocrity. We feel instinctively that the truly satisfying life would be spanned by one great overarching bridge of purpose. This was the instinctive recognition that was slowly transforming the world at the beginning of the Dark Ages.

in the concept of life as a pilgrimage

Let us look more closely at the way this craving for 'long term solutions' expressed itself in the life of one of the most remarkable of all visionaries: the prophet Mahomet.

A few miles from the eastern shore of the Red Sea, in the Sirat mountains of Saudi Arabia, there is a sandy and inhospitable valley. It contains a well that is fed from a deep underground source, and which consequently never runs dry. Long before the Romans set foot in north Africa it had become a regular stopping place for

eye-to-business vs eye-to-purpose

caravans and for wandering Bedouins. The well – called Zem-zem – acquired a reputation for healing the sick, so that it became a place of pilgrimage. A cube-shaped house or temple was built over it, incorporating in one of its walls a black meteoric stone that was regarded as sacred; tradition declared that this House of God, the Ka'ba, had been built by Abraham; the historian Diodorus Siculus mentions that it already existed in 50 B.C. A town called Mecca sprang up around the sacred well.

In the time of Justinian, the Arabs like most ancient peoples were pagans who worshipped many gods. It is true that they regarded Allah as the creator of the universe, but they also believed that he was surrounded by a host of minor gods and demons. Some five or six years after the death of Justinian – around 570 A.D. – a boy was born into a poor household in Mecca. His father died before his birth, and the baby was handed to a wet nurse from a nomadic desert tribe – which suggests that his health was giving some concern. (Mecca was regarded as unhealthy.) His mother died when he was six, and the child – whose name was Mahomet (or Muhammad) – fell to the charge of his grandfather, a man who was a hundred years old and who seems to have doted on the handsome and lively boy. But the grandfather died after only two years, and Mahomet was brought up in the household of his senior uncle, Abu Talib, the head of the clan.

Little is known of Mahomet's early years except that he probably worked as a shepherd. He also accompanied his uncle on trading journeys, and on one of these journeys to Syria, when he was fourteen, is said to have made the acquaintance of 'Sergius, a Nestorian monk', who told him something of the Christian religion. He must have been already acquainted with the basic elements of Christianity and Judaism; on the Ka'ba itself there was a portrait of Abraham carrying a bundle of arrows (for divination), and on a column nearby, the virgin Mary with the child Jesus.

As a young man, Mahomet became the agent and steward of a wealthy woman named Khadijah, who was some fifteen years his senior; when he was twenty-five, he married her. Their married life was a happy one, and it was to last for twenty-five years.

Both Mahomet and Khadijah were deeply religious. During the month of Ramadan, held sacred by the Arabs, they moved into a cave on the edge of the desert and spent the time in prayer and meditation. And when Mahomet was in his fortieth year, he entered a period of inner crisis. We know little about it except that it was a 'dark night of the soul', during which he experienced profound depression and believed himself to be possessed by a demon. He told his wife that he saw lights and heard noises – there were sounds like bells and a humming like a swarm of bees. He spent much time alone in a cave on Mount Hara, or wandering on the edge of the desert, calling upon God for help; he was several times tempted to commit suicide by throwing himself from a cliff. In this state, he must have wondered to which of the pagan gods he could turn for aid. And finally, there crystallized out of his torment the conviction that there was only one God, the creator of the universe – that same creator who was proclaimed by Abraham and by Jesus Christ. One day, Mahomet had a vision of a majestic being – whom he later concluded to be the angel Gabriel – who told him: 'You are the messenger of God.'

He told his wife what he had seen and heard: she believed him. But the rest of his family found it frankly incredible. Only his cousin Ali and his friend Abu Bekr were convinced. For the next three years – from 610 until 613 – Mahomet discussed his beliefs in private. Few were interested, and he made only thirty-nine converts, mostly from the young men of the town, who were impressed by his total conviction and by the force of his personality. He continued to behave like a man in torment. He would become depressed and fatigued, and begin to shiver. He would sweat like a man in a fever. Then he would speak the words he felt rising in his heart, and they were written down by his followers (Mahomet himself could not write). These early *suras* of the Koran came to birth with severe labour – Mahomet said that producing three of them, one after another, had turned his hair grey. In 613 A.D. he began to preach openly, and encountered immediate hostility.

Mahomet's uncle, Abu Talib, was head of the clan and therefore its protector; if Mahomet was killed, it could mean a blood feud. Some of the leading Meccans went to Abu Talib and offered him the price of Mahomet's blood; Talib curtly refused. But when, in 619, Abu Talib died, Mahomet found himself without a protector. The new head of the family was hostile. His wife Khadijah died at about this time – his sons had already died. He must have felt himself to be a man under a curse, who brought misfortune to all he cared for. At one point, the angry Meccans besieged Mahomet and his followers in their homes; he was forced to withdraw to a nearby oasis.

And now there came hope from an unexpected direction. The town of Yathrib – later Medina – was three hundred miles to the north. It had a large Jewish population, and the Jews were intolerant of their pagan fellow townsmen; they spoke of the coming of the Messiah who would crush the unbelievers underfoot. In 621, twelve citizens of Yathrib came to Mecca on pilgrimage, heard Mahomet preaching and became Muslims (a word meaning 'those who submit to God'). Even more came in the following year. There was a suggestion that Mahomet should go to Yathrib; but after ten years of derision and hostility, he was understandably cautious – he was, at least, making slow headway in Mecca. Some of his followers emigrated to Yathrib and were well-received; the inhabitants of the town listened to the message of Islam (meaning 'surrender'), read the verses of the Koran and decided that they would back the Prophet against the Jewish Messiah. Mahomet's enemies in Mecca heard that he had been invited to Yathrib and saw their danger; as the dictator of another town (for that is what it amounted to) he could represent a real threat. The situation was desperate enough to make them decide to ignore the prohibition against shedding blood in the sacred city. On the night of 16 July 622 A.D., assassins burst into the Prophet's house and rushed to his bedroom. They were too late. Mahomet had slipped away earlier and was now heading towards a cave in Mount Thaur, accompanied only by Abu Bekr. His flight to Yathrib – the *hijra* (or hegira) – was the turning point in his life. He arrived there two months later, on 20 September 622.

It must have been a strange and bewildering experience, to be received with interest and enthusiasm instead of angry derision. Mahomet was given a piece of land and had a house built. And he now became aware that the first business of a conqueror is organization. Legal and other ties were instituted between his followers; he himself contracted a number of marriages for this reason (tradition says ten), one of them to Abu Bekr's infant daughter. He also realized that one day his followers were going to have to fight for the right to be Muslims and began to think in military terms.

It was clear, for example, that sooner or later there would be a confrontation with Mecca. In his new, aggressive frame of mind, Mahomet decided to provoke one by sending out his followers to raid Mecca caravans returning from Syria. In fact, the year after his arrival in Medina, he himself went out on three such raids. They were unsuccessful, possibly because their movements had been betrayed. So Mahomet sent out a raiding party in the sacred month of Rajab, a time when Arab hostilities were normally suspended; the Muslims intercepted and plundered a caravan coming from Yemen. The Meccans were scandalized at this violation of the sacred month, and prepared for action. A month later, in March 624, Mahomet led a raid on another Meccan caravan; its supporting force of eight hundred men, led by Mahomet's old enemy Abu Jahl, engaged Mahomet's force – of around three hundred – at a place called Badr. And the Meccans learned what other armies would learn in the years to come: that men who fight with religious conviction may be outnumbered more than two to one and still win an overwhelming victory. Forty-five Meccans were killed, including Abu Jahl; the Muslims lost only fourteen. Although the engagement was a small one, it was perhaps the most significant in Islamic history, for it convinced the Muslims that Allah was fighting with them. It engendered the confidence that enabled the Arabs to conquer the Mediterranean.

This confidence was shaken, but not badly eroded, the following year, when a force of three thousand Meccans engaged a thousand Muslims at Uhad, near Medina. The Meccans were thrown back, but Mahomet's forces suffered heavy losses, and neither side could claim a victory. Two years later, a force of ten thousand Meccans besieged Medina, but their cavalry was unable to cross a deep trench dug by the Muslims. After a night of storm, the besiegers lost their enthusiasm and left. It was after this siege that the Muslims turned on the Jewish clan of Qurayzah, suspected of intriguing with the Meccans; the men were all executed and the women and children sold into slavery. In due course, all Jews were ejected from Medina.

Two years later, in 629, Mecca surrendered quietly as Mahomet approached with a force of ten thousand. By that time, many leading Meccans had already deserted to Medina, and Mahomet had smoothed the way to a settlement by marrying the widowed daughter of his chief Meccan opponent, Abu Sufyan. Eight years after leaving Mecca as a fugitive, Mahomet returned as a conqueror.

In the following year, Mahomet led thirty thousand men on a raid on Syria. He was demonstrating to the Arabs that, now they had achieved unity, anything was possible. It was a lesson they had learned well by the time of the Prophet's death (probably from malaria) in 632.

To understand Mahomet's achievement we have to grasp that before his time the Arabs of the Hejaz consisted mainly of wandering tribes of Bedouins who spent much of their time raiding one another; it was murderous anarchy. This explains the blood feud; it was the only way of making a man feel that if he killed some of your tribe, some of his own tribe would eventually pay the price. But it was a wasteful method of maintaining some kind of law. It meant that the Arabs stayed permanently divided.

Yet the Arabs were formidable fighters. Both the Romans and the Persians used them as mercenaries. As we have seen, the Roman and Persian empires had been at each other's throats since the time of the Seleucids around 200 B.C. And while Mahomet was establishing himself as the despot of Medina and leading raids against Meccan caravans, the new Roman emperor of Constantinople, Heraclius, was at war with the Persian monarch Chosroes II. In 626, the year after the battle of Uhad, the Persians besieged Constantinople but were thrown back. In the following year, Chosroes was murdered by his own troops. His successor soon died of plague, and then for five years there was a mad scramble of pretenders to the throne of Persia and the usual intrigues and murders. History was, of course, repeating itself. And while Romans and Persians wore one another out, the Arabs flourished and grew strong.

History also repeated its now-familiar patterns after Mahomet's death. When he died, he was master of Arabia. He was succeeded by his disciple Abu Bekr, who became first Caliph of Islam. What do successful conquerors do when they have time to sit down and survey their gains? Again, history provides us with the answer: they either squabble amongst themselves or look for more lands to conquer. The followers of the Prophet proceeded to quarrel. Many felt that Mahomet's son-in-law Ali – married to his daughter Fatima – was a more suitable candidate for Caliph. The Muslims split into followers of Abu Bekr – the Sunni – and followers of Ali, the Shi'a. Besides, many of the nomad tribes who had offered allegiance to Mahomet felt that his death ended their obligations. So the new Caliph had to go to war. It was a political as well as a religious decision; if Arabia was allowed to split apart again, it would lose its strength. If it lost its strength, then it was no longer an effective force for conquest. And if it ceased to conquer, then there would be no flow of booty back to Mecca and Medina. So there was a bitter struggle that lasted for two years, until the rebel tribes were finally brought to heel. Then Abu Bekr died and was succeeded by another close associate of the prophet, Omar. He was faced with the same alternative: expand or stagnate. He had no hesitation about throwing his energies into expansion.

The obvious enemy was the 'unbeliever' – in this case, Rome *and* Persia. And these two empires were exhausted by war. Omar's great general, Khalid, known as 'the Sword of Allah', defeated the Byzantines near Damascus and took Syria in 635. Jerusalem fell three years later. Iraq – occupied by the Persians – fell in 637, Mesopotamia in 641, Egypt in 642. And after a struggle of sixteen years, Persia itself fell to the Muslims. The citizens of most of the conquered lands welcomed the Arabs; they were tired of paying taxes to a ruler in a distant city; the Arabs at least were neighbours. Their conquest of Alexandria, and its subsequent loss when a Byzantine fleet appeared on the horizon, made the Arabs aware that they also needed ships. So they built their own fleet, and in 655 annihilated the Byzantine fleet.

Now only one major stronghold remained: Constantinople itself. In 673, the Arabian fleet blockaded Constantinople. The walls built by Constantine and his successors proved impregnable, so the Arabs prepared to wait until they had starved the city into submission. Its fall seemed inevitable.

And at this point, a single invention altered the tide of history. It was the brainchild of an architect named Callinicus, who came from Heliopolis, in Syria. He had decided that he preferred the Christian emperor to the Muslim Caliph, and moved to Constantinople – now ruled by Constantine IV. Callinicus seems to have been interested in chemistry, and in explosives. He discovered that a mixture of saltpetre, bitumen, naphtha, sulphur and quicklime could produce a flame that was almost unquenchable. The secret formula is now lost, but it seems clear that the naphtha, bitumen and sulphur were the inflammables, while the saltpetre provided the oxygen to keep it burning. When water is added to quicklime (calcium oxide), the result is immense heat. This seems to have been the basic secret of the substance that became known as 'Greek fire'. The startled Arabs found themselves facing ships that came towards them belching fire like dragons. When the fire landed on the water, it went on burning. It could be hurled through the air with catapults, in the form of balls of flax soaked in the chemical, or it could be made to roar from a copper or iron tube like a flamethrower. If Callinicus had stayed in Syria and given his invention to the Caliph, the Arabs would have been invincible. Now the Byzantines used it to scatter the Arab fleet. Men who were struck by the flames writhed in agony as their flesh bubbled and melted. When Greek fire landed on wooden decks, it burned its way through them; water only made it seethe and spit more violently. Gibbon says it could be extinguished by urine, but it is doubtful whether any Arab kept his head enough to try that interesting remedy.

The Arab navies continued returning for five years, but they never learned the secret of Greek fire. And so long as Constantinople could obtain its supplies by sea, it was impregnable. It would be several more centuries before the invention of gunpowder and cannons made the city wall obsolete.

So the Arabs retired from the fray, and in 677 A.D., the Byzantine navy destroyed the Arab fleet at Syllaeum. All Europe heaved a sigh of relief; for it had seemed by this time that the Arabs were unconquerable, and tales of their massacres had terrified everybody. (These were mostly exaggerated; when the Arabs conquered, they usually showed themselves to be tolerant rulers.) After the defeat at Syllaeum, the myth of Arab invincibility was at an end.

Unfortunately, the Arab conquests did nothing to heal the splits within Islam. The Caliph Omar was assassinated in 644; his successor, Othman, twelve years later, by followers of Ali. Muawiyah, the governor of Syria, swore to revenge Othman and led an army against Ali, who was now the Caliph. They eventually made peace, but Ali was assassinated in 661 by a dissident. Muawiyah became Caliph, and it was he who besieged Constantinople. When he died in 680, his son Yazid succeeded him, but the Shi'a – followers of Ali – felt he had no right to the position. Ali's eldest son Hasan had died some years before under mysterious circumstances, believed poisoned by Muawiyah. Now his second son, Hussein, was invited to become Caliph by dissidents in Iraq. Yazid's army defeated him in battle and his head was sent to Yazid in a basket. In 680, most of Ali's family was assassinated, including Fatima, the prophet's daughter. But the murderers missed one sickly child, who lived to continue the dynasty.

So Islam itself was torn by the same violent internal dissensions as ancient Rome, and the average life expectancy of a ruler or pretender seemed much the same as under the Caesars. Muawiyah and his son Yazid were the founders of a dynasty – the Ummayads – but this also led to further divisions and slaughter. Yazid died after only two years, and his son shortly after this. The Ummayads chose Marwan, a cousin of Muawiyah, while another candidate was favoured in Syria, Egypt and Iraq. There was a battle in 684, with tremendous slaughter of the rival candidate's forces. Marwan became Caliph, but it was the beginning of a disastrous feud which would eventually cause the downfall of the Ummayads. The Shi'a continued to hold the Ummayads in contempt, regarding them as worldly and corrupt – which, on the whole, was true. Meanwhile, Arab expansion went on slowly – rather more slowly than before the siege of Constantinople, but surely nevertheless. In 711 they invaded Spain, and others reached India – in 713 there was even an incursion into China. By 715, the Arabs were masters of Spain. Their expansion north continued until the fateful year 732, when they were finally halted at Tours by Charles the Hammer – Charles Martel. The Muslims retreated back over the Pyrenees and never reappeared in Europe. The battle of Tours was as decisive for Europe as the battle of Chalons, where Attila the Hun had been defeated in 451.

Understandably, the Christian world loathed and feared the Arabs; Mahomet's name was corrupted to Mahound and became a synonym for the Devil. And we might well raise our eyebrows at the notion that a great religious movement, whose central belief was that man should surrender himself totally to the will of God, should lead its devotees to impose their beliefs with fire and sword. This would be naive. Man is a creature with a thorn in his side, with a perpetual will to 'go somewhere'. At least, he must have the *feeling* that he is 'getting somewhere'. This is why human beings sweat and struggle and strive, instead of browsing peacefully like cows in a field. This is why all human children seem to have a perpetual craving for toys, and why human adults continue to need their own grown-up toys: colour televisions, video-recorders, fast cars etc. And when masses of men are united – particularly when these men are 'have-nots' – they instantly begin to look around for something to conquer.

will-to-meaning

many kinds of expansion

266
268

Expansion is a basic law of history. It is very regrettable, but it is so. It means, in effect, that man is a natural burglar. When a nation takes to the sea and invades another country, it is committing burglary just as surely as the thief who forces open your back window with a jemmy. The Arabs did not even have the excuse that they were converting pagans. The Persians and the Spaniards believed in God as much as they did themselves, and some small disagreement about prophets – Zoroaster or Mani or Jesus – was neither here nor there, since Mahomet himself always acknowledged these prophets as genuine. The truth is that religion only provided the cement that gave the Arabs unity; the laws of history did the rest. An Arab poet admitted as much in a poem addressed to a young Bedouin: 'No, not for paradise did you forsake the nomad life. Rather, I think, it was your yearning after bread and dates.'

So the Arabs, like the Romans and Persians before them, committed burglary all over the Mediterranean. And then, as with these earlier civilizations, the laws of history began to operate in favour of the conquered peoples – or at least, to offer them some compensation. When a 'have not' becomes a 'have', the need to commit burglary begins to evaporate and is replaced by a desire for interesting acquisitions. To begin with, the Arabs were as destructive as the Vandals; when they conquered Alexandria in 640, the general pointed to the library and said: 'If these books agree with the Koran, they are useless; if not, they are infidel. Burn them.' And the library was set on fire. When they captured Rhodes in 654, they sold the famous Colossus to a Jewish merchant. But a century later, the Ummayads were replaced by the family of the Abbasids. As usual, it was a vicious and treacherous business. Some of the Abbasids – a family who belonged to the same Koreish tribe as Mahomet – were descendants of the murdered Ali, and they gained the support of the Shi'ites by promising that, if they came to power, they would appoint a Shi'ite Caliph. From 747 until 749 there was a murderous civil war; but the rebels finally triumphed. An Abbasid named Abu-al-Abbas proclaimed himself Caliph, although he was no descendant of Ali. In 750, he invited eighty prominent Ummayads to a banquet and, while his guests were eating, signalled his men to kill them. Then the corpses were covered over and the remainder of the terrified guests instructed to go on with their meal. In his first speech as Caliph, Abu proudly referred to himself as al Saffah, the Shedder

– meaning thro' growth/expansion

+ √ will → meaning

of Blood. But under the Abbasids, the Arab state entered its equivalent of the golden age.

Its Augustus was the Bloodshedder's brother, al-Mansur, who came to power on the death of the Bloodshedder five years later. He built himself a new capital, Baghdad, in Iraq, the city of the Arabian Nights. It became the Rome of the Dark Ages, a city of silks and porcelains, linens and furs, ivory, gold and jewels, honey and dates and sherbets. And it also came to replace Alexandria as the world's centre of learning. One day in 765, al-Mansur fell ill with a stomach complaint, and was cured by a Christian monk from a monastery a hundred and fifty miles away. He was asked by the Caliph to set up a hospital in Baghdad, which he did. He also brought to Baghdad many of the books from the monastery of Jundi Shapur, Greek classics on astronomy, philosophy and ancient science. The Arabs had a practical reason for being interested in astronomy: they wanted to know in which direction Mecca lay, since all mosques had to look towards Mecca and believers had to prostrate themselves in that direction five times a day. The compass was unknown, but the Greek astronomer Ptolemy had invented an instrument called the astrolabe, for measuring the position of the stars on a rotating dial. Now al-Mansur recognized the value of this infidel science and had the Greek books translated into Arabic. Then, eight years later, a traveller from India arrived, bringing more astronomical texts, and with a new way of writing figures that was far more convenient than the Latin method. It was our modern system of placing the units in one column, the tens in the next, and so on. We still speak of 'Arabic numerals' although it would be more correct to say Indian numerals; but the Arabs brought the method to Europe.

The Arabs did far more than reawaken interest in astronomy and mathematics; they stimulated the European intellect to new labours. The ancient Greeks had been the last intellectual adventurers of Europe; the Romans had added little but their genius for engineering. And when Rome fell to Alaric in 410 A.D., Bishop Augustine of Hippo – later St Augustine – made it the occasion for a lengthy sermon on the vanity of human achievement called *The City of God*. Earthly cities are bound to fall, said St Augustine, but the aim of the Christian is to build the city of God. And he warned Christians to shun science and intellectual enquiry: 'a certain vain desire and curiosity . . . to make experiments . . . cloaked under the name of learning and knowledge.' *The City of God* became the most popular of all Christian books next to the Bible, the great bestseller of the Middle Ages, and the Christian church agreed wholeheartedly with its distrust of science. Five centuries after al-Mansur, the unfortunate Roger Bacon, a scientist of remarkable originality, was condemned to prison for daring to introduce 'certain novelties' (i.e. new ideas) into his work. The Church believed that Aristotle was the last word in scientific and philosophical knowledge.

But for these men of the desert, the works on astronomy, science, medicine, philosophy, astrology were an exciting new experience; they fell on them and devoured them ravenously. Arab mathematicians delighted in problem-solving. And although the Church was suspicious of 'novelty', it had to admit that Ptolemy's great work on astronomy, the *Almagest*, seemed to be a landmark in human knowledge. (In fact, it was basically nonsense, since Ptolemy was convinced that the earth is the centre of the universe and had to make all his calculations fit that mistaken assumption; however, it started Europe thinking about astronomy again.) So the Arabs who had burned the library of Alexandria made amends by re-awakening the European appetite for learning.

After al-Mansur died in 775 A.D., his son al-Mahdi continued his policy of encouraging the arts and sciences, and of building schools. He reigned for ten years; then came Haroun al-Raschid of Arabian Nights fame, whose reign was mostly taken up with a lengthy war with the Byzantines, who were forced to retire, licking their wounds. And Arab history in the Middle Ages reached its climax with the twenty-year reign of Haroun's son, al-Mamun the Great, in whom the Arab desire for conquest turned into a passion for knowledge. He built two observatories and a 'House of Knowledge' containing a vast library. He also became curious about that mysterious monument, the Great Pyramid, particularly when he heard a legend that it contained star maps of the ancients. His workmen hacked their way in and discovered the pyramid's various passages, and the King and Queen's Chambers; but they found no secret room with star maps. Nevertheless, al-Mansur's scholars constructed the first complete map of the heavens and another of the earth. (Both have, unfortunately, disappeared.)

The general chaos of the Dark Ages can by no means be laid at the door of the Arabs. It came about, quite simply, by the fall of Rome,

protection rackets

which left Europe to the barbarians. Apart from the Ostrogoths, Visigoths, Huns and Vandals, there were the Slavs, the Burgundians, the Franks, the Lombards and the Saxons. Many of these barbarians were basically nomads, who disliked settling in towns even when they had conquered them, and preferred to move around restlessly from area to area, exacting their taxes in food and other goods. This hardly made for stable administration. The first of the great Frankish kings (the Franks were a German tribe), Clovis, became leader of his tribe in 481 A.D. at the age of fifteen, invaded Gaul and became converted to orthodox Catholicism. Having defeated Burgundians, Visigoths, Alamanni and the Romans occupying Gaul, he set up his capital in Paris. His dynasty became known as the Merovingians, after his grandfather Merowech. But his successors soon found that it was hard work being a king if you had no real power or wealth. Without the magnificent Roman civil service, it was practically impossible to run the country and collect taxes. The next best thing was to hand over various estates to local magnates, 'counts', making them promise to supply a small army if it was needed. But this meant that the counts, in effect, became little local kings and the central king had to live off his own estate and eat his own produce. 'Taxes' were impractical, even if the counts had been willing to pay them, for there was little money in circulation; the counts would have had to pay in eggs and cabbages. When the king went for a drive, it was in an ox-cart driven by his ploughman. So in the Dark Ages, the whole of Europe was rather like Ireland in the seventeenth century: poor, barren and very provincial.

In fact, Ireland in the seventh century A.D. was a great deal ahead of most of the rest of Europe. In the fifth century, a Briton named Patrick had been captured by Irish pirates and learned their strange tongue; he went to Ireland and converted the country. The Irish, who were Celts, took to learning as avidly as the Arabs would a few centuries later, and their monasteries became miniature universities. All over Europe, it was the monasteries that preserved books and kept learning alive. Now that the Roman emperor was in Constantinople, the pope had virtually become emperor of the west; he enthusiastically encouraged rulers such as Clovis (later Latinized to Louis), who conquered in the name of the Church. The various bishops and abbots were naturally granted land; so the monks and churchmen of the Dark Ages were among the few who could count on eating a square meal every day and drinking a glass of wine. Otherwise, life in the Dark Ages was as harsh and difficult as it had been since human beings began to build cities in Mesopotamia. Most people were chronically undernourished – as disinterred skeletons show – and an enormous percentage of babies died at birth or soon after. Robber bands roamed what was left of the roads. If anyone could have remembered the good old days of Roman occupation, they would have sighed with nostalgia.

It was the 'law of expansion' – expand or perish – that destroyed the Merovingians. Clovis divided his realm between four sons, which was a mistake. The historian Morris Bishop says: 'The realm would soon have been subdivided into numerous tiny principalities had not the excess of heirs been diminished by illness (poison) and accident (murder).' (*The Penguin Book of the Middle Ages*, p. 20.) But there was nowhere for these feeble kings (*rois fainéants*) to expand to. They began to rely increasingly on their major domos – or 'mayors of the palace' – so that the real power fell into their hands. One of them engineered the kidnapping of the heir to the throne in 656, and the child, named Dagobert, was brought up in Ireland while the major domo's son occupied the throne. Dagobert managed to get back to France and take his throne back – only to be murdered as he took a nap under a tree when out hunting. Charles Martel, the man who drove the Arabs out of France, was a major domo. It was his son, known as Pépin the Short, who sent a message to the pope asking whether the throne ought to be in the hands of a hopeless incompetent; the pope answered no. So Pépin held an election and seized the throne. And Pépin repaid the pope by taking an army to Italy and inflicting a number of defeats on the barbarian Lombards, who were making life difficult for the pope. He then handed over the captured cities; they became the basis of the Papal States, and of the tremendous power and wealth that the Church would accumulate in the coming centuries.

Pépin had grasped the basic law of history, the law of expansion. He went on to expand his domain until it extended as far as the Pyrenees. And the lesson was also grasped by his son Charles, who came to the throne in 768, ruled for the next forty-six years and became known as Charlemagne, Charles the Great. He was a giant of a man, six feet four inches tall, with a drooping blond moustache, a

is the material or spiritual plane

powerful physique, and an appetite for women that compares with that of Attila the Hun – it is possible to detect a distinct note of envy in H. G. Wells's account of him in the *Outline of History*. He understood the law of expansion so well that he spent most of life fighting – his fifty-four campaigns including expeditions against Lombards, Saxons, Frisians, Danes, Avars, Gascons and the Arabs in Spain. The Saxons of north-east Germany proved particularly hard to subdue. They were pagans, who still held human sacrifices. Like most barbarians, they spent much of their time raiding and often crossed into Charlemagne's northern territory, looting and burning. Charlemagne had much the same experience with the Saxons that the Romans had had with their German ancestors. He would conquer them, set up garrisons and force them to agree to pay tribute; as soon as his back was turned, the Saxons massacred the garrisons and sacrificed some of the defenders to their pagan gods. Whereupon Charlemagne would return with his forces and inflict blood-curdling punishments. When this had been going on for more than twenty years he finally lost patience, beheaded every Saxon leader he could capture – several hundreds – and deported whole tribes to his own territories. Then he colonized Saxony with Franks. When he told the Saxons that they could choose between Christianity and execution, the English monk and scholar Alcuin – who lived at Charlemagne's court – objected that this was no way to make good Christians. But Charlemagne was right and Alcuin was wrong; the Saxons were 'converted'.

If we compare Charlemagne with some of his great predecessors – such as Constantine or Justinian – it seems clear that evolution had at last thrown up a higher type of man. He knew Latin and Greek and worked on a grammar of his native language. He was fond of music and books, collected old ballads, and filled his court with scholars and artists. He was huge, hearty, loved inviting people to dinner, and announced that anyone could come to see him to complain about injustice. During his periods at home he toured his dominions, organized local government, took an active interest in education and established new abbeys. Yet, oddly enough, he had no capital. A typical descendant of barbarians, he preferred to keep on the move – although he had a special fondness for Aachen (Aix-la-Chapelle – so named after a superb chapel Charlemagne built there). He even had a half-mile-long bridge constructed over the Rhine at Mainz.

While Charlemagne was making himself the emperor of the north, the popes continued to have problems in Rome. Placed between the still-flourishing Byzantine empire and the new Frankish empire, they seemed – and were – rather insignificant. Pope Leo III was undoubtedly something of a weakling, and was detested by the relatives of the previous pope, who felt they could provide better candidates for the throne of St Peter. In 799, some of these rowdies seized Leo in the street, announced their intention of gouging out his eyes and cutting out his tongue and, while the pope writhed and struggled, slashed at his eyes with a sword – he bore the scar on his eyelids for the rest of his life. They were interrupted by some of Charlemagne's envoys, and Leo escaped to the domain of his most powerful ally. Charlemagne heaved a sigh of exasperation; in his late fifties, he was getting tired of fighting, and probably felt that the pope was not worth fighting for anyway. But he sent Leo back to Rome with a suitable escort, the attackers were brought to trial and exiled, and order was finally restored. To signal his gratitude, Leo crowned Charlemagne emperor of the west in St Peter's on Christmas Day 800 A.D. Charlemagne became the first Roman emperor since the boy Romulus was deposed more than three centuries earlier. But he seems to have regarded the position as something of a liability. He went back north, ruled for another fourteen years, and died at his favourite palace in Aachen.

And – the refrain becomes tiresomely predictable – as soon as he died, his empire began to fall to pieces. Nothing could provide a more emphatic contradiction to the argument that Tolstoy puts forward in *War and Peace* that 'great men' are not really the driving force behind history than this constant refrain: 'As soon as so-and-so died, his empire began to collapse . . .' And the cause is usually the same: the heirs quarrel amongst themselves, newly-conquered subjects take the opportunity to revolt, and weakness turns into chaos. Two of the three sons among whom Charlemagne proposed to divide his empire actually died before they could succeed; but Charlemagne's ineffectual son Louis the Pious compensated by dividing the kingdom between four sons. At a time when it desperately needed unity, Europe was again split apart.

Even before the death of Charlemagne, there were new menaces on all frontiers. Fierce Slavic warriors swept across the Balkans and into Greece. The Arabs continued to make inroads from the south, and Charlemagne's attempt to drive them from Spain was his least successful campaign. And from the north came the most terrifying and ruthless of the new barbarians, the Vikings. These were the most frightening invaders since the Huns. To begin with, they fought like madmen – their own word for the mad frenzy they displayed in battle was to go 'berserk' – it has been suggested that they took some kind of drug before battle. Like the Saxons, they also sacrificed their enemies to their northern gods, with a particularly nasty ritual called 'the blood eagle', which consisted of sawing out a man's ribs while he was still alive, then tearing out his lungs and spreading them apart like an eagle's wings. They seemed to have no conscience and no mercy. Possibly sheer hardship made them brutal. Their long, narrow ships were scarcely bigger than large rowing boats, by modern standards, and they were quite open, with no decks, so that the thirty or so men on board had to sleep in the open. The compass had not been invented, so in cloudy weather they had to steer by instinct. When they found a promising-looking settlement near the coast, they slaughtered, raped, burned and pillaged as if to take revenge for their long nights of hardship. Our modern view of them as noble warriors would not be shared by a traveller returning to his native village and finding every house burnt to the ground and every man, woman and child murdered. Nowadays we should regard them as vermin who had to be exterminated at any cost. The Franks, English, Italians and other nations who suffered from their raids no doubt took the same view. But there was no medieval Pompey to flush the rats out of their nests. Charlemagne is said to have cried as he saw the black sails of the Vikings in the Channel, and he built forts against them. But he was dead by the time the Vikings became the scourge of Europe, and his grandsons were too weak to organize adequate resistance. Villages and monasteries simply had to be rebuilt inland, as in the days of the Mediterranean pirates.

And what was it that made the Vikings into 'criminal rats'? The question itself offers the clue: overcrowding. The forefathers of these robbers were farmers who lived in the bleak lands of the north. They cultivated the ground – where possible – but the soil was poor and thin. Their main food was meat – reindeer meat. With a few tame reindeer they could catch the wild ones. As their farms were divided amongst their children, there was not enough land to

smash & grab 'artists'

provide crops. Since they were living in a country of fiords and waterways, they took to the sea and became traders. But there was always danger from pirates, so they went heavily armed. And quite suddenly – probably within a space of a decade or so – they realized that their prosperous Frankish neighbours could be plundered . . . For Europe, the fateful 'year of the Viking' was the year Charlemagne was crowned emperor – 799.

These 'heroic adventurers' depended on a technique of hit-and-run. In head-on battles, they were usually beaten. But their swift boats had them out of harm's way before the defending army arrived. And when the army was weak, they moved in. They descended on England in the middle of the ninth century and burnt York to the ground; the king of the Northumbrians, Aelle, suffered the blood eagle sacrifice; so did Edmund, king of the East Angles. In 870 they attacked the West Saxons and marched up the Ridgeway to the Berkshire downs, where a great white horse had been cut into the turf by the Celts. The king's younger son, Alfred, led an impetuous charge against them, and by nightfall the white horse was stained with Viking blood and the ground was covered with their bodies. But the men of Wessex had no standing army; they were farmers who had to leave their land to fight the invader. So Viking forces, under their leader Guthrum, penetrated into Wessex, and Alfred – now the king – had to take refuge in the swampy country around Athelney in Somerset. English history hung in the balance. If Alfred had decided to give up at that point, England would have become an outpost of Scandinavia, and the language of modern England and America would be Danish. In fact, Alfred built a fort and began to make forays against the Norsemen. His messengers went out to call Englishmen to his standard. And in May 878, his army attacked the Norsemen at Edington, not far from the white horse, and inflicted total defeat.

The sequel is completely typical of the Middle Ages. Alfred knew the Danes were in England to stay. Three weeks after the battle, Guthrum came to Athelney with his leading men and was baptized as Alfred's godson. There followed days of feasting. When Guthrum left, he was a friend and ally. The Danes went back to East Anglia and shared out the land as farmers – their portion of England became known as the Danelaw. And Alfred went on to build himself a navy and fortified towns and to become a small scale Charlemagne of southern England.

Criminality & abstract vision

Now in a sense, the most decisive part of this story is the last part – the baptism and feasting. It was the establishment of a personal relationship that turned 'criminal rats' into good citizens. Like all criminals, the Vikings had regarded their victims as abstractions, non-persons; it was the law of xenophobia in operation. So they could pretend that moral laws were non-existent – or at least, that they did not apply to these foreigners any more than to the reindeer they ate. The moment the foreigners became 'people', the time for rape and pillage was over.

Charles the Simple of France was finally forced to adopt the same remedy in 911 A.D. The Vikings had sailed up the Seine in 845, 851, 861 and 885, pillaging Paris three times and burning it twice. In 885, they besieged the city, which held out grimly under the leadership of Odo, count of Paris; the Parisians were forced to eat dogs, cats and even rats. Finally, the king, Charles the Fat, arrived on the scene with a vast army, but was too cowardly to fight the Vikings; so he offered them 'Danegeld' and bought them off, to everybody's disgust. Naturally, the Vikings took the money and then went on to burn and loot the rest of the country. Understandably irritated, the Franks deposed Charles and made Odo king; but Odo's luck was little better and he was also forced to the humiliating expedient of Danegeld. His successor, Charles the Simple, offered the Danish leader, Rollo, the land we now call Normandy (Normans were originally Norsemen), and it was their descendants who invaded England in 1066 under William of Normandy.

Oddly enough, these same Vikings became the people we now know as Russians. They raided and traded to the north, and in 850 a Viking called Rurik made himself ruler of Noygorod. The inhabitants of Russia were Asiatics, of Mongol stock, with a tendency to lethargy and dreaminess. A combination of this Asiatic stock with Viking blood produced what we today regard as the typical Russian with slanting eyes and high cheekbones.

During this period, Europe was a bloody chaos of 'criminal rats' fighting for supremacy. The Slavs, under King Sviatopluk, held an empire that stretched from Germany to the Carpathians. Arnulf, one of the German Carolingians, resisted the Slavs with the aid of a Russian people called the Magyars (or Hungarians); it proved to be a mistake, for the Magyars were as savage and predatory as the Vikings. They were superb horsemen who could shoot accurately with a bow and arrow from the back of a galloping horse. Like the Vikings, they were cruel and destructive, burning villages and setting fire to the harvest for the sheer pleasure of spreading terror. When they raided a village, they killed all the men, mutilated the children, then tied the women on the backs of cattle and drove them off for rape and slaughter. It was the Hungarians who put an end to Sviatopluk's empire. They invaded northern Italy in 899, and when the emperor Berengar led fifteen thousand troops after them they defeated him, forced him to pay ransom money and spent another year plundering.

In the south, the threat still came from the Muslims, now known as the Saracens, who now occupied Sicily. The Abbasid empire was falling apart, but the Muslims had learned the art of seafaring and were the chief pirates of the Mediterranean. Like the Vikings, they raided and plundered far from home – although, being in the slave trade, they were less likely to slaughter their victims. In 846 they even reached Rome and sacked St Peter's. They established themselves a base on the coast of Provence and even became a menace on the Alpine passes, taking particular pleasure in seizing Christian prelates on their way to Rome and demanding large ransoms. The pilgrimage to Rome, which had been popular since the seventh century, became more dangerous than ever before. The Church tried to forbid women pilgrims to go, since males who put them up for the night were likely to demand payment in kind and the lady usually ended as the local prostitute in some remote part of France or Italy. The Arab pirates made the sea more dangerous than it had been since the days of the Cilician pirates. They practically strangled trade between Rome and Byzantium. In northern Italy, the pirates had established a fortified camp on the river Garigliano and raided as they felt inclined from Rome to the Alps. Finally, the warrior pope John X formed alliances with various princes and persuaded the Byzantine fleet to bottle up the river mouth. They besieged the impregnable fortress, starved the Arabs into submission, then went in and slaughtered every one of them. It must have been a satisfying moment, and princes and counts all over Europe must have day-dreamed grimly about doing the same to the Slavs or Magyars or Vikings on their own doorsteps. In fact, the German emperor Otto the Great did succeed in inflicting a crushing defeat on the Magyars at the battle of the Lechfeld, in 955. The Magyars then decided to settle down, occupied the land we now call Hungary, and became a nation of peaceful farmers and horsebreeders.

All this explains why, when we think of the Middle Ages, we think of castles and towers and walled cities with battlements. Walls were the only defence against the raiders. Yet gradually the raids ceased as Vikings, Magyars and Slavs settled down to farming. The Normans continued to raid all over the Mediterranean, although even they settled down after William the Conqueror became king of England – not, however, before they had retaken Sicily from the Arabs and sacked Rome (1084).

The Arabs were also in retreat. By the year 1000 – the year the early Christians believed the world would end – their power was coming to an end in Spain; in 1034 and the following year, the Byzantine fleet, manned by Scandinavian mercenaries, decimated the Arab pirates and raided Moslem strongholds in north Africa. Yet, oddly enough, this downfall of the Arabs was not particularly beneficial to Byzantium. As Baghdad grew less important, the trading routes from the east into Europe began to pass it by; and since Byzantium had been on the trading route to Baghdad, it also suffered. Besides, a new and dangerous power was arising to the east of Byzantium: the Turks. They were swiftly becoming the Vikings – or the Huns – of the Mediterranean. The reason, as usual, was the growing population. The Turks were a tough nomadic people who had few towns; but in the late tenth century they overthrew their Persian overlords and, by the year 1000 Turkestan was ruled by the 'mighty Mahmud, the victorious lord' (as he is called in the *Rubaiyat of Omar Khayyam*), who extended his empire as far as India. After the death of Mahmud in 1030, a strong clan called the Seljuks made a bid for power. They took over Baghdad, conquered Armenia from the Greeks, and finally controlled all of Asia Minor – so that the land that had been the home of Helen of Troy, and the refuge of the Cilician pirates, finally became Turkey. The clash with Byzantium was inevitable, and in 1071 the Turks inflicted total defeat on the Byzantine army at the battle of Manzikert, in Armenia. The Byzantine emperor, Romanus, was captured and ransomed, but was murdered later that year; the great Turkish leader, Alp Arslan, was also assassinated in the following year. By that time, Jerusalem had fallen to the Turks without a struggle; Damascus and Antioch followed. The Byzantine emperor, Michael IV, saw the Turks at his gates and made an agonized appeal to the pope in Rome for help. Meanwhile, Spain was again under attack, this time from a fanatical Muslim sect, the Almoravids. So just as the Christian world was getting used to the idea that the Saracens were on the run, they learned that things were worse than ever.

Two men were chiefly responsible for bringing the news to Europe (for in those days of poor communication, it might have taken years). One was the pope himself Urban II, a Frenchman. He hurried to France in 1095, asked many bishops to meet him at Clermont, and there, in a great open field, stood on a platform and told the vast crowd of Turkish atrocities against Christians in the Holy Land. In fact, there is little evidence that the Turks mistreated Christians; they were far harsher against their own dissident sects. But it was undoubtedly true that pilgrimages to the Holy Land had now become much more dangerous. When the pope called for a crusade, hundreds of noblemen fell on their knees and dedicated themselves and their property to the service of God.

The other great preacher of the crusade was a dirty, flea-infested monk called Peter the Hermit, a short, dark-haired man who rode around on a donkey. But he possessed what we would now call 'charisma', that curious power of swaying a crowd that was later to be Hitler's most remarkable asset. Men were doubly eager to listen to him since life was hard and miserable, and the idea of a visit to the Holy Land seemed a welcome alternative to ploughing for sixteen hours a day.

What followed was something of a grim farce. Most of these ignorant peasants were not quite sure who they were supposed to fight; they had a vague idea that all foreigners were heathens. In the Rhineland, thousands of men set out to join a certain Count Emich, who claimed to have wakened up one morning and found a cross branded on his flesh. Some of the pilgrims had apparently decided to follow a god-inspired goose, although it is not clear how they recognized its inspiration. Count Emich felt that butchery may as well begin at home, and ordered his followers to attack the Jews of Spier – they were to become Christians on pain of death (or, in the case of women, rape). They went on to Worms and massacred the Jews there for two days, then on down the Rhine, slaughtering Jews wherever they found them. Many now decided that they had done their Christian duty and returned home. In Hungary, other crusaders obtained permission of the king to revictual, provided they behaved themselves. They took this to be permission to pillage the countryside; a young Hungarian boy was impaled to teach him a lesson. The king declared that if the crusaders wanted to pass through his domain they must agree to be temporarily disarmed. Then the Hungarian army got its own back by massacring them. Emich himself was refused permission to enter Hungary, so the crusaders fought the Hungarians until they were all routed and massacred – Count Emich managed to escape and went back home.

Peter the Hermit's army reached Constantinople in August 1096, having stormed a town in Hungary on the way and killed four thousand inhabitants. The emperor Alexius looked at this undisciplined rabble with dismay and recognized that the pope had made a mistake in calling the crusade. His guests proceeded to loot, steal and remove the lead from church roofs. Alexius shipped them across the Bosphorus as quickly as he could. Once in enemy territory, they decided that it was time to begin converting the heathen. They stormed into several villages of Greek Christians and began torturing the inhabitants and roasting babies on spits. Another group captured a castle and discovered, to their delight, that it was full of provisions. It seemed an ideal headquarters from which to raid the countryside. A Turkish army surrounded them and made them aware that their only source of water was a spring below the castle. The crusaders were finally forced to drink the blood of their own horses, and one another's urine. Then they surrendered. Many of them agreed to become Muslims; the others were killed. The other crusaders – the ones who had successfully converted the Christian Greeks – marched off to avenge their colleagues, were ambushed in a valley and virtually wiped out. Since they had their women and many children with them, they were at a disadvantage. The Turks spared pretty girls and boys, who were carried off into slavery. Only three thousand of the twenty thousand army managed to fight their way into a disused castle, and held out against besieging Turks while a Greek sailed back to Constantinople for help. The emperor sent several men o' war and rescued them; but once back in Constantinople their arms were taken from them. That was virtually the end of the 'first crusade'.

It was obvious that something more organized was required, and the following year an army led by Godfrey of Bouillon arrived in

Constantinople. The crusaders, accustomed to the discomfort of their draughty, smoke-filled castles and rat-infested villages, surveyed this magnificent city with envious suspicion, concluded that its inhabitants must be effete and corrupt, and were with difficulty dissuaded by their leaders from trying to seize it for themselves. After some mutual hostility, the crusaders were made to swear loyalty to the emperor and were packed off across the Bosphorus. With constant skirmishes, and many deaths from heat and thirst, they struggled across Syria and laid siege to Antioch. It fell after seven months, and the crusaders massacred every Turk in the town. Then – their original army of thirty thousand reduced to a mere twelve – they marched on Jerusalem and besieged it in the heat of July. Siege towers enabled them to climb the walls. They poured into the city and began a massacre that lasted for several days. No one was spared. The Jews of the city had taken refuge in their synagogue; it was set on fire and they all burned. As Salomon Reinach says, with mild irony, in *Orpheus, a History of Religions*: 'It is said that seventy thousand persons were put to death in less than a week to attest the superior morality of the Christian faith.'

In the light of history, we can see that the success of that first crusade was actually a disaster for Europe. It convinced Christendom that the Holy Land could be turned into a kind of Papal State. The result was that over the next two centuries there were eight more crusades, most of which failed miserably. The original success was never repeated; but it inspired all the later efforts. When Turks captured Edessa in 1144, Louis VII of France led a disastrous Second Crusade. In 1174, a brilliant Arab leader named Saladin preached a jehad, or Holy War, against the Christians, and Jerusalem was retaken in 1187. A third crusade failed to retake it, but King Richard I of England succeeded in negotiating a truce allowing Christians access to the Holy Sepulchre – which had been available in any case before the first crusade. The most absurd and pathetic of all the crusades was the Children's Crusade of 1212. A twelve-year-old shepherd boy named Stephen, from the town of Cloyes, went to King Philip of France and handed over a letter which he claimed had been given to him by Christ, who had appeared to him as he was tending his sheep. The king was understandably suspicious of a letter written in modern French by a first-century Hebrew, and probably recognized the boy as an exhibitionist or a liar; at all events, he sent him away. Undeterred, Stephen began to preach, declaring that the sea would turn into dry land as the children approached, and that children, supported by God, would overthrow the Saracen army. Thirty thousand children under twelve years of age gathered at Vendôme – girls as well as boys – and, surrounded by crowds of sorrowing parents, marched off triumphantly towards Marseilles, preceded by Stephen in a gaily-painted cart. The weather was hot; many died of thirst on the way. Those who arrived safely rushed to the harbour to see the sea divide; when nothing happened, some denounced Stephen and turned back towards home. Most stayed on, hoping for a miracle. After two days, two kindly merchants offered to provide ships to take them across to Palestine. Seven vessels set sail, and the children vanished forever. Eighteen years later, a priest who had accompanied the expedition told what had happened. Two of the ships were wrecked in a storm. The other five were met by arrangement by Saracen merchants, who handed over a large sum of money to their French colleagues and carried off their purchases to the slave markets of Alexandria and Baghdad.

A German children's crusade, led by a boy named Nicholas, was slightly luckier. Fifteen thousand of the twenty thousand children died on their journey to Italy; when the sea failed to open, they were received by the pope, who told them to go home. Very few survived the return journey, and Nicholas was among those who disappeared. When the survivors straggled back to the Rhineland, angry parents demanded the arrest of Nicholas's father, who was hanged. The story deserves a place in this criminal history of mankind largely on account of the criminal stupidity of the parents in allowing the children to go.

The Children's Crusade inspired a fifth crusade. 'The very children shame us . . .' the pope declared. So an army embarked for Egypt, rejected excellent terms from the Saracens, including the surrender of Jerusalem – the Christians wanted money too – and forced the sultan to fight them. His army proved stronger than the Christians, so the crusaders were forced to make terms and go back to Europe. And sixth, seventh, eighth and ninth crusades were equally abortive. Far from freeing the Holy Land from the Saracen, the crusades ended with the Turks entrenched in the Danube Basin.

The Saracens conquered in another way. Those ignorant peasants and equally ignorant nobles who left their homes in 1096 had never looked beyond the boundaries of their own villages. When they were not fighting with the heathen, they were now learning that the Muslims were as honourable and courteous as good Christians, and a great deal more cultivated than most. For thousands of country-bred louts, the crusades were a kind of university. When they came to an end, Europe had ceased to be a provincial backwater.

Six

ASSASSINS AND CONQUERORS

In September 1298, a few years after the end of the ninth crusade, there was a sea battle between two fleets belonging to the rival trading ports of Genoa and Venice. It ended in the humiliating defeat of the Venetians – the commander committed suicide by dashing his head against a bench – and the capture of their fleet. Among the captured sailors was a man named Marco Polo, who was thrown into jail in Genoa. There he found himself sharing a cell with a Pisan called Rusticiano, who had been there since some earlier battle. Rusticiano was a writer of romances, and when Marco Polo began telling him stories of his extraordinary travels in China – the land of the great Kubla Khan – Rusticiano begged him to write it down. So Marco sent for his travel notebooks and, with the aid of Rusticiano, wrote an account of his adventures. He took the manuscript with him when he left prison, and – in spite of the fact that printing had not yet been invented, and books had to be copied by hand – it was soon being read from end to end of Italy.

Regrettably, it was not read for educational reasons. No one believed Marco's tales of his travels with his father and uncle; his contemporaries assumed it was a novel. Marco was called sarcastically 'Marco Millions', because his book mentioned such vast distances and huge sums of money; the book itself became known as *The Million*. On his deathbed a quarter of a century later, Marco's friends begged him to admit that the book was mostly lies. 'I have not told half of what I saw,' he said irritably. And in carnivals thereafter, there always appeared a clown called Marco Millions who told preposterous lies. It was many centuries before scholars recognized that Marco Polo was a painstakingly truthful man.

One of Marco's least credible stories concerned a sinister being called the Old Man of the Mountain. This old man, whose name was Aloadin, lived in Persia, and was regarded by his people as a prophet. He inhabited a fortress at the head of a valley, and was rich enough to turn the valley into an enormous and beautiful garden, full of pavilions and palaces, trees bearing every kind of fruit and brooks flowing with wine and milk as well as water. The pavilions were inhabited by beautiful dancing girls. It was, in fact, a very passable imitation of the paradise promised by the prophet Mahomet.

When the Old Man wanted somebody killed – Marco Polo does not explain why – he would order one of his followers to carry out the assassination, promising that his reward would be an eternity in paradise. And the man would unhesitatingly sacrifice his life to carry out the order; for he was convinced that he had already tasted paradise. The cunning old man had all his trainee assassins drugged and carried into the garden; when they woke up they found themselves surrounded by beautiful girls, who plied them with food and wine and offered their favours. After a few days, the young man was drugged and carried back to the castle. He would now be impatient to sacrifice his life to regain paradise . . .

The would-be killers, says Polo, are called 'Ashishin', and that word provides the clue to the real identity of Aloadin, the Old Man of the Mountain. The castle really existed; it was called Alamut, meaning Eagle's Nest, and is perched on a rock in the Elburz mountains of Iran. There *was* probably some form of landscaped garden below the castle, in the valley, for a narrow slit in the rock of Alamut leads to a green enclosure with a spring. The Old Man of the Mountain was called Hasan bin Sabah, and it was through him that the word 'assassin' entered the European vocabulary. It is derived from 'hashishim', for it was also widely believed that his followers nerved themselves to kill – and be killed – by smoking hashish.

Hasan bin Sabah was born about the year 1030, in the town of Rayy, near modern Teheran; his family were Shi'ite Muslims – that is, Muslims who believed that the prophet's cousin Ali should have become the first Caliph instead of Abu Bekr. Hasan was deeply interested in religion, and became involved with a sect called the Ismailis who had broken away from the Shi'ites.

We have seen that the Abbasids – who were orthodox Muslims – had gained power by promising to support a Shi'ite Caliph, then failed to redeem the promise. By the year 1000, the Shi'a and the Sunnites – orthodox Muslims – were no longer so bitterly opposed.

The real opposition came from the Ismailis, who had set up their own rival dynasty, the Fatimids, with its own Caliph. (Fatima, the prophet's daughter, had been killed in the massacre of Shi'ites in 680 A.D.; but a sick boy named Ali ibn Husayn had survived to carry on the line). By the time of Hasan bin Sabah's birth, it looked as if the Ismailis were going to be the winners in the Islamic power struggle – but this was before the Seljuk Turks appeared on the scene and lent their support to the Abbasids.

Hasan seems to have been a late developer. He was in his thirties when a serious illness made him decide to become an Ismaili; he took the oath of allegiance in 1072. Four years later, he had to leave his home town – no doubt for preaching Ismaili doctrines – and made his way to the newly-built Ismaili capital, Cairo. There he became a supporter of the Caliph's eldest son – and presumptive heir – Nizar. Political – and/or religious – intrigues led to his expulsion from the capital. One biography says that he was sentenced to death, but that just before his execution one of the towers of the city collapsed; it was seen as an omen and he was exiled instead. The ship on which he was deported ran into a violent storm; Hasan stood calmly on the deck and declared that he could not possibly die until he had fulfilled his mission. In fact, the ship was wrecked in Syria, but Hasan escaped. He finally arrived back in Persia in 1081. By now in his late forties, he had become an impressive figure, a man with a ravaged face, burning eyes and a tone of total conviction. For the next nine years he travelled and preached, gaining an increasing horde of followers. And in 1090 he came to the castle of Alamut and decided that this was the fortress he was looking for. If political intrigues prevented Nizar from becoming the next Fatimid Caliph – as seemed likely – then Hasan would need a firm base from which to conduct his own campaign.

He achieved his aim with remarkable ease. The castle was owned by an orthodox Muslim. Hasan's preaching converted the surrounding villages, then his preachers became guests at the castle and converted the servants. Hasan was smuggled into the Eagle's Nest in disguise. One morning, the owner woke up to be told that he had been dispossessed. He was politely shown the door and handed a generous sum in compensation.

Hasan ruled like a patriarch. His followers seldom saw him. The rule was strict. One of his sons was caught drinking wine and executed. Hasan lived frugally, wrote books, and plotted how to overthrow the Abbasids in Baghdad. The first problem was to undermine the Seljuk Turks who supported them, and who were now the masters of Persia. Little by little, Hasan extended his religious empire. He proved to be as good a general as the prophet himself – his greatest ally being the hatred of the Persians for the Turks. His preachers – called *dais* – won over the surrounding villages. He extended his influence to an area called Quhistan in the south-east, and the Turks were overthrown in a popular uprising. The Turks besieged him in Alamut, but it was impregnable – as he had known it would be.

As a general he had one major problem. His followers were devoted – fanatically so – but they were few in number compared to the Turks. In 1092 he decided upon the answer: to strike down his enemies one by one, making use of the total obedience of his disciples.

We have seen that the Seljuks established their power when they defeated the Byzantine army at the battle of Manzikert in 1071; but their leader, Alp Arslan, died a year later and his son Malik Shah came to the throne. Malik's Grand Vizier was a man called Nizam al-Mulk – who, as it happened, had been at school with Hasan bin Sabah, as well as with the mathematician and poet, Omar Khayyam. Nizam had set Omar to the task of revising the calendar. The Arab chroniclers tell a story to the effect that when Nizam became Vizier in 1073, both Omar and Hasan came to him asking for jobs, and Hasan was given a position at court; but his thirst for power soon became apparent, and Nizam sacked him. It is just possible, for in 1073, Hasan had not yet set out on his travels to Cairo.

Twenty years later, Nizam was Hasan's most dangerous enemy, the man he would most like to see dead. In October 1092, during Ramadan, Nizam had finished giving audience to various suppliants and was carried out of the tent towards the tent of his womenfolk. A man in the garb of a Sufi – a holy man – came forward and was allowed to approach the litter. He pulled a knife from his clothes and drove it into Nizam's heart. A few moments later, he was himself killed by Nizam's guards. When Hasan heard the news, he chuckled with elation. 'The killing of this devil is the beginning of bliss.'

It seems likely that when Hasan planned the murder he had no other aim in view than to get rid of a 'traitor', but that now he suddenly realized that he had an infallible method of extending his power. Marco Polo was no doubt mistaken: it was unnecessary to persuade his followers to kill with a 'glimpse of paradise'. They were delighted to offer their lives for their prophet.

Hasan's assassins (or, of course, as they called themselves, Ismailis) were the first terrorists. To their enemies, they were vicious criminals trying to overthrow society; to their supporters and converts, they were a small but highly trained army, overthrowing oppression by the only means at their disposal. And in the years that followed, the list of victims was a long one, and included anyone who had dared to speak openly against their doctrines – princes, governors, generals and religious opponents. A point came where no one in authority dared to go out without armour under his robes. One victim was stabbed as he knelt in the mosque at prayers surrounded by his bodyguards. A chief opponent woke from a drunken sleep to find a dagger driven into the ground close to his head, and a note saying 'That dagger could just as easily been stuck in your heart.' He decided to reach an understanding with Hasan.

With successes like this, we might assume that Hasan would become master of Persia, possibly even the new Caliph in Cairo. In fact, everything went against him. When the Caliph died, it was the younger brother of Nizar – Hasan's candidate – who came to the throne, and Nizar and his sons were killed in the squabbles that followed. Ismailis infiltrated the armies of the new Turkish sultan Berkyaruq, who had formed an uneasy alliance with Hasan; in self-defence, he began to persecute the Ismailis. When Hasan's other major stronghold was taken and the Ismaili leader flayed alive, it had to be all-out war – a war Hasan was bound to lose. During the last thirty years of his life, he watched his empire crumble. The assassinations continued – he even extended his arm as far as Syria and Egypt – yet his situation remained basically unchanged; he was virtually taking on the whole Arab world. And the sequel to one of his last assassinations reveals the extent of that failure. In 1121, Hasan finally succeeded in getting his revenge on the vizier al-Afdal, the man who had frustrated Nizar's chances of becoming Caliph. Oddly enough, the new Caliph was delighted – he had grown tired of the vizier's overbearing manners. So he sent Hasan a letter asking him why he did not return to the fold. In addressing such a suggestion to a man of Hasan's fanatical conviction he might be seen as inviting a rebuff. Yet Hasan seized on the idea with relief. In a sense, it was his admission of defeat. The reconciliation never took place – the new vizier assured the Caliph that he was next on the assassination list, which was almost certainly untrue, since Hasan had no motive for killing a man who was offering him friendship. But it served to make the Caliph change his mind. Hasan died three years later, in 1124, at the age of ninety. The sect continued in existence and established a base in Syria – one of its most spectacular successes was the murder of the crusader Conrad of Montferrat, king of Jerusalem, in 1192; but eventually they were stamped out – in Persia by the Mongols, in Syria by the Sultan of Egypt, Baybars.

Hasan's greatest mistake was to order the assassination of Nizam al-Mulk. This was the real turning point in his career. For a man who kills by stealth cannot be trusted. He inspires the same kind of exaggerated horror as a poisonous snake or spider. And the comparison establishes precisely why the terrorist method carries the seed of its own downfall. The snakes developed poison because they are among the most defenceless of creatures. Anyone who has ever kept snakes will know that they are, in fact, rather amiable and unaggressive creatures who do not deserve their reputation as vicious monsters. But a poisonous snake will strike if stepped upon or frightened, so human beings cannot afford to lose their fear of snakes. Once a man has placed himself in this category – labelled 'dangerous and untrustworthy' – he can abandon all hope of achieving his aims by normal means. If he is a politician, he has guaranteed his own failure. The story of the assassins is a parable in how *not* to go about achieving power.

But the lesson of the assassins goes beyond the mere question of ends and means and allows us to grasp the basic question of the nature of criminality. Hasan was, by any definition, a Right Man. His religious sincerity is not in question; but he placed his grimly obsessed ego at the service of his religion. He was personally convinced that he was right; everything else followed. Those who opposed him were wrong and deserved to die. It is a moot point whether it made the slightest difference whether Nizar or his younger brother became Caliph; it is even a moot point whether it makes the slightest difference that a believer refers to his deity as Jehovah, Allah or Ahura Mazda. But even this is not the issue. The issue is that man is capable of reaching out towards a freedom that

the threshold creature

transcends his everyday limitations, and that saints and prophets, poets and artists, scientists and philosophers, all share this aim to a greater or lesser degree. The greatest enemy of this transcendence is the ego with its petty aims and convictions. It is true that we cannot live without the ego; a person without an ego would be little more than an idiot. Another name for ego is personality, and in artists, saints and philosophers, the personality is a most valuable tool. Neither St Francis nor Beethoven nor Plato would have achieved much impact without their personalities. But the personality is a dangerous servant, for it has a perpetual hankering to become the master. Every time we are carried away by irritation or indignation, personality has mastered us.

And this, we can see, is the basic theme of history, its most constant pattern. Civilization was the outcome of man's religious urge – for the first cities grew up around temples. Religion has continued to be perhaps the most dominant theme in human history. Yet practically every major religious movement has changed its nature as its followers have fought amongst themselves. Why could those early city-dwellers not have lived in peace and prosperity, tilling the ground and worshipping their gods? They had what all animals crave most – security. But sooner or later, some minor squabble would blow up between small groups of rival citizens, and then all their fellow citizens would feel outraged to hear about the affront; every ego would rise up on its hind legs and cry out for revenge. (Rabelais satirizes it in *Gargantua* when a war flares up over a quarrel between shepherds and bakers about cakes.) And the human ability for sympathy and communication instantly becomes a disadvantage as everyone feels that he himself has personally received the insult. Nothing heals more slowly or festers more persistently than a bruised ego. New resentments supplement the old ones, and soon both sides are convinced that the only answer lies in the total humiliation of the other.

The Assassins furnish a typical example, but the history of Christianity could offer a thousand more. As soon as Pépin gave the popes a basis of power by making them a present of the first Papal States, the popes became as violent and predatory as any emperor. Two and a half centuries later, the German emperor Otto the Great set out to create the Holy Roman Empire, and pope and emperor instantly came into head-on collision; the pope lost, and was deposed

ego must be servant not master

identifying with evolutionary perspective

Nb factor in history

civilization & religion

by Otto, who replaced him with his own man. The struggle with the popes was continued by Otto's successors. A century later, a pope named Hildebrand – Gregory VII – came to the throne with the conviction that the pope should be the temporal as well as the spiritual head of Christendom, and that he ought to choose emperors rather than vice versa. He could, said Gregory, interfere as he liked with the laws of any Catholic country, and his papal decrees should automatically overrule any decree of king or emperor. He sent messengers to all the European courts informing the kings and emperors of these new rules. Henry IV of Germany, the Holy Roman Emperor, was outraged by this presumption. He called a synod of German bishops at Worms and informed Gregory that he had been deposed. Whereupon Gregory used the most formidable weapon in his armory: excommunication. In the Middle Ages, it was the most terrifying penalty the Church could impose. For the medieval intellect was curiously static (this was before the crusades); every Christian accepted without reservation that the wicked would suffer an eternity of horrible torments in hell, and also that if a man sinned, only the Church could remove the burden of sin and guarantee that he would still get to heaven. This was not regarded as philosophy or speculation or religion, but simply as fact, like the wetness of water. And since priests spent a great deal of time telling their congregations about the unpleasantness of hell, most people were terrified of the idea, and duly grateful to the Church for guaranteeing that they would avoid it. To be governed by an excommunicated king was almost the equivalent of being governed by the devil. The nobles began to plan Henry's overthrow. He had no alternative than to climb down, swallow his pride and humbly beg the pope's forgiveness. Gregory was spending January in a castle at Canossa, near Parma. Henry went there in the garb of a pilgrim, barefoot, to beg forgiveness. The pope kept him waiting in the snow for three days before he let him in and granted absolution. To add insult to injury, the pope gave his support to a Swabian duke who had revolted against Henry. This was too much. Henry fought the duke and killed him, then marched to Rome with an army; Gregory was forced to flee to Salerno, where he died in exile. Henry replaced him with his own candidate.

All this violence did no one any good. When Henry marched into Italy, Gregory called upon the aid of a Norman ally – the adventurer

1c. *the Germans always chafed against the papacy*

Robert Guiscard, who was in the process of freeing Sicily from the Arabs. Guiscard marched on Rome with a huge army which included Saracens, and when the Romans rose in an anti-papal riot, Guiscard's army sacked Rome again (1084), with the usual bloodshed, rape and looting: a large part of the city was burned. As a consequence, Gregory became so hated that he was forced into exile.

The violent and unpleasant consequences of the quarrel reverberated on for another century. The popes were convinced that their spiritual power ought to involve earthly dominion; the German emperors thought – rightly – that earthly dominion was their affair. The quarrel became fiercer still under the emperors of the Hohenstaufen family (the 'Staufer emperors'). Frederick I (known as Barbarossa, or Redbeard) tried to add Italy to his empire, and might have succeeded if he had not been drowned on the third crusade with King Richard of England. His grandson Frederick II – known as *stupor mundi* (wonder of the world) because he was one of the greatest scholars of his day – tried even harder to seize the pope's power for himself, and was twice excommunicated as well as being denounced as the Antichrist. But to the pope's delight, he died of a sudden fever in 1250; to the pope's even greater delight, his son Conrad died when he was invading Italy. The pope now presented Sicily to the Frenchman Charles of Anjou. The Sicilians had not much liked the 'Staufer emperors', but they disliked the French even more and rebelled in favour of a Staufer descendant. Charles won the fight. A boy called Conradin, grandson of *stupor mundi*, tried to regain his inheritance but was also defeated; he was publicly beheaded – an act that shocked the whole of Europe. And rebels in Sicily were crushed with particular violence, an act that made them loathe the French with a deep and unquenchable hatred.

The bloody climax erupted on Easter Monday 1282, in Palermo, Sicily. The Sicilians were in a rebellious mood; the king's men were touring the island and seizing all stores of grain to supply an expedition against Constantinople. In front of the Church of the Holy Spirit, people were waiting to attend Vespers. Some French officials wandered into the square; they had been drinking and were in a merry mood. The crowd glared at them but did nothing. Then a sergeant named Drouet threw the match into the powder keg by grabbing a pretty married woman and trying to take liberties. Her enraged husband snatched out his knife and stabbed Drouet to death. The other Frenchmen drew their swords; the Sicilians drew their daggers, and within minutes, all the French were dead. The Sicilians realized that this would mean more executions. So they rushed through Palermo shouting 'Death to the French'. Frenchmen were killed on the streets; then the Sicilians poured into inns frequented by the French. Women and children were killed too; the Sicilians were in a mood in which they wanted to exterminate every Frenchman in the world. They even broke into the monasteries and dragged out all foreign friars; they were ordered to pronounce '*ciciri*', a word the French found difficult; anyone who stumbled or stuttered was slain. The French soldiers were easy to kill because most of them had been out drinking all day. Two thousand men, women and children were killed that night. Ironically, the French flag was replaced by the German eagle – the Sicilians had hated the Germans when they were rulers. The governor escaped to a nearby castle, but as he was parleying about surrender someone shot him dead with an arrow and the rest were massacred. Palermo declared itself a Commune. So did other towns as their citizens heard of the massacre and rose up against their French occupiers. Charles of Anjou was forced to call off his expedition against Constantinople. The citizens of Messina – descendants of those ancient pirates who had slit the throats of all the men and married the women sixteen centuries earlier – beat off all the French attempts to repossess the island and eventually offered the throne to a Spaniard who was related by marriage to the Staufer emperors. So a hundred-year-old squabble came to an uneasy resolution.

But if we look for a moment past the endless complications of loyalties and territorial claims and go straight to the heart of the matter, we can see that this was not really an ideological struggle between spiritual authority and the ambition of emperors. The underlying reality of the quarrel is also the underlying reality of the rise and fall of the assassins: grimly inflated egos convinced that they are arguing about spiritual issues or matters of principle when they are simply dominated by their own emotions.

As we have seen, the Christians were fully aware of this problem. They had always recognized the dangers of the ego, with its sins of pride and self-righteous resentment. From the time of Constantine, there had been movements within the Church that warned about the dangers of worldly power and tried to show by example how

Christians ought to live: the hermits and desert fathers, the whole early monastic movement and dozens of solitary rebels – both women and men – who were later recognized as saints. In the tenth century, the papacy reached its lowest point so far – a period of fifty years that is known as the 'pornocracy'; the office was simply bought and sold. Pope Sergius III had a mistress called Marozia, who made sure her bastard son became Pope John XI; both she and the pope were thrown into jail by another of her bastards; but in due course, her grandson became Pope John XII. (He was the one who asked Otto the Great for help, then promptly betrayed him and was deposed.) All this brought about a strong reaction. In France, a new monastic order was founded at the Abbey of Cluny that called for new standards of spirituality. But it also recognized that a monk's duty was not simply to plant potatoes and make cider; he ought to devote himself to prayer and study – even study of the pagan writers – and to bringing Christian ideals to the common people. So just at the time that the election of popes fell into the hands of the German emperors, a great new movement of religious reform spread all over Europe.

And here we encounter the real absurdity. When the abbots of Cluny insisted that a monk should devote himself to prayer, meditation and study, they had recognized instinctively that human evolution is a matter of inner-development. This is the only true answer to the murderous violence of the power-hungry ego. When a man is totally absorbed in intellectual – or spiritual – discovery, the ego relaxes and then falls asleep.

Yet the Church was totally opposed to intellectual discovery. Convinced that man is a wicked sinner whose only salvation lies in the grace of God, the popes and bishops denounced intellectual speculation as a waste of time. It could only make a man proud of his own abilities and endanger his eternal salvation. It was not that the Church was afraid of losing its hold on the human mind. It genuinely believed that the message of Jesus – as interpreted by St Paul – was the total, self-sufficient answer to the riddle of human existence. Humankind was miserable because Adam had sinned, and the result was death and misery. But the Son of God had died on the cross to redeem mankind from original sin. The Church was an organization established by Jesus to make sure that all men had a chance of salvation, of getting to heaven when they died. That was all that mattered. Book-learning was quite irrelevant. Philosophy and natural philosophy (as they called science) were both a waste of time. In fact, they encouraged man to think that he had the power to make up his own mind on questions of morality, and so endangered his soul. Leaders like Hildebrand believed sincerely and deeply that all men were ignorant children and that they were the spiritual fathers of mankind.

So the Church gave with one hand and took away with the other. Man must try to live the 'inner life', but he must on no account try to think for himself. The result was that the human intellect marked time for a thousand years. When the Church rediscovered the works of Aristotle – through the Arabs – in the eleventh century, he was seized upon with delight and voted a kind of honorary Christian. The reason was simply that he had apparently explained practically everything, from physics to morality, and the existence of his works gave no one any excuse for indulging in speculative thinking. The answer to every possible question could now be found either in the Bible or Aristotle. Aristotle explained the physical world; the Bible explained the spiritual world. What more was there to know? And if monkish philosophers – such as Peter Abelard – still felt the need to exercise their minds, they could apply themselves to explaining how the two worlds fitted together, and how God revealed His eternal goodness by making everything exactly as it is and not otherwise.

So the medieval world was a strangely static place, rather like a waxworks. People stayed in the place where they were born – unless they happened to be peddlers – because there was no reason to go anywhere else. Besides, travel was very difficult because there was almost no money in circulation. Only the great lords handled gold – and even they only occasionally. In his own castle he had no need for gold; his tenants brought him the produce he needed, and the beef came from his own herds. The common people made their own clothes, ate their own eggs and cabbages, drank their own milk and cider. It was the crusades that changed all that. If a crusader was making his way to the Holy Land, he needed gold – he could hardly take a dozen cartloads of cabbages and eggs to pay his way.

Italy, of course, had gold, for – apart from Byzantium – it was the most cosmopolitan place in the world. The pope owned vast estates – far too vast for his tenants to pay him in produce; he had to be paid in gold. So when the crusaders made their way through Italy, they

Frederick the II

took advantage of the Italian banking system. A bank (or banc) was a table, behind which sat a moneylender prepared to give gold (or, as the system became more sophisticated, letters of credit) in exchange for mortgages or documents that promised repayment with interest. Some crusaders paid for their passage by placing their soldiers and horses at the disposal of the banker. In the fourth crusade, the crusaders first of all stormed the city of Zara, an Adriatic port, and returned it to the Venetians, then went on and stormed Constantinople, sacked the city and gave half the spoils to Venice. The cities of Italy that lay on the route of the crusaders became very rich during the nine crusades. But their development was not entirely to the advantage of the popes. For riches bring luxury and leisure – as in ancient Rome – and leisure brings a need for excitement, for travel, for new ideas. The 'wonder of the world', emperor Frederick II, had spent his childhood and youth in Sicily acquiring his taste for learning and freethinking in that island where Arabs and Christians had lived in harmony for two centuries. This is why he was not unduly perturbed when the pope excommunicated him; he was relatively certain that the Church is *not* essential to salvation – for if it is, then all those highly intelligent Muslims are damned, and that cannot be true.

And now we can begin to see what an extraordinary cataclysm was about to occur. Scepticism like Frederick's was as far as it could be from the total belief of the popes. Absurd as it sounds, Frederick's guardian during his early years had been Pope Innocent III, one of the most fanatical of the crusading popes. He believed in his spiritual mission with a grim, humourless intensity, and took it for granted that one of his major tasks was to crush all unbelievers. He reserved his deepest loathing for a sect called the Cathars – one of those 'purist' reform movements that had sprung up in opposition to the obvious corruption of the Church. Cathars were not unlike the Quakers of a later century; their observances were simple, their lives rather ascetic. Like the Persian prophet Mani, they believed that everything to do with the spirit is good and everything to do with the world is evil. In which case, of course, God could never have created the world; it must be a creation of the Evil One. Jesus could not have had a physical body, and the crucifixion must have been some kind of mirage. These doctrinal differences, which strike us as harmless enough – there are a dozen modern Christian sects with far stranger views – seemed to Innocent III a guarantee of damnation. Toulouse was the centre of this heresy, and the pope excommunicated its ruler, Count Raymond. He sent inquisitors to sniff out heresy, and one of Count Raymond's men assassinated the papal legate (or ambassador). For two days, the pope was so angry that he could not speak (a sure sign of a Right Man). When he recovered his voice, he shouted for a crusade against the heretics. This was unheard of – a crusade against Christians. The king of France refused to have anything to do with it. But dozens of knights thought it would make excellent sport – especially as it was only to last forty days. They besieged the town of Béziers and massacred its twenty thousand inhabitants, although many were not Cathars. Town after town was reduced in the same way – including Toulouse itself. The 'crusade' dragged on for decades, and ended with the siege of the fortress of Montségur in 1243 and the burning alive of two hundred people who refused to renounce their faith. The Church stamped out Catharism as the Nazis tried to stamp out the Jews – by mass extermination.

So it is one of the ironies of history that Innocent III should have been the guardian of the young Frederick, and no doubt direct contact with that dogmatic and narrow-minded old man convinced Frederick that the Church could not possibly be the only repository of truth. Frederick was the first sign of a new intellectual attitude; he was, in fact, the first of the 'Renaissance men'. His attitudes and those of the pope were as far apart as fire and ice. Sooner or later, there was bound to be an enormous explosion. It is satisfactory to record that when Frederick came to power he flatly declined to burn heretics, or even to allow priests freedom from taxation and from the jurisdiction of civil courts.

This particular battle ended, of course, with the death of Innocent in 1216, but continued a decade later with equally violent clashes between Frederick and Gregory IX then with his successor Innocent IV. But the real struggle was between two different currents of human evolution: religious authoritarianism and scientific enquiry. There can be no doubt that the great religions – Buddhism, Christianity, Islam – had taken mankind an immense step beyond the kind of mindless materialism that had been the downfall of Rome. But all religions begin like a mountain stream, and slowly turn into a rather muddy river. The 'crusade' against the Cathars was a sign of how far Christianity had turned into a kind of 'closed shop', a merely authoritarian dogma. Innocent III was the first pope to establish Inquisitors – the Dominicans – to root out heresy and burn the rebels. He was, in effect, screwing down the lid of a pressure-cooker. Sooner or later, it was bound to explode.

Another 'purist', St Francis of Assisi, succeeded in remaining within the fold – although it was touch-and-go for a while and some of his followers were later burnt as heretics in Marseilles. But one of the stories concerning St Francis helps to pinpoint precisely what was happening in the final years of the Middle Ages. Francis Bernadone was the son of a rich businessman of Assisi – a member of the newly rising class that would undermine the Church. Legend declares that he fell in love with a beautiful woman, but that when he pressed his suit she pulled down her dress and revealed that one of her breasts was eaten away with cancer. It made him aware of the vanity of human desires and took him a step closer to recognizing his mission. We find it easy enough to understand his reaction. He had, in effect, been converted from frivolity to seriousness. He felt an urge to turn his back on his futile life of dandyism and find some purpose into which he could channel his enormous energies. We can also see that his reaction *might* have been to seek out the best physician he could find and study the problem of cancer. (As it was, he spent three years tending lepers.) Instead, he created his movement of 'poor friars'; he had, in effect, taken a backward step to the hermits in the desert. And this same retrogressive tendency is also symbolized by his positive loathing of money; when his friars brought donations, they had to bring them in their mouths and drop them into a heap of dung, to remind themselves that money was no more than excrement. We can understand his point – his father was probably obsessed by money and he took the opposite stance – and we can also see that he was taking his dislike too far. The circulation of money was the greatest single factor in freeing the mind of man from the stagnation of the Middle Ages. Francis's heart was in the right place; it was his head that needed examining.

And while popes were hurling excommunications, Dominicans were torturing suspected heretics and Franciscan friars were walking the roads, the really important changes were taking place on another level. Inventions were transforming human existence. The plough of the ancient world was basically a pointed stick, which was attached to some kind of frame behind an ox; then it was pulled along to scratch the surface of the ground. In the Middle Ages, someone realized that a knife would cut much deeper. A deep cut on its own would be of no particular use, but if some kind of twisted board could follow behind the knife, it would split open the cut and turn the earth sideways. And the long furrows that resulted allowed the water to drain away, so that a field could be ploughed even when it was wet.

The chief problem with the new plough, which had wheels on the front, was that the harness – which passed around the ox's chest – was liable to strangle the animal. Around 900 A.D. someone thought of the answer: a rigid collar or frame that would transfer the strain from the chest to the shoulders. Together, these two inventions revolutionized agriculture, and so provided food for an increasing population. Increasingly large horses were developed – for war as much as agriculture – and this presented another problem: their hoofs tended to split when they were heavily loaded or pulling a great weight. The metal horseshoe provided the answer, at about the same time the horse collar came to Europe.

One of the biggest problems for early sea traders was that they had to wait for the wind to blow in the right direction. In the Mediterranean, the Carthaginians had taken advantage of the fact that the wind blows six months one way and then six months the other, to make their voyages in the proper season. The old sails were, of course, strips of square canvas. Then the Arabs invented a triangular sail that could be fixed to a movable boom; it could be moved around to catch the wind so the ship was no longer forced to sail the way the wind happened to be blowing. Mariners soon made the incredible discovery that they could actually sail into the wind by allowing the wind to strike the back of the sail. The triangular – or lateen – sail arrived at about the same time as the crusades, and it meant a sudden dramatic increase in commerce.

There was still the problem of steering. In the year before the birth of Francis of Assisi – 1180 – a travelling English monk came upon a magnetized needle that floated on a cork, and always pointed the same way. A century later, the Spanish king Alfonso the Wise – who had also commissioned a great chart of the stars – decreed that all his ships should carry the 'magnetic compass'. Sailors no longer had to rely on the stars to navigate.

In the time of Charlemagne, someone realized that a handle could be attached to a circular grindstone, and that this device greatly assisted the sharpening of knives, scythes and ploughshares. This may have stimulated people in looking for new ways of using wheel-power. The simple watermill had been known since Roman times – the wheel with buckets, or slats of wood, to catch the water that poured down a sluice and turned the wheel. The Romans even knew about gears – that if a wheel had spikes sticking out of its circumference it could be made to interact with the spikes on another wheel. If the wheels were at an angle of ninety degrees, the second wheel could be made to turn a grindstone that would turn corn into flour. And the power could be varied by varying the size of the wheels. Around 900, the new interest in wheels led to the discovery that levers and cams could be attached to the drive-shaft, and that they could work a pump, power a trip-hammer or even drive a saw. So processes such as crushing sugar cane, hammering flax, pounding leather, grinding ore, could all be 'automated'. It could even drive a bellows for a blast furnace.

Even the Church played its part in the story of invention. Monks had to wake at all hours of the night to say their prayers. One way of telling the time was to make a small hole in the bottom of a bucket and fill it with water; divisions could be marked on the side of the bucket to give a more accurate idea of how much water had dripped away. It was not too difficult to make the empty bucket tilt on a lever and ring an alarm bell. By the time of Marco Polo, there were highly elaborate water clocks with dials and scales. It was only a matter of time before someone realized that water was unnecessary. A heavy lead weight on a string could be made to turn a wheel, and this could be geared to other wheels to control the speed at which the weight fell. By the time Marco Polo's memoirs were the latest sensation among cultured Italians, this new type of clock was already in use.

Now it is impossible for the human mind to solve a complicated problem and not to feel a certain delight in its own ingenuity and persistence. And this sense of delight, as we all know, is accompanied by a curious ripple of triumph and optimism, an exciting presentiment that obstacles are going to be overcome and that tomorrow will be in every way more interesting than yesterday. This is the feeling that marked the end of the Middle Ages. We call the period that followed the Rebirth – Renaissance – meaning that it was a rebirth of the ancient learning. In a more fundamental sense, it was the birth of the modern era.

So it seems typical that the most influential of the new discoveries – so far as the future of mankind was concerned – was a force of destructiveness: gunpowder. Gunpowder was invented in China some time around the year 1000, and seems to have been used for fireworks, but not, so far as we know, for destructive purposes. It is interesting to speculate how the discovery came about. Its chief ingredient is nitre – saltpetre. And in Europe at least its discovery came about by a rather curious process. Walls of farm buildings were often built with mud in which the hardening ingredient was cattle dung. Men would go and urinate against these walls, with the consequence that white streaks would form on the wall. This was nitre – potassium nitrate. Someone no doubt tried the experiment of tossing some of this crystalline substance on a bonfire, and observed that it made the wood burn with a new fury – it releases oxygen. The next step, which was probably made by some Chinese alchemist – for they had been at work trying to make semi-magical drugs and elixirs since the fifth century B.C. – was to find that, in certain proportions, nitre, sulphur and powdered charcoal will burn with a single bright flash, or – if confined in a tube – explode. (Joseph Needham has a long account of Chinese chemical experiments with saltpetre in Vol. 5 (part 4) of *Science and Civilization in China*, but does not explain how its discovery came about. He promises more information in the so-far unpublished Volume 6.) So the Chinese made fireworks, and the Mongol hordes of Genghis Khan seem to have learned about it from them and brought gunpowder to the west when they invaded the Kharismian empire in 1218 A.D. By about 1250 the Arabs had invented the first gun, a bamboo tube reinforced with metal bands which would fire an arrow. And so man's most dangerous invention before the atomic bomb reached Europe around 1300, and helped to blow apart the last remnants of the Middle Ages.

The warrior who was probably responsible for bringing gunpowder to the west has been described by one historian as 'the mightiest and most bloodthirsty conqueror in all history.' The Mongol Temujin, known to history as Genghis Khan, was born in 1167 in the wild steppe country to the north of China. The Mongols were not unlike the Red Indians of North America when the whites first encountered them: a large number of separate tribes, usually at war with one another. Temujin was the son of a famous warrior, Yesugei, who was killed by treachery on his way back from arranging his son's betrothal to a girl called Börte (or Bertha). Yesugei's tribe took the opportunity to expel the widow – fortunately a woman of strong character – and her children, including the nine-year-old Temujin. For years they lived in the wilderness, and it hardened them and made them ruthless – in his teens Temujin quarrelled with one of his brothers about a fish, and cold-bloodedly murdered him. Then their former tribesmen decided to forestall vengeance by taking him captive; after great hardship Temujin made a daring escape. He emerged from these experiences a formidable warrior whose strength was matched by cunning and foresight.

The steppe was full of feuding kings – or 'khans' – and Temujin made an ally of an old friend of his father, Torghril, khan of a tribe called the Kereits (a man who had achieved his position by murdering two of his brothers). And when, one morning, wandering horsemen descended on Temujin's camp and stole his wife Bertha, Torghril rose to the occasion, and his warriors helped track down the kidnappers, who were surprised by a night attack. When Temujin discovered that Bertha was pregnant, he ordered the massacre of the whole tribe, including women and children. But – typically – he brought up the child as his own son.

This expedition made Temujin's reputation, and in due course he was elected chief of his tribe. This led to a quarrel with his 'blood brother' Jamuqa, who felt he had a better claim. Temujin triumphed eventually, but in the meantime suffered a heavy defeat in battle, after which Jamuqa had seventy of his followers boiled alive in cooking pots; later tradition ascribed the atrocity to Genghis Khan, a reflection of the terror that his name – which means mighty ruler – came to inspire.

By the beginning of the twelfth century, China was governed by the great Sung dynasty, whose first emperor, T'ai Tsu, had united most of the country. But the Sung emperors kept their armies small, for fear of rebellion, and this brought a worse evil – attacks by the barbarians, chief among whom were the Mongols. When Manchurian nomads called the Chin (or Golden) forced the Sung emperor to retreat south, the 'Golden Emperors' took over the court at Peking.

The Golden Emperor heard about this new and powerful khan and decided to suggest an alliance against the Tartars. Genghis Khan was delighted; the Tartars were traditional enemies. He and Torghril descended suddenly on their makeshift fortress and massacred the defenders. His old enemies among the Mongols decided that it was time to unite to destroy him before he became too powerful. They were too late. In a spectacular battle during a storm – raised, according to the Mongol historian, by tribal sorcerers – he defeated the rival army and put all the chieftains to death. This defeat is also the subject of a typical story of Genghis Khan. One of the enemy chieftains escaped and was taken prisoner by one of his own servants, who had decided to change sides. On the way to Genghis Khan, he relented and freed his prisoner; then he went to offer Genghis Khan his loyalty, apologizing for not bringing his master as a prisoner. 'If you had,' said Genghis Khan, 'I would have put you to death.' As it was, he made the man a trusted retainer. The story gives an idea of why he inspired such powerful loyalty.

The conqueror now turned back to the Tartars and defeated them in a decisive battle in 1202. He executed all prisoners but took two beautiful daughters of a Tartar chief as his wives – like most world conquerors, he seems to have been sexually insatiable.

In the spring of the year 1206, Genghis Khan called together all the tribes of Mongolia to a great assembly near the headwaters of the river Onon; there, once again, he was proclaimed khan of all the Mongols. This event was to be as significant for Asia – and Europe – as Mahomet's flight to Medina. At last, the dozens of warring tribes were united under one ruler. Now they were prepared to conquer the world.

In which direction should they expand? To the north lay Siberia, on the other side of the Altai mountains: there was nothing to attract them in that vast, empty land. To the south-west lay the Persian empire, now ruled by the Seljuk Turks. South lay China, whose northern half was ruled by the Golden Emperor. This became Genghis Khan's first objective. But for the moment, he was not ready to attack the emperor. Instead he directed his attention to the only part of northern China not under the emperor's domination: the fertile province now called Kansu, ruled by a semi-Tibetan people called the Tanguts. Genghis Khan began raiding them and his armies caused as much inconvenience as terror. The great Silk Road, the trading route between Kansu and Persia, was at their mercy and their threat strangled the economic life of north-west China. So after four years of harassment, the Tangut decided to beg for peace. As a special inducement, they offered Genghis Khan one of their princesses – Tangut girls, with their delicate features, were regarded by the Mongols as particularly desirable. There was also a large tribute that included a herd of rare white camels. The great khan made peace. Now he could turn his attention towards the Golden Emperor.

The old Golden Emperor – Genghis's former ally – was dead, and his successor he regarded as an imbecile. In 1211, Genghis began his attacks against northern China. But it was well-fortified and most of his attacks were thrown back. Then a subject people called the Khitai decided to rebel against their Chinese masters. They were Mongols, and Genghis was glad to send them a task force under his lieutenant Jebe. They besieged the town of Liao-Yang, in Manchuria, and Jebe used a technique that was to bring the Mongols many later successes: he pretended to retreat, allowed the defenders to relax, then reappeared suddenly and took the town in a surprise attack. The Khitai were installed on the throne – but as vassals of Genghis Khan.

Now the Mongols began to fight their way grimly into China, through the northern passes. They besieged and conquered town after town. They took the Great Wall by storm. Sheer nomad cunning was as important as weight of numbers. They would reach the entrance to a pass where the enemy were in an impregnable position, pretend to run away and then suddenly turn and cut down the enemy as he foolishly pursued them. Then came the khan's reward – the sight of the towers of Peking, and the Great Plain that stretched to the Yellow River with its beautifully cultivated fields of rice, millet and maize. To these barbarians of the Steppe, it must have looked like heaven on earth. They gleefully trampled the crops into the ground and burnt harvests. They besieged and sacked town after town. In Tsi-nan, the principal town of the Shantung province – famous for its silk – they were amazed by the palaces, enormous fountains, lakes of giant lotuses and parks with statues of the

Buddha. But the Mongol response to palaces was to burn them down. They looted and burned for most of a year, then let the Golden Emperor buy them off with a huge bribe. But when Genghis heard that the Golden Emperor had decided to move farther south, he hastened back into China, took Peking and proceeded to burn down its palaces – the imperial palace smouldered for a month.

Yet it is here that Genghis Khan reveals the difference between his mentality and that of the Huns or Vandals. Among the ex-courtiers still in Peking was a scholar named Yelui Choutsai, a tall, bearded man with a sonorous voice and pleasing manner who also happened to be a nobleman. Genghis Khan was charmed by his honesty; when he told Choutsai that he was now 'liberated' from his previous master, the sage replied smoothly that he would have been disloyal if he had felt hostility to his former sovereign. Soon, Choutsai became one of the khan's chief advisers. No matter how formidable they were on horseback, the Mongols became good natured and peaceable in their own tents, and Choutsai found he was able to speak firmly and frankly. He pointed out that it was simply bad policy to leave behind burning crops and palaces; it would be more sensible to leave them untouched and collect a yearly tax. Genghis Khan saw the sense of this and followed Choutsai's advice. This did not mean that the Mongols ceased to burn, loot and massacre – particularly when Genghis was elsewhere – but that they did so only when it was not to their advantage to do otherwise.

Now northern China was conquered, and southern China – the retreat of the Sung emperors – looked disconcertingly far; Genghis decided to look to the west. For news had come that one of his subject-kings had been murdered by a prince named Kuchlig. He told Jebe (known as the Arrow) to go and execute Kuchlig, and Jebe did precisely that. Kuchlig took flight as soon as the Mongols invaded; Jebe, with all the nomad's skill of tracking, followed him high into the Pamir mountains, caught up with him and cut off his head. And now Genghis Khan discovered – probably to his mild astonishment – that he was master of a new country full of Turkish Muslims who were all delighted to see him (for Kuchlig had persecuted Islam). Moreover, he was peering through the passes that led into the land of the Arabian Nights.

In this land, the Turks had become the main rulers – not the Seljuks but a family from Khiva in Turkestan. These sultans, the

Kharismians, had recently completed vast conquests, from the Ganges to the Tigris, and were settling down to enjoy their new possessions. Genghis was impressed by what he heard about them. He had no desire for war – he already had more territory than he could possibly handle, and the Turkish emperor, Mahomet, had sent an ambassador to encourage peaceful relations. Genghis responded by sending him three emissaries with a message saying 'We have equal interest in fostering trade between our subjects – I shall look upon you as my son.' Mahomet was no doubt mildly irritated by this presumption, but nevertheless sent back a diplomatically friendly reply. So Genghis ordered a caravan to set out for Turkestan, loaded with treasures – all stolen – and money to buy Turkish goods. It reached the border town of Otrar; but through some failure of communication – or perhaps simply out of contempt for these upstart barbarians – the governor ordered it to be seized. All the Mongols – a hundred of them – were killed.

When Genghis Khan heard the news he was outraged, but had sufficient self-control to send another ambassador to the sultan to ask for the extradition of the governor of Otrar. Mahomet made the miscalculation of his life – the miscalculation that released the 'yellow peril' on Europe. He had the ambassador put to death.

There is no rage like that of a Right Man who has been insulted – and Genghis Khan was, beyond all doubt, a Right Man. This is the only way in which we can explain the appalling revenge he took for the death of his hundred caravaneers and his ambassador. He marched into Turkestan with his full forces. Just before setting out, his rage was inflamed by another insult. The Tanguts had been the first people of China to swear allegiance to Genghis Khan; now, as he prepared for war, he sent to them for a contingent of soldiers. With astonishing stupidity, a minister who detested the Mongols sent back a reply which said, in essence: If you don't have enough troops, perhaps you'd better call off the expedition. Genghis Khan ground his teeth, but had to put off revenge until a later date.

The Turkish sultan had, in fact, a far larger army than Genghis Khan – he could undoubtedly have marched into Mongolia and conquered it. But now he had no idea where the Mongols would attack. He had to dispose his army at strategic points over a long frontier. Otrar, of course, was an obvious guess – which probably meant Genghis would avoid it. But the great khan, in his fury, did nothing of the sort. He crossed the mountains to the north and appeared before Otrar, on the north bank of the Syr Darya River. The governor defended the town with a courage born of the grim certainty of the horrible death that awaited him; it was a difficult siege; even when the Mongols broke in, the governor took refuge with his best troops in the citadel and it took another month to starve and storm them out. The Turks had run out of arrows; as the Mongols broke in, the governor and his women took refuge on the roof and the women tore bricks from the walls and handed them to the governor, who hurled them down on the Mongols. It was useless; he was captured, still fighting frenziedly, and dragged in front of Genghis Khan. Now was the moment the conqueror had dreamed about. He ordered the man to be executed by having molten metal poured into his ears and eyes.

And so it went on, the grim business of mass slaughter of innocent people whose only crime was to be the subjects of a king who had dared to insult Genghis Khan. In fact, the Mongols spared any town that voluntarily threw open its gates to them. The inhabitants were merely ordered to move outside the walls while the Mongols pillaged for days. Anyone found still in the town was killed. If a town resisted and then surrendered, clemency was doubtful; Benaket, west of Tashkent, asked to surrender after three days and the defenders were promised their lives. In fact, all the soldiers were executed. The craftsmen were given to the Mongol chiefs – in the Middle Ages, a craftsman was a more valuable commodity than ten horses – and all the young males were taken away to help the Mongols in other sieges. The Mongol method was to drive the hostages ahead of them as they besieged a town, as a living shield. It was a trick they had discovered in China: taking hostages from the surrounding country-side and using them as 'shock' troops – troops who received rather than administered the shock.

Bokhara resisted, but its mercenaries tried to make off during the night; the Mongols caught them and killed them. Then they marched into the town and ordered all the inhabitants outside while they looted. But they were not to escape with this punishment. Women were raped in front of husbands who did not dare to intervene; the few who did were committing suicide. Some women did commit suicide rather than submit. Then the town was burnt to the ground.

Samarkand was besieged in May 1220. There was a very large Turkish force there – fifty thousand. The walls looked impregnable. So Genghis Khan drove prisoners in front of him as he attacked. The townspeople came out to fight. The Mongols pretended to break and flee. The defenders poured after them – and the Mongols suddenly turned and hacked them to pieces – fifty thousand of them. Half the mercenaries in the town deserted to Genghis Khan, and the townspeople decided to surrender. The remaining mercenaries were besieged in the citadel, starved out and killed to a man. Then the men who had deserted to the Mongols were also executed – Genghis Khan loathed treachery. Thirty thousand craftsmen were taken away; another thirty thousand men had to accompany the Mongols as 'shock' troops. Other prisoners were allowed to ransom themselves.

Urgenj also decided to fight. The Mongols made their prisoners fill in the moat, which took ten days. Then they began to mine the walls – it is possible that gunpowder was used here. Inside the town, they used buckets of oil to set fire to the houses. Poor relations between two of the khan's sons led to some early defeats in this siege, and the Mongols were now determined to take revenge – they regarded it as an insult when people defended themselves. District by district, house by house, they took the town, killing everyone. Women and children helped the defenders, knowing they would die in any case. Finally, when a few thousand defenders were left in one fortified area, they asked for mercy. The reply was ambiguous – which should have made anyone acquainted with the Mongols suspicious. The population was made to stand outside the city walls, then all the men were massacred – with the exception of the craftsmen. The women and children were taken as slaves. Then the Mongols breached the dykes holding back the river and submerged the charred ruins.

The Turkish sultan was appalled at the total ruin brought about by his own stupidity. He fled, and Genghis Khan ordered Jebe the Arrow to hunt him down. The sultan was too panic-stricken to do the sensible thing and collect troops. He still had millions of loyal subjects. Instead, he fled south into Persia, hoping to get to Baghdad, changed his mind and doubled back towards the Caspian Sea and was only one step ahead of his pursuers as he leapt into a boat – arrows followed him out to sea. He reached the island of Abeskun and died soon after – probably of exhaustion.

Meanwhile, Genghis Khan was slaughtering indefatigably. After a

pleasant summer at a quiet oasis near Samarkand, he marched on a
town called Termez on the Amu-Darya (Oxus) river. It refused to
surrender, was stormed, and all the inhabitants massacred. As one
old woman was about to be killed, she cried out that if they would
spare her she would give them a pearl. They asked her where it was
and she said she had swallowed it. They immediately disembowelled
her and found several pearls. Genghis Khan told his men to open up
all the dead to inspect their stomachs.

Balkh (Bactria) surrendered quietly – in fact, it had already made
token submission to Jebe the Arrow. Its inhabitants were told to
assemble outside the walls and then massacred. It seems to have
been an act of pure sadism – or possibly it was intended as a warning
to the other forts and towns of the region. These were also taken by
the now familiar method of using local people as a kind of human
shield.

And so the murder and pillage went on and on. Genghis Khan
swept down through Afghanistan, and the heir to the Kharismian
empire was pursued to the border of India. With an oddly typical
gesture of generosity, Genghis Khan ordered his archers not to fire
as the prince plunged into the Indus near Ghazni, and told his sons
that this was a man on whom they should model themselves. But
then, he had by that time killed hundreds of thousands of innocent
people in Afghanistan – when his grandson was killed in one siege at
the valley of Bamiyan, he ordered that every living thing there
should be slaughtered, down to children in the mother's womb and
the household pets. It was the completely irrational reaction of a
Right Man who has convinced himself that he is a kind of god, and
that anyone who shows the least sign of defiance is unutterably
wicked.

It is equally typical that as he again crossed the Oxus on his way
back home in 1222, Genghis took with him Muslim scholars to
explain to him the meaning of Islam, and listened with deep interest
as two Muslim jurists taught him about the meaning and importance
of towns and how to administer them – he made the two men
administrators of a large area. It is also typical that when he returned
home and found awaiting him a saintly Chinese monk called Kien
Changchun (for whom he had sent three years earlier hoping he had
an elixir for prolonging life), he enjoyed engaging in long conversations about Taoist philosophy. But then he was on horseback again,

preparing to take revenge on the Tanguts, who had refused to send him an army before he set out to reduce the Kharismian empire. It was the usual story, although the people in mountain areas avoided the usual torture and massacre by going into hiding before he arrived. 'Tanguts being of an age to bear arms he slaughtered, the lords being first to die.' But he allowed his Chinese counsellor Yelui Choutsai to dissuade him from simply laying waste the whole country, seeing the good sense of accepting taxes instead. (Similarly, in China, his general Muqali – who was still warring with the Golden Emperor – allowed himself to see the good sense of not torturing and oppressing captive populations but allowing them once again to become prosperous and productive.)

Genghis was still capturing and burning Tangut towns in 1227 when he began to feel ill and, with the instinct of a nomad, realized that death was near. A hunting accident in the previous year had weakened him; now, with typical Right Man logic, he blamed the Tanguts for bringing him on a punitive expedition when he was less than fully recovered and so causing his death. He was besieging the capital, Ning-hsia, and gave orders that by way of punishment every human being should be exterminated 'so that men of the future will say: the Khan has annihilated their race'. And then, not a moment too soon for the good of the human race, this remarkable monster died, in August 1227, at the age of sixty.

Yet it has to be acknowledged that, by the standards of his time, Genghis Khan was by no means a mere homicidal maniac. As a human being, he possessed many excellent, even lovable, qualities. He was like Aksakov's uncle – mentioned in an earlier chapter: 'And this noble, magnanimous, often self-restrained man – whose character presented an image of the loftiest human nature – was subject to fits of rage in which he was capable of the most barbarous cruelty.' This could have been written about Genghis Khan.

The explanation, clearly, is that he was a man of quite exceptional dominance – several degrees above the rest of the 'dominant five per cent' – who happened to find an ideal field for his self-expression. Mongolia was ready for a man who could bring unity; and once unity was achieved, Genghis Khan became subject to the 'law of expansion' which controls all newly-triumphant nations. They cannot suddenly cease to grow and conquer. He had to lead his people towards delights that they had always wanted – in this case, endless sex and plunder. His success, fortunately, was enough to satisfy both his people and his own immense craving for power. And within the limitations of his rapacious ego and his innate barbarism, he showed a considerable capacity for personal evolution. There seem to be very few cases in which he failed to live up to his own strict code of barbarian honour.

This stands out by contrast to the behaviour of his generals (of whom four were his sons). When an army under his fourth son Toluy broke into Nisa, in Khorassan (with the use of immense Chinese catapults), they ordered all the inhabitants to go outside the city walls and tie themselves together with their hands behind their backs; then the Mongols surrounded them and massacred them with arrows – if they had scattered for the hills, most would have escaped. When Merv fell, Toluy had all the inhabitants beheaded as he watched, and had two hundred merchants tortured until they revealed where they had hidden their treasures. But Toluy was told later that some people in Merv had escaped death by lying down among the dead; so when Naishapur – home of Omar Khayyam – fell he ordered all corpses to be decapitated, and three pyramids of heads were built up – one of men, one of women, one of children. This strikes us as sick sadism, and no excuses about 'barbarism' can deodorize from it the smell of evil. Jebe the Arrow, although less murderous, was equally free from scruples. He had been sent on a kind of reconnaissance expedition into the Caucasus and Russia. This was certainly no part of the Kharismian empire, but he burned towns, and depopulated those that resisted just as the Mongols had in Turkestan. In the steppes to the north of the Caspian, he was attacked by a coalition army of mountain people of three different races. One of these groups, the Kipchaks, were Turkish nomads, and Jebe managed to buy them off with large quantities of plunder and with persuasive words about nomad brotherhood. Then when he had defeated the other two tribes he pursued the Kipchaks, massacred them and took everything back. Later, he defeated a Russian army of eight thousand in the Dnieper valley near present day Alexandrovsk. One Russian prince managed to withdraw to his fortified camp and made terms for a safe passage home. The Mongols agreed – then massacred them. It is unlikely that Genghis Khan's strict code of barbarian morality would have allowed him any of these betrayals.

* * *

during Crusade times

The Mongol empire continued to expand for another half century after the death of Genghis Khan – under his sons and grandsons – and even then took another century to fall apart; but the remainder of this story must be told in summary.

Genghis Khan's eldest son Jochi had died of natural causes six months before his father; it was the third son, Ogodai, who was elected khan. He immediately pursued his father's war with the Golden Emperor, and persuaded the southern Sung emperor – who had lost his northern provinces to the Golden emperors – to become his ally. The 'Golden' (Chin) were subdued in 1234, whereupon the Mongols, with their usual lack of loyalty, went to war against the Sung. Other Mongols set about the conquest of Russia; Kiev was destroyed in 1240; the Mongols poured into Poland, encountered an army of Germans and Poles at Liegnitz, and wiped them out. Fortunately, they found the woods and mountains of Lower Silesia unattractive – they preferred the open steppe. (It was just as well they were not tempted to push on another hundred miles into Germany: they might have found the countryside beyond the Moldau or the Elbe altogether more to their taste.) So they retraced their steps over the Carpathians and into Hungary, where they slaughtered the Magyars (who had been raiding Europe since the time of Charlemagne).

Meanwhile, in Asia, Ogodai had died in 1241, and Genghis Khan's grandson Mangu became khan. He went on fighting the unfortunate Sung and ordered his brother Hulagu west to attack the cities of Islam. The reason for this was not any rebellion of their Persian subjects, but Mangu's nervousness about the sinister descendants of Hasan bin Sabah, the order of Assassins.

It seems to have come about in this way. When the Kadi of Qazvin came to pay his respects to the new khan in his capital Karakoram, he was wearing a shirt of mail; he explained that he had to wear it all the time and told the story of the assassins, now led by an Imam called Rukn al-Din. He probably emphasized the power held by this relatively small sect through the fear it inspired and pointed out that the khan himself was undoubtedly on their list. When Ismaili ambassadors came to present themselves at the khan's court, they were turned away, and the khan probably felt the danger was getting closer (although, of course, Ismailis were not necessarily assassins). The khan redoubled his guard, which seems to suggest he was now losing sleep and brooding on stories of the assassins' ability to creep under doors and down air vents. This is why, in 1256, Hulagu was ordered to go and stamp out the menace.

The assassins had a series of impregnable castles, and might have been in a good position to hold out indefinitely, as they had against the Seljuks. But their new Imam Rukn al-Din was a pacifist. He made a submissive reply to Hulagu's demand that he destroy his own castles, and even sent his seven-year-old son as a hostage. Fortunately, Hulagu returned the boy; for this demand to offer their necks to the Mongols had the assassins understandably worried. Hulagu prepared to attack the castle in which Rukn was staying, and Rukn hastily made his submission. Hulagu received his treasures condescendingly, but treated Rukn well and gave him a hundred white camels and a beautiful Mongolian girl for his bed. He needed Rukn to help him subdue the other castles without bloodshed. And this is precisely what the new Imam did. A whole string of forts surrendered, including – finally – the Eagle's Nest itself, at Alamut. The Mongols burned it; they would probably never have entered as besiegers.

Now that the Mongols no longer needed Rukn, his family was murdered. Rukn himself managed to buy a little more time by asking permission to go and present himself to the khan at Karakorum; but Mangu refused to receive him and he was murdered on the way back, he and his followers being 'kicked to a pulp' according to the Arab chronicler Juvaini.

So the assassins had finally ceased to exist in Persia, as they already had in Egypt, where the sultan Baybars had annihilated them. It was the price the Old Man of the Mountain paid for his terrorist methods.

Hulagu, who seemed to be as stupidly sadistic as most of the Mongol conquerors, now marched on Baghdad, held by Mustasim, last of the Abbasid Caliphs. They reached there in January 1258 and laid siege to the great city of al-Mansur and Haroun al-Raschid. After a few weeks, Mustasim begged for mercy. It could easily have been granted – Baghdad had committed no wrong against the Mongol khan. But Hulagu must have been disappointed at the tame surrender of the assassin strongholds; possibly his men were growing restive for a little rape. He stormed the city and ordered a total massacre. It was probably one of the largest the Mongols had ever undertaken. So Baghdad, the most beautiful and exciting city since Byzantium and Alexandria, was left a smoking ruin full of corpses. The sultan himself was trampled to death by horses. Hulagu surveyed his work with satisfaction, and prepared for new conquest.

His object was Africa, and the gateway was Syria and Palestine. It looked as if nothing would prevent conquest of the whole north coast of Africa; there were no armies strong enough to oppose him except those of Baybars, sultan of Egypt. He took Aleppo in 1258, and moved on Egypt. But at this point he received word of the death of his brother Mangu; and this was serious news. For Hulagu's elder brother Kubla was the next in line for succession, and he and the youngest brother were in strong disagreement on a vital matter – whether the Mongols should remain horsemen of the steppes or move into a more civilized country. Arigboge, the youngest, agreed with Genghis Khan that the Mongols should remain nomads – civilization would soften and corrupt them. Hulagu agreed with Kubla that corruption could be enjoyable, and was inevitable in any case. Now Kubla needed his support in the argument, for Arigboge had strong supporters. And so, to the relief of all the Mediterranean, Hulagu turned his army homeward.

But Baybars was unwilling to allow him to escape so easily. His army caught up with the Mongols at Ain Jalut, near the Sea of Galilee, in September 1260, and the Mongols sustained their first real defeat. The main body of the army was put to flight, although, with the injustice of history, the Mongols managed to avoid massacre. And Hulagu, nursing his wounds, hurried back to Mongolia.

His intervention was timely. Arigboge lost the argument when he was seized and thrown into prison, where he died. Kubla Khan became the Great Khan in 1260. He decided that his chief task was to complete the conquest of China and start a new dynasty. And in the next thirty-four years, this is precisely what he did.

He was warring against the Mongols' former allies, the Sung, and it was altogether more difficult than overthrowing the Chin in the north. The terrain consisted mainly of flooded rice fields, which made cavalry useless. The hot, damp climate was hard on the Mongols. But they made good use of the great siege catapults they had used to destroy the Kharismian empire – some required a hundred men to work them – and in less than twenty years, the last of the Sung emperors had flung himself in despair from a high cliff into the sea. Kubla Khan was master of China.

In the year Kubla Khan became leader of the Mongols, Marco Polo's father and uncle set out from Venice and sailed to Constantinople. (It was still in the hands of the Latins – since the siege by the crusaders – but would become Greek again the following year.) Marco himself was only six at the time, and so too young to travel. The two men journeyed overland to Bokhara, and there met envoys who had been sent by Kubla to Hulagu, no doubt to tell him of Mangu's death and the struggle for succession. The envoys pressed them to return with them to Cathay (which was the nearest Europeans could get to pronouncing Khitai – China) to meet the khan, and the Polos allowed themselves to be persuaded. It was fortunate that they knew the language of the Tartars, and so did Kubla Khan. When they arrived (presumably at Karakoram) the great khan received them affably and engaged them in long conversations. He liked them so much that he asked them to go back to the pope and ask him to send a hundred scholars to come and teach western ways to the Mongols. They returned to Europe, where they discovered that the pope had just died – as had Polo's wife – leaving a fifteen-year-old boy, Marco; they decided to return to 'Cathay' with Marco. They went through Cilicia and Armenia to Persia, then over the Pamirs to Kashgar, and so by stages on to Kubla's capital, Peking. Kubla Khan again received them graciously, was much taken with the bright young man who spoke Tartar so fluently, and sent him on various diplomatic missions. All this is described by Marco Polo in the famous *Milione*, one of our most remarkable and vivid glimpses into past history.

No doubt one of Kubla's reasons for welcoming the Polos was that he himself was a far from welcome guest in China. The Chinese saw the Mongols as something rather like Tolkien's Orcs – filthy, smelly creatures with no manners, no morals and a revolting taste in food and drink. (The Chinese would not have dreamed of drinking milk; they still prefer lemon in their tea.) But, then, in Europe – even Venice – in the thirteenth century no one bothered about washing more than once a week.

For seventeen years Marco remained in the service of Kubla Khan and travelled all over the empire, to realms as distant as Burma and Japan (and possibly to India). For three years he was the governor of the city of Yang-Chow. Whenever he returned from his travels, he told Kubla stories about the people he had seen, and the khan made notes; he was endlessly curious. When the Polos finally intimated their desire to return, he was sad and reluctant; but finally he gave them leave to accompany a princess who was to wed the khan of Persia. The Polos delivered her safely and at last made their way back to Venice. They were so ragged and dusty on their return that they were refused admittance to their own house. Later, they invited all their friends to a banquet, then had their dirty old clothes brought in and cut open the seams to extract rubies, sapphires and diamonds. And so the Polos lived – more-or-less – happily ever after (except for Marco's brief period in a Genoa prison). Their benefactor Kubla Khan – the man Coleridge made the subject of a famous dream-poem – had died in the year before they reached Venice.

Kubla Khan had done his best to live up to the vision of his grandfather. He pressed on south into the Vietnam peninsula and sent armies into Burma, but his soldiers found the tropical heat and the flies too much for them. He even tried to conquer Japan; this required fleets, and the Mongols had never seen the sea before they came to China. The first warships disembarked their troops at Hakata Bay, in North Kyushu, in 1274, but Samurai warriors proved too much for the sea-sick Mongols who had not yet regained their land legs. Seven years later, an immense force of 140,000 Mongols made the mistake of landing in the same bay. But the Japanese had used the interval to build a considerable wall around the bay, and they kept the Mongols penned in until a typhoon blew up and destroyed half the fleet and the Mongol morale. The soldiers who could make it scrambled back to their ships and sailed for home; the Japanese picked off the rest at their leisure. Less than half the force returned to China.

In a sense, the defeat was the end of the Mongol empire. The formidable Kubla continued to administrate China until his death thirteen years later. But his 'Yuan dynasty' (it meant 'new beginning') had no real chance of establishing itself in China; it was too much hated. When Kubla's heirs fell to quarrelling amongst themselves, it was clear their days were numbered. The country was divided by civil wars; then the Chinese rose up, took the Mongols by the scruff of the neck, and firmly ejected them. This was a mere seventy-four years after Kubla's death. And then, like a corpse, Genghis Khan's great empire decayed and fell apart.

Seven

TRAVELLERS AND ADVENTURERS

There was one chapter of Marco Polo's travels – the forty-sixth of Part Two – that caused immediate and intense excitement all over Italy. There he speaks of the Tartars of the steppe 'who had no sovereign of their own, and were tributary to a powerful prince who . . . was named in their language Unc Can, by some thought to have the same signification as Prester John in ours.' But in subsequent chapters he refers to this leader simply as Prester John – undoubtedly encouraged by his amanuensis, Rusticiano, who realized what a sensation these comments would cause. For more than a century, the legend of Prester John – the Christian priest (hence the name) who ruled a country in India – had been as famous in Europe as that of King Arthur's magician Merlin.

It had all started around the year 1165, with the appearance in Italy of a mysterious *Letter of Prester John*, describing his remote and exotic kingdom – a kind of twelfth-century Shangri-La. Like the story of Merlin – concocted at about the same time by a notorious romancer called Geoffrey of Monmouth in his history of Britain – the legend of Prester John made an enormous appeal to the romance-starved imaginations of the Middle Ages. Pope Alexander III took the Prester John letter so seriously that he wrote a long reply in 1177, and despatched his personal physician, 'Master Philip', to deliver it somewhere vaguely in the direction of India. No one knows what became of Master Philip, but a copy of the pope's letter survives.

Prester John tells in his *Letter* how he lives in a magnificent palace, with gates of sardonyx that give some kind of warning if anyone tries to introduce poison. He has a magic mirror that can show him what is going on anywhere in the land, and a fountain whose waters have the property of the Elixir of Life, and can keep a man looking thirty for ever. Prester John has a ring containing a precious stone that can make him invisible, and there follow descriptions of many other marvels: a sea of sand in which there are various edible fish, a river made of rolling stones, and worms called salamanders who can only live in fire – Prester John has robes made of their skin, and they can only be cleaned by holding them in fire. The country itself has no crime, falsehood or poverty – although, oddly enough, Prester John still feels it necessary to make war.

So it was understandable that Rusticiano became very excited when Marco Polo told him about a Christian potentate called Unc Can, which signified Prester John. Any fragment of gossip about Prester John guaranteed that a book would reach a wide audience.

Polo's account sent many romantic travellers on the road to Samarkand and Kashgar in the century that followed publication of the travels. They never, of course, found Prester John. But this was not because Prester John never existed. Polo's account of Prester John is, indeed, inaccurate – for example, he makes him Genghis Khan's enemy and kills him off in a battle for the hand of a beautiful princess. In fact, Prester John was Genghis Khan's closest friend and ally – Torghril, khan of the Kereits. The Kereits were Nestorian Christians, members of that heretical sect who believed that Christ was first and foremost a man, and who had been driven eastward into Asia in the early days of the established church.

The legends of Merlin and King Arthur, blown up to grotesque proportions by Geoffrey of Monmouth – a Welsh bishop – were largely responsible for that tradition of chivalry, of knights in armour wearing their lady's kerchief on their helmets, that we regard as so typical of the Middle Ages. And the legend of Prester John, blowing like a spring breeze into that stagnating waxworks, was as important as the crusades in stirring the minds of men and making them dream of distant horizons. For once again, we must make an attempt to grasp an almost impossible concept: that there was a time when a man took it for granted that he would die in the same hovel in which he was born, and in which his great-great-grandfathers had died, and in which his great-great-grandsons would die in their turn. It was not that people had no ambition to better themselves; it was that they believed that the world was a perfectly stable and static place which would never change. Life was hard – but then, it was supposed to be, for man was expelled from Eden for Adam's sin. Now, at least, that problem was solved; the Church would take care of everybody's salvation, and guarantee an eternity of blissful relaxation. Meanwhile, reminders of death and mortality were everywhere. Beggars exhibited their deformities outside churches, lepers walked the streets in processions, sounding their rattles, criminals were gibbeted and burned in public, and rats waddled through the refuse in the street like pet cats and dogs. Every church had its tableau of the Dance of Death with its grim reaper. One result of all this was the famous 'anonymity' of medieval craftsmen. It strikes us as strange, and rather admirable, that there should be no signature on a beautiful rood screen or statue of the virgin and child; historians tell us that this is because the work was done solely for the greater glory of God, and we are suitably impressed. But everyone in the small community knew exactly who the craftsman was, and would be happy to mention his name to any visitor who happened to enquire. What they were *not* much concerned about was a visitor in a hundred years time, for 'posterity' was a concept that did not really exist. These people lived in the present; they knew practically nothing about yesterday. (Herodotus was not even translated into Latin until 1452.) Their apparent humility was simply another outcome of the waxworks mentality.

And it was at this point – say, around 1150 – that people began to whisper that the return of King Arthur was about to take place or that the pope had received a letter from an emperor called John the Priest, who could make himself invisible, and who possessed a magic mirror that could show him distant places – he might even be looking at them at this very moment, informed by spirits that he was being talked about . . . And the result must have been a frisson that was only partly superstitious terror; for the idea brought an intimation that interesting changes were in the air, like the first smell of spring. What no one could guess was that the changes, when they came, would be brought by hordes of trained killers who would leave behind deserted cities and headless corpses.

It was undoubtedly fortunate for Europe that Genghis Khan's forces never reached farther than Poland. China and Russia were ravaged by the Mongols, eastern Europe by the Turks, then the Mongols. The Arabs – one of the most promising civilizations in the western world – were also devastated by Turks and Mongols. (Their own caliphs had a desire for wealth and display that was just as ruinous.) They had been the inventors of banking; but since Islam forbade usury, this was taken over by Christians and Jews. (And, as

Christians began to look with increasing disfavour on usury, more and more by the Jews.) But after the Vikings had settled down, northern Europe was enviably stable. When the Mongols opened up the roads from Germany to China, it was the merchants and explorers of Europe who reaped the benefit. And the lure was romance as much as commerce – as late as 1488, Bartolomeu Dias set out to look for Prester John, and ended by discovering that it was possible to sail around the Cape of Good Hope.

The Church, as usual, remained blissfully unaware of these tremendous changes until too late. We can see, in retrospect, that ever since it became a political power, the Church had suffered from an exaggerated idea of its own importance. Instead of quietly trying to suffuse the people with its own ideas, like all the other great religions, it wanted to rule and give orders – that episode when St Ambrose had bullied the emperor Theodosius into public repentance for having seven thousand people killed in the circus had made every pope dream of humiliating earthly kings. The papacy's two most spectacular successes were when Gregory VII excommunicated Henry IV of Germany and made him wait in the snow for three days to beg forgiveness, and when Innocent III – the greatest medieval pope – placed all England under interdict in 1209 and finally bullied King John – under threat of a crusade against him – to hand over England as a papal fief. (But all the pope's objections to Magna Carta later failed to destroy it.) The execution of the boy Conradin, the last of the Staufer emperors, in 1268, seemed to prove that the Church could win any battle in the end. (It must have given the pope additional satisfaction that it took place in the square at Naples, where Frederick II, the 'wonder of the world', had founded a university to try to undermine the power of medieval superstition.)

In the year the Polos were making their way back from Cathay, a new pope was elected. Boniface VIII was a big, florid extrovert who was vain about his good looks and enjoyed drinking in low company; he preferred the dress of an emperor to papal vestments because he found it more becoming. Boniface enjoyed giving orders, and in 1290, before he was pope, told the assembled university of Paris that its teachings were trivial and poisonous, and that they were all forbidden to discuss such inflammatory subjects as the mendicant orders (like the Franciscans) in public or in private. To us it seems absurd to forbid anyone to discuss something in private; to the future Boniface VIII it came naturally.

It was power that interested Boniface. After the downfall of the Staufers, he saw no reason why he should not realize the dream of Gregory VII and become the true ruler of all Europe's kings and emperors. Innocent III, we may recall – guardian of the young Frederick II – had persuaded the 'wonder of the world' to remit all taxes on the clergy; but Frederick went back on his word when he became emperor. Now Boniface decided it was time to try again, and in the year he became pope made the matter the subject of a bull. This was a papal edict (so called because of its ball-like seal – the Latin word was preferred because to refer to papal balls would obviously give rise to misunderstanding), and it was regarded as un-contradictable. No priest, said *Clericis Laicos*, could be taxed without direct permission of the pope.

In France, this notion caused rage and dismay. The king, Philip the Fair, was in character not unlike the pope – vain, aggressive and inclined to display and extravagance. As a result, he was permanently in need of money, and to cut off his church revenues caused him acute distress. He reacted promptly by cutting off all the pope's revenues from France – that is, by issuing an edict forbidding money to leave the country. At the same time, the English king Edward I outlawed the clergy. Within a year, Boniface was practically compelled to withdraw *Clericis Laicos*. He tried to placate Philip by canonizing his ancestor Louis IX.

Once again dreaming of power and grandeur, the pope proclaimed the year 1300 a 'Jubilee Year', a year for rejoicing, when anyone who came to Rome would receive automatic remission of sins. Hundreds of thousands of pilgrims flocked to Rome; hundreds of thousands of pounds flowed into the papal treasury. It was, says Frederick Heer in *The Medieval World, 1150–1300*, 'the first example of the manipulation of the masses for a political end'. The great procession itself was like a combination of a Roman triumph and a Nuremberg Rally. The pope was preceded by two swords, symbolizing his spiritual and earthly dominion, and heralds went ahead crying: 'I am caesar, I am emperor!' Gold coins were showered on the tomb of St Peter at such a pace that two croupiers had to pull them in with rakes. All this money was intended by the pope for the subjection of Sicily – that old quarrel still dragged on – and to press his claim as the real emperor of Europe.

The quarrels between Boniface and Philip the Fair began to blow up again. A haughty papal legate gave great offence to Philip with his insolent manners, but since he was the pope's ambassador, there was nothing the king could do about it. However, the legate happened to be a French bishop, and as soon as his term as ambassador expired, Philip had him arrested, tried for blasphemy and disrespect for royalty, and thrown into prison. The pope was outraged – and began to be alarmed when Philip spoke about appointing future bishops himself instead of leaving it to Rome. In 1302 he issued a bull called *Unam sanctam* that went farther than anything before in asserting the pope's superiority to kings and emperors. (It has since become something of an embarrassment to the Church, which has been obliged to declare that nothing in it is 'divinely inspired' except its last line – about there being no salvation outside the Church). He went on to threaten to depose Philip and excommunicate him.

Philip's response was to call a meeting of the French equivalent of parliament, the Estates General, which denounced the pope as a heretic and said many other harsh things about him. (Modern research has shown that the heresy charge was not unfounded – it seems probable that Boniface did not believe in the immortality of the soul.) Then Philip sent off a kind of commando unit to Italy to kidnap the pope. This was done with the aid of an Italian family that the pope had offended, the Colonnas. The conspirators went to the pope's town of Anagni, where he was spending the summer of 1303. With the complicity of the townspeople – who also seem to have had their grudges – they besieged him in his palace, and burst in as he was about to issue the bull excommunicating Philip. During the next few days, it seems fairly certain that the pope was roughly handled by his captors, although he refused to give way to their demands. They were prepared to drag him back to France to stand trial when the townspeople of Anagni experienced a change of heart and rescued him. But the sudden recognition of his own vulnerability had broken the pope's will. He went back to Rome – where he was made prisoner by some of his enemies – and died soon after.

What we can see – and what the vainglorious and arrogant Boniface was entirely unable to see – is that he never stood the slightest chance of success in realizing Hildebrand's dream of papal domination. He had not even noticed how much the world had changed. Frederick II might be dead, but his spirit was alive and was transforming the world. It was against that spirit that Boniface had broken his head – not against the arrogant stupidity of Philip the Fair. The whole of France was behind Philip in telling the pope to keep his nose out of foreign affairs. And as the news of the 'kidnapping' and its sequel spread, the rest of Europe smiled sarcastically.

Philip's rather underhand schemes continued to prosper. The next pope died – probably of poison – within a year. And Philip made sure that his successor was a Frenchman – a Gascon, Clement V. And Philip bribed or persuaded him not to go to Rome but to transfer the seat of the papacy to Avignon. There he lived in a huge and luxurious palace. This 'Babylonian captivity' of the papacy lasted for seventy-three years, during which time most of the popes thoroughly enjoyed themselves – in fact, gave the papacy a bad name for self-indulgence – and, naturally, lent a sympathetic ear to the demands of the French king.

With the pope in Avignon, Philip turned his attention back to the question of how to make money. Somebody's pocket had to be picked, and one obvious candidate was the wealthy order of knights known as the Templars. They were very rich – they had often lent the king money – and very powerful. Founded in the Holy Land after the success of the first crusade, they had originally been housed in a wing of Solomon's temple in Jerusalem. The Holy Land was, as we have seen, a dangerous place during the Middle Ages, and the Knights Templar had been decimated again and again in battles with the Saracens and finally ejected by the sultan Baybars in 1303. Their immense wealth had been bequeathed to them mainly by grateful crusaders whom they had nursed through sickness or injury. Philip had applied to join them, and had actually been rejected. For a man of his childish temperament, this was an insult that had to be avenged.

Ex-Templars were interrogated, and the king soon had a list of hair-raising accusations, such as homosexuality, worshipping a demon called Baphomet (in the form of a wooden penis) and spitting on the cross. The accusations were an imaginative compilation of the medieval ideas about black magic and demons, complete with naked virgins, female demons and endless sodomy.

Secret orders went out, and at daybreak on 13 October 1307, the authorities swooped, and almost every Templar in France was arrested. It was important to work fast, in case there was a public outcry – a matter like this could so easily turn into a boomerang that would make Philip a laughing stock. Disappointingly, there proved to be no documentary evidence of the abominations of which they were accused, and the treasure of the Templars was not found either – it seems fairly certain that they had advance warning and spirited it away. So Philip had the knights tortured horribly – so horribly that thirty-six of them died within a day or two. The new pope in Avignon issued a bull ordering the arrest of all Templars in all lands, and for three years Templars were tortured and tried. It was a nauseating farce, and Philip had not gained by it a fraction of the wealth he had expected. But it had to be carried through. In 1312, the pope admitted that there was not enough evidence to prove heresy; nevertheless, he dissolved the order. The tragedy came to an end in March 1314. Jacques de Molay, Grand Master of the Templars, who had been in prison for seven years, was exposed in front of Notre Dame to make a public confession. To everyone's dismay, he declared that his only offence was to lie under torture; he insisted that the order was pure and that the charges were false. Nevertheless, at sunset, on the Ile de Palais in the Seine, he was slowly roasted to death over a fire. The story went around that the last words of the dying man had been a summons to the pope and the king to meet him in front of God's throne one year hence, for judgement. Oddly enough, both the pope and the king died within that year.

And so, after the long halt of the Middle Ages, like a train waiting for hours in a country station, history began to rumble forward again. Now that the temporal power of the popes was broken, and the new universities – Oxford (founded 1264), Bologna, Paris, Naples –were beginning to revive the learning of the ancients, the world seemed set for exciting changes. A university was not necessarily a conglomeration of professors, each teaching his own subject; it might, like the University of Paris, spring up around one man – the controversial theologian Peter Abelard – as the Academy of Athens had sprung up around Socrates; what mattered was that it was vitally interested in *ideas*. For the first time since the ancient Greeks, people were thinking again. Oddly enough, the legal system

i.e. Thinking critically

of Justinian became the subject of enthusiastic study. But this was because men no longer took it for granted that the Church was the one and only authority on matters of right and wrong; they wanted to discuss the whole concept of justice.

Since the west, unlike the east, had largely escaped the scourge of the Mongols, there might seem to be every reason for optimism about the future of Europe. In fact, to the average peasant, things had never looked worse. All the trade and commerce that had been stimulated by the crusades had brought prosperity, and prosperity brought a steep rise in the population. It is now a drearily familiar story, although no one gave it much serious thought until the Reverend Thomas Malthus turned his mind to the problem in the last years of the eighteenth century. Prosperity means that more children come into the world, and that of those, more survive into adulthood. New land has to be cultivated to feed them. By the time the Polos set out for Cathay, Europe was already becoming uncomfortably overcrowded. Methods of agriculture had improved, but not enough to produce anything like abundance. In most years, everybody got by. But as soon as there was a bad harvest, people starved and died. In 1315, the year after the death of Philip the Fair, there was a disastrous harvest all over Europe. The lack of sun not only meant that corn stayed unripe; it also meant a lack of salt – which was produced by evaporation of sea water – and this in turn meant that meat could not be stored for the winter. (This particular problem eventually led the Portuguese to sail around the world in search of spices, and pepper and nutmeg became the most valuable commodities in the world; but that time had not yet arrived.) There was mass starvation; people ate dogs, cats, rats, bird dung, even other human beings. It was a problem that no one seemed to be able to understand; the world was full of new prosperity, and people were dying by the thousand.

The earth itself seemed to be going through a period of convulsions. In 1281, a typhoon had wrecked Kubla Khan's fleet off Japan. In 1293, thirty thousand Japanese were killed when a seismic wave hit the coast. In 1302 Vesuvius erupted, and in 1329, Etna. And England, in the midst of its starvation, experienced a violent earthquake in 1318, killing hundreds of people already scarcely alive from undernourishment. (Scots were eaten at the siege of Carrickfergus in 1316.) In 1304, the Holy Land itself was subjected to floods, and Damascus was inundated – as if nature itself had gone mad. In 1359, a hailstorm with lightning devastated the army of Edward III in France and killed six thousand horses.

But a disaster that was greater than all of these put together began in China in 1333, when drought on the plains between the Kiang and Hoai rivers brought famine, and then nature went to the opposite extreme and poured down non-stop rain in such torrents that a mountain called Tsincheou collapsed and left a vast hole in the earth; the floods killed four thousand. Another immense convulsion in the earth in the Ki-Ming-Chan mountains created a lake a hundred miles across; the dead in the surrounding area were estimated at five millions. And the enormous heaps of dead began to incubate the bubonic plague.

Plague is, in fact, a disease that is carried by fleas, who are in turn carried by rats. The disease has always existed in certain areas, so it is still not clear why it should break out at specific times, or why rotting corpses should encourage it. But by 1340 it had spread over much of China; then it went on to India and Mongolia, Persia and Asia Minor. In 1346, it killed eighty-five thousand in the Crimea. When it reached the shores of the Black Sea, the Tartars seem to have decided to look for scapegoats – the old human tendency to 'magical thinking' – and settled upon the local Christian traders. The Genoese merchants in the city of Tana were attacked and driven to their trading base, the town of Caffa (now Feodosia), which was fortified for just such an emergency as this. The Tartars prepared to starve them out. And at this point, the plague struck; half the Tartar besiegers were thrown into convulsive agonies of misery and thirst, with the typical large swellings of the groin and armpits and the black spots on the skin that led to the disease being called the Black Death. They decided to abandon the siege; but first of all they used some of their huge catapults – the ones that had been brought from China by Genghis Khan – to toss some of their corpses into the fortress. The defenders immediately carried them to the sea; but the plague took a hold. They scrambled into their ships and sailed back for the Mediterranean. The ships put in at Messina – on Sicily – and Genoa; and within days, people in both places were dying by the thousand. The plague reached Messina in October 1347; by the following year, it had reached England, and quickly killed nearly half the population.

Again there was a search for scapegoats. In Germany, it was rumoured that Jews had been poisoning the wells, and fleeing Jews were seized at Chillon and tortured. Under torture, they confessed to the charge. They were executed, and there were massacres of Jews in Provence, at Narbonne and Carcassone, then all over Germany: Strasbourg, Frankfurt, Mainz and the trading towns of the north belonging to the Hanseatic League. Here Jews were walled in their houses and left to starve; others were burnt alive.

Another scapegoat was the leper. In the Middle Ages, lepers were usually regarded with considerable tolerance and allowed to form grimly picturesque processions; now they were stoned to death, or simply refused entry into the walled towns.

One of the stranger phenomena that flourished under the Black Death was the movement known as Flagellants. These had originated about a century earlier in Italy, when various plagues and famines convinced the Italians that God wanted them to show repentance, and took the form of pilgrimages in which people walked naked to the waist, beating themselves with whips or scourges tipped with metal studs. On that occasion it had seemed to work, and had been tried periodically since then. Now the Black Death convinced increasing numbers of people that desperate remedies were necessary. A letter, supposed to have fallen down from heaven, declaring that only Flagellants would be saved, was first published around 1260, but reappeared in 1343 in the Holy Land – it was supposed to have been delivered by an angel to the Church of St Peter in Jerusalem. Now waves of flagellation swept across Europe with all the hysteria of religious revivals. The Flagellants – mostly fairly respectable 'pilgrims' of both sexes – would arrive in a town and hold their ceremony in the main square: they would strip to the waist, then flog themselves into an increasing state of hysteria until blood ran down to their feet, staining the white linen which was the traditional dress on the lower half of the body. The pilgrimage would last for thirty-three days, and each flagellant would have taken a vow to flog himself, or herself, three times a day for the whole of that time. A Master also moved among them, thrashing those who had failed in their vows.

As Flagellants themselves carried the plague from city to city, public opinion suddenly turned against them. The magistrates of Erfurt refused them entry, and no one objected. It was best not to

mental changes wrought by the Black Death

wait until the Flagellants were within a town to raise objections, for their own frenzy made them violent, and they were likely to attack the objectors – one Dominican friar in Tournai was stoned to death. Human beings seem to be glad of an excuse to change their opinions, and only a year after they had been generally regarded with respect and admiration, the Flagellants were suddenly attacked as outcasts and cranks. The pope issued a bull against them, and the hysteria vanished as abruptly as it had begun.

The horrors of the plague did as much as the crusades or the spread of commerce to end the state of mind known as the Middle Ages. It created a desperate sense that something important had to happen, that the world must be changed. Monks ran away from their cloisters; serfs ran away from their estates. Oddly enough, the Black Death did nothing to increase the prestige of the Church; the fact that so many priests died seemed to prove that they were no holier than anyone else. In England, the priest John Wycliffe translated the Bible into English – the Church had always tried to keep it from the common people because it liked to play the role of interpreter – and denied that the Church had some absolute right to rule man's conscience. The pope issued bulls condemning Wycliffe and ordered his arrest; but since the clash with Boniface, the pope was not much liked or respected in England – it was a matter of national pride. So even when the Archbishop of Canterbury was persuaded to prosecute Wycliffe for heresy in 1377, he came to no harm. His followers were later forced to recant. But it was a turning point in European intellectual history when an Englishman could describe the pope as a 'limb of the devil' and the clergy as 'ravening wolves' and still remain at liberty.

The fire of revolution that was now sweeping through the English countryside was not entirely due to misery and oppression. In fact, peasants were better off now than they had ever been. The Black Death had killed off so many that labour was short, and they could demand – and get – higher wages. The Hundred Years War with France, which started ten years before the Black Death and continued for another century, brought a new prosperity as soldiers returned from Normandy with plunder; shipbuilders and military suppliers made a fortune. By 1350, twenty-five million people – a third of the population of Europe – had died, and landlords were forced to sell land – which was useless to them – to the peasants. But the peasants were irritable and dissatisfied; after the Black Death, it all seemed an anticlimax. Besides, some of these new merchant-adventurers – like Richard Lyons of London – used their power to fix prices of some essential goods and created scarcity where there was none. Men began to listen with enthusiasm to the teachings of the 'mad priest of Kent', John Ball, who told them that 'things won't go well in England until everything is held in common, without serfs or lords . . .' Ball, who has been greatly admired by modern socialists, was a muddled thinker whose ideas were quite simply a form of 'magical thinking', the tendency to allow emotion to distort logic. 'What right have they to be on top? They wear velvet and rich stuffs, with ermine and other fur; we must dress cheaply. They have wines, spices and good bread; we have rye and husks and only water. Fine manor houses for them, but wind and rain for us toiling in the fields.' The emotion is that of a child who feels that another child has more toys, and that it would be pleasant to give him a black eye and take them away.

But Kent was ready to listen to such teachings. There the Black Death had been worse than elsewhere; there was a desire for major changes. The war with France was going badly, and the king's attempt to raise money through a poll tax caused intense ill feeling. Riots broke out in Essex in May 1381 and six jurors were killed. In Kent, the rebels set out to march on London, led by an ex-highwayman named Wat Tyler. John Ball was in Maidstone jail; they rescued him and took him with them. Then they marched to Canterbury and Rochester, burning castles and manor houses on the way.

London was a walled city, but the rioters had friends within; London Bridge was undefended, and the gate at Aldgate was opened to the rebels from Essex. While the fourteen-year-old King Richard II took refuge in the Tower of London, the rioters threw open all the gaols and began beheading the people they felt were responsible for their problems – like the merchant Richard Lyons, the Treasurer and the Archbishop of Canterbury. A whole colony of Flemings were executed merely because they were foreigners. The leaders made lists of people they wanted to execute, and the axe in Cheapside rose and fell. On 14 June 1381, Tyler presented the king with a list of their demands – that serfdom should cease, that their rebellion should be pardoned, and that land should be rented at fourpence an acre. The king agreed. Rebels and courtiers came face to face in Smithfield Market, the peasants holding their bows ready. Wat Tyler rode forward alone to speak to the king. What happened next is uncertain. The usual account is that his manner was so insolent that the outraged mayor of Walworth struck him violently and another of the king's followers then ran him through. It sounds plausible; it hardly seems likely that the king would plan the betrayal of Wat Tyler in front of all his followers. The French chronicler Froissart tells the rest of the story – how the rebels raised their bows, how the young king walked alone towards them, muttering over his shoulder to his courtiers 'Let no man follow me.' Then he called to the rebels: 'Would you kill your king? I will be your leader.' And he persuaded them to adjourn to the fields of Clerkenwell. The king's men now mobilized their forces and restored order. The peasants drifted home, some convinced that Wat Tyler had been knighted – in spite of the evidence of his head on London bridge; in any case, they all trusted their king.

Now that the forces of order had triumphed they had no intention of sticking to their agreement. They immediately revoked their promises, declaring that they had been made under duress. Other rebellions elsewhere were nipped in the bud by experienced soldiers. The king's authorities went into the countryside, placed rebels on trial and executed them – the number, though, was relatively small, less than two hundred. The authorities, aware what a close thing it had been, sat back with a gasp of relief. As they regained confidence, they proceeded to tighten the screws. But things had changed, and everyone knew it; the execution of John Ball could not put back the clock.

Richard's success in retaining his kingdom might be expected to have been the prelude to a long and prosperous reign. In fact, success went to his head. Two years later, he asserted his total independence as a ruler and, by way of underlining the point, had one of his uncles, the duke of Gloucester, murdered. He became as despotic as any Roman emperor, had his cousin exiled and, when the father – John of Gaunt – died, seized his inheritance. At this point he made the mistake of setting out on a punitive expedition to Ireland, whose natives were even in those days causing the English endless trouble. His cousin seized the opportunity to return to England and by the time Richard hurried back his power was in ruins. He was imprisoned in Pontefract Castle, where he died – history claims he

or a sense of it, is vital in human affairs

starved himself to death. And his cousin proclaimed himself King Henry IV. The whole drama was to intrigue William Shakespeare – who, like Arnold Toynbee, was fascinated by the 'horrifying sense of sin manifest in the conduct of human affairs' and its root in human weakness, but whose sense of history was insufficiently developed to allow him to respond with anything more than a facile pessimism.

Pessimism was also the response of the greatest poet of his time to the new chaos that was destroying the Middle Ages. Dante Alighieri was unfortunate enough to be born in Florence – in 1265 – a city that was permanently divided by political squabbles. The old quarrel between followers of the pope and of the emperor – Guelphs and Ghibellines – had become endlessly complicated by feuds between families. Four thousand Guelphs – the party to which Dante's family belonged – were killed at the battle of Montaperto five years before he was born. Ghibellines re-entered the city in triumph six years later, but were almost immediately driven out again when their champion, the Staufer emperor Manfred, was defeated at Benevento.

Dante was in his mid-thirties when the pope – Boniface VIII – sent in a 'referee' to investigate the latest outbreak of bloodshed between the factions; one of the results was that Dante, who had changed sides, was sent into exile, blamed for problems with which he was completely unconnected. For the last twenty-one years of his life he wandered from city to city, dreaming of the family from which he was separated, and of Beatrice, a girl with whom he had fallen in love at the age of nine and who had died in her twenty-fifth year. It was during this time that he wrote his long poem, *The Divine Comedy*.

The poem is the story of a kind of dream voyage, in which Dante is guided through hell and purgatory by Virgil, then through paradise by Beatrice. It is the first – and greatest – epic poem of the Middle Ages, and a revelation of the medieval mind. But the reader who expects it to be a revelation of the religious spirit of St Francis and Cluny will be disappointed. Most of the poem is a piece of savagely satirical journalism, concentrating on personalities and events of the day – rather as if a modern poet had written an epic called the Nixonad about Watergate and modern American politics. And for most of its length, the tone is relentlessly negative, a mixture of spite and self-pity. Dante seems to be completely in the grip of vengeful daydreams about people he hates – precisely the kind of vengefulness we have come to associate with the criminal. The *Comedy* makes us aware that there was something stuffy and petty about the medieval mentality. The human race was still trapped in a kind of suffocating literal-mindedness.

The irony is that this poem created a new form of literature, and showed a way out of the trap. What appealed to Dante's contemporaries was not the unhappy politician, spluttering bile about his enemies; it was the unhappy lover, dreaming about the dead woman he had never even kissed. With unerring instinct, Dante had chosen the precise image that would appeal to a sentimental age: the great poet, bowed down with the weight of unjust exile, separated by death from the woman he loved. In the fourteenth century, the image of Dante had much the same kind of appeal as that of Rudolph Valentino in the twentieth. Unintentionally, Dante had created the romantic cult of the individual.

Other poets learned quickly. Francesco Petrarch, the son of a lawyer, also made literary use of unconsummated love – for a woman he called Laura, whom he saw in a church in Avignon when he was twenty-three – and became the most popular poet in Europe. Out of his personal life he created a new kind of poetry – direct, intimate, full of images of nature. His significance in European history is that he was the first 'romantic'. As a child he preferred books to real life – at one point his father threw them all on the fire – and when his father died he gave up his law studies to devote himself to literature and archaeology. It was Petrarch who made Italy aware of the great monuments of its past. He lived in his imagination, and taught other people to live in theirs. And the hunger for what he had to offer was so great that the whole population of a town often came out to meet him on his travels.

Equally interesting is his own confession of the cause of his lifelong melancholy. In a work called *My Secret*, he admits that his deepest dissatisfaction is with the feebleness of his will-power, which prevents him from achieving the kind of noble life he can imagine. The poet who has been called 'the first Renaissance man' had identified our basic human problem: our inability to control the movements of consciousness.

His younger contemporary Boccaccio also turned his back on a business career to write poetry, and wrote naturally in the 'personal' manner. He has been called the first writer – since he did nothing but write and became famous solely for his writing (even Petrarch was a canon of the Church). But his major contribution to the new freedom of expression was his collection of bawdy tales, *The Decameron*, which celebrated love and sexuality with a frankness that had not been known since Catullus. It is unlikely that Boccaccio would have felt free to write *The Decameron* if the pope had been in Rome instead of Avignon; as it was, he kept the book a secret from his friend Petrarch. But legend has it that he presented a copy to the British ambassador, Geoffrey Chaucer. In due course, Chaucer had no hesitation in placing himself in the centre of *The Canterbury Tales*.

Boccaccio lived in Florence – a city whose importance in the history of the Renaissance is out of all proportion to its size. Its wealthy merchants hired great artists – Giotto, Masaccio, Ghiberti, Uccello, Brunelleschi, Donatello – and turned it into the most beautiful city in Europe. It was also the scene of one of the earliest experiments in a kind of socialism. In 1378, the chief justice, Salvestro de Medici, set out to curb the power of the merchants, and the lower paid wool-workers rebelled and demanded higher wages. They were successful, but the result was an immediate disastrous increase in unemployment. The guilds might be ruthless, but they kept the cash flowing in. The new government soon collapsed. But later, when Florence again felt the need for leadership with a democratic flavour, they recalled that a Medici had helped them against the rich and turned to the head of the family, Cosimo de Medici. The Medicis would be the masters of Florence for most of the fifteenth century – the city's golden age.

As Florence expanded, and Rome again became the city of the popes, the rest of the Mediterranean was aware of the rise of a more sinister force: the Turks. They had been crushed by the Mongols under Genghis Khan, but after Hulagu was chased out of north Africa by the Mamelukes, they resumed their slow expansion. In 1290, the Ottoman dynasty was founded by Osman I. In 1331, Nicaea was taken by the Turks; seven years later, Nicomedia. In 1365, Adrianople – in Thrace – fell and was made the Turkish capital. Now the Turks were established on the western side of Constantinople, and it could only be a matter of time before the capital of eastern Christendom fell. In fact, they besieged Constantinople between 1391 and 1398, and finally withdrew after exacting an enormous tribute. A crusade was called against them in 1396, led by Sigismund of Hungary; an army of twenty thousand Christian knights tried to press forward too quickly and was totally defeated.

At this point, Europe was provided with one more breathing space by yet another incursion of the Mongols. Their leader was another descendant of Genghis Khan – on the female side – called Timur Lenk, Timur the Lame – better known in the west as Tamurlane, the hero of an immensely popular Elizabethan play by Christopher Marlowe. He spent nineteen years (from 1362 to 1380) making himself master of Transoxania, fighting invading nomads; then he spent another seven years conquering Iran. But Tamurlane, while undoubtedly a great general, seems to have been slightly insane. He was a mad, obsessive killer who felt that a conqueror's chief business was to commit murder on a massive scale. His violence was pointlessly sadistic: when he conquered Sabzawar in 1383 he had two thousand prisoners built into a living mound, then bricked in. Later the same year, he had five thousand captives beheaded at Zirih and their heads made into an enormous pyramid. In 1386 he had all his prisoners at Luri hurled over a cliff. In Delhi he massacred a hundred thousand prisoners. This extraordinary madman invaded Anatolia in 1400, took the garrison of Sivas and had its four thousand Christian defenders buried alive. He stands out in world history as the most spectacular sadist of all time. Yet in the pageant of world history, he is very much a sideshow. If he had been another Genghis Khan, he would have consolidated his home base and then spread very slowly to the north, into Russia, the land of the Kipchak nomads. *This* was the country that was then awaiting unification and a strong ruler. If he had done this – as Arnold Toynbee has pointed out – Moscow might now be ruled from Samarkand instead of vice versa.

But Tamurlane seemed to lack even a grain of political good sense. Russia was a bare land of empty steppes. He felt that a conqueror's business was to besiege wealthy cities and decapitate all the inhabitants, and Persia and India were more suitable for this purpose than Russia. In 1395, he even went into Russia on a punitive expedition against Toqatmysh nomads and came within a few days march of the squalid little wooden town called Moscow; but he failed to recognize the prize that lay within his grasp – Russia was still struggling against the Tartars – and turned back towards Samarkand, then to India. His own soldiers objected to attacking their Turkish kinsmen in northern India; but for Tamurlane, it was the only thing worth doing and his will prevailed. In 1405 he set out on an expedition against China, but fortunately died on the way. He was, in a sense, a kind of dinosaur, the last of the old Assyrian-style conquerors who thought in terms of mass-murder and torture. Inevitably, his empire collapsed within half a century of his death.

In 1402, Tamurlane had brought the Ottoman empire to the point of dissolution; but in the following year he retired, and the Turks were able to return to the business of capturing Constantinople. It took them until 1453, and then it was done with the aid of incredibly powerful guns. One cannon fired a ball weighing a quarter of a ton; when it was tested, the cannonball went for almost a mile and buried itself six feet in the ground. The Turks burst into the city on 29 May 1453; the emperor was killed, and the Christian population was dragged off into slavery.

In fact, the taking of Constantinople by Mahomet II proved to be an error of gigantic proportions. It had been the gateway to the east, the great international crossroads where cultures and merchants intermingled. As soon as Mahomet became its master he recognized the danger of killing the goose that laid the golden eggs and tried to persuade the Greeks to stay on. It was too late; the life had drained out of the city of Constantine.

It was still not the end of Turkish ambition. They were masters of Greece; they dreamed of becoming masters of Italy. When Cosimo de Medici was in Venice – in exile from Florence – the Venetians had only just concluded a peace with the Turks after sixteen years of war; they paid for it by handing over some of their trading stations. Half a century later, the war broke out again, and Venice was forced to hand over more trading stations and pay an immense annual tribute to be allowed to trade in the Black Sea. In 1480, the Turks invaded Italy and took Otranto, and in the following year they besieged the knights of St John in Rhodes – fortunately, Mahomet II died and the siege was called off.

In short, the Turks were now expanding all around the Mediterranean, and strangling trade. There had even been a point when they commanded the gateway to the Mediterranean itself, a north African town called Ceuta which looked across the narrow Strait of Gibraltar. If the Turks had been – like the Arabs before them – willing to exchange ideas and trade, it would have made no serious difference; but they seemed to be particularly difficult and bloody-minded – for centuries afterwards, the phrase 'to play the Turk' meant to behave with stupid ferocity, like a dog in a manger.

So in 1415 the Portuguese sent an expedition against Ceuta. Portugal was a young country which had been founded by common-ers during the second crusade. It had a fairly small population and a long sea coast, and it was natural they should become sea traders. Ceuta threatened its livelihood. King John of Portugal sent his son, Prince Henry, with a fleet of ships, and they were lucky enough to be driven by favourable winds and to take the Turks by surprise. Prince Henry sank their fleet, then systematically destroyed Ceuta. Now, at least, European merchants could come and go as they pleased into the Mediterranean.

But the Turks continued to play the Turk, and to block the overland trade routes to the east – to Persia, India, China. And since the Europeans of the fifteenth century had developed a taste for silks and spices, this was disastrous. They had discovered that spices would preserve meat through the long winter, and leave behind a rather more interesting taste than salt. They also believed – quite erroneously – that the smell of spices could prevent the plague, and every nobleman carried an orange stuck with cloves of cinnamon to sniff when he had to walk through a slum quarter. The east was full of cheap spices. But the Turks blocked the route, or charged such enormous duties that it was not worth the long journey.

Europe had still not forgotten Prester John, that great Christian monarch who lived somewhere on the other side of the Turks. If they could find a direct sea route to *his* lands, the problem would be solved. But no one had any idea of whether such a route existed.

The Portuguese had sailed down the west coast of Africa for a thousand miles or so, to Cape Bojador, south of the Canaries; but there the water turned white and looked very dangerous – it was called the Boiling Sea. No one had ventured farther south than that.

Fortunately, Prince Henry of Portugal had money to spare, since he was the Grand Master of the Order of Christ, which had replaced the Templars. He hired map-makers, navigators and ship-designers, and opened a school to train sailors for long-distance exploration. This problem of the sea route to the realm of Prester John became his obsession, so that he earned himself the title of Henry the Navigator. In fact, all his navigating was done from an armchair – he had no desire to risk his own life. His shipwrights built a new type of vessel called a caravel, designed for the open sea instead of (like most ships of his time) the Mediterranean. And in 1427 his caravels sailed out into the Atlantic nearly eight hundred miles from the shores of Portugal. They discovered the islands called the Azores, and Portuguese settlers were soon on their way there.

Cape Bojador still remained a barrier to the south. In 1433, the sailors on a caravel refused to venture into the Boiling Sea, and turned back. Henry, from his armchair, insisted that they had nothing to be afraid of; the boiling seas were probably due to shallows, and all they had to do was to sail out into the ocean and round them. He proved to be correct; the following year, the same ship sailed beyond Cape Bojador and landed on the other side. The sailors found a pleasant land with vines and flowering plants and took samples back to Portugal. Soon Henry's ships were exploring the coast of Africa and setting up trading posts.

Henry the Navigator died in 1460, his dream of finding the route to India still unrealized. Twenty-eight years later, Bartolomeu Dias rounded the Cape of Good Hope. His successor, Vasco da Gama, reached the mouth of the Zambesi and discovered that the Arabs had preceded him by the overland route. But an Arab pilot guided him across to Calicut, in India. When he finally returned home, he had lost three-quarters of his men from scurvy and several of his ships. The Portuguese sent warships to deal with the hostile Arabs and built trading posts all round the coast of Africa.

Meanwhile, a Genoese adventurer named Christopher Columbus had also been in Portugal trying to raise money for his own pet project – finding a way to China and India by sailing west across the Ocean Sea (as the Atlantic was then called). The Portuguese turned him away and he took his project to Spain. Here his luck improved when the Spanish queen, Isabella, became his patroness. Delays were interminable; it was six years before he was ready to start. But on the morning of 3 August 1492, the *Santa Maria*, the *Pinta* and the *Nina* sailed from Palos.

According to the maps of that time, the island of Japan (Zipangu) should be due west of the Canaries, so Columbus began by turning south, then west. Luck had taken him in the right direction – into the north-west winds that roared up the coast of Africa. For weeks, these winds carried them into the Atlantic. The sailors became increasingly nervous – some believed they might fall off the edge of the world. Columbus kept two log books, one showing the real distance and the other a greatly reduced distance, to keep his officers quiet. But when the crew threatened mutiny, he had to promise that if there was no land within three days they would return to Spain.

On the third day – 11 October – a branch with green leaves drifted past the ship. By mid morning of the following day, the delighted sailors were splashing ashore towards a group of naked human beings who looked at them curiously. Columbus had landed on one of the Bahamas; he called it San Salvador. He went on to discover Haiti and Cuba. Then, leaving behind a colony to search for gold, he sailed back to Spain. The total voyage had taken seven months. Columbus was received like a hero and loaded with honours and riches. Yet it is typical of him that he also claimed the large reward that was supposed to go to the first sailor who sighted land. The persistence that enabled Columbus to discover America was partly the sheer manic obsessiveness of the typical Right Man. It was to be responsible for most of his later misfortunes.

When the second ship, the *Pinta*, arrived back in Palos, it brought a rather more dubious gift to the old world – a sexual disease that the captain, Martin Pinzon, had picked up from a native woman. It was called syphilis, and within ten years had spread all over the ports of Europe and the near east – an ironic testimony to how far communications had improved.

Columbus made three more voyages – on the third of which he discovered the mainland of America, landing at the place now called Colon on the isthmus of Panama. But the remainder of his life was something of an anticlimax. His arrogance and stubbornness caused endless trouble, and at one point he was loaded with chains and sent back to Spain. Totally blind to his own shortcomings, he remained convinced that he was a misunderstood saint. He died, exhausted and embittered, at the age of fifty-five.

Absurdly enough Columbus was quite unaware that he had discovered a new land; he thought he had landed in Asia. It was an Italian scholar named Pietro Martire who made a calculation based on the size of the earth (which Eratosthenes had worked out) and realized that Columbus had found an unknown continent – which he christened the New World. Another explorer, Amerigo Vespucci, who crossed the Atlantic soon after Columbus, gave his name to the new continent: America. On a map of 1507, 'America' was shown as a curiously shaped island about a quarter the size of Africa.

Many of these early explorers lost their lives. John Cabot, who explored the coast of north America, vanished with his whole fleet somewhere in the Atlantic; Ponce de Leon, who discovered Florida, was killed by an Indian arrow; Vasco Nunez de Balboa, who crossed Panama and saw the Pacific, survived hostile Indians to be executed by a governor sent out from Spain; Juan Dia de Solis was killed by hostile natives after discovering the River Plate; and Fernando Magellan, who is credited with the first circumnavigation of the globe, never actually completed the two-year voyage (1519–21); he tried to convert the natives of the Philippines to Christianity by pointing guns at them and was killed. *a criminal history*

Most of the rest of this story of the opening of America is a saga of trickery, bad faith and cruelty. In 1519, the governor of Hispaniola sent Hernando Cortez to explore inland. By a curious coincidence, Cortez landed on the coast of Central America at a spot where the Indians expected certain mysterious 'white gods' to return. The legend said that fair-skinned men had landed in the remote past, brought a knowledge of science and engineering, and gone away promising to return. The natives of Mexico – called Aztecs – mistook the Spanish for the benevolent white gods. Cortez had an additional advantage: the natives had never seen horses, and they thought that the horse and rider were one entitity. So the Spaniards, with less than five hundred men, were able to advance to the Aztec capital, Tenochtitlan. The king, Montezuma, received them with courtesy and treated them well. When they saw rooms filled with gold treasures, they decided to seize them for Spain. The king was taken and held captive; Cortez, in effect, became king. But while he was away from the capital, the people rose up in revolt, killed Montezuma and drove out the Spaniards; Cortez had to retake the city with heavy artillery. There was a bloodbath and widespread destruction; then Cortez set out to systematically destroy the power of the Aztecs all over Mexico. Within three years of his landing, the Aztec empire had been destroyed.

The conquest of Peru by Francisco Pizarro followed much the same pattern. Like Magellan, Pizarro was financed by the emperor

– he missed the truly criminal treatment of the natives

overcoming his sense of weakness

Charles V. In 1532, with a mere hundred and eighty men and twenty-seven horses, he marched south from Panama. The Incas, led by their king Atahualpa, came to meet him with an army. Pizarro invited the king to a friendly conference, and the king arrived – unarmed – with a large retinue of noblemen. At a signal, they were attacked by the Spaniards, who killed hundreds. The Indians agreed to ransom Atahualpa with a roomful of gold, and the Spaniards watched it being carried in – more than five million pounds worth. Then the king was strangled. The catastrophe seemed to have paralysed the will of the Incas, and they made no real resistance when the Spaniards occupied their capital, Cuzco. The Inca empire was destroyed as easily as that of the Aztecs. But the Spaniards quarrelled amongst themselves about the spoils, and Pizarro was eventually murdered by plotters.

In the ninety-nine years between the time Henry the Navigator's caravel braved the Boiling Sea and the day Pizarro's men murdered Atahualpa, the world had changed more than in any preceding century. For these were far more than voyages of geographical discovery. They were man's discovery of his own capabilities. The Church could still curb intellectual speculation and convince man that he was a sinner who ought to wait patiently until it should please God to remove him from this wicked world. The spirit of independence was, according to the Church, the spirit of Lucifer; it had caused the downfall of Adam, and on the intellectual level, men were still willing to be convinced. But these voyages of discovery were a practical lesson in the virtue of courage and independence, and there was nothing the Church could do to disguise *their* message. Columbus and Magellan taught men that they should have no fear sailing into unknown seas of the mind. In 1517, two years before Magellan's voyage, Martin Luther proclaimed the new spirit of independence when he nailed his ninety-five theses to the church door in Wittenberg. *Luther/Columbus – the same spirit of daring*

There was another form of revolution that the Church was helpless to suppress: invention. Luther's revolt would have remained confined to Wittenberg if it had not been for a quiet revolution that had taken place in the German town of Mainz. In the 1430s, a silversmith named Johann Ganzfleisch – John Gooseflesh, better known to posterity by his mother's family name of Gutenberg – experimented with a scheme for manufacturing cheap bibles. The

monks of the Middle Ages knew how to carve letters out of wood or
soft metal and use them for printing initial letters on manuscripts.
Gutenberg was working on a method of casting letters in a brass
mould. The main problem was that the mould had to be broken to
get each letter out, so it was wasted. He invented a mould in three
parts, held together by a spring so that it could be taken apart
undamaged. In the 1440s, he went on to use movable type to print
the Bible. It should have made him a rich man; but one of his
partners became impatient for the return of his investment and
ruined the inventor. Gutenberg died blind and forgotten in 1468.

But printing was the invention that Europe had been waiting for;
the proof is that within a mere twenty-three years there were presses
in a hundred and ten towns. By the time Luther nailed his theses to
the church door, all the Greek and Roman classics were available in
cheap translations. The Church tried hard to prevent the reading of
the Bible – on the grounds that people were close to salvation when
they were ignorant – but that battle had already been lost.

The printing revolution would have been impossible without
another revolution: the making of cheap paper. In the Middle Ages,
monks copied out their manuscripts on parchment or vellum, the
skins of animals. The Arabs brought papermaking from China
(where a form of printing had already been invented), and also
invented the horizontal loom, in which the threads could be
separated by merely pressing a foot pedal. When people began to
wear linen instead of wool, old linen was suddenly in plentiful
supply. The result was a good and cheap paper: the paper that
helped to bestow fame on Dante, Petrarch and Boccaccio by
bringing a hand-copied book within the means of everybody who
could read.

In terms of its impact on the European mind, the most influential
of these early printed books was not the Bible or Dante but a
compilation of old tales of chivalry called the *Morte d'Arthur*. Until
the mid-1920s, very little was known about its author, Sir Thomas
Malory, except that he had been born about 1400 in Warwickshire
and been a member of parliament. Then an American scholar,
browsing through an old bundle of manuscripts in the public record
office, came upon the startling information that Malory had been
virtually a one-man crime wave, and had spent the latter part of his
life in prison – where he had written the famous book. After fighting

in the French wars under the Earl of Warwick, Malory had apparently found life in rural Warwickshire too tame and had become the leader of a gang of brigands. In 1451, they broke down the doors of an abbey at Coombe and made off with money and valuables. The records showed that Malory had broken into the house of one Hugh Smyth, and 'feloniously raped Joan, wife of the said Hugh'; a few months later he went back and raped her again. Several accounts of his extorting money 'by threats and oppression' make it clear that he could be regarded as a predecessor of some of the gangsters we shall later consider in the chapter on the Mafia. He was also, according to the records, a cattle rustler and horse thief.

Back in Newgate prison in 1463 – for the third or fourth time – he whiled away the hours compiling the *Morte d'Arthur*, possibly with the aid of the nearby library of Grey Friars. That he was still in prison when he finished it seems to be proved by the words in the final chapter praying God to 'send me good deliverance'.

The handwritten manuscript might well have found its way on to some library shelf and been forgotten. (In fact, such a manuscript – its beginning and end pages missing – *was* found in the library of Winchester school in 1934.) But fortunately, in 1485 – fourteen years after Malory's death – it fell into the hands of the English printer William Caxton. He launched it on the world, and it instantly became almost as popular as the Bible. The rapist and cattle rustler had achieved a belated immortality. But, more important, the *Morte d'Arthur* carried the ideals of knightly chivalry to the far corners of Europe. The great explorers gave man a taste for romance and adventure; it was Malory who carried it into every literate household.

For the Church, this liberation of the human imagination would eventually prove more dangerous than any number of heretics and infidels. But that day had not yet arrived.

Eight

THE CHURCH OVER-TRIUMPHANT

In the week before Easter 1478, a group of would-be assassins arrived in Florence: their intended victims were two of the Medici family: Lorenzo – already called the Magnificent – and his younger brother Giuliano. The plotters included the Archbishop of Pisa, Francesco Salviati, and two leading bankers of Florence, Francesco de' Pazzi and Bernardo Baroncelli. And in Rome, providing moral support for the plot, was the pope, Sixtus IV.

The notion of a pope and an archbishop being involved in a murder plot strikes us as startling: in the fifteenth century it was almost commonplace. The pope was, in effect, the Roman emperor, the Caesar. With enormous revenues flowing in from all over the civilized world, he built palaces, employed great artists, hired armies, poisoned rivals, fathered bastards and gave away important Church appointments to members of his family. Italy was full of rival cities that tried to gobble up all the small towns in their area; the popes made sure that Rome did her share of the gobbling. This is partly what had caused the present coolness between the pope and Lorenzo de' Medici. They both wanted a little town called Imola, which happened to be under the protection of the duke of Milan; the duke had promised it to Lorenzo. Then the pope bribed the duke with an advantageous marriage between his own nephew and the duke's bastard daughter; so Imola became part of the Papal States. Lorenzo took it philosophically – he was that kind of a man. But he got his own back when the Archbishop of Florence died, and the pope wanted to appoint one of his favourites, Francesco Salviati. Lorenzo blocked the appointment and gave it to his own brother-in-law; Salviati had to be contented with a second best – Pisa.

The Medicis were, of course, the leading family of bankers in Florence, although their chief rivals were the Pazzis. The Pazzis were popular with the common people of Florence, but not quite as popular as the Medicis, who were naturally friendly and democratic. When the pope was trying to raise the cash to buy Imola, Lorenzo de' Medici asked the Pazzis not to lend him any money. He thought he could trust their loyalty. Instead, Francesco de' Pazzi went straight to the pope and told him what Lorenzo had suggested. As a result, the pope got his money, and the papal bank account was transferred from the house of Medici to that of Pazzi.

Lorenzo now made the mistake that almost cost him his life. He was young and impulsive, and irritated by Francesco's treachery. A rich man called Giovanni Borromeo was on his death bed; he had no sons, but his daughter was married to a Pazzi. Lorenzo quickly passed a law that said male heirs should be preferred over females; the result was that his own nephews inherited Borromeo's fortune. And it was at this point that the pope and his nephews (the Riario family, who also hated the Medicis) and Archbishop Salviati and Francesco de' Pazzi entered into a conspiracy to remove the Medici brothers and make the Pazzis the rulers of Florence. The pope, in fact, announced that he would not countenance bloodshed; but he knew as well as anyone that the Medicis could not be removed without bloodshed.

The head of the Pazzi family, Jacopo, was brought into the plot; he disliked it, but agreed anyway. Another member, Renato de' Pazzi, thought it would be easier to destroy the Medicis by ruining them financially and opposed the risks of assassination. He was overruled. The duke of Milan had recently been murdered by three noblemen as he entered the cathedral; they did it with such smooth efficiency that no one realized for a few minutes that the duke had been killed – everyone thought he had fainted. Killing the two Medici brothers would be slightly more complicated, since it had to be done at more or less the same time; but at least the Medicis walked about unarmed and without bodyguards.

A condottiere – a professional killer – named Montesecco was hired to carry out the assassination, and he was introduced to Lorenzo de Medici so that he would know his man on the day. Lorenzo was charming and courteous, and Montesecco began to have twinges of conscience about the murder. But it was too late for a change of plan. Two armies of mercenaries were due to arrive outside the gates of Florence on the morning after the killings, and when that happened the cat would be out of the bag anyway.

The plot was simple. A boy named Raffaello Sansoni, one of the Riario family, was staying with the Pazzis for a few days on his way to take up an appointment as the governor of Perugia; he also happened to be a cardinal and a brilliant student at the university of Pisa. Lorenzo was sure to ask the boy to dinner – together with the Pazzis. Lorenzo and his brother Giuliano would be stabbed as they rose from the table.

The invitation went according to plan; when Lorenzo heard that the brilliant boy was in Florence, he invited him to dinner on the evening of Saturday 25 April 1478. But at this point, a hitch arose. Giuliano had hurt his knee, and had to stay in bed. The assassinations had to be postponed. If Giuliano was in bed, it seemed unlikely that he would come to his brother's house the next day. But he might just possibly be persuaded to attend mass in the great cathedral, the Duomo.

And now Montesecco's conscience got the better of him; he had no objection to stabbing a man at dinner, but it was another thing to do it as he knelt at Mass. The archbishop assured him that it was perfectly legal and moral, and that the pope would give him absolution, but Montesecco still refused. The plotters had to turn to the two priests of the Duomo, Antonio Maffei and Stefano de Bagnone, who felt there could be no possible religious objection to killing someone on their own premises.

The boy Raffaello was told nothing about the plot. He was due to collect Lorenzo at his house on Easter Sunday and then go on to the cathedral to perform Mass. When the plotters arrived at Lorenzo's house, they were told that he had already gone ahead with Raffaello. But his brother was still in bed. Pazzi and Baroncelli asked to see Giuliano, exerted their powers of persuasion, and finally got him to dress and accompany them to the cathedral. As they walked in, Pazzi gave Giuliano a friendly squeeze around the waist: he was actually feeling to see if he had brought his dagger. Giuliano was unarmed.

At the given signal, Baroncelli shouted 'Traitor' and plunged his dagger into Giuliano's side. Then other members of the Pazzi family rushed forward and stabbed him another eighteen times. Giuliano died almost immediately. But the priest Maffei was less successful with Lorenzo. Instead of striking first, he placed a hand on Lorenzo's shoulder to steady him for a powerful blow. Lorenzo, more alert than his sick brother, turned quickly, and received a stab wound in the neck. As Pazzi and Baroncelli rushed up to stab him, Lorenzo was surrounded by his friends and hustled into the sacristy, which had bronze doors. The assassins battered on these in vain, then decided it was time to leave. Lorenzo waited until the cathedral was empty and was led home by his friends.

Meanwhile, the head of the Pazzi family was riding around outside waving his sword and shouting 'Liberty and the republic' at the top of his voice. The angry crowd shouted 'Balls', not a reference to that part of the anatomy but to the balls on the Medici coat of arms. When the crowd showed signs of turning ugly, Jacopo rode out of the city gate to his country estate.

Archbishop Salviati's part of the plot was to hurry to the Signoria Palace, where the town councillors – the priors – were meeting and announce that he was taking over the government of the city. His crowd of hired bravos were to rush in shortly afterwards to intimidate the priors. But having entered the courtyard, and let Salviati into the palace, they closed the door behind him, unaware that it had recently been fitted with a spring lock, so that they could not get in. So when, stuttering and stammering, Salviati tried to make his announcement – looking anxiously over his shoulder and wondering what had happened to his bravos – the head of the town council called his guards and arrested the archbishop.

Meanwhile news of Giuliano's murder had spread, and an angry crowd gathered outside the palace. When the gate was forced open they found the trapped bravos and massacred them. Some of the crowd rushed to the Pazzis' house, where Francesco had retired to bed with a wound in his leg; he was dragged back to the palace. Then, as the crowd below screamed 'Balls!', the body of Francesco shot out of the upstairs window, a rope around the neck, and stopped with a grotesque jerk. There was a sound of screaming, and Archbishop Salviati fell out of the same window; he was actually seen to bite Pazzi in the breast as he dangled on the end of the rope, then try to bite through the rope with his teeth. Two more of the plotters followed him. In the square, anyone who was suspected of being in the plot was hacked to death. The boy cardinal had to be escorted back home, while the crowd shouted threats about lynching. Finally, Lorenzo himself appeared at the window of the Signoria, his neck bandaged, and asked the crowd to go to their homes. They obeyed him.

The other two Pazzis – Jacopo and Renato – were caught two days later. Jacopo was tortured and then hanged naked. The innocent Renato, who had opposed the plot, was also hanged on Lorenzo's orders. Such sternness was uncharacteristic of Lorenzo; but he had loved his brother very deeply. The two priests who had tried to stab him were found in hiding; their ears and noses were sliced off, then they were hanged. The hired killer Montesecco was also caught and tortured; he made a full confession implicating the pope, and as a result was allowed a soldier's death by the sword.

Pope Sixtus was understandably furious at the failure of the plot, and the murder of Salviati seemed a direct challenge to his power. He ordered that Lorenzo should be sent to Rome to be tried for the crime. Florence, of course, refused. So the pope excommunicated the city and called for a crusade to destroy it. There were many rival cities who were delighted to answer the call: Siena, Urbino, Naples. The Sienese began to raid Tuscany as did the dukes of Calabria and Urbino. And, most dangerous of all, so did the armies of King Ferrante of Naples, known as one of the toughest and least scrupulous rulers in Italy. Florence's half-hearted mercenaries allowed themselves to be driven back; soon Ferrante commanded most of the Mediterranean coast. Then, as Florence fought with its back to the wall, the plague suddenly arrived, and people began to die at the rate of eight a day. Lorenzo knew his Florentines just as well as Dante knew them; it could only be a matter of time before they decided to hand him over.

But he fought back grimly. His ally the French ambassador managed to stop Lucca from declaring war by threatening to freeze the city's goods in French ports. Florence's allies, Venice and Milan, were persuaded to attack the forces of the pope and King Ferrante in the rear, which at least created a diversion. The pope countered by hiring Swiss troops to cross the Alps into Italy. Things began to look desperate.

And at this point, Lorenzo played the masterstroke of his career. As a man who kept his ear to the ground, he gathered that King Ferrante would like to see Florence humbled, but not destroyed. Besides, the French King Louis XI believed he had a claim to the throne of Naples. As a friend of Lorenzo's, he would be sure to try to avenge his death by turning his armies against Naples. It was not good sense for Ferrante to place his head on the block merely to oblige a thoroughly treacherous pope.

And so Lorenzo walked straight into the lion's mouth – into Naples. It was a dangerous thing to do – Ferrante was known as a man who would offer a safe conduct and then stab his guest in the back. Lorenzo was, quite simply, relying on his famous charm, and on the fact that he knew more about Italian politics than any other man. It took three months, but finally Lorenzo's charm and good sense carried the argument. King Ferrante agreed to peace. The pope was furious and helpless. As Lorenzo returned to Florence, crowds cheered until they were hoarse and every bell in the city rang all day.

In the fluid state of Italian politics, the tide would no doubt have turned against Lorenzo sooner or later – in fact, the king of Naples regretted his decision as soon as he made it, and tried to get Lorenzo to return when he was on the high seas. Then, in 1480, Florence received aid from an unlikely ally – the Turks. They had taken Constantinople in 1453; now they besieged Otranto, in the 'heel' of Italy. And the man behind it – so everyone believed – was Lorenzo; he had casually told King Ferrante that he had some influence with the Turks, and now it looked as if he was telling the truth. Otranto fell, and there was a general belief that Mahomet II intended to march on Rome. The pope decided it was time to make peace. He received an embassy from Florence – naturally, Lorenzo stayed away – and granted the city absolution, while a crowd outside screamed orchestrated abuse at the 'Florentine dogs'. Mahomet II died the following year, and Florence entered on a well-deserved period of peace that lasted until Lorenzo's death in 1492.

By that time, Pope Sixtus had been dead for eight years, replaced by a belligerent nonentity called Innocent VIII. He died in the same year as Lorenzo the Magnificent. It was known that his own choice as a successor was the nephew of Pope Sixtus, Giuliano della Rovere; in fact, at the first ballot, the cardinals unhesitatingly elected him. Then the rival candidate proceeded to distribute enormous bribes – not just money but palaces and promises of high office. At the second ballot, he won easily. He became Pope Alexander VI, and historians show a rare unanimity in agreeing that he was the most corrupt, ungodly and ambitious man who had occupied the throne so far. His name was Rodrigo Borgia.

Rodrigo had a passion for young girls, and since – like most of the Borgias – he had charm and good looks, he was able to lead a life that

Casanova would have envied. The previous pope had to reprimand him for holding an open-air orgy in his garden with crowds of expensive courtesans. (These were the days before Columbus brought the clap back from America and even mass promiscuity was perfectly safe.) His favourite mistress was a virtuous lady named Vannozza Cattanei, who regarded herself as his wife. On her Rodrigo fathered three bastards in succession: Juan, Cesare and Lucrezia. Juan was the eldest and most handsome; he inherited his father's easygoing nature. Cesare was less handsome (although, like all the Borgias, he had nothing to complain about), but more passionate and self-assertive. The youngest, Lucrezia, born in 1480, was pretty and gentle, with a receding chin and a temperament that seemed to beg to be dominated. Both brothers obliged enthusiastically, and vied in teaching their sister erotic games. She was probably the mistress of both of them before she reached her teens.

At the time she was pregnant with Lucrezia, Vannozza was in her late thirties, and felt that her position ought to be legalized. Rodrigo was unable to marry her, but he found her a husband – who became the pope's secretary as a reward. Rodrigo seems to have specified that she should not be unfaithful to him with her new husband, and when she produced a son named Joffré in 1482, suspected she had broken her side of the bargain; nevertheless, he gave the boy the same lavish affection as his brothers Juan and Cesare. One of these two would have to become a soldier, for Rodrigo had secret plans of becoming the master of all Italy. The other, of course, would have to enter the Church, because he would in due course become pope. To Cesare's furious disgust, Juan was chosen for a military career while he was made a priest.

By the time his father became Pope Alexander VI in 1492, Cesare was already displaying signs of that peculiar temperament that would make him the most hated man in Italy. He was a youth of immense self-assertiveness, and he had been spoiled from birth, adored by his mother, later worshipped by his sister, loved and protected by his immensely powerful father. It was the kind of background that had created Caligula and Nero. Cesare was handsome, intelligent and athletic. He could see no earthly reason why his wishes should ever be frustrated. If they were, he exploded into rage. He never forgave an insult or slight. At sixteen, he put off his clerical vestments and rode around Rome fully armed, often with the current mistress by his side. He openly behaved like a lover towards his sister, who was just emerging into her teens, putting his arm round her in public. It may have been this that made the new pope decide that it was time Lucrezia got married. The husband he chose was a minor princeling, Giovanni Sforza, related to the family who governed Milan. Sforza seems to have been delighted at the prospect of an alliance with the most powerful family in Italy. But when he caught the look of brooding hostility on the face of his new brother-in-law, and heard of his reputation for disposing of his enemies with untraceable poisons, he must have realized that he had made a mistake. For the time being, in any case, he could not consummate the marriage, because Lucrezia was under age. At an early opportunity, he slipped off back to his estates at Pesaro.

The pope had fallen in love again, with a young girl named Giulia Farnese, who had long blond hair strikingly similar to Lucrezia's. Giulia was betrothed to the pope's nephew, Orsino, a child with a bad squint. Giulia did not resist the handsome Rodrigo for long; she became Orsino's wife and Rodrigo's mistress. The alliance was the beginning of the immense fortunes of the Farnese family. The boy Orsino did not seem to mind being cuckolded by his uncle, or if he did, he had no choice. As a reward for the Farnese family, the pope decided to make Giulia's brother a cardinal – although he was aware that this was a move that would meet with strong opposition. While he was about it, it seemed good sense to make Cesare a cardinal as well. He waited until half the cardinals were out of Rome, then called the other half together and bullied and threatened them into creating the two new cardinals.

When the much-hated King Ferrante of Naples died in 1494, his son Alfonso came to the throne, and the pope decided to confirm his friendship by marrying his twelve-year-old son Joffré to Alfonso's pretty illegitimate daughter Sanchia. At sixteen, Sanchia already had a reputation for promiscuity; she seemed a suitable addition to the Borgia clan. Besides, the pope liked young girls. But his bargain caused another menace to loom on the horizon. The French King Charles VIII – successor to Louis XI – felt he had a claim on Naples. In 1494, the worst happened, and Charles invaded Italy to claim his throne. It was to be the beginning of four centuries of foreign invasions and foreign domination.

For the Medicis in Florence, the invasion was disastrous. The new ruler of Florence was Lorenzo's son Piero; but he was not half the man his father was. He had inherited the chief of his father's troubles – a fiery monk called Savonarola, a kind of mad puritan who seethed with rage at the carnivals organized by the Medicis, and who had refused to give Lorenzo absolution on his deathbed. As the French army marched into Italy – defeating Alfonso at Rapallo – Savonarola went to meet the king at Pisa and announced that he was God's agent who had come to restore the Church to its old virtues. As Charles drew near to Florence, Piero began to suffer convulsions of guilt and bad conscience; he had been partly responsible for the invasion by supporting Alfonso. Charles was not interested in Florence, but he was glad to accept the gold that Piero offered him, and the use of Florentine fortresses. The people of Florence were enraged at this pusillanimous conduct; they stoned Piero in the streets and chased the Medicis out of Florence. Then Florence declared itself a republic. In fact, Savonarola was its ruler. He encouraged the destruction of all 'vanities', including books and art treasures. The Medici palaces were attacked and priceless books, paintings and sculptures destroyed. During the carnival in 1497, a great bonfire was built in the square outside the Signoria palace, piled high with all of the usual carnival apparel – false beards and wigs, masquerade dresses – as well as books, paintings and other vanities; as the bonfire blazed, the people sang a Te Deum. But they soon grew tired of wearing sober clothes and singing hymns. Savonarola had gained his influence by telling them that the old times were the best, that the men of the past had all the virtues of decency; the Florentines were always susceptible to sentimental nostalgia. Now they had a chance to make a realistic assessment of the 'old ways' and their response was to have Savonarola arrested. The man who was really behind this was the pope, Rodrigo Borgia; he was growing nervous as Savonarola denounced the corruption of the Church. He ordered Savonarola to be tortured continually until he confessed something that would allow them to sentence him to death: on one single day, the monk was placed on the rack fourteen times. On the morning of 23 May 1498, Savonarola was taken to a scaffold that stood on the exact spot where the 'bonfire of vanities' had been held the year before and hanged with two companions; then his body was burned in front of the crowd. Rodrigo Borgia had once again silenced the opposition.

The pope himself had been humiliated by the invasion of Charles VIII. His mistress Giulia and her sister had been captured by the French, and had to be ransomed for a huge sum; fortunately their captor was a man who held high ideals of chivalry, so they were not violated. But the women of Rome were less fortunate when the French army arrived in January 1495 on its way to Naples. The pope took refuge in the Castel Sant Angelo, and the French plundered and raped for several days. The king issued orders that all looters were to be hanged, but this did not prevent them from breaking into the house of Cesare's mother a few days later. (Cesare later managed to lay his hands on these looters – Swiss mercenaries – and tortured them horribly.) The pope was forced to sue for peace. He even agreed to hand over Cesare as a hostage. So when Charles rode out of Rome towards Naples, Cesare Borgia accompanied him. He was dressed in his cardinal's robes and had seventeen velvet-covered wagons behind him – he said these were his travelling clothes. Cesare managed to compel the respect of the French officers with his skill in wrestling; but at the first opportunity he slipped away and returned to Rome. His seventeen wagons were found to be empty. For the first time, Rome laughed with approval at one of Cesare's exploits.

The foreign invasion had served to unite various warring factions against the French, and Charles had to retreat back across the Alps. Alfonso of Naples had been forced to abdicate; but when Charles was driven out he returned. The pope thereupon invited Alfonso and his beautiful daughter Sanchia to Rome. He was anxious to take another look at this dazzling teenager. In fact, Sanchia found she could twist the pope around her finger. Cesare, who was totally unable to resist any attractive girl (or youth, for that matter, for he was bisexual) lost no time in luring her to his apartment. Sanchia had heard of his reputation as the most dangerous man in Italy; therefore it was only a matter of prudence to submit. They were both sensualists, and neither felt any pangs of conscience about becoming lovers. The pope showed no jealousy; it seems fairly certain that he was also enjoying her favours.

Rodrigo was wondering how he could use the war to further his own schemes of expanding the papal territories. When Charles VIII returned to France, he decided to attack Charles's ally, the Orsini family. His son Juan – the one who was supposed to be the soldier – was in Spain, where he had inherited the title of Duke of Gandia. His father sent for him to come back to Italy, and placed him in charge of the army. But he proved to be a poor general. When the papal troops were defeated near Bassano in January 1497, the pope had to sue for peace, and Juan – to his brother's unconcealed delight – returned to Rome in disgrace.

Lucrezia's husband, Giovanni Sforza, seemed to realize that his days would be numbered if he stayed within reach of Cesare; so he was now a permanent absentee and the pope decided that Lucrezia should be divorced. It was scandalous, but it seemed to be the only way. The grounds chosen were non-consummation of the marriage on account of her husband's impotence. Sforza was enraged by this slur on his virility, but when he was told that in order to legally disprove it he would have to perform the sexual act with a courtesan in front of a panel of churchmen, he reluctantly decided to allow himself to be divorced.

Lucrezia was placed in a convent, to silence rumour. But no one objected when her brother Cesare went to see her there. Six months later, to the pope's deep embarrassment, Lucrezia was found to be pregnant – six months pregnant. Cesare was not the kind of man who could resist possessing his sister under the nose of a mother superior. In the event, the skill of Lucrezia's dressmaker concealed her condition, and she behaved so demurely in front of the judges that no one doubted she was a virgin. In due course, Lucrezia gave birth to a son. Three years later, a three-year-old child was brought to the Vatican, given the name of Giovanni Borgia, and made an heir to the Borgia fortune. Roman gossip declared that he was not merely the pope's grandson but also his son – for Rodrigo was as sexually experimental as Cesare and enjoyed sharing his son's mistresses. Meanwhile, the pope decided that if Lucrezia was to be prevented from causing further embarrassment, she urgently needed another husband. With his policy of keeping these things in the family, he decided that Sanchia's brother Alfonso would be an ideal candidate.

Meanwhile, Rome had a baffling mystery to gossip about. It was a murder mystery, and the victim was Juan Borgia, the pope's eldest son. On Wednesday 14 June 1497, Juan and Cesare went to supper with their mother. They left before dark, accompanied only by two footmen, and by a mysterious masked man who had joined them during supper. Juan had been seen in public with this masked man on a number of occasions recently, and seemed fond of him – Juan, like Cesare, was bisexual. Now they rode off, with the masked man sharing the saddle of Juan's horse. At a certain point, Juan announced that he was going off on his own; Cesare apparently warned him that it was dangerous at this time of night. But the pope's guards had made the streets of Rome safer than for many years, and Juan shrugged off the objections and rode into the night with his masked friend. He was never seen alive again. A boatman on the Tiber reported seeing a man leading a horse, with what appeared to be a body across the saddle, and heard someone address the horseman as 'My lord'. Then there was a splash.

The river was dragged and Juan's body was recovered; he had nine stab wounds, and his money was untouched. The pope was shattered, locked himself in the Vatican, and cried and fasted for three days. Most Romans believed that Juan had been killed by enemies of the pope – perhaps by the Sforzas or the Orsinis. It was only later that people began to put two and two together. While his brother was alive, Cesare was doomed to remain in the Church; but what Cesare wanted above all things was to prove himself as a soldier. After the death of Juan, Cesare was finally released from his vows and given a French title, the Duke of Valence (it was all part of a package deal with the new French king, Louis XII, who wanted a divorce). Cesare usually succeeded in getting his own way.

Cesare's new dukedom served a double purpose; it cemented the pope's relationship with the French king, and it gave the pope an opportunity to get rid of Cesare for a while. He went to France, asked the French king to find him a bride, and set about making himself thoroughly disliked. It was not difficult; he had been spoilt and he was very arrogant. The French began inflicting minor humiliations, and Cesare was thrown into fits of rage. Finally, he was married to the sixteen-year-old daughter of the king of Navarre; in a letter to his father, he described the sexual details of their wedding night at length; this was the kind of thing the pope appreciated. Cesare seems to have acquitted himself manfully, although he was by this time suffering from the disease that Columbus's sailors had brought back. The syphilis seemed to be improving with treatment, but its signs were already apparent on Cesare's once-handsome face.

Then, with the pope's approval, the king of France invaded Italy and Cesare came with him. Back in Rome, he began a curious campaign of murder against people who had been with him in

France, paying back the slights and insults he had been forced to swallow in the French court. Young men with whom he had had intimate relations died suddenly after banquets, or were found stabbed to death in the Tiber. The Romans recalled the death of his brother Juan, and began to see the light.

Meanwhile, Cesare had at last achieved his ambition of being a successful general. There had been a rather incompetent plot to poison the pope; Caterina Sforza was suspected of being behind it. She was a widow of a Riario, and as governor of Imola and Forli, one of the pope's bitterest opponents. She was also still a beautiful woman. Cesare set out with the hope of conquering more than her two towns.

In fact, his victories were almost a walkover. Caterina had been a harsh ruler, and her subjects were delighted to surrender to Cesare Borgia. Imola fell; so did Forli. Caterina took refuge in the castle of Forli, but was finally forced to surrender. Cesare made sure she surrendered absolutely everything, and he wrote his father a detailed account of his night in her bed. Well pleased with himself, Cesare went back to Rome. In his conquering mood, he longed for the soft embraces of his sister. It seemed intolerable that she should still be married to Alfonso – and apparently in love with him. In July 1500, Alfonso was crossing St Peter's square after eating supper with the pope. Some pilgrims approached him and he reached into his pocket for money. Suddenly he was surrounded, and daggers rose and fell. He was strong, and fought furiously. Papal guards ran towards them and the attackers took to their heels. Alfonso, bleeding badly, was carried to his wife's apartment in the Vatican, and there his wife and his sister Sanchia worked tirelessly to save his life. When he began to recover, the pope gave him a room close to his own, to make sure there would be no further attacks. Just a month after the original attack, Lucrezia and Sanchia left him alone for an hour. They came back to find him strangled. Cesare, accused of the murder, openly admitted it; he said it was self-defence – that Alfonso had fired a cross-bow at him as he walked in the garden.

The people of Naples demanded an enquiry into the case. The pope promised it – then forgot about it. Lucrezia, grief-stricken, went off to her castle at Nepi. Cesare also prepared to set out on another military expedition. He made sure that he called at Nepi on the way. And although Lucrezia knew that her brother was her husband's murderer, she flung her arms round his neck when they met. Cesare had to demonstrate that she belonged to him again.

After establishing his right to his sister, Cesare marched off to further conquests. He had the kind of dash and boldness that can bring swift victories. The aim was to subjugate Romagna, the area to the south of Venice. The pope provided the money by selling cardinal's hats to twelve completely unsuitable but wealthy candidates. Cesare captured Rimini, Fano and Pesaro; Faenza, under its young master Astorre Manfredi, held out for months but surrendered in March 1501. Cesare had the bit between his teeth. It looked as if nothing could stop him. In chapter 7 of *The Prince* his friend and adviser Machiavelli tells a typical story, with obvious approval. When Cesare had subdued Romagna – and been created duke by his father – he decided that the province needed stern laws; there was too much brigandage and general disorder. So he appointed the most ruthless man he knew – Remirro de Orco – with full authority to do anything he liked to restore law and order. Orco carried out the task with ferocity, and soon had the whole region cowering. At which point, Cesare – who wanted to avoid the blame for this cruelty – had Orco seized, hacked into two pieces and left out in the public square at Cesena. It looked as if Cesare had meted out a brutal end to someone whose brutality he detested; so everyone was satisfied.

Machiavelli tells another story with equal approval: how when Cesare learned of a plot against him he charmed the plotters – all noblemen – with offers of good will and future alliances. They were invited to come and discuss their problems at a friendly banquet, and arrived without weapons. As they sat down to talk, they were seized from behind and strangled.

In the summer of 1502, Cesare displayed the same qualities on the field of battle. His latest objective was the town of Camerino. This lay well to the south of his other conquests in Romagna, and the major town of Urbino lay between the two. Its duke, Guidobaldo, was a friend and ally, so felt he had no reason to worry about his exposed position. Cesare marched on Camerino from the south – and then, unexpectedly, swung north and seized Urbino – Guidobaldo had to flee to Mantua. Then Cesare turned south and took Camerino. If anyone had accused him of treachery, he would probably have replied that if an ally is in a position to stab you in the back, then it is commonsense to get in the first stab.

Meanwhile, Lucrezia had married again. Considering the risk involved in forming an alliance with the Borgias, it is surprising that anyone was willing to accept her. But the pope was aware that his magnificent vitality was failing; he wanted to see his favourite daughter settled. For an enormous dowry, the duke of Ferrara agreed to permit the alliance of the pope's bastard daughter with his son, Alfonso D'Este. It was Cesare himself who suggested the alliance, and this seems to be evidence that his military successes had given him a new self-confidence and drawn some of his venom. But before his sister left for Ferrara, Cesare made sure she spent her final nights in his bed. As a kind of farewell party he brought fifty courtesans into his apartments in the Vatican, then made them scramble, naked, for hot roasted chestnuts. Lucrezia presented the prizes.

And then, with shattering suddenness, the whole edifice of power came tumbling down. On Friday 11 August 1503, the pope and Cesare attended a party at a vineyard just outside the city; their host was cardinal Adriano Castelli da Corneto. Roman gossip later declared that the Borgias wanted the cardinal's wealth and had taken along a jar of poisoned jam; the cardinal got wind of the plot and poisoned the food of his guests. It could be true – the list of cardinals who had died at convenient moments and left the pope their estates is a long one. On the other hand, it is just as likely that the damp vineyard harboured some kind of fever. The next day, the pope, the cardinal and Cesare were all ill in bed. For a few days, the pope and his son were both on the point of death; then both began to recover, and the pope sat up and played a game of cards. On 18 August he had a relapse and died.

Cesare, still lying ill in bed, was in trouble, and he knew it. If one of his father's enemies became pope, his career would be at an end. From his sickbed he frantically plotted and pulled strings. When a harmless and aged cardinal was elected Pius III, he heaved a sigh of relief; at least he had a breathing space. But it proved to be too short. The shock of becoming pope was too much for the old man, who died within a month. And the man who replaced him – as Julius II – was a member of the Rovere family, those old enemies of the Borgias. On the day Julius was elected, Cesare told Machiavelli grimly that 'he had thought of everything that might happen on the death of his father, and provided against everything, except that he never thought that at his father's death he would be dying himself'.

It was a realistic assessment. Like the Old Man of the Mountain, Cesare had created so much hatred and disgust that he was regarded as a poisonous spider. Three years earlier the Venetian ambassador had reported: 'Every night, four or five murdered men are discovered – bishops, prelates and others – so that all Rome is trembling for fear of being destroyed by the duke Cesare.' Now that the pope was dead, Rome was determined to have no further cause to tremble. Cesare took refuge in the Castel Sant Angelo to avoid the daggers of his enemies. Lucrezia, safe in Ferrara, wrote to the king of France to ask him to allow Cesare to take up his dukedom there; but for the French, Cesare was now an embarrassment. For a while it looked as if his star was rising again; the new pope was forced to confirm him as head of the papal armies and sent him off to quell rebellions. Then he changed his mind and had Cesare arrested and brought back to the Vatican as a prisoner – he was kept in the room where Lucrezia's second husband had been strangled. The Spaniards, who had been backing Cesare, realized that he was too dangerous to be allowed to raise an army. When Cesare escaped from Rome and hurried to his allies in Naples, the Spanish king Ferdinand had him arrested and put in prison on the island of Ischia. After two months there, he was forced to agree to give up his conquests in Romagna. Everything he had gained was now lost. Then he was allowed to go to Spain. But he had forgotten that his brother Juan had left a widow, and that she was determined to revenge her husband's murder. Cesare was arrested again and imprisoned at Cincilla. The Spaniards had only one reason for keeping him alive: he was a valuable pawn to use against the pope. To have Cesare in prison was like having a plague germ in a bottle. In 1506, Cesare escaped, and succeeded in joining his brother-in-law, the king of Navarre, who was engaged in a territorial dispute in Spain. Cesare again became a commander – of a mere hundred troops. Determined to demonstrate that he was as bold as ever, he rode ahead of the rest of the army and engaged the enemy. Luck had deserted him. He was badly wounded and left to die of thirst, stripped naked. It was 12 March 1507, and Cesare Borgia was still under thirty-one years of age.

Cesare had only three mourners: his mother Vannozza, his sister Lucrezia, and his one-time adviser, Niccolo Machiavelli. Machiavelli was a Florentine diplomat who began to make his mark *a new attitude in a culture*

shortly after the execution of Savonarola; the son of a poverty-stricken lawyer, he felt – like most of these Renaissance men – that success was the only thing that mattered. Being interested in power, he studied the gigantic chessboard of Renaissance Italy with fascination. When the Medicis came back to power, aided by the pope and the Spaniards, Machiavelli fell from favour and decided to write a book to try to ingratiate himself with the younger Lorenzo de Medici. Arrested, tortured and finally released, he spent his retirement producing *The Prince*, a work that has baffled generations of scholars. Its advocacy of cynical opportunism is so extraordinary that it seems inconceivable that he wrote it without some ulterior motive. It has been suggested that it is intended as satire – like Swift's pamphlet suggesting that the people of Ireland should overcome starvation by eating their own children – or that he hoped to lure the younger Lorenzo to his own downfall. Both suggestions overlook the essential simplicity of Machiavelli's outlook. He had no more inclination towards religion than Cesare Borgia had – or Rodrigo. Therefore, life was a question of how to achieve your objectives as economically as possible. For Machiavelli, the only worthwhile political objective was Italian unity. Cesare had brought that closer by conquering Romagna, and if it had not been for his bad luck in falling ill in 1503, he might have conquered the whole of Italy. With objectives as important as this, what did a little poisoning and a little treachery matter?

The argument sounds quite plausible – until we study the life of Cesare Borgia. Then we see that Machiavelli's argument has one serious flaw. Cesare was a half-insane sadist, a Right Man driven by an outsize ego. Whatever success he achieved, the inner worm would have finally destroyed him – the total inability to control his own negative emotions. Even his political policies were short-sighted; his ruthlessness made him dangerous and therefore hated. Cesare *was* a symbolic figure; but not, as Machiavelli thought, of the ideal Renaissance Prince. He was, quite simply, the archetypal criminal, the man who spends his life taking short-cuts. Nothing is worse for a criminal than early success; it trains his reflexes to develop the lightning-grab. And without a counterbalancing self-control, he is bound to go too far. On one occasion when Cesare lost his temper with a cardinal in front of the pope, he drew his sword and actually stabbed the man so that blood splashed on the pope's robes. (The

man oscillates between religions a Chine [?] (handwritten)

cardinal survived.) This was not the quality of a 'man of iron'; it was mere lack of self-control. The death of his father made him realize that he had never possessed real power; he had been standing on his father's shoulders. This is what he meant when he told Machiavelli that he had died on the same day as his father. The megalomaniac dream was over.

It becomes possible to see why reformers all over Europe were longing for the downfall of the Church. It was not simply that it had become corrupt – that could be remedied. It was that the Church had nothing whatever to do with religion. Rodrigo Borgia was not a particularly bad man. Apart from conniving at the murder of a few cardinals, he did nothing very wicked. But he had no more to do with the teaching of Jesus than Tiberius had. He was simply an updated Caesar. The Church was on to a good thing, and he knew it.

We have seen that history seems to be a story of the pendulum-swings of the human spirit between evolutionary purpose and mere materialism – that is, between religion and crime. Man needs material prosperity; it is basic to his survival. But when he has achieved material security, he finds himself oddly dissatisfied and confused. An instinct tells him that it is now time to turn to more important matters. This instinct aims ultimately at control: control of his own conscious processes. He recognizes intuitively that such control can only be achieved if he can attach himself to some greater purpose, like a water-skier to a speedboat. And, absurdly enough, that he could achieve this aim more satisfactorily in a monastery cell or on a mountain top than in a palace. This is why Petrarch and Boccaccio became famous all over Europe, in spite of the fact that their books had to be copied by hand. Petrarch is remembered as the first man who climbed to a hilltop merely to look at the view. And when Boccaccio described his young men and women telling their risqué stories in the midst of trees and flowers, he was giving expression to a new form of human longing – the same longing that had swept the Mediterranean world thirteen centuries earlier when the preacher from Nazareth announced the end of the world and a 'new deal' for the human race. What man wanted instinctively was a 'new deal'. The plague only focused and intensified that longing. And the soul of man could begin to grasp its meaning on mountain tops or in the midst of woods and streams. Yet no one could deny the practical need for palaces – and hovels.

It must have seemed to these men of the late Middle Ages that the Persian prophet Mani was obviously right when he said that man consists of two warring principles, body and spirit. And this is why movements like the Cathars were so dangerous to the Church, and were stamped out with such murderous ferocity. To us, it seems obvious that the Cathars had oversimplified the problem to the point of absurdity. We know that man *does* possess two egos, that they appear to be associated with the double-brain, and that their purpose is to co-operate with each other like two lumberjacks at either end of a double-handed saw. The Cathars believed that the two principles were engaged in a war to the death, and that religion demanded that we should starve and humiliate the conscious ego. Naturally, then, they believed that the popes, with all their wealth, were on the devil's side without knowing it. The popes were more reasonable and, in a logical sense, closer to the truth. They felt that man must learn to balance on a tightrope between body and spirit, and try to give each its due. They also recognized that man is ignorant and undisciplined and needs some kind of authority to give his life a basic semblance of order. Since the Cathars wanted to destroy that authority, they could not be treated with tolerance.

John Wycliffe was another spiritual reformer, the religious equivalent of Petrarch, expressing the same craving for simplicity and deeper purpose. It was on a visit to Bruges in 1374, as an ambassador to the papal court, that he was shocked by the worldliness of the Catholic clergy. The impulse that drove him was identical to the impulse that drove the abbots of Cluny and St Francis of Assisi – a desire to give people a sense of religious purpose. In Rome, he might well have started his own religious movement within the Church and ended by being canonized. But he happened to be an Englishman who lived in a time when the pope was a pawn of the king of France, and England was at war with France. John of Gaunt used him as a pawn in his own political machinations. So Wycliffe, by a historical accident, became the first 'Protestant'. He happened to concentrate his attack on what was, for the Church, a particularly dangerous point: the notion that the consecrated wafer does not really turn into the flesh of Christ. For Wycliffe, it was self-evident

institutional crime

nonsense. But for the Church it meant that, if the blessed sacrament is a fraud, then a priest is not necessary to administer it. The priest would be superfluous. This is why the Church wanted to burn Wycliffe – who, fortunately, being in England, was beyond its reach. Besides, with two popes, the Church was too divided to do much harm.

The Bohemian reformer Jan Hus was less lucky. He was deeply influenced by Wycliffe, and ten years after Wycliffe's death (in 1384) was delivering lectures at the University of Prague in which he called for Church reform. The Church leaders were horrified, but the common people agreed it was a time for change. In 1410, the archbishop of Bohemia became so incensed at the constant use of Wycliffe's name that he had two hundred copies of his books burnt on a bonfire. But two years later Hus became rector of Prague university and went on repeating his heresies. There were, he pointed out, now three popes claiming to be the head of Christendom – not all of them could be infallible.

In 1414, the Church itself recognized that this farce of too many popes had to be brought to an end as quickly as possible; so a council of bishops was convened at Constance. Hus was asked to go and explain himself. He refused until the Holy Roman Emperor, who also happened to be king of Bohemia, gave him a solemn promise that he had nothing to fear and a safe conduct. Hus went to Constance, and was immediately arrested. Dragged into the council hall, he was ordered to renounce his heresies. He refused, although he knew it meant death. The Church made this as horrible as possible by burning him alive. The Church council went on to declare Wycliffe a heretic in retrospect and ordered that his bones should be dug up and burned.

The Council of Constance finally healed the breach within the Church; Martin V was made pope. He proclaimed a crusade against Hussites and Lollards (Wycliffites), and an army marched into Bohemia, where the murder of Hus (and his friend Jerome of Prague) had aroused powerful national feelings. But three 'crusades' all failed to break the resistance of the Bohemians; their land was ravaged; all kinds of atrocities were committed; but the invaders were driven out.

In Italy, crime had become as commonplace and as widespread as in England before the Black Death. In its state of constant war, things could not have been otherwise. In Parma in 1480, the governor was intimidated by threats of murder into throwing open all the public jails and letting out the criminals; the natural consequence was an epidemic of burglary and murder – some houses were even besieged and demolished by the armed gangs. One priest called Don Niccolo de Pelagati carried the materialistic principles of Pope Rodrigo to an absurd extreme. On the day he celebrated his first mass he also committed a murder, but received absolution upon a suitable payment. He then began a career of crime that included killing four men and marrying two wives, with whom he travelled. As the historian Jacob Burckhardt says in his *Civilization of the Renaissance in Italy*: 'He afterwards took part in many assassinations, violated women, carried others away by force, plundered far and wide, and infested the territory of Ferrara with a band of followers in uniform, extorting food and shelter by every sort of violence.' Don Niccolo was caught and hung up in an iron cage outside San Giuliano in Ferrara in 1495. Yet he had done nothing that Cesare Borgia had not done on a far larger scale.

In the year 1500, Pope Rodrigo Borgia declared a Jubilee, a year in which all pilgrims who made the journey to Rome should receive total absolution for their sins. The idea, we may recall, had been devised by Pope Boniface VIII, who needed croupiers to rake in the coins from the tomb of St Peter. In 1500, Rodrigo Borgia needed money for Cesare's wars and decided that some new attraction should be provided. He ordered that a special door, a Holy Door, should be made in St Peter's, and circulated the story that it had always existed but that it was bricked up after every Jubilee and reopened a century later . . . The result was that the Jubilee of 1500 brought in larger sums than ever before, all of which instantly vanished into the Borgia coffers.

The Jubilee also involved a minor drawback that the pope had overlooked. Pilgrims who arrived in Rome and discovered that it was virtually a sixteenth-century Las Vegas or Monte Carlo – a city geared to making money at top speed – were bound to feel disillusioned about the Church. They were bound to compare these Roman churches with their small church at home, with its underpaid priest. Why *should* Rome be the automatic recipient of a river of gold? It was the feeling that had fuelled the Hussite revolt of a century ago; now it began to smoulder again.

In the year 1510 a young German monk named Martin Luther came to Rome on a mission to the pope. The man on the papal throne at the time was the Rovere – Julius II – who had imprisoned Cesare Borgia. Julius lacked Rodrigo Borgia's charm; he was a man of strong opinions and fiery temper. But he was the kind of pope Italy needed at the time. His method of dealing with the French invaders – encouraged by Rodrigo – was not to call for a crusade but to put on armour and lead his troops into battle. In ten years, the 'warrior pope' drove the foreigners from Italian soil. It was Julius II who hired a young man named Raphael to paint murals in the papal palace, and Michelangelo to paint the ceiling of the Sistine Chapel. (The two had endless clashes – one day the pope was heard roaring from the top of a ladder: 'Do you want me to throw you off this scaffolding?') He also wanted to complete St Peter's, and this required an enormous sum of money. Rome hummed with the sound of priests gabbling masses at top speed and hurling money into their coffers.

At twenty-seven years of age, Martin Luther had his own problems. He was a manic depressive who experienced sudden fits of deep misery, even of panic. Convinced that he was under direct assault by the devil – he still experienced twinges of sexual desire – brother Martin longed to feel confident about his own salvation. The prospect of a journey to Rome – to ask the pope to settle some minor religious dispute – filled him with immense expectation; surely the sight of the bones of St Peter, of the actual stairs that Jesus had climbed to appear before Pilate, of the crown of thorns and the fragments of the cross, would dissipate the fog of indifference that numbed his senses?

In the event, Luther was enough of a realist not to be too horrified at the reality of Rome; but he was disappointed. The priest who heard his general confession did not really seem to understand; he certainly didn't care. Luther wanted to say mass at the entrance to the Sancta Sanctorum chapel, but it was too crowded, and irritable priests muttered 'Passa, passa' – 'Move on.'

All the same, it was not the journey to Rome that undermined Martin Luther's faith. He knew that religion is a spiritual reality and that the man of God must learn to see through the world of matter as if it were made of glass. When he returned to Saxony – this time to the monastery at Wittenberg – this feeling was confirmed by his new vicar, Johann von Staupitz, who was a mystic. He had read the writings of the great German mystics – Eckhart, Suso, Tauler, Mechtild of Magdeburg – all of whom taught that the soul can achieve ultimate union with God. But all mystics have passed through a 'dark night of the soul', a period in which they were unable to feel, even to pray. 'If it had not been for Dr Staupitz,' said Luther, 'I should have sunk in hell.'

Staupitz encouraged Luther to preach and lecture – in August 1513 he began lecturing on the Psalms. By 1515, he was preparing his lectures on St Paul. His problem, he found, was to understand the phrase 'the justice of God'. He assumed that it meant the punishment meted out to sinners. So God was a just and angry God – admirable, but hardly lovable. He wanted to be able to drop his defences, to experience emotional catharsis, a sense of reconciliation. And one day, as he wrestled with this problem of the justice of God, it came. 'I grasped that the justice of God is that righteousness by which through grace and sheer mercy God justifies us through faith.' The significant words here are 'through grace and sheer mercy'. Luther had succeeded in breaking through the psychological barriers of fear and mistrust, into a perception of an all-loving God. 'Thereupon I felt myself to be reborn and to have gone through open doors into paradise.'

As with Wycliffe, the historical accident of being born far from Rome prevented Luther from using his new insight for the good of the Church. If he had been born an Italian, he might, like St Francis, have appealed to the pope to allow him to form a movement to carry his message directly to the people. There was nothing in it that was contrary to the teachings of the Church. He wanted to assure people that they were not damned, that this medieval world of devils and demons was a lie, or at least, only a half-truth. It was the other half that mattered: the grace and mercy of God. Faith itself was enough to ensure salvation. This was the message Luther poured into his sermons of 1515 and 1516.

Unfortunately, it contained the germ of a disagreement with the present policies of the Church. In 1513, Julius the warrior-pope had been replaced by Leo X, the son of Lorenzo the Magnificent. Leo shared with Rodrigo Borgia the feeling that life was intended for enjoyment, and spent so much time in his hunting boots that pilgrims found it hard to kiss his feet. He ate well, drank well, kept

individualism

individual qualities replace salvation mad money

court jesters, and spent enormous sums of money on art and entertainment – for example, on the newly invented entertainment called opera. Leo was the pope of whom it was said that he spent three papal treasuries – his predecessor's, his own and his successors'. Inevitably, he needed money, and since he could not proclaim a Holy Year for another ten years or so, he encouraged the sale of indulgences. These were bits of paper, handed out by a priest, that stated that the recipient was, for the time being, freed of all his sins. Since everyone believed literally in the picture of the afterlife described in Dante, with each minor sin costing, perhaps, a century in Purgatory, most people felt that indulgences were a good bargain. But they were, of course, expensive – a prince could expect to pay twenty-five gold pieces, and even a commoner was expected to find one gold piece – perhaps a year's income.

If Luther was correct about faith, then these highly profitable indulgences were useless, or at least, irrelevant. A piece of paper was no substitute for faith. Besides, religious experience demanded suffering – Luther knew this from personal experience. 'God works by contraries, so that a man feels himself to be lost at the very moment when he is on the point of being saved . . . Man must first cry out that there is no health in him. He must be consumed with horror. This is the pain of Purgatory.' Luther was not saying anything with which the desert fathers would not have agreed wholeheartedly. But for the pope and the German princes, it was being said at the worst possible moment.

For example, Prince Albert of Brandenburg was already a bishop of two cities, and when the archbishop of Mainz died, he recognized that this appointment would be a valuable addition to his income. The problem was that three archbishops had died within ten years, and the parish could not afford the vast fee demanded by Rome to install a new one – ten thousand ducats. Albert borrowed this from the German banking house of Fugger. Their interest rates were enormous, and he had to repay the debt as quickly as possible. The answer lay in the sale of indulgences. The pope would grant the right to sell indulgences in Brandenburg if Albert would agree to pay over half his proceeds to the Church . . .

If indulgences were to be sold, there was no point in doing it half-heartedly. Albert chose a Dominican named Tetzel, a skilled salesman. He would approach a town preceded by a trumpeter and a drummer, and would be met by the town dignitaries, who walked with him in solemn procession, preceded by the papal cross. Then Tetzel would preach a hellfire sermon in the market place until everybody was shuddering, and old ladies rushed home to count their pennies and see if they amounted to a gold piece. Monks collected the cash and handed over the pieces of paper.

In fact, indulgences were not to be sold in Wittenberg. This was not due to religious scruples, but to the fact that Luther's own prince, Frederick the Wise of Saxony, held the franchise for that area. Nevertheless, many of Luther's parishioners hastened to cross into Prince Albert's territory to take advantage of the offer. Luther was disgusted. To Frederick's embarrassment, he preached against this blatant commercialism, this cut-price salvation. And on the eve of All Saints, 1517, he posted on the door of the Castle church in Wittenberg a placard, written in Latin, containing ninety-five theses which he challenged theologians to debate. His first point was that Rome was too rich. 'Before long . . . Rome will be built of our money.' He was, of course, mistaken. The pope *was* rich, but he was always broke. Papal indulgences do not remove guilt, said Luther, and they endanger the soul by generating a sense of false security . . .

Luther's chief target was Albert, so he sent him a copy of the theses. Albert, naturally, sent a copy to the pope, who is reputed to have remarked: 'Luther is just a drunken German; he will feel different when he is sober.' The problem did not strike him as particularly serious. Indeed, it was not particularly serious. A papal bull correcting the worst abuses of indulgences would probably have satisfied everyone, including Luther. Instead, the pope decided to do nothing for the time being. If Luther wanted theological argument, he should get it in due course. Meanwhile, he could be ignored. And back in Wittenberg, Luther continued quietly with his duties. Most of his fellow townsmen disagreed with his attack on indulgences – they felt that the Church could not be entirely wrong about how to go about saving souls. Meanwhile, someone had spread the controversy by having Luther's attack translated into German and printed in the form of broadsheets. This made it a subject of debate all over Germany. On the orders of the pope, Luther's superiors ordered him to repudiate his ninety-five theses; he refused politely – pointing out that they were not, in any case, dogmatic assertions, but subjects for debate. The Augustinians were unwilling to condemn Luther, for he was under attack from their chief rivals, the Dominicans, the detested order who became 'Inquisitors' and burned witches and heretics. Meanwhile, Luther was preparing to defend himself by studying the Bible, and concluded that the text ordering 'penitence' was a mistranslation; it did not say '*do* penances' but simply 'be repentent'. So the argument gradually became warmer. The preacher Tetzel attacked Luther; Luther replied; their arguments were rushed into print. Germans who had long felt resentful about the wealth of the Church began to nod in agreement. A Dominican named Prieras described Luther as a leper with a brain of brass and a nose of iron, and Luther retorted with an attack on Boniface VIII, calling him a wolf. Everybody could understand abuse, and the broadsheets achieved a new popularity. Suddenly, everyone in Germany had heard of Martin Luther.

Eighteen months after he had nailed the theses to the church door, the Church decided to grant Luther's request for a debate. It was to take place in Leipzig, and the Church was to be defended by a scholarly monk named Johann Eck. In 1519, Luther walked into Leipzig, followed by two hundred of his students with battle axes. They remembered what had happened to Jan Hus, and were willing to put up a fight if the bishops tried to do the same thing to Luther. When the debate began in the great hall of the castle, Eck immediately accused Luther of holding some of Hus's 'heresies'. To Eck's delight, Luther replied that he was not so sure they *were* heresies. The debate continued for several days, until the duke said he needed the hall for a ball. But Eck had got what he wanted – admissions that amounted to heresy. Meanwhile Luther, now a national hero, was cheered by crowds along his route back home.

Pope Leo sent Luther an ultimatum: recant, or be excommunicated. The stubborn German was now too angry to care. He replied with a pamphlet, written in German – so that everybody could read it – criticizing the Church and proposing reforms. Leo replied with a bull of excommunication. In German cities, Luther's pamphlets were burned publicly on the orders of the bishops. In Wittenberg, defiant students burnt the pamphlets that denounced Luther.

The emperor of Germany – and of Spain, the Netherlands and many other places – was Charles V, the man who had financed Magellan's voyage round the world and would later finance Pizarro's conquest of Peru. He certainly had the power to suppress Luther, and the inclination as well. But he was also in continual need of money. And if the German princes – many of whom were 'protestants' – withdrew their support, his position would be seriously weakened. So when the pope appealed to him to suppress Luther, he could only reply, unhappily, that it would be done eventually, but that for the moment they must proceed with caution. It was decided that Luther should appear in front of the German parliament – the Diet – when it met at Worms in April 1521.

Luther was accompanied by a cheering crowd of two thousand when he came to Worms. But in front of the Diet, he was obviously nervous. When asked whether he stood by all he had written, he asked for time to think it over and was given an extra day. But when he returned the next day, he replied firmly that he would be glad to recant if he could be shown his error. Then he left the Diet to decide whether he was a heretic. Under the gaze of Charles V, they decided that he was. But by that time, Luther had disappeared, apparently kidnapped by bandits. In fact, Frederick the Wise had ordered him to be taken to the Wartburg Castle for his own safety.

Luther spent a year in the half-empty castle, and whiled away the time by translating the Bible into German. Meanwhile, his revolt spread. Monks and nuns left their monasteries and married. Priests began to recite the mass in German. Reformers began smashing sacred statues in churches (which, after all, was nothing new – the early Christian Church had also had its iconoclasts). Finally, public disorder in Wittenberg grew so dangerous that the townspeople asked Luther to return. Ignoring Frederick's order to stay in the castle, he went back in March 1522. The disorders subsided. Luther was allowed to continue with his work unmolested.

And, without any further effort from Luther, the new 'protestant' movement snowballed. This was not entirely a compliment to its spiritual conviction; the German princes soon realized that, if they became Lutherans, they could lay their hands on the wealth of the Church – particularly of rich monasteries. In a few years time, Henry VIII would make the same discovery. Then there was a general social dissatisfaction, of the kind that had caused Wat Tyler's revolt in England. Religious revolt tended to develop into primitive communism – as it had in Bohemia after the death of Hus. So the name of Luther was used to justify two diametrically opposite revolutions.

Things came to a head in south Germany in 1525, when the peasants revolted, plundering castles and cloisters. They wanted their share of the immense wealth they imagined to be in the hands of the Church and the aristocracy. Contemporary pictures show them guzzling wine and eating the monastery's trout and chickens. An evangelist named Thomas Müntzer, who believed himself to be the new Daniel, led one group from Mulhausen. Nearly six thousand of them were surrounded by a professional army and massacred. The peasants had appealed to Luther, but he was horrified to hear his name used as an excuse for pillage and murder; he wrote a pamphlet 'Against the Murderous and Thieving Hordes of Peasants', in which he advised the princes to 'smite, slay and stab'. At the time he wrote it, the bloodshed had not started; by the time it appeared, mobs of peasants were being wiped out all over Germany. The peasants cursed Luther as a traitor to their cause.

Yet Luther's opposition to the peasants was a guarantee of the survival of his Church. If he had lent his name to the revolt, the nobles would have set out to destroy Protestantism. As it was, they regarded him as an ally. In 1526, the Diet passed a law saying that each German state could make up its own mind whether to be Protestant or Catholic. Three years later, Charles V tried to force them to change their minds, but it was too late. Protestantism was now 'legal' in Germany. Luther's part in the drama was now played. He married a nun who had escaped from a convent, had six children and died at the age of sixty-three, nearly thirty years after he had accidentally started a revolution by nailing up his ninety-five theses.

During those early years of the Lutheran revolution, no one seemed a more unlikely candidate for conversion to Protestantism than England's Henry VIII. To begin with, he was not even remotely interested in religion. Henry liked to regard himself as a kind of ideal Renaissance man: a fine athlete and horseman, a good shot with a bow, a skilful tennis player and a very passable poet and composer – his courtiers naturally assured him that he was equal to the best. He was interested in theology in an amateurish kind of way, largely because friends like Sir Thomas More encouraged him to believe that he was a profound thinker. (It was More who wrote most of the book against Luther that led the pope to call Henry 'Defender of the Faith'.) In short, his character had certain distinct affinities with that of Nero. He was also as spendthrift as Leo X. During the course of his life he wasted his subjects' money building twenty or thirty palaces and vast ships that would not sail. When he had squeezed all the money he could get by way of taxes, he debased the coinage so that inflation rose steadily during his reign – by the time his daughter Elizabeth came to the throne prices had risen by four hundred per cent.

He began his career as king – at the age of twenty – with a truly Machiavellian stroke. His father's chief tax collector was John Dudley, a conscientious civil servant who was, naturally, much hated by the people. Henry achieved easy popularity by having him arrested and executed on a trumped-up charge.

His troubles with the pope began six years after he had been acclaimed Defender of the Faith. Henry was married to Catherine of Aragon, daughter of Ferdinand and Isabella of Spain who had sent Columbus to America; diplomatically, it was an excellent match. But Catherine provided her husband with no male heir. Henry had frequent affairs with ladies of the court, and Catherine pretended not to notice; but when, in 1526, he met the nineteen-year-old Anne Boleyn, he had begun to think it was time to look for another wife. He asked his lord chancellor, Cardinal Wolsey, to approach the new pope, Clement VII, about a divorce.

Clement – the former Giulio de Medici – was not a man to make up his mind quickly. Besides, he had other problems on his mind. He was tired of the Emperor Charles V marching his troops through Italy whenever he felt inclined, even though Charles could point to a treaty with Leo X to justify it. Besides, the Vatican was expected to disgorge money for the emperor's soldiers, and the pope felt this was totally against the laws of nature. Encouraged by the French king, Francis I, he declined to pay any more and created an alliance of Italian cities to fight the Spaniards. It was a tragic mistake. Francis I failed to send the army he had promised. Charles V had no money to pay a good professional army and had to raise an army of ruffians with promises of plunder. Too late, Clement tried to buy them off. On 6 May 1527, the mercenaries threw scaling ladders against the walls of Rome and burst into the city. The result was the most horrifying sack of Rome so far – worse by far than that of Alaric. It was simply murder, rape and torture, and it went on for months. They killed pointlessly, without reason. They were determined to get paid if it involved dismantling every house in Rome and torturing every man and woman to force them to give up their hidden treasures. As far as Rome was concerned, it was the end of the Renaissance. In fact, it was very nearly the end of Rome. And this violence was not the fault of Charles V – who tried hard to stop it – or the vacillating pope. The blame must be laid squarely at the door of Martin Luther. Most of these mercenaries were Lutherans who were delighted to try to destroy the 'eternal city'. They regarded it as a duty as well as a pleasure to rape nuns, to throw priceless statues into cesspools, to slash religious paintings, to stable their horses in St Peter's. For these Catholics were robbers and plunderers and deceivers; they deserved to be exterminated. The sack of Rome of 1527 was an expression of the new religious spirit of the north.

It also explains why Charles V – a good Catholic – should have developed a particularly virulent loathing for Protestants; as the 'second Charlemagne', he itched for the opportunity to repay them in kind.

Charles also had something to say about the divorce of Henry VIII and Catherine of Aragon. Catherine was his aunt; her only daughter Mary – who would become queen of England – his cousin. He brought pressure to bear on the pope – who would have been perfectly willing to grant Henry his divorce. Clement vacillated. Francis I sent his armies into Italy and won victories; Clement now felt independent enough to send an envoy to England to try the case. Then, in 1529, Charles beat the French army at Landriano and the war ended in a treaty that was humiliating for France. Henry put the blame on Wolsey – he was the kind of man who had to have someone to blame – and the cardinal only escaped execution by dying of illness. Then the king secretly married Anne Boleyn – who was withholding her sexual favours pending wedlock – and a new Archbishop of Canterbury, Cranmer, declared that Henry was now divorced from Catherine of Aragon.

In 1530, the king suddenly realized that this quarrel with Rome could be highly profitable. Using the same trumped-up treason charge that he had used against Wolsey – that of recognizing the pope's authority above the king's – he blackmailed Canterbury into paying £100,000 and York into paying £19,000. Then, like a tiger who has tasted blood, he surveyed the abbeys and monasteries of England, computed their wealth and ordered his chief minister,

Thomas Cromwell, to squeeze them dry. Glastonbury Abbey was a typical example. Its abbot, Richard Whyting, had entertained Henry magnificently, which was a mistake. In 1539, Whyting was accused of treason, sentenced to death by Cromwell and hanged on Glastonbury Tor. The beautiful abbey building – whose grounds had held the body of King Arthur – was then reduced to a ruin.

Henry went on to marry four more times. When Anne Boleyn presented him with a daughter (later Queen Elizabeth I) and then a stillborn son, she was beheaded on an accusation of adultery. Jane Seymour, the next wife, died after giving birth to a son, Edward. Henry was pushed into marrying the unattractive Anne of Cleves for political reasons by Cromwell – who paid for the mistake by his own downfall and execution. When Charles V and Francis I made the marriage unnecessary by starting to quarrel again, Anne was quickly divorced. Meanwhile, Henry had fallen in love with a sexually desirable teenager named Catherine Howard – he was unaware that she had already had several lovers, including her two cousins Francis Dereham and Thomas Culpepper. After marrying Henry in 1541, she appointed Dereham her secretary and had several clandestine meetings with Culpepper – although it was never proved that she committed adultery with either. Denounced by Cranmer, she was executed on the same spot as Anne Boleyn. Henry married his last wife, Catherine Parr, in 1543, and was considering having her executed for contradicting him when he died himself at the age of fifty-five.

In his final years, Martin Luther experienced pangs of doubt about the revolution he had fathered – not because he regretted the break with the Catholics (his hatred of popery was almost paranoid), but because of the bloodshed it had already caused. In July 1523, two Augustinian monks were burnt at Brussels, the first victims of the Reformation. But large-scale problems were incubating in Zurich, where the Protestant opinions of a young Swiss pastor, Ulrich Zwingli, had already persuaded the town council to support him. Zwingli – who had arrived at his views quite independently from Luther – was altogether less emotional than the German reformer. Some of his followers felt that he was too reasonable, too inclined to seek a compromise with authority, and they formed into a communistic movement that believed that men should be baptized a second time – hence their name, Anabaptists. For some reason, they aroused a rage and detestation out of all proportion to their harmfulness. Even the American historian John Lothrop Motley, writing *The Rise of the Dutch Republic* in the mid-nineteenth century, lost his temper when talking about them, and wrote: 'The leaders were among the most depraved of human creatures, as much distinguished for licentiousness, blasphemy, and cruelty as their followers for grovelling superstition. The evil spirit driven out of Luther seemed, in orthodox eyes, to have taken possession of a herd of swine . . .' (Everyman edition, Vol. 1, p. 79). In fact, the Anabaptists simply believed in accepting the New Testament as a literal guide to living – in many ways they resembled the Cathar heretics of two centuries earlier. A mass 'second baptism' that took place outside Zurich in 1525 led the town council to ban them and pass sentence of death on any who were caught. After that, the Anabaptists were driven out of city after city. Thomas Müntzer, one of the leaders of the peasants' revolt, was an Anabaptist. After the revolt had been put down, the Anabaptists continued to look for a city where they could put their principles into action. In 1532, they took over Münster, in Westphalia, and, according to Motley, 'confiscated property, plundered churches, violated females, murdered men who refused to join the gang, and . . . practised all enormities . . .' Their prophet John Boccold, known as John of Leyden, preached polygamy and married fourteen wives. In 1535, the Bishop of Münster besieged the city, which held out until its inhabitants were forced to practise cannibalism, then surrendered. The bishop then had the Anabaptist leaders tortured horribly, and hung in cages from a church tower. In Amsterdam, a mixed crowd of men and women who ran naked through the streets claiming to represent 'the naked truth' were all executed.

In Brussels in 1535, an imperial edict was issued 'condemning all heretics to death'. And so, more than ten years before Luther's death, the slaughter began. Catholics murdered Protestants; Protestants murdered Catholics; and both of them murdered Anabaptists. Since Charles V was perhaps the most powerful monarch in Europe, the Protestants would undoubtedly have suffered some serious reverses had it not been for the non-stop quarrel that raged between Charles V and Francis I. They went on fighting war after war, mostly about territorial claims in Italy and Burgundy. It was not until 1544 that they concluded their fourth major war with the Treaty of Crespy and Charles could turn his mind to his long-cherished dream of smashing the Protestants once and for all. Besides, the Catholic Church was no longer quite so indefensible. In 1534, a young Spaniard named Ignatius Loyola had founded the Order of Jesus – or the Jesuits – whose purpose was to reform the Church from the inside. He was successful beyond everyone's wildest hopes; Jesuit missionaries and Jesuit schools carried Catholicism from China to America. If Loyola had started his movement twenty years earlier, Protestantism would probably have been nipped in the bud. And at the Council of Trent the Church showed its determination to reform itself by remaining in session for eighteen years.

So by the year of Luther's death, 1546, Charles V felt ready to complete the Counter-Reformation by killing every Protestant in Europe. He had had a great deal of practice in suppressing revolts. He was the grandson of Ferdinand and Isabella, who had brought unity to Spain. Unfortunately, when they had driven the Moors out of Granada, they had also founded the Spanish Inquisition to make sure that everybody in Spain – including Moors and Jews – became good Christians; the name of their chief inquisitor, Torquemada, became a by-word for cruelty. Charles inherited the bigoted Catholicism of his grandmother, and approved of her notion of burning heretics. When he came to Spain from Ghent at the age of seventeen (in 1517) he could not even speak Spanish and soon had a widespread revolt on his hands. Luck was with him; the rebellion turned into a kind of peasants' revolt – they even called themselves 'comuneros' – and the nobles who had supported it went over to Charles's side. So in 1521 there was a mass execution of rebels after they were defeated in battle, and Charles was confirmed as king of Spain. He spent most of the rest of his life fighting the king of France, but in 1522, when he realized that Protestantism was spreading fast, he introduced the Inquisition in the Netherlands; and in 1523, two Protestant martyrs were burnt at the stake, singing hymns and shouting defiance.

But by the time the treaty of Crespy left Charles free to try and stamp out the Protestantism, the Protestant princes had formed their own defensive alliance, the Schmalkaldic league.

As his chief commander, Charles appointed the ambitious and

sadistic Duke of Alva – who has strong claims to being the most wholly vicious character to make his appearance in this criminal history of mankind. (The only attractive episode in his life is a mad seventeen-day ride he made from Hungary – where he was fighting Turks – back to Spain to spend a few hours with his newly-married wife; the rest of his life is a saga of bigotry and torture.) But he was also a man of undoubted brilliance and courage. Making a dangerous crossing of the Elbe, Alva's army swooped on the Protestants at Muhlberg and inflicted a shattering defeat. It was one of the most glorious days in the life of 'the second Charlemagne'. Charles then marched his armies on to Wittenberg, no doubt regretting that his arch-enemy Luther had died in the previous year. After a siege, Wittenberg surrendered, and for a few days Charles must have believed that he had defeated Protestantism single-handed. Then he took a closer look at the German scene and his optimism evaporated. These people were grimly and fanatically Protestant; they hated the Catholics. A war would be a war to the death. And eight years later, after many battles and sieges, Charles had to acknowledge that he was never going to batter the Protestants into submission; he concluded the peace of Augsburg, allowing the Protestants freedom of worship within their own territories. In the same year, the exhausted and dispirited emperor abdicated and retired to a monastery, where he spent the remaining two years of his life flogging himself with a rope whose knots gradually wore away.

His empire was divided between his brother Ferdinand and his son Philip. Philip got the Netherlands – and this was to have far-reaching consequences, for Spain and for the rest of Europe. Two years before Charles abdicated – in 1544 – Philip had married the queen of England, Mary Tudor – later to become known as Bloody Mary. This thirty-six-year-old virgin, the daughter of Henry VIII and Catherine of Aragon, had fallen in love with Philip as soon as she saw his portrait. Philip said he would rather not reign at all than reign over heretics; so Mary restored the laws against heresy and declared that, from now on, England was once again a Catholic country. Two weeks later, the first married priest was burnt at the stake in Smithfield.

Mary was probably insane when she started her campaign of persecution; in the previous year she had been convinced she was pregnant and her stomach swelled convincingly. Then doctors discovered it was a phantom pregnancy, induced by hysteria. It was after this that she ordered the persecution of Protestants; three hundred of them were burned at the stake – the story is told in Foxe's *Book of Martyrs*, which the English adopted as a second Bible. No one mourned Mary when she died at the age of forty-two. But the people of England went mad with joy when her half-sister Elizabeth was proclaimed queen.

Philip's first act in becoming ruler of the Netherlands was to tell the Inquisitors to get on with their job. The chief of these was a man called Titelman, and the pleasure he took in torture suggests that he was mentally deranged. He enjoyed personally dragging suspects from their beds and hitting people on the head with a large club. This kind of thing aroused Protestants to a frenzy. One man called Bertrand de Blas snatched the consecrated wafer from the hands of a priest and trampled on it, shouting: 'Fools, do you take this thing to be Jesus Christ?' It seemed impossible to devise a suitable punishment for such a crime. He was dragged to the market place on a hurdle, and his hand and foot were twisted off with red hot pincers. Then his arms and legs were tied together in the small of his back and he was suspended over a slow fire on a chain and allowed to swing back and forth as he roasted. Another family called Ogier was arrested for holding prayers at home – they included a teenage son and a child. At the hearing, the child answered with such simplicity that the judges had tears in their eyes and decided to sentence only the father and the teenager. As the boy burnt to death, he screamed aloud 'Eternal father . . .' and a monk who was present screamed back 'God isn't your father – you're the devil's children.' A week later, they decided to burn the wife and younger child, wiping out the family.

In the first two years of his reign, Philip encouraged the Inquisition to burn thousands of people. Then, in 1567, he decided that real firmness was needed and sent in the Duke of Alva. It was, we can see in retrospect, the supreme mistake of Philip's career, the mistake that was to cost Spain the empire built up by Charles V. In February 1568, the Holy Office issued a statement declaring that everybody in the Netherlands was a heretic and therefore sentenced to die. Since the Netherlands had three million inhabitants, it was an impossible task, even for a man as efficient as Alva. In Holy Week, eight hundred people were executed. The method was to seal their mouths with a kind of iron gag that allowed the tongue to protrude, then the end of the tongue was sliced off and burned with a red hot iron, so it swelled and could not be withdrawn. Then they were thrown into the flames. But as a method of genocide, this was too slow. People were made to lie on the ground and had their backs broken with a tremendous blow of an iron bar or axe, then they were left to die. But this required a great deal of energy from the executioners, whose arms became tired. So Alva ordered prisoners to be tied together three at a time and tossed into the river to drown. By this method, he managed to execute eight thousand people in one session in Antwerp. But it was still slow work. Alva himself later said that he had ordered about nineteen thousand executions for heresy. But there were tens of thousands of others for rebellion.

In spite of all the cruelty, Alva was unable to crush the revolt. An attempt to impose a kind of 'value-added tax' of ten per cent on everything bought and sold brought matters to a head and he had to climb down. (The inhabitants of Europe have grown more docile since those days.) William of Orange, driven out by the Spaniards, invaded with his brother Louis, while a league of nobles who were contemptuously known as 'the beggars' raised a revolt in the north. In 1573, the duke of Alva was withdrawn from the Netherlands at his own request. He knew that, for all his ruthlessness, he had failed to stamp out the spirit of Protestantism.

Meanwhile, the English, under their Protestant queen Elizabeth, were delighted to see the Spaniards getting themselves into so much trouble. She lent secret support to the Dutch, arousing the hostility of Spain. And when British mariners such as Sir John Hawkins and Sir Francis Drake committed acts of piracy against Spanish ships, she turned a blind eye. And Philip, who began by proposing marriage to Elizabeth, ended by hatching a plot to invade England and murder her. He planned to put her cousin, Mary Queen of Scots, on the throne, and the unfortunate Mary lost her head as a consequence. Drake and Howard's total defeat of Spain's attempt to conquer England with an armada in 1588 was the beginning of the end of the empire of Charles V.

In France, Protestantism had arrived via Switzerland, and the teachings of a reformer named John Calvin. Calvin was a French version of Savonarola, intended for the Catholic priesthood, converted by some kind of 'revelation' at twenty-one, and convinced that he was the direct instrument of God. He arrived in Geneva in 1536, at the age of twenty-seven, just after that city had become Protestant. His bigotry led to his being expelled two years later; but he was recalled in 1541. Calvin's religious creed could be summarized in Groucho Marx's words: 'Whatever it is, I'm against it.' A merchant who smiled during a baptism ceremony was sent to prison; so was a man who dozed during a sermon. In the four years after he returned to Geneva, fifty-eight men were executed for objecting to Calvin's narrow theology. In 1553, a Spaniard named Servetus, who held the Arian view that God is one and not three, made the mistake of coming to Geneva and was swiftly burnt at the stake. In 1555, Calvin won an argument with the city government about the right to excommunicate 'heretics', and from then on began a kind of religious reign of terror. The Genevans did not show the same good sense as the Florentines, and allowed this maniac to continue to bully them until his death at the age of fifty-five.

But during Calvin's lifetime, Geneva had become a place of refuge for persecuted Protestants, many of whom returned home to preach his doctrines of damnation and hellfire. Scotland, with its grey skies and damp climate, found the idea of any kind of fire appealing and swallowed the doctrine whole. So did France, where the Protestants called themselves Huguenots. They were particularly strong in the south, where the Cathar heresy had been so successful. Francis I had persecuted heretics, and in 1545 even allowed twenty-four villages in Provence to be burnt to the ground and everyone in them slaughtered. His son, Henry II, married an Italian, Catherine de Medici; but he was killed accidentally when a lance at a tournament went into his eye. (Oddly enough, the French prophet Nostradamus had described the death with startling accuracy in one of his 'quatrains'.) As the Huguenots became stronger, it seemed a good idea to try to reach some settlement with them; so after a particularly unpleasant civil war, Henry's widow Catherine decided to marry off her daughter Marguerite to the head of the French Huguenots, Henry of Navarre. All the major Huguenots in France poured into Paris to attend the wedding in August 1572. It looked as if Catherine had found the way to peace. Yet at the same time she was plotting murder. The man she hated most was a leading Huguenot, Admiral Coligny, who was becoming remarkably friendly with her son, the young king Charles IX. Catherine called upon the assistance of the chief Catholic family, the Guises. Four days after the wedding, a gun exploded as Coligny walked past and he fell to the ground. He was not killed – only wounded – but the Huguenots were furious and talked of revenge. Catherine decided to anticipate them. On the morning of 24 August, six days after the wedding, armed men battered at Coligny's door. He was stabbed to death, then his body was dragged into the street and hacked into pieces. In the Louvre, the Huguenot nobles who were guests of the king were dragged from their beds and murdered. As St Bartholemew's Day dawned, the bell of the Hotel de Ville gave the signal for the massacre. The people of Paris were told it was the open season for Huguenots. The mobs poured into Huguenot houses and killed everybody inside. Babies were thrown out of windows and tossed into the river. Catholic shopkeepers who disliked the Huguenot shopkeeper next door were delighted to get rid of a competitor. And so it continued for three days; between three and four thousand Huguenots died. Henry of Navarre saved his own life by agreeing to re-convert to Catholicism.

It was the Catholics' dream – the dream of Charles V and Francis I, of Bloody Mary and Philip of Spain – to get rid of the Protestants by exterminating them. They all had to learn that it was impossible – just as the English under Elizabeth had to learn that it was impossible to get rid of the Catholics by executing them. Death by martyrdom merely fuelled the flames, and twice as many heretics sprang up as before. The massacre of St Bartholomew also led to another bloody civil war – for Henry of Navarre managed to escape and lead his Protestants against the Catholics. Eventually, he became king of France – Henry IV – and issued the Edict of Nantes declaring that Huguenots were free to worship in their own way. That satisfactory and logical solution was, of course, the last thing that anybody wanted; twelve years later Henry was stabbed to death by a fanatical Catholic, and the bloodshed in the name of religion continued.

To the eye of the historian, the situation is replete with irony. An orthodox Jew suffering from the delusion that the world is about to come to an end creates a new form of Judaism. His followers, who have now put off the end of the world to the year 1000, go on to conquer half the world. In the process, they become as corrupt and tyrannical as their early persecutors and are finally routed by a neurotic German monk who suffers from constipation. The result is a long-drawn out religious war that causes more misery and more deaths than the conquests of Attila, Genghis Khan and Tamurlane put together. And the only thing that is clear is that all this has nothing whatever to do with the teaching of the Jew who started it all.

Nine

HISTORY CHANGES ITS RULES

At ten o'clock in the morning on 30 May 1593, four men sat down to a meal at a tavern owned by Mistress Eleanor Bull, overlooking the river Thames at Deptford: a notorious swindler, a robber, a government spy and a great dramatist. The dramatist was twenty-nine-year-old Christopher Marlowe, who had achieved fame with his *Tamburlaine the Great* at the age of twenty-three. His *Jew of Malta* and *Doctor Faustus* had been equally successful; he had even tried his hand at a play about the St Bartholomew Day slaughter called *The Massacre at Paris*.

On this day in May, Marlowe must have been feeling a certain anxiety; two weeks before, his friend Thomas Kyd had been arrested by officers of the queen, who had searched his room. They were looking for 'treasonable materials' – verses inciting Londoners to riot against foreigners. What they actually found among Kyd's papers were certain 'atheistical' writings, 'vile heretical conceits denying the deity of Jesus Christ'. Kyd was taken to Bridewell prison and tortured on the rack. This consisted of a powerful oak frame, rather like a table with its top removed, with rollers attached to the legs at both ends. The prisoner was stretched out on the floor, ropes tied around his wrists and ankles, then the rollers were turned so he was drawn up level with the 'table top'. If he still refused to talk, the pulleys were turned still farther until his arms and legs came out of their sockets. Under this torture, Kyd confessed that the 'vile heretical conceits' belonged to his friend Christopher Marlowe. Kyd was then released, a broken man – he died about a year later. Marlowe was arrested at Scadbury, the country home of his patron Thomas Walsingham, where he had fled to escape the plague in London. He was taken to prison, but quickly released on bail – undoubtedly due to the influence of powerful friends. (Walsingham, who was the cousin of Queen Elizabeth's secretary of state, Sir

Francis Walsingham, was virtually the government's spymaster general.) But the case was by no means at an end. Marlowe was due to appear in front of the Star Chamber, a kind of Inquisition whose interests were political rather than religious.

Marlowe and his friends spent the day eating and drinking, and probably discussing the business of spying – all four had been at some time employed by Walsingham. They may have walked along the bank of the river, which would have been pleasantly green and open to the fields. Then they went back to the room and did some more drinking. Around six in the evening, they decided to pay the bill, and a dispute arose between Marlowe and a man called Ingram Frizer. According to the evidence given at the inquest, Marlowe was lying on a bed, behind the other three, who were sitting at the table. Marlowe grabbed Frizer's dagger and slashed at his head, inflicting two wounds on the scalp. The others then grappled with Marlowe to disarm him; Frizer got possession of the dagger, and stabbed Marlowe above the right eye. It penetrated about two inches, and Marlowe died instantly.

Many Marlowe scholars have raised doubts about this story. Marlowe's wound would have been consistent with a man who was attacked as he lay with his eyes closed. It would then have been easy enough to inflict the scalp wounds on Frizer and concoct the story of the quarrel – Frizer was, in fact, acquitted and taken back into Walsingham's employment. And why should Marlowe have been murdered? He was certainly something of a liability to his friends. Four years before, he had been involved in a fight that ended in the murder of a man called Bradley. In the previous year he had been arrested on a charge of coining – an extremely serious matter in the Elizabethan age, when coining was regarded as petty treason, and the coiner could be hanged, drawn and quartered. He escaped by pleading that it was merely an experiment 'to see the goldsmith's cunning', and since only one coin had been made, Burghley – Elizabeth's chief adviser – decided to take a lenient view.

A week after Marlowe's second arrest, an informer named William Baines prepared a document for the queen 'containing the opinion of Christopher Marlowe concerning his damnable opinions', which lists various heterodox opinions on religion – such as that Moses was a conjuror, that Jesus deserved to be crucified, and that all Protestants were hypocritical asses. In another document, Baines speaks of 'the horrible blasphemies uttered by Christopher Marlowe', and goes on to state that 'in every company he cometh he persuades men and women to Atheism, willing them not to be afeard of bugbears and hobgoblins and utterly scorning both God and his ministers'.

Even fifty years earlier, such opinions would have been unthinkable. Frederick II, the 'wonder of the world', is reported to have said that Jesus, Moses and Mahomet were imposters; but then, he had the advantage of personal acquaintance with one particularly bigoted pope, as well as with many Moslems. As Hugh Thomas pointed out in his *Unfinished History of the World*, he is the only man reported to have held such views between 400 and 1400 A.D. Even men of classical culture – like Petrarch – would never have dared to think such a thing. They took the existence of God and the devil so completely for granted that it would have seemed a very poor gamble to harbour such thoughts – after all, if hell really did exist, you might find yourself in it as a punishment for doubting its existence. The undermining of the Catholic faith by Luther caused intellectual shock waves all over Europe. It seemed that the unthinkable, the impossible, had happened. It was as if a mountain had collapsed and revealed that it was made of painted cardboard. Even the efforts of Ignatius Loyola and the Council of Trent made no real difference. Calvin and Bloody Mary could go on burning as many heretics as they liked: Humpty Dumpty could never be put back together again. We can see this new attitude of irreverence in Marlowe's *Jew of Malta*, where someone says: 'Look, look, master, here comes two religious caterpillars.'

That is why, when we read the Elizabethans, we feel that their minds are akin to our own. Dante, Chaucer, Petrarch, even Malory, seem to be strangers, inhabitants of another universe. They accepted that there was some great scheme of things, of which they were a tiny part. The Elizabethans were the first generation to grow up in a new climate of religious scepticism. The English had never really been interested in religion. As Conyers Read says, 'in thirty years they accepted five distinct changes in their religion without any great fuss about the matter.' (*The Tudors* p.138.) A people who could accept these swings from Protestantism to Catholicism and back again as a matter of course were not likely to feel that either had a monopoly of religious truth. They might not be in the least inclined towards atheism, but the new religious climate was bound to make them willing to discuss such questions as predestination – the doctrine upheld by Calvin – and the immortality of the soul. (Marlowe's contemporary Sir Walter Raleigh acquired a reputation for atheism because of his eagerness to discuss such topics over the dinner table.) And men who cease to feel that such subjects are forbidden have begun to take responsibility for their own consciences. They are thinking and behaving like individuals.

Christian dogma was also being undermined from another direction – but so gradually and gently that at first no one paid any attention. In 1506, eleven years before Luther nailed up his theses on the church door, a quietly-spoken physician named Nicholas Copernicus became secretary and medical adviser to his uncle, the bishop of Ermland, between Prussia and Poland. Copernicus was a canon of the Church, and his hobby was astronomy. Six years later, when his uncle died of food poisoning, Copernicus had more time to devote to the stars, and he wrote a small book suggesting that the sun is the centre of the universe and that the earth is a ball that travels round it once a year. This amazing assertion contradicted everything believed by the Church throughout the Middle Ages, which accepted the complex system of Ptolemy in which the earth is the centre of the universe. To anyone who observed the heavens closely, Ptolemy's system had enormous disadvantages, in that it had to explain why the planets travel around the earth in such strange and complicated orbits – sometimes even going backwards. Copernicus, who was a timid little man and in no way a revolutionary, saw that these contradictions vanished if he assumed that the earth goes round the sun, like all the other planets. No one was shocked by Copernicus's ideas, even when he published *On the Revolutions of the Heavenly Bodies* in 1542; in fact, the pope's right-hand man, Cardinal Schoenberg, suggested that the book ought to be published, and no one paid much attention when it appeared. Copernicus died shortly after it came out, and was soon forgotten. Half a century later, the greatest astronomer of his time, the Dane Tycho Brahe, was convinced that Copernicus was mistaken and that the earth was the centre of the universe. His reason had nothing to do with religious prejudice. He saw that if the earth moved round the sun, then it must travel millions of miles every year. In that case, the stars ought to change their positions – as a church tower changes its position when seen from a moving train. And they don't. Tycho did not realize that the stars are so many billions of miles away that we would not notice the small changes in their position – it would be many years before someone would invent an instrument delicate enough to measure it.

Although Tycho had no magnifying telescope – they had not yet been invented – he made thousands of minute observations of the position of the planets. When he died in 1601, his young assistant Johannes Kepler, who believed in Copernicus's theory, studied Tycho's figures and tried to understand the laws that governed the planets. What baffled him was that Tycho's figures showed that every planet travels at different speeds at different times. That seemed absurdly complicated. Then, one day, he succeeded in working out the shape of such an orbit, and saw that it was not at all complicated. It was a simple ellipse – a shape like an egg. He published his theory in a book called *The New Astronomy* in 1609. Astronomers read it with interest; no one else paid much attention.

One of these astronomers was a brilliant but self-assertive Italian named Galileo Galilei, the professor of mathematics at Padua university. In the year Kepler's book came out, Galileo heard about a new invention that had become fashionable in Holland. Lenses had been around for about three centuries – in fact, primitive rock-crystal lenses have been found in ancient Nineveh and Carthage. Now a Dutchman had discovered that if two lenses are put into opposite ends of a cardboard tube they will magnify distant objects. Galileo quickly made himself a telescope. Then he stepped outdoors one fine night in the autumn of 1609 and looked at the moon. What he saw amazed him. Instead of a smooth surface, he saw a landscape covered with pockmarks; closer examination showed he was looking at mountains and valleys. Then he looked at the Milky Way – which to the eye looks like white gas – and saw that it was made up of millions of stars.

It was when he turned his telescope on Jupiter that he received the most exciting revelation. He saw three tiny white 'stars' close to the edge of the planet, and the next day, they had moved around to the other side – proving that they were not stars. Jupiter had moons, like the earth. But our moon had always been used by opponents of Copernicus as the chief objection to his theory. If the earth went round the sun, then why should the moon go round the earth? Surely it could not be an exception to the law of nature? Now Galileo could see that our moon is not an exception – other planets have them too. In a state of great excitement, Galileo wrote a book called *The Starry Messenger*. It made him instantly famous, and became the seventeenth-century equivalent of a bestseller. It was like Marco Polo's travels, a book about strange, distant regions, and everybody wanted to read it. At forty-five, Galileo suddenly found himself famous.

Galileo was, in fact, a great scientist; but his discoveries had so far not been of the kind that cause widespread interest. At the age of eighteen, he had been sitting in the cathedral at Pisa when he noticed the lamp swinging back and forth from the ceiling. He timed the swings, and observed that they always took the same time. A few years later, he went to the top of the leaning tower and dropped a heavy and a light cannon ball at the same moment; he observed that they struck the ground at the same time – disproving Aristotle's assertion that heavy objects fall faster than light ones.

But as a human being, Galileo had serious shortcomings; from early on in his academic career, he displayed a crude self-assertion that gave much offence. And his sudden fame at forty-five acted as an intoxicant. The Academy of Science made him a member; at a banquet in his honour the new invention was christened 'the telescope'. The pope, Paul V, gave him an audience. The Jesuits honoured him with ceremonies. For a man with Galileo's thirst for fame, it must have been a heady experience. It made him more arrogant than ever. When scientific opponents raised objections to his theories, he treated it as a personal affront, and tried to crush them with sheer rudeness. It must be admitted, of course, that in most cases, he was right and they were wrong; but this does not excuse his bad manners. And the Church began to worry about the sheer dogmatism with which he asserted his opinions.

This was, in fact, a matter in which the Church had right on its side. Cardinal Robert Bellarmine, one of the soundest thinkers of his time, said that if Galileo thought that Copernicus was right, then it was up to him to prove it. And this was precisely what Galileo could not do. For he still lacked one essential insight: a theory of gravitation. Only gravity could explain why the planets circled around the sun as if attached to strings, and why they had reacted on one another until their orbits ceased to be circular and turned into ellipses. In fact, an English doctor named William Gilbert had stumbled on this essential clue in writing a book called *On Magnets* in 1600; he had suggested that the earth itself was an enormous magnet, and that this explained why things stuck to its surface as it spun round instead of flying off into space. But Galileo failed to grasp the importance of Gilbert's idea. Instead, he wrote a book called *Dialogue on the Two Chief World Systems* in which he continued to insist that Copernicus was obviously correct. The new pope, Urban VIII, read it in manuscript and insisted that Galileo should stop asserting what he could not prove; he ought to present the two systems (Ptolemy and Copernicus) and leave the reader to make up his own mind.

To a man of Galileo's headstrong temperament, this was intolerable. In a thoroughly underhand way, he had the book printed with a papal seal of approval, which he persuaded out of a good-natured but ignorant priest. It came out in 1632. And when the pope read it, he exploded with rage. It was not Galileo's opinions that annoyed him so much as the fact that Galileo had quite openly defied him. He was as headstrong as Galileo, and he had a great deal more power. So the book was confiscated, and Galileo had to appear in front of the Inquisition. He had virtually no defence. He had promised the pope that he would teach the Copernican hypothesis *as* theory, not as proven fact, and he had broken his word. Galileo was forced to retract his statement that the sun was the centre of the universe, although legend adds that he muttered under his breath 'It moves all the same' (meaning the earth). Then he was allowed to go free. Historians of science like to assert that the episode reveals the bigotry of the Church and the honesty of the man of science. In fact, the Church emerges from the trial of Galileo with considerable credit; it was the scientist who was entirely to blame.

This was not how the rest of Europe saw it. Before the end of the century, Isaac Newton's *Principia* had demonstrated beyond all shadow of doubt that Copernicus was right, and did so with such a tremendous apparatus of mathematical calculation that few people dared to raise doubts. Newton, of course, had discovered the missing piece of Galileo's jigsaw puzzle: gravity. He had done what Galileo was unable to do: proved the Copernican theory, which is exactly what Pope Urban VIII had asked Galileo to do; *he* should have received the credit for being an open-minded man of science.

Instead, the Church was once again left looking discredited. The spirit of Christopher Marlowe must have chuckled sarcastically.

The century of Galileo and Newton saw the disappearance of another piece of medieval superstition: the witchcraft craze. Witches have been known since ancient times; the evidence suggests that they were people who happened to be possessed of what we would now call 'paranormal powers', the most common being the ability to heal. But it is worth noting that witches themselves have always, in all times, claimed that their abilities are somehow involved with the control of spirits. The so-called spiritualist movement of the nineteenth century was, in the most precise sense, a revival of witchcraft. And the parallel of the spiritualist movement – and some of the extraordinary effects produced by the 'spirits' during seances – should warn us against making the simplistic assumption that witchcraft was pure superstition and self-delusion. (I have discussed these questions at length elsewhere, notably in *Mysteries*, Part 1, chapter 3, and *Poltergeist*, chapter 6.)

In ancient Greece, Rome, China, India, Egypt, Japan and Sumeria, witches (or magicians) were regarded with fear; yet it would probably be true to say that in most rural communities, the witch or 'seer' was taken for granted and regarded as a useful member of the community.

When Pope Innocent III ordered the massacre of Cathars in the thirteenth century, the survivors took refuge in remote valleys in the Alps and Pyrenees, where they could worship in peace. But in 1320 the paranoid Pope John XXII, who was convinced that his enemies were plotting to take his life by magic, authorized a cardinal in Carcassone (the original centre of the Cathar heresy) to take action against magicians, sorcerers and heretics. The Dominican inquisitors had the muddled idea that, because the Cathars thought the world of matter was created by the devil, they must be devil worshippers. And witches were supposed to owe their supernatural powers to a compact with demons. So the inquisitors began trying Cathars on charges of witchcraft and heresy. The first witch trial had already taken place in Toulouse in 1275, when an old woman named Angèle de la Barthe was accused of having sexual intercourse with a demon and giving birth to a monster – a confession wrung from her by torture. But it was not until 1390 that the first secular trial for witchcraft – quite unconnected with heresy – took place in Paris: a woman named Jehanne de Brigue was accused by a man of saving his life by witchcraft when he was on the point of death; Jehanne confessed under threat of torture and implicated the man's wife, claiming she caused the illness by putting a spell on her husband. Both women were burned.

Witch persecutions continued sporadically for the next century, then they were given a new impetus by a book called *Malleus Maleficarum* (the Hammer of Witches) by two Dominican inquisitors, Heinrich Kramer and Jacob Sprenger. By that time, common-sense was beginning to prevail, and the Parlement of Paris had declared that witchcraft was a delusion; Sprenger and Kramer passionately opposed this view, insisting that witchcraft is performed with the aid of demons. Printing – which had been invented four decades earlier – gave this book an enormous circulation; it became one of the most widely read books of its time – its popularity undoubtedly due to its description of the 'foul venereal acts' committed by demons on witches. This piquant combination of sex and demonology went into many editions in many languages.

By the late sixteenth century, the witch craze had begun to move to a climax all over Europe. In Toulouse, forty witches were burned in 1557, and in 1582, eighteen witches were burned in Avignon; between 1581 and 1591, nine hundred witches were sentenced in Lorraine, and in 1609, four hundred witches were burned in four months. In Germany it was the same story: in 1572, five witches burnt at Treves; between 1587 and 1594, more than three hundred people tried for witchcraft; then, in the early seventeenth century, there were literally thousands of burnings. One 'witch-finder', Franz Buirmann, burned half the population of one village of three hundred inhabitants between 1631 and 1636; in Bamberg, sixteen hundred people were burned; in Würzburg, seven hundred and fifty-seven – these included children whose ages ranged from three to fifteen. But the Thirty Years War called a temporary halt to the persecutions. By the end of the century, revulsion at all the torture had caused the trials to slow down to a trickle again; in 1714, King Frederick William of Prussia ordered an end to all such trials.

In England, the same revulsion was caused by the career of Matthew Hopkins, the 'witchfinder general', a lawyer who became convinced that his village – Manningtree, in Essex – was infested with witches. An old woman was stripped and searched for devil's marks, and when they found that she had a kind of extra teat, they tortured her until she confessed that she used it for suckling her 'familiars' – a spaniel, a rabbit, a greyhound and a polecat. Thirty-two women were arrested, and nineteen of them hanged.

Hopkins suddenly found himself in great demand as an expert in sniffing out witches; at an average of £6 per witch, he found it a profitable occupation. During the next year, he made over £1,000; in Bury St Edmunds alone, sixty-eight people were hanged. His method was to strip the victim and prick her all over for 'devil's marks' – spots that were supposed to be insensitive to pain after being touched by the devil, or to toss the suspected witch into a pond and see whether she floated – if not, she was condemned.

But after only a year of this, commonsense reasserted itself. A clergyman named Gaule attacked Hopkins from the pulpit and published a pamphlet pointing out that it was still illegal in England to torture witches. Hopkins suddenly became unpopular, and when an angry crowd tossed him into a pond, he decided it was time to retire on his profits. Later the same year, he died of tuberculosis. And in England, the witchcraft craze was at an end.

In America, it reached its climax in Salem in 1692. A neurotic and unpopular clergyman named Samuel Parris became convinced that the black maid Tituba (from Barbados) was teaching the children to practise voodoo – which was probably true. The children, aged nine, eleven and twelve, began having strange convulsions and declaring that spirits were pinching them. Tituba was beaten, and confessed to being a witch. She implicated various other old women, who were arrested and tortured. The whole area was suddenly possessed by witchcraft hysteria, believing that the witches turned themselves into birds and animals at night. In a few months, twenty people were tried and executed, including a sceptical farmer named Proctor, who denounced the trials as nonsense, and a man named Corey, who was pressed to death under heavy weights; his wife was also hanged.

Like Matthew Hopkins, the children who had started the whole thing were now regarded as experts on witchcraft, and were called to the neighbouring town to identify witches. Forty arrests were made in Andover, and the magistrate himself had to flee when he refused to order more.

At this point, the girls overreached themselves, naming the wife of the governor as a witch. When the governor, Sir William Phips, returned from fighting Indians, he dismissed the court and released most of the accused. The witch hysteria ended as abruptly as it began. The Rev. Samuel Parris had to leave Salem with his family.

In France, as in England and America, the witchcraft craze blew itself out in a storm of extraordinary violence: the Chambre Ardente affair. And in this case, there is evidence that it was not entirely a matter of smoke without fire. In 1673 – in the reign of Louis XIV – two priests informed the authorities that many of their penitents had asked absolution for murdering their spouses by poison. What was happening, it seemed, was that a ring of fortune tellers and witches were supplying poisons – euphemistically known as 'succession powders' – to men and women who wanted to get rid of their current spouses in favour of lovers or mistresses. The chief of police, Nicholas de la Reynie, asked his agents to begin making cautious enquiries. A fortune teller named Marie Bosse was reported to have said that she would be able to retire when she had arranged three more poisonings; Reynie sent a disguised policewoman to consult her on how to get rid of her husband. The fortune teller sold her poison, and was arrested.

It soon became clear to Reynie that this case concerned more than a few unscrupulous old women. There was a widespread 'poisons ring', dealing in undetectable poisons – rather as a modern drugs ring deals in drugs – and many wealthy and influential men seemed to be mixed up in it; but there was also an element of black magic, and here he found that many priests were involved. Abortions were performed and the unwanted babies 'sacrificed' on an altar, their blood often falling on to the breast of a naked girl who was lying there.

Now France may be said to have had something of a tradition of monastic misdemeanours connected with black magic. In the 1630s, there was a scandal involving Franciscan nuns in a convent at Louviers, when it became clear that two successive father confessors had made a habit of debauching the nuns and holding black masses, during one of which a newborn baby was crucified. Two priests were publicly burned. Now de la Reynie revealed how one woman, a Madame de Poupaillon, wanted to get rid of her aging husband and was given a potion containing arsenic in which she was to soak his shirt; it could cause a skin inflammation resembling syphilis. She was also given 'healing salves' to rub on the sores – actually, more poison. Her husband became suspicious and retreated out of harm's way into a monastery.

The king ordered the creation of a special court – it became known as the Chambre Ardente, the lighted chamber, because the room was draped in black and lit by candles. More old women were arrested – one, called La Voisin, was an abortionist who had got rid of 2,500 unwanted babies. She was burnt alive in an iron chair.

The king became alarmed when he learned that his mistress, Madame de Montespan, had often served as the naked 'altar' for a sacrifice. Another of his mistresses, Madame des Oillets, had bought a love charm for the king, which had been concocted by a priest from menstrual blood – from the lady – and sperm from a man, who masturbated into a chalice. Another priest had copulated with the girl who served as an altar in view of the congregation. After seven years of investigation, it became clear to the king that more public scandal would cause a major political upheaval. A hundred and four people were sentenced – thirty-six to death; then Louis decided to suspend the Chambre Ardente. Fortune tellers were banned by law. But witchcraft was declared to be a superstition. In 1709, the king attempted to consign the whole affair to oblivion by having all the papers destroyed; but the official transcripts were overlooked. They reveal quite clearly that, unlike earlier cases of witchcraft, the Chambre Ardente affair involved a very large number of people who believed they were taking part in black magic ceremonies, and that their criminal projects had received the active support of the devil.

Another public scandal of the same period indicates that poisoning was as popular in seventeenth-century France as in Rome under the Borgias. When a young libertine named Sainte-Croix died in 1672, a small box was found among his effects; it contained a number of vials containing colourless liquids – which turned out to be poisons – and letters from the Baroness de Brinvilliers, which made it clear that she and Sainte-Croix were lovers, and that they had been involved together in various poisonings. When she heard that the box had been found, Madame de Brinvilliers fled to England, then to the Netherlands, then took refuge in a convent. She was at large for three years; and when finally arrested was found to be carrying a confession which was so frank in its erotic detail that it had to be printed in Latin.

The Baroness – Marie Madeline d'Aubray – had been born in

1630, the daughter of a nobleman who was civil lieutenant of Paris. She seems to have been highly sexed from the beginning, and by the time she reached her teens had had sexual intercourse with her brothers. She married the Baron de Brinvilliers at twenty-one, and he soon spent the enormous dowry she brought him. Then she met Sainte-Croix and became his mistress. The baron had no objection; but when Marie's father found out, he had Sainte-Croix arrested and thrown into the Bastille. Here the young man met an Italian poisoner named Exili, and learned something of the art of administering 'inheritance powders'. When Sainte-Croix was released from the Bastille after two months, he told his mistress that he had discovered a foolproof method by which they could be avenged on her father. They bought poisons from an apothecary, and Marie tried them out by visiting poor patients in the hospital and presenting them with bottles of wine and baskets of fruit. These tests convinced her that the poisons were efficient and undetectable. When she was at home with her father during Whitsun 1666, he fell ill, and was carefully nursed by Marie. He died that September.

In the following year, her two brothers died. Poison was detected in the body of one of them, but no accusation was made. The man who administered the potions was a professional poisoner named Hamelin, who later blackmailed Marie and became her lover. Sainte-Croix was also extorting money from her on the strength of her letters and two promissory notes she had signed when he agreed to help her murder her brothers.

An attempt to poison her sister and sister-in-law came to nothing when a tutor in whom she had confided sent a warning to the sister. She next tried to poison her husband, in order to marry Sainte-Croix; but Sainte-Croix had no intention of marrying her, and kept frustrating her plans by administering antidotes. All this did the baron's health no good, but he survived.

At this point, Sainte-Croix died of an illness. When Marie heard about it, she exclaimed: 'The little box!' And in fact, the contents of the little box were to bring her to the headman. The poisoner Hamelin was arrested and tortured; he was sentenced to be broken alive on the wheel. By this time, Marie de Brinvilliers was in England; when attempts were made to extradite her, she fled to the Netherlands, then back into France, then to Antwerp and Liège. In his *Celebrated Crimes*, Alexandre Dumas tells a delightful story of how the agent who was sent to arrest her discovered that the police had no jurisdiction within the walls of a convent, and was compelled to disguise himself as an abbé and seduce her, then persuade her to meet him outside, where he was able to arrest her. The true story seems to be that she was arrested by a political agent who was given a key of the convent, so that he had only to let himself in and take her by surprise.

She was tortured by having buckets of water poured in her mouth through a funnel, and sentenced to death after a court case that lasted three months, between April and July 1676. On the scaffold she behaved with dignity and courage. The executioner severed her head at one stroke, after which the body was burnt. But some of her relics were sold as charms – the story of her repentance made many consider her a saint. Like the Chambre Ardente affair, the Brinvilliers case has an odd air of belonging to an earlier century. In fact, both cases reveal that France was only just emerging from the Middle Ages.

Before we plunge back into this increasingly fast-flowing stream of modern history, let us pause to survey the long road that mankind has travelled in eight thousand years.

The first great landmark in the story of man is the establishment of the cities, more than eight thousand years ago. The next was the invention of writing, about three millennia later. Within a mere two thousand years, this had led to the achievement of Greece – to Plato, Aristotle and the Greek dramatists, and of great scientists like Aristarchus and Eratosthenes.

Unfortunately, this development of the human spirit is paralleled by a development in the spirit of war. From the time of Sargon of Akkad, military leaders have expressed their sense of destiny – that is, their evolutionary appetite – by trying to build empires – the Assyrians, the Minoans, the Achaeans, the Persians, the Babylonians, the Spartans – even the Athenians themselves. The collapse of Athens is perhaps the most interesting tragedy in human history in that here we see the downfall of the spirit of intellectual evolution at the hands of the spirit of war.

For two thousand years, science and philosophy lie dormant. Instead, the spirit of religion becomes the spearhead of evolution. Ancient Rome is the purest expression of aggressive militarism; it produces no art, literature, philosophy or religion worth mentioning. Rome invited its own destruction by spreading its boundaries too far, until even the most warlike of emperors could not maintain peace for more than a year or two at a time; Diocletian collapsed with exhaustion after holding it together for twenty years. And we see this as a recurrent pattern of military history. Even if a great conqueror can contain his newly-won empire, his sons or grandsons find it too much for them, and it disintegrates.

The Church, in the absence of any counterforce, dominated the western intellect for more than a thousand years. In that time it created an immense, static 'order of nature', in which thinking was regarded with distrust and suspicion. It seemed to be like one of those immense rocking stones that are found in remote places, where a weight of many tons is balanced on a single point; it can be made to sway backwards and forwards, but no amount of effort seems to be able to move it from its place. At first, it looked as if Martin Luther had done precisely that. But within a few years, the Church was as stable as ever, calling for crusades – like the one that defeated the Turks at Lepanto in 1571 – burning heretics, like Giordano Bruno (1600), and forcing scientists like Galileo to recant. Besides, Protestantism was only Catholicism under another trade name; it did not burn quite as many heretics as the Catholic Church, but it did its share. As a version of Christianity, it was certainly no improvement on Catholicism.

The real change was due to other causes: to the broadening of the mind that came with the crusades, to the increasing use of money, which created a new class, and to the opening of the seas by Henry the Navigator, Dias, Columbus, Magellan, Cabot, Drake. In the sixteenth century, the Turks continued to be the major threat in the Mediterranean – they came close to taking Vienna in 1529 – but they became slightly more amenable after their defeat at Lepanto, and the British under Queen Elizabeth were able to form a Levant Trading Company to trade with them and the East India Company (1600) which had to cross Turkish territory on its overland route to India. (The Portuguese were still guarding the sea route.) Even the Church allowed itself to be swayed by this new spirit of adventure and tolerance. Matteo Ricci, the pioneer Jesuit scholar in China, was adopted by Chinese Confucians as one of themselves; the Jesuits made Christianity more palatable for the Chinese by translating

'God' as 'Heaven' (T'ien). Unfortunately, the Church intervened and ordered that Chinese converts should be taught that the Christian God is personal, and that their ancestor worship was anti-Christian. The inevitable result was that the Christians were thrown out of China in 1723.

But meanwhile, Europe was entering a new Athenian age. Francis Bacon, born three years before Christopher Marlowe (1561) was the first great imaginative visionary of science. In his *New Atlantis* (1627) he envisaged the first science institute, known as Salomon's House, with laboratories dug into the hillsides, skyscrapers half a mile high, huge marine laboratories and strange machines; twelve of its fellows travel into foreign lands and collect reports on experiments and inventions. Francis's central thesis was the one that had landed Roger Bacon in prison three centuries earlier: that science should be based on observation and on reason, not on the writings of lazy philosophers like Aristotle who could not be bothered to test their observations. Bacon's own doctor, William Harvey, discovered the circulation of the blood. In France, René Descartes was teaching that all knowledge should be founded on reason, and on the principle of doubting everything until it can be proved. (But since he lived in a Catholic country, he took care not to risk prison by doubting the dogmas of the Church.) Bacon's secretary, Thomas Hobbes, was the first philosopher of history; it was he who remarked that human life in the state of nature is 'solitary, poor, nasty, brutish and short'. His solution to this problem was not religion, but the social contract by which men agree to live together under a strong ruler. Man created society and government out of his craving for order: therefore, no king rules by divine right, but by a general agreement. In Holland, the philosopher Spinoza was expelled from his Jewish congregation for insisting that religion should be based on reason, and that all the truths of religion can be grasped through reason. John Locke, born in the same year as Spinoza (1632), taught that man is by nature good, and that again, the only principle he can finally trust is that of reason.

These men were the true heirs of Plato and the Italian humanists, and clearly, they were more dangerous to authority than Wycliffe, Luther, Zwingli and Calvin all rolled into one. What made them more dangerous was that they had no intention of challenging organized religion. They were too fascinated by the immense new vistas that were being opened up by the use of reason and imagination. Descartes invented analytical geometry, Newton and Leibniz the differential calculus – mathematical instruments of immense power in uncovering the secrets of nature. Yet all three would have regarded themselves as orthodox Christians – Newton even spent years of his life working out a 'history of the earth' based on the chronology of the Bible. In *A Short History of the World* H. G. Wells expresses the situation in one of his brilliant images: 'The history of mankind for the last four centuries is rather like that of an imprisoned sleeper, stirring clumsily and uneasily while the prison that restrains and shelters him catches fire, not waking, but incorporating the crackling and warmth of the fire with ancient and incongruous dreams . . .' (Chapter 52). Yet in a sense, it hardly matters that Descartes, Newton and Leibniz are sleepers. What matters is that Leibniz dreamed of a society of scholars who would investigate all branches of science and combine them into one great system of truth, and that Newton's *Principia* provided all future scientists with a key to the mechanics of the universe. Anyone who has grasped the meaning of human history will realize that mankind is still far from awake.

While the scientists and philosophers dreamed of truth, the rest of the world pursued its favourite occupation of mass murder. Yet even this was gradually changing. One of the last of the old-style world-conquerors, Babur, was a descendant of Genghis Khan and Tamurlane. In the year Columbus returned from his first American voyage, Babur came to his father's throne in Ferghana (in Genghis Khan country) and, by the time he was twenty, had twice taken and twice lost Samarkand. Driven out of Transoxania by the Tartars, he made himself master of Afghanistan, then decided that he wanted to be emperor of India. His first invasion in 1519 ended in failure, but five years later he was back again at the head of a force of twelve thousand and made himself master of Delhi. When his favourite son, Humayun fell ill, Babur prayed that his own life should be taken instead; Humayun recovered and Babur fell ill and died (1530). Humayun lost his empire for a while to an Afghan adventurer, but returned after fifteen years of exile and recaptured Delhi. He died shortly afterwards in an accident, and was succeeded by his son, Akbar the Great Mogul. Akbar went on to build a vast empire in northern India and Afghanistan. But he was no mere Tamurlane – in

fact, he was altogether closer to Kubla Khan. With an empire full of
Moslems and Hindus – even Christians – he insisted on treating
them all alike and allowing all equal opportunities. His court was
famous for its learning as well as for its magnificence. So while
Europe was torn with religious wars, and the duke of Alva was
burning Dutchmen by the thousand, Akbar the Great Mogul was
revealing a kind of greatness that had been rare since the days of
Asoka. Significantly, a representative of the East India Company
arrived in Akbar's domains in 1603, and was granted a concession
five years later. Akbar died in 1605, and religious tolerance continued in northern India for more than sixty years, when the emperor
Aurengzeb began a mass persecution of Hindus.

In China, the old order continued to prevail, since the Chinese,
like the Japanese, were averse to change. The Mongols were thrown
out in 1368, and replaced by the Ming dynasty, which gave the
country three centuries of relative peace and order. This was
founded by a beggar who became a rebel, Hung-wu, a despot who
made a habit of having his ministers tortured. His successors were
little better, but at least maintained order, in spite of Mongol raids in
the north and attacks from Japanese sea pirates. His people were so
distrustful of foreigners that they massacred the first Portuguese who
landed in China. Then, in 1644, Peking was captured by a brigand
who called himself 'the dashing general', and the last Ming emperor
hanged himself on a hill over the city. He was soon replaced by a new
'barbarian horde', the Manchus, who became masters of China and
ruled until the twentieth century. Their power was gradually
undermined by foreign traders – particularly the British, who
introduced opium to China. We can regard China as a kind of last
outpost of the ancient world, obeying the old law of history – of
conquerors gradually becoming effete and lazy, and being driven out
by new barbarians.

Meanwhile in Europe, the game was being played according to a
new set of rules. Under the old rules, a king as powerful and as rich
as Philip II of Spain – with wealth pouring in from the Americas –
would have conquered half Europe. His problem was that he lacked
the kind of simple-minded drive that could have made him a worthy
successor to his father, Charles V. He was an uncomfortable mixture
of hard-working bureaucrat and religious fanatic. A sensible king
would have pacified his Dutch subjects – ignoring their Protestan-

tism – leaned over backward to maintain friendly relations with England, and turned his full military strength against the Turks. Instead he persecuted the Dutch and quarrelled with the English, while still trying to crush the Moslem menace in the Mediterranean. He had weakened himself by dividing his forces; so that when the English fleet and the bad weather destroyed the Armada in 1588, his schemes collapsed like a house of cards. And the Turks, although defeated at Lepanto, went on expanding for another century. Philip's bull-in-a-china-shop behaviour would have made him a world conqueror, in an earlier age; but in Europe, the china shop was getting too small and too overcrowded, and a world conqueror was likely to end up on the floor surrounded by broken crockery.

Queen Elizabeth's successor, James I, was not at all a bull in a china shop. He was a strange, feeble man, a homosexual who was given to bursting into tears, who slobbered as he talked, and whose legs were so weak that he had to lean on people's shoulders when he talked to them. But he sensibly kept England out of further conflict with Spain, and also aloof from the conflict – which began with the Dutch revolt – that became the Thirty Years War. James believed firmly in the divine right of kings – that kings were appointed by God – and seemed to be in an excellent position for forcing his opinion on his subjects. But here too he discovered that the game was not being played according to the old rules. His problem was that his subjects were not openly rebellious; they merely had quite definite ideas about their rights. When he summoned his parliament to vote him funds, they insisted on talking about their own rights, and later on, flatly refused to vote him money, declaring that he was wasting it on his favourites – such as the tall and handsome Robert Carr, who shared the king's bed. Moreover, at a Church conference at Hampton Court, a new group of religious reformers known as Puritans – because they wanted to purify the Church of Roman Catholic rituals – presented a demand for more control over the rich and powerful bishops. Once again there were clashes, and the king had to recognize that his subjects might be obedient but they had minds of their own. There was more trouble when James announced a plan to marry his son Charles to a Spanish princess. This eventually fell through – because the Spaniards also hated the idea – and parliament voted him some of the money he wanted. But most of James's life was spent in frustrating struggles with parliament. He was forced to learn that there was a new spirit abroad, that people felt they had a right to think for themselves and to assert their individuality. His son Charles I learned this greatly to his cost when his parliament went to war against him, and eventually cut off his head.

In France, the situation looked altogether more stable, closer to the world of the Middle Ages. After the murder of Henry of Navarre by Ravaillac in 1610, Henry's wife, Marie de Medici, became regent – since the heir, Louis XIII, was only nine years old. Marie showed herself an expert in intrigue, and ruled with the aid of her lady-in-waiting, Leonora Galigai, and her husband Concini. The shy and introverted boy-king, whose only pleasure was hunting, poured out his heart to this chief falconer, Luynes. One day, the commander of the guard pushed his way through a crowd of courtiers, walked up to Concini, and signalled his men, who raised their guns and killed Concini on the spot. 'Now I am really king,' said Louis proudly, while his mother had hysterics in bed. Three-quarters of a century earlier, the young king of Russia, Ivan the Terrible – who was thirteen at the time – ordered his servants to murder his enemy Prince Shuisky and throw his corpse to the dogs; it was the beginning of a bloody but highly successful reign. But Louis was living in the new century. Luynes turned out to be greedy and corrupt as an adviser. The queen mother had to be recalled from her exile, together with her chief adviser, Cardinal Richelieu. And it was Richelieu who became head of the royal council, made bargains with England, Holland and Denmark, plotted against the descendants of Charles V – the Hapsburgs – and eventually involved France in the disastrous Thirty Years War. Unlike Russia, France had no place for a tsar; it needed a diplomat capable of turning double somersaults.

The Thirty Years War is another demonstration of how the rules of history were changing. It started as the great culminating clash between Protestants and Catholics, when Ferdinand of Bohemia – another Hapsburg – tried to crush Lutherans and Calvinists in his dominions. The Protestants of Bohemia rebelled, and threw two leading Catholic governors out of the window of Prague Castle – the famous 'defenestration of Prague'. (Amusingly, one of the attackers shouted angrily: 'Now let's see if the Virgin will help him'; then looked out of the window and said: 'My God, she has! He's crawling away . . .') The Spanish sent troops to help Ferdinand put down the rebellion, and a Protestant German prince, Frederick of the Palatinate, marched in on the side of the rebels. Hungary was dragged into the war, then Sweden. The history of the conflict resounds with great names: Tilly the Fighting Monk, Wallenstein, Gustavus Adolphus. If Ferdinand had not mistrusted his great general Wallenstein so deeply, he would probably have won the war; as it was, Wallenstein was murdered by his own side, to the delight of the Protestants. Then the Catholic Richelieu came into the war on the side of the Protestants, for he had no desire to see a Hapsburg become the most powerful ruler in Europe. So the war dragged on to its indecisive end in 1648, and neither side could claim victory. In retrospect, it was a pure waste of time.

Thanks to Richelieu, France came out of the Thirty Years War stronger than ever, so that the next king, Louis XIV, was able to behave like a Roman caesar. If anyone stood a chance of recalling the ways of an old-time conqueror, it was the Sun King, who had so much money that he was able to bribe half the monarchs of Europe. He was certainly strong enough to revoke the Edict of Nantes in 1685 and outlaw Protestantism in France. He built Versailles and had the sense to choose as his chief minister a shopkeeper's son – Jean Baptiste Colbert – who revolutionized France's industry and made it rich. Then, powerful and secure, he began to behave like an emperor. He flatly declined to entertain Colbert's idea that the nobles ought to pay taxes like everybody else, since he felt that wealthy and idle nobles ought to decorate the court of a truly great king. The result is that Louis drained the national wealth as fast as Colbert created it. Then, deciding that a great king ought to be a great conqueror, he found an excuse to pick a quarrel with Spain, marched 120,000 troops into the Spanish Netherlands and ended with vast tracts of land and important trade concessions. But the Dutch cities revolted and, under the leadership of William of Orange, gradually forced Louis to withdraw. When William of Orange became king of England by deposing the bigoted Catholic James II, the English and the Dutch, joined by Sweden, Spain and Savoy (on the Swiss-Italian border) so harassed Louis's forces on land and sea that he was forced to sue for peace. He was learning that, in this complicated modern world, there is no room for absolute emperors. When his grandson, Philip of Anjou, became king of Spain in 1701, Louis saw the chance of a masterstroke – of permanently uniting France and Spain into one empire. This was the last thing the rest of Europe wanted, particularly the Dutch, who had suffered so much from Spain. Louis marched again into the Netherlands to try to force the Dutch to agree, but in 1702, England and Holland declared war on France, and half Europe joined in. The war dragged on until 1713, when Louis finally made peace – having been forced to agree that his grandson Philip could never become king of France. So twelve years of effort was wasted, and Louis felt old and tired and oddly let-down – just as Charles V had in his last years; he died two years later, in 1715. If he had concentrated on trade and expansion in the colonies, the French empire would have spread across the world, and the people of the United States would today probably be speaking French. As it was, France lost its American possessions within a few decades, and the king of France lost his head before the end of the century. If Louis XIV had not been so determined to play at being Charlemagne, the French Revolution would never have taken place.

If our visitors from space could have revisited the earth at any time between 1450 and 1650, their first impression would have been that things have not changed greatly since the days of ancient Rome. There are still one or two major powers – such as the pope and the Holy Roman emperor – who dominate most of Europe. The barbarians – the Turks – are still battering at the gates and making inroads. The scene is, admittedly, rather more complex than in the time of Diocletian; but Europe is still a mass of armies marching and countermarching. Christianity, the religion of love and reconciliation, has had no noticeable effect. And perhaps there is no reason why it should, for human nature cannot be expected to change in the course of a thousand years or so. Whole cities are still being wiped out by invading armies, just like Carthage. And there are still plenty of Caligulas and Domitians – men like Sultan Selim I (father of Suleiman the Magnificent), Vlad the Impaler, Ivan the Terrible. In fact, in this respect, mankind seems to have achieved new levels of sadism. Vlad the Impaler – the historical Dracula – was a minor king of Wallachia (now in Rumania), who spent most of his life fighting the Turks, displaying immense bravery and resourcefulness; he was also one of the most appalling monsters in history, deriving tremendous pleasure (undoubtedly sexual) from watching people die slowly. On a lightning raid into Transylvania in 1457, Dracula had his captives – men, women and children – taken back to Wallachia so that he could watch them being impaled – his favourite method of execution. Old woodcuts show the victims impaled through their stomachs, but it seems certain that the wooden stake was driven into the anus or vagina so that the victim's own weight made him sink down on to it; he gave orders that the end should not be too sharp, so that it would take longer. In a quarrel with Saxon merchants around 1460, he held a mass impalement, and also burned alive four hundred apprentices. The impalements were regarded as an entertainment during meals; one Russian boyar had the misfortune to hold his nose when the smell of blood sickened him; he was immediately impaled on a particularly long stake. Irritated by the number of beggars and sick people in his domains, Vlad invited them all to a banquet, then locked them in and set fire to the building. When he was imprisoned in Hungary for twelve years, and unable to satisfy his taste for torture of prisoners, he tortured animals. He was killed in battle – against the Turks – in 1476, probably by his own men.

Ivan the Terrible – born in 1530 – was a fairly normal Russian tsar – except for a tendency to rape any woman who took his fancy – until the death of his wife, when he was twenty-seven. He then became pathologically suspicious, subject to insane rages and a devotee of cruelty and violence. Here we can see the typical 'Right Man' syndrome in its most naked form. When he became convinced that the citizens of Novgorod were planning rebellion – which was almost certainly untrue – he had a wooden wall built round the city to prevent any of the inhabitants from fleeing. Then for five weeks he sat and watched them being tortured to death; husbands and wives were forced to watch each other being tortured; mothers had to watch their babies being ill-treated before themselves being roasted alive. Ivan looked on with insane satisfaction as sixty-four thousand people were killed in this way. But his blood-lust had been sated; when he marched on Pskov to inflict the same punishment, the inhabitants received him on their knees, and he was placated. When he besieged a castle in Livonia, the defenders preferred to blow themselves up with gunpowder rather than fall into his hands.

But as we have seen, the pathology of such cases is relatively simple. A man with a natural 'spoilt' temperament is placed in a situation where he can indulge every whim. He could be compared to a glutton who is placed in a situation where he can eat himself to death. Every one of us wants 'his own way' as a child, but contact with adult discipline forces us to learn restraint. The Caligulas and Draculas and Ivans are allowed to grow like unpruned trees until they are a tangled mass of overgrown emotions. Their inability to discipline the negative aspect of themselves intensifies their problems. The ego turns into a kind of cancer that consumes them.

Yet fortunately the circumstances that produce these freaks are rare. Most of us are enslaved – and disciplined – by material circumstances from the moment we are born. Our fathers and mothers have to discipline themselves to stay alive, and they make sure that the lesson is passed on to us. The result is that nearly all the 'monsters' of history are to be found amongst absolute rulers. They are rare even among the barons and dukes, for people who have daily contact with other people have to learn some kind of restraint. Most of us realize, for example, that to encourage our own anger is one of the lesser forms of self-destruction. Dracula's contemporary Gilles de Rais is an interesting landmark in the history of crime, for he is one of the first known examples of a man whose political power is limited, yet who developed all the characteristics of the sadistic egoist. But then, he was one of the richest men in France – probably in Europe – and was thoroughly spoilt and pampered as a child. In his twenties – he was born in 1404 – he fought bravely at the side of Joan of Arc and helped to drive the English out of France. Then he went back to his estates and proceeded to spend money with spectacular abandon. He also began to indulge his favourite perversion – the torture and murder of children. His method was to have the children kidnapped, or lured to his castle on some pretext. He would commit sodomy – even with female victims – while strangling the child or cutting off the head. He also enjoyed disembowelling his victims and masturbating on the intestines. Dismembered bodies were then thrown into an unused tower – about fifty bodies were found there after his arrest. Gilles's downfall came when he beat and imprisoned a priest; he was arrested and tried as a heretic. He had undoubtedly been attempting to practise black magic to repair his fortunes. Threat of excommunication led him to confess, and he was executed – strangled, and then burned – in October 1440. But although Gilles retains a place as one of the first 'non-political' monsters in history, his psychology is not really so very different from that of Cesare Borgia. It is again a simple case of the 'cancerous ego'.

It is this natural tendency of the unconstrained ego to develop criminal tendencies that Christian theologians called 'original sin'. They saw in it evidence that there is some fundamental weakness – or sickness – in human nature. It also explained why the authority of the Church was necessary. We have seen that the problem can be explained more simply in terms of 'divided consciousness', of the fact that man tends to become trapped in his left-brain ego. We have also seen that a great deal of the cruelty in history – for example, of the Romans – was not due to sadism but to an overdeveloped sense of purpose. Like the emperors who built the Great Wall and the great canals of China, they were so obsessed by their purpose that they treated individuals as if they were as unimportant as flies.

All this explains why the kind of crime we find recorded up to the end of the Middle Ages has a curiously non-individual quality. Robbers murder travellers just as a butcher kills cattle; it is a way of making a living. When they are caught, the robbers are executed; but no one bothers to record their deeds. The crimes that the chroniclers feel worth recording are the crimes against authority – treason, conspiracy, coining. Crime on lower social levels is as uninteresting as the activities of rats or fleas.

With the Renaissance, this slowly begins to change, because it is an age of developing individualism. But the individualism only affected the educated classes – and the Church. So it is not surprising to come across a case like that of the priest, Don Niccolo de Pelagati (mentioned on p. 360) who went in for rape, murder and robbery. He was merely following the lead of the pope himself.

Almost a century after the exploits of Don Niccolo, the Nuremberg public executioner, Master Franz Schmidt, kept a rough diary of the people he executed. A very large number of the entries read simply: 'A thief hanged'. There are also many women who have killed illegitimate children soon after birth. One maidservant is beheaded simply because she had had children by both the father and son of the house where she worked. But the great majority of the murderers who are executed have committed their crimes in the course of robbery. 'Elizabeth Rossnerin of Leibsgrüen, a day labourer and beggar, who smothered and throttled her companion, also a field worker, and took 4 pounds 9 pfennigs from her.

types of crime

Beheaded with the sword as a favour because she was a poor creature and had a wry neck . . .' 'Frederick Werner of Nuremberg . . . a murderer and robber who committed three murders and twelve robberies . . .' And many of the worst crimes are committed by partners or gangs. 'Kloss Renckhart of Feylsdorf, a murderer who committed three murders with an associate. First he shot dead his companion, secondly a miller's man who helped him to attack and plunder a mill by night. The third case was again at a mill, called the Fox Mill, on the mountains, which he attacked at night with a companion. They shot the miller dead, did violence to the miller's wife and the maid, obliged them to fry some eggs in fat and laid these on the miller's body, then forced the miller's wife to join in eating them . . .' 'Niklauss Stüller of Aydtsfeld . . . a murderer. With his companions Phila and Görgla von Sunberg, he committed eight murders. First he shot a horse soldier; secondly he cut open a pregnant woman alive, in whom was a female child; thirdly, he again cut open a pregnant woman in whom was a female child; fourthly he once more cut open a pregnant woman in whom were two male children. Görgla von Sunberg said they had committed a great sin and that he would take the infants to a priest to be baptized but Phila said he would be himself a priest and baptize them, so he took them by the legs and dashed them to the ground. For these deeds he, Stüller, was drawn on a sledge at Bamberg, his body torn thrice with red hot tongs, and then he was executed on the wheel.' But cases like this, involving sadism, are rare. So are sex crimes — not more than half a dozen in twenty-five years. 'Hans Müllner, a smith, who violated a girl of thirteen years of age, filling her mouth with sand that she might not cry out . . .' (Evidently the girl was not killed.) 'A man beheaded for violating a girl of fourteen.' Two homosexuals are executed for committing sodomy, and a farm labourer for buggery with cows and a sheep. Apart from the sadism of the robbers, most of the crimes seem to be curiously anonymous; they seem to spring out of circumstances rather than out of a criminal disposition.

From Luke Owen Pike's *History of Crime in England* we learn that at the same period in England the commonest crimes were robbery and – oddly enough – perjury. 'Perjury . . . was the most thoroughly ingrained of all the English crimes.' This refers to the perjury of witnesses and jurors in court cases. Corruption was widespread, starting with government ministers; everyone was expected to take bribes, and jurors were only following the custom of their betters. Pike remarks significantly: 'During the reigns of the Tudors, men in the highest positions still resorted to those mean arts which have now, at any rate, descended to a lower grade of society.' The poor committed the occasional theft and murder; the rich indulged in conspiracy and corruption.

Yet society is now changing fast, and it is inevitable that crime will follow it sooner or later. This is the age of the Elizabethan drama, and the plays of Shakespeare and Marlowe are full of clearly individualized characters – not the wooden types of the *Morte d'Arthur* and *Orlando Furioso* – even of *Don Quixote*. 'In Shakespeare's time,' says Erich Kahler, 'the destiny of peoples coincided with the destiny of their monarchs and nobles' (p.500 of *Man the Measure*). And, what is more, the ordinary individual began to feel that he was, in some obscure way, the equal of the monarch and noble. We only have to look at the popular journalism of the time – pamphlets by writers such as Robert Greene and Thomas Nashe – to see that they assumed a very high degree of mental alertness in their readers. Indeed, as Q. D. Leavis argues in *Fiction and the Reading Public*, 'By modern standards they show an insulting disregard of the reader's convenience: the dashing tempo, the helter-skelter progress, the unexpected changes of direction and tone so that the reader is constantly faced with a fresh front, the stream of casual allusion and shifting metaphor, leave us giddy as the Elizabethan dramas leave us stunned' (p.88). People who were capable of plunging into this foaming whirlpool of prose were not afraid of using their minds. Like the ancient Greeks, they loved to go to the theatre and be told a fascinating story of murder and intrigue. But they loved too the simple, almost characterless novels of the time such as Sidney's *Arcadia*, Greene's *Card of Fancy* and Nashe's *Unfortunate Traveller*; in these they didn't want character – only to be told an interesting story. Yet as soon as men are capable of spending an hour or so in 'another world', they have also learned to daydream and to detach themselves from their own narrow lives.

This explains why, when James I called his first parliament in 1604, he found himself faced with a houseful of respectful but strong-minded individuals, determined to stand by their rights. And the new religious Puritanism was not the expression of a grim and joyless morality; it was an assertion of religious individualism, a defiant rejection of both Bloody Mary's Catholicism *and* Queen Elizabeth's new Anglican church, which looked like Catholicism with an English accent. We find the new spirit in John Milton's 'masque' *Comus*, presented in 1634, in which the wicked enchanter Comus tries to seduce a girl lost in the forest. One of her two brothers – searching for her – makes a long speech about chastity, and about how a noble idea enters

> The unpolluted temple of the mind,
> And turns it by degrees to the soul's essence,
> Till all be made immortal . . .

and the second brother exclaims:

> How charming is divine Philosophy!
> Not harsh and crabbed as dull fools suppose,
> But musical as is Apollo's lute.

The girl, naturally, defeats the sorcerer's wicked designs without the slightest effort – so easily that the contest seems unfair. But Milton is not being merely 'moral'; he had discovered that ideas can be as bracing as a cold wind, and that the individual's conscience is the most powerful weapon he possesses.

The English enjoyed their Puritanism; it tasted of freedom. *The Pilgrim's Progress* (1678) expressed this new sense of individual responsibility. 'Do you see yonder shining light? He said, I think I do. Then said the Evangelist, Keep that light in your eye, and go up directly thereto . . .'

So when King Charles assured his people that God had made him king, and that in obeying him they would be obeying God, they replied that they had their own shining light, and cut off his head. When King James II tried to reintroduce Catholicism twenty years later, they sent an invitation to the Protestant William of Orange to come and take his throne.

We find it hard to understand why the English responded with such enthusiasm to this rather joyless religion of Puritanism. The answer is simple. When a man possesses any kind of deep inner conviction, he is happy; what is more, his happiness is founded on a rock. When he lacks conviction, he is a drifting ship without a rudder. It is impossible to study human criminality for long without realizing that it is a history of rudderless ships.

— *opportunists* —

A few years before William of Orange invaded England, a certain Professor Sylvius of Leyden invented a new medicine which he called geneva, from the French word *genièvre*. It was made of cheap alcohol – distilled from corn mash – but given a sharp and pleasant flavouring with berries of the *genièvre* – or juniper. It was sold in small bottles in chemists' shops, and the Dutch soon realized that geneva was as potent as good brandy, and far cheaper. When William and Mary installed themselves on James's throne in 1688, their countrymen began to export the new drink to England. Since England was quarrelling with France, and was therefore reluctant to buy French brandy, geneva – or gin – quickly became the national drink. Because of the brandy embargo, a law was passed permitting anyone to distill his own drink, and the English soon improved on the Dutch original, distilling an even cheaper grade of corn mash, and producing a powerful spirit that would now be called moonshine. (It is also probably a safe bet that this was when someone discovered that beer could be distilled to produce whisky.) Gin shops opened all over England – one London street had six of them.

Queen Elizabeth's subjects had drunk sherry (Falstaff's 'sack'), beer and wine, which were cheap – wine cost fourpence a quart. Then James I had succeeded in raising some of the money parliament refused to grant him by taxing various commodities, including wine and sherry, so that the English working man of the seventeenth century could only afford beer. By 1688, the English working classes were alcohol-starved. The consumption of gin rose steadily, from half a million gallons around 1690 to three and a half million by 1727 and – by the middle of the century – to nineteen million gallons.

The result was a crime wave. Many gin shops carried the notice; 'Drunk for a penny, dead drunk for twopence, clean straw for nothing.' Crimes to obtain money for gin became as common as crimes to obtain money for drugs in our own society. Theft became so common that, in 1699, a particularly savage act was passed that made almost any theft punishable by hanging, provided the goods were worth more than five shillings. At the same time, anyone who helped to secure the apprehension of a thief could obtain various tax exemptions and rewards. The measures were desperate; but so was the situation. Quite suddenly, England was virtually in a state of war with criminals. The diarist Narcissus Luttrell mentions an endless series of highway robberies and similar crimes. On one Saturday in 1693, a highwayman named Whitney had been arrested after resisting for an hour, and another highwayman was arrested in St Martin's Church. A gang of seven broke into Lady Reresby's house in Gerard Street, tied her and her family up and then rifled the house. Three coaches were robbed coming from Epsom, and three rowdies had caused an affray in Holborn, broken windows and run a watchman through with a sword, leaving it in his body. The invasion of houses by robber gangs had become as common as it was before the Black Death. A few years later, the famous robber Dick Turpin – whose exploits were far less romantic than his legend – led a gang that specialized in breaking into country houses, torturing the householders to force them to disclose valuables and raping any maids. Turpin's fame rested on the flamboyant manner of his death, bowing and waving to the mob from his cart, and finally voluntarily leaping from the gallows ladder.

All this makes an interesting contrast with crime in the age of Queen Elizabeth. It had been just as widespread, but far less serious. London was then full of thieves and confidence men (known as 'cony catchers', a cony being a rabbit). The thieves used to meet once a week in the house of their leader, who also happened to be the brother-in-law of the hangman; there, like an alderman's meeting, they discussed 'prospects' and exchanged information. In contemporary descriptions (Robert Greene wrote several pamphlets about it), the London criminal scene in the time of Elizabeth sounds rather like Damon Runyan's New York, deplorable but fairly good-natured. A century later, this had changed. Highwaymen infested the country roads, burglars operated in the towns, and women and children appeared as frequently in the courts as men. Children were trained as pickpockets, and were also sent out to earn gin money by prostitution – the novelist Henry Fielding, who became a magistrate in 1740, wrote of the large number of children 'eaten up with the foul distemper'. The government's reaction was to execute almost every offender who appeared in court. In 1722, a gang of Hampshire poachers had murdered a keeper who had interrupted them; they had blackened their faces so as to be less visible in the dark. Landowners in the Waltham area (where it took place) were so

drugs & crime

alarmed that the government was prevailed upon to pass an act – the 'Waltham Black Act' – which enabled almost any poacher to be hanged. (If the act had been in existence when Shakespeare was arrested for poaching from Sir Thomas Lucy, his works would have remained unwritten.) The act included a list of more than three hundred other offences – including catching rabbits – for which a man could be hanged.

Yet these measures had no effect on the rising crime rate. It could hardly be expected to when a large proportion of the population was permanently drunk. Henry Fielding reckoned that a hundred thousand people in London alone lived mainly on gin. Another observer stood outside a gin palace for three hours one evening and counted 1,411 people going in and out. These 'palaces' usually consisted of a shed, full of barrels of gin; the customers merely came to buy a pennyworth of gin, which explains the enormous number. Whole families, including, father, mother and children then sat on the pavement and drank themselves unconscious; with gin at a penny at quart, it was not difficult. The artist William Hogarth engraved two famous pictures, 'Beer Street' and 'Gin Lane', to expose the evil. In Beer Street, a lot of jolly-looking men and women are drinking outside a tavern and obviously engaging in intelligent political discussion (there is a copy of the king's speech on the table). In Gin Lane, a drunken mother allows her baby to fall out of her arms into the area below, a madman impales a baby on a spit, and a man who has hanged himself can be seen through the window of a garret. Fielding remarked that the gin 'disqualifies them from any honest means to acquire it, at the same time that it removes sense of fear and shame and emboldens them to commit every wicked and dangerous enterprise.' The result was that pickpockets who had once relied on skill and light fingers now knocked down their victims with bludgeons in broad daylight. The novelist Horace Walpole was shot in the face by a highwayman in Hyde Park in 1752.

Punishments, both in England and on the continent, had always been barbarous; now they became sadistic. The sentence of being hanged, drawn and quartered was usually reserved for political criminals, although it might be applied to some particularly violent robber. The victim was dragged to the place of execution behind a cart; he was then half-hanged, and his bowels were torn out while he was still alive and burned in front of him. After this the body was cut into four pieces. Female criminals were often burned alive, because it was regarded as more 'decent' than allowing them to risk exposing their private parts as they swung from a rope. (In this respect our ancestors were remarkably prudish.) But it was common for women – as well as men – to be stripped to the waist before being whipped through the streets to the pillory or gallows. After the 1699 act, thieves were branded on one cheek to make their offence public knowledge – this was probably regarded as an act of clemency, since most thieves were hanged. Prisoners accused of offences that involved speech – perhaps preaching false religious doctrines – would have a hole bored through the tongue as they were held in the pillory. A confidence man named Japhet Crook was sentenced to have both ears cut off and his nose slit open then seared with a red hot iron; the hangman, known as 'Laughing Jack' Hooper, cut off both ears from behind with a sharp knife and held them aloft for the crowd to see, then cut open Crook's nostrils with scissors; however, when he applied the red hot iron to the bleeding nose, Crook leapt out of his chair so violently that Hooper – who was a kindly man – decided not to carry out the rest of the punishment. On the Continent, sentences were even crueller; red hot pincers were used to tear out the tongues of blasphemers. A madman called Damiens, who tried – rather half heartedly – to stab Louis XV of France in 1757, was executed by being literally 'quartered'. He was carried to the execution because his legs had been smashed with sledgehammers. His chest was torn open with red hot pincers, and lead poured into the wounds. Then his hands and feet were tied to four dray horses, which were whipped off in opposite directions. They were not strong enough to tear off his arms and legs, so more horses were brought; even so, the executioner had to partly sever the arms and legs before they could be pulled off. Damiens remained conscious until he had only one arm left – during the early part of the proceedings he looked on with apparent curiosity – and his hair turned white during the course of the execution.

But then, punishment was intended as a public spectacle. The underlying notion was to deter; in fact, it seems to have had the effect of making the spectators sadistic. This was perhaps an extreme example of the 'xenophobic' reaction discussed in an earlier chapter. The English had always been inclined to treat foreigners as an object of mirth – in 1592 the duke of Würtemburg noted that London crowds 'scoff and laugh' at foreigners and are likely to turn nasty if the foreigner shows any sign of being offended. At public spectacles, the criminal became the despised 'foreigner'. When placed in the stocks or pillory, he was likely to be pelted with stones and dead cats until he died. A woman named Barbara Spencer was sentenced to be burnt alive for coining in 1721; at the stake she wanted to say her prayers, but the mob wanted to get on with the entertainment and booed and threw things at her as she tried to pray; she had still not succeeded in saying her prayers when the hangman applied a torch to the faggots. Days when notable public executions were held at London's main gallows – Tyburn, at Hyde Park corner – were usually public holidays. They became known as 'gallows days', which in turn became 'gala days'. On the day when James Whitney –the highwayman who resisted capture for an hour – was taken to Tyburn, he was one of eight men who were sentenced to hang simultaneously on the triangular shaped scaffold that had been erected in the time of Queen Elizabeth. (The older type, consisting of two uprights and a cross bar, was less efficient in that it would only hang one or two at a time.) Only seven men were hanged on that occasion; Whitney was reprieved at the last moment for offering to betray his accomplices. Whitney was lucky enough to be popular; he was driven back through a cheering crowd with the rope still round his neck. But he was hanged a week later, having told all he knew.

In 1735, it struck a bookseller named John Osborn that the lively interest excited by criminals could be turned to his advantage, and he issued three volumes of *Lives of the Most Remarkable Criminals*. Pamphlets about famous criminals had been popular since the time of the Elizabethans; but they usually concerned people in the upper ranks of society and dealt with only one case at a time. By the time of Osborn, most criminals were ordinary highwaymen, footpads, housebreakers and pirates. But he recognized that the public had an insatiable appetite for the details of the lives of the people they loved to see hanged. Almost every one of the *Lives*, two hundred or so cases, begins with a moral preamble: 'It is an observation that must be obvious to all my readers, that few who addict themselves to robbing and stealing ever continue long in the practice of those crimes before they are overtaken by Justice . . .', and so on. And this was not because Osborn felt the need to justify himself in publishing tales of crime. It was because he recognized that his readers enjoyed

421 growth of empathy / social feeling

422, 2427, 474

art & emotion combined

congratulating themselves that they were not in the hands of the law. The pleasure of watching an execution was based on the feeling that you were in the crowd, not on the gallows. The public of Henry Fielding's day had very little imagination, very little capacity to *identify* itself with another person's suffering. This is why one of the popular entertainments was going to 'Bedlam' to laugh and jeer at the mad people. It would take another century before novelists like Dickens could persuade people to enjoy putting themselves in the place of the 'unfortunates' of society.

The most striking thing about Osborn's *Lives of the Criminals* is the utterly commonplace nature of most of the crimes, and their curious lack of *personal* interest. We live in an age of personalities, of gossip columns, of 'people in the news'. It is true that ninety-five per cent of the crimes that now take place in London or New York are commonplace and 'impersonal'. But the remaining five per cent help to fill scandal sheets with titillating details. We are accustomed to crimes having a strong 'individual' interest, the element that makes them suitable for film or television treatment. In Osborn, not even one per cent of the crimes would be suitable for dramatic treatment.

One of the few possible exceptions is the case of Catherine Hayes, a housewife who conspired with her two lovers to murder her husband, a retired moneylender. They lived in lodgings not far from the Tyburn gallows, and Catherine's relations with her husband were poor – she declared that he was pathologically mean, which is probably true. A young tailor named Thomas Billings came to the house and became her lover while her husband was away on business. Soon afterwards, a man named Thomas Wood moved in and also became her lover. She offered to share her husband's fortune of fifteen hundred pounds – a vast sum for those days – with her lovers if they would help her get rid of John Hayes. They did this one evening in 1725, after all four of them had drunk bottle after bottle of wine between them. (They were rich enough to drink wine, not gin.) One of the lovers hit Hayes with a hatchet and fractured his skull. The next problem was to get the body to the river. Catherine suggested that they cut off the head, so that if they were forced to abandon the corpse en route, it would be unrecognizable. With a great deal of retching, the two men sawed off the head with a carving knife, leaving the headless body to bleed into a pail. Then the two men walked down to the river and tossed the head in. It landed on mud – the tide was out. The following day, they dismembered the corpse, put it into a trunk, and threw it into a nearby pond under cover of darkness.

Meanwhile, the head had been found in the mud, and the parish officers of Westminster decided to put it on public exhibition to try to discover its identity; the blood was washed off, the hair neatly combed, and the head set on a pole in St Margaret's churchyard. One apprentice immediately recognized it and rushed off to inform Catherine Hayes. She told him sternly that her husband was in bed and that he would get into trouble if he spread such reports. When the head began to decay, it was placed in a jar of spirits and exhibited to anyone who was interested. Inevitably, someone reported his suspicions to the law; when the officers arrived, Catherine Hayes was in bed with Billings. Both swore stoutly that they were innocent; when Catherine was shown the head, she kissed it passionately and shed tears, still insisting she had no idea how her husband had died. Then Wood was arrested and confessed everything. The two men were sentenced to be hanged. Catherine was sentenced to be burned, since her crime was 'petty treason' – the husband being regarded as the lord and master. She screamed all the way back to prison. When she was tied to the stake, the hangman tried to strangle her as an act of mercy, but the flames burned his hands and he had to jump back; it took three hours for the body to be consumed.

The outstanding feature of the case is the personality of Catherine Hayes; there is a distinct resemblance to Marie de Brinvilliers. But unlike Marie, she was no aristocrat; she was the daughter of poor parents and had become a military trollop – the collective mistress of several officers – then a maidservant on a farm. It is clear she was a nymphomaniac, and that her dissatisfaction with her husband was basically sexual. He certainly knew that Billings was her lover, but made no objection, probably glad to see someone else taking on a share of the work. Both lovers were many years her junior – she was thirty-five, and they seem to have been teenagers. Any number of parallel cases could be cited from the twentieth century; but in the first half of the eighteenth century, she is unique: a woman who wanted something badly – to live openly with two lovers – and who was willing to commit murder to get it. She was, in fact, as much a criminal product of the individualism that produced *The Pilgrim's*

Progress as Caligula was a criminal product of the individualism that built ancient Rome. She seems to exemplify one of the 'laws' that has emerged during the course of this study: that the genius of each age produces its own characteristic type of criminality.

[handwritten annotation: nb observation i.e. the evolution of crime]

Ten

FROM INDIVIDUALISM TO REBELLION

In the year that Catherine Hayes and her husband moved to London – 1719 – the literary sensation was a work called *The Life and Strange Surprising Adventures of Robinson Crusoe of York, Mariner*. Its author is an interesting example of the relationship between genius and criminality.

Daniel Foe was born in London in 1660, the son of a butcher of St Giles, Cripplegate. His family were 'dissenters', that is, nonconformists who disagreed with Catholicism and Protestantism. Foe was so much a dissenter that in 1683, at the age of twenty-three, he enraged his fellow dissenters by publishing a pamphlet in which he said the Turks had no business besieging Vienna (as they were now doing under the leadership of Kara Mustapha), and that he hoped they wouldn't succeed, even if the Viennese *were* Catholics. In 1685, Foe was involved in the Duke of Monmouth's rebellion against James II and was lucky to avoid being condemned to death by the sadistic Judge Jeffreys. He married well – the lady brought him a dowry of £3,700 – set up in business as a wholesaler of stockings, and made a quick fortune. Extravagance and bad management led to bankruptcy, and he was forced to flee from his creditors. He went to Bristol, where he became known as 'the Sunday gentleman', that being the only day he dared to venture out of his lodgings without fear of arrest. By this time, William of Orange was on the throne of England. 'Dutch Billy' was not a popular king; he was a lonely, introverted man who seemed to have a knack of getting himself disliked. The poet Dryden was offered a large sum of money to dedicate his translation of Virgil's *Aeneid* to the king, but preferred to issue it without a dedication. But Daniel Foe saw his chance and offered his services to the government as a pamphleteer. The first result was a tract, issued in 1694, defending the unpopular war with France, which William was losing, 'and serving King William and

Queen Mary and acknowledging their Right'. William, whose popularity was lower than usual because of the treacherous massacre of the MacDonalds at Glencoe, was glad of a supporter, and Foe was given a profitable government post. He also took advantage of the new fashion for Dutch tiles to start a tile factory at Tilbury, and was finally able to pay off all his creditors.

In 1701, Foe issued a poem called *The True Born Englishman*, which enjoyed enormous success; its argument was that it was unfair to abuse Dutch Billy for being a foreigner, since all Englishmen are a compound of nationalities – Celts, Saxons, Vikings, Normans and Picts. Unfortunately, William of Orange died in the following year, and Foe found himself temporarily without a patron.

In *The True Born Englishman* he sneers at people who pretend their family came over with William the Conqueror. But shortly thereafter he began signing himself D. Foe, then De Foe, then Daniel De Foe. When he next came to public notice, a year later, he was Daniel Defoe. The occasion was a pamphlet called *The Shortest Way With Dissenters*, although this was not actually signed. Under William of Orange, dissenters had been allowed to hold public office, provided they were willing to pay occasional lip-service to Anglicanism. After the king's death, reactionaries – known as 'high fliers' because of their high principles – began to demand that dissenters should be banned from public office. Oddly enough, Defoe agreed with the high fliers; he thought the kind of dissenters who were willing to compromise were a poor lot. His pamphlet satirized the high fliers by suggesting that all dissenters should be banished or hanged. It was rather as if an American liberal wrote a book suggesting that all negroes should be sent back to Africa, and that those who refused to go should be burned alive, and signed it with the name of some well-known reactionary. Many high fliers were taken in and greeted the pamphlet with enthusiasm – one clergyman said he valued it above all books except the Bible, and prayed that Queen Anne would carry out its suggestions. The dissenters were at first terrified – haunted by visions of being burnt at the stake. Then it leaked out that this was one of Defoe's hard-hitting jokes, and everyone was furious. Parliament issued a warrant for Defoe's arrest on a charge of libelling the high fliers by making them out to be bloodthirsty maniacs. Defoe went into hiding and tried to apologize, but it was no good; he had to give himself up. In

July 1703, he was sentenced to stand in the pillory for three days and to be detained during the queen's pleasure.

It was, in fact, his best stroke of luck so far. Overnight, he became a popular hero. The crowds who gathered at the pillory shouted 'Good old Dan' and threw bunches of flowers. There would be nothing like it for another fifty years, when John Wilkes would find himself a popular hero through a similar accident.

Defoe was then confined in Newgate for a year, where he mingled with pickpockets and footpads – accumulating material for future novels – and continued to write pamphlets. He was now so popular that no government could silence him. He started his first newspaper in jail – it was called *The Review* and was full of political commentary, lively interviews with thieves and murderers, and gossip about current scandals. He was becoming a power with his pen.

He obtained his freedom by approaching the Lord Treasurer with a scheme that was worthy of Machiavelli. He suggested that the government needed a network of informers to point out potential critics and enemies: in short, an army of spies. The Lord Treasurer was just the man to approach with such a sinister idea; Robert Harley was a born schemer, a man of whom a contemporary wrote: 'He loved tricks, even where not necessary, but from an inward satisfaction he took in applauding his own cunning. If any man was ever born under the necessity of being a knave, he was.' It is a description that applies equally well to Defoe.

The result was that Queen Anne was prevailed upon to release Defoe from prison, and Defoe proceeded to travel the country and build up a network of agents. It would hardly be an exaggeration to call him the father of the police state. He laid down the basic rules for spying. Each agent had to appear to be an ordinary citizen; every one had to be unknown to the others. The aim was unobtrusive thought-control of the people of England. And the scheme was amazingly successful – in fact, Defoe's network became the foundation of the British Secret Service. And he quickly established its value by playing a significant part in the union of England and Scotland into one country called Great Britain. The English liked the idea; the Scots were dubious. Defoe went off to Scotland in 1706, with half a dozen plausible cover stories – that he was a ship-builder, a wool merchant, a fish merchant, and so on. He became intimate with various government ministers in Scotland, and quietly influenced opinion. In May 1707, Scotland and England became Great Britain, and Defoe returned home well satisfied.

In 1710, the Whig (i.e. liberal) government fell; Defoe, who had made his reputation as a fighter for liberal principles, quickly switched sides, declaring, with his usual glibness, that he cared more for his country than for party prejudice. But in 1714, Harley – who had become an alcoholic – was dismissed; Queen Anne died a few days later, and a Whig administration came into power under George I. Defoe was thrown into prison, and although he obtained his freedom, he was soon back in jail again on a charge of libelling the Earl of Anglesey. Once again, he offered his services as a spy. And the Whigs, who knew his abilities, decided that a discredited Tory might make an excellent spy – particularly if everyone assumed he was still in disgrace. He might, as an 'enemy' of the government, find out what their opponents were planning. And at the moment, their opponents were not the Tories so much as the Jacobites – supporters of the house of Stuart. Under the guise of a government opponent, Defoe gained the confidence of various anti-government newspapers, and was soon using his Machiavellian skills to suppress anything the government disliked.

Sooner or later, he was bound to be found out. One of his dupes was a man called Mist, who ran a Jacobite newspaper. Mist printed a letter criticizing the government without showing it to Defoe, and when he was summoned before government ministers tried to put the blame on Defoe. The Whigs began to suspect that Defoe was doubly treacherous. The breach was healed, but Defoe seems to have realized that his days as a double-dealer were numbered. He had to find some other way of making a living. He recollected that he possessed the material for an interesting narrative. In 1704, a Scottish pirate named Alexander Selkirk had quarrelled with his pirate captain and been marooned, at his own request, on an uninhabited island called Juan Fernandez. He spent five years there before he was rescued, and when he returned to England, became a celebrity. Defoe probably went to see him in Bristol in 1713, and bought his papers for a trifling sum. Using this material as a basis, Defoe dashed off *Robinson Crusoe*. The book appeared in 1719, and immediately became a classic. Unfortunately for Defoe, it instantly appeared in several pirated editions, so he made less from it than he might. But he went on to write more novels – *Captain Singleton, Moll*

Flanders, Colonel Jack, Journal of the Plague Year and others. By the early 1720s, his credit as a spy had collapsed completely, and he lived mainly from his novels. But these were highly popular – particularly novels of 'low life' like *Moll Flanders*, which may well have inspired Osborn to bring out his *Lives of the Notorious Criminals*.

His end was typical. In August 1730, at the age of seventy, he suddenly disappeared. Until recently, the reason has been a mystery, but research has revealed that old debts – his tile factory had gone bankrupt while he was in prison for his dissenters pamphlet – were catching up with him. He could almost certainly have paid them off with the money from his novels. Instead, he preferred to abscond again. He died in the April of the following year in an obscure lodging house, not far from the spot where he was born.

For us, Defoe is a figure of symbolic importance. Shaw remarked that we judge the artist by his highest moments, the criminal by his lowest. It is rare to find a man who combines elements of both, and it enables us to see clearly the relationship between these two elements in human nature itself.

As a human being, Defoe was essentially a compromiser, a man who was always on the lookout for short-cuts, who believed that it is impossible to prosper in this world unless you cheat – in short, a crook. Yet we only have to look at his career to see that he was totally mistaken. Like all crooks, he suffered from a peculiar form of stupidity that made him unaware that bending the rules is not the best way of achieving what you want. In creating the secret service Defoe undoubtedly thought he was being brilliantly Machiavellian, placing his natural immorality at the service of his craving for security and influence. In fact, he gained neither security nor influence; he merely placed himself at the mercy of the political weather. His eventual downfall – after the Mist affair – strikes us as completely inevitable, the obligatory third-act downfall of any comedy villain. (It seems odd how often the lives of criminals seem to follow the pattern of a morality play – until we recognize that this is not divine retribution but the inevitable consequence of stupidity.)

What Defoe *did* possess was a certain wry honesty about his own dishonesty. This probably explains why *Moll Flanders* – the story of a woman with no principles – is his best novel; like Moll, Defoe was an honest whore. And it is *this* element in Defoe that made him a

*both 'break'
rules, but different
in different ways*

great novelist, and led to the only real success he ever achieved. He gained security only when he made honest use of his writing talent, without any attempt to be Machiavellian.

So in Defoe we can see with exceptional clarity the two great opposing tendencies of human nature which are also the two main currents of human history, crime and creativity, violence and intelligence, expediency and integrity. We can also see that the real objection to crime is that it is basically a mistake, a miscalculation. It is, quite simply, the wrong way of going about the business of survival. If dishonesty achieves its immediate aims, it does so at the cost of a long-term self-undermining.

The irony about Defoe is that his core of honesty – the instinctive honesty of the artist – not only brought him his only real success, but changed the direction of European culture. We could say that Defoe's career symbolizes the conflict between the outer and the inner man, the personality and the soul. His dubious personal morality died with him; his artistic integrity went marching on, and created a revolution whose importance it would be impossible to underestimate. This is why we must now consider it in some detail.

Robinson Crusoe was not, of course, quite the first novel – possibly the *Morte d'Arthur* deserves that title; and there had been many others, from Sidney's *Arcadia* to *Don Quixote* and Lesage's *Gil Blas*. But most of these works would be described as sophisticated fairy stories, relying almost wholly on fantastic plots to hold the reader's interest.

By contrast, *Robinson Crusoe* is a sustained flight of imagination. When Crusoe struggles ashore, then builds a raft and removes food, ammunition and wine from the wrecked ship and constructs a tent of sailcloth, the reader is there on the island with him. *Robinson Crusoe* is a long book, and the story is extremely simple. But no one objects to the slowness of the narrative because the reader's time scale has changed. Crusoe has been there for twenty-four years before he finds the footprint of Man Friday. Why did Defoe extend Selkirk's five years to decades? Because he had become so fascinated by his own narrative that he felt it would be a pity to shorten it. Unlike earlier novels, unlike *Don Quixote* and *Gil Blas*, *Robinson Crusoe* is one single sustained narrative, like a flight from London to New York.

In the history of European culture, *Robinson Crusoe* is perhaps the

lit/art enhances/extends man's inner life

412

most important single event since Thespis invented the Greek drama in the sixth century B.C. Like the drama, it was a kind of magic carpet, making human beings aware that life is *not* 'solitary, poor, nasty, brutish and short', that the material reality around us is not the only reality. All animals feel themselves to be at the mercy of the material world, so that when serious problems arise, they are inclined to run away or surrender. Human beings have emerged from the purely animal stage far too recently not to be victims of this instinctive assumption. The result is that we habitually underestimate ourselves and our strength. But when a man can explore a desert island without leaving his armchair, when he can charge into battle without risking his life, when he can cross Africa – in company with Defo's Captain Singleton – without fatigue or thirst, then he also begins to experience a new courage to face his own problems. More: he begins to experience a desire to explore the unknown. Defoe enabled his middle-class reader to share the excitement of Columbus and Magellan, of Galileo and Newton. He revealed that human beings do not have to be limited by the narrowness of their physical experience.

412

Three years after *Robinson Crusoe* there appeared his novel of 'low life', *Moll Flanders*. It was certainly read by a London printer and publisher named Samuel Richardson, who had been apprenticed to the trade since he was seventeen. Now in his early thirties, Richardson enjoyed doing a little scribbling in his spare time; but he was too busy making himself a fortune to take it seriously. Like many others, he must have been impressed, perhaps a little shocked, by Moll's frank description of her seduction. The seed lay dormant for almost twenty years; then, when he had reached the age of fifty and had more spare time, a publisher asked him to write a Teach Yourself book on the art of correspondence. Richardson decided to give his 'familiar letters' a moral flavour: he composed letters from deserted women to their unfaithful lovers, from anxious fathers to daughters living in London, and letters of advice to pretty girls who were engaged as maidservants. Suddenly, he found himself carried away by a flood of creation: the letters began to pour out from him. At this point, he recalled a story he had once heard of a virtuous servant girl who had resisted her master's attempts at seduction and ended by marrying him. It was too good an idea to waste on a few familiar letters; he turned it into a separate novel called *Pamela*. It

empathy H12

poured out so fast that he had written two hundred thousand words – twice the length of the average novel – in two months.

Pamela came out in November 1740. It was an instantaneous success, sweeping across England and to the Continent in a matter of months. It tells the story of an attractive servant girl whose mistress dies; her master, Mr B, tells Pamela she can remain in the house in charge of the linen. Then he begins his attempts to seduce her. In one scene he leaps out of a cupboard just as she has got undressed and throws her on the bed – here the debt to Defoe seems evident. Pamela is saved by the entrance of the housekeeper. Then Mr B sends her to a country house and places her in charge of a procuress; next time he tries to rape her, the procuress holds her hands; but Pamela goes into convulsions and he gives up again. Nothing like this had ever appeared before. Under the guise of a moral tale, Richardson was writing something very like pornography. But pornography itself was quite unknown in 1740; it was invented five years later when a poverty-stricken young man named John Cleland dashed off a novel of seduction called *Fanny Hill* to get himself out of debt. It was true that *Pamela* moved at a snail's pace – Dr Johnson remarked that 'If you were to read Richardson for the story your impatience would be so fretted that you would hang yourself.' But people were not reading it for the story. They were reading it to *enter the world* of a girl who is in constant danger of being raped. (And in parts of England they rang the church bells when the last part appeared and it became clear that Pamela had retained her virtue to the altar.) Like *Robinson Crusoe*, the novel had the effect of transforming the reader's time scale, so that he left behind the world of everyday necessities and entered the world of imagination. It would hardly be an exaggeration to say that Richardson had invented the literary equivalent of the religious experience, a kind of secular nirvana. In fact, before *Pamela*, the most popular literary fare was volumes of sermons, and this was because a sermon can have this effect of suspending the reader above his own life to contemplate the business of living from a bird's eye view. *Pamela* did it far more efficiently and dramatically, and volumes of sermons quickly became a drug on the market.

Richardson followed up *Pamela* with *Clarissa*, and revealed his insight into the reasons for *Pamela*'s success by making the new novel another long-drawn-out study in seduction; this time the

good

heroine *is* raped, and dies of shame and humiliation. It was twice as long as *Pamela*, and became even more popular. Once again, clergymen praised the novel from the pulpit for its moral perception, while readers experienced strangely mixed sensations of pity, indignation and erotic excitement.

In 1760 there appeared in Paris a novel called *Julie, or the New Héloïse* that achieved a success that made even that of *Pamela* seem trifling by comparison. Public lending libraries – which had sprung up in the past twenty years – hired it out by the *hour*. The philosopher Kant, who took the same walk every day so punctually that local residents could set their watches by him, forgot to go out on the day he read *The New Héloïse*.

The author was a Swiss vagabond named Jean Jacques Rousseau, who had fallen in love with a countess who rejected him, and who sublimated his misery in the novel. *The New Héloïse* is the story of a handsome young man named Saint-Preux, who is hired as a tutor to two young girls. He falls in love with one of them – Julie – and goes away to place himself beyond temptation. But Julie's father is so pleased with her progress that he recalls him. One night, Julie admits him to her bedroom, and they become lovers. But the ending is moral; Julie dies in an accident, after marrying the man of her father's choice, and Saint-Preux devotes his life to becoming the tutor of her children.

What made the book a sensation, of course, was the episode of the seduction – and Rousseau's argument that if a couple are in love, they have a right to consummate it in defiance of social conventions. In fact, *The New Héloïse*, like *Pamela* and *Clarissa*, was taking advantage of the enormous sexual frustration that existed everywhere in the eighteenth century. How did this frustration come about? It is true, of course, that sexual frustration is inherent in the nature of society, since social beings are obliged to restrain their desires. But in the age of Boccaccio or Malory, it was taken as natural that a couple should have sexual intercourse if they fell in love. Shakespeare and his contemporaries also took it for granted. Then came the change in the 'rules of the game'. Society became more stable because it *had* to become more stable. The old chaos could no longer be tolerated in this world of increasingly powerful nations: the England of Cromwell, the France of Louis XIV, the Spain of Charles II, the Prussia of Frederick William – and later of

Frederick the Great – the Russia of Peter the Great, the Sweden of Charles XII. These changes were reflected in English Puritanism, in German Lutheranism, in French Protestantism – with its roots in Calvinism. The foundation of the Bow Street Runners in 1750 is symbolic; society *had* to learn to become more orderly.

The result of increased restraint is an increase in the left-brain's power of veto. Automatic controls inhibit natural responses, and sex develops an increasing aura of 'forbiddenness'. If Rousseau had been writing about a French Moll Flanders, no one would have been shocked; Moll is a throwback to the Elizabethan age. But he was writing about a baron's daughter who lives in a mansion and takes a bath every day. So what Saint-Preux was seducing was not simply a girl; it was a social symbol. By 1760 it was taken for granted that an upper-class girl preserves her virginity as a valuable part of her dowry. Rousseau, with his arguments for free love, was undermining the fabric of society as much as Luther undermined it when he challenged the Catholic Church. Yet, like Samuel Richardson, Rousseau did it all with a demure air of morality. He was, in fact, appealing to another morality that had remained dormant just below the surface since the publication of *Pamela*: the morality of sentiment, the morality of Tristan and Isolde, Aucassin and Nicolette and Romeo and Juliet. What was so shocking – and piquant – was to bring it up to date. Even the celibate Immanuel Kant must have enjoyed identifying himself with Saint-Preux, and relished the sensation of vicariously seducing Julie. Kant's philosophy was achieving new depths of perception into the human mind; Rousseau was achieving new depths of perception into the human heart. They had as much right to call themselves explorers as Columbus and Drake; and their readers accompanied them on their travels and shared their sensation of discovery.

In 1774, another frustrated lover poured his miseries into a novel about an unhappy love affair, and the book made his name famous all over Europe. Goethe's *Sorrows of Young Werther* was about an artist who falls in love at first sight and commits suicide when the girl marries another man. There is no rape or seduction: not even the satisfaction of kisses. Then why did *Werther* become a literary sensation – as well as causing an epidemic of suicide? Because it is about a man whose love becomes a fever, an obsession. It was a blast of intense feeling, like hot air from a furnace. In effect, it convinced the intelligentsia of Europe that they were not feeling enough. It encouraged people to pour out their emotions and to burst into tears. When we read the letters written during the next few decades, we feel a little bewildered to read phrases like 'My friend, I watered your letter with my tears', or 'I could not restrain the sobs that rose in me as I recalled our farewell' – particularly when the correspondents are men. But Goethe had convinced people that they ought to let their feelings go. He also convinced them that they ought to feel ecstasy as they looked at mountains and forests – something that had been almost forgotten since Petrarch startled his friends by climbing a hill to look at the view. The result was that poets suddenly noticed that nature was beautiful – something no one would have guessed from the poetry of Pope and Dryden. Novels of unhappy love affairs poured from the presses, and Europe sobbed convulsively. One of the most popular was Henry Mackenzie's *The Man of Feeling*, whose sole purpose is to harrow the emotions with a series of sad tales and hard-luck stories; beggars, madwomen, prostitutes, all tell their stories of the hard-hearted world. The hero himself is shattered by the news that his lady-love is to marry another, and there is an affecting scene in which she tells him she loves him just before he dies. He is, says the narrator, the victim of 'too keen a sensibility', and this was regarded as being entirely to his credit. Groups of people used to read *The Man of Feeling* aloud to have the satisfaction of shedding tears in public. Fifty years later, a correspondent of Sir Walter Scott describes how she recently attended a reading of *The Man of Feeling* and everyone roared with laughter. Yet this was not a sign that people were becoming more callous: only that they had become inured to Mackenzie's pathos. A little more than ten years later, they were crying just as uninhibitedly over the death of Little Nell.

In *Fiction and the Reading Public*, Q. D. Leavis has argued that the change was entirely for the worse; that sugary sentimentality and second-hand morality had replaced the racy vigour of *The Pilgrim's Progress* and *Tom Jones*. But this is only half the story. Bunyan, Defoe and Fielding were objective because they had no alternative; it never entered their heads that literature was a medium for discussing their feelings. For them it was a kind of mirror that reflected the world they saw around them. Compared to Rousseau and Goethe they were in a state of primal innocence. In fact, it would hardly be inaccurate to describe them as 'pre-bicameral'. It is true that they are bicameral in the sense that they are self-conscious; they are aware of questions of religion and morality. Yet their sense of identity is simple and unambiguous. As you read *Pilgrim's Progress*, you feel that in spite of his agonies about his salvation, John Bunyan felt he was John Bunyan and nothing but John Bunyan. He accepted his left-brain sense of identity as the total truth about himself. Young Werther, on the other hand, is already concerned about the difference between his identity when he is alone with nature and his identity when he is among other people. And Goethe's Faust sees his social identity – the grey-bearded professor who is respected by his students – as a kind of grotesque mask, like the *persona* of the ancient Greek actor.

But what is most important about Faust is his underlying conviction that he is not an actor or a professor, but a god:

> I, image of the gods, who thought myself
> Close to the mirror of eternal truth,
> Who bathed in heaven's light and clarity,
> Leaving the earthly part of me behind;
> I, more than angel, I whose boundless strength,
> Seemed even then to flow through nature's veins,
> And revel in creation like the gods . . .

(My own free translation.)

This is the essence of romanticism: the paradoxical feeling that man might, after all, be a god. This is what Mrs Leavis is failing to grasp when she criticizes the romantics for retreating into a sickly world of fantasy. Three centuries after the Renaissance, man has again begun to suspect that he has the power to alter the course of nature and to grasp eternal truth.

What has happened, of course, is that man has begun to suspect that 'other identity', the being in the other half of the brain. That sense of time flowing at half its proper speed which we experience on reading *Robinson Crusoe* and *Pamela* is 'right brain awareness'. The left brain is obsessed by time; the right is indifferent to it. In his early letters, young Werther expresses a floating sense of timelessness:

The solitude in these blissful surroundings is balm to my soul . . . My whole being is filled with a marvellous gaiety, like sweet spring mornings . . .

When the mists in my beloved valley steam all around me, when the sun rests on the surface of the impenetrable depths of my forest at noon, and only single rays steal into the inner sanctuary, when I lie in the tall grass beside a rushing brook, and become aware of the remarkable diversity of a thousand little growing things on the ground, with all their peculiarities, when I feel the teeming of a minute world amid the blades of grass and the innumerable, unfathomable shapes of worm and insect closer to my heart and can sense the presence of the Almighty, who in a state of continuous bliss bears and sustains us – then, my friend, when it grows light before my eyes and the world around me and the sky above come to rest wholly within my soul like a beloved, I am filled often with yearning, and thinking that if I could only express it all on paper, everything that is housed so richly and warmly within me, so that it might be the mirror of my soul as my soul is the mirror of Infinite God . . . ah, my dear friend, but I am ruined by it, I succumb to its magnificence.

This interminable sentence, with its failure to reach a proper conclusion, nevertheless conveys a sense of floating in blissful ecstasy. It is almost like a radio set that has tuned in to some frequency whose existence we never even suspected.

But the new awareness brings its own problems, for Werther, like Mackenzie's Man of Feeling, suffers from 'too keen a sensibility', and it brings him to suicide. This was the dilemma of the romantics. Should they try to pursue these new sensations to their limits, and risk insanity, or would it be more sensible to try to come down to earth and get on with the practical business of living? The new sensibility had turned the artist into a social misfit, an 'outsider' who seemed doomed to peer at life through a keyhole. He was, in a word later coined by Karl Marx, 'alienated' from his society.

While Defoe, Richardson, Rousseau and Goethe were creating their inner revolution, another kind of revolution was transforming their society.

Because the English had kept out of the Thirty Years War, England in 1700 was already more prosperous than France or Germany, and farmers and businessmen began to concentrate on more efficient ways of production. In 1733 came an invention that revolutionized weaving more than anything since the invention of the flat frame in the fourteenth century: the fly shuttle. On the old loom, two men had to stand on either side to toss the shuttle back and forth. A weaver named John Kay invented a method that would send the shuttle – on small wheels – flying back and forth under blows from wooden hammers. It increased the speed of weaving, but it robbed the two men of their job. Kay became intensely unpopular in Colchester, where he introduced the fly shuttle, and had to move to Leeds. There his fly shuttle was eagerly adopted, but the manufacturers refused to pay him for its use and forced him into expensive litigation that ruined him. In his native town of Bury, his house was wrecked by a mob; he moved to Manchester and was forced to escape hidden in a wool sack. He died a pauper, the first victim of the 'restrictive practices' that have continued into the late twentieth century.

Mining was becoming an increasingly important industry; but mines tended to flood with water. In the 1650s, Otto von Guericke had invented a vacuum pump. By the end of the century, a Frenchman named Denis Papin had discovered that a pump could be worked with steam power. The pump was attached to one end of the see-saw, and at the other there was a piston in a cylinder; the piston would be driven up by steam from a boiler and then would descend – driven by a heavy weight – as the steam condensed. Naturally, this was a slow business. Around 1700, an ironmonger named Thomas Newcomen was experimenting with a pump when there was an accident; melting solder allowed cold water to leak into the cylinder, and the piston descended with such a bang that it wrecked the pump. But Newcomen realized that he had discovered a better method of making the piston descend; a little cold water was sprayed into the cylinder at the end of every upward-stroke, and the new engine worked at twice the speed. Newcomen engines were soon in use all over Europe.

In 1763, a young Scott named James Watt was repairing a model of the Newcomen engine at Glasgow university when he saw how it could be improved. By cooling the cylinder down and heating it up again, three-quarters of the energy was being wasted. What was needed, he saw, was a pump with two separate chambers – a cooling chamber, and a permanently hot piston chamber. He found a rich partner named Boulton, and in 1769 was able to patent his new engine. And the world entered the industrial age.

It so happened that large numbers of people were available to work in the new factories. Landowners had perfected better methods of farming – fertilizers, the drill-seeder, the horse-drawn hoe. What now stood in the way of efficiency was the enormous amount of 'common land' that surrounded most villages. This was usually poor land on which everyone had a right to pasture their animals or grow low-yield crops; moreover, it was often interspersed with the land on which the farmers wanted to carry out their new experiments. Landowners petitioned parliament, and parliament responded by passing 'Acts of Enclosure', which required common land to be divided up between various owners, every one of whom had to fence off his portion. The small owners usually preferred to sell out. And the poor who had lived on the commons in wooden huts found themselves homeless. This is why increasing numbers of country folk found their way into the towns and the new factories.

Here conditions were often appalling. Children from five upwards were taken from workhouses and orphanages to labour in the cotton mills for twelve hours a day. The smallest could pick up cotton from the floor. No one was forced to go – they were lured by promises of good food and pleasant working conditions; once in the mills, they were underfed, beaten and even tortured. Those who tried to escape were chained up. Some children even committed suicide. Adult workers laboured for fourteen hours a day, and lived in damp cellars provided by the employers. A labourer from the country might find himself assigned to a straw mattress on which a man had just died of fever. Workers had to watch their wives and children drawn into these conditions and working beside them in the mills and factories. Most of the children died young, or grew up permanently stunted.

Worse still, the new inventions began to make many workers unnecessary, so they were turned out to starve. When new power looms threw Yorkshire workers out of their jobs in the early nineteenth century, their reaction was to form secret societies whose aim was to blackmail the employers into getting rid of the machinery. They called themselves Luddites, after a man called Ned Ludd, who was supposed to have smashed stocking machines in the 1780s. They operated like the Ku-Klux-Klan, sending warnings to mill owners, threatening to smash windows or burn down their mills unless they got rid of their machinery. Many gave way to this intimidation. In 1812, the Luddites intercepted two weaving frames that were on their way to the mill of a man named William Cartwright; they smashed the frames and left the drivers tied up in a ditch. Cartwright appealed to the government for help, and they sent a small consignment of troops. On 11 April 1812, a mob of Luddites smashed down Cartwright's gates and poured into the mill yard with axes. As they began to chop their way into the building, soldiers fired from upper windows. The mob fled, leaving their wounded behind. But this was only one victory in a bitter war that dragged on for another year. An employer named Horsfall who employed similar tactics was murdered in reprisal; in 1813 there were mass trials of Luddites, with many executions and transportations. It was a tragic and pointless conflict; the workers were unaware that the enemy was not the mill owners but the current of history itself. Almost two centuries later, the British trade unions are still fighting the same Luddite battle.

To understand the bitterness of these industrial conflicts, we need to go back to the age of Louis XIV. Like the Luddites, Louis was equally determined to make time stand still. When his minister Colbert brought prosperity to France by encouraging trade and industry, the king undid the good work by exempting the nobles from taxes and wasting the money on futile wars. Louis died in 1715; and things improved under the regency of the duke of Orleans, then under Louis XV and his minister Fleury, but the disastrous Seven Years War in 1756 led to the loss of most of the French overseas empire. There was a steady rise in the population – from sixteen millions in 1715 to twenty-six millions by the time of the Revolution – which flooded the towns with unemployed farm labourers and beggars. The more enterprising formed into robber bands that terrorized the countryside. While the poor died of starvation, the rich still managed to avoid taxes. So while England became the 'workshop of the world', France was torn by social conflicts.

But the major problem was not economic but psychological. The real conflicts of history are caused by men behaving like spoilt children. What infuriated the French peasantry was not the prosperity of the rich, but their arrogance. Louis XIV had never understood that history was being played according to new rules; he behaved as if he were Charlemagne, and his nobility followed his lead. Typical of his Right Man attitude was an event that took place in 1661, when the French ambassador in London announced to the Spanish ambassador that if he drove up first to the palace gates his horses' reins would be severed. The Spanish ambassador reacted by having them reinforced with chains. There was a fight and bloodshed. Louis XIV dismissed the Spanish ambassador in Paris, sending him back to Madrid with a message saying that if the French ambassador was not given precedence at all court ceremonies, there would be extremely serious consequences (meaning war). Spain under Philip IV was not strong enough to defy France; so an envoy was despatched to Louis to concede his demands and make a public apology in front of the assembled court. Louis was behaving like a headstrong brat, as we have come to expect monarchs to behave throughout history. But the world was changing, and Louis's determination to have his own way led directly to the French Revolution.

It is even possible to suggest a precise date for the origin of the Revolution: December 1725. It was in that month that the thirty-year-old dramatist Voltaire was talking rather too freely at the Comédie Française about his prospects of becoming prime minister. An aristocrat, the Chevalier de Rohan, insulted him, and Voltaire replied sharply. A fight was avoided when a lady fainted. A few days later, Voltaire was dining with the Duc de Sully when he received a message that someone wished to see him outside. He went out, and was beaten up by hired ruffians, while Rohan stood in the background and jeered.

Voltaire was mad with rage; he rushed indoors and asked the duc to sign a statement about the assault; his host refused to get involved – after all, the aristocracy had a perfect right to have a commoner chastised. And although Voltaire was a favourite at court – the queen was fond of him – nobody was interested in helping him obtain justice. Voltaire took fencing lessons, mixed with ruffians, and dreamed of revenge – which demonstrates that the psychology of men of genius is not so very different from that of criminals like Carl Panzram. The Rohans, one of France's most powerful families, had him followed by police spies. When they appealed to a minister for 'protection', Voltaire was arrested and thrown into the Bastille; he was released only on condition he left the country. He was forced to go into exile in England.

Voltaire's experience filled him with a seething hatred of the *ancien régime*, a hatred that turned him into the most witty and venomous satirist in Europe. His criticism of religion and society inspired other reformers – notably, Jean Jacques Rousseau; and it was Rousseau's book *The Social Contract* (1762) that was mainly responsible for the French Revolution, in which many members of the Rohan clan lost their heads.

Another member of the Rohan family precipitated the scandal that led to the Revolution. Bishop Louis de Rohan was tall, suave and handsome, with a reputation for seduction as formidable as that of Pope Rodrigo Borgia. In 1770, he was bishop of Strasbourg when the next queen of France, Marie Antoinette, passed through the city on her way to meet her future husband. She was a beautiful fifteen-year-old ash-blonde, and Rohan's susceptible heart was smitten. Unfortunately, it became clear over the course of the next ten years that the queen disliked him – Rohan had been ambassador at the court of Marie Antoinette's mother Maria Theresa of Austria, and the Austrian queen had taken a strong dislike to him. Between 1770 and 1780, Marie Antoinette did her best to block various appointments, although she was unable to prevent Rohan being made a cardinal.

In 1780, Rohan became the dupe of a beautiful adventuress who called herself Countess de la Motte Valois – she was married to a penniless army officer named la Motte. The countess became his mistress, and somehow convinced him that the queen wanted him to act as intermediary in buying a very expensive diamond bracelet – it cost one million four hundred thousand livres – from two jewellers named Boehmer and Bassenge. In fact, the queen knew nothing of the scheme. Rohan was in raptures at the thought that the queen had changed her mind about him – who knew what was possible now? – and purchased the necklace on credit. At a secret meeting with 'the queen' in a garden, he was allowed to kiss her foot – in fact, it was a young courtesan who had been hired to play the part. When the first payment – of 400,000 francs – fell due, Rohan sent the demand to the queen through the countess, and received in reply a forged letter asking him to meet the payment himself. The countess thought Rohan a millionaire; in fact, his extravagance kept him permanently in debt. When he was unable to raise the whole sum, the jewellers applied direct to the queen, whose reaction was to fly into a rage and demand Rohan's arrest. It was typical of her spoilt stupidity; it would have been better for everyone if she had allowed the matter to be hushed up. As it was, Rohan was arrested, together with the 'magician' Cagliostro, in whom he had confided; the countess and her lover were also arrested. (Her husband was in London selling the necklace.) The court case made Rohan a laughing stock, although both he and Cagliostro were acquitted. It also caused deep hostility towards Marie Antoinette, who was booed and hissed by the Paris mob. (No doubt they had heard her famous remark 'Let them eat cake' when told that the poor had no bread.) The countess was publicly branded and whipped, arousing widespread sympathy. (She died in London five years later, after falling out of a window when trying to escape her creditors.) The affair of the necklace totally discredited the monarchy – Napoleon later referred to it as the starting point of the Revolution.

By 1787, the problems had become acute, and the Marquis de Lafayette, who had taken part in the American revolution, suggested that the king should call a parliament – or Estates General. Louis XVI refused, but as the idea was taken up by newspapers and pamphleteers, finally gave way. Now he suddenly became unpopular with the aristocracy, who suspected – rightly – that he meant to force them to pay taxes. Parliament met, but the representative of the people found they were being blocked at every turn by the bishops and the aristocracy. In 1788, there was a crop failure that led to famine. Peasants began to revolt and burn the houses of the rich. The people of Paris heard rumours that the king had sent for troops to attack them. On 14 July 1789, they surrounded the Bastille – where large numbers of soldiers were supposed to be hiding – and began shooting. The governor agreed to surrender, but as he marched out with his soldiers (in fact, only a hundred and ten), he was seized and beheaded with a butcher's knife. The prisoners in the Bastille were all freed, including a dissipated nobleman called the Marquis de Sade . . .

For the time being, the king and queen were safe; in fact, if Louis had behaved sensibly, he would have kept his throne. But he decided to try and escape and return at the head of an army. He and the queen were caught at Varennes, returned to Paris, and sentenced to death. By a gruesome coincidence, the king himself was responsible for the manner of his own death. Not long before his flight, the new assembly had asked the king's physician, Dr Antoine Louis, to look into a new beheading machine that had been designed by a humanitarian called Dr Joseph Guillotin. The lower cutting edge of the blade was curved. As Louis and Dr Guillotin were studying sketches of the machine in the Tuileries Palace, the king strolled into the room, looked at the sketch, and said: 'That wouldn't suit every neck – what you need is something like this.' He took a pencil and drew a blade with a cutting edge that sloped upwards. Guillotin decided to test both types of blade. The king proved to be right. The curved blade failed to sever the neck of a corpse, but the sloping blade decapitated two corpses the first time. Two years later, the king was decapitated by the same sloping blade; the queen was executed in the following year.

The man who was directly responsible for the queen's death was Maximilien Robespierre, an extreme leftist who regarded himself as a humanitarian – he invented the slogan 'Liberty, equality, fraternity.' By 1793, Robespierre was suggesting that the only way to save the Revolution was to execute everyone who might betray it. He ordered the trial and execution of all potential 'traitors'. In Paris alone, 2,600 suspects, mostly nobles, were tried and executed. Victims included the chemist Lavoisier, discoverer of oxygen, and the poet André Chenier. Moderate leftists (Girondins) were guillotined for being moderate. When Robespierre had his close associate Danton executed, he became dictator of France. The port of Toulon had been handed over to the British fleet by 'traitors'; a young captain named Napoleon Bonaparte was despatched with an army to retake it. He succeeded brilliantly; but the extreme reds – the Jacobins – went on to execute hundreds of its citizens as traitors. Marseilles, which had also shown itself unfriendly to the Jacobins, was also 'purged'. Lyons executed its Jacobin leader and suffered the same fate. So did Bordeaux and Nantes. At Nantes, a sadistic madman named Jean Baptiste Carrier was placed in charge of the executions. He had five hundred children taken to meadows outside the town and shot and clubbed to death. He had many children publicly executed – some of them so small that the blade would not reach their necks and sliced their heads in two. The public executioner had a breakdown and died after executing four children, all sisters. Then Carrier invented a new and more efficient method of execution: drowning, or 'noyades'. Barges filled with prisoners were towed into the middle of the river, then sunk while men waited on the banks with hatchets in case any escaped. One man and woman were tied together naked, face to face, and drowned.

Just as in ancient Rome, terror led to more terror. The humanitarian Robespierre was actually worried by the bloodbath, and felt his followers were going too far; yet he failed to grasp that both he and they had fallen a victim to one of the basic laws of criminality: what might be called 'the snowball effect'. Mass murderers usually commit widely-spaced crimes, then commit them with increasing frequency until they are caught or commit suicide. The Revolution had filled France with mass murderers like Carrier. Even humanitarian judges were afraid to be lenient in case they were arrested and executed. (Amusingly enough, the Marquis de Sade, now 'Citizen Sade' and secretary of an assembly of revolutionaries, resigned when they proposed acts that were 'horrible and utterly inhuman'; he was arrested later that year – 1793 – and spent much of the rest of his life in prison.) In 1794, Robespierre agreed that the Terror had to be intensified, and that anyone who disagreed with the government should be sentenced to death. In one month, 1,300 were beheaded in Paris. All this bloodshed finally sickened the citizens of Paris. On 28 July 1794, in the midst of the new Terror, Robespierre and his friends were planning more mischief in the city hall when troops burst into the room. There was a shot, and Robespierre fell forward with a shattered jaw. Some of his friends jumped from windows, and were horribly injured on the pointed railings below. Later the same day, Robespierre and nineteen of his followers were guillotined. Soon after, Carrier, the butcher of Nantes, was tried and guillotined. All over France, Jacobins were killed by mobs. The French Revolution, one of the most extraordinary outbreaks of mass murder in human history, was over.

We can see, in retrospect, that the French Revolution was caused by individuals rather than by economic conditions; by nobles who believed they had a divine right to their riches and titles, and by individuals like the king (who secretly regarded the people as scum, and who trampled the tricolour flag underfoot at a banquet of his officers). If Louis had been capable of reason, he would have accepted the new Assembly, endorsed its declaration of the Rights of Man, and quietly waited for the storm to blow over. Instead, he dreamed of returning to Paris at the head of an army and suppressing the scum. It was pure ego-assertion, the same kind of ego-assertion that had made Louis XIV humiliate Spain, that had made the Chevalier de Rohan humiliate Voltaire, that had made Voltaire direct his venom at the *ancien régime*, that had made Marie

Antoinette demand the arrest of Cardinal Rohan – and that later made Robespierre establish himself as dictator of France.

In England there was no revolution – although the poor had as much ground for complaint – because there were no nobles like Rohan to arouse hatred. The king had been executed in 1649, and the idea of 'divine right' had died with him. In fact, George III had made a determined attempt to rule without parliament; but the American Revolution had undone him. In France, a labourer touched his hat as a gentleman passed; in England, he might well spit. Foreigners were amazed at the lack of deference shown by the English poor. When they felt dissatisfied, they rioted, and on two occasions – in 1795 and 1820 – they even mobbed the king. When Voltaire returned from England and published letters in favour of English liberty, he had to flee Paris; towards the end of his life he chose to live at Ferney, conveniently close to the Swiss border. But an English rabble-rouser like John Wilkes could be hated by the aristocracy and the middle classes and still rely on the support of the London mob to keep him out of prison while he continued to defy parliament. In 1791, Tom Paine, an Englishman who had helped inspire and guide the American Revolution, was able to publish his revolutionary *Rights of Man*, praising the French Revolution, in England, and follow it up in the next year with a second part that contained precise proposals for cutting the army and navy, remitting taxes and creating a welfare state. In 1792, he left England hurriedly, convinced he was about to be arrested. But it was Robespierre's police who arrested Paine in the following year; only Robespierre's own execution in 1794 saved Paine from the guillotine. And *The Rights of Man* continued to be the Bible of the new working-class movement in England, endlessly discussed at meetings. The poverty and misery of the industrial revolution in England were worse than anything on the continent; but while the working classes could argue about *The Rights of Man* there was no danger of revolution. Fortunately, there was no English Louis XVI and no English Robespierre either.

By the early years of the nineteenth century, both the poets and the political idealists were in agreement that crude ego-assertion was the curse of mankind. This is why William Blake welcomed the American Revolution, why Wordsworth, Coleridge and Southey supported the French Revolution, why Shelley and Byron denounced tyranny. Suddenly, the solution to mankind's problems seemed marvellously simple. All were caused by authority – by authority gone mad. Get rid of the kings, the despots and the governments and mankind would enter a golden age. For man, as Rousseau said in the first sentence of his *Social Contract*, was born free, but was everywhere in chains. Shelley's analysis of what was wrong with the world in *Queen Mab* and *Swellfoot the Tyrant* was in many ways similar to Van Vogt's Right Man theory. When a stupid man is given power, his ego becomes inflated, and he behaves as if he were the centre of the universe. The simple and obvious solution is to destroy the tyrants like mad dogs, and mankind will again be happy and free – for Rousseau had argued that there had been an age in the past when mankind was innocent, self-sufficient and happy. Then society had created the idea of private property, and all the machinery of oppression and injustice.

For the poets, freedom *was* a marvellously simple thing:

> The mountains look on Marathon –
> And Marathon looks on the sea;
> And musing there an hour alone,
> I dreamed that Greece might still be free . . .

All that was necessary was to drive out the Turks, and Greece would be free; and in this context, the word means more than merely political freedom; it means what Byron meant in his Sonnet on Chillon:

> Eternal Spirit of the chainless Mind!
> Brightest in dungeons, Liberty! thou art.

It was an alluringly simple idea, and it became the basis of the philosophy of socialism. Free man from political tyranny, and Reason will do the rest. Certainly, if we grant Rousseau's premise that man is born free, then everything else follows. Unfortunately, the theory is dangerously oversimplified. Man is born with certain potentialities for freedom, but he seldom realizes them. He is born a slave to his biological appetites and to his emotions. And this means that he may *be* free without experiencing his freedom. This is Fichte's paradox: 'To *be* free is nothing; to become free is heavenly.'

That is to say, man's greatest enemy is not tyranny, but his tendency to mechanicalness, to take things for granted.

De Sade was himself a walking demonstration of Rousseau's fallacy. When the king was guillotined, he wrote a pamphlet entitled: 'Frenchmen, one more step if you wish to become Republicans!' In it he argued that, now they had got rid of the king, the next step was to get rid of God. Then they would be free of the greatest tyrant of all, superstition, and man could at last enter the Age of Reason. De Sade printed this discourse in a book called *Philosophy in the Bedroom*, which is about the defloration and corruption of a virgin. And it is perfectly obvious that the male's pleasure in deflowering a virgin is the pleasure of the ego asserting its supremacy. The girl lies passively, all her defences down, and the male experiences a sense of triumph as he enters her. There is no difference between this ego-assertion and the ego-assertion that led to the French Revolution. The execution of the king and the rejection of God are irrelevant; they left things exactly as they were before.

This is the problem the idealists were shirking: the problem of power. Their argument was based on the tacit assumption that, if ego-assertion is bad, then the ego itself must be wicked. It ought to be somehow abandoned – allowed to dissolve in the Brotherhood of Man, or in Nature, or in scientific knowledge. But the ego is merely our sense of selfhood, and it seems to reside in the left hemisphere of the brain; it cannot be simply deprived of its share of the partnership. To begin with, the right would find it impossible to operate without it. And, unfortunately, the ego is by nature a tyrant, since its chief task is to get things done. When King Frederick William I of Prussia was walking through Potsdam one morning, he saw a crowd waiting outside the post office – the postmaster had overslept. Frederick smashed the windows to awaken the man, then thrashed him with his own hands. Shelley and Byron would have seen this as an appalling example of tyranny. But Frederick was only concerned with efficiency; he wanted to make Prussia powerful, so that it would never again be reduced to misery by a Thirty Years War. The result was that he became obsessed by his army and by the problem of law and order. Lazy officials were flogged; thieves were hanged. One man who had stolen a few shillings pleaded that his wife and children were starving; Frederick replied: 'I forgive him the debt; but he must be hanged.' But he achieved his aim; Prussia became the second most powerful nation in Europe.

The problem is that the ego can easily overreach itself. Frederick William's son, also called Frederick, was a lover of literature and music, and hated the army. His father treated him with unremitting hostility, and when his son tried to escape to England, had him thrown into prison and the officer who had tried to escape with him decapitated in front of his eyes. But when he became king of Prussia, Frederick II was old enough to feel nostalgic about his early training, and increased his army by ten thousand men. It seemed pointless to have such an army and not to use it; so Frederick picked a quarrel with the empress Maria Theresa of Austria – mother of Marie Antoinette – and invaded Silesia. With Austria finally beaten, Frederick decided to devote his life to art and philosophy, and built himself a palace called Sans Souci – Without a Care. There he wrote music, played the flute, and entertained scientists, poets and philosophers, including Voltaire. But a man who has annexed someone else's country cannot expect to be left in peace. He was attacked simultaneously by Austria, Sweden, Russia and France. After more than twelve years of war he beat back his enemies and signed a peace treaty, but Prussia was in ruins, and Frederick an exhausted and disillusioned man. He devoted the remainder of his life to rebuilding his country and adding to it, until he had created the foundation of modern Germany. But it was a kind of modern counterpart of ancient Rome, a land without freedom, without democracy, without joy. And within two decades of Frederick's death, the great Prussian state had collapsed, undermined by Napoleon. There was not enough vitality in it to hold it together. Hermann Pinnow writes in his *History of Germany* (Everyman edition, p. 271): 'The work of the "crowned Friend of Man", which had been conceived on such generous lines, was soon shattered through his complete neglect of the accomplished facts of history.' Like Louis XIV, Frederick failed to grasp that, in the modern world, the rules of history have been changed.

The tragedy of Frederick the Great makes us aware that Rousseau and Paine, Shelley and Byron were oversimplifying when they denounced authority as the major curse of mankind. Frederick was not a tyrant; he was one of the most enlightened monarchs of his time. He began his reign by throwing open the state granaries to the poor, abolishing flogging and reducing the punishment for crimes. He was a sincere admirer of Voltaire and Rousseau. If a man as well-intentioned and as enlightened as Frederick could become a tyrant against his will, then there was clearly something wrong with the socialist belief that tyranny was the outcome of human wickedness and could be abolished by dethroning the tyrants and replacing them with idealists.

The history of Napoleon Bonaparte underlines the same point. Napoleon regarded himself as a successor of Frederick the Great; when he visited his tomb he told his officers: 'Hats off, gentlemen – if he were still alive we should not be here.' His rise to power is one of the most remarkable success stories in history. As a young officer he was sent to fight the Austrians in Italy; his purpose was only to harass them while the main French forces converged on Vienna. In fact, his victories were so brilliant that he was soon the hero of France. He next persuaded the government to let him take an army to Egypt, to cut off the British trade route to India, and again there was a series of astonishing victories before Nelson trapped the French in Egypt by destroying their fleet. Napoleon hurried back to France, took part in the overthrow of the government, and was elected first consul. He went on to end the civil war in France, win a victory against the Austrians, and bring Britain, Austria and Russia to the peace table. During the next two years, he showed himself to be an admirable peacetime ruler, establishing public schools, reducing unemployment, and establishing the Code Napoleon which gave all men equal rights under the law. Many believed him to be the saviour of Europe, and Beethoven dedicated his Eroica symphony to him. In 1804 he was crowned emperor in Notre Dame by the pope.

Napoleon now had a chance to make France the most prosperous nation in Europe and establish peace for a generation. Instead, he revealed that he was no better than all the other brainless conquerors since Alexander the Great. The conqueror must prove his greatness by making himself feared. Napoleon assembled a fleet to invade England. Nelson destroyed it at the battle of Trafalgar, losing his own life in the process. The major European powers formed an alliance against Napoleon; he revealed his military genius by luring the Austrians and Russians into a trap and defeating them at the battle of Austerlitz. Once more he had security; once more he threw it away, like a compulsive gambler. This time the enemy was

Prussia; he shattered them at the battle of Jena, went on to defeat the Russians at Friedland, and signed the treaty of Tilsit in 1807. Once again he had the chance to become Europe's greatest statesman; once again, the criminal desire to play at soldiers led him to throw it all away. And this was the pattern for the remainder of his life. There were battles against the Spanish, the Portuguese, the Austrians. In 1812, Napoleon marched into Russia with an army of half a million men. The Russian winter did him more damage than the Russian army; only eighteen thousand men staggered back to France. The enemies of France marched into Paris, and Napoleon was sent into exile on Elba.

That should have been the end of the story; but the compulsive gambler can never rest while he still has a thousand to one chance. Napoleon escaped back to France, raised another army, and made himself emperor again. And now, for the first time, he showed signs of having learned from experience and appealed to his enemies for peace. It was too late; they regarded him as a habitual offender who ought to be hanged to save further trouble. The English and the Prussians combined to defeat him at Waterloo; then they packed him off the the remotest spot they could think of – the island of St Helena, in the south Atlantic, where he died six years later, probably of poison.

Reading the story of the Revolution and the career of Napoleon, it is again difficult to avoid the feeling that some invisible spirit of history was doing its best to teach the human race commonsense. When we look back over the past eight thousand years, it is clear that the most irritating characteristic of human beings is their passivity. The mass of people accept whatever happens to them as cows accept the rain. It is true even of the great rulers and generals; we have seen how, again and again, they achieve some triumph, relax for a brief period, then begin to feel oddly bored and dissatisfied, and look around for fresh adventures. There is no evidence that Alexander the Great really wept when he had no more worlds to conquer; but whoever invented the story had a profound understanding of human psychology. So for more than seven thousand years of civilized history, the human urge to escape boredom found its way into armed aggression, while the common people huddled together and waited for the storm to pass over. Then came the crusades, which taught the upper classes of Europe that the world was not quite static after all.

Luther's revolt against the Catholic Church taught the common people the same lesson. Then a series of catastrophes – like the Thirty Years War, the War of the Spanish Succession, the wars of Frederick the Great – made Europe aware that it ought to be looking actively for peace, while the rise of science and industry showed the world that there *were* interesting alternatives to war. The old cow-like spirit was vanishing. The British Civil War under Cromwell and the French Revolution taught the common people that they could also influence the course of history. So when the Revolution was over, and the French became aware that this massive bloodletting was not what they wanted, they elected as first consul a young general who seemed capable of giving them what they dreamed about: peace, prosperity *and* justice. The Americans, with their own revolution behind them, and delighted to be at peace again, were displaying a vitality that was reminiscent of the early days of Rome. When Napoleon revealed his limitations: that he was a mere replica of so many past 'conquerors', and that his idea of greatness was to play chess with the lives of thousands of his fellow countrymen, all Europe shouted 'No!' and combined to get rid of him as a modern police force might combine to hunt down a Public Enemy Number One.

And with the nuisance finally on St Helena, everybody could sit back and take stock of this remarkably changed world. What did they really want? In China and Japan they had already made up their minds: they wanted to slow down the pace of change and stick to the old ways. India felt the same, but had no choice as the East India Company became master of Bengal, then spread across the rest of the continent. But Europe was fairly sure that it wanted to have done with war, and to share the benefits of progress and the industrial revolution. So as soon as Napoleon was safely on his way to St Helena, the major nations of Europe met together and tried to decide how peace could be maintained. What they decided was, in effect, to put back the clock. If there is really a spirit presiding over history, it must have groaned and cast its eyes up to heaven.

What happened is that England, Austria, Prussia and Russia decided to go back to the principle of the divine right of kings. They called it 'legitimacy', but it meant the same thing. Louis XVIII was restored to the French throne, and the remainder of the old aristocracy got out its silk dresses and embroidered waistcoats.

England was inclined to go its own way – it didn't really care about legitimacy, for its markets were undamaged, and it was still more interested in the future. But the rest of the leaders who gathered at Vienna simply wanted to go back to the past. A Quadruple Alliance soon turned into a Triple Alliance of Russia, Prussia and Austria, which they preferred to call the Holy Alliance. And they proceeded to create police states in their own countries. Louis XVIII, having been forced to flee on one occasion, was determined not to rock the boat and sat as still as possible; but he died only three years after Napoleon, and his brother, Charles X, did his best to suppress all traces of the Revolution. When the republicans resisted, he dismissed his Chamber of Deputies by royal decree and took away the freedom of the press. The result was that he had a minor revolution on his hands. The streets of Paris were barricaded for three days. Finally, Charles lost his nerve and fled to England. It was the clearest possible warning of what would happen if the aristocracy tried to turn back the tide of history. But the Holy Alliance continued as before; it would be another eighteen years before the revolutions of 1848 would teach them the same sharp lesson.

What we are now discussing is, of course, the greatest ideological conflict of modern times, and the third great ideological conflict in the history of mankind. The first was the clash between Christianity and paganism, which ended with the victory of Christianity. The second was the clash between the Catholic Church and the various protestant movements – beginning with the Cathars – which ended in a draw between the two sides. The third is the clash between socialism and old-fashioned individualism. This continues to rage as bitterly as ever in the closing years of the twentieth century, with no sign of victory for either side. But historical perspective enables us to make one basic observation. Christianity began as an *individual* protest movement against state-supported paganism. Almost as soon as it achieved power, it abandoned its individualism and became another state-supported religion that persecuted individualism. Protestantism challenged it in the name of individualism, and its protest was successful. Protestantism has maintained its individualistic flavour down to our own time; but it must be admitted that in most of the countries in which it has taken root it has merely replaced Catholicism as the state-supported religion. And even in the time of

Calvin, it had become merely another form of dogmatic orthodoxy. The great protest ideologies have a tendency to turn into their opposites. Socialism also began as a movement of individual protest; but even in the time of Robespierre, it showed a tendency to change into a murderous dogmatism that refused to tolerate individualism.

So it would be a mistake to follow the lead of writers such as H. G. Wells and Hendrik van Loon – who both wrote histories of mankind – and condemn the men who created the Holy Alliance – Metternich, Talleyrand and Alexander of Russia – as old fashioned reactionaries who failed to grasp the lessons of history. All three were realists, who could see that this new ideology was based upon muddled idealism. The world was not really made up of wicked tyrants and free-born men who were kept in chains. The example of America proved that. After their revolution, the Americans had quarrelled amongst themselves for a few years about whether the country should be run by the upper classes – known as Federalists – or the people, who called themselves Democratic republicans. Hamilton, the secretary of the treasury, believed that America needed a strong government supported by bankers. Thomas Jefferson believed in complete freedom of speech and a people's democracy. In 1801, the Democrats won, and America continued to nurture individualism and to allow complete freedom of expression where politics was concerned. No one preached that the rich were wicked, or that the wealth of the country ought to be distributed equally among every man, woman and child. There was no need, since everyone had equal opportunities. So the Americans went their cheerful, materialistic way and grew prosperous. Obviously, this conflict between socialism and individualism was quite unnecessary.

England was another case in point. It is true that the French Revolution had frightened the governing classes, so that they banned Paine's *Rights of Man* and tried to repress radicalism. But they were sensible and moderate about it. In fact, after Napoleon had been beaten, young Tories took the lead in abolishing some of the horribly repressive laws which had been enacted to deal with the great crime wave of the previous century, and to allow greater political freedom. While Charles X was trying to take away the vote from the French middle classes, English reformers were doing their best to extend it to anybody who paid a rent of ten pounds a year; in 1832 they succeeded, and the first Reform Bill was passed. In 1867, a new reform bill gave workers in the cities a right to vote. By 1884, every male had a right to vote. So although there were agitations and riots in Britain, there was no explosion. By 1800, Robert Owen had set up his own socialist community at New Lanark and demonstrated that co-operative principles actually work. And in the second half of the century, upper class socialists such as John Ruskin, William Morris and H. M. Hyndman had turned socialism into something almost as respectable as Methodism or Quakerism.

Unfortunately, for better or for worse, society in Russia, France, Prussia and Austria was far more polarized. It was divided into the aristocracy and the people in rather the same way that society on a farm is divided into people and animals. This, unfortunately, was a fact. Socialists, out of the goodness of their hearts, stood for the working man. But they then went on to make rather silly assertions, such as Pierre Joseph Proudhon's dictum that 'Property is theft', which made the ruling classes grind their teeth. No zoologist had yet observed that all living creatures have their own 'territory', and that therefore property, far from being theft, is deeply embedded in animal instinct. But the non-socialists felt in their bones that these arguments about a past Golden Age, when Adam delved and Eve span and everybody loved one another, were woolly-minded non-sense. And meanwhile these socialists – or, as they were now calling themselves, revolutionaries – were asserting that society would never be peaceful and stable until all the rich had been robbed of their wealth and all the land was held in common. It was impossible to take them seriously. All that could be done was to banish them or shoot them. But that only made things worse. In 1825, a group of Russian officers known as the Decembrists – because that was the month of their revolt – tried to overthrow the new tsar, Nicholas I, and obtain a constitution; Nicholas was forced to shoot the ringleaders and exile the rest. Russia had been drifting in the direction of liberalism, but after the Decembrist revolt, she became more reactionary than Prussia or Austria. Nicholas's successor, Alexander II, actually took the tremendous step of abolishing serfdom (1861), and was assassinated by a revolutionary for his pains.

So it would be an oversimplification to regard Metternich, Talleyrand and the rest as reactionaries who wanted to suppress all freedom of speech. They wanted what everyone else wanted: peace and prosperity. And they honestly regarded the socialists as criminals who were using a specious false logic to justify their attempts at robbery. They recalled what had happened during the French Revolution, when the power had simply fallen into the hands of a new set of tyrants, and assumed that what the socialists wanted was to seize the power for themselves.

They were by no means entirely wrong. A case in point was the German agitator Karl Marx, whom the tolerant English had allowed to settle in London. He was the son of a wealthy Jewish lawyer (who in turn was the son of a rabbi), and had spent his childhood in pleasant and elegant surroundings in Trier, in the Rhineland. He also became engaged to the girl next door, Jenny, the daughter of Baron von Westphalen. His father wanted him to be a lawyer; Marx believed he was destined to be a great poet, a second Goethe. He studied first at the university of Bonn, then at Berlin. Here there was great intellectual ferment, and Marx plunged into it with delight. The philosopher who interested the younger generation more than any other was Georg Wilhelm Friedrich Hegel. Hegel had studied world history, and had reached the conclusion that, in spite of the cruelty and misery, mankind was slowly evolving towards a deeper sense of freedom. That is, history shows the struggles of 'spirit' to impose itself on a world of matter. Marx, who was never one to accept second place, tried to carry Hegel's philosophy one stage farther. The problem was that he was profoundly and savagely pessimistic, and believed that the soul had no existence. So his own version of Hegel's evolutionism was totally materialistic.

What Marx hoped was to become a professor of philosophy, and to play a leading role in the intellectual ferment of his time – like his friend Bruno Bauer, whose 'rational theology' was causing intense controversy. Unfortunately, most of central Europe at the time was in the grip of the 'Metternich system' – police spies, rigid supervision of anyone in government service or education, and suppression of 'new' ideas. Bauer soon lost his job as a professor, and Marx's hopes of a comfortable academic career faded. He became the editor of a liberal newspaper, and soon had the circulation soaring with his articles attacking various injustices – such as the punishment of peasants who picked up dead wood in the forest. When Marx attacked the government of Tsar Nicholas of Russia, the newspaper was banned.

Marx moved to Paris in 1843, became a friend of the poet Heine,

right concept *but* The cause is greater than this

and continued writing about socialism – or, as he preferred to call it, communism. He was undoubtedly a man of powerful intellect, and impressed everyone with whom he came into contact. He was also a bully, a tremendously dominant man who felt that he deserved to be famous and was already deeply embittered about the oppression that was forcing him into poverty. (His father by now was dead and Marx soon spent his inheritance.) Like Voltaire, he was determined to teach his own country a lesson. It was in Paris that he evolved one of his most fundamental concepts – alienation, the worker's total sense of non-participation in society. Alienation, says Marx in a manuscript of 1844, is the inevitable lot of man because of the institution of private property; only when this has been abolished will he feel free and happy. This was, of course, an absurdly unrealistic assessment of the human condition, combining Rousseau's fallacy about the past 'golden age' with Proudhon's zoologically inaccurate notion that property is somehow 'unnatural'. But then, Marx's philosophy was an expression of his violently emotional temperament; he was not interested in philosophical truth, but in achieving results. In his *Theses on Feuerbach* of 1845, he stated: 'The philosophers have only *interpreted* the world in different ways; the point is to *change* it.' It was the kind of statement that appeals to every young man who has not yet found his natural place in the world. Marx also defined what he meant by man. 'The essence of man is not an abstraction inherent in each particular individual [i.e. a soul]. His real nature is the ensemble of social relations.' This is to say, man is not just a social animal – as Aristotle had stated; he is *nothing more* than a part of a vast web of social relations. He has no existence apart from other men. And what of other men? They have no existence apart from him. Society is like a house of cards, all leaning against one another. But if men have no free will, if they are no more than twigs floating on a stream, then what is the stream? Marx's answer – which certainly had the merit of originality – was: economic forces. Throughout history, men have imagined they are driven by ideals of truth and justice and religion; in fact, the philosophy of Plato was merely an expression of the economic forces in the Mediterranean in 500 B.C.; Christianity was an expression of the economic forces in the Roman empire in 100 A.D.; Luther's revolt was an expression of the economic forces of 1500 A.D. – the proof being that Luther was enraged by the Church's financial skulduggery, and that the peasants

used Lutheranism as an excuse to revolt against the landowners . . .
Marx's new friend Friedrich Engels, son of a wealthy textile
manufacturer, later admitted wryly that Marx had gone too far in his
emphasis on economic factors, but by that time it was too late.

emotional

Marx's mainspring was hatred; in a book called *The German
Ideology* he wrote gleefully about the coming revolution, 'when the
reflection of burning cities is seen in the heavens . . . and the
guillotine beats time, and the maddened crowd screams "It's going,
it's going", and "self-consciousness" is hanged on lamp-posts.'
Oddly enough, he hated many of his fellow revolutionaries almost as
much as he hated the bourgeoisie. Their love of mankind filled him
with rage. In 1846, Marx conducted his first 'purge'. The victim was
an idealistic socialist called George Weitling, son of a laundress who
had spent some time in prison and lived among workmen in slums.
At a meeting of the revolutionaries in Brussels, Marx launched a
violent attack on Weitling, saying that his idealism had only caused
workers to lose their jobs, and that his socialism was sentimental and
woolly-minded. Weitling retorted that he had nothing to learn about
socialism from a man who spent all his time theorizing in his study.
The barb went home. Marx rushed up and down the room roaring
with rage – he was never noted for self-control – and Weitling
became aware that the rest of the comrades were looking at him with
grave disapproval. Marx never afterwards lost an opportunity to
denounce Weitling as 'an abject fraud'. Soon afterwards Marx
turned all the force of his invective against a friend of Weitling's,
Hermann Kriege, who favoured brotherly love and women's rights.
Kriege also regarded private property as natural. Marx thundered
against Kriege in a pamphlet which had the desired effect of making
many socialists feel Kriege was a traitor to the movement. If not,
why should Marx denounce a fellow-socialist? The answer was that
Marx was cast in the same mould as Savonarola and Calvin; anyone
who preached socialism without accepting his 'scientific' doctrines
was obstructing the course of progress.

In 1844, Marx became acquainted with Proudhon, another mild
and idealistic revolutionary; soon Marx was trying hard to 'purge'
Proudhon, who replied reasonably to one of Marx's blasts: '. . . for
God's sake . . . let us not try to instil another kind of dogma . . . Let
us not fall into the contradiction of your compatriot Martin Luther
who, after overthrowing Catholic theology, immediately set himself

nor, the dogmatic attitude

the task of founding, with all the apparatus of excommunication and anathemas, a Protestant theology.' But that was precisely what Marx was intent on doing.

At this point in the nineteenth century, history was on Marx's side. The Church was back in power, the Jesuits were teaching again (they boasted that if they could have a child for the first few years of its life, it would remain a Catholic for ever), and scientists who taught that the world might be more than four thousand years old had to watch their step. In France, the 'citizen king' Louis Philippe was far from popular. The liberals were forbidden to hold meetings, but they got round this by adopting a British custom of 'political banquets', at which no one could forbid speeches. The government banned such a banquet on 22 February 1848, and the people became restless. A crowd set out on a peaceful protest march to the ministry of justice; troops were called out, and someone accidentally fired a shot. Then the troops fired directly into the crowd, which scattered, leaving behind dead and wounded. The church bells of Paris rang; barricades were thrown up in the streets, just as in 1830. And the 'citizen king', like Charles X before him, fled to England.

News travelled slowly in those days, but when it reached Austria there were riots in Vienna. Metternich was forced to flee the country. In Hungary, Kossuth led a revolution. The Czechs demanded a constitution. In Dresden, the young opera composer Richard Wagner fought on the barricades, and then had to flee the country as the police and army regained control.

Marx was exultant; at last, the revolution had arrived. He had published his *Communist Manifesto* in the very month of the French uprising, in which he explained that the real enemy was the 'bourgeoisie', the middle classes. Communism would abolish the bourgeoisie as well as property. (But he was careful to explain that in the future communist state, personal freedom would be respected.) Now Marx rushed from Brussels to Paris – only to find that the revolutionary fever was already subsiding now that the king had gone. But it had reached Germany, where King Frederick William IV had been forced to grant a parliament, a free press and a constitution. Marx moved to Cologne and set up a revolutionary newspaper. It was popular, but disappointingly, no one seemed to want to disembowel the bourgeoisie or hang them from lamp-posts. In a few months the newspaper collapsed. Marx returned to Paris, and was quickly expelled. He and Jenny left for London with their three children; Jenny was pregnant with a fourth.

From the personal point of view, the remainder of Marx's life was a long, frustrating anticlimax. He lived in poverty – at one point they were even evicted into the street – and his baby son died. Engels, now running one of his father's mills in Manchester, provided the money that supported them. A police spy who was set to watch Marx reported: 'The dominating trait of his character is a limitless ambition and love of power.' But after observing Marx for some time, the British authorities decided he was a harmless German intellectual.

Marx joined the Communist League in London, and was soon engaged in his favourite activity of trying to purge it of 'traitors'. Two more children died, while the maidservant, Hélène Demuth, became pregnant by Marx; to preserve his dignity as a revolutionary leader, Marx spread the story that Engels was the father. He became increasingly domineering, increasingly resentful. A comrade named Techow wrote of him: 'The impression he made on me was that of someone possessing a rare intellectual superiority, and he was evidently a man of outstanding personality. If his heart had matched his intellect, and if he had possessed as much love as hate, I would have gone through fire for him . . . Yet it is a matter for regret . . . that this man with his fine intellect is lacking in nobility of soul. I am convinced that a most dangerous personal ambition has eaten away all the good in him.' This is a perceptive summary of Marx's chief defects. He hungered for fame, for success, for influence. And since the only circles in which he had any influence were socialist, the dominance expressed itself in the form of violent denunciations and 'purges'.

In 1864, the field of that influence suddenly expanded. French workingmen had come to London in 1863 to see the Industrial Exhibition, and had made contact with English socialists. Someone thought of the idea of an international organization of socialists. Marx was voted on to the committee by London's German socialists, and, in his usual manner, he had soon taken charge. He drew up the rules and made sure the subjects discussed were dictated by himself. With bullying, effrontery and various subterfuges, he usually succeeded in getting his own way.

During all these years, Marx had been labouring on his major work, his own Hegelian system; the first volume appeared in 1867 under the title *Das Kapital*. Hegel was trying to demonstrate that history was moving towards the complete expression of spirit. Marx set out to demonstrate that history was moving inexorably towards communism. But how could such a proposition be sustained in view of the obvious fact that history is the story of a continual struggle for power among *individuals*? How could anyone who studies the progress of civilization from the first cities of Mesopotamia believe that mankind is moving towards the abolition of private property? According to Marx, the answer lay in a concept which he called 'surplus value'. What is the value of, say, a table or chair? It is obviously the value of the materials, and of the *labour* that has gone into it. If a carpenter asks a certain sum for a table, *this* is what he is charging for. If the carpenter is working for an employer, and the employer pays him exactly as much as his labour is worth, then he must add something extra to the price of the table when he sells it in a shop – otherwise, he will not make a profit, and he will soon be unable to employ anybody. This 'extra' profit is what Marx calls surplus value. But the public are not going to pay more for the table than it is worth; if they think he is overcharging, they will go to the shop next door. The employer's only way of making a profit is to force the workers to do more work than he pays them for – to pay a man for eight hours and make him work ten or twelve.

This method of exploitation works well enough in a pre-industrial society. But in the industrial society, most of the work is done by machines. And – here is the core of the argument – a machine cannot create 'surplus value'. You cannot make it work longer hours than you pay it for. Of course, we do not pay a machine wages; but we have to pay for it in the first place. And the manufacturer will make sure he charges exactly what the machine is 'worth' in wages. So in the new industrial age, machines will gobble up all the profit and manufacturers will go bankrupt. And if the workers have been replaced by machines, who will buy the products of the machines? The result is bound to be widespread economic crisis, which in turn will bring the inevitable Revolution. The workers will take over the means of production; the profit-motive will vanish, and mankind will live happily ever after in a free communist state. In fact, it will not even be a state, for, according to Marx, the 'state' (i.e. the machinery of legislation) will gradually wither away as men live in perfect harmony and friendship and laws become unnecessary.

Anyone who examines the above argument closely will quickly note its central fallacy: that a machine cannot provide a profit because its manufacturer will charge as much for it as it is 'worth' – that is, as much as the employer would have to pay workmen to do the same amount of work. This is obviously untrue. Let us suppose I am a painter and decorator, and I employ a workman who takes a whole day to paint two rooms by hand. For his day's work I pay him £10. At the end of the week, I have paid him £50 for painting ten rooms. Then someone invents a spray-gun that costs £50, and which will spray a room with paint in an hour. My workman can now spray forty or so rooms a week, and I have made a large profit. Moreover, I still have the spray-gun, which can be used next week and the week after that. If the spray-gun manufacturer works out that it will make me a thousand pounds profit during its working life, and tries to charge me a thousand pounds for it, I shall smartly tell him what he can do with his gun.

A machine *can* produce 'surplus value'. In fact, it is a device for doing precisely that. It takes advantage of the laws of nature to make work easier and quicker. And its cost is *not* related to how much profit it will make for me, but to the labour (and materials) that went into its production. Marx's demonstration of the inevitable downfall of capitalism is based on a fallacy that is little more than a schoolboy howler.

The rest of his theory deserves little more attention. Even if the profit-motive is *made* to vanish by repression, as in Soviet Russia, the result is not a state of loving brotherhood and innocent freedom. In no communist country has the state shown the slightest sign of disappearing. Marx indignantly denied that his communist state would be a regimented system that would undermine the freedom of the individual. In fact, the freedom of the individual has always been the first thing to vanish in a communist-controlled country.

In short, *Das Kapital* is full of promises that could never be fulfilled because they are based on a false view of human nature. The central fallacy lies in the mechanistic concept of human nature: the notion that man's ideas and values are totally governed by his economic circumstances. This in turn means that Marx's philosophy ignores a basic reality of human nature: that man works best when he is driven by *a sense of purpose*: that is, by 'the profit-motive' in its broadest sense. A man who badly wants anything, from the girl next door to a new car, will pour an enormous amount of concentrated effort into obtaining it. Place him in a commune and tell him he is working for 'the common good', and even if he is a good communist, some of his enthusiasm will evaporate. In communist countries, the result has been almost permanent economic crisis due to inefficiency. China and the Soviet bloc are the most powerful living argument against the doctrines of *Das Kapital*, a demonstration that Marx's blueprint for Utopia has no relation to actuality.

Then why did *Kapital* come to exercise such widespread influence? Because Marx possessed Savonarola's talent for emotional invective. He himself told a correspondent 'It is certainly the most terrible missile that has ever been aimed at the bourgeoisie.' Marx could always marshal his 'economic facts', his starving Irish, his miners dying of silicosis, his foundrymen scalded to death with boiling metal, his seamstresses coughing away their lungs. And the tone of scientific precision proved irresistible to a new generation of socialists, from Bernard Shaw to Lenin and Trotsky. Marx, like Luther, had arrived at precisely the right moment in history.

He almost came too late. By 1867, when *Kapital* appeared, he was fifty years old, and was an exhausted and embittered man. His aggressive and domineering nature meant that he was not greatly loved. And there were certainly no signs that history was moving obligingly towards the revolution. The German prime minister, Bismarck, was as determined as Frederick the Great to increase the power of Prussia. He and Austria had defeated Denmark in 1864 and divided Schleswig-Holstein between them; then he picked a quarrel with Austria and defeated her in the 'seven weeks war' of 1866. Having united the German states, he granted them a constitution, 'to keep the liberals quiet', then went on to allow France to pick a quarrel with Prussia about the throne of Spain. It took only a few weeks for the Germans to defeat France in the Franco-Prussian War of 1870. The defeat set off a civil war in France, and the working men of Paris set up their own government, or Commune. It was put down with brutal ferocity, with the deaths of 20,000 'communards' and the arrest of 40,000 more. Then France returned to prosperity, the era of Maupassant and Zola and the post-impressionists, and all threat of revolution receded. Fortunately for world communism, Russia remained as backward as ever, and its tsars continued to behave like Louis XVI, denying even the most reasonable demands of the liberals. So eventually, *Das Kapital* provided the match that lit the Russian revolution of 1917.

By then, Marx had been dead for thirty-four years. His last years were slightly more comfortable; Engels settled an annuity on him, and Marx was able to send his daughters to a ladies' seminary, go abroad for holidays, and gamble on the stock exchange. If he had been able to live like that forty years earlier, he would never have become a revolutionary. For Marx, like Voltaire, thirsted for revenge. Like Voltaire, he never lived to enjoy it.

Eleven

A CENTURY OF CRIME

mythologies of the criminal

Daniel Defoe died in the age of Dick Turpin; Karl Marx in the age of Jack the Ripper.

This statement symbolizes the immense social changes that had taken place in a century and a half. Turpin was a popular hero, who played to the crowd as if his execution were a first night. The Ripper was a public enemy who frightened everybody, like some nightmare creature from the collective unconscious; one old lady collapsed and died when she heard the news of his latest murder. The criminals of the age of Defoe were outside the law, but they were not outside the sympathy of the London poor. In the Victorian age, even the common burglar had become an alarming, half-mythical creature – due largely to Dickens's portrait of Bill Sykes in *Oliver Twist*. The criminal had become 'alienated' from society, and society regarded him as a dangerous outcast.

Yet the crimes of the eighteenth century were worse than anything the Victorians had to endure. In the summer of 1751, a farmer named Porter, who lived near Pulford, in Cheshire, engaged some Irish labourers to help with the harvest. One August evening, there was a crash at the door as someone tried to force his way in; the farmer evidently kept it locked as a precaution. Five Irishmen smashed their way into the house, grabbed the farmer and his wife – who were sitting at supper – and tied them up. Porter was ordered to reveal the whereabouts of his cash box, and tried delaying tactics; at this the gang threatened to torture them both. A daughter who had been listening outside the door now rushed into the room, flung herself on her knees, and begged for her father's life; she was also tied up and threatened. She gave way, and told the gang where the valuables were kept.

The youngest daughter, a girl of thirteen, had hidden herself; now she escaped out of the rear door, tiptoed to the stable, led out a horse and rode across the fields to the village. She went to the house of her brother and told him what was happening. The brother and a friend armed themselves – probably with knives and hatchets – and hurried to the farm. A man was on watch; they managed to approach so quietly that he was taken unawares, and promptly killed. Then they rushed into the parlour, and found the four men holding the farmer – who was naked – and trying to force him to sit on the fire to reveal where he kept his savings. One robber was promptly knocked senseless; the other three fled through the window. The rescuers organized a pursuit, and caught up with two of the robbers on Chester bridge; another man, the ringleader, was caught on a ship at Liverpool. All four men were tried and sentenced to death, but the sentence of the youngest was commuted to transportation for life. The ringleader, Stanley, managed to escape on the eve of his execution. On 25 May 1752, the other two – named M'Canelly and Morgan – were hanged, 'their behaviour [being] as decent as could be expected from people of their station'.

This kind of house storming was commonplace during the crime wave of the eighteenth century. The robbers organized themselves like military units. A house that was to be attacked was watched for days until the gang knew when they could burst in, and when they were likeliest to be safe from interruption. Stealth and skill were unnecessary in the actual operation; it was conducted like a siege of a town. The M'Canelly and Morgan case shows that the burglars of the mid-eighteenth century had already discovered a method of torture that became common in France at the time of the Revolution – when the robbers were known as *chauffeurs* – warmers. (Professional drivers were later called chauffeurs because the earliest cars were steam driven, so that the driver was literally a stoker, or 'fireman'.) We have seen that the streets of London were unsafe even by day; footpads operated openly in all the parks and open spaces, while highwaymen waited in every wood and thicket along every main road.

In the year after the execution of M'Canelly and Morgan, the novelist Henry Fielding, who had been a magistrate for thirteen years, declared that he could halt the London crime wave if the treasury would place £600 at his disposal. The secretary of state took him up on his offer. Fielding was a magistrate at Bow Street, so the force he created became known as the Bow Street Runners. Their job was simply to patrol central London, get to know the gangs – who had become accustomed to operating quite openly – and try to catch them in the act. Good intelligence work was more important than actual detection, because ever since the Elizabethan age, London's thieves and criminals had behaved as if they were one of the medieval guilds. During the reign of Queen Anne, the city marshal of London, a man named Charles Hitchin, was a notorious transvestite and sodomite who acted as a receiver of stolen goods and blackmailed thieves for sexual favours. When a bucklemaker named Jonathan Wild, who had spent four years in prison for debt, regained his freedom in 1714, he decided to model himself on Hitchin, and was soon the most prosperous receiver of stolen goods in London. When a thief stole a watch he came straight to Wild. So did the watch's owner. For a sum of money, the watch was restored, and Wild and the thief split the fee. No one complained because the victims were glad to get back their property. Thieves who refused to co-operate were sent to the gallows. Wild prospered for ten years, but in 1725 – the year Catherine Hayes was burned – he was arrested on a minor charge of assisting a thief to escape. The authorities succeeded in convicting him on another minor charge – restoring stolen goods without prosecuting the thief – and he was hanged on 24 May 1725. Fielding wrote his first novel about Wild. And he also saw clearly that the London crime network could be smashed by anyone who took the trouble to get to know the thieves. This is what the Bow Street Runners did, and the criminals had become so accustomed to immunity that they were captured by the dozen. Fielding says he had the immense satisfaction of reading the morning papers, and watching the reports about murders and street robberies diminish day by day until they ceased altogether. He had only used a half of the £600 voted by the government.

Highway robbery proved just as easy to halt. All that was needed was the equivalent of the modern patrol car on the lonely roads around London – a heavily armed policeman on horseback. When the highwaymen and burglars knew they might be interrupted at any moment, they moved to remoter parts. Since England had never been policed before, the introduction of the patrols caused wide-spread alarm in the criminal fraternity and crime fell dramatically.

Naturally, this could not last. The old gangs were replaced by new ones who employed new methods and tried not to advertise their operations. This was the first major step towards the 'alienation' of the criminal. He had to employ more stealth and cunning, to develop the arts of a fox raiding a chicken farm. When Henry Fielding's blind brother John took over his job at Bow Street, he had to do the work all over again – hang dozens of highwaymen and housebreakers, and send hundreds of pickpockets and petty thieves to prison. Fielding tried some famous cases, yet in few of these are the crimes themselves of any interest. A clergyman named Dr Dodd forged a bond for £4,200 and was hanged; another clergyman, the Rev. James Hackman, shot a woman he adored (the mistress of the Earl of Sandwich) in a fit of hysterical jealousy, and was hanged. And an unprepossessing and sadistic old woman named Sarah Metyard was charged with killing two girls who had been sent to her from the workhouse to learn to be seamstresses. It is not clear whether Sarah Metyard was merely evil-tempered, or whether she derived sexual pleasure from ill-treating the many girls who became her apprentices, but she beat one girl so badly, after an attempt to run away, that the child died; the other girls were told she had had a fit. The girl's sister was suspicious, so she was murdered. Sarah Metyard cut up the bodies when they began to decay, and dumped them in a sewer, with the aid of her daughter. A coroner who saw the remains thought they were bodies from a churchyard that had been dissected by a surgeon. Then the daughter became the mistress of a man called Rooker, and Mrs Metyard began to cause disturbances at his house in Ealing. The daughter told her lover about the murders, and he told the authorities, assuming that the daughter would not be indicted, since she was under age at the time. He was mistaken, and both women were hanged.

But the Fieldings died, and no magistrates of comparable energy took their place. The eighteenth-century crime wave continued unabated.

Things began to change as the industrial revolution at least provided jobs for anyone who wanted to work. As Luke Owen Pike has said in his *History of Crime in England* (Vol. 2, p. 406): '. . . there began to be drawn a broader line than had ever existed before between the criminal classes and the rest of the community.' Roads were improved, and better communications meant that highwaymen had less chance of remaining uncaught; in 1805, the horse patrols were revived in the London area, with uniformed officers guarding the roads for ten miles around London from five in the evening until midnight. There was still no regular police force, because the English remained convinced that policemen were people who spied on you, searched your home and dragged you off to jail. So methods of detecting a crime after it had been committed were still hit-and-miss.

But then, the crimes themselves continued to be of a curiously commonplace nature, as we can see by studying the *Newgate Calendar*, a compilation of criminal cases from 1700 onward published in 1774 by J. Cooke. We read: 'executed for sheep stealing', 'executed for forgery', 'executed for an unnatural crime' (sodomy), 'executed for housebreaking', 'executed for robbing a poor woman', 'executed for highway robbery', and so on. There are, of course, dozens of cases of murder, most of them family murders – husbands murdering wives – and murders in the course of robbery, many involving smuggling. The language seems absurdly inappropriate to the crimes: 'this atrocious monster', 'this abandoned wretch', 'this brutal villain'. Rape is relatively rare, and most of these cases concern upper-class males, such as Colonel Francis Charteris, 'a terror to female innocence', who made a habit of seducing his servant girls, and who 'used violence' against a girl called Anne Bond who declined his offer of a purse of gold to sleep with him. Charteris was hanged. We observe the incredible cruelty involved in many of the murders: a gang of smugglers who beat two customs men to death in 1749, crushing the testicles of one of them, and a smuggler called Mills who flogged a customs man to death in the same year. Elizabeth Brownrigg used to obtain servant girls from the parish workhouse, then strip them naked and flog them to death – often hanging from a hook in the ceiling. She was hanged in 1767, but her husband and son, who had been equally responsible for a number of deaths, were given six months each on the technicality that they were not the girls' employers. But all this brutality was merely a reflection of the Age of Gin, when London's gutters were full of drunks, and life was cheap. The *Newgate Calendar* gives the impression that ten times as many murderers escaped as found their way into Newgate prison.

In 1811, there was a case that made a sensation through the length and breadth of the country, and caused householders everywhere to bolt and bar their shutters. It took place in a house in the Ratcliffe

Highway, in the East End of London. On the night of Saturday 7
December 1811, someone broke into the house of a hosier named
Timothy Marr, and murdered Marr, his wife, their baby and an
apprentice boy of thirteen. A servant girl who had been sent out to buy
oysters discovered the bodies. The incredible violence of the murders
shocked everyone; the family had been slaughtered with blows of a
mallet that had shattered their skulls, then their throats had been cut.
The killer was obviously a homicidal maniac, but the motive had
probably been robbery – which had been interrupted by the girl's
return. In an upstairs room, a constable of the river police found the
murder weapon – a 'maul', a kind of iron mallet with a point on one
end of the head; they were used by ships' carpenters. The head had
the initials 'I.P.' punched into it. Two sets of footprints were found
leading away from the house.

Twelve days later, there was a second mass murder at a public
house called the King's Arms, in Gravel Lane, close to the Ratcliffe
Highway. The pub was run by a Mr Williamson and his wife, with
help from their fourteen-year-old granddaughter, Kitty Stilwell, and
a servant, Bridget Harrington. There was also a lodger, twenty-six-
year-old John Turner. After the bar had closed at 11 P.M., Williamson
served a drink to an old friend, the parish constable, and told him that
a man in a brown jacket had been listening at the door, and that if the
constable saw him, he should arrest him.

A quarter of an hour later, the lodger had gone to his bed in the attic
when he heard the front door slam very hard, then Bridget
Harrington's voice shouting 'We are all murdered.' There were blows
and more cries. Turner crept downstairs – naked – and peered into the
living room. He saw a man bending over a body and rifling the
pockets. Turner went back upstairs, made a rope out of sheets tied
together, and lowered himself out of the window. As he landed with a
crash on the pavement – the 'rope' was too short – he shouted
breathlessly 'Murder, murder!' A crowd quickly formed, and the
parish constable prised open the metal flap that led into the cellar. At
the bottom of some steps lay the body of the landlord, his head beaten
in by a crowbar that lay beside him. His throat had been cut and his
right leg fractured. In the room above lay the bodies of Mrs
Williamson and Bridget Harrington. Both their skulls had been
shattered, and both had had their throats cut to the bone. The
murderer had escaped through a rear window.

Dozens of sailors and men in brown jackets were arrested on suspicion, among them a young sailor named John Williams, who lodged at the Pear Tree public house in nearby Wapping. He was a rather good-looking, slightly effeminate youth with a manner that sometimes caused him to be mistaken for a 'gentleman'. There was no evidence against him. But when handbills with pictures of the maul were circulated, John Williams's landlord, a Mr Vermilloe (who happened to be in Newgate prison for debt) said that he recognized it as belonging to a Swedish sailor named John Peterson. Peterson was now at sea, so had a watertight alibi, but had left his chest of tools behind, in the care of Vermilloe.

John Williams was now suspect number one. He had been seen walking towards the King's Arms on the evening of the murders, and had returned to his lodgings in the early hours of the morning with blood on his shirt – he claimed this was the result of a brawl. The stockings and shoes he had worn had been carefully washed, but bloodstains were still visible on the stockings. Williams's room mates said he had no money on the night of the murders, but had a great deal on the following day.

Williams cheated the executioner by hanging himself in prison on 28 December 1811. An inquest declared that he was the sole murderer of the Marrs and the Williamsons – a verdict that may be questioned in view of the two pairs of footprints that were found leaving the Marrs' house. He was given a suicide's burial at a cross roads in East London, with a stake through his heart – the old superstition being that suicides could become vampires.

The details of the Ratcliffe Highway murders are rather less interesting than the effect they produced on the public. It was the first time in English history – probably in European history – that a crime had created widespread panic. Why? Because it was generally accepted that they were committed by one man. In fact, it is rather more probable that they were committed by two, or even by a gang – one witness who lived near the Marrs said he heard several men running away. If that had been believed, there would almost certainly have been no panic – gangs of thieves were still a familiar hazard in 1811. It was this notion of a lone monster, a man who stalked the streets on his own, lusting for blood, that terrified everybody. Jack the Ripper turned this nightmare into reality seventy-seven years later. But in 1811, the 'alienated' criminal had still not made his appearance.

Three more cases would produce this same widespread, feverish public interest during the next two decades. The first was the murder of a sportsman and gambler named William Weare by two more members of the sporting fraternity, John Thurtell and Joseph Hunt. Thurtell, a man of strong character and imposing physical presence, was familiar on the race courses and at barefist boxing matches. Weare had won from him a considerable sum of money at billiards, and Thurtell was convinced he had cheated. So Weare was invited for the weekend to a cottage belonging to a man called William Probert, near Elstree. The four set out from London in two horse-drawn gigs – two-wheeled carriages – and as they arrived, Thurtell shot Weare in the face; the bullet bounced off his cheek-bone and Weare begged for his life. Thurtell threw him down, cut his throat with a penknife, then jammed the pistol against his head so hard that it went into the brain, filling the barrel with blood and tissue. The body was then dumped in a pond, and the three men went into the cottage and had supper with Probert's wife and sister-in-law. The next morning, Thurtell and Hunt went to look for the pistol and penknife, without success; but as they left, two labourers found the weapons on top of a hedge. They reported the find to the Bow Street Runners, who soon discovered Weare's body in another pond, into which it had been moved. Probert quickly turned king's evidence, and so escaped. Thurtell was hanged, while Hunt was transported for life.

This commonplace murder aroused such widespread interest that it was quickly turned into a play that was performed before crowded houses. A popular ballad of the time – which was sold at the execution – had the well-known stanza:

> They cut his throat from ear to ear
> His head they battered in.
> His name was Mr William Weare
> He lived in Lyons Inn.

But why *did* it arouse such horrified fascination? It may have been partly because Thurtell was such a well-known character in the sporting world. But it was more probably the violence of the murder – the cut throat, the pistol filled with brains. Again, the crime touched a sense of nightmare: the ruthless criminal who ignores the laws of God and man. Yet the sensation it caused is also evidence

greater sensitivity to crime

that society was changing fast. In Defoe's time, the murder of Weare would have been merely one more case to add to the *Newgate Calendar*. But things were different in 1823. Luke Owen Pike says:

England in the beginning of the year 1820, when George III died, was already the wealthiest and, in many respects, the most civilized country in Europe . . . Stage coaches now traversed all the main roads, which were at length beginning to deserve comparison with the great engineering works given to us by the Romans . . . Canals intersected the country . . . All these changes were, in the main, opposed to crime.

History of Crime in England, Vol. 2, p. 407.

In fact, crime was rising steadily – Major Arthur Griffiths estimates in *Mysteries of the Police and Crime* (Vol. 1, p. 84) that there was a ratio of one criminal to every 822 members of the population in 1828. But most of these crimes were the result of misery and poverty, of half-starved factory workers and out-of-work farm labourers. What shocked people about the crimes of John Williams and John Thurtell was that they were not the outcome of desperation. They were deliberately committed for personal gain, for self-satisfaction; in other words, they were acts of ego-assertion, like the crimes of Caligula or Gilles de Rais. The age of individual conscience, inaugurated by Bunyan and Wesley, was changing into the age of individual crime.

This was, in fact, something of an illusion. Williams – and possibly a companion – had merely committed murder in the course of robbery: a hundred similar cases could be cited from the previous century. Thurtell's murder was a commonplace gangland execution; Weare was a scoundrel, and all four of them were gamblers and crooks. But the public *wanted* to believe that these were monsters; it stimulated some nerve of morbidity, in an age that was becoming increasingly prosperous and increasingly mechanized.

This also explains the excitement generated by the 'Red Barn murder' of 1827. William Corder, a farmer's son who became a schoolmaster, allowed himself to be bullied into marrying Maria Marten, a mole-catcher's daughter who was known in Polstead, Suffolk, as the local tart. She had lost her virginity to one gentleman ('an unfortunate slip' says the *Newgate Calendar*) and then bore a bastard child to another. She also became pregnant to William's brother Thomas, but the child died soon after birth. After Thomas

abandoned her, Maria had an affair with a 'gentleman' named Peter
Matthews, who thereafter paid her an allowance of twenty pounds a
year.

William seems to have been an oversensitive mother's boy who
was harshly treated by his father and made to work on the farm for a
minimal wage. His response was to become something of a petty
crook – on one occasion he borrowed money from a neighbour 'for
his father' and spent it; on another, he secretly sold some of his
father's pigs. He was sent away to London in disgrace, but returned
to the farm when his brother Thomas was accidentally drowned
trying to cross a frozen pond. He soon became Maria's lover, and
they spent their evenings making love in the Red Barn on the farm.
Maria's quarterly five pound note disappeared mysteriously, probably into Corder's pocket, indicating that he continued to look for
the easy way out of his problems. Maria became pregnant again in
1827, and gave birth to a boy; but the child was sickly, and soon
died. Maria's father evidently felt that it was time she became an
honest woman, and pressed Corder so hard that he agreed to be
married. At which point, he seems to have experienced regrets, and
looked, as usual, for the easy way out. He told Maria that they must
be married in secret, and persuaded her to meet him in the Red
Barn, dressed in a suit of his own clothes. On 18 May Maria kept her
appointment in the Red Barn, and was never seen again. Corder
returned home and told Maria's family that he had placed her in
lodgings in Ipswich for the time being. He told other stories to other
enquirers. Then, tired of the gossip, Corder slipped away to
London, where he advertised for a wife in a newspaper. The result
was a meeting with a young woman called Mary Moore, whom he
married. She had enough money to set up a girls' school in
Ealing; Corder bought himself some spectacles and became head-
master.

Meanwhile, in Polstead, Maria's mother had been having lurid
dreams in which she saw Corder shoot Maria in the Red Barn and
bury her there. Her husband recalled that Corder had been seen with
a pick and shovel on the day his daughter disappeared, and went and
dug at a spot where the earth had been disturbed; he soon unearthed
his daughter's body in a sack.

Corder was arrested and hanged – it was an open-and-shut case.
His defence – that Maria had committed suicide during a quarrel –

deceived no one. Before being hanged, in August 1828, he confessed to murdering Maria Marten.

A book and a play about the murder became instantly popular, and remained so into the twentieth century. Why? Men who killed their pregnant mistresses or wives were by no means uncommon. What thrilled the British public was the piquant mixture of sex and wickedness – the combination that still sells many Sunday newspapers. The *New Newgate Calendar* adopts an almost breathless tone: 'The murder for which this most diabolical criminal merited and justly underwent condign punishment, rivalled in cold-blooded atrocity that of the unfortunate Mr Weare, and was as foul and dark a crime as ever stained the annals of public justice.' Then it goes on to describe what a beautiful and 'superior' young lady Maria was. In short, it has little or no relation to the actuality – a sluttish countrygirl of loose morals and a weak young man of criminal tendencies. But it was the story everybody wanted to believe, just as they wanted to believe that the 'unfortunate Mr Weare' was a respectable businessman who had been lured to his death by two monsters.

What has happened is quite simple. It is a question of two distinct forms of 'alienation'; alienation by the new world of industry, with its dreariness and impersonality, and alienation by the novel, which has now become a kind of fairy story, with only the most tenuous links with reality. The first 'Gothic' thriller, Horace Walpole's *Castle of Otranto*, had appeared in 1765, a mere five years after Rousseau's *New Héloïse*, and from then on, the struggle was on to see who could invent the most blood-chilling and preposterous story. In 1795, Ann Radcliffe's *Mysteries of Udolpho* headed the field, to be eclipsed a year later by Matthew Gregory Lewis's *The Monk*, that had everything from murder and demonology to rape. The Gothic romance had to be set in an old castle, and be full of ghosts and hints of monstrous cruelty – early Hollywood films such as *Frankenstein* and *Dracula* took over the medium and surpassed it. In 1820, the Rev Charles Maturin produced his *Melmoth the Wanderer*, which, as *Everyman's Dictionary of Literary Biography* remarks, 'outdoes his models in the mysterious, the horrible, and indeed, the revolting.' By 1840, these horror stories had become so popular that publishers issued them in weekly parts, the 'penny dreadful', and tales such as Rymer's *Varney the Vampire* petrified readers from Land's End to John o' Groats. (In America they were called 'dime novels'.)

And this, combined with the sheer boredom of the ten or twelve hour day in factories, explains why the murder of William Weare and Maria Marten aroused a morbid excitement out of all proportion to the facts of the case. The world had become 'unrealistic'. Defoe had written with plodding realism, like a newspaper report; the scribe of the mid-nineteenth century had to talk breathlessly about 'diabolical criminals' and 'cold-blooded atrocities' to produce any impression on an audience fed daily on gore and cruelty.

But at least cases like this made the British public aware of the need for a real national police force, instead of local parish constables. And the trial that, more than any other, brought this home to even the most anti-authoritarian liberals was that of the Edinburgh body-snatchers, Burke and Hare. These two Irish labourers met in 1826, and moved into a 'beggars' hotel' in Tanner's Close, Edinburgh, together with their common-law wives. Somehow, Hare succeeded in taking over the house when its owner died. And when a tenant called Old Donald died owing his rent, Hare decided to recover the money by selling his corpse to the medical school. The dissection of bodies was forbidden by law; so when someone offered the medical schools a corpse – usually stolen from a newly-dug grave – no one asked any questions. Dr Knox, of 10 Surgeon's Square, paid Hare £7.10s for the corpse, which was more than twice what Old Donald owed. It struck Burke and Hare that this was an easy way of making a living – if only they could come by enough corpses. But graveyards were usually guarded to prevent the theft of bodies. The solution seemed to be to 'make' corpses. So when a tenant called Joe the Mumper fell ill, Burke and Hare hastened his end by pressing a pillow over his face. The ten pounds they received for his body convinced them that they had stumbled upon a more profitable occupation than labouring.

In February 1828, a female vagrant named Abigail Simpson was lured to the house and made drunk. On this first occasion, Burke and Hare lost their nerve, and she was still alive the next morning. But they got her drunk again, and Hare suffocated her, while Burke held her legs. Again, the corpse was sold for ten pounds. And over the next eight months, they despatched eleven more victims by the same method. Some of the victims were never identified – like an Irish beggar woman and her dumb grandson; Burke strangled her and broke the boy's back over his knee. Dr Knox probably became suspicious when he was offered the body of an attractive little prostitute named Mary Paterson and one of his students recognized her as someone he had patronized. His suspicions must have become a certainty when Burke and Hare sold him the body of a well-known idiot called Daft Jamie, but he preferred to keep quiet.

The downfall of Burke and Hare came through carelessness; they left the corpse of a widow named Docherty in the house while they went out, and two of their lodgers located it. On their way to the police, they were met by Burke's common-law wife, who saw from their faces that something was wrong and fell on her knees to beg them to keep quiet. The tenants allowed themselves to be persuaded over several glasses of whisky in a pub, but finally went to the police anyway. A search of the house in Tanner's Close revealed blood-stained clothing. Hare quickly turned king's evidence and was not tried. Burke was sentenced to death, and hanged in January 1829. Hare left Edinburgh, and died, an old blind beggar, in London.

This was by far the most gruesome case in British criminal history; yet it was perhaps a little too horrifying for the British public, which preferred tales in which beautiful girls were seduced. So the case of Burke and Hare never achieved the same widespread popularity as the Red Barn murder, or the case of Ellie Hanley, the 'Colleen Bawn' ('white girl'), a pretty Irish girl who had been married and then murdered by a young rake in 1819. But it undoubtedly helped to reconcile the British public to the first appearance of the British bobby (so called after the founder of the force, Sir Robert Peel) in September 1829. The new police were told to be firm but conciliatory, respectful, quiet and determined, and to maintain a perfectly even temper. They followed these instructions to the letter, with the result that the public gradually lost its distrust of its new guardians.

But it took some time. During these early years, the major problem for the British bobby was simply that he wore uniform and looked 'official'. This tended to arouse automatic resentment in the slums of England's major cities. In June 1830, Police Constable Grantham saw two drunken Irishmen quarrelling over a woman in Somers Town, north London, and when he tried to separate them was knocked to the ground and kicked in the face with heavy boots. He died soon afterwards, the first British policeman to die in the execution of his duty; the murderers walked away and were never caught. Six weeks later, a policeman named John Long became convinced that three suspicious-looking characters in London's Gray's Inn Road were contemplating burglary, and accosted them. Two of them grabbed him by the arms and one stabbed him in the chest. There was a hue and cry, and another policeman who came on the scene caught a man who was running away. He proved to be a baker called John Smith, who had a wife and six children, and he protested that he had heard a cry of 'Stop thief' and joined in the chase. His story was disbelieved and he was hanged a few days later. Under the circumstances, it seems likely he was innocent, and that the early police felt it was better to hang an innocent man than no one at all.

In 1833, the murder of another policeman revealed that the English attitude towards authority remained ambivalent. A mildly revolutionary group called the National Political Union called a meeting in Coldbath Fields, which was promptly banned by the police commissioner. The ban was ignored, and a crowd gathered around a speaker on a soap box. Eight hundred policemen and troops looked on suspiciously. A police spy slipped away from the crowd to report that sedition was being preached, and the man in charge of the police ordered his men to advance slowly, their truncheons at the ready. The crowd booed and pelted them with stones; the police got angry and began hitting out wildly, knocking down women and children as well as men. A man drew a knife as a policeman tried to capture an anarchist banner, and stabbed him in the chest. Police Constable Robert Culley staggered a few yards and fell dead.

A coroner's jury, considering the death, was obviously unsympathetic to the police, feeling they had no right to interfere with freedom of speech. When the coroner was told the jurors were unable to agree on a verdict, he replied that they would have to stay there without food and drink until they *did* agree. Whereupon the jury – which consisted of respectable tradesmen – produced a verdict of justifiable homicide against the unknown person who had stabbed Constable Culley. The spectators cheered, and the jury found themselves treated as heroes. The short-term result was to increase the hostility between police and public; but the long term-result was to allow Englishmen to stand on a soap box and say whatever they liked.

In France, the whole situation would have been regarded as preposterous. They had had their official police force since the time of Louis XIV and the policeman took it for granted that he represented the king's authority and could say and do as he liked. One result of this attitude, of course, was the French Revolution. But the infamous Chambre Ardente affair, with its revelation of mass poisoning and child-sacrifice (see p. 389) was evidence that the French needed a police force rather more urgently than the English. (This was, of course, before the introduction of gin caused the English crime wave.) The French chief of police was also the censor of the press, and could arrest newspaper publishers and anyone who printed a 'libellous book'. (Prohibited books were actually tried, condemned, and sent to the Bastille in a sack with a label – specifying the offence – tied to it.)

The French concentrated on the spy system to keep crime in check – a vast network of informers. M. de Sartines, the police minister under Louis XV, once had a bet with a friend that it would be impossible to slip into Paris without knowledge of the police. The friend – a judge – left Lyons secretly a month later, and found himself a room in a remote part of the city; within hours, he had received a letter by special messenger, inviting him to dinner with M. de Sartines. On another occasion, de Sartines was asked by the Vienna police to search for an Austrian robber in Paris; he was able to reply that the robber was still in Vienna, and give his exact address – at which the Vienna police found him.

The French underworld was also more organized than the British could ever hope to be. When Louis XVI married Marie Antoinette in 1770, a gang stretched cords across the street under cover of darkness, and crowds attending the celebrations stumbled over them in large numbers. Two thousand five hundred people were trampled to death in the confusion, and the pickpockets moved around rifling the corpses. But the next day, de Sartines's men swooped on known criminals and made hundreds of arrests. They did it so swiftly that they recovered enormous quantities of stolen goods – watches, rings, bracelets, purses, jewellery – one robber had two thousand francs tied up in his handkerchief. It was an inauspicious beginning for a marriage that ended on the guillotine.

After the Revolution of 1789, the police force was disbanded – only to be formed again by Robespierre, who wanted to know what his enemies were doing. Napoleon appointed the sinister Joseph Fouché his police minister, and Fouché's spy network became even more efficient than that of de Sartines.

Under Fouché, the chief of police in Paris was a certain M. Henry. One day in 1809, he received a visit from a powerfully-built young man called Eugène-François Vidocq, who offered information about certain criminals in exchange for immunity. Vidocq was totally frank with Henry; his life had been adventurous, and a hot temper and a love of pretty women had brought him more than his share of trouble with the law. He had been a smuggler, and had escaped from prison, and even from the galleys. Now he wanted a quiet life. Henry could see Vidocq felt trapped; but he wanted him to feel still more trapped, until he would do anything that was asked of him. So M. Henry declined his offer and allowed him to go.

What Vidocq had not told Henry was that he was now involved with a gang of coiners. They denounced him to the police, who called when Vidocq was in bed; he was arrested, nearly naked, on the roof. When M. Henry saw the prisoner, he felt pleased with himself; now Vidocq was well and truly trapped. Henry was now able to state his own terms. And they were that Vidocq should become a police spy and betray his associates. It was hard, but Vidocq had no alternative than to accept. He was taken to the prison of La Force, with the task of spying on his fellow prisoners. It was dangerous work, but freedom depended on doing it well. He did so well, reporting undetected crimes to M. Henry, and the whereabouts of stolen goods, that M. Henry decided to give him his freedom – as a police spy. Vidocq was loaded with chains for transfer to another prison; on the way he was allowed to escape. It made him the hero of the criminal underworld of Paris. His first task was to track down a forger named Watrin, who had escaped and totally disappeared. Cautious enquiries revealed that Watrin had left some possessions in a certain room. Vidocq waited for him to reappear, captured him after a desperate struggle, and dragged him off to M. Henry. There was a large reward. Soon after, Watrin was guillotined. So was another forger named Bouhin – the man who had denounced Vidocq to the police two years earlier. He had been arrested on Vidocq's information.

During the next few years, Vidocq showed himself to be the most determined, efficient and enterprising police agent in Paris. His success aroused intense jealousy in the Police Prefecture, and his colleagues often denounced him as a man who was really in league with the criminals. M. Henry knew better; he knew Vidocq was too attached to his new-found security. He also knew that the rivalry between his men was the greatest threat to the efficiency of the Paris police. Every area in the city had its local station, and there was little co-operation between them. So when Vidocq suggested forming a small force of men who could move freely anywhere in the city, Henry immediately seized upon the idea. Vidocq was allowed four helpers, all chosen by himself – naturally, he chose criminals. There was fierce opposition from all the local police departments, who objected to strangers on their 'patches', but Henry refused to be moved. Vidocq's little band was called the Security – Sûreté – and it became the foundation of the French national police force of today.

In 1833, Vidocq was forced to retire, because a new chief of police objected to a Sûreté made up entirely of criminals and ex-criminals. He immediately became a private detective – the first in the world – and wrote his *Memoirs*. He became a close friend of writers, including Balzac, who modelled his character Vautrin on Vidocq.

For the modern reader, the most astonishing thing about Vidocq's *Memoirs* is that the crimes were so singularly un-vicious. This is not to say that criminals were not perfectly capable of murder; only that there was a complete absence of the kind of anti-social resentment that distinguishes so many modern criminals. Burglary or robbery with violence was simply a profession, usually embraced by people who drank too much and liked to keep more than one mistress. Many robbers swore to 'get' Vidocq when they came out; no one actually tried it, for their resentment evaporated quickly. During his early days as an informer, Vidocq met two hardened criminals he had known in jail, spent twenty-four hours drinking with them, and agreed to take part in a robbery which would include cutting the throats of two old men. He managed to get a note to M. Henry, and the police were waiting for them as they climbed over a garden wall. Someone fired; Vidocq dropped to the ground, pretending to be hit. And one of his fellow burglars had to be restrained from flinging himself in sorrow on Vidocq's 'body'. It is again a matter of the 'xenophobic' reaction – 'them' and 'us'. W. S. Gilbert was perfectly correct when he pointed out that 'when a felon's not engaged in his employment' he is as human and sentimental as anyone else. Vidocq often took the trouble to get to know men he had been instrumental in sending to the guillotine or life-imprisonment, performing small services – like taking messages to families – and formed genuinely warm and close relationships with them. He even instituted a custom of standing in the prison yard to watch the men being chained together before they were led off to the galleys. On the first occasion, they raged at him like wild beasts and dared him to come among them. Vidocq did precisely that – while prisoners looking out of barred windows urged the convicts to kill him. Yet no one touched him; they respected his bravery. Vidocq accepted various small commissions – final messages to wives and sweethearts – and parted from the convicts on the friendliest of terms. The socialists were obviously not entirely mistaken to argue that crime was largely a question of social conditions. The criminal with a 'grudge against society' had not yet made his appearance.

He made it, in fact, in 1834, the year after Vidocq's retirement, in the person of Pierre François Lacenaire. In December of that year, an old woman and her son were found murdered in their room in Paris, stabbed and hatcheted. A few weeks later, there was an attempt to murder a bank messenger who had been summoned to a room to collect money from a 'M. Mahossier'. Although badly wounded, he managed to shout, and his two assailants fled. He was able to describe 'Mahossier', and Vidocq's successor Canler, who was placed in charge of the case, discovered that Mahossier was really a crook named Lacenaire, who used many aliases. Two of his accomplices were arrested and confessed. Finally, Lacenaire himself was arrested as he tried to negotiate a forged bill; infuriated that his companions had betrayed him, he also made a full confession – to the murder of the old woman and her son, as well as the attempt on the bank messenger. In prison, he wrote his *Memoirs*, and became something of a celebrity. For Lacenaire was far more educated, and far more intelligent, than the average criminal. He wrote poetry, studied anarchist literature, and regarded himself as a rebellious outcast of society.

Lacenaire's *Memoirs* tell a story that is familiar today, but was in those days unique: the oversensitive child who was jealous of the attention his parents gave to his elder brother, and who developed an immense capacity for resentment and self-pity. 'A victim of injustice since infancy, I had . . . created a view of life quite different from other men's.' He stole to gain attention, and found that it only made his parents furious. After two boring years in a bank he came to Paris and tried to live by his pen, found this impossible and joined the army, then grew bored and deserted. He turned his talent to forging bills of exchange. In Italy, he discovered that one of his fellow hotel guests had told the police that Lacenaire was probably a fugitive from justice; Lacenaire invited the man out for a walk in the woods, ordered him to fight a duel, and then, when the man refused, shot him through the head. Another spell in the army ended in disgrace. And when he began to feel weary and desperate, his self-pity suggested that someone must be to blame, and that the someone was Society. 'I determined there and then to be the scourge of Society . . .' He was reasoning in the same manner as Carl Panzram, but half a century before Panzram's birth. Like Panzram, he was convinced that other people deserved the blame. 'Some people will say to me "What are you complaining about? . . . Forger in France, murderer in Italy, thief in Paris, meditating sinister projects against Society – had you a right to its charity?" Yes, because I thought my father's fortune would enable me to pay it all back. Murderer in Italy? Yes, because I had been betrayed in a cowardly fashion . . . Meditating sinister projects against Society? Yes, because in 1829 it refused me not a place in its ranks – which I had done nothing to win – but bread, to which the whole world has a right, good and bad alike . . .' But within a few pages he is admitting that when he has money in his pockets, he has to squander it as soon as possible. It is 'magical thinking'. His misfortunes are always 'no fault of his own': 'But when I found myself penniless, through no fault of my own, when . . . I found myself rejected and disdained on every side . . . then hatred followed contempt, deep, gnawing hatred, in which I eventually included the whole of humankind.' Rousseau convinced him that the rich were to blame. So he went and killed a poor old woman and her homosexual son, a petty moneylender . . . What he really meant was that self-pity led him to make the decision to abandon all restraints, to be 'out of control', to allow himself to sink to the level of a beast of prey, while assuring himself that it was not really his fault. In prison, he received the kind of attention he had always craved, and he revelled in it. At this point, he must have recognized that he had made the wrong decision: that it *would* have been worth the effort of self-discipline to achieve the fame he had

evolution of empathy

always wanted. Like Vidocq, he would have been glad of a second chance. But it was too late, and he did the next best thing: went to the guillotine with cool bravado.

One of the most interesting comments in Lacenaire's *Memoirs* occurs in a passage where he is discussing virtue. 'I know only one virtue, which is worth all the rest: it is Sensibility.' By sensibility he meant what we would call sensitiveness, the ability to feel deeply, like Young Werther and the hero of *The New Héloïse*, the ability to go into ecstasies and write poetry.

The concept enables us to grasp what was happening to society, and why the nature of crime was changing steadily. The uneducated poor might still be living under much the same conditions as the poor of Defoe's day. But hundreds of thousands of men like Lacenaire were absorbing cheap fiction and living inside their own heads rather than in the material world. Their ability to enter the world of imagination made them more sensitive than the unlettered poor. But it also subjected them to fits of gloom and discouragement, to 'nervous prostration', to fits of self-pity. In short, it turned them into victims of the 'emotional body' – of their own feelings. So instead of reacting to stress with cheerful pragmatism, they conjured up non-existent problems. 'I lived ten years in an hour,' says Lacenaire, describing one of his own fits of despair. 'I wanted to kill myself . . . Henceforth, my life was a long drawn-out suicide . . .' In America, at the same time, a young army cadet who bore a certain physical resemblance to Lacenaire was behaving in much the same way; he was writing poetry, neglecting his duty, drinking heavily, alienating friends and relatives. Edgar Allan Poe was nine years younger than Lacenaire, and he turned to literature rather than crime. But a comparison of their two lives shows startling similarities, and makes us aware that they were extreme examples of a type that was becoming increasingly common. The majority of them lacked the talent of Lacenaire and Poe; but novels had filled them with the vague feeling that they deserved more out of life than they were likely to get. The writings of the socialists seemed to justify this feeling; they diffused the vague idea that the majority were under-privileged because a small minority had seized all the riches of society for themselves. This notion convinced Lacenaire that he should be stabbing people in the back rather than making any effort, and that anybody who *had* achieved anything through effort must be a crook who deserved to be murdered and robbed. So although socialism began as a doctrine of compassion and concern, it soon degenerated into a 'magical' justification of criminality. Proudhon and Marx dreamed of a society of strong and self-sufficient individuals; in fact, they did more than all the politicians to create a society of self-pitying egoists.

American society had always believed in the importance of individual enterprise; it is therefore no surprise that American crime began to exhibit this individualistic tendency long before crime in Europe. In 1776, a beautiful eighteen-year-old girl, Bathsheba Ruggles, was married to Joshua Spooner, a wealthy landowner who was many years her senior – the marriage having been arranged by her father, General Timothy Ruggles. Spooner owned a great deal of Massachusetts. Bathsheba soon began having affairs with local men. In 1776, Bathsheba, like her father, was an ardent supporter of King George, while her husband favoured secession. One day, an emaciated young soldier passed the front door, and Bathsheba invited him in for a meal. Sixteen-year-old Ezra Ross had soon joined the list of her lovers. In February, 1778, Bathsheba offered a meal to two British soldiers who had escaped from an American prison camp. She then set about persuading Ross and the two guests to murder her husband. On 1 March 1778, they waited for him as he returned from a tavern, strangled him and threw his body down a well. The following morning, Bathsheba gave a very passable imitation of an anxious wife; a search party found Spooner's body, which had been stripped of most of its clothes. The three killers had stopped in a tavern in the nearby town of Worcester, where they spent some of the money Bathsheba had given them and showed off a watch that had been taken from Spooner. They were arrested, and immediately confessed. Sentenced to death with the others, Bathsheba tried to delay the sentence by insisting that she was pregnant, but was disbelieved. After all four had been hanged on the same scaffold, she was dissected, and found to be five months pregnant.

It could be argued that Bathsheba Spooner had been anticipated by half a century by Catherine Hayes. But John Hauer, of Heidelberg, Pennsylvania, displayed an enterprising originality that surpasses anything in the *Newgate Calendar*. When he married Elizabeth Shitz, he expected her to inherit part of her father's considerable fortune but when Peter Shitz died in 1795, he left most of his estate to his two sons, Francis and Peter; Elizabeth inherited only a thousand dollars. Hauer challenged the will in court, without success. He then went to the Shitz brothers and told them that the ghost of the old man had appeared to him in a dream and declared that the inheritance should be divided equally. They declined to believe him. Hauer warned them that their father had said he would haunt them if he ignored the request. Soon afterwards, the brothers were awakened with the sound of footsteps in the attic, a clanking of chains and a hollow voice announcing itself as their father. They rushed up to the attic and caught Hauer holding a chain – he insisted that he had been summoned there by the old man's ghost. This time they threw him out.

The next time the younger of the Shitz boys – seventeen-year-old Peter – visited his sister, Hauer got him drunk and bet him five gold dollars that he would not dare to jump from a beam in the loft with a rope tied round his neck. Peter took the dare. Fortunately, the rope broke.

At this point, Hauer ran out of ideas. Two years later, in 1797, he went into a tavern, got into conversation with four Irish labourers, and persuaded them to murder the Shitz boys with a promise of sharing in his future fortune. Three days after Christmas, the Irishmen broke into the Shitz house, found Francis in bed, and shot him through the ear, then struck him with an axe. They then forced their way into Peter Shitz's room and attacked him; Peter succeeded in jumping from the window and escaping.

The ease with which the burglars had found their way to the correct bedrooms made the authorities suspicious. The pistol that had killed Francis was found and identified as belonging to one of the Irishmen. They implicated Hauer, and all five were tried. Only Hauer and M'Manus – the man who owned the pistol – were found guilty. Hauer then made a determined attempt to convince the police that he was insane, stripping himself naked and biting anyone who came into the cell. It made no difference; he was hanged in July 1798.

By comparison with Europe, America was a law-abiding country at the end of the eighteenth century. The puritan ethic was still strong, and in small rural communities serious crime was unusual. Inevitably, there were robbers and badmen; but their life span was

Why?   *?*

usually short. In the Ohio wilderness, two robbers named Big Harpe
and Little Harpe killed dozens of trappers, but were finally hunted
down by a posse; Big Harpe was killed and beheaded; Little Harpe
escaped and vanished. In the following year, a killer named Sam
Mason was tracked down and beheaded by a bounty hunter named
Bill Setten; unfortunately for Setten, he was mistaken for Mason – in
spite of being able to exhibit his head in a jar – and hanged.

A surprising number of the crimes of this period were committed
by slaves. Pomp, a slave of Andover, Massachusetts, killed his
master Charles Furbush with an axe in 1795 after Furbush had
flogged him and tied him to a rafter overnight. Edmund Fortis raped
and killed Pamela Tilton of Vassalborough, Maine, in 1794. In 1803,
Cato, a slave on a farm near Charlestown, New York State, raped
and murdered May Atkins. In 1800, a Haitian slave named Gabriel
mustered an army of a thousand blacks near Richmond, Virginia,
intending to massacre the white population, and committed various
murders of whites before his army was broken up by militia. In New
Jersey, Cyrus Emlay killed his master, Humphrey Wall, with a
hatchet, then burned the house down. In 1831, a slave named Nat
Turner led a negro revolt in Virginia and killed fifty white people
before being captured. He told the jury at his trial that he had
viewed his mutilated victims, including children, 'with silent satisfaction, and immediately went in search of other victims'.

What we have here, in fact, is an early version of the 'resentment
murder'. The negroes, as a class, had more to resent than the whites,
so it is not surprising that some of them should develop an attitude
towards society that resembles Lacenaire's. This is probably true
even of the rape murders listed above; white women represented the
forbidden, the whole world of which the negro felt himself deprived;
therefore a rape murder was a social as much as a sexual crime.

America's first mass murderer, Samuel Green, was also motivated
by resentment, and the case bears some remarkable resemblances to
that of Carl Panzram. Born in Meredith, New Hampshire, about
1800, Green was a natural delinquent who began stealing early.
Apprenticed to a blacksmith, he was caught stealing, and whipped;
sent home, he was whipped again. His reaction was to throw the
family dog into the well, so that it polluted the water. Punished
again, he reacted by stabbing the family pig. He moved into
Newhampton to live with a man named Dunne, and the old cycle of

stealing and being flogged was soon re-established. He made two attempts to kill Dunne with a booby-trap, both of which failed; this time he was beaten until his back was a mass of blood and torn flesh. Eventually, Green joined up with another rebel named Ash, and the two began working with a counterfeiter who used them to pass dud money. An event of this period is typical of Green's vengeful mentality. He hurled a baulk of timber under a fast-moving sleigh full of schoolchildren, which overturned and caused some injury. The schoolmaster attacked Green and Ash and left them bruised and battered. Later, they lay in wait for him, knocked him unconscious and left him bound and naked to freeze to death – fortunately, he was found in time.

Green's first murder seems to have been of a jewellery salesman whom he and Ash encountered in a tavern in New Hampshire. They waylaid him later and robbed him; then discussed whether it would be safer to kill him. 'A dead cock never crows,' said Ash, and Green winked and dashed out the man's brains with his club.

Green then turned into a version of the later Western badman, specializing in burglary but killing when he was interrupted. The precise number of his murders is unknown, but he was soon the most wanted man in America. His career came to an end in Danvers, Massachusetts in 1820, when he was arrested for stealing goods from a store when drunk. He was sentenced to four years in prison and sent to Boston. He made various escape attempts, after each of which his sentence was increased. Finally, he heard that a negro prisoner named Williams had alerted the guards before his last escape attempt; he managed to corner Williams one morning, then knocked him unconscious with an iron bar and systematically smashed his arms, legs and ribs. Williams died of his injuries, and Green was hanged in April 1822. Unlike Panzram, he wrote no detailed confession, so we know little about his two-year crime-spree from 1818 to 1820. What seems very clear is that he was a man of exceptionally high dominance who, like Panzram, refused to be beaten into submission. He was an 'assassin' in the same sense as Lacenaire, a man for whom killing was a twisted form of self-expression. And since he was executed fourteen years before Lacenaire, he may be regarded as the first 'assassin' in modern criminal history.

The type became increasingly common during the rest of the

nineteenth century, and almost commonplace in the twentieth. Towards the end of the century, Nietzsche discussed a killer called Prado in a letter to the playwright Strindberg: '. . . the history of criminal families . . . always leads one back to an individual too strong for his particular social environment. The latest major criminal case in Paris, Prado, is a classic example. Prado was more than a match for his judges, even his lawyers, in self-control, wit and bravado. This in spite of the fact that the pressure of the trial had already affected him so much physically that several witnesses recognized him only from old portraits.' Prado was, in fact, another Lacenaire, a robber who was prepared to murder if discovered. In 1887, he had been arrested as he fled from the scene of a robbery in a hotel; he fired two shots from a revolver and seriously wounded one of the policemen chasing him. Some time later, his two mistresses were also arrested for complicity, and placed in the same cell. One of them told the other that she believed Prado to be responsible for the murder of a prostitute named Marie Agaetan in the previous year; the killer had cut her throat and made off with her jewellery. This story was repeated to an examining magistrate, and the police were able to track down jewellers who recognized Prado as the man who had sold them Marie Agaetan's jewellery. In court, Prado decided to be his own advocate, and, as H. B. Irving put it in his *Studies in French Criminals of the 19th Century*, 'shows himself well-read, prodigal of words, and inexhaustible in protestations, overwhelming his judges with denunciations.' It was all to no effect, of course, and he was executed. From the death cell he wrote a letter to a friend in which he declared: 'For the wise man, there are no such things as laws. Since all laws are subject to errors or exceptions, it is for the wise man to judge for himself whether he shall obey them or break them.'

But then, Prado, like Lacenaire, was a born actor. Nietzsche is perceptive when he describes him as an 'individual who is too strong for his particular social environment' but at the same time, he is romanticizing when he says that Prado is more than a match for his judges in self-control. The transcript of the trial shows that he simply talked too much; he sounds like a man who has at last succeeded in getting on television and is determined to make the most of it. His comments about the 'wise man' make him sound like a criminal Marcus Aurelius; we have to remind ourselves that he is in court merely for slitting the throat of a prostitute.

What strikes us most about the 'assassin' is this element of *miscalculation*. Lacenaire remarked on his own lack of feeling when he committed murders; he seemed to be observing himself from a distance. This is basically 'schizophrenia', separation from reality. We can observe the same thing in another remarkable case of the period: that of Jean Baptiste Troppmann. Born in Alsace in 1869, Troppmann was the son of a poor mechanic who – like Samuel Green and Lacenaire – was ill-treated by his father and defended by his mother. He grew up a homosexual. At school he was bullied, but showed such violence when he was attacked that they finally stopped. At work in his father's workshop, he was bullied by his brother until one day he seized a hammer and hit Edward in the face. After that, Edward let him alone.

Troppmann performed athletic exercises until he gained a remarkable bodily strength. He read and re-read Eugene Sue's absurd concoction of Gothic horrors *The Wandering Jew*. He studied chemistry in secret, probably to learn about poisons. Everything about him indicates the typical 'loner' who is determined to make his mark in the world.

His method of making his mark was to plan the murder of an entire family. When he met a wealthy businessman named Kinck, he tried to persuade him to invest in various moneymaking schemes, all of which Kinck wisely turned down. Finally, Troppmann persuaded Kinck to accompany him on some kind of business trip; as soon as they were in the country, he gave Kinck a glass of wine laced with cyanide; Kinck died immediately. Troppmann buried the body in a forest, and lured the eldest boy, Gustave, into the countryside; he was stabbed in the back and buried. Finally, Troppmann persuaded Madame Kinck – who was pregnant – and her five children to accompany him to meet her husband. They took a cab to Pantin, near Paris, where Troppmann claimed her husband was staying. He persuaded them to alight in a lonely spot, paid off the cab, then killed them all in a field.

The next morning a workman noticed blood on the road, tracked it to a spot where the earth had been newly dug, and gave the alarm. The bodies of the Kinck family were unearthed. The ferocity with which they had been hacked suggested a sadist – the two-year-old girl had been disembowelled. A label in a child's coat enabled the family to be identified. Troppmann was arrested in Le Havre, where he was hoping to escape to America with the money he had taken from the Kincks. He was publicly executed, and the novelist Turgenev was allowed to accompany him from his cell to the guillotine. His description makes it clear that Troppmann was determined to die well. Turgenev was impressed by the good-looking, twenty-year-old youth, and obviously felt that this execution was a barbarity. One of his companions remarked that he felt they were not watching the execution of a common criminal, but that this was the year 1794 and they were present at the death of an aristocrat. Yet Turgenev took care not to mention the nature of the crime for which Troppmann was condemned.

Troppmann, then, was another 'assassin', another 'man who was too strong for his particular social environment'. Yet again, the most puzzling thing about the crime is that element of miscalculation; it seems as absurd, as excessive, as the Ratcliffe Highway murders. How did he come to plan anything so stupid? We discover the answer by glancing into the novel that Troppmann read again and again – *The Wandering Jew* by Eugene Sue. It is about the brilliant and evil Father Rodin, a Jesuit priest who is determined to secure for his order the vast legacy that should go to the last seven members of the Simon family – descendants of the wandering Jew who mocked Jesus and was condemned to walk the earth until the second coming. So he sets out to prevent them from being present to claim the legacy: one is drugged, one declared insane, one jailed for debt, and so on. The wicked priest is finally killed by poisoned holy water that he accepts from someone's fingers. *The Wandering Jew* became Troppmann's Bible; it explains, for example, why he took up the study of undetectable poisons. But he decided to go one better than Father Rodin and kill all his victims. Troppmann was a victim of his own fantasies – or rather, those of Eugene Sue.

What is happening, in fact, is that the nature of crime is slowly changing in a manner that suggests Maslow's 'hierarchy of needs'. According to Maslow, the basic need is for food and drink, and the majority of crimes described in the *Newgate Calendar* are committed for food and drink – some quite literally. The next level of the hierarchy is the need for security, for a roof over one's head. America, with its pioneering spirit and its farming communities, achieved this level a decade or so earlier than Europe, where, particularly in the large cities, the majority of criminals remained on the bottom rung of the ladder. The crimes of Burke and Hare, committed in 1826, are still 'bread and butter' murders, while the crimes of Bathsheba Spooner, John Hauer and Samuel Green are crimes that aim at security; they also have a note of individual self-assertion, of the criminal making his own decision about right and wrong.

In fact, this type of crime becomes the typical crime of the nineteenth century; not, in terms of statistics, its most frequent, but at least the kind we instantly remember when someone mentions nineteenth-century crime. We think of Dr John Webster, in the Massachusetts Medical College, striking his colleague Dr George Parkman on the head with a chunk of timber, then burning his body piecemeal in the laboratory furnace; of Constance Kent, the sixteen-year-old schoolgirl who cut the throat of her four-year-old half brother and stuffed his body down an outside lavatory; of Dr Pritchard, poseur and Don Juan, who poisoned his wife and mother-in-law in Glasgow; of Florence Bravo, accused of poisoning her husband with antimony; of Marie Lafarge, accused of murdering her husband with arsenic; of Lizzie Borden, accused of murdering her father and step-mother with an axe; of Dr William Palmer of Rugely, who poisoned his wife, children and several unfortunate business associates; of Madeleine Smith, who poisoned an importunate lover who refused to accept that she was tired of him. All these crimes have a typical Victorian flavour. They are essentially 'domes-tic' murders – committed for various purposes, but always to preserve the killer's domestic peace and security. The only possible exception on the list is Constance Kent, another strong-minded 'resentment killer', who finally unburdened her soul with confession and spent a lifetime in prison. Her case is also remembered for the careful investigative work of Inspector Jonathan Whicher of Scotland Yard, which so impressed both Dickens and Wilkie Collins that they used him as a model for policemen in their novels. In *Bleak House*, Dickens described Inspector Bucket as a 'detective officer', so introducing a new word to the language.

What had happened is that, for a large proportion of the population, the old violent world of the *Newgate Calendar* had been left behind. The industrial revolution had created wealth, and wealth has created a new sense of security – a feeling that domestic stability is the very foundation of existence. The typical novel of the eighteenth century was about wanderers and vagabonds: *Tom Jones*, *Robinson Crusoe*, *Peregrine Pickle*, *Gil Blas*. The typical novel of the nineteenth century has a solid, four-square domestic setting. The Victorians loved to read about substantial, respectable people: Squire Brown and Bishop Proudie, Mr Pickwick and John Halifax, Gentleman. Their ideal seemed to be a world rather like that of Tolkien's hobbits, drowsing in their warm hobbit holes, or John Betjeman's small boy tucked up in bed, 'safe inside his slumber-wear'. Dickens catches the feeling better than anyone in his descriptions of Christmas, whether the setting is the farm at Dingley Dell or Bob Cratchit's shabby four-room cottage. All this explains why the typical Victorian murder is not the 'bread and butter' crime, but murder committed for domestic security.

It also explains the rise of socialism. The poor of the eighteenth century had taken it for granted that they were not born 'gentlemen', and accepted their lot; but the poor of the nineteenth century wanted to know why they lacked a home and regular income when everybody else – even the Bob Cratchits – seemed to have them. This is what created the sense of 'alienation' observed by Marx, and the unrest that led to riots.

What the Victorians failed to notice – even perceptive Victorians like Dickens – was the increasing number of alienated individuals – 'outsiders' like Lacenaire, who no longer felt themselves a part of society. The first literary expression of the phenomenon occurred in 1888; it was in the October of that year that a sketch called *Hunger* appeared in the Danish literary monthly *My Jord*. Its author, a twenty-year-old Norwegian named Knud Pedersen, described a man living alone in a bleak room in Christiana (Oslo) almost delirious from hunger. He speaks of himself as 'an exile from existence', as isolated as a city dweller in a jungle. Two years later, Pedersen expanded the story into a novel, changed his name to Knut Hamsun, and achieved overnight fame. But his novel was regarded as an indictment of an uncaring society; no one recognized it for what it was, the first 'outsider' document.

But it was in that same year, 1888, that England was suddenly shocked into an awareness of the alienated 'loner'. In the early hours of 31 August, a carter on his way to work noticed a bundle lying on the ground in Bucks Row, in the Whitechapel district of east London. It proved to be a woman, whose skirt had been pushed up around her waist, and the man's first thought was that she had been raped – an indication of the increasing frequency of this crime. He touched her face and realized she was dead. At the mortuary, it was seen that the woman had been disembowelled. She proved to be a prostitute named Mary Ann Nicholls, who had been wandering around trying to find someone to give her a few pence for a bed in a doss house.

A week later, another body was found in the back yard of a lodging house at 29 Hanbury Street, in the same area. The body was in a rape position, with the legs apart and the knees raised. She had been killed – like Mary Ann Nicholls – by strangulation and then having her throat cut; then the killer had cut her open from the chest downward and removed some of the inner organs. The mutilations seemed to reveal a certain medical knowledge – or at least, a knowledge of where the organs were located.

London became aware that there was a sadistic maniac on the loose. The first murder had caused shock; this caused a sensation. It was recollected that another woman had been murdered in the George Yard Buildings, Whitechapel, in early August, stabbed thirty-nine times. The murders caused the same universal fear that had been experienced in 1811 at the time of the Ratcliffe Highway murders. The police made dozens of arrests – anyone who was denounced by the neighbours as eccentric was a suspect; dozens of unbalanced men walked into police stations declaring that they were the killer. In late September, the murderer acquired a nickname when the Central News Agency received a letter threatening more murders: 'I am down on whores and shant quit ripping them till I do get buckled'; it was signed 'Jack the Ripper'. Confessions to being 'Jack the Ripper' continued to pour in, mostly from drunks and mental defectives.

Two days after the 'Ripper' letter was received, the killer struck twice on the same night. In the back yard of an International Workers Educational Institute in Berner Street he cut the throat of a Swedish prostitute called Elizabeth Stride, but was interrupted by the arrival of a horse and cart and escaped from the yard as the alarmed driver rushed into the club. He walked half a mile or so towards the City, picked up a prostitute called Catherine Eddowes, who had just been released from the Bishopsgate police station where she had been taken in drunk and disorderly, and took her into the corner of Mitre Square. A police constable who passed through the square every quarter of an hour found the body lying there. The face had been badly mutilated; the left kidney and entrails had been removed and taken away. The next morning, before the news had had time to reach the newspapers, the Central News Agency received another 'Jack the Ripper' letter, regretting that he had been interrupted, and so could not send the victims' ears as promised. (There had been an attempt to remove the second victim's ear.)

Six weeks later, on 8 November 1888, the Ripper committed his last murder. This time he picked up the woman – a twenty-five-year-old Irish prostitute named Mary Jeanette Kelly – outside her lodgings in Miller's Court, Dorset Street. She was killed in her room at about 2 A.M. – neighbours heard a cry of 'Murder' at this time but paid no attention – then the Ripper spent the remainder of the night mutilating her, burning rags in the grate to provide light. When she was found the following morning, the head had been almost severed from the body. Some of the entrails had been hung over a picture frame. The heart lay beside her on the pillow, but her breasts were on the table. One arm had been almost removed, and the killer had spent some time cutting the flesh from the face – including the nose – and the legs. These mutilations must have taken him at least an hour.

Then the murders ceased. The killer was never identified, although Sir Melville Macnaghten, the Commissioner of Police, later declared that the chief suspect had been a young and unsuccessful barrister named Montague John Druitt, who had committed suicide by drowning three weeks after this last murder. There have been many other candidates, from a sadistic midwife to the heir to the throne, the Duke of Clarence. But most of the books about the Ripper are based upon what is probably a false assumption: that the Ripper must have been known to many people as a maniac, and that he (or she) would have stood out from the crowd as an unusual personality. The truth is probably that the Ripper was some anonymous unknown, a street sweeper or market porter, whose sadistic obsession was totally unsuspected by those who knew him. But the assumption tells us a great deal about the impact of the murders. They seemed to be a deliberate outrage, like some terrorist bombing, an 'alienated' man screaming defiance at society and taking enormous pleasure in the shock he produces. The double murder, followed by the elaborate mutilation of the last victim – the photograph makes it look like a butcher's carcase – gives the impression of someone shouting: 'There – what about that?'

The odd thing is that the Victorians were only dimly aware that these were sexual murders. No contemporary newspaper refers to them as sex crimes, although the murderer is often described as 'morally insane'. Bernard Shaw said jokingly that the killer was probably a social reformer who wanted to draw attention to the appalling conditions in the East End of London; but the comment was more apposite than he realized. The Ripper was clearly a man who was insanely obsessed with blood and stabbing and who was particularly fascinated by the womb. He was obsessively neat – the bodies were always carefully arranged, sometimes with the contents of the pockets placed symmetrically around them. But the most significant thing about him was that he felt totally *separated* from society. Like Lacenaire, he probably experienced a state of detachment, a sense of unreality, which vanished only when he killed or daydreamed about killing. Although he was probably indifferent to the social conditions in the East End of London, he was nevertheless an extreme product of Marx's 'alienated' society.

The most sensational American case of the same decade was in some ways more remarkable than that of Jack the Ripper. Hermann Webster Mudgett was born in 1860 in New Hampshire, became a medical student at eighteen, got married, and practised his first swindle – an insurance fraud involving the faked death of a patient – while still at medical school. He practised medicine in Mooers Forks, New York State until 1886, then moved to Chicago, where he became 'H. H. Holmes'. There he began his career of murder, killing a friend, Dr Robert Leacock, for his life insurance. He married a second time – bigamously – but ran into trouble when he forged his wife's uncle's signature. He became an assistant in a drug store run by a Mrs Holden on 63rd Street, Englewood, and in 1890 became a partner. There was some talk about rigged books and prosecution, and Mrs Holden vanished. Holmes became sole owner of the store. He was soon doing so well that he built himself a house opposite – it later became known as 'murder castle'; one of its peculiarities was a chute leading to the basement; others were glass pipes with which he could flood rooms with gas, and peep holes into all the rooms. One of his tenants, Dr Russell, was killed with a blow from a chair; the body was sold to a medical school which apparently asked no questions about the injuries.

A Mrs Julia Conner and her daughter moved into the house, and Mrs Conner became pregnant by Holmes, so her husband left her. Mrs Conner died in the course of an operation for abortion, and Holmes poisoned the daughter, afraid she might talk about her mother's death.

Holmes next killed a companion on a fishing trip, discovering he was carrying a great deal of money; the man – named Rodgers – was killed with blows from an oar. A southern speculator named Charles Cole was also killed for his money – his skull was so damaged by the blow that his corpse was useless to the medical school. After that, Holmes killed a domestic servant called Lizzie because he was afraid the janitor was about to run away with her and he wanted to retain his services. Holmes was preparing to ship this corpse to the medical school when his secretary, Mary Haracamp, walked into the room together with a pregnant woman named Sarah Cook. Holmes swiftly pushed them into the tiny room he called 'the vault', to be suffocated.

A girl named Emily Cigrand became his new secretary and also his mistress. When she told him she was getting married, Holmes lured her into the 'vault' and ordered her to write a letter to her fiancé breaking off the engagement. The girl wrote the letter, but Holmes nevertheless turned on the gas and watched her die a lingering death. His later confession makes it clear that he was now beginning to take considerable pleasure in watching people die.

Ten more victims followed within months. Holmes began using poison; the motive was normally to extort money, but when – as in most cases – the victims were women, they usually became his mistresses too. One of these mistresses was a girl called Minnie Williams, from whom Holmes had swindled several thousand dollars. Holmes murdered her sister Nannie in the vault, and also somehow persuaded her brother to make him the beneficiary of an insurance policy; the brother was later shot 'in self defence'. By that time, Minnie had also been murdered; she had confessed to an insurance representative that a fire in the 'castle' had been deliberate arson.

Soon afterwards, Holmes acquired a partner in crime, a man named Benjamin Pitezel. This may seem out of character; but in fact, Holmes planned to murder Pitezel from the beginning. Their first joint venture in crime landed Holmes in jail for the first time. He bought a drug store in St Louis, mortgaged the stock, then let Pitezel remove it. He spent ten days in jail before being bailed out by his current 'wife', a girl named Georgiana Yoke. It was in prison that Holmes met the famous train-robber, Marion Hedgepeth, and confided in him that he had worked out a perfect insurance swindle. It involved insuring a man's life, getting him 'killed' in an accidental explosion, and substituting another body for that of the victim. Hedgepath gave Holmes the name of a crooked lawyer to deal with the insurance company, and Holmes promised to give him five hundred dollars if the plan was successful.

In August 1894, the police were called to a house in Philadelphia where a body had been discovered; it was that of a man who had apparently died in an explosion involving chloroform. The corpse was, in fact, Pitezel. Holmes was the beneficiary, and the insurance company paid up ten thousand dollars. But he failed to pay either Hedgepeth or the crooked lawyer. Hedgepeth denounced Holmes; the insurance company realized they had been defrauded, and Holmes was suddenly a wanted man.

In fact, Holmes was engaged in disposing of the rest of Pitezel's family, Mrs Pitezel and her five children. He had somehow persuaded Mrs Pitezel to allow him to take three of the children to 'join their father'. Fortunately, he was located while Mrs Pitezel and two of the children were still alive. He was taken back to Philadelphia, where a post mortem had revealed that Pitezel had died of chloroform poisoning. A detective named Geyer succeeded in tracking down the remains of the three missing children, two girls in Toronto – buried in a cellar – and the nine-year-old boy in a house near Indianapolis, where only a few charred bones were left.

After he had been sentenced to death, Holmes published a full confession of his murders – twenty-seven in all. This is so horrifying that it has been suggested that the confession was partly fabricated – although Holmes had made no attempt to suggest he was insane and it is difficult to imagine any other motive. Moreover, where it was possible to check, the confession was found to be accurate. He claimed to have starved the janitor to death in the 'vault'; in fact, bricks had been torn from the wall by someone attempting to dig his way out. He claimed that Nannie Williams had marked the door of the vault by kicking it in her death struggles; this footprint was found. He claimed that he had killed Pitezel by tying him up and burning him alive with benzine, in spite of his screams for mercy; the injuries were consistent with this, and since the later inquest showed that Pitezel had died from chloroform poisoning, they must have been inflicted before death. Holmes declared in his confession that he committed his crimes 'for the pleasure of killing my fellow beings, to hear their cries for mercy and pleas to be allowed even sufficient time to pray . . .' Instruments of torture were found in the 'castle', including a rack, barrels of acid, a dissecting table and surgical knives. One room had been lined with asbestos, and the gas pipe that entered it seemed to be designed as a kind of blow torch.

What seems clear is that, unlike Pieydagnelle, Baker or Pomeroy (see the next chapter), Holmes was not a born sadist. He seems to have spent eight years in practice in New York state, living with his wife and child and behaving perfectly normally. He was a petty swindler, no more. He became a mass murderer and torturer by slow degrees. His only 'abnormality' during the early stage is his appetite for women, and it seems probable that the peepholes in the rooms of the 'castle' were constructed with a view to voyeurism – during the Chicago Exhibition of 1880 he had many female guests.

Oddly enough, Holmes became convinced that his increasing callousness was accompanied by increasing physical degeneracy – he was obviously acquainted with the now-discredited theories of Cesare Lombroso, who postulated the existence of a criminal 'type' distinguishable from a normal man. He was also convinced of a theory that has been revived in our own time: that the two sides of the face reflect different aspects of the character, the left reflecting the 'natural' character and the right the 'acquired'. This means that if a mirror is placed down the centre of a photograph of a face, and a photograph taken of the two left halves, it should have a different character from a similar photograph taken of two right halves. (In an early issue of *The Criminologist* – November 1966 – Nigel Morland printed two such photographs of the mass murderer Peter Manuel, and the difference between them is startling.) Holmes was convinced that one side of his face – and body – had developed various signs of 'degeneracy', a comment that David Franke in *The Torture Doctor* (New York, 1975) takes to be an indication of 'the primitive state of the science of criminology in 1886' (p. 183). But a photograph of

Holmes reveals that the two sides of his face *are* quite different, and that it is the right that looks degenerate – the side that is governed by the left cerebral hemisphere, the ego. Holmes speaks of 'the malevolent distortion of one side of my face and of one eye – so marked and terrible that . . . Hall Caine [a contemporary novelist] . . . described that side of my face as marked by a deep line of crime and being that of a devil . . .'

Like Jack the Ripper, Holmes is a kind of grim landmark in social history. But his sadism was far more cold and calculated than that of the Ripper. Why, then, has he never aroused the same horrified fascination as the Whitechapel killer? The answer is partly, of course, that the Ripper was never caught, so we are free to fantasize him into a monster. But it is also because Holmes's contemporaries failed to grasp his motivations. The account of the case in Thomas S. Duke's *Celebrated Criminal Cases of America* (1910) – the American equivalent of the *Newgate Calendar* – treats him as a swindler who murdered for money. The confession was disregarded – Holmes had already made one lengthy confession in which he insisted that he was innocent of murder, and the second was considered just as untrustworthy. Later writers on the case have been inclined to believe he exaggerated his 'wickedness' to make it more saleable to the newspapers. But we have seen other cases in which a criminal who has been sentenced takes pleasure in describing his crimes in detail. The whole point of such a confession is that he enjoys telling the precise truth, without excuses or exaggeration.

And what the confession enables us to understand is that Holmes represents a supreme example of the criminal tendency that seems to be a part of mankind's inheritance. Certain episodes give us a clue: for example, locking the janitor in the 'vault' – a huge safe with a heavy metal door – and allowing him to starve to death. The janitor had tried to extort money from Holmes. Holmes's response was murderous rage – the rage a Roman emperor would have felt if his slave had insulted him. In the same way, his response to Emily Cigrand's announcement that she meant to marry was to push her into the vault, force her to sign a paper swearing that she would abandon the idea, and *then* to kill her slowly with poisonous gas. (Holmes seemed to have several varieties of poisonous gas – detectives who opened one tank were almost overpowered by an evil-smelling vapour.)

We know nothing about Holmes's early development; but it is safe to say that he was always a person who wanted his own way. But even Right Men have to learn to conceal the overweening ego and appear normal to most people; only a Domitian or Ivan the Terrible can afford to indulge every flash of rage. Holmes set out to realize the Right Man's fantasy – total and uninhibited ego-indulgence. His 'murder castle' was the realization of his dream. With its elaborate machinery for torture, murder and destruction of bodies (he had a furnace that could reduce a body to ashes without producing tell-tale black smoke) it became an extension of his 'remorseless ego'. When Holmes had watched Emily Cigrand choke to death, then destroyed her body in the furnace, he could look at himself in a mirror and tell himself that he was one of the most powerful and dangerous men in the world. As he strolled amongst the crowds at the Chicago Exhibition, he could feel that he was a god in disguise. All he had done, in fact, was to turn himself into a super-spoilt child. Only in the last months of his life did he recognize that the fantasy had destroyed his own self as surely as any of his victims.

Part Three

THE AGE OF MASS MURDER

One

THE RISE OF SEX CRIME

We have already noted that sex crime was rare before the mid-nineteenth century; among all the hundreds of cases in the *Newgate Calendar*, only about half a dozen concern rape. This was not because people were less interested in sex; it is clear from *Moll Flanders* and *Pamela* and *Tom Jones* that they thought about it all the time. But their attitude was somehow more realistic. They regarded sex as they regarded a good dinner. The first pornographic novel, John Cleland's *Fanny Hill*, appeared in 1749, nine years after Richardson's *Pamela*. Cleland's description of a rape could hardly be more down-to-earth:

The first sight that struck me was Mr H— pulling and hauling this coarse country strammel towards a couch that stood in a corner of the dining room; to which the girl made only a sort of awkward hoidening resistance, crying out so loud that I, who listened at the door, could scarcely hear her: 'Pray, sir, don't . . . let me alone . . . I am not for your turn . . . You cannot, sure, demean yourself with such a poor body as I . . . Lord, sir, my mistress may come home . . . I must not indeed . . . I will cry out . . .' All of which did not hinder her from insensibly suffering herself to be brought to the foot of the couch, upon which a push of no mighty violence serv'd to give her a very easy fall, and my gentleman having got up his hands to the stronghold of her VIRTUE, she, no doubt, thought it was time to give up the argument, and that all further defence would be vain; and he, throwing her petticoats over her face, which was now as red as scarlet, discovered a pair of stout, plump, substantial thighs, and tolerably white; he mounted them round his hips, and coming out with his drawn weapon, stuck it in the cloven spot, where he seemed to find a less difficult entrance than perhaps he had flattered himself with (for, by the way, this blouze had left her place in the country, for a bastard), and indeed, all his motions shew'd he was lodg'd pretty much at large. After he had done, his DEAREE gets up, drops her petticoats down, and smooths her apron and hankerchief. Mr H— look'd a little silly, and taking out some money, gave it her with an air indifferent enough, bidding her be a good girl and say nothing.

Cleland's attitude towards sex is the attitude of the eighteenth century: commonsense and earthy. We find it again in Boswell's *London Journal* – written for only his own eyes:

I picked up a girl in the Strand; went into a court with the intention to enjoy her in armour [contraceptive sheath]. But she had none. I toyed with her. She wondered at my size, and said if I ever took a girl's maidenhead, I would make her squeak. I gave her a shilling, and had command enough of myself to go without touching her.

This seems to explain why *Fanny Hill*, in spite of its wide popularity, found no imitators; Boswell's contemporaries were less interested in reading about sex than doing it.

Then came the Victorian age. With an eighteen-year-old virgin on the throne – Queen Victoria was crowned in 1837 – England felt the need to mend its morals – or, at any rate, its public attitudes. In the early years of Victoria's reign, men and women still bathed nude at many seaside resorts; all that soon changed. The undergarment known as drawers (because they could be drawn on) was soon being referred to as underpants (in the case of the male) and knickers – short for knickerbockers – in the case of women; the embarrassment, it seemed, was that the word 'drawers' might evoke an image of them being drawn off. This kind of thing was, naturally, self-defeating; the more there was a sense of taboo, the more people found to blush about. Women became embarrassed if they had to refer to a chest of drawers; table and piano legs were swathed in frills because a naked leg – even of wood – might invoke impure thoughts. By the late Victorian age, even 'knickers' had acquired a faint air of naughtiness, and the frills on table-legs – which suggested long knickers – were replaced by long table cloths. Prudery induced a kind of galloping inflation in euphemisms.

By the law of reverse effort, the taboos made sex seem wicked and attractive, with the result that there was suddenly a market for 'forbidden' books. On the Continent, there had always been a brisk trade in what might be called 'anti-clerical pornography' – books about priests who seduce their penitents and monks who indulge in sodomy or bestiality. These now began to be imported into England, together with some of the classic works of outstanding sexual frankness – Boccaccio, Margaret of Navarre, Aretino, Casanova. But by 1830, a new tone had begun to creep into the sexual literature. It can be seen in a work called *The Ladies' Tell-Tale*, an undisguised imitation of *The Decameron*, containing various descriptions of seduction; the opening story, 'Little Miss Curious', tells of an eleven-year-old girl who watches the butler masturbate through a crack in his bedroom door, and who finally allows – indeed, encourages – him to seduce her. Here we can sense the influence of de Sade, with his obsession with 'the forbidden'. It is no longer a matter of straightforward couplings, as in *Fanny Hill*, but of peeping through doors, surreptitious fingerings, unlikely accidents that provide the excuses for intimacy (the girl loses her virginity by falling on a stick when chasing a butterfly). The influence of de Sade is also apparent in *The Lustful Turk* (published in 1828) about two middle-class English girls who are captured by Moorish pirates and deflowered in the Dey's harem by the masterful Turk. The emphasis is all on the pain: 'he unrelentingly rooted up all the obstacles my virginity offered, tearing and cutting me to pieces, until the complete junction of our bodies announced that the whole of his dreadful shaft was buried within me.'

In 1853, an obscenity act enabled the British customs authorities to seize indecent books and pictures. The result, of course, was an increase in home-produced pornography. By the mid 1870s, there were enough books with titles like *Chastity Deflowered*, *Peregrine Penis* and *Female Flagellants* to enable a pornophile named H. Spencer Ashbee to devote a three-volume work – *Index Librorum Prohibitorum* – to listing and describing them. In July 1879 there appeared in London a 'journal of facetiae and voluptuous reading' called *The Pearl*, which continued for a little over a year. This is no mere attempt to imitate *The Decameron*, where the sex and humour are equally balanced, or even *The Lustful Turk*, with its touches of geographical authenticity; *The Pearl* is quite simply intended as an aid to masturbation. One of its models is the tale of 'Little Miss Curious'; in fact, a serial called 'Lady Pokingham, or They All Do It' contains a lengthy episode in which a butler allows himself to be persuaded to seduce a twelve-year-old girl:

'I don't care if I die in the effort,' she whispered softly. 'Never mind how it hurts me, help all you can, Willie dear, this time,' as she raised herself off him again, and he took hold of her buttocks, to lend his assistance to the grave girl. Clenching her teeth firmly, and shutting her eyes, she gave another desperate plunge upon William's spear of love, the hymen was broken, and she fairly impaled to the roots of his affair. But it cost her dear, she fell forward in a dead faint, whilst the trickling blood proved the sanguinary nature of Love's victory.

The stories in *The Pearl* are wish-fulfilment fantasies, with no relation to reality. They can also be seen as reaction to Victorian prudery. Victorian girls were expected to blush at the least suggestion of indelicacy; so most of the young ladies in *The Pearl* are an impossible mixture of demure schoolgirl and nymphomaniac.

Her face was crimson to the roots of her hair, as her hand grasped my tool, and her eyes seemed to start with terror at the sudden apparition of Mr John Thomas; so that, taking advantage of her speechless confusion, my own hand, slipping under her clothes, soon had possession of her mount, and, in spite of the nervous contraction of her thighs, the forefinger searched out the virgin clitoris. 'Oh, oh, oh! Walter don't! what are you about . . .'

A moment later she is gasping:

'Oh, Walter, I'm so afraid; and yet – oh yet, dearest, if I must die I must taste the sweets of love, this forbidden fruit . . .' She lay before me in a delightful state of anticipation, her beautiful face all blushes of shame.

And so the conquest is completed. And in story after story, for the next eighteen issues, the same kind of thing happened, varied with floggings and mixed orgies. It seems probable that the magazine expired because the writers could think of nothing new to say.

Spencer Ashbee, the author of the *Index of Prohibited Books*, is also suspected of having written the enormous sexual autobiography *My Secret Life*, published in eleven volumes in Amsterdam between 1888 and about 1892. It reveals a mind totally obsessed by sex from a very early age. As a small boy, 'Walter' seizes an opportunity to look at his baby sister's genitals, hides behind lavatories to watch elder sisters urinate, and creeps into the bedroom of female cousins on a hot night to spy on their nakedness. While still a schoolboy he seduces a maidservant, then the cook. He and his cousin Fred hide in a basement to peer up women's skirts through a grille in the pavement. This enormous work – of over four thousand pages – gives the impression that 'Walter' thought about sex for every waking moment of his life. He obviously found it all so delicious and exciting that he settled down to describing it in detail when he was in his early thirties.

It is instructive to compare *My Secret Life* with the memoirs of

Casanova, written a century earlier. Casanova loved sex; but he also loved travel (preferably in his own carriage), mixing in society, eating good food and conversing with intellectuals (such as Voltaire and Rousseau). He loved attractive women because they were essential to his picture of himself as the complete man of the world; but his attitude towards them was as straightforward as that of a hungry man towards a good dinner. By contrast, Walter is apparently interested in very little besides sex, and his attitude towards it is that of a *thief*. Every woman has a secret, which he longs to steal. They can be fat or thin, tall or short, dark or fair; he still longs to know the exact appearance of their genital organs. As a lover, he has no finesse; his idea of seduction is 'entreating her to let me see and feel her cunt, using all the persuasion and all the bawdy talk I could.' 'I watched my opportunities; my conversation . . . was one repetition of lustful wants and prayers; I used to pull my prick out, beg her to see and feel it.' And once he has achieved his objective, he needs to tell himself he has achieved it. 'I put my hand down and felt around. What rapture to feel my machine buried! nothing but the balls to be touched, and her cunt hair wetted with my sperm, mingling and clinging to mine; in another minute nature urged a crisis, and I spent in a virgin cunt, my prick virgin also. Thus ended my first fuck.' He enjoys making the girls describe what is happening: 'What's that inside you?' 'Your prick.' 'What am I doing?' 'Fucking me.' We can see that he is trying to make himself *more conscious* of what is happening; in fact, sex is simply a means to an end: to making himself more conscious. He writes about it because he feels that the experience has not engraved itself deeply enough on his consciousness. His attitude is as far as possible from that of Casanova or the Elizabethans. They accepted sex as a pleasure, but then went on to something else; for Walter sex is the most deliciously intense of all experiences because it is the most forbidden.

It is interesting to note that this feverish interest is not simply a matter of a physical need. From the beginning, his obsession has a distinctly romantic element that relates it to the raptures of Young Werther and Rousseau's St Preux. He describes reading novels as a schoolboy, 'thinking of the beauty of the women, reading over and over again the description of their charms, and envying their lovers' meetings.' As absurd as it sounds, Walter is a true worshipper of the 'eternal feminine'. His passion may express itself in the crudest physical forms, but it springs from the imagination. And, like all idealists, he finds it hard to reconcile dream and reality: 'These feelings got intensified when I thought of my aunt's backside, and the cunts of my cousins, but when I thought of the heroines, it seemed strange that such beautiful creatures should have any.' His lifelong craving for women is based on a feeling that there is something untouchable, unpossessable, about them. His quest for ultimate sexual satisfaction is a kind of mystical pilgrimage, like Parsifal's search for the Holy Grail.

And here we come to the heart of the matter. Walter lacks the self-confidence for knight errantry. He sees himself – with some slight justification – as coarse, boring and stupid. If he possessed the panache of a Don Juan or Casanova, he would devote himself to pursuing the beautiful, slim-waisted girls he sees riding in the park, who are closer to the romantic heroines who fire his imagination. But he lacks the courage, and so is willing to settle for less – far less. In order to satisfy the itch in his loins, he deliberately *lowers his aim*. This lowering of the aim, this decision to take a short-cut, also constitutes the essence of criminality.

The Pearl makes it clear that Walter's attitude to sex was not unique; the Victorian male was subject to all kinds of obsessions. He longed for virgins and under-aged girls, for incest and rape, for spanking and flogging. How had this change come about in a mere century? Victorian prudery cannot be wholly to blame, for these trends were apparent a decade before Victoria came to the throne; moreover, the *Index of Prohibited Books* makes it clear that this was also true of France, which was far less inhibited than England.

The answer begins to emerge if we think of the most basic differences between the Europe of Dr Johnson and Voltaire and the Europe of Tennyson and Flaubert: the factories and railways. Casanova lived in an age of adventure; Walter lived in an age where adventure was fast disappearing. Walter, like Casanova, travelled all over Europe; but wherever he went, he was surrounded by Victorian domesticity, and his travels seem tame by comparison. Casanova hardly strikes us as a fully mature adult; but Walter seems a permanent adolescent. He devotes his life to sex because it is the only thing left to conquer, the only satisfactory outlet for his *will*.

Zoologists have observed that monkeys in zoos copulate far more than monkeys in the wild; it is the only thing left to do. The same is true of a civilization that has achieved a high level of security. Chesterton remarked that an adventure is only an inconvenience rightly considered, and that an inconvenience is only an adventure wrongly considered. The aim of civilization is to do away with inconvenience; in doing so, it also does away with adventure. Adventurous individuals may even turn to crime – like Hornung's Raffles or Chesterton's Flambeau – because they find civilized life unbearably dull. Unadventurous individuals, like Walter, may seek 'adventure' in seduction and the quest for sexual variety. The element of danger may be absent, but the 'forbidden' provides the excitement.

All this enables us to see that the stories in *The Pearl* are, in fact, a form of imaginary sex crime. Victorian pornography only magnified a process that had been taking place since man built the first cities. When a man lives a complex social life among his fellow men, he can no longer allow free expression to his spontaneous impulses. He could be compared to someone who has become accustomed to driving at ninety miles an hour on the open highway, and then has to get used to the heavy traffic in a city. Our minds have a brake as well as an accelerator (and, for practical purposes, we could say that the right brain is the accelerator, the left the brake). The more civilized we become, the more we have to learn to stamp on the brake. Every impulse has to be monitored and checked.

We can see the result in any shy adolescent. The tendency to blush and stammer springs out of a nervous habit of applying the accelerator and brake simultaneously. And ten thousand years or so of civilization have turned us all into permanent adolescents. We do not all blush and stammer; nevertheless, at almost any point in our daily lives, we are equally ready to apply the accelerator or the brake. This also means that we have a 'double' view of any challenge. Part of us is inclined to go ahead; part holds back. Part of us sees it as a wonderful opportunity; part sees it as a dangerous trap.

In effect, it is as if every one of us contained a kind of Faust and Mephistopheles. Goethe's Mephistopheles describes himself as 'the spirit that negates'. He is the perpetual doubter. But, as William Blake remarked:

> If the sun and moon should doubt
> They'd immediately go out.

Man's life is a permanent state of 'ambivalence', a continual attempt to negotiate minor hurdles and overcome inhibitions. This explains why man is the only creature who goes insane and commits suicide.

In many of us, 'ambivalence' is so much a way of life that we are not really sure we want to go on living. We do, of course. Any sudden danger makes us aware that the desire to live constitutes the very foundation of our being. And this is why human beings voluntarily expose themselves to dangers – drive racing cars, pilot single-handed yachts, climb mountains. Danger raises them above the 'ambivalence' and fills them with the certainty that life is strange and beautiful.

This also explains why the history of civilization is largely a history of wars; war is like driving at ninety miles an hour. And when man is not at war, life becomes a search for what William James called 'the moral equivalent of war' – forms of excitement, of *purpose*, that sweep away our doubts.

These 'doubts' have become purely automatic reflexes, like a knee-jerk or the salivation of a Pavlov dog. The Norwegian writer Agnar Mykle has a novel, *The Hotel Room*, that enables us to see this point very clearly. The hero has gone to the bedroom of a woman he knows slightly, and tries to force her to make love. They struggle for a long time, and he finally succeeds in gaining entrance. At this, she decides to give way. 'But already, as he was undressing, he had caught the faint smell from her loins that told him she had made herself sterile for the occasion. For a brief instant that had excited him, but the next moment . . . the effect had been damping, fatal.'

Why? The girl who has introduced the spermicide is the same girl who excited him so frantically a few minutes earlier. But because she has ceased to resist, she has 'normalized' the situation. His will has been allowed to relax, and this has produced a certain automatic reflex, like a hypnotic command. He has ceased to be a man with a clear objective; her acceptance has transformed him once again into 'ambivalent man'.

We once again confront this basic fact about human beings: that they have a confident sense of their own identity only when the will is firmly connected to its objective, like a water-skier to a motor boat. As soon as that connection is broken as the sense of urgency disappears, 'mechanicalness' supervenes, and we become victims of doubt and ambivalence.

The connection may also be broken by sheer fatigue. Civilized life is as complicated as juggling a dozen cups and saucers; in our frantic attempt not to break them, we often drive ourselves to the point of sheer exhaustion. Crime is an attempt to solve the problem by smashing the cups and saucers. That is, an attempt to reduce life to simplicity instead of trying to develop the self-control to cope with its complexity.

There is, of course, a less harmful way of reducing life to simplicity. In imagination, juggling a dozen cups and saucers becomes as easy as tossing a coin. In the past two thousand years, man has deliberately developed his imagination as a counterbalance to his tendency to left-brain obsessiveness. Imagination is a deliberate attempt to allow us to relax by short-circuiting reality. It offers a unique combination of relaxation and fulfilment. It also serves the important purpose of restoring our strength and courage. In short, it is an intoxicant. Samuel Richardson and Jean-Jacques Rousseau discovered that when imagination is combined with sexual desire, the result is twice as intoxicating. In *Fanny Hill*, John Cleland carried the process one stage farther, and distilled a kind of raw alcohol. Victorian prohibition turned this form of bootlegging into a major industry.

Sooner or later, the 'imaginary' sex crime was bound to be translated into reality. This began to happen towards the middle of the nineteenth century. In *Psychopathia Sexualis*, Krafft-Ebing mentions that between 1851 and 1875, 22,017 cases of rape came before the courts in France, that is to say, about nine hundred a year. He also mentions the astonishing fact that three-quarters of these involved children. It is possible, of course, that sexual offences against children were more frequently reported than those against adult women; even so, it seems clear that sexual violence in the nineteenth century was directed more at children than at adults. It was a question of 'forbiddenness'. In the streets of Victorian London or Paris, women were fairly easily available – not just prostitutes but (as we can see from *My Secret Life*) shopgirls, factory girls, maidservants. So the aura of 'forbiddenness' clung to children more than to adults. In the twentieth century, increased prosperity meant that an increasing number of working-class girls ceased to be sexually available; so the rape of adults increased.

What seems strange is that, in spite of this increase in the crime of rape, the Victorians were still slow at recognizing the sexual element in crimes involving sadism. On a Saturday afternoon in July 1867, three children were playing in a meadow near the town of Alton, Hampshire, when they were approached by a young man named Frederick Baker. Baker was known to be subject to depressive fits, and was the son of a man who had attacks of 'acute mania'; but he was generally regarded (according to the *Illustrated Police News*) as a 'young man of great respectability'. Baker gave the children a ha'penny each, and persuaded eight-year-old Fanny Adams to go for a walk. It was two hours before the children told Fanny's mother that she had gone off with Baker (whom they knew). She met Baker returning to the town, and asked him what he had done with her daughter; he seemed perfectly calm and self-possessed, and assured her that Fanny had gone off to buy sweets. It was many hours later that a search party found the body in a nearby hop garden; it had been hacked into fragments and scattered over a wide area. Baker was arrested; he continued to protest his innocence. But his diary was found to contain the entry; 'Killed a young girl today. It was fine and hot.' He was sentenced to death, and a huge crowd watched his hanging at Winchester gaol.

The *Illustrated Police News* was a scandal sheet that catered for the public appetite for gore and violence; it was full of hair-raising pictures of horrible murders and accidents: men hacking up corpses or being bitten in two by sharks. Yet its account has no hint that this is a sex crime. Not only does it omit to mention that the child's genitals were missing (which is perhaps understandable in a Victorian journal); it also says nothing about the crucial diary entry. So far as its reporter was concerned, Baker was simply suffering from an attack of 'mania'. (Krafft-Ebing added the sexual details in his account of the crime twenty years later.)

In fact, there are enough clues even in the *Illustrated Police News* account to enable us to play the detective and piece together the story. We observe, first of all, that when Baker met Mrs Adams he seemed perfectly calm, and there was no sign of blood on his clothes. Yet he should have been soaked in blood. This suggests that he removed all his clothes before killing the child – he had probably throttled her into unconsciousness. It also suggests premeditation. A man who has given way to a sadistic impulse on the spur of the moment would be shaken and frightened afterwards. Baker's calm suggests that he had thought this out in advance. Few sex killers commit a crime of this sort without either leading up to it with minor offences, or fantasizing about it long in advance. Since Alton was a small town, and there is no mention of previous offences – Baker was 'a young man of great respectability' – we may assume that he was a fantasist. He was a solicitor's clerk in a dull country town; his family background had probably been difficult – since his father suffered attacks of 'acute mania' – and he must have found life boring, frustrating and lonely. He is a paedophile, his sexual fantasies are sadistic, involving decapitation. (Fanny's head was the first part of her to be found.) He finally convinces himself that he can only achieve the kind of full sexual satisfaction he craves by killing a child. This is dangerous – in a small town – but he feels that the satisfaction will be worth the risk. He persuades Fanny to go with him, and completes the crime, finding it as satisfying as he had expected. ('It was fine and hot.') If he had not been caught, he would certainly have killed again. In fact, if he had taken the precaution of committing the crime in a city, where no one knew him, he would probably have killed many times, and England would have had its 'Jack the Ripper' twenty years earlier.

What made the Victorians incapable of understanding a crime like this was their rigid and inflexible idea of 'normality'. Even a man as intelligent as John Stuart Mill believed it ought to be possible to reason madmen out of their delusions; he felt that the delusions were *consciously held beliefs* – like the notion that the earth is flat. He was incapable of understanding the inner turmoil of a schizophrenic. In the same way, the average Victorian believed that the attraction of men for women and vice versa was a law of nature, like hunger and thirst and protection of offspring. So a man who felt sexual desires for members of his own sex must be wilfully perverse; he had *chosen* to be wicked, like a burglar or murderer. Lesbianism was not a crime under Victorian law because they held a fixed idea of the 'normality' of women; women were therefore incapable of anything as perverse as sexual desire for their own sex.

In short, the Victorians were crude realists in all matters pertaining to psychology – it was all part of their obsession with domesticity and security. Life had to be sane and predictable. As a result they failed to grasp that all experience is fifty per cent 'mental'. (And this explains why even intelligent Victorians found the philosophy of

Kant – which is based on this recognition – so difficult to understand.) In fact, experience varies greatly from day to day because of the varying amount we 'put into it'. I may do the same thing – say, take the identical walk – on two successive days, and feel bored and irritable one day, wide-awake and receptive the next; in which case, the scenery will strike me as *self-evidently* dreary one day, and delightful the next. Experience has to be chewed and swallowed and digested, just like food.

Lonely, frustrated men like Frederick Baker have a poor stomach for real experience, which they have learned to mistrust; it usually gives them indigestion. But in the nineteenth century, European man had stumbled upon the pleasures of the imagination. Poets and novelists used it to create an extraordinarily rich fantasy world, and fifteen-bob-a-week clerks used it to taste the pleasures of being a 'toff' and having ten thousand a year. But for a bored depressive like Baker, it could also be dangerous. As he fantasizes about women, he discovers that the sexual emotion can be sharply intensified by adding a dash of cruelty – say, tying her up and gagging her. As his imagination becomes accustomed to sexual aggression, he adds further refinements. Eventually, by Pavlovian conditioning, he associates sexual pleasure with the idea of violence – in Baker's case, apparently, decapitation and dismemberment. And one day, as his imagination again begins to flag, he begins to toy with the breathtaking idea of turning the fantasy into reality . . .

It is interesting to note how often this kind of extreme violence is associated with the sex crimes of this period. Four years after the murder of Fanny Adams, a young man named Eusebius Pieydagnelle gave himself up to the police in his native village of Vinuville, confessing to seven murders involving stabbing and mutilation. Since childhood he had lived opposite a butcher's shop and had become fascinated by the sight and smell of blood. He persuaded his parents to apprentice him to the butcher, a M. Cristobal, and enjoyed drinking blood and wounding the cattle. His father decided that he ought to have a more respectable profession and apprenticed him to a lawyer; Pieydagnelle plunged into depression. One day he crept into a room where a girl was sleeping, intending rape; then he noticed a kitchen knife, and felt a compulsion to stab her. He achieved orgasm at the sight of the blood, and went on to commit six more murders – his final victim being his ex-employer Cristobal.

In Italy in the same year – 1871 – the twenty-three-year-old Vincenz Verzeni committed two sex murders – of a fourteen-year-old girl and a twenty-eight-year-old married woman. Both were attacked in the fields and strangled; then the intestines and genitals were torn out. He was arrested after trying to strangle his cousin, a girl of nineteen, who succeeded in persuading him to let her go. Verzeni admitted that he began to experience sexual pleasure as soon as he began to choke a woman; in three earlier attempts he had achieved orgasm while pressing the throat, and allowed the victim to live.

In 1874, a fourteen-year-old youth named Jesse Pomeroy received an exceptionally savage sentence for the murder of two children – solitary confinement for the rest of his life. (In fact, he spent fifty-eight years in prison, dying in 1932.) Pomeroy was a tall, gangling boy with a hare lip, and one of his eyes was completely white. At the age of twelve, he had already been arrested for attacking two boys – he stripped both and flogged them with a rope end. He spent two years in a reformatory, and was out again in 1874. In March of that year, a ten-year-old girl named Katie Curran vanished from the area near Pomeroy's home in Boston. The following month, a four-year-old boy was found dead with thirty-one knife wounds. The police searched Jesse Pomeroy's house and found a knife with blood on it; a further search revealed the body of Katie Curran buried in the cellar. Pomeroy admitted that he derived pleasure from torturing children. His crimes aroused the same kind of widespread horror as those of Jack the Ripper in London the following decade and – like the Ripper murders – were the subject of much exaggeration. An account in *Boston Murders*, edited by John Makris (New York, 1948) says he committed twenty-seven murders. *Knife, Rope and Chair* by Guy Logan (London, 1930) mentions more than a dozen. There were acrimonious discussions about whether Pomeroy was insane, or merely subject to 'blood lust'. Yet at the time it occurred to no one that the crimes were sexual.

In April 1880, a four-year-old girl named Louise Dreux disappeared in the Grenelle quarter of Paris. The following day, neighbours complained to the police about an unpleasant black smoke pouring from the chimney of a retarded twenty-year-old youth named Louis Menesclou, who lived on the top floor of the same building as the Dreux family. They entered his room and looked in the stove; a child's head and entrails were burning there. In Menesclou's pockets they found both the child's forearms. Menesclou admitted killing her, and sleeping with the body under his mattress overnight. He indignantly denied raping the girl, but became embarrassed when asked why the genitals were missing. A poem found in a notebook began 'I saw her, I took her', and talked about 'the joy of an instant'. Menesclou was executed. The similarities to the Frederick Baker case are striking.

It was the Jack the Ripper murders of 1888 that made the world suddenly aware of the emergence of a new type of crime. We have already noted that they were not generally recognized as sex crimes – there was still a tendency to regard the killer simply as a homicidal maniac. (Zola based a novel, *The Human Beast*, on the murders, and the title summarizes the contemporary attitude to the Ripper: he was a human being with the appetites of a tiger.) But from the fact that the victims were prostitutes, and that the killer left them naked from the waist down, it was impossible not to realize instinctively that some form of twisted sexuality was involved. The murders caused such a sense of outrage because there was an obscure feeling that the killer had somehow 'broken the rules' – as we might feel if terrorists started bombing schools.

For the Ripper himself, the sense of outrage he caused was an obvious motivation; in the two letters that are generally accepted as genuine, he gloats over the murders, and heads one of the letters 'From Hell'. The idea of this 'human beast' prowling the streets made everyone shudder; he *wanted* to make everyone shudder. In fact, he was probably a shy, repressed, sensitive little man – like Richard Speck, the killer of eight nurses in Chicago in 1966, or the Boston Strangler, or the Yorkshire Ripper, Peter Sutcliffe – for whom this slashing and stabbing was an orgasmic release from his usual sense of inferiority and 'ambivalence'.

It is a reasonable assumption that Jack the Ripper would have lost his legendary status if he had been caught and tried. The 'French Ripper', Joseph Vacher, *was* caught and executed; so that although his crimes were very similar to those of Jack the Ripper, he never achieved anything like the same notoriety. Vacher, born in 1869, was given to fits of sudden violence. But what emerged at his trial in 1897 was that he was another self-pitying, oversensitive 'outsider', whose crimes were partly motivated by resentment towards a world that he felt had treated him badly. He blamed all his troubles on being bitten by a mad dog at the age of eight, but this seems to have been merely an excuse. At one point he became devoutly religious and entered a monastery; but he was thrown out for making sexual advances to other novices. In the army, during his national service, he was so upset when his promotion to corporal failed to materialize that he tried to cut his throat. Discharged on medical grounds, he proposed to a young girl, and when she refused him, tried to kill her and himself. He only wounded her, and a bullet that entered his own right ear made him deaf and paralysed the facial muscles on that side. He was committed to an asylum, and discharged as cured in April 1894. It was at this point that he became a tramp, and began to commit sex murders. On 20 May 1894, he encountered a twenty-year-old girl, Eugenie Delhomme, near Besançon, and throttled her unconscious. He then cut her throat, severed the right breast, and trampled on her belly; after this, he had intercourse with the body. She was the first of eleven victims, five of them boys. Most of these were disembowelled, and, in many cases, he removed the genitals. On 4 August 1897, he attacked a woman gathering pinecones in the Bois des Pelleries; she proved to be stronger than he expected, and her shouts brought her husband and children, who overpowered Vacher. He was taken to a local inn, where he played his accordion until the police arrived, and realized that he was the black-bearded tramp who was suspected of being the 'Ripper of the south-east'. But witnesses failed to identify him, and he was only sentenced to three months for indecent assault. In prison, he wrote to his judges, confessing to the series of mutilation murders of the past three years. In spite of his insistence that he was insane, a panel of doctors judged him to be of sound mind, and he was executed in December 1898. Vacher's trial might have excited more attention had not the Dreyfus trial been taking place at the same time.

While Vacher was still being tried, two schoolgirls disappeared on their way home from school in the village of Lechtingen, near Osnabrück. The bodies were later found in nearby woods. The limbs had been amputated and the intestines scattered over a wide area. A travelling carpenter named Ludwig Tessnow came under suspicion, and was taken in for questioning. He insisted that various stains on his clothes were brown wood-stain, and was released.

Three years later, on the Baltic island of Rügen, two young

brothers vanished. Their remains were also found in nearby woods, the limbs hacked off and the intestines scattered. The next day, a woman reported to the police that she had seen the children talking to the carpenter Tessnow, who lived in the village of Baabe and who had only just returned from his wanderings around Germany. Tessnow was arrested, and spots resembling dried blood were found on his clothes – there had been some attempt to wash them off. Tessnow again insisted that they were wood-stain. This reminded the examining magistrate of the Lechtingen murder of September 1898, and he sent to Osnabrück to enquire the name of the suspect who had been held; when he found that it was Tessnow, he had no doubt that he had caught the killer of the two boys. He also recalled that, shortly after Tessnow had returned in June 1901, half a dozen sheep had been killed and mutilated in a field on Rügen.

But there was no concrete evidence against Tessnow. At this point, the prosecutor heard that a young doctor named Paul Uhlenhuth, of the University of Griefswald, had discovered a test that would not only distinguish blood from other substances, but could actually distinguish the type of blood; the test depended on the defensive properties that are developed by blood when it is injected with foreign protein. Tessnow's clothes were sent to Uhlenhuth, who cut out various stains and dissolved them in salt water. His test showed conclusively that the stains on the clothes were not wood-stain; they were of blood – both human and sheep's. This evidence was conclusive. Tessnow was executed.

The most striking thing about the cases mentioned above is their sadistic violence. It seems odd that so many of the major sex crimes in the latter half of the nineteenth century should involve this frenzy. The answer undoubtedly lies in the social attitudes of the period. At most levels of society, relations between men and women were stiff and formal. So when sheer sexual lust overcame these inhibitions, the result was a violent explosion that went beyond mere rape.

Of course, there *were* a large number of ordinary rapes, and no doubt it would be possible to disinter these from the police court records of the time. But they were not recorded by writers of crime (such as Major Arthur Griffiths, whose *Mysteries of the Police and Crime* is still the best general introduction to nineteenth century villainy.) Thomas S. Duke's *Celebrated Criminal Cases of America* is the American equivalent of the *Newgate Calendar*, and was published as late as 1910; yet among its hundred or so cases, there are only three sex crimes. In all three, we observe this same 'explosive' element. One is the case of Jesse Pomeroy, already described. Another concerned a 'degenerate' named Hadley, who lured a fifteen-year-old girl to a rented house, claiming he needed a baby sitter; she was raped and 'frightfully mutilated'. The crime was obviously carefully planned – the house had been specially rented – and Hadley was never caught.

The third case is in some ways the most typical. In 1895, twenty-four-year-old Theodore Durrant was a Sunday school superintendent and a prominent member of the Emanuel Baptist Church in San Francisco. He was also in his final year at the Cooper Medical College. He was deeply interested in pretty, twenty-one-year-old Blanche Lamont, a highly religious girl who 'seldom went to places of amusement'. On 3 April 1895, Miss Lamont left her cookery class and accompanied Durrant to the Emanuel Baptist Church on Bartlett Street. He had the church keys. There he strangled her, and dragged her body up to the belfry, where he stripped and, presumably, raped her. (When the body was later examined, decomposition made it impossible to be specific about this.) He placed two small wooden blocks under her head as a pillow, crossed her hands on her breasts, and left her. He had been alone in the church with her for more than an hour. Downstairs he encountered the church organist, nineteen-year-old George King, a close friend. King observed that Durrant looked pale and shaken. Durrant explained that he had been searching for a gas leak, and had been almost overpowered by escaping gas. King sympathetically went off to buy a bottle of bromo-seltzer; but the story of the gas leak puzzled him, for he could smell no gas, and he knew that plumbers had checked all the fittings recently.

Blanche's disappearance caused wide excitement; but no one suspected Durrant, whose piety seemed to place him above reproach. Durrant confided to Blanche's aunt and uncle – with whom she lived – that he suspected she had allowed herself to be lured to a 'house of ill-repute'; he even made sure he was seen travelling to outlying areas, searching for her.

One week after the murder of Blanche Lamont, Durrant persuaded twenty-year-old Minnie Williams – another regular churchgoer – to accompany him into the church library. What happened next can be tentatively reconstructed from medical evidence. Durrant went out of the room, and reappeared naked. Then he grabbed Minnie, pulled her skirt over her head, and rammed the cloth into her mouth to choke her screams. He raped her, then took a knife and slashed and stabbed her so violently that blood spurted over the walls. When the blade broke off in her breast, he raped her again. Then he went to a meeting of young church members – which Minnie had been due to attend – arriving two hours late. At midnight, after the meeting, he went back to the church again; what he did there will never be known.

Early next morning, Durrant left San Francisco to do some training with the state militia. Women who went to decorate the church for Easter Sunday found Minnie's mutilated body in the library; the dress had been rammed down the throat so violently that the medical examiner had difficulty in pulling it out. Police searched the rest of the building and found Blanche Lamont's body, looking 'white as marble'; but downstairs in the church, it quickly turned black and began to decompose, so the doctor was unable to say whether – or how often – she had been raped.

Durrant was arrested. His friends and colleagues were simply unable to believe that he could be the murderer; they insisted that he was a 'good man'. But a reporter discovered that another young lady, a Miss Annie Welming, had narrowly escaped becoming a rape victim. She had gone into the church library with Durrant, who had left her alone. Then he walked in, naked, and the girl had screamed and fled.

Many witnesses had seen both girls with Durrant just before they disappeared. His appeals lasted for three years, but he was eventually hanged in 1898. The case caused a sensation all over America, and was reported in European newspapers (an indication that sex crime was still a rarity).

Durrant's case provides us with a great deal of insight into 'Victorian' sex crime. There is no reason to suppose that his supporters, who regarded him as a 'good man', were mistaken. All the indications suggest that he was genuinely religious. One close friend – and fellow student – testified that Durrant had certainly been 'pure' up until two years before, since they had discussed the matter at length. The story of Annie Welming suggests that he was an exhibitionist with a compulsive desire to appear naked in front of women. (Miss Welming told a friend about her experience, and there was some gossip; however, Durrant's reputation stood so high that it soon died away.)

This in turn suggests that he knew precisely what he intended to do on the day he took Blanche to the church. He had even established an alibi, asking a friend to answer his name in the roll-call at the medical school. Blanche and he had been 'keeping company' for some time; at one point, she had refused to speak to him for several weeks after he made some kind of advance. The evidence suggests that he wanted her badly. She was prim and respectable and would allow no 'liberties'. On 3 April 1895, he decided that the pleasure of throwing off all his sexual inhibitions and frustrations was worth the risk. When he walked in naked, she probably screamed; he throttled and raped her. Then he carried the body up to the belfry and undressed it. He spent a considerable time – at least half an hour – alone with the body. He may have hinted to Minnie Williams that he had killed Blanche – a witness testified that Minnie had said 'she knew too much' about Blanche's disappearance. It is even possible that Durrant lured Minnie to the church to silence her. If so, the temptation of being alone in the church with a pretty girl was too great. The clothes Durrant was seen wearing on the day of Minnie's disappearance had no bloodstains, which suggests not only that he took them off before stabbing her, but that he took them off in another room, since her blood spurted so far. Marks on Minnie's neck showed that she had been throttled unconscious before the dress was thrust down her throat; at this point, she must still have been alive. After raping her, Durrant was still in such a frenzy that he slashed and stabbed her until the knife broke off in her breast. The medical examiner testified that there was evidence that Durrant then raped her again – although this could have happened when he returned at midnight.

The Durrant case, then, is a textbook Victorian sex crime, and it makes us aware of the inhibitions and frustrations that caused the element of explosive violence in so many cases of the period. Most young men – and women – are biologically prepared for sexual intercourse from the age of thirteen or so, and experience sexual curiosity many years earlier than that. In an age when even a glimpse of a woman's ankle was regarded as sexually provocative, the frustration of young men must have been enormous. In *My Life and Loves*, Frank Harris describes how, as a child, he used to allow the pencil to roll under the table so that he could crawl on all fours and look at the girls' legs. But when he mentions seeing 'the legs up to the knees', we realize that they wore long skirts; it was their ankles and calves that caused Harris so much excitement.

It is clear, therefore, why sex crime suddenly made its appearance in the second half of the nineteenth century: it was due to a combination of imagination – fed by the new habit of novel-reading – and of frustration due to Victorian prudery. Suddenly, sex was no longer the down-to-earth occupation it had been for Cleland and Boswell; it had become something to brood about and gloat about. Baudelaire remarked that unless sex was sinful, then it was boring and meaningless; what he meant was that, in the crucible of the imagination, sex could be turned into something that was at once wicked and delicious. In the works of the new 'sexologists' such as Krafft-Ebing and Havelock Ellis, we read of various kinds of fetishism – of men who were sexually excited by women's shoes, stays, knickers, aprons, even crutches. The sheer pressure of desire had imbued these objects with sexual 'magic'. Havelock Ellis himself had once seen his mother urinating in Regent's Park, and for the rest of his life, wrote poetically about 'golden streams' and persuaded his mistresses to urinate in front of him.

All this explains why, although Victorian prudery was fast disappearing by the year 1901 (when Queen Victoria died), the problem of sex crime showed no sign of going away. It is true that the old, morbid sense of 'forbiddenness' gradually leaked away as sex became a subject that could be discussed openly, and that one result was that violent sex crimes – like those of the Ripper and Vacher – became increasingly rare. But there could be no return to the realistic sexual attitudes of Defoe and Cleland. For better or worse, sex had been taken over by the human imagination.

This meant, of course, that sex had become slightly unreal. Shakespeare idealized Juliet; but he knew precisely what she was like as a human being. The heroines of Dickens and Thackeray and Wilkie Collins lack a whole dimension of reality. 'Professor' Joad once remarked that he became interested in women when he discovered they were not solid below the waist. The Victorian novelists give the impression that their heroines *are* solid from the waist down (no wonder 'Walter' found it impossible to imagine them having female organs like his cousins). So the new sexual frankness – and the alarming theories of Professor Freud – made no real impact on the romanticism of the Edwardians. They continued to be avidly interested in seduction and adultery, even when they were convinced they were being shocked.

Newspaper proprietors – like William Randolph Hearst – soon made the discovery that sex sells newspapers; so the public had to be told the details of every divorce scandal. Murder cases involving adultery received headline treatment for as long as the case lasted. In America in 1904, the sensation of the year was the trial of *Floradora* girl Nan Patterson for shooting her lover in a hansom cab when he announced he was leaving her (she claimed it was suicide). In 1906, journalists labelled the murder of architect Stanford White 'the crime of the century'; White was shot by a rich playboy named Harry Thaw, who had discovered that his wife – another *Floradora* girl – had been White's mistress. Both were utterly commonplace crimes of passion; but they had the necessary element of adultery and glamour.

Even glamour was not essential; it was the sex that mattered. The sensation of 1908 was the case of the sinister Belle Gunness of Indiana, who advertised for husbands and then murdered them. 1910 was a good year. In London, Dr Crippen was tried for the murder of his wife (yet another ex-showgirl); he dismembered her and eloped with his mistress, who was disguised as a boy. In Venice, there was the trial of Countess Marie Tarnowska, who had persuaded one lover to murder another in order to collect his insurance money and run away with a third. We would now describe her as a scheming nymphomaniac; but a contemporary book about her calls her 'the strange Russian woman whose hand slew no man, but whose beauty drove those who loved her to commit murder for her sake.' (Even Belle Gunness, who weighed twenty stone and whose features were distinctly porcine is depicted in contemporary sketches as slim and beautiful.)

But a case of 1913 revealed that a genuine sex crime could eclipse all other scandals. On a Saturday morning in April, fourteen-year-old Mary Phagan went to collect her wages from a pencil factory in Atlanta, Georgia; on her way out, she called at the ladies' toilet in the basement, where a negro named Jim Conley was sleeping off a hangover. The next day, her body was found in the basement, her dress around her waist, and a cord knotted round her throat so tightly that it disappeared into the flesh. She also had teeth marks on her bare shoulder. Two notes lay by the body, stating that she had been attacked by 'a tall, sleam negro' – an obvious attempt to throw suspicion on the nightwatchman who found the body. (Conley was short and squat.)

The manager of the pencil factory, a Jew named Leo Frank, was arrested. Conley at first escaped suspicion by asserting that he could not read or write; later, when it was proved that he could do both, he insisted that Leo Frank had made him write the notes on the day before the murder. Oddly enough, the citizens of Atlanta preferred to believe that a Jew was guilty; public indignation would not be satisfied with the mere hanging of a negro. Negros were lynched every day on the slightest pretext – in the week after Mary Phagan's murder, one was lynched for firing off a gun when drunk, one for speaking disrespectfully to a white man, and one for ogling Sunday-school mistresses at a picnic. In 1906, an unfounded rumour that blacks had killed two white women led to some of the worst race riots in American history, and many black men, women and children were killed by a rampaging white mob. If one white life was worth a dozen blacks, then obviously there was no mathematical logic in arresting a black for Mary Phagan's murder; a Jew made an altogether more satisfactory culprit.

It was the newspapers who were mainly responsible for Frank's eventual conviction. They discovered that the public appetite for stories about the Phagan murder was insatiable; any new fact about the case would sell 'extras'. If facts were lacking, they could be invented – like the story that the walls of Frank's office were covered with photographs of nude girls. If they pointed in the wrong direction – for example the discovery that the bite marks on Mary Phagan were not made by Frank's teeth – they were ignored. For over two years, the Phagan story went on selling newspapers, until the day in August 1915 when Frank was dragged from jail by a lynch mob and hanged on a tree near Mary Phagan's home. Even then, public interest remained as strong as ever; there were several books about the case, and three movies. The death of Mary Phagan touched some chord of public morbidity, like the murder of Maria

Marten a century earlier. But in Maria's case, it was the brutality that shocked; in Mary Phagan's, it was the thought of rape. It is something of an anticlimax to learn that the medical evidence showed the assault was never completed, and she remained a virgin.

It seems somehow symbolic that the Frank case occurred on the eve of the First World War. It was the war that swept away the last vestiges of the Victorian outlook, and introduced our modern age of violence.

In fact, the violence had been gathering for more than three decades.

Two

REVOLT

On 1 March 1881, the tsar of Russia, Alexander II, was returning to the palace after an inspection of his troops. In his pocket he was carrying a document that he had worked out with his advisers: a tentative plan for some kind of Russian parliament – the first step towards the English style of representative government. Although Alexander had freed the serfs, socialist agitation was increasing, and in the previous year, an anarchist bomb had destroyed the dining room of the Winter Palace a few minutes before the tsar and his family came in for dinner. Now, at last, he was prepared to relinquish a little of his absolute power.

As a precaution, the carriage was returning to the palace by an unaccustomed route. Suddenly, there was a tremendous explosion. The carriage rocked, and its door was blown in, but the tsar was unharmed. Shakily, he looked out, and saw a man and a boy lying in the road, both bleeding. Alexander was a kindly man; he got out of the carriage to see whether they were badly injured. As he did so, there was another tremendous explosion – so great that it smashed the windows many streets away. The tsar was hurled on to his face, both his legs shattered. The bomb had been made of nitro-glycerine enclosed in a glass ball, and it had killed the assassin and twenty bystanders. Fragments of bloody flesh hung from trees and lamp-posts. The tsar was rushed back to his palace; an hour later, he died.

The assassin belonged to a group who called themselves Narodniki, or the Party of the People's Will. They were followers of the revolutionary Michael Bakunin – who had been Marx's chief rival for leadership of the First International and had been out-manoeuvred by Marx. Bakunin, in turn, was a follower of Pierre Joseph Proudhon – Marx's pet detestation and the man who invented the phrase 'property is theft'. It was Proudhon, in fact, who had coined the word 'anarchy', meaning the opposite of hierarchy: no government. But as this came to be used as a synonym for chaos, its devotees preferred to use the form 'anarchism'. Bakunin had died in 1876, a disillusioned and disappointed man – 'a Columbus who had never seen his America' as his friend Alexander Herzen put it.

The Marxists believed that socialism would come about of its own accord, as the rotten structure of capitalism collapsed. The anarchists were less optimistic. They were firmly convinced of the basic goodness of human nature, of man's ability to live in peace with his fellows in an ideal world. But in the meantime, power was in the hands of kings and police chiefs. And, since they were determined to hold on to it, the only way to bring about the Revolution was to 'remove' these enemies of the people. Even the gentle Prince Peter Kropotkin, who had been converted to anarchism out of the goodness of his heart, had begun to preach bombs and bullets in the late 1870s: 'A single deed is better propaganda than a thousand pamphlets.' And in the 1870s, the anarchists had made four unsuccessful attempts on crowned heads: two on Wilhelm I of Germany, one on the king of Spain and one on the king of Italy. The assassination of Tsar Alexander II was their first major success. It was also a signal for a period of total repression in Russia. The police swooped; revolutionaries were arrested by the dozen, and either hanged or thrown into the Peter and Paul fortress. Censorship was reintroduced. The new tsar, Alexander III, detested the very word reform, and made a determined attempt to put back the clock to the days of Peter the Great. But it meant that he became virtually a prisoner in his own palace. He died prematurely in 1894, and was succeeded by his son Nicholas II, who was to be the last of the tsars.

Anarchism arrived in America in the late 1870s, and the city where it found most response was Chicago, a minor trading post that had turned into a major city overnight with the wealth from blast furnaces and cattle stockyards. It was full of immigrants, and the new entrepreneurs, true to the methods of their British counter-parts, paid starvation wages. (Even three decades later, conditions were still so bad that an accurate description of the Chicago stockyards in Upton Sinclair's novel *The Jungle* (1906) shocked the whole nation.) The result was that the workers tried to form trade unions, the bosses tried to break their strikes with blacklegs, and Chicago was in continual industrial ferment. A German immigrant, August Spies, founded a German-language anarchist newspaper

called the *Arbeiter-Zeitung* – Workers Times – and urged the workers
to stand up for their rights. He became particularly embittered when
his brother was shot dead by a policeman for 'creating a disturbance'
at a picnic, and cried in his newspaper: 'Revenge! Revenge!
Workingmen to arms!' There was mob violence on 3 May 1886, when
police and strikers clashed in front of the McCormick Harvester
Company, and the following morning, the *Arbeiter-Zeitung* announced that there would be a mass meeting in the Haymarket that evening
at 7.30. By 8 o'clock, three thousand people had assembled, and were
listening to an inflammatory speech by Spies, urging them to arm
themselves to meet the aggression of government hirelings. When
another anarchist began to shout: 'Kill the law, exterminate the
capitalists, and do it tonight,' the police decided it was time to
intervene. The police chief ordered the mob to disperse. At that
moment, a large black bomb went whizzing through the air, hissing
like a skyrocket, and there was an explosion that could be heard far
away. The police began to shoot. So did the crowd. When the mob
finally dispersed, the anarchists carrying away their dead and
wounded, it was found that seven policemen had been killed by the
explosion. The police swooped on the office of the *Arbeiter-Zeitung*
and five men were arrested, including Spies. Two days later, the
police located a bomb factory; one of the men they arrested claimed
that the anarchists had planned to bomb all the Chicago police stations
simultaneously. The bomb maker, Louis Lingg, was also arrested. In
August, eight anarchists were tried; seven were sentenced to death,
the other to fifteen years in prison.

The verdict was obviously a miscarriage of justice in the sense that
no one knew who had thrown the bomb. Splinters removed from dead
policemen suggest that it was of the same type as those manufactured
by Lingg. But there was no proof that any of the eight had been in any
way responsible for the deaths of the seven policemen. However, the
jury was in no mood for this kind of legal hairsplitting; as far as they
were concerned, the American way of life was being threatened by
homicidal maniacs who were taking advantage of American freedom
of speech. Lingg succeeded in committing suicide in his cell with a
capsule of fulminate – the explosive that detonates a bullet – and four
others, including Spies, were hanged the next day. Lingg had written
with his own blood 'Long live anarchy!' in his cell. The two other
condemned men had their sentences commuted to prison terms.

Now that anarchism had martyrs, the movement became more powerful. Their basic mythology – that rulers and 'bosses' were criminals who had robbed the working man – was pure 'magical' thinking, a thin rationalization of the 'xenophobia' of primitive tribes. Their basic philosophy – that when the rulers had been murdered, men would live together in perfect harmony – was completely untenable. We have seen how the Fielding brothers halted the crime wave in eighteenth-century London with a few Bow Street runners and horse patrols, and how it instantly started up again when the patrols were withdrawn. But the anarchists insisted that police were only necessary because of poverty, and that as soon as the Revolution had destroyed all authority, there would be more than enough of everything for everybody; people would only have to go and help themselves from the goods taken from the rich. As to work, five hours a day would be enough to support everybody in comfort . . . No one even suggested that if everybody was allowed to help themselves, the warehouses containing the goods of the rich would soon be empty; that would have been regarded as a libel on the nature of the poor. But Bernard Shaw sounded a note of realism in a Fabian pamphlet when he asked how, if human nature was so perfect, the oppression and corruption had arisen in the first place.

Anarchist disturbances came to France in the early 1890s. On May Day 1891, three anarchists were arrested for taking part in a demonstration and badly beaten up by the police. At their trial, the prosecuting attorney demanded the death sentence – an absurd demand, since the men were only accused of incitement to violence. The judge was more reasonable; he acquitted one, and sentenced the others to three and five years respectively. In the following year, there was an explosion at the home of the judge, which demolished a stairway but fortunately injured no one. Two weeks later, the home of the prosecuting lawyer was blown up. A left-wing professor who was arrested after the first explosion – and no doubt subjected to the vigorous interrogation methods of the French police – admitted that he had planned the attack, but said that it had been carried out by a man named Ravachol. This Ravachol, it seemed, was already known to the police – not as a political revolutionary, but as a burglar and suspected murderer. His real name was Konigstein, and he was believed to have killed four people – an old man and three old women – in the course of robberies.

On the evening of the attack on the home of the prosecutor, a gaunt, bearded man in his forties had dinner at the Restaurant Véry on the Boulevard Magenta, and talked to the waiter, a man named Lhérot, about the explosion – which no one yet knew about. When the same man came back two days later, Lhérot tipped off the police and he was arrested. But was he Ravachol? Fortunately, the police had a new method of identification, invented by a police clerk named Bertillon. He believed that certain measurements were unique – the circumference of the head, length of hand, foot and so on – and had talked the police into giving his system a trial. Konigstein-Ravachol had been briefly under arrest after the murder of an old miser at his hut in the forest, but released for lack of evidence: however, Bertillon had taken his measurements at the time. They now proved that this man who had talked of bombing *was* Ravachol himself. (As a result, Bertillon became world-famous, and his system was adopted by every major police force in the world – only to be replaced in a few years by fingerprinting.)

The waiter Lhérot talked a little too triumphantly about his part in the arrest; the evening before the trial, there was a bomb explosion at the restaurant, which killed the proprietor, Lhérot's brother-in-law.

Ravachol himself was a figure who gave the French public nightmares. Born forty-two years earlier, he had become the bread-winner of the family when his father – named Koenigstein – had deserted them when his son was eight. Like Troppmann, he became devoted to Eugene Sue's *Wandering Jew*, and its revelations of the wickedness of the Jesuits had turned him into an atheist. When he became interested in anarchism, both he and a younger brother were dismissed by their employer. He watched the family starve – his young sister died – and dreamed of revenge. He took up robbery to supplement his income. He felt no remorse about his four victims because, he said, they were 'middle class'.

The explosion in the restaurant intimidated the judges, and they sentenced Ravachol to a prison term – although bombing was a capital offence. But when the police were able to produce evidence for the four other murders, Ravachol was tried again and sentenced to death. He cried 'I shall be avenged!'

In November of that year, a bomb was found in the Paris office of a mining company that was involved in a strike; a policeman

political terrorist crime

carefully carried it off to the local station, where it exploded, killing five. Paris, suddenly, was thrown into panic; restaurants suffered as no one dared to venture into one. There was a rumour that the anarchists intended to poison the city's reservoirs. But many of the younger poets and painters revelled in all the excitement and declared their support for anarchism.

In December 1893, another embittered member of the unemployed, August Vaillant, who had been put out on to the streets at the age of twelve, threw a bomb in the Chamber of Deputies. It was a small bomb, intended to alarm rather than kill. A poet named Laurent Tailhade was enthusiastic, and exclaimed: 'What does it matter about the victims if it is a fine gesture?' The judges disagreed, and Vaillant was executed. A week later, a bomb exploded in the restaurant of the Gare St-Lazare, killing one and injuring twenty. Two more explosions in Paris streets killed only one passer-by; and when a bomb exploded in the pocket of a Belgian anarchist named Jean Pauwels, killing him, he was found to be responsible for the two street explosions. A bomb in the Restaurant Foyot put out the eye of the poet Laurent Tailhade. The man who was finally arrested and tried for the Gare St-Lazare explosion, Emile Henry, said it was aimed against the bourgeoisie who could afford to eat in restaurants.

On 24 June 1894, the president of France, Sadi Carnot, was driving in an open carriage through the streets of Lyons, where he was visiting an exhibition; he told the police to allow people to approach him if they wanted to. A young man holding a rolled-up newspaper stepped forward, then removed a knife from the newspaper and plunged it into Carnot's stomach, shouting 'Vive la révolution! Vive l'anarchie!' He proved to be a young Italian, Santo Caserio. Carnot died soon after. Caserio was executed shouting 'Vive l'anarchie!'

The anarchist scare in France ended abruptly. The government put thirty anarchists on trial, accused of conspiracy. The jury refused to be stampeded, and acquitted them all, except three burglars. This rational gesture deprived the anarchists of more martyrs and took the steam out of their propaganda. Besides, leaders of the movement, such as Kropotkin and Malatesta, were already beginning to doubt the wisdom of violence when it attracted undesirables like Ravachol. The French socialist movement became theoretical once again.

In America, two events helped to take some of the bitterness out of the anarchist struggle. The most articulate and passionate spokesman of revolution, Johann Most (who had been expelled from Germany for liberalism, then from England for praising the Irishmen who assassinated Lord Frederick Cavendish in Phoenix Park, Dublin) suddenly announced that he had ceased to support 'the propaganda of the deed'; he denounced a young anarchist named Alexander Berkman who had made an attempt to kill the manager of the Carnegie Steel Works during a strike. The denunciation may have been prompted by the fact that Berkman had supplanted Most as the lover of a young Jewish revolutionary, Emma Goldman; nevertheless, it influenced large numbers of American anarchists. Then the governor of Illinois, John P. Altgeld, re-examined the case of the Chicago anarchists and announced that the jury had been 'packed' with men who were specially chosen to convict. Altgeld's motives were also not entirely disinterested – he had a personal grudge against Judge Cary, who had been in charge of the trial. Altgeld was defeated at the next election; but his gesture helped to restore the good name of American justice, and to undermine the anarchists' insistence that everyone in authority was a crook.

In Spain, it was a grimmer story. The Spaniards are strangers to moderation. In January 1892, there was a minor peasants' revolt in Andalusia. Farmworkers marched to try and free four men who had been imprisoned for taking part in labour agitations ten years before; police broke them up and four ringleaders were killed by garrotting. In September 1893, the Spanish prime minister, Martinez de Campos, was attacked by an anarchist as he reviewed troops in Barcelona; two bombs thrown by a man named Pallas killed his horse and six people, but left him only bruised. Pallas was garrotted. Seven weeks later, two bombs were thrown in a theatre in Barcelona, causing panic and leaving twenty-two dead and fifty injured. The police now began to make indiscriminate arrests – the figure ran into thousands – and tortured suspects to extort confessions. Seven people confessed and were executed, including the man who had admitted the theatre bombing.

In June 1896, a bomb was thrown at a religious procession in Barcelona, killing eleven and injuring forty. The premier, Antonio Canovas del Castillo, ordered more mass arrests and torture. Four suspected terrorists were executed, seventy-six sentenced to prison terms. An account of the tortures published in a Paris newspaper caused an international outcry. In August 1897, Castillo was taking a holiday at a spa in the Basque mountains when he was approached by a pleasant-looking blond young man, who produced a revolver and killed him. Madame de Castillo hurled herself on him screaming 'Assassin.' 'I am not an assassin,' replied the young man gravely, 'I am an avenger.' He was in due course garrotted.

In September 1898, the empress Elizabeth of Austria, wife of the emperor Franz Joseph, was stabbed to death by a young Italian named Lucheni. He had remarked to a fellow workman: 'Ah, how I'd like to kill somebody. But it must be somebody important, so it gets in the papers.'

The next victim was the last of the nineteenth century. King Humbert of Italy had escaped one assassination attempt in 1897, when a man tried to stab him in his carriage; he moved too quickly. But in July 1900 he was distributing prizes to athletes in Monza when a man stepped up to the carriage and killed him with four revolver shots. The assassin was an Italian named Bresci, who had travelled from America. He was sentenced to life imprisonment – since Italy had no death penalty – but committed suicide in prison.

In America, an unbalanced young Polish immigrant named Leon Czolgosz carried a clipping about the assassination of King Humbert wherever he went. He attended anarchist meetings, but seemed so muddled and strange that the comrades suspected him of being a police agent. In September 1901, Czolgosz stood in a line in Buffalo, New York State, to shake hands with President McKinley, who was visiting the American Exposition. He shot McKinley, who died eight days later. McKinley was the third American president to die at the hands of an assassin, the previous two being Abraham Lincoln and James Garfield – the latter shot by an unbalanced religious maniac named Charles Guiteau who liked to describe himself as the premier of England. Czolgosz was electrocuted, although one psychiatrist diagnosed him as suffering from delusions. And McKinley's successor, Theodore Roosevelt, pushed Congress into amending the Immigration Act to exclude anyone who taught disbelief in or opposition to organized government.

In England they had the good sense not to get too excited about anarchism. This was perhaps due to the fact that the English have never shown much interest in ideas, unable to accept that they could make the slightest practical difference. So every variety of anarchist and revolutionary was able to find refuge in London, and be reasonably sure of receiving only minimum surveillance from the police. The club in Berner Street in which Jack the Ripper committed the first of his double-murders was a well-known meeting place for foreign revolutionaries, one of many in London. Because they were allowed to talk as much as they liked about violent revolution, they made no attempt to practise it. The only 'anarchist outrage' of the 1890s in London was an attempt by a feeble-minded youth, Martial Bourdin, to blow up the Greenwich Observatory (February 1892); the bomb exploded prematurely, blowing him to pieces, but the Observatory was untouched. Eighteen years later, in December 1910, a group of Russian anarchists broke into a jeweller's shop in Houndsditch, east London, and opened fire when the police knocked on the door, killing three policemen. A nationwide man-hunt led to the arrest of several of the gang, and in early January of the following year, two more members were surrounded by police at a house in Sidney Street. After an all-night siege and a shooting match that lasted all morning, the house burst into flames and both anarchists were burnt to death. Even this failed to provoke the government into trying to suppress anarchist ideas. So in England, the ideals of anarchism faded away gently, suffocated by the British failure to take them seriously. In Spain, where repression continued (and another premier, Canelejas, was assassinated in 1912), they lived on, to play a major role in the civil war of the 1930s.

The anarchists were not entirely mistaken to believe that governments have been responsible for some of the world's worst problems. But they failed to grasp that it is not a question of individual wickedness; merely of policies that, at the time, struck honest men as reasonable. The blame for 'the horrifying sense of sin manifest in the conduct of human affairs' cannot be laid at the door of a few wicked individuals, or even a few thousand. England is an interesting case in point. By 1900, the British empire was several times larger than the Roman empire had ever been. But the British did not regard themselves as conquerors; merely as a civilizing influence, like missionaries. The upper-class Englishman of the 1890s saw himself reflected fairly accurately in Conan Doyle's portrait of Dr Watson: decent, honest, not very bright, but infinitely loyal. He would have found it difficult to believe that the empire's foreign subjects saw him as an oppressor and exploiter.

Yet this, in practical terms, is what the British were. In Ireland, there had been political problems since the time of Henry VIII, when England became Protestant and Ireland remained Catholic. The English solution to every outbreak of dissatisfaction was to send an army to massacre the Irish. They called this 'pacification'. The *Encyclopaedia Britannica* remarks: 'Ireland was now so "pacified" that even in the year of the Armada it scarcely moved.'

In 1607, the old Irish earls fled in disgust and died abroad, and the English decided to try a radical solution: taking Ulster away from the Irish and settling English Protestants there. In 1641 the Irish rebelled again and massacred the Protestants in Ulster. Eight years later, Cromwell went to Ireland and massacred a great many Catholics in revenge – so many that it more or less settled the Ulster question once and for all. James II asked the Irish to help him recover his throne, but was defeated at the battle of the Boyne and fled abroad. Again, the Irish had to bear the brunt of another 'pacification'.

When the Irish rebelled in 1916, the trouble-makers were a few cranky nationalists who had little general support; the English suppressed the rising without difficulty. But instead of putting the rebels in jail – or better still, letting them go free to live with their unpopularity – they decided to shoot them. Old wounds re-opened; there was a full-scale rebellion; British troops went in to suppress the Irish Republican Army. Eventually, the British public itself became disgusted by the bloodshed, and in 1921, Southern Ireland became a republic. But the old problem of the 'plantation' of Ulster with Protestants refused to go away and, in the last decades of the twentieth century, is causing as much trouble as ever. We can see that, in the case of Ireland, the British have constantly over-reacted to their difficulties, and non-stop bloodshed has been the result.

In India, it was a similar story. From the British point of view, 'conquest' had been thrust upon them. The East India Company only wanted to trade with India. The Portuguese, French and Dutch had to be firmly discouraged by the British navy. When a local nabob, Saraj ud-Daulah, attacked the British settlement in Calcutta in 1756 and threw 146 English prisoners into the notorious Black Hole, the British under their commander Clive defeated Daulah at the battle of Plassey, placed their own man on the throne, and the British were the rulers of Bengal. This brought them into conflict with the Marathas, the leading power in India since they had overcome the Moguls; the British finally crushed the Marathas in 1818, and so became rulers of an even larger portion of the subcontinent. In 1856, a particularly bloody mutiny broke out when Hindu troops – known as Sepoys – heard a rumour that the fat that covered their cartridges came from pigs and cows. Since they had to bite the end off the cartridges to load, and since pigs were sacred to Mahommedans and cows to Hindus, they would be committing sacrilege. The Sepoy troops at Meerut reacted by massacring the British officers and their families. Various native princes who objected to British rule took the opportunity to rebel. Delhi fell to the mutineers, then Cawnpore. The atrocities were appalling: women and children disembowelled and burned alive. When the British re-took Cawnpore, they found a well full of dismembered corpses of women and children, while in the nearby house two women had been tied to pillars, their throats cut, and a child impaled by his chin on a hook. When the British finally subdued the rebels three years later, they took an equally appalling revenge; rebels were executed by the thousand – tied over the mouths of cannons and blown in two. And the British crushed the remaining maharajahs and became masters of India. No one was to blame but the rebels. But the Indians saw it differently. They had been subjected to the abuses and oppressions of the East India Company since Clive's victory, and for them the mutiny was as justifiable as Boudica's rebellion against the Roman forces in Britain. It has to be acknowledged that the British displayed unusual stupidity in trying to force the Sepoys to bite the cartridges and allowing the rebellion to begin at all.

The East India Company also played its part in the 'pacification' of China. In India, they had discovered the drug called opium made from poppies, and in the form of laudanum it became a popular drug in England for soothing colds and toothaches. At first it was thought to be no more harmful than alcohol, but by the early nineteenth century, it was known to be addictive. This did not prevent the East India Company offering to trade China opium in exchange for tea in the 1830s. The Chinese, like the Japanese, wanted nothing to do with 'foreign devils', and kept their doors closed to Europeans. But the Cantonese were induced to try opium, and were soon demanding it in large quantities. To trade with the west, it was necessary to play an elaborate game. A wealthy group of Cantonese called the Hong merchants acted as go-betweens. The British (and American) ships would anchor down-river at Macao. The Hong merchants would go on board and do their business, then hordes of junks would take the chests of opium – weighing more than a hundredweight each – back to Canton. The foreign devils would then set sail, chased by vessels of the Chinese navy, which fired salvos after them. And the emperor would be told that once again the foreigners had been repelled by the Chinese navy.

In 1838, the emperor appointed a rigidly honest official to stop the traffic, as a consequence of which, more than a thousand tons of opium was dumped into the river. The enraged British government sent in the British navy, which went up and down the coast bombarding Chinese towns, and captured the island of Chusan. The humiliated emperor had to back down and pay six million dollars in compensation; he also handed over the port of Hong Kong, so that the British were now able to flood China with opium. Canton, Shanghai and other ports were also opened to foreigners, who could live in their own settlements and move around China subject only to their own laws. Various foreigners annexed slices of territory – the British, the French, the Russians, the Germans, even the Japanese. In 1899, a patriotic secret society called the Order of Harmonious Fists – which the British derisively nicknamed the Boxers – began tearing up railways and killing foreigners and Chinese Christians. The Boxer rebellion was as bloody and cruel as the Indian mutiny, and was stamped out as ruthlessly – by an international force that included the Japanese. The Chinese government had to pay a third of a billion dollars in compensation, and to make more concessions. The result was an upsurge of Chinese nationalism, which led to the overthrow of the Manchu dynasty in 1911, by rebels headed by Sun Yat-sen. When Sun tried to get the foreigners out of China, most of them flatly refused to co-operate. Sun turned to the Soviet Union for aid. The long-term result was present-day communist China – another product of western stupidity and western greed.

Japan had similar problems with the west. In 1853, America established peaceful contact with Japan, when American warships steamed into Yedo (later Tokyo) harbour. Trade links were formed, and the Japanese also opened 'treaty ports'. They soon found, like the Chinese, that foreigners expected to live according to their own laws, and to impose their own rules of trade. In 1862, an Englishman who had accidentally broken a rule of politeness was killed by the followers of a local lord. With one voice, the western powers – British, American, French and Dutch – protested, and sent a naval force to bombard coastal towns; they also humiliated the emperor – who was regarded by the Japanese as a god – by threatening to bombard Kyoto unless he signed treaties. The Japanese decided it was time to modernize. So began the remarkable success story which resulted in modern industrialized Japan. But the humiliations which the west had inflicted – and continued to inflict – on Japanese pride led eventually to the attack on Pearl Harbor in December 1941. To the west it was an appalling example of Japanese treachery and ruthlessness. To the Japanese, it was an attempt to avenge a century of insults and humiliations.

In the second half of the nineteenth century, the western powers also parcelled out Africa. The Dutch had already discovered that its southernmost tip had a pleasant climate and settled there. The Spanish and Portuguese had settled an area of the west coast, which became known as the Gold Coast, the Ivory Coast and the Slave Coast. In the late 1870s, King Leopold of Belgium financed the American explorer Stanley, who presented the king with a large area of the Congo Basin, which became known as the Belgian Congo. The cruelties committed in the rubber plantations there became legendary; natives were flogged to death and, if they tried to escape, tortured and mutilated. The French claimed portions to the north of the Congo; the Portuguese seized a stretch from the east to the west coast; while the Germans concentrated their attention on the east coast around Zanzibar. Italy seized Somaliland, Eritrea and Ethiopia in the north. The British, more ambitious than any of the others, schemed to make Africa British from the Cape to Cairo, and succeeded in taking a large area from the Dutch – known as the Boers – in the Boer war 1899–1901. Clearly, it never struck anyone for a moment that the Africans themselves had a certain right to their own country. But when, after the Second World War, some African states succeeded in achieving independence, many became communist simply because communist ideology seemed to be at the opposite extreme from western imperialism.

* * *

he misses the point

All this then, seems to support the anarchist view that government is to blame for mankind's problems. But the anarchist view rests on the notion that there are two classes in the world: the oppressed and the oppressors. And anyone with the slightest knowledge of history knows this to be untrue. When the oppressed are given the opportunity, they become the oppressors. For the real problem lies in human nature itself. Governments are oppressive only because they behave exactly like individuals. When an individual is offended, he thinks in terms of 'getting his own back'. So do governments. According to the anarchists and socialists, the ordinary people love peace; it is the rulers who want war. In fact, when national pride is hurt, *everybody* wants war, and the common people are more belligerent than most. This is the cause of international conflict, and it is also the cause of crime. Man is a creature who easily works himself up into a state of righteous indignation, and his indignation places him at the mercy of negative emotions. His rational self is tossed around like a small aeroplane in a storm. Suddenly, nothing matters but soothing the outraged feelings, the bruised ego. If he is successful, and the offender is suitably humiliated, the storm subsides and he is once again capable of kindliness and reason. But while the fury lasts he is, in effect, mildly insane.

We might say that a person who behaves in this way was 'possessed'. But the behaviour could be compared to another medical condition that is rather less rare: hypnosis. Hypnosis consists of a narrowing of the field of attention until the subject is 'locked' in a state of narrowness, unaware of anything beyond it. This is precisely what happens to human beings when they are gripped by rage or indignation. The problem is that the effect of that rage, when directed against other people, is to produce in them the same state of 'hypnosis'. The two combatants are then likely to remain locked in this state of mutual-provocation until the original cause of the quarrel has ceased to be important. The hypnosis has become a self-propagating condition, which may continue until both are exhausted or one is destroyed.

The history of the twentieth century may be seen as a continuous illustration of this process. We may take as a convenient starting point an event that occurred shortly after the accession of the tsar Nicholas II in 1894. Rumour had spread that the new tsar was anxious to modernize Russia and permit his subjects more liberty. He was, in fact, a gentle and charming person, totally unlike his autocratic father, who had the temper of a bull. Local councils (known as *zemstvos*) were told that the new tsar would be glad to receive deputations. A deputation from Tver arrived in St Petersburg and presented the tsar with expensive presents and with an address expressing their loyalty. It contained the innocuous phrase: 'We expect, gracious sovereign, that these local councils will be allowed to express their opinions in matters which concern them . . .' The result startled them. The writer of the address was dismissed from the public service with ignominy, and an official reproof was sent to the governor of Tver, who knew nothing about the matter. A few days later, the tsar addressed the assembled deputations, and told them sternly that it had come to his knowledge that some local councils were indulging in 'the senseless dream that they might participate in the government of the country'. 'I want everyone to know,' shrieked the tsar, 'that I intend to maintain the principle of autocracy, like my father,' and he raised his hand as if shaking his fist. The audience went out looking shaken and cowed. And Nicholas's wife, the tsarina Alexandra, looked at him with adoring admiration.

The tsar's reaction to revolutionary ferment was to order his chief of police, von Plehve, to arrest anyone suspected of leftist sympathies. Plehve, who had organized the mass executions after the assassination of Alexander II, approached his task with enthusiasm. One of these arrested was a beautiful young student named Marie Vietrov – a few 'forbidden books' had been found in her room. Instead of being merely suspended from the university – the usual punishment – she was incarcerated in the Peter and Paul fortress. What took place during the next two months is not certain, although both torture and rape have been suggested. On 10 February 1897, Marie Vietrov committed suicide by soaking her mattress in paraffin and lying on it as she set it alight. She died after two days of horrible suffering. Her parents were not told until two weeks later. A secret press printed a document denouncing the government for her death, and asking what kind of tortures or humiliations had driven her to kill herself when her friends had already secured an order for her release. It was distributed in thousands. Vast crowds attended her funeral service, in spite of warnings from the police to disperse. A year later, industrial workers formed the Social Democratic Party which became the Communist Party.

The tsar was indifferent to all this agitation; he was more interested in trying to extend Russia's influence in the far east – particularly China and Korea. Japan had just won a war against China and wanted territorial concessions. So did Russia. In 1901, Japan's greatest statesman, Hirobumi Ito, came to St Petersburg to discuss the problem. He was ignored and snubbed; answers to his official communications were delayed for weeks. The tsar regarded the Japanese as irritating foreigners who should be taught their place. The result was that the Japanese helped themselves to the disputed territory in north Korea. The Russians were outraged, and declared war. In 1904, the Russian fleet was ordered to sail halfway round the world to destroy the Japanese fleet. Russia was in for a painful surprise. The Japanese had been industrializing and modernizing for several decades; they had even introduced the kind of democracy that Russia was still dreaming about. And they defeated the Russians in battle after battle. Finally, the Russian navy arrived, at Tsushima, where the Japanese sank all but two ships within a few hours. The Japanese had demonstrated that their chief minister could not be insulted with impunity.

After the war, one Russian statesman remarked: 'It will not be the Japanese who will walk into the Kremlin, but the Russians.' He understood that a national humiliation was the worst thing that could have happened to the tsar. In fact, while the war was still going on, the chief of police, von Plehve, was assassinated when a bomb was thrown under his carriage; the explosion was so great that he was literally atomized.

The government's response was to appoint a liberal, Prince Sviatopolk-Mirsky, in his place. To the tsar's fury, Mirsky held a conference of newspaper editors and asked for public support. A meeting of *zemstvo* delegates asked for more civil liberties. On 22 January 1905, a priest named Father Gapon led a delegation of workers to the Winter Palace to present a petition to the tsar. They were joined by more workers and by crowds of women and children. As they stood in front of the palace, calling for their 'little father', troops opened fire, then Cossacks charged the crowd, slashing with their swords. There was panic, and children were trampled underfoot. One hundred and fifty people were killed and two hundred wounded. When the tsar heard about it, his first question was: 'Do you think they've killed enough?' And when he was told that another regiment had fired on unarmed workers, he commented, 'Fine fellows.'

What was happening in Russia was that one single man, deluded by the idea that he was still the absolute ruler, was behaving in a way that seemed to justify everything that Marx and Kropotkin had ever said about monarchs. The strange thing is that the tsar was not personally an autocrat or dictator. He was a gentle soul who loved to spend his days quietly with his wife and family. He found it totally impossible to be unpleasant to anyone, even when he was angry, so that all who talked to him went away dazzled and charmed; ministers would be stunned when they received their dismissal by post the next day. Nicholas was a weakling, a weathercock who changed his mind from moment to moment. In short, he was basically a child who had no intention of leaving his own subjective dream world for the difficult world of reality. When Russia urgently needed a realist, it found itself ruled by this man who was totally unfitted for responsibility.

The tsarina was the worst possible wife for such a man. She was a morbidly sensitive German, who would have made an excellent *Hausfrau*, but lacked every single quality needed by an empress. She doted on the healer and mystic Rasputin, a 'monk' of genuine religious inspiration, but who also possessed an insatiable appetite for wine, women and song. When popular demand forced the tsar to grant a form of parliament – called the Duma – it was the unworldly Rasputin who kept assuring him that he was still autocrat of all the Russias and ought to behave accordingly.

But the first decade of the twentieth century was an extremely dangerous time for a ruler who lacked all sense of reality. The current of history was flowing more swiftly than ever before; there was a sense of foreboding, like approaching rapids. And unfortunately for Europe, the tsar was not the only ruler who lived in a dream world. With his bristling moustaches and arrogant stare, Kaiser Wilhelm II of Germany looked a typical Prussian officer. In fact, he was an over-sensitive, over-emotional man who was much given to play-acting and self-pity. 'Once in the middle of a fervent complaint that he was always misunderstood . . . he contrived to let a large tear fall upon his cigar.' He was born with a withered arm, and the disability increased his determination to look tough and formidable; the fierce upturned moustaches symbolized the front he presented to the world. In character, he was more like Nero than Julius Caesar. 'The greater part of his life . . . was an illusion, a sort of perpetual sleight of hand to bolster his ego.' (Both quotes are from Michael Balfour's *The Kaiser and his Times*, chapter 4.)

This neurotic weakling found himself living in a society that was fast going out of date. The Germans had been terrified by the revolution of 1848, and were determined not to let it happen again. But by 1900 the world had changed too much to treat liberals and socialists as dangerous madmen. People wanted change; they were sick of militarism and despotism. And the Kaiser, like the tsar and the emperor of Austria, was frantically trying to hold back history.

If the tsar had been a realist, he would have appreciated that he needed the full support of the Russian people. The defeat by Japan had revealed Russia's weakness. The army was run by corrupt politicians and generals who put the money intended for munitions into their private bank accounts; so half the soldiers had old fashioned rifles and the rest had none at all. Moreover, Russia was surrounded by aggressive powers. Germany was building up its navy to try to grab territory in Africa. The French, who had recovered from the humiliation of the Franco-Prussian war, had taken Morocco. The British were in Egypt. In Turkey, the government had been seized by a group called the young Turks who were determined not to allow their empire to crumble any further. Austria, under Franz Joseph, seemed to be one of the most stable countries in Europe, and had its eye on the Balkans – determined to frustrate the efforts of the tiny Bosnia, Serbia, Croatia and Slovenia to unite into one large country called Southern Slav Land (Yugoslavia).

The Austrians had occupied Bosnia since 1878, and were looking for an excuse to annex it permanently. When they did this – in 1908 – there was a European crisis, and Russia was tempted to go to war. (Rasputin dissuaded the tsar by telling him the Balkans were not worth fighting about.) Even the Italians felt it was time to expand, and in 1911 annexed Tripoli and the Dodecanese. It was the old game of land-grabbing, as played by the major powers in the nineteenth century. What now made it so dangerous was that it was being played in such a tiny space. Moreover, the major powers had formed various alliances with one another, promising to defend one another in the event of attack.

On 28 June 1914, the son of Franz Joseph of Austria, archduke Franz Ferdinand, was paying a state visit to Sarajevo, the capital of Bosnia – now part of the Austro-Hungarian empire. It was a rash thing to do, for today was Vidovdan, the anniversary of a Serbian defeat which was celebrated as a holiday. The archduke was gloomily certain that he would sooner or later be assassinated, and had told his children's tutor: 'The bullet that will kill me is already on its way.' At ten o'clock that morning, a bomb was thrown at his carriage; although it wounded several members of the crowd, the archduke and his wife were uninjured. The bomb thrower was captured and prevented from swallowing a cyanide capsule. The archduke attended a ceremony in the town hall, and remarked to his wife as they left: 'I have a feeling there may be more bombs around.' The carriages made a wrong turn at an intersection, and stopped to turn round. A young man walked forward, raised a revolver, and fired two shots. The archduke and his wife were killed instantly.

It soon proved that some high officials in the Serbian government knew about the plot to kill the archduke. Angrily, Franz Joseph demanded the right to interrogate them. Serbia refused, and Austria declared war. Russia had an agreement to help Serbia, but the position was risky, for the Kaiser would be sure to support the Austrians. Meanwhile, the Russians seethed; the Serbians were brother Slavs and the Austrians intended to steal their country. The tsar was torn between his desire for peace and his desire to avenge the insult. He compromised and ordered a partial-mobilization. In Germany, the Kaiser was having one of his 'nervous crises', convinced that England, Russia and France had agreed among themselves to crush Germany. At one of the most critical moments in modern history, he behaved like a hysterical female. He sent the tsar a message ordering him to stop the mobilization immediately. Nations stared one another in the eye and blustered. For just a moment, everybody seemed to have second thoughts; Serbia tried to soothe Austria with talk of compromise, and the tsar suggested that the dispute should be referred to an international tribunal. Then the Austrians shelled Belgrade, the capital of Serbia. The Russians continued to mobilize. Germany declared war. And suddenly, for the first time in his life, the tsar was the most popular man in Russia – for the people were, as always, more belligerent than the generals.

The Kaiser sent an insulting ultimatum to France and Belgium,

Russia's allies. They responded angrily, and Germany felt it had to save face by marching into Belgium. Britain entered the war in defence of Belgium, and because it had no desire to see Germany acquire more sea ports. Japan declared war on Germany, and Italy sided with Great Britain.

The war was the tsar's downfall. His troops fought bravely, but they lacked ammunition and proper clothing. Food intended for the army rotted in railway sidings. As the Russians suffered defeats and heavy casualties, the tsar sacked his commander-in-chief and took over that position himself. It made no difference. Russians starved and the war fever evaporated. In December 1916, Rasputin was murdered by a group of liberal conspirators, and his body was found under the ice of the river Neva. The tsar returned from the front and seemed to become curiously apathetic. The government was obviously disintegrating, and the country was paralysed by strikes. On 8 March 1917, disorders broke out in St Petersburg (then called Petrograd) to protest about the lack of bread. Policemen fired on crowds. Regiments began to mutiny. And the parliament decided that it had to step in and form a provisional government. The tsar watched his fantasies disintegrating around him. His own soldiers ordered him back into the palace when he tried to leave.

The Germans were delighted with the news, and sent the revolutionary Lenin back to Russia by sealed train. He was greeted by huge crowds and a brass band. But his own party, the Bolshevists, were not in power, and Lenin had to flee temporarily to Finland. He came back in disguise, and planned a *coup d'état*. In November 1917, the Bolshevists seized key buildings in Petrograd.

The tsar's family were already in exile in Siberia, in Tobolsk. The tsar himself turned down a plan of escape, hoping to recover his throne. When the Bolshevists took over, they transferred the family to Ekaterinburg, in the Urals. As loyal troops were not far away, the Bolshevists ordered their execution. On 16 July 1918, the tsar and his family – the tsarina, four daughters and his thirteen-year-old son – were taken down to the cellar and shot with revolvers. They were thrown down a mineshaft. The next day, the tsar's brother, the tsarina's sister and four nephews were taken to the same mineshaft and thrown down alive; dynamite was tossed in after them. In the rest of the country, the civil war between loyalists and communists continued, with appalling atrocities on both sides. The whole of

Russia was paying for the tsar's delusion that he could rule like his father.

If humankind were capable of learning from history, the First World War would have taught them that war had become an absurdity.

The German general von Schlieffen had devised a plan that should have overwhelmed the allies within months. It was to hurl a huge German force into France, big enough to overrun the country within weeks, then to turn his attention to destroying the Russians. Unfortunately for the Kaiser, von Schlieffen died, and his successor, von Moltke, failed to grasp the importance of the time element. He nervously divided his forces between Russia and France, with the result that the German offensive bogged down along the Marne river. Both sides then dug trenches, and slugged away at one another for the rest of the war – four years of it – killing millions on both sides, but each failing to dislodge the other. Churchill, the British lord of the admiralty, tried to break the deadlock by launching an attack on Turkey from the Dardanelles, to open a new supply route to Russia; this also bogged down, with tremendous loss of life.

We find it hard to understand how two enormous armies could sit down opposite each other for four years, launch offensives and counter-offensives which lost and gained the same piece of ground, and kill one another by the million. When the British launched an attack in north-eastern France in 1915, they lost a quarter of a million men and gained three miles. When the Germans attacked Verdun in 1916, there were two million men engaged on both sides, and half of these were killed; Verdun was left a ruin but the Germans failed to take it.

Then why did they go on? Why did the leaders of both sides not open peace negotiations, since the failure of the Schlieffen plan had made all the Kaiser's other aims irrelevant? Because both sides were dominated by their emotions, and national pride demanded some kind of victory to make up for the suffering. It came, eventually, only because the Germans made a second incredible blunder, and began sinking American shipping to prevent supplies reaching Britain. Sensibly, America had been determined to keep out of the war; but when American ships were sunk by German U-boats (the U standing for 'undersea'), their national pride also demanded revenge. A telegram – probably forged – purporting to be from the

German foreign secretary Zimmerman and offering Mexico large slices of American territory when Germany won the war, supplied the necessary element of indignation and outrage; America entered the war in 1917. Her weight turned the scales. The Kaiser was shocked and distressed when his generals told him there was no alternative to surrender.

Europe was a wreck. Half its young men had been killed, hundreds of its towns devastated. Three major dynasties had collapsed: the Romanovs in Russia, the Hapsburgs in Austria and the Hohenzollerns in Germany – the Kaiser was forced to abdicate, and went to live in Holland (where he died in 1942). As the world took stock of its losses, it was perhaps the most traumatic moment in the history of the human race. It was also clear evidence that there was something badly wrong with mankind. Ever since civilization had arisen in Mesopotamia, man had been fighting his own kind about territory. Now the latest quarrel about territory had led to this shattering devastation. The situation could be compared to a household whose members constantly get drunk and squabble; then one day, the disagreements become so violent that every window is smashed, several walls are demolished, and the garden is trampled into a morass. In these circumstances, the most drunken family would recognize that something drastic has to be done. But the human problem is rather more complicated than drunkenness. The simple animal need for territory cannot be easily reconciled with civilization. Animals merely snarl at one another at their boundaries; but armies cannot restrict their activities to snarling. The war problem is fundamentally a territorial problem, and can probably only be solved when the last vestige of the empire-building mentality disappears.

The American president, Woodrow Wilson, recognized this intuitively when he suggested the foundation of the League of Nations to deal with future 'boundary disputes'. Europe accepted his suggestion with relief. Yet the victors failed to grasp how far these boundary disputes – 'territory' – had been responsible for the Great War – in fact, for all wars in history. So they proceeded to re-draw the map of Europe in a way that would almost certainly guarantee another war within decades.

Three
THE MAFIA

War is a deliberate release of the aggressions of society. Unfortunately, it is easier to let the genie out of the bottle than to induce him to go back again. This is why every war in history has been followed by an outbreak of crime. The crime wave that followed the First World War was – like the catastrophe that caused it – the most violent in history. It differed from all previous outbreaks in one ominous respect: instead of quietly receding, it gathered strength, and became the most organized system of corruption since the days of Rodrigo Borgia.

Organized crime had, of course, been a feature of civilization since the days of the Greek pirates. But compared to the forces of law and order, the criminals lacked efficiency and foresight – which is why Pompey was able to destroy the pirates in a matter of weeks. In the London of Shakespeare and Jonathan Wild, or in the Paris of Vidocq, organized crime managed to maintain a precarious existence by keeping a 'low profile'. This meant chiefly that violence had to be kept to a minimum; for it was violence that outraged the citizens and forced authority to take action. In countries where banditry was an accepted fact of life, it existed with the aid and approval of most citizens. That could only happen in places – such as nineteenth century Greece and Sicily – where the citizens detested their rulers and regarded the bandits as 'freedom fighters'. Even so, violence could produce a ferocious backlash. In 1870, Greek brigands – led by the notorious Arvanitákis brothers – captured a party of distinguished English tourists near Marathon and demanded a ransom of £50,000 or, alternatively, an amnesty. (They had grown rich on banditry and wanted to return to society.) The Greek government categorically refused, and soldiers advanced on the bandit hideout. The four captives were promptly murdered as the brigands fled towards the village of Dilessi. Seven brigands were killed and six captured. The British government was outraged and threatened to invade Greece; the Russians threatened to fight on the side of the Greeks. The Greek government fell; most of the bandits who had escaped were finally killed or captured. And in Greece, kidnapping ceased to be a more-or-less acceptable custom.

Italy was another country where political unrest and foreign rule made organized crime respectable. In Sicily in the Middle Ages, the word *mafia* meant disdain for anything foreign; over the centuries it came to mean criminals who defied the foreign authorities (in the nineteenth century the letters were believed to stand for: *Morte Alla Francia Italia Anela* – Death to France is Italy's Cry). In Naples, organized crime went under the name of the Camorra; in Calabria, the *Fibbia*; the *Stoppaglieri* in Monreale. (Anyone who wants to understand how this kind of lawlessness developed should read Manzoni's novel *The Betrothed – I Promessi Sposi* – set in the 1620s.) The Italian tendency to indulge in blood feuds that sometimes went on for generations fostered the spirit of lawlessness. Yet, oddly enough, it was Garibaldi's unification of Italy in 1860 that turned the Mafia into a full-scale criminal organization. One reason was that the Mafia placed itself at the disposal of Garibaldi when he invaded Sicily (because, as one historian says, it could not afford to be on the losing side), and so achieved a kind of respectability. Besides, the Mafia constituted a sort of private army of mercenaries that could be hired by landowners – or the central government – to keep the peasants in order. And now that Italy at last belonged to the Italians, the mafiosi could forget political quarrels and concentrate on the business of extortion and intimidation. The criminal was no longer a social outcast, living in the mountains; he had become a force in society. By the late 1860s, the Mafia had organized itself into a society with its own rules and initiation rites. (On the west coast of America, the same thing was happening with the Chinese 'tongs'.) In fact, the aim of all these criminal brotherhoods was to be a kind of secret local government. They made farmers and small landowners pay taxes (later to be called 'protection'), destroyed the property of those who refused, and corrupted judges and police officers to prevent criminals from being successfully prosecuted. They developed the rule of Omertà – meaning the code of silence, the refusal to talk to authority, even when dying from an assassin's bullet or a stiletto.

The Mafia leaders soon discovered that crime was not the best way to make a living. It was far easier to rent an estate from an absentee landlord, then let it to peasants at an extortionate rate. By the 1890s, the Mafia had become a kind of criminal aristocracy in Sicily. By the turn of the century, the leader, Don Vito Cascio Ferro, was a kind of benevolent despot.

It is Ferro who is suspected of organizing the importation of the Mafia into America. The most popular city for Italian immigrants was New Orleans, which had a climate much like that of southern Italy. It was there that one of Sicily's best known brigands, Giuseppe Esposito, decided to settle in 1880. Esposito had also made the discovery that, even for a mafioso, violence must be used with caution. In November 1876, his gang had kidnapped an English curate named John Forester Rose and demanded a £5,000 ransom. Rose's wife declined to pay, and Esposito sent her one of her husband's ears. A week later, she received his other ear, and a note telling her that unless she paid up the next package would contain his nose. She paid, but there was an international scandal like the one that followed the Dilessi murders; the Italian government sent its *carabinieri* looking for the gang, and after a battle nine were killed and fourteen captured. Esposito succeeded in bribing his way out of jail, but decided that Sicily was no place for him and sailed for New York. Soon New Orleans, with its large Italian population, proved more attractive than the inhospitable north. But Esposito was filled with contempt for the relatively unambitious scale of lawlessness in New Orleans, and began to apply rules of Mafia organization. He would undoubtedly have become America's first 'godfather' if it had not been for the persistence of the Sicilian authorities, who instituted extradition proceedings. In July 1881, two police officers – Mike and Dave Hennessey – arrested Esposito, who was betrayed by a friend named Tony Labousse. A few days later, Labousse encountered a friend of Esposito's named Gaetano Arditto, and shots were exchanged which resulted in the wounding of Arditto and the death of Labousse. It was probably America's first Mafia killing. Arditto was tried and sentenced for the murder, and Esposito was returned to a Sicilian jail. But the Mafia organization in New Orleans persisted, and led to many more killings before the end of the century.

After Esposito's departure (he spent the rest of his life in prison), the New Orleans criminal fraternity – at least, its Italian section – was organized by two brothers, Charles and Tony Matranga, the latter a saloon keeper. Like their Sicilian counterparts, the Matrangas angled for political power, and expanded cautiously into 'legitimate' business. Apart from the Matrangas, one of the most influential Italian families in New Orleans was headed by three brothers named Provenzano; their contracts with shipping companies gave them a monopoly on loading and unloading fruit at the docks; they employed several hundred Italian workers, and paid them relatively high wages – forty cents an hour for day work and sixty cents for night work. In 1886, a new shipping firm called Matranga and Locascio appeared at the docks and began competing with the Provenzanos. With their strong-arm methods, the Matrangas took only two years to wrest control from their rivals. The Provenzanos decided to retaliate. On 5 May 1890, Tony Matranga, Tony Locascio and three other men finished supervising the unloading of a banana boat and drove off in a fruit wagon; suddenly, shots were fired from ambush, and three men, including Matranga, were wounded – Matranga's leg had to be amputated.

The chief of police, Dave Hennessey – who had arrested Esposito nine years earlier – took charge of the case. The Provenzanos were his friends, but the evidence indicated that they were responsible for the ambush, and two of the brothers – and three of their employees – were arrested and put on trial. But Hennessey was aware that the Matrangas were just as much to blame. He determined to end the power of the Mafia in New Orleans, and wrote to the police in Rome for photographs of Esposito bandits who were believed to be members of the Matranga gang. He received an anonymous letter warning him that he would be killed if he persisted, but he ignored it. The Provenzanos were found guilty, but their lawyer succeeded in winning a retrial. Hennessey announced that he would appear as a witness in favour of the Provenzanos, and would produce evidence about the Mafia in New Orleans. (His brother Mike had been killed – allegedly by the Mafia – in Houston, and Dave Hennessey was out for revenge.) On the night of 15 October 1890, Hennessey was walking home through heavy rain, accompanied by a police captain; he and his companion said goodnight, and a few seconds later, several shots sounded. The police captain rushed back to find his chief dying. Asked 'Who did it?' Hennessey answered: 'Dagoes.' He died a few hours later in hospital.

New Orleans was outraged. There was talk of lynching, and some eminent Italian families published advertisements in the newspapers, disavowing all connection with the killing. Mayor Shakespeare took over the case, and told the police: 'Scour the Italian neighbourhood – arrest every Italian if necessary.' Nineteen Italians were arrested, including a fourteen-year-old boy who was alleged to have signalled Hennessey's arrival. Their trial opened in February 1891. With a single exception – Huembert Nelli in *The Business of Crime* – writers on the case agree that the evidence against the Italians was overwhelming. The chief witness for the defence was a shady private detective named Dominick O'Malley, who had been indicted several times for bribing jurors and intimidating witnesses. One of the accused admitted in court that he had been present at a meeting where the death of Hennessey had been decided. Yet in spite of this, the jury declared an acquittal. There was helpless rage among the American population of New Orleans, and rejoicing among the Italians, whose market stalls were adorned with bunting. The accused were taken back to prison for their own protection, but allowed to wander freely; they celebrated that night with Chianti and spaghetti. Two days later, angry citizens marched on the jail, overcame the guards and found eleven of the fourteen Italians. Most were clubbed to death; one was hanged from a lamp-post. Whether or not they were guilty of the murder, their end caused an abrupt reduction in Mafia activities in New Orleans.

The case served to make Americans aware that the Mafia had imported Italian methods of extortion and intimidation; for now, with the Mafia's power in New Orleans temporarily broken, many New Orleans businessmen of Italian origin admitted that they had been blackmailed into paying 'protection'. Meanwhile, the Italian crime syndicate was spreading quietly all over America. In 1903, it acquired a new name when a Brooklyn contractor, Nicola Cappiello, went to the police to report that he had been receiving threatening letters signed 'The Black Hand' (*mano nera*). He had already paid a thousand dollars, but the friends who had agreed to act as intermediaries had returned saying that the criminals were demanding another three thousand. Realizing that they intended to bleed him dry, Cappiello secretly contacted the Brooklyn police. Their investigation revealed that the 'friends' were also the extortioners, and all were tried and found guilty.

On 14 April 1903, a barrel on a vacant lot in Manhattan proved to contain a corpse that was almost decapitated; the man had been stabbed seventeen times. One of New York's best detectives, Joseph Petrosino, finally identified the corpse as a small-time crook named Benedetto Madonia. When Madonia's watch was found in a pawn shop, the man who pawned it – Tomasso Petto, known as Petto the Ox – was arrested. It emerged that both Petto and Madonia were working for a ring of Italian counterfeiters, and that their job was to distribute the forged money. Madonia had been pocketing more than his share of the proceeds; so he had been murdered and left in a public place as a warning to other members of the gang. The nature of the crime attracted wide publicity. And once again, the public felt thoroughly frustrated when the case against the accused collapsed because witnesses suddenly became forgetful – even the dead man's wife and son declined to testify.

The problem, of course, stemmed from the fact that the criminal syndicates had been tolerated in Italy because they were opposed to rulers that the people hated. This anarchistic spirit transplanted well to America, where the 'dagoes' were looked down on by white Anglo-Saxon Protestants. And in America, the land of opportunity, many previously poor Italians became relatively affluent, and so aroused the envy of those who remained poor. Extortion was an easy – and almost foolproof – way of parting the better-off from their money. A threat to kidnap a child or dynamite a home was enough to make most Italians feel that money was a small price to pay for peace of mind. Even criminals were not immune. The head of the counterfeit gang, Ignazio Saietta (known as Lupo the Wolf) divulged at one point that he had paid $10,000 over the years for 'protection'. He was as vulnerable as anyone because his own criminal activities made him unwilling to go to the police.

In 1907, the New Orleans Mafia was again in the national press. Seven-year-old Walter Lamana, son of a successful undertaker and landlord, walked off with a man who promised him ice-cream; a few hours later, his father received a ransom demand for $6,000. Italian businessmen decided it was time to put an end to the power of the Black Hand and formed a committee. Various arrests were made, but the men had to be released for lack of evidence. Then another

Italian businessman who had received an extortion letter – demanding $2,000 – brought it to the police, telling them that he was sure it had been written by a man named Tony Gendusa. The police compared it to the Lamana ransom note and decided they were in the same handwriting. Tony's brother Frank was arrested and, under a certain amount of 'persuasion' from the police, admitted that Tony had been involved in the kidnapping. A group of vigilantes called on a farmer named Campisciano – whose name had also been mentioned – and induced him to talk by the use of a time-honoured method: they bound his hands, placed a noose round his neck, and pulled it tight over the branch of a tree. Campisciano broke down and led them to the small corpse that was wrapped in a blanket, lying in the water of the swamp. The child had been crying, he said, and one of the men had strangled it. (In fact, Walter Lamana had been killed by a hatchet blow.)

Campisciano, it now emerged, inspired terror in the area, and until his arrest, few people dared to tell all they knew. The result was that six people came to trial – including Campisciano's wife. Four more – among them Tony Gendusa – had escaped. Two brothers named Gebbia were sentenced to death – the noose that hanged one of them was given to Walter Lamana's father. At a separate trial, the remaining four were found 'guilty without capital punishment'. For a while, it looked as if angry citizens meant to organize a lynching party; but the governor called in the militia and the threat was averted. In New Orleans, the power of the Mafia was broken.

Other cities were less fortunate. In 1908, more than four hundred Black Hand threats were reported to the police, and one reporter estimated that for every one of these, there were probably two hundred and fifty that went unreported. In Chicago in the following year, the highly successful racketeer Big Jim Colosimo received so many Black Hand threats that he sent for his wife's nephew, Johnny Torrio, to come from New York to protect him. Torrio's remarkable efficiency and intelligence eventually made Colosimo the most powerful gangster in Chicago. The Black Hand also operated with impunity in Boston, Philadelphia, Baltimore, Pittsburgh, Cleveland, Kansas City and San Francisco. In Chicago in 1908, Black Handers even succeeded in extorting money from parents by threatening to blow up schools.

New York was particularly successful in these early years in its fight against the Mafia. This was largely due to the courage and resourcefulness of one man – detective Joseph Petrosino, the man who had arrested Petto the Ox. When the singer Caruso received a Black Hand extortion note, Petrosino tracked down the sender, broke both his arms, and put him on a boat back to Sicily. When he heard that Enrico Alfano, a Black Hander who had killed and mutilated a whole family in Naples, was in New York, Petrosino went straight to his room, intimidated Alfano and two gun-carrying bodyguards, and led them back to the police station linked together with their own ties and a sheet. Petrosino's luck held until he persuaded his boss, Commissioner Theodore Bingham, to send him to Sicily to look for Black Handers in the Italian police files. In Palermo, he found dozens of wanted files on men he knew to be in America, and sent them back to New York. But Sicily's leading mafioso, 'Don' Paulo Marchese, invited Petrosino to an expensive restaurant, and Petrosino was rash enough to accept. When the 'don' realized how much Petrosino knew, he ordered his death. Petrosino was told to meet an informant at the base of the Garibaldi statue on 12 March 1909; from the darkness, guns opened up and riddled his body with more than a hundred bullets. The Italian government apologized, but no one was ever arrested for the murder. Another Mafia boss, Don Vito Cascio Ferro, was one of many who claimed to have been the executioner – alleging that he killed Petrosino with one shot, then hurried back to the dinner table of a member of the Chamber of Deputies who had agreed to provide an alibi.

Petrosino's murder caused widespread dismay in America; it seemed to prove that the criminals were immune. And it struck many poor but intelligent young men that crime was a better way of achieving 'upward mobility' in a democratic society than hard work. Some – like Frank Costello and Charles 'Lucky' Luciano – were Italian; others, like Meyer Lansky, Hymie Abrams and Charles 'King' Solomon, were Jews. Some of the most successful – like Dion O'Banion and Bugs Moran in Chicago – were Irish. Such men realized that petty crime was a waste of time, and that real success could only come through corrupting police officers and politicians and acquiring a 'power base'. The result was that – like the 'godfathers' in Sicily – they became respectable members of society, while the risks were taken by their hired thugs. In Akron, Ohio, in 1918, a racketeer named Rosario Borgio became so incensed when the police kept raiding his houses of ill fame that he called a meeting of gangsters and announced that he would pay $250 for every policeman who was murdered, the aim being to eliminate the entire Akron police force. The petty crooks were delighted at this prospect of easy money, since nothing was easier than walking up behind a patrolman at night and shooting him in the back. Akron policemen began to die with disturbing regularity – and there seemed to be no obvious motive. Early in 1919, Lieutenant Michael Fiaschetti – who had been trained by Petrosino – was told that two of the suspected police-killers were in New York. He arrested them, and persuaded one of them – Tony Manfredi – to talk by convincing him that the gang had ordered his execution and that his companion was the chosen killer. Rosario Borgio and three other gangsters were sentenced to death.

In New York, the top gangsters were discovering that the philosophy of socialism could be turned to their advantage. During the first decade of the century, New York crime was dominated by various gangs of thugs, many with membership of more than a thousand. The best known of these was the Five Points gang, led by an ex-prize fighter named Paul Kelly – who was, in fact, a Neapolitan called Paolo Vaccarelli. There was a bitter rivalry between the Five Pointers and the Lower East Side Gang led by Monk Eastman and – later, when Eastman was sentenced to ten years – by 'Kid' Twist. Twist was murdered in 1908 at Coney Island fairground, but the battles between the gangs had exhausted both sides by that time. Kelly moved to Harlem and became a labour racketeer – or, as he would have preferred to express it, a Union organizer. He organized the rag-pickers, and used his position to 'shake down' employers. Since this was a far safer way of making a living than dealing in stolen goods and prostitution, Kelly extended the field of his activities to other forms of labour; he became president of the International Longshoremen's Union and a member of the American Federation of Labour. The New York waterfront was controlled largely by the Irish; under Kelly's leadership, an increasing number of Italians became longshoremen. By 1919, three-quarters of the longshoremen were Italian. A man who wanted a job had to be prepared to 'kick back' a percentage of his earnings to Kelly. Kelly remained a respectable union leader until 1953, when he was expelled for taking bribes.

By 1919, New York was the criminal capital of America. The Mafia existed in most other major cities but it remained an underground criminal organization; only in New York had it achieved something like political control. And New York was regarded by the rest of America – particularly the rural communities – as a pit of corruption and wickedness. America was a religious country, and the forces of law and order were well in control. And then, in 1920, the law-abiding citizens handed the gangsters a mandate for unlimited expansion. It was called the Volstead Act.

Prohibition was not a sudden visitation of the spirit of religious intolerance. The crusade for total abstinence had been launched as early as the 1840s – largely by Methodists. It sprang up in the frontier towns, on the great plains of the west. In most small towns, the saloon was a shack that sold cheap whiskey and gin, and the men who used it were prone to drink themselves unconscious because they might not be back in town for another month. The women who could be picked up in such places were usually worn out drabs suffering from venereal disease. When the face of vice was so ugly, the Anti-Saloon League had no difficulty persuading the virtuous that the answer lay in total prohibition. Boredom and sexual frustration also played their part in the psychology of the temperance crusader. Carrie Nation, who used to wreck Kansas saloons with a hatchet around the turn of the century, was always stirred to additional destructiveness by the sight of 'immoral' pictures over the bar. As Americans became more aware of the growth of organized crime, the abolitionists used it as an additional argument for prohibition; if alcohol was banned, the vices that depended on it would wither away.

But in spite of this aggressive puritanism, America would probably never have taken the fatal step if it had not been for the First World War, when many states banned the manufacture of alcohol merely in order to conserve grain for food. This caused no problems, since Americans were ready to take any measures to defeat the Kaiser. The 'dry' lobby in Congress saw success within its grasp and pushed through the eighteenth amendment, banning all alcohol; Senator Andrew J. Volstead proposed an act for its legal enforcement, and it was promptly passed. On 17 January 1920, America became 'dry'; the Anti-Saloon League declared that it presaged an 'era of clear thinking and clean living'.

What Congress had done was to create in America the same conditions that had made Italy the most lawless country in the world. Government suddenly became the enemy of the people. Americans had always been inclined to cynicism about politicians – the comedian Will Rogers remarked: 'With Congress, every time they make a joke it's a law, and every time they make a law it's a joke.' Now Congress had made a particularly bad joke, and commonsense revolted. The gangster who was willing to defy the new law suddenly ceased to be a public enemy and became a benefactor. By the time America realized its mistake – after ten years of murder and violence – it was too late. Organized crime had come to stay.

The greatest mistake of the Anti-Saloon League was in failing to work out how total prohibition could be enforced. 'Near-beer' – beer containing less than one half per cent alcohol – was still legal, so breweries were allowed to continue operating. But in order to manufacture near-beer, ordinary four per cent beer had to be brewed, then de-alcoholized. There was nothing to stop the brewers diverting kegs of real beer, or providing their customers with some pure alcohol – distilled from the beer – to add to their unpalatable near-beer. An alternative was to add industrial alcohol, which was still legal – American production of industrial alcohol shot up in the 1920s from 28 million gallons to 180 million. Drinkers who could afford it had no difficulty in buying real Scotch or brandy from smugglers who brought it in from Canada – which was soon providing the American market with more than five million gallons a year. Apart from these large-scale commercial concerns, thousands of ordinary citizens were willing to take the risk of distilling alcohol on cheap apparatus – 'alky-cookers' – and selling the results to criminal syndicates who paid up to $15 a day – a sum that would once have represented a week's wages for many of them.

In Chicago, 'Big Jim' Colosimo – also known as Diamond Jim because of his habit of carrying pockets full of diamonds – already had the criminal organization to launch into large-scale traffic in illicit alcohol. (It quickly became known as bootlegging, because a boot was a good place to conceal a bottle or a hip flask.) He already ran a chain of brothels, with the aid of his chief lieutenant, Johnny Torrio, who was an ex-member of the Five Points Gang. Torrio was small, well-dressed and quietly-spoken; he was also intelligent enough to know that violence usually rebounds against those who employ it. When it came to gangland disputes, he preferred diplomacy to assassination. At the beginning of Prohibition, he was in his mid-thirties; Colosimo was fifty – too old to take advantage of the magnificent opportunities that had been placed in his lap by the Anti-Saloon League. Torrio chafed impatiently; but on 11 May 1920, he suddenly inherited Colosimo's empire when his employer was mysteriously shot through the head as he went to take delivery of a consignment of alcohol. Rumour had it that Torrio paid the assassin – a man named Frankie Yale – ten thousand dollars.

Colosimo's funeral was magnificent, attended by five thousand mourners. And as soon as it was over, Torrio settled down to the business of organizing Chicago's crime. There were too many gangs engaged in bootlegging, and even at this early stage they were inclined to shoot at one another for violations of territory. Torrio called the gangs together, proposed a peace treaty – pointing out that there was more than enough for everybody – and suggesting that the gangs should reach strict agreements about territory. And when the various gang leaders – Dion O'Banion, the Gennas, the O'Donnells (two gangs of that name), 'Terrible' Touhy and Terry Druggan – had agreed to co-operate – or at least suspend hostilities – Torrio turned his attention to expanding the former Colosimo empire, searching out locations for roadhouse-brothels in Cook County (which had been allotted to him) and bribing the local police and civic authorities. Torrio preferred to avoid threats and violence; instead he relied on persuasion and judicious gifts. Most of Chicago's most influential businessmen and politicians were happy to co-operate. Torrio went into partnership with a wealthy brewer, and was soon making more money in a week than Colosimo had made in a year.

Minor criminals viewed his success with envy. A safe-blower named Joe Howard decided to join the bootleg business by holding up a truck loaded with alcohol and leaving the driver to walk home – a practice that became known as hijacking, presumably because the gunmen stopped the trucks with a shout of 'Hi, Jack!' When two of Torrio's consignments vanished in this manner, Torrio decided to suspend his prejudice against violence. On 8 May 1924, Joe Howard was in Heinie Jacobs' bistro on South Wabash Avenue, explaining to some acquaintances that all dagoes were cowards, when an overweight young Italian walked in through the door. 'Hi, Al,' said

Howard, and was shot through the head six times. The next morning, Chicago newspapers carried photographs of Torrio's chief lieutenant, Alphonse Capone, who was wanted for questioning by the police.

In 1924, Capone was twenty-five years old. He had known Torrio in New York, and had always regarded him with hero worship. When Capone was nineteen – in 1918 – Torrio had invited him to come to Chicago to work as a bouncer in the Colosimo Café on South Wabash; his wages were $75 dollars a week. It was widely believed in Chicago that Capone murdered Colosimo. What is certain is that by 1922 he was earning $2,000 a week by running the brothels. He also slept with the most attractive of the girls, and at some point acquired syphilis.

When the police were searching for Capone, he was nowhere to be found. Meanwhile, the witnesses to the Howard shooting all began to develop doubts about whether the killer *was* Capone. One of them simply vanished. A month later, Capone walked into a police station, saying he had heard a rumour that he was wanted for questioning. The police were forced to drop the case for lack of evidence.

By 1924, the Torrio-Capone gang was also at cross-purposes with Dion O'Banion, whose territory was the North Side. The Irishman had been a choir boy, and disapproved of brothels; he was also inclined to take every opportunity to grab more than his share. The last straw came when he sold Torrio one of his breweries for half a million dollars, then tipped off the police when Torrio went to view his acquisition; Torrio was arrested.

On 8 November 1924, three gangsters walked into O'Banion's flower shop on North State Street. O'Banion felt no misgivings; a leading mafioso had died, and he was selling flowers to all the leading gangsters. He held out his hand to Frankie Yale, who had come from New York. Yale held on to it while the other two men emptied their guns into O'Banion. Again, the funeral was magnificent, with O'Banion in a solid silver coffin (costing $10,000), lined with white satin. Capone sent flowers.

O'Banion's chief lieutenant, Hymie Weiss, swore vengeance. A few days later, Capone was sitting in a restaurant talking to its proprietor, Tony the Greek, who was a close friend; some customers came in and Tony went forward to greet them. He never came back; the next day his body was found encased in quicklime. Capone is said to have sobbed when he heard the news. In January, he missed death by seconds when he left his car to go into one of his speakeasies – so-called because customer's were urged not to speak loud. Another car drove past slowly, and Capone's car was riddled with machine-gun bullets. Twelve days later, Torrio narrowly escaped death as he and his wife were entering their apartment building; a sub-machine gun opened up, wounding Torrio's chauffeur; Torrio dropped on all fours and ran towards the building. A bullet hit his left arm and spun him round; then a shotgun blast broke his jaw and punctured his lungs and abdomen. The gangster who stood over him – 'Bugs' Moran – to fire the final shot into his head discovered that his gun was empty; before he could reload, the driver of their getaway car hooted, and they ran off. Torrio decided it was time to resign his share of the business; he returned to Italy, a millionaire, leaving his ex-protégé in charge.

Capone became increasingly nervous as Weiss continued to shoot his friends and allies. Angelo Genna, a rival beer baron, was the next. Then, on 20 September 1926, an eleven-car cavalcade came into the heart of Capone territory, in Cicero, drove past the Hawthorne restaurant, where he was eating lunch, and riddled the place with machine-gun bullets. No one was hurt, but Capone was worried. He suggested a truce. Weiss agreed – on condition that Capone handed over the killers of O'Banion. Capone declined. He posted some of his men in a rented room opposite the flower shop (which continued to be Weiss's headquarters). On 11 October 1926, three weeks after the Cicero incident, Weiss was entering the shop when machine-gun fire raked the street and he fell, riddled with bullets.

When O'Banion's other aide, Vincent Drucci, was killed by a policeman, the only member of the gang who remained a threat to Capone was George Moran, known as 'Bugs' because when he lost his temper he seemed to go insane.

On 13 February 1929, a bootlegger told Moran he had a truckload of alcohol for sale; Moran told him to deliver it to a garage in North Clark Street. The next day – St Valentine's Day – a car drew up in front of the garage just before 11 A.M., and five men got out, two in police uniforms. A few minutes later, they emerged from the garage, the policemen pointing guns at the other three; it seemed to be an arrest. Someone walked into the garage and found seven men lying on the floor near the wall. The 'police' had lined them up – they were mostly Moran gangsters – and then mowed them down with machine-gun fire. Then they were shot in the head with shotguns. One of the seven was a doctor who merely happened to be in the garage.

Moran escaped the massacre; he arrived while the shooting was going on and waited until the 'police' drove away. He told the real police: 'The only man who kills like that is Al Capone.' But Capone was sunbathing by his swimming pool in Palm Island, Florida, at the time of the massacre. Moran died in 1957 of lung cancer.

The St Valentine's Day massacre caused a public outcry, and the authorities decided it was time to show that Capone was not above the law. A month after the massacre, on 16 March 1929, Capone and his bodyguard were leaving a cinema in Philadelphia when he was stopped by police and arrested on a charge of carrying a concealed weapon. He was quickly brought before a judge and sentenced to a year in prison. It was not an uncomfortable year – a man with fifty million dollars can usually buy small luxuries in jail. But when Capone came out, the twenties were over; the depression had set in. When the Inland Revenue Department had Capone arrested on a charge of failing to pay income tax, he tried to buy his way out of trouble with an offer of four million dollars. The tax authorities turned it down, and Capone was sentenced to eleven years in jail and costs of $80,000. He was paroled in 1939, and died in 1947 of paresis of the brain, due to the syphilis he had contracted years earlier. He was forty-eight at the time of his death.

Although Capone's notoriety has led to an automatic association between Chicago and 1920s gangsterism, every major city in America had its bootleggers and gangsters – New York, Boston, Philadelphia, Denver, Cleveland, Detroit, Kansas City, Los Angeles – and in every one of them, the struggle for power between the gangs was as violent as in Chicago. In 1928, Torrio returned to America – driven out by Mussolini – and went back into the bootleg business in New York; together with Lucky Luciano, Longy Zwillman and Meyer Lansky, he quickly built up another booze empire. (He would also be jailed for income tax evasion in 1936.) Other leading bootleggers in New York were Dutch Schultz and the gambler Arnold Rothstein, who, as early as 1923, had also diversified into drugs. Rothstein was murdered in 1928 when he declined to pay a gambling debt of $320,000.

In October 1929, Lucky Luciano was himself 'taken for a ride' – probably by members of the gang of a rival bootlegger, Legs Diamond. They beat him unconscious and stabbed him repeatedly in the back with an ice pick, leaving him for dead. Rushed to hospital, 'Lucky' survived. Thereafter, members of Diamond's gang began to disappear; Diamond himself was killed by persons unknown in December 1931.

By that time, it was clear to most people in America that Prohibition had been an appalling mistake, and that it had turned the country into a gangsters' paradise. In 1932, the Democrats made repeal of Prohibition one of their major campaign promises; Roosevelt defeated Hoover by an immense majority, and in February 1933 Prohibition was repealed.

By that time, Luciano had established himself as New York's leading mafioso, just as Capone had been Chicago's. Luciano's boss had been an old-style gangster called Joe Masseria. In 1930, another gang boss named Salvatore Maranzano started a gang war against Masseria. As gunmen on either side were killed or 'taken for rides', Luciano decided that he might be in a better bargaining position without his boss. On 15 April 1931, Masseria and Luciano had just finished a game of cards in a restaurant when Luciano excused himself to go to the toilet; in his absence, four men shot Masseria to death. (All were famous gangsters: Vito Genovese, Albert Anastasia, Joe Adonis and Bugsy Siegel.) Luciano quickly offered a truce to Maranzano on Maranzano's own terms. But Maranzano had scarcely had time to accustom himself to his new role as the 'godfather' of New York when he was superseded. Five men walked into his office, flashing police identification badges; a dozen witnesses who happened to be present were made to line up with their faces to the wall. Then Maranzano was shot and stabbed to death. None of the killers belonged to the Mafia; their leader was Bo Weinberg, Dutch Schultz's chief lieutenant. But it is impossible to doubt that this was a Mafia killing; for on the same day – 11 September 1931 – more than thirty old-style Mafia bosses – 'moustache Petes' as they were known disrespectfully to their juniors – also died in a nationwide purge. It was a remarkable feat of planning, and reveals how far Prohibition had turned the Mafia – now known as Unione Siciliano – into a giant corporation. And its president was now Lucky Luciano.

Prohibition had turned small-time mobsters into multimillionaires, and so made them practically ineradicable. 'Ever since the purge of '31, Unione has been no more Mafia than a processed shot of heroin is the original poppy.' (Sid Feder and Joachim Joesten in *The Luciano Story*, chapter 4.) With so much money, the Mafia could buy immunity and choose their own political appointees. After the Maranzano murder, the incumbent district leader (i.e. local councillor in Tammany Hall) was warned that, if he valued his life, he would resign. A Luciano candidate, Albert Marinelli, was elected. In July 1932, Marinelli was present at the Democratic Convention in Chicago for the presidential nomination; the leading Democratic candidate was Franklin D. Roosevelt. Also present were Lucky Luciano and his friend Frank Costello. Luciano kept well in the background – it would have benefited no one if some political commentator had wondered what leading gangsters were doing at a Democratic Convention – but the delegates were kept well supplied with good liquor. It made no difference that Marinelli was supporting one of Roosevelt's rivals and that Roosevelt gained the nomination; Luciano had friends on both sides.

So the end of Prohibition made little difference to the gangs. They had diversified into other businesses – such as drugs, gambling and labour racketeering. Luciano's friend Louis Buchalter – known simply as Lepke – dominated the garment industry. Frank Costello was the gambling boss, with a sideline in gem smuggling. Luciano had by this time decided that the future lay in the drug trade, although he owned brothels all over the country.

The chief problem remained inter-gang rivalry. Capone's arrest had taught the New Yorkers that it was unwise to arouse public protest by conducting feuds in the streets. The point was driven home at a meeting in the latter half of 1932, chaired by gangland's respected elder statesman, Johnny Torrio. All New York's leading gangsters were invited: Costello, Joe Adonis, Lepke, Longy Zwillman, Bugsy Siegel, Meyer Lansky and Dutch Schultz. Luciano was in the chair. Torrio pointed out that when Prohibition was repealed, politicians would cease to depend on the gangsters for alcohol, and the gangster would cease to be regarded as a social benefactor. They would lose valuable 'contacts'. Therefore, they should decide in advance to stick together. Inter-gang warfare must cease, and to achieve this, the gang leaders must keep in close contact, like the board of a public corporation . . . After Torrio and Luciano had put the case, resistance melted. In effect, the gangs were forming a cartel, and the strength of one was the strength of all. By 1934, the advantages of this mutual-protection society were so obvious that gangs from all over the country suggested joining. A meeting was called in Kansas City; gangsters from Kansas City, Chicago (the Capone gang), Cleveland (the Mayfield mob) and Detroit (the Purple gang) attended, together with delegates from Boston, Miami, New Orleans, Baltimore, St Paul and St Louis. Luciano and Meyer Lansky – known, because of his stature, as 'The Little Man' – were the organizers. The result of this meeting was the formation of the Syndicate – sometimes known as Murder Incorporated.

Whenever a body is found in the gutter or a doorway today, it is still more or less casually dismissed by press and public as the result of differences of mob opinion, just as it was in the trigger-happy twenties. It doesn't work that way any more. Not one top boss in the underworld has been slain since 1934 unless the execution has been sanctioned, approved, and in fact directed, by the gang lords of the nation.

From *Murder Incorporated* by former District Attorney Burton B. Turkus and Sid Feder, 1951.

Dutch Schultz was one of the first to fall foul of the new Syndicate. Now Prohibition was over, Schultz ran a highly profitable form of racing lottery called the numbers racket. He was an eccentric individualist who was never much liked by his fellow gangsters, and Luciano deplored his bad manners. On one occasion, Luciano called a meeting of gangsters at his flat, and provided girls for the entertainment of his guests. Schultz was so taken with one of them that he hauled her into the bedroom before the meeting began, and shouted his own occasional contributions through the open door. When he emerged he tossed a hundred dollars at Luciano, saying 'That's for the girl,' and went out.

When the Federal authorities decided that Schultz was open to charges of income tax evasion, his lawyers succeeded in having his trial moved to Syracuse, in upstate New York. Schultz moved there, mixed in local society, became involved in charitable activities, and, according to one historian, hired a public relations firm to improve his image. The result was that the jury acquitted him. But during his absence from New York, Lepke had moved in on Schultz's profitable numbers business in Harlem; Schultz's chief lieutenant, Bo

Weinberg, was persuaded that his boss would be spending a long time in jail and agreed to work for new masters. But Schultz did return, and Weinberg was mysteriously stabbed to death. Schultz was embittered about the loss of his rackets, but recognized that he stood no chance against the rest of the Syndicate. He decided to bide his time.

However, Schultz was too much of an individualist to be able to escape notice. New York's new mayor, Fiorello La Guardia, had announced that he would make war on the racketeers, and was photographed smashing up gaming machines with a sledge hammer. For the time being, Schultz was safe, since the District Attorney, William C. Dodge, had received large contributions from Schultz to his election campaign. But when a grand jury investigating the numbers racket realized that the D.A. was actively impeding the investigation, they demanded his removal, and a formidable young lawyer named Thomas E. Dewey was appointed in his place. It was Dewey who, in his previous role as Federal Attorney, had indicted Schultz for income tax evasion. Schultz's reaction to his appointment as District Attorney was manic rage. He proceeded to arrange for Dewey's assassination. One of his gunmen began to watch Dewey's movements, and established that he made a habit of calling at a local drug store every morning to use the telephone while his two bodyguards waited outside. The Syndicate heard of the proposed killing and summoned Schultz to a meeting. Lepke pointed out that the murder of the District Attorney would create precisely the sort of unwelcome public outcry that they all wished to avoid. Schultz's arguments were overruled. Dewey must be allowed to live.

Schultz declined to accept the verdict. And it soon came to the notice of the Syndicate that he was still observing Dewey's movements, with the obvious intention of presenting the Syndicate with a *fait accompli*. And when their information network established that Dewey had less than two days to live, they decided to act. Schultz had moved to Newark, New Jersey, and ate his meals in the Palace Chophouse. On the night of 23 October 1935, Schultz and his aides were in a backroom of the Chophouse, having a business meeting. Schultz went out to the men's lavatory. The Syndicate killer, 'Charlie the Bug' Workman, strolled into the Chophouse, walked into the lavatory and saw Schultz bent over the washbasin. Assuming him to be a bodyguard, Workman drew his gun and shot him in the back. Then he went back to the bar to wait for Schultz – a bar that had suddenly emptied at the sound of the shot. It was some time before it dawned on Workman that the man in the toilet – who had seemed vaguely familiar – was the man he was hired to kill.

Schultz was not dead; he spent twenty-four hours babbling in delirium before he died in hospital. It was many years before Dewey learned how close he had been to death.

The Schultz assassination caused very nearly as much of a scandal as the killing of Dewey might have done. One of the things Schultz revealed in his final delirium was that the man responsible was 'the boss himself'. Dewey began looking for Luciano. He was in Arkansas, but as soon as his whereabouts was known, Dewey demanded his extradition. He began a round-up of the brothel madames who now worked for the Syndicate; many of them had been independent before Luciano obliged them to become his employees, and were delighted to talk. Torrio was also arrested, and charged with income tax evasion. Luciano was charged on ninety counts of extortion, and his bail was set at $350,000. Torrio went to prison for two and a half years. Luciano received a term of from thirty to fifty years. Realizing that many of those who had testified against him would be in danger of their lives, the judge warned that if any of these witnesses was harmed in the future, he would instruct that Luciano and his fellow defendants should spend the maximum term in jail without parole.

It looked, then, as if law and order had won after all. Dewey certainly thought so. What he did not realize was that the crime syndicate now spread across the country and could operate just as smoothly without Luciano. Small operators were forced out of business and their rackets taken over by the Syndicate. If a murder was necessary, a hired gunman arrived from out of town, killed him with quiet efficiency, and left town the moment the job was done. Burton Turkus estimates that about a thousand murders were committed by 'Murder Incorporated' in the first five years of its existence. The fee for a killing ranged from a thousand to five thousand dollars. (Pittsburgh Phil, one of the best known contract killers, is believed to have murdered five hundred persons between 1930 and 1940.) In most cases, the corpses were never found – they were dumped in swamps or rivers.

The law learned about the existence of Murder Incorporated in

1940. A prisoner named Harry Rudolph sent for Turkus – then assistant District Attorney – and told him that he had been present when another gangster was killed in 1933; the killers included a much-wanted killer named Abe Reles, known as 'Kid Twist'. Reles was so confident that the law was unable to touch him that he gave himself up the moment he heard the police wanted to talk to him. Then, when he found out that Harry Rudolph had 'fingered' him for the gang murder, he realized his mistake. The D.A.'s office was determined to put as many gangsters behind bars as possible, and judges were co-operative. With the evidence against him, Reles knew it meant the electric chair.

Oddly enough, Reles was a good family man; and at the time of his arrest, his wife was expecting another baby. To the amazement of the District Attorney's office, he suddenly offered to 'sing' – turn State's evidence – in exchange for immunity. A bargain was struck. When Reles told them about Murder Inc., the D.A. and his staff could hardly believe their ears. Until that time, the police had had no suspicion of the existence of the Syndicate. Now Reles told them that he belonged to a 'troop' in Brownsville whose chief business was assassination, and that similar troops existed all over the country.

Reles continued to 'sing' for two years, and as a result of his testimony, Lepke went to the electric chair; so did his chief executioner Mendy Weiss, Louis Capone, Pittsburgh Phil (Harry Strauss), Happy Maione and Dasher Abbadando. The transcript of Kid Twist's testimony makes some of the most horrifying reading in the history of gangsterism: how, for example, Pittsburgh Phil set fire to the body of a murdered mobster, purely for the pleasure of seeing him burn. These men were, in the most literal sense, human butchers. Reles also described how, when Lepke was hiding from the police in 1939, he ordered Reles to kill eleven witnesses who meant to testify against him; Reles succeeded in killing seven before Lepke went on trial.

As Reles continued to 'sing', an increasing number of gangsters became nervous. Then, on the morning of 12 November 1941, Kid Twist mysteriously fell from his sixth-floor window in the Half Moon Hotel on Coney Island. Six policemen were guarding him, but all alleged they were out of the room or looking the other way. The body was so far from the wall of the hotel that it seemed reasonably certain that Reles had been given a vigorous push. But no one was ever indicted, and the death remains a mystery.

During all this time, Luciano was making strenuous and unsuccessful efforts to get himself paroled. Then, on 9 November 1942, the French liner *Normandie* was burned down to the waterline at a Hudson River pier; it was about to be converted to a troopship, and it was obviously an act of sabotage. The waterfront was still controlled by the Syndicate – in fact, by Luciano, from his prison cell. Naval Intelligence decided to approach Luciano and ask for his co-operation; Meyer Lansky – now the Syndicate's banker and chief accountant – agreed to act as intermediary. The full story has still not been told; Luciano himself later claimed that he and Dewey arrived at an agreement: he would contribute $90,000 to Dewey's campaign fund (Dewey was intending to run for President), and would help Naval Intelligence keep the waterfront free of sabotage; in exchange, he would be paroled at the end of the war and sent back to Italy. Meanwhile, he would be transferred to the relative comfort of Great Meadow Prison, in Comstock, New York State. Luciano even suggested arranging for Hitler to be assassinated by the gangster Vito Genovese, who was at present in Italy. This ambitious plan came to nothing, but for the remainder of the war the New York waterfront remained free of sabotage. At the end of the war, Dewey kept his part of the bargain; Luciano was paroled and deported to Italy (although he was an American citizen). Dewey ran as Republican candidate twice (in 1944 and 1948) but lost both times. But he became governor of New York state.

Ironically, the American occupation of Italy had restored power to the Mafia, who had been crushed by Mussolini. As a result of a message from Luciano to the 'godfather' in Sicily – Don Calogero Vizzini – the Mafia had given American forces full co-operation when they landed. It was only natural that these 'patriotic' Italians should then be allowed a leading role in restoring the country to normality – for example, in nominating leading 'anti-fascists' for key posts in cities like Naples. The Americans handed Italy back to the godfathers.

Luciano was deported in February 1946. Precisely one year later he was in Havana, Cuba – a city whose crime was controlled by Meyer Lansky, 'the Little Man'. There, in the best hotel, Luciano sent for his aides from all over America – Frank Costello, Willie Moretti, Bugsy Siegel – the man who had founded the gambling industry in Las Vegas – and the Fischetti brothers from Chicago. When Siegel was asked to repay some of the vast sum of money he had borrowed to build the Las Vegas gambling casino and the Flamingo Hotel, he lost his temper and stormed out of the room. His friend Meyer Lansky was deputed to talk sense into him, but failed. On 20 June 1947, Siegel was shot to death in the Beverly Hills apartment of his mistress, Virginia Hill. Lansky is reported as saying: 'I had no choice.' Lansky himself denied being behind the killing, and attributed it to Luciano.

When an enterprising newsman revealed Luciano's presence in Havana, the Batista government felt obliged to order him out of Cuba. Luciano returned to Italy. Banned by the government from Rome – where he had established various rackets – he settled in Naples. He gave many interviews, insisting that he had been much maligned, and that he was not a gangster. In 1961, when he was sixty-four years old, Luciano decided to set the record straight by allowing a film producer to make a film of his life. Then orders arrived from America: 'The Little Man wouldn't like it.' Luciano summoned the producer, Martin Gosch, and told him regretfully that they would have to drop the idea; when Gosch pointed out that everyone knew that Luciano's word was his bond, Luciano replied that if he kept his word they would both end up dead. By way of compensation, he talked at length to Gosch about his life, and these conversations formed the basis of *The Last Testament of Lucky Luciano* by Martin Gosch and Richard Hammer, published in 1975. In January 1962, Luciano died suddenly of a heart attack; he was sixty-four.

Luciano's close associate Vito Genovese had fled from America in 1937, when the 'heat was on', and spent the war in Italy. If Mussolini was embarrassed to learn that his millionaire friend was a wanted gangster, he decided it was worth a little embarrassment when Genovese spent a quarter of a million dollars on a new fascist headquarters in Nola. When the Americans landed, Genovese persuaded them to take him on as an interpreter for army Intelligence. When a CIA agent discovered that he was a wanted killer, Genovese was escorted back to New York. Then one of the chief witnesses against him, Peter La Tempa, died of poison in his jail cell; in June 1946, Genovese was acquitted. He lost no time in reasserting his authority over the New York mobs. In October 1951, the New Jersey Mafia boss Willie Moretti was murdered. He was a close associate of Genovese's chief rival, Frank Costello, who had taken over Bugsy Siegel's gambling empire in Las Vegas; and Genovese was determined to 'cut himself in'. In June 1953, another Costello ally, Steven Franse, was murdered. In February 1955, it was the turn of Longy Zwillman, who was found hanged in the basement of his home in Orange, New Jersey, in a wire noose; the verdict was suicide. And on 2 May 1957, Costello was entering his apartment building when someone yelled 'This is yours, Frank,' and shot him in the head. The shout probably saved Costello's life; he lost a great deal of blood, but survived. In his pockets, police found gambling receipts from a Las Vegas casino, and when Costello declined to answer questions about them, or to name his would-be killer, he was jailed for contempt of court. The doorman picked out the gunman from a police photograph; it was Vincent ('The Chin') Gigante, a Genovese lieutenant.

Two months later, Frank Scalise, a Mafia underboss (second-in-command) was shot down at midday on a Bronx street. He was killed, according to underworld gossip, because he had been selling Mafia membership to non-Italians; but it seems altogether more likely that he was another victim in the gang war.

With Costello out of the running, Albert Anastasia, the Syndicate's chief executioner, stood in the way of Genovese's bid for power. Anastasia was known as the 'Mad Hatter' of crime because he became insanely homicidal when angry. It was Anastasia who had ordered the murder of a public-spirited citizen named Arnold Schuster who had recognized a famous bank robber, Willy Sutton (Willy the Actor) and informed the police. Schuster's murder – in March 1952 – was intended to warn all other public spirited citizens to mind their own business. Anastasia subsequently had Schuster's executioners killed, to cover his tracks.

Genovese heard that Costello had been conferring with Anastasia, and that the subject was almost certainly himself. He decided to strike first. His own gunmen were too well known to Anastasia, so Genovese approached the underboss of Anastasia's 'family', Carlo Gambino, and made him a proposition. Anastasia was one of the most wanted men in New York – Burton Turkus said he had been getting away with murder for thirty years – and his notoriety was bad for the Mafia. On 25 October 1957, Anastasia was lying in a barber's chair in the basement of the Sheraton Hotel, his eyes closed, when two men walked in and shot him at close range; Anastasia jumped up and fell into a mirror, which shattered as more shots hit him in the back of the head. The men ran out, threw away their pistols, and vanished.

This killing was arranged by a minor Mafia figure, Joey Gallo, an intensely individualistic gangster who was determined to become a *capo* in his own right. Gallo and his brothers were, at the time, members of another leading 'family', the Profacis; the assassination of Anastasia consolidated Gallo's position in the Profaci family, and during the next two years he is credited with about a dozen more 'hits'. When Gallo appeared in front of a senate committee on crime in 1959 – interrogated by Robert Kennedy – the hearing was televised, and Gallo became what his biographer Donald Goddard called in *Joey* (published in 1974), 'the matinée idol of organized crime'. A few months later, Judge Samuel Leibowitz sentenced him to three years in prison for 'coercion'; he was out within three months.

Gallo was becoming tired of being a mere 'hit man'; he may also have sensed that the family boss, Joe Profaci, was nearing his end (he died in 1962). In 1961, Gallo decided on a bold move – to kidnap the leading members of the Profaci family. His 'soldiers' grabbed four Profaci gangsters, including Frank, the Don's brother. Joe Profaci agreed to talk, provided the hostages were released. Soon after this, there was a murder attempt on Joey's brother, Larry Gallo, providentially interrupted by a routine visit from the police. By the time Gallo realized he had been outmanoeuvred by Profaci, he was under arrest for an attempt at extortion – trying to 'cut himself in' on the business of a moneylender named Theodore Moss. Gallo drew a seven-to-fourteen-year jail sentence, and the Profaci war came to an end. A few months later, Profaci died of cancer.

By this time, Vito Genovese's attempt to become the 'boss of bosses' had also ended in failure, largely due to the Syndicate's 'banker', Meyer Lansky. Lansky had been one of Luciano's closest associates; he owned enormous gambling interests in Florida. When Zwillman and Anastasia died, Lansky was aware that his own turn was imminent. In November 1957, Genovese summoned all America's top mafiosi to a meeting at the estate of a businessman named Joe Barbara, at Apalachin, in New York State. Lansky sent word that he was unable to attend because he had 'flu; oddly enough, none of his close friends attended either. That day, the local police called on Barbara, observed the dozens of expensive limousines in his driveway, and decided to investigate. Dozens of alarmed gangsters leapt out of windows and took to the woods. This happened minutes after the meeting had voted to appoint Vito Genovese the new head of the Syndicate for the whole country. It was an inauspicious beginning. No charges were made as a result of the Apalachin round-up – all the gangsters had perfectly legitimate reasons for being there – but the story made nationwide headlines, and Genovese lost face.

When Lansky heard that Genovese was planning to kill Luciano – even though Luciano was now living in 'retirement' – he decided it was time to take more serious action. One of Lansky's men was serving time in Sing Sing; his name was Nelson Cantellops. Lansky offered Cantellops a life pension and a promise of protection if he would testify against Genovese to the Narcotics Bureau. Cantellops decided he had nothing to lose. He 'sang' to such effect that Genovese was sentenced to fifteen years in jail.

Even in prison, Genovese remained a force in the underworld. It is alleged that he ordered a number of executions from his prison cell. Fellow mafiosi came to report to him every day. Other prisoners were not allowed to address him unless he spoke first. One of these prisoners was a gangster named Joe Valachi, who had worked for a *capo* named Joe Bonanno – known as Joe Bananas. Genovese seems to have believed that Valachi was one of those who was responsible for landing him in jail. Valachi was not a man of iron nerve; when he became convinced that his execution had been ordered, he asked to be placed in solitary confinement. There he decided that his only chance of escape lay in killing the executioner. On 22 June 1962, Valachi seized a piece of iron pipe, and killed a fellow prisoner named John Saupp, a forger. He discovered too late that Saupp bore a striking resemblance to a Genovese henchman called Joe DiPalermo, who had been the intended victim. Faced with execution, Valachi decided to try and strike a bargain with the authorities. The result was the most detailed revelation of Mafia crimes – and organization – since the days of 'Kid Twist' Reles. Valachi began by revealing that the term 'Mafia' was long out of date; it had been superseded first by 'Unione', then by 'Cosa Nostra'. He went on to confirm what the justice department had long suspected: that Dewey's intensive campaign against the Syndicate, culminating in the execution of Lepke and Pittsburgh Phil and the deportation of Luciano, had left the basic organization untouched. Robert Kennedy called Valachi's testimony 'the biggest intelligence breakthrough yet in combatting organized crime'.

This time the authorities did not make the same mistake as in the case of 'Kid Twist'. Valachi was kept under close guard in a comfortable jail cell; although Genovese offered $100,000 for his murder, he survived to die of a heart attack in his cell in Texas in 1971. Genovese himself had died in jail in 1969.

With Genovese behind bars, Carlo Gambino became the most powerful member of 'Cosa Nostra'. He soon found himself facing a challenge rather more dangerous than Gallo's attempt to take over the Profaci family. Joe Bonanno was a 'family' *capo* who had 'retired' to Tucson, Arizona, although he continued to have interests in New York, mainly in 'loan sharking' (usury). Bonanno was part of the nine-member Commission – elected from America's twenty-four leading Mafiosi – that governed Syndicate affairs. When Joe Bonanno's son Bill was also elected to the Commission, fellow members began to feel that the Bonanno family was acquiring undue influence. About this time Valachi's revelations caused Joe Bonanno some embarrassment, and he moved temporarily to Canada. There he heard rumours that other Commission members were planning to get rid of him. Bonanno decided to strike first, and ordered the killing of four leading mafiosi, including Carlo Gambino. Bonanno was closely allied to the Profaci clan – his son Bill was married to Rosalie Profaci – and the order was passed on to a Profaci 'hit man', Joe Colombo. And Colombo – no doubt recognizing that his chances of killing four leading gangsters were minimal – contacted Gambino and told him: 'It's war. Bananas is trying to take over.'

On 21 October 1964, Bonanno was walking towards the entrance of his New York apartment when two men pushed guns in his ribs and dragged him into a car. Bonanno was taken to a Catskill resort, where his fellow Commission members demanded explanations. They were not anxious to kill Bonanna; with his son still alive, that would mean all-out gang war, and much unwelcome publicity. What they really wanted was to persuade Bonanno to surrender his 'business' interests, and agree to vanish into retirement. Bonanno had little alternative. In exchange for his own life, and a promise that his family would be left untouched, he agreed to leave the country. Gloomy but philosophical, he retired to Haiti. The newspapers referred to the affair as 'the Banana split'. Joe Colombo was appointed head of the Profaci 'family' as a reward for loyalty.

Bill Bonanno was understandably upset by his father's kidnapping and subsequent retirement, and was indisposed to accept the demotion it implied. Clashes with rival factions led to an offer of a truce in January 1966; but as Bill Bonanno made his way towards the agreed location – the house of one of his own relatives – he was fired on from a doorway and had to run for his life. No one was hurt; but when Joe Bonanno heard about the attack in Haiti, he decided that his rivals had terminated their agreement by breaking it. In May 1966, he returned to America. It was the signal for what became known as 'the Banana war'. In November 1967, three ex-Bonanno gangsters, who had defected to the other side, were eating in a Brooklyn restaurant when a man approached their table and mowed them down with sub-machine-gun fire. In March 1968, another ex-Bonanna gangster was parking his car when he was hit in the throat by a bullet. A few days later, Bill Bonanna's chauffeur and body-guard was murdered by the rival faction. The killing was still going on twelve years later when, in July 1979, Carmine Galante – another Bonanna associate – was shot to death in a Brooklyn restaurant.

But perhaps the most interesting development of the 1970s was the Mafia's attempt to convince the American public that it did not exist. The architect of this audacious scheme was Joe Colombo, the ex hit-man who was now *capo* of the Profaci family. When his son was arrested in 1970, on a charge of melting coins into silver ingots, Colombo formed the Italian-American Civil Rights League to pro-test at the way good citizens were always being accused of being mafiosi. The Mafia, he said, was a myth invented by the police; there was no organized crime in America; and if there was, it was certainly not organized by Italians. He discovered, to his surprise, that he had tapped a vein of resentment in his fellow Italian-Americans, who felt they were a persecuted racial group. Hollywood was persuaded to abandon the term 'Mafia' – with the result that it was cut out of the script of *The Godfather*. The League threw a picket around the FBI headquarters; 50,000 people attended a rally in Manhattan's Columbus Circle. Colombo was voted League man of the year. Suddenly, he was a national figure. Politicians began to listen respectfully. Mafia gangsters became accustomed to posing for photographs with civic leaders. One reporter wrote of 'Colombo's magical hat trick by which the Mafia had been made to disappear like a magician's white rabbit'.

At first, older 'godfathers' – like Carlo Gambino – were willing to wait and see what came of it all. They had always hated publicity, but Colombo's seemed to be of the right kind. But things began to go wrong in December 1970, when Colombo's bodyguard Rocco Miraglia was arrested outside the State Supreme Court. He was carrying a black attaché case, which Colombo insisted belonged to him and contained papers of the Civil Rights League. Intrigued by his obvious concern, the FBI agents examined its contents, and found that it appeared to contain accounts of various financial transactions involving huge sums of money, and relating to various well-known Mafia figures, such as Carlo Gambino. The Mafia suddenly found itself again the subject of police harassment. And Colombo's League was blamed.

On 28 June 1971, Colombo stood up in front of a vast audience at Columbus Circle to review the results of the League's first year. As he moved through the cheering crowd towards the rostrum, shots rang out and he dropped to the ground; the man who had fired them was a negro photographer, Jerome Johnson. Within seconds, Johnson was dead, shot by a Colombo bodyguard (who was never identified). Colombo recovered after five hours of brain surgery, but his active role as a *capo* was over; he was paralysed.

One of the chief suspects behind the Colombo shooting was Joe Gallo, the lone 'individualist' who had gone to jail in 1961 and who came out ten years later. Gallo had spent his years in prison trying to make things difficult for the authorities, alleging persecution and being persecuted as a consequence. Back in his old territory, South Brooklyn he had immediately underlined his lack of respect for Joe Colombo by tearing down posters for the Civil Rights League and ordering Rocco Miraglia out of the district.

Ten years in jail had made Gallo decide that he was sick of being a gangster. After seeing a film called *The Gang That Couldn't Shoot Straight* – a spoof on the Mafia – he telephoned one of its leading actors, Jerry Orbach, and introduced himself. As a result, he became the friend of the Orbachs, and was soon being introduced to their society friends. Mrs Marta Orbach was impressed by his intelligence and his wide reading – he talked about Sartre, Camus, Céline, Kafka and Wilhelm Reich. 'He needed people who were as bright as he was,' Mrs Orbach said. The result was that Joey Gallo suddenly found himself a social celebrity. His new friends insisted that this was not the usual morbid interest in gangsters, but because he impressed them as genuinely intelligent and perceptive.

In March 1972, Gallo married a pretty divorcee with a young daughter. On 6 April he went to eat in a restaurant in Mulberry Street, which was on Joe Colombo's territory. It was either an act of rash bravado, or an indication that he felt he had nothing to fear – in spite of being chief suspect in the attempted assassination at Columbus Circle. The following evening, Gallo was rash enough to return there to celebrate his forty-third birthday; he had his new wife and stepdaughter with him. A Colombo henchman who was in the restaurant when the party arrived hurried out to a telephone. Joe Yacovelli, the Colombo family 'counsellor', agreed that it was time to punish these incursions. Half an hour later, three men walked into the restaurant and began shooting. Gallo was killed by the first bullet, although it took him some time to die.

Although more gang murders followed Joey Gallo's death – there were sixteen within a short period – his assassination seems to mark the end of an era. The Mafia had come to America more than ninety years earlier, when Giuseppe Esposito arrived in New Orleans from Sicily, and for the next fifty years it stamped its own vicious brand of individualism on American life. With the Luciano takeover and the formation of the Syndicate, it became a business organization; but the men behind it still belonged to the old tradition of ruthless individualism. By the time of Colombo's shooting, most of these figures were either dead or in 'retirement'. Meyer Lansky had been forced to leave the country on tax evasion charges; Carlo Gambino had succeeded in avoiding a deportation order by collapsing with a heart attack. The new leaders of the Mafia have grown up in the Syndicate, and have acquired the mentality of members of a national corporation. Even if Gallo had decided to 'go straight' – as he insisted he had during the final months of his life – he would have remained a disturbing anachronism. He was a walking affront to the

Organization Man mentality. His death underlines a paradox: that in less than a century, the Mafia – a word that once signified contempt for authority – has itself turned into precisely the kind of authority it once rebelled against.

It seems equally paradoxical that, in this century of scientific crime fighting, the Mafia should have defied every attempt by the authorities to destroy it. The solution is that, where there are vast sums of money to be made, <u>the wealthy criminal has no shortage</u> of <u>allies amongst the authorities.</u> And by the 1970s, drug smuggling had become one of the world's most prosperous industries. In 1960, a kilo of heroin cost about $2,500 in Marseilles, where it was manufactured from morphine base; in New York, it sold at about $6,000 a kilo wholesale, and at over $600,000 street price. By 1980, a kilo of grade four heroin cost about $12,000 from the supplier, and was worth a quarter of a million dollars in New York at wholesale prices. 'Cut' with mannite or lactose powder, its street price runs to many millions. No other business in the world provides such profits.

In 1962, a swoop by the New York Narcotics Bureau (dramatized as 'the French Connection') dealt a crippling blow to the Marseilles drug traffic. Palermo, the original home of the Mafia, became the centre of the world's drug traffic. Sixty per cent of America's heroin came through Palermo. The result is that between 1973 and 1983, Palermo has become one of the richest cities in Italy. One result is that in the 1980s, Palermo has had an average of two gang murders per week.

Anybody who took an anti-Mafia stand was in danger. In 1982, the victims included two judges, two police chiefs and a leading Christian Democrat politician. And at this point, the Mafia apparently overreached itself. Pio La Torre, the Sicilian Communist Party leader was a relentless campaigner against the Mafia and a member of the Parliamentary Anti-Mafia Commission; he had sponsored a bill to give the police special powers to deal with the Mafia, including access to private bank accounts and tapping telephone conversations. The 'La Torre law' failed to reach the statute book. On 30 April 1982, La Torre was ambushed and shot to death.

General Alberto Dalla Chiesa, the policeman who had defeated the Red Brigades, was appointed prefect of Palermo. When he arrived with his new young wife, he had a foreboding that he would be killed.

Dalla Chiesa pressed hard for the La Torre law to be passed, but the government dragged its feet. In a country as poor as Italy, it could be politically dangerous to destroy an industry that brings wealth.

Then on 3 September 1982, Alberto Dalla Chiesa was shot dead, together with his wife and his police escort. The result was that the Church launched a violent campaign against the Mafia; the Pope denounced it on a visit to Palermo. And the 'La Torre law' was passed by a guilt-ridden Parliament. The result has been Italy's most successful campaign against the Mafia so far. In November 1982, sixty-five defendants came to trial in Palermo in what became known as the Spatola trial – after Rosario Spatola, the alleged Mafia 'accountant' whose multi-million-dollar 'laundering' operations had been opened to investigation by the new law. But with at least twenty backroom heroin refineries in Sicily capable of producing half a billion dollars' worth of heroin a week, it seems doubtful whether even the anti-Mafia law can get to the root of the problem.

Compared to America and Italy, there is something engagingly amateurish about organized crime in Britain. After the trial of the Kray twins in 1969, it was revealed by their defence counsel that, at one point, the twins went to New York and tried to make some business arrangement with the Mafia, explaining that they ruled London, that the police were in their pay, and that they were immune from arrest. The Mafia sent an envoy to London – who was promptly arrested in the Mayfair Hotel and placed in Brixton jail to await deportation. 'I thought you told me you ran this place?' he said with disgust when the twins came to see him in prison.

Gangsterism came to Britain after the First World War; by the end of the 1920s, the slums of most major cities had their mobs of criminal hooligans. But the kind of gang warfare described in *No Mean City* (see pp. 181–2) has more in common with the present-day violence among gangs of Mexican teenagers in Los Angeles than with the American Mafia. That is to say, it is essentially a phenomenon of 'territory' – the 'overcrowded rats syndrome'. Overcrowding heightens tension; tension heightens aggression. In a 'normal' social situation – without overcrowding – the dominant five per cent naturally find various outlets for their need for self-expression, from daydreaming to competitive sport. But in a society that teems with aggression, even the intelligent find themselves unable to ignore the challenge; their self-respect demands the ability to respond aggressively to aggression. So normal competition comes to express itself through violence.

In Glasgow in the 1920s there were dozens of gangs with names like the Norman Conquerors (from Norman Street), the Briggate Boys, the Beehive Gang and the South Side Stickers. Norman Lucas has argued in his book *Britain's Gangland* that Peter Williamson, the leader of the Beehive Gang, was Britain's first true gangleader. He enlisted various criminals, such as burglars and safebreakers, and ran a profitable business. Since guns are difficult to obtain in Britain, the Glasgow gangs used razors and broken bottles. Violence was casual and instantaneous. A newspaper reporter, Arthur Helliwell, told a story of a young man who saw someone being attacked in the street, and intervened; he was knocked unconscious with a bottle. He woke up to find a kindly-looking man asking anxiously: 'Are you all right, son?' When he nodded, the man said: 'Well, next time, mind your own business,' and slashed his cheek to the bone with a razor.

Even in the 1920s, football hooliganism was common in Glasgow. When a footballer named William Fullarton scored a winning goal in a match between two local Glasgow teams, he was afterwards battered unconscious with a hammer. He was so enraged that he formed his own gang – called 'The Billy Boys' – which took violent reprisals against the rival supporters. Fullarton's natural leadership qualities made his gang one of the most formidable in the Gorbals, and he provoked some spectacular street battles with rival gangs. Fullarton was a Protestant, and he often marched through Catholic territory with a band playing Orange marches. He was arrested in 1934 after he led his gang into battle when drunk, clutching a baby girl in his arms. The danger to the child led the police to arrest him – with many broken heads – and he was sentenced to a year in prison. He fought in the Second World War and, when he came back, found that he had outgrown the need for violence. For the remainder of his life, he worked in a Clydebank shipyard. But when he died in 1962, vast crowds followed his coffin, and the floral tributes and brass band were reminiscent of a Chicago funeral of the 1920s; the inhabitants of Bridgeton – his old territory – remembered his days as a gangleader with affection.

The case is interesting because it is clear that, in less aggressive surroundings, Fullarton would have expressed his 'dominance' by becoming a well-known footballer; the beating turned him into a gangster.

Even more instructive is the more recent case of Jimmy Boyle, another gangster from the Gorbals. Boyle spent his first period in a remand home at the age of thirteen; by his late teens, he had become a Glasgow character, a 'man of respect' (to use the Mafia term) who made a more-than-adequate living out of the 'protection' racket. When a fellow gangster called Boyle an obscene name, Boyle slashed him with a razor; the man died, and Boyle was sentenced to fifteen years in jail. He became known as one of the most difficult prisoners ever held in a Scottish jail, a 'mad dog' – like Carl Panzram – who would attack a guard even when he knew it meant being beaten unconscious and spending months in solitary confinement. He ate with his fingers and smeared the walls of his cell with excrement. When news of his exploits reached the Glasgow public, there was a general feeling that he ought to have been 'put down' like a mad dog. After years of defiance, Boyle was finally transferred to the Barlinnie Experimental Special Unit, where prisoners were allowed an unusual degree of freedom. Boyle found it a shattering experience when a guard casually handed him a knife to cut the string of a parcel. He began to express himself through sculpture and writing. His auto-biography, *A Sense of Freedom*, was an immediate success. Now released from prison – and working actively for prisoners' welfare – it is clear that Boyle has also outgrown his violence. The dominance that once found its expression in violence has been re-routed into creativity. Unlike Panzram, Boyle was able to turn back before he had gone too far.

It seems clear that the gangster mentality is usually created by slum conditions in which 'territory' becomes a matter for dispute. Without subscribing to the view that criminals are unfortunate victims of an unfair society, we can nevertheless recognize that men like Joey Gallo and Jimmy Boyle would never have become gangsters if they had been born into a middle-class environment and attended high school and university. Then why, since Britain has as many slums as America, have the gangs never succeeded in infiltrating British society in the way that the Mafia has infiltrated America? The answer seems to lie in the British 'genius for compromise'. The temperance movement in Britain was as powerful as in America in the early twentieth century; but it would have been inconceivable for the British Parliament to vote for Prohibition. In America, Cosa Nostra derives a huge part of its income from drugs. In Britain, a drug addict can get his drugs on the National Health, provided he agrees to treatment; so the opportunities for a British drugs syndicate are circumscribed.

In the 1920s and '30s, it looked for a while as if Mafia-style gangsterism had come to England. With the end of the First World War, England turned its back decisively on Victorianism. There was a new sexual freedom, and a determination to have a good time. Race meetings became more popular than ever before; and since vast sums of money changed hands, one inevitable result was the formation of race gangs. The bookmakers were expected to pay 'protection', and to purchase various other services and amenities – stools, race cards, even chalk – from the gangs. A Birmingham gang, known as the Brummagem Boys and led by a man named Bill Kimber, dominated most of the Midlands and much of the north. But when they attempted to move south, they encountered a rival gang from London's Italian quarter, the Sabini Boys, led by Charles, Harry and Joseph Sabini. These were reported to be connected with the Sicilian Mafia. Throughout the 1930s, there were violent clashes between the Brummagem Boys and the Sabini gang. One battle in London's Mornington Crescent ended with the arrest of Joseph Sabini and five of his men; the police also collected a number of revolvers and other dangerous weapons. At the trial at the Old Bailey, witnesses failed to appear, or had suffered lapses of memory. A member of the Brummagem gang was found shot in the street near the flat of Charles Sabini, but claimed he had no idea who fired the gun. It began to look as if there was nothing to stop the Sabini Mafia from becoming as powerful as its counterpart in New York – particularly after a tremendous battle at Bath race course, which ended with the permanent retreat of the Brummagem Boys back to the Midlands. A rival gang from Hoxton began to invade the Sabini territory, and their battles at various race tracks so inflamed public opinion that the police decided on tough action. When sixteen members of the Hoxton gang were arrested after a battle at Lewes race course, all were given stiff jail sentences. And by the beginning of the Second World War, when the Sabini brothers were interned as enemy aliens, the race gangs had ceased to enjoy immunity, and dozens of their members were in jail for long periods. There was no national Syndicate to ensure 'business as usual' while the gang bosses were in jail.

Prostitution, unlike racing, continued to flourish during the war – particularly in London, which was full of sex-starved servicemen – and ensured the continued prosperity of another family of Italian gangsters, the Messina brothers. Their father, Giuseppe Messina, had left Sicily in the mid-1890s to become an assistant brothel keeper in Valetta, Malta. In ten years he had enough money to move to Alexandria, and to set up a chain of brothels all over the Mediterranean. Five sons were born between 1898 and 1915. In 1932, the family was expelled from Egypt, and – since Giuseppe Messina could claim British citizenship from his long residence in Malta – they were able to move to London. There they found the vice scene old fashioned and inefficient, with drab-looking females soliciting on street corners. The brothers imported glamorous-looking girls from the Continent, and made them British citizens by marrying them to down-and-outs who were willing to go through a registry office ceremony for a few pounds; these girls were installed in flats, and paid the brothers ninety per cent of their takings – which, during the war years, amounted often to £100 a night.

The brothers recognized that 'non-professionals' – the kind of girls who would not normally drift into prostitution – are more desirable to the male than the usual tired-looking streetwalker, and developed their own efficient methods of recruiting a higher class of girl. She would be courted by one of the brothers, seduced, and installed in an expensive flat. When she realized that her lover was getting tired of her, and that the life of luxury was about to end, she was usually in the right frame of mind to agree to receive a few selected male guests. Within weeks she was a full-time prostitute.

During the Second World War, the Messina brothers became very rich. They were also very discreet, and their habit of moving between England and the continent made them elusive as well. They first came to the attention of the police when another gangleader, Carmelo Vassalo, tried to exact 'protection' from three Messina girls; there was a fight in South Kensington in which Vassalo lost the tips of two fingers. Vassalo and his gang were charged with demanding money with menaces, but Eugenio Messina also found himself in the dock for wounding Vassalo. He was sentenced to three years in prison. While he was awaiting his appeal in jail, one of his brothers tried to bribe a guard to 'look after' Eugenio, and received a sentence of two months.

In 1950, a newspaper reporter, Duncan Webb, 'exposed' the brothers in the *Sunday People*, and four of them hastily left the country. The fifth, Alfredo, made the mistake of remaining in his home in a respectable district of Wembley, convinced that the police had no evidence against him. Two policemen called on him, and when one left the room, the other alleged that Alfredo tried to bribe him with bundles of £100 notes. A judge disbelieved Alfredo's defence that the policeman had asked to see into his safe, and extracted the notes himself, and Alfredo received two years in jail. A large proportion of London's underworld was convinced that he had been 'framed'.

Two of the brothers, Eugenio and Carmelo, established themselves in Brussels; but the Belgian police were determined not to allow them to establish a foothold, and in 1955 both were charged with carrying loaded revolvers. At their trial in Tournai, one indignant middle-class mother told how her daughter had been seduced by Eugenio, who had then proposed that she should go to London to 'work'. The mother accused Eugenio of being a white slaver and persuaded her daughter not to go. Evidence like this led the judge to sentence Eugenio to seven years. Carmelo, whose health was poor, received two.

Attilio Messina, who had returned to London, was also brought to bay by angry parents. Edna Kallman, a woman in her early forties, told how she had been returning home from her job as a dressmaker in 1947 when Attilio had offered her a lift in his car. He took her to dinner, seduced her, and installed her in a flat in Knightsbridge. After two years, he told her that she either had to get out, or work as a prostitute. Cowed and miserable, she agreed. She was moved to a flat in Bond Street, and made to solicit in the street. As her health began to fail and her looks to deteriorate, she attracted a poorer class of customer; Attilio made her work twice as hard. One night, she called the police to help a fellow prostitute who was being beaten up by a client. Attilio told her grimly that he would deal with her the next day. Convinced that this meant something worse than the usual beating, she fled to the home of her mother and stepfather in Derby, and told them the whole tragic story. They went to the police, and Attilio was arrested. Although he insisted that he was a respectable antiques dealer, he was found guilty, and sentenced to four years in prison. This was virtually the end of the Messinas as a power in the underworld.

Gang life in England was always violent; but until the 1960s it was far less ruthless and dangerous than its American counterpart. The case of Jack 'Spot' is typical. Spot – whose real name was Comer – ran a race ring that specialized in fraud; when punters returned to collect their winnings, the bookie had absconded. In 1955, in Soho, a quarrel broke out between Spot and a bookmaker named Albert Dimes, a friend of a rival gang boss named Billy Hill. Spot produced a knife and chased Dimes into a fruit shop, slashing at him; in his excitement, he dropped the knife, and Dimes picked it up and slashed Spot. When the police arrived, Spot had fainted from loss of blood and Dimes had left in a taxi. At the trial, Spot insisted –against all the evidence – that Dimes was the aggressor, and received unexpected support from an eighty-eight-year-old retired clergyman named Basil Andrews. Andrews claimed that he had happened to be in Frith Street when the fight broke out, and saw Dimes draw the knife on Spot. It was only later, when he read about the case in the newspapers, that he decided to come forward out of a sense of fair play. His evidence was instrumental in getting Spot acquitted; but there was evidently some doubt in the jury's mind, for Dimes was acquitted too. The British public was outraged by this verdict; how could two men who had slashed each other both be innocent? The Rev. Basil Andrews found himself the object of unwelcome attention, and when he let slip that he was frequently broke because of 'harmless flutters in the sporting world', suspicion increased. Finally, Andrews admitted that he had accepted a few pounds to testify in Spot's favour. The three men accused of bribing him went to prison. Six months later, Spot was out walking with his wife when he was beaten to the ground with a crowbar and slashed with a razor. He preserved the underworld code of silence, insisting that he had no idea of who did it. But his wife named Billy Hill and several of his men. Two of these were arrested, and sentenced to seven years each. The British public was left with the vague impression that justice will always triumph in the end.

A case that took place in 1960 threw some doubt on that

proposition. The manager of a Soho club, Selwyn Cooney, decided to pay a visit to the Pen Club in Duval Street, Stepney; he was accompanied by his girlfriend, the barmaid, Joan Bending. In the Pen Club, he was approached by a gangster named James Nash, who accused him of 'having a go' at his brother Ronnie. Cooney was knocked to the ground; his nose was broken and some teeth knocked out. Then two shots were fired. The doorman, Billy Ambrose, collapsed with a bullet in his stomach; Cooney was also shot. When the police arrived, he was lying dead on the pavement outside. Nash was nowhere to be found, but two other men, John Read and Joseph Pyle – who had helped Nash to beat up Cooney – were arrested.

The chief prosecution witness was to be Mrs Fay Sadler, part-owner of the Pen Club. But she vanished, and all attempts to locate her failed. Cooney's friend John Simons had to be kept under constant police surveillance because the gangs were determined to silence him. His girlfriend, a twenty-year-old blonde named Barbara Ibbotson, had her face slashed in Soho. The prosecution pressed the judge to bring the trial forward because of the danger to witnesses; the same day, Barbara Ibottson was in her bath when three men broke into the flat, held her head under water, and slashed her face again. She fled from London. At the trial in April 1960, Simons testified that it was Nash who murdered Cooney; but Fay Sadler had still not appeared. Then, unexpectedly, the judge stopped the trial and discharged the jury; one of the jurors was later said to have discussed the case with a prisoner on remand. When the new trial opened, a surprise witness insisted that Joan Bending had been drunk at the time of the affray, and that Simons was in another bar. The charges against Read and Pyle were dropped, and James Nash was acquitted. All three were later charged with causing grievous bodily harm to Cooney; Nash received five years, and the others, eighteen months. Simons was later attacked and left bleeding from razor slashes. Fay Sadler reappeared after the trial, alleging that she had been ill. Cooney's girlfriend, Joan Bending, was forced to flee from London; during the course of the next few years, she changed her address repeatedly. The general impression left by the case was that British justice had been slightly less than triumphant.

In 1956, when sentencing two gangsters for a knife attack, the judge remarked: 'It sounds like the worst days of Prohibition in Chicago rather than London in 1956.' The remark showed prescience. Although the police were still unaware of it, London already had two gangs who had consciously modelled themselves on the Mafia: the Richardsons and the Krays.

Charles Richardson, born in Camberwell in 1934, spent his first term in approved school when he was fourteen – the year in which his father deserted the family. In 1956, he set up the Peckford Scrap Metal Company in south London; it was, in fact, a front for receiving stolen goods. Richardson had considerable talent as a businessman, and could probably have made a fortune by legitimate means. Instead, he and his younger brother Eddie practised large-scale fraud. The method was to open a wholesale business and order goods from a manufacturer. These were promptly paid for. So were subsequent orders – each larger than the last. Finally, they would place an enormous order – for perhaps £20,000-worth of goods – and then disappear. The goods were then sold at cut rates, usually to market dealers.

Even in 1956, the police were aware of the fast-growing empire of the Richardsons. But none of the West End club owners to whom they hired out one-armed bandits – and from whom they exacted 'protection' – dared to complain. Charles Richardson made sure of that by terrorizing anyone he even suspected of crossing him. The evidence suggests that he was a sadist who enjoyed inflicting physical injury. A childhood friend named Laurence Bradbury described his methods. When Richardson asked him to use his trucks to move stolen goods, Bradbury became nervous and made excuses. One night, Charles and Eddie Richardson came to the club that Bradbury was running for them, and stayed on until it was closed. Then Bradbury was held down on a table and his sleeve rolled up. His forearm was cut from the elbow to the wrist with a razor, which was run up and down in the cut several times. Bradbury abandoned all idea of trying to leave the Richardson gang. In 1966, he was accused of killing a business associate of Richardson's in South Africa – a man Richardson believed had double-crossed him – and was sentenced to life imprisonment.

At these torture sessions, Charles Richardson dressed himself up in judge's robes, and conducted a mock trial. Then the victim was stripped naked, and a device known as 'the box' was produced. This was an electric generator with clip-on leads. These were attached to various parts of the body, including the genitals, and the handle was turned. Buckets of cold water were thrown over the victim to lower his electrical resistance. Teeth would be pulled out with pliers, and cigarettes would be stubbed out on the bare flesh. An electric fire would be held close to the body, and slowly moved around. One man named Harris was tortured for an hour in an attempt to make him reveal the whereabouts of a man the Richardsons wanted to interview. Finally convinced that he did not know, Richardson allowed him to put his clothes on; then he suddenly plunged a knife through his foot, pinning him to the floor. Then, unexpectedly, Richardson admitted he had made a mistake and said he was sorry; he handed Harris £150. All this suggests that Richardson was deriving pleasure from the torture, and was unable to resist driving the knife through his foot; then, with the urge satisfied, he became conciliatory.

In July 1965, a man named James Taggart was asked to visit the Richardsons to discuss 'business'. He was, in fact, accused of holding back £1,200 on a business deal. Taggart was stripped, beaten, cut and given electric shock treatment. An associate named Alfred Berman, who walked in while Taggart was being tortured, described being appalled at the sight of a naked man tied to a chair and covered in blood while Richardson screamed at him and kept hitting him with a heavy pair of pliers – the pair used for pulling teeth. After being untied, Taggart was made to clean up his own blood – including splashes on the wall.

He went to the police, who were shocked at his injuries, and even more shocked at his story. Bradbury was at this time under arrest for the murder of the businessman, Thomas Waldeck, in South Africa, and a detective flew out from London to question him. What he heard convinced him that the Richardsons were at least as dangerous as their more notorious rivals, the Kray brothers. But by this time, Charles Richardson was a wealthy businessman with large offices in Park Lane. It was necessary to proceed with caution, and Commander John du Rose – who later trapped the Krays – was appointed to look into the brothers' business activities. It was suspected that Richardson had police officers in his pay, and every man on the investigation squad was ordered to total secrecy. Even so, the Richardsons heard about the investigation, and they began to make preparations to leave the country. By this time, the enquiry had been under way for a year, and it was necessary to act quickly. The Assistant Chief Constable Gerald McArthur – who was in charge of the investigation – went on holiday to Austria, to allay the suspicion of the gang, and returned secretly a few days later. The police swooped at dawn on July 1966, and arrested the Richardson brothers and another eight men; Charles Richardson's common-law wife was also arrested. At the trial, victim after victim came forward to describe torture, and it became clear that this was something more than the normal intimidation practised by the underworld; Charles Richardson did it for pleasure.

After a trial of forty-two days, Charles Richardson was sentenced to a total of fifty-eight years in jail; his brother Eddie received a ten-year sentence. Roy Hall, the man in charge of the electric generator, also received ten years. Other gang members received various sentences.

In prison, Charles Richardson showed every sign of being a reformed character, and by 1980, was working with handicapped prisoners and had become a 'trusty'. Then, angered by eight parole rejections, he absconded from his open prison. An offer to give himself up came to nothing, and at the time of this writing, he is still at large, allegedly living in Paris.

The Richardson gang, like the American Mafia, believed in keeping a low profile. They were not interested in notoriety, only in money and power. The Kray twins, their chief rivals, were as flamboyant as Big Jim Colosimo or Al Capone. Oddly enough, their methods kept them out of jail rather longer than the Richardsons.

Ronald and Reginald Kray were born in the East End of London in October 1933; at school, they acquired a reputation as formidable fighters. In their teens, both became professional boxers; then, after a period in the army – much of it spent in detention – they worked for Jack 'Spot' at a night club in Covent Garden. They had soon moved into the 'protection' racket, and 'cut themselves in' on a billiard hall in the Mile End Road and a club called the Green Dragon in the East End. Business prospered; with their reputation for violence, they were soon known and feared from Woolwich to the City.

In 1956, Ronald Kray landed in serious trouble; with two companions, he strode into the Britannia pub in Stepney, and shouted at a man named Terrence Martin, 'Come on outside or we'll kill you in here.' Outside, without paying attention to many witnesses, they beat Martin and stabbed him with a bayonet. As a result of this affair, Ronald Kray and one of his companions were sentenced to three years; the man who had actually used the bayonet, Robert Ramsey, received seven.

In Winchester jail it became clear that Ronald Kray was mentally unstable, and he was transferred to a mental hospital in Epsom. One day, Reggie came to visit him. It was Ronnie who walked out with the other visitors. Then Reggie established his own identity, and had to be allowed to go. The journalist Norman Lucas finally persuaded the Krays that Ronnie should give himself up. He was sent back to the mental hospital. Freed in the spring of 1959, he went back into partnership with Reggie, and they opened the Double R club – the initials intertwined like those of a Rolls Royce – in Bow. They also opened a West End night club and restaurant called Esmeralda's Barn, off Knightsbridge, and began to acquire a certain celebrity as they mixed with show business people and politicians. The food was excellent (I once ate there myself), but their hospitality was too lavish, and it collapsed. A venture called the Kentucky Club in the East End was more successful. In 1959, Reggie was sentenced to prison for eighteen months for demanding money with menaces; but he was soon out again, and the life of celebrity – and violence – continued as before.

The twins seemed to be dual personalities. Their cousin Ronald Hart, who had spent some time in prison, went to work for them in the mid-1960s, and described his impressions to Norman Lucas. Socially, the twins were charming; they dressed well, their manners were excellent, and their famous friends found it impossible to believe any ill of them. Yet both were capable of unprovoked violence; Ronald, in particular, was given to fits of hysterics in which he seemed to become half insane. One man who placed a hand on his shoulder and said jokingly that he was getting fat had his face slashed open so that it needed seventy stitches. A customer in a pub who asked for change was beaten up. A man who was suspected of cheating the twins was shot in the leg; Reggie Kray told Hart, 'You want to try it some time. It's a nice feeling when you shoot someone.' Hart told Lucas: 'I saw beatings that were unnecessary even by underworld standards and witnessed people slashed with a razor just for the hell of it.'

In 1965, Reggie Kray married his childhood sweetheart, Frances Shea, seven years his junior. The marriage was a disaster from the beginning. On their honeymoon, he locked her in the bridal suite in Athens and went to get drunk. She claimed that the marriage was never consummated. Two years later, she left him, and two months after that, killed herself with an overdose. She was twenty-three.

It was also in 1965 that the Krays were arrested and charged with demanding money with menaces; they were refused bail on the grounds that they might 'seek to interfere with prosecution witnesses'. Lord Boothby – an acquaintance of Ronald Kray's – caused something of a sensation by asking in the House of Lords how much longer they were to be held without trial. After ninety days and two trials, the twins were acquitted.

The chief rival of the Krays were the Richardson brothers, Eddie and Charles, who dominated crime on the south side of the river. The rival gangleaders had nothing but contempt for one another. The chief lieutenant of the Richardsons, a man named George Cornell, was also hated by Ronald Kray; he had openly taunted Ronald with being a homosexual, and had warned the father of Kray's nineteen-year-old boyfriend of the nature of the relationship. By March 1966, most of the Richardson gang was in custody. Only one prominent member had escaped arrest – George Cornell. And on the evening of 6 March he walked into a pub called the Blind Beggar, in Bethnal Green – the heart of the Krays' 'manor'. Half a mile away, at the 'Lion', in Tapp Street, Ronald Kray was informed that Cornell was on his territory. He left immediately, in company with a henchman named John Barrie, a Scot. At 8.30, he walked into the bar of the Blind Beggar. It was a quiet evening and the bar was almost empty. As Barrie fired warning shots at the ceiling, Ronald Kray drew a 9 mm Mauser pistol and shot Cornell above the right eye. Then the two gunmen walked out. When Reggie – back in the 'Lion' – was told that Ronald had just shot George Cornell, he remarked: 'Ronnie does some funny things.'

Questioned at the Commercial Road police station, Ronald Kray denied all knowledge of the shooting; he repeated his denial soon afterwards to a crowd of reporters. Everyone in the East End knew that the 'colonel' (as Ronald was known) had killed George Cornell; but there seemed to be no witnesses to the shooting.

The murder of Cornell seems to epitomize what Van Vogt calls 'the decision to be out of control'. It served no purpose; Cornell was in no way a threat to the Kray gang. But Ronald Kray had become accustomed to being allowed to lose his temper and commit violence. When he heard that Cornell was on his territory, he felt that he 'deserved' to die – it was the Nero syndrome. Besides, a killing would confirm his reputation as Britain's leading gangster.

This is precisely what it did. As the months went by, and the police made no attempt to arrest him, it began to look as though the twins were – as they boasted – above the law. When witnesses failed to pick out Ronald Kray in an identification parade, the brothers threw a party and invited the press. And, incredibly, Ronnie now convinced his brother that it was *his* turn to do a murder. 'He was very proud that he had murdered,' Hart told Norman Lucas, 'and was constantly getting at Reggie and asking him when he was going to do his murder. He used to goad him. Whenever Reggie got drunk he brooded on Ronnie's remarks . . . He could not, he pointed out, just kill anyone without a reason, but Ronnie didn't seem to think of that.'

So in order that Reggie could also boast of being a murderer, a victim was selected. This was a small-time crook called Jack McVitie, known as 'the Hat' because he was ashamed of his partially bald head and wore a hat most of the time. McVitie had a cutting sense of humour, and when his remarks were reported back to the Krays, they decided that something had to be done. In fact, McVitie sent them an apology, assuring them that he had not intended any harm. Then more satirical insults were reported. The twins decided that, since a victim was needed, McVitie was the obvious choice.

On 28 October 1967, the Krays and several henchmen arrived at the Regency Jazz Club in Hackney – one of the establishments they 'protected' – and informed the proprietor that they intended to kill Jack 'the Hat' on his premises; he begged them to do nothing of the sort, and they finally agreed to do it elsewhere. They moved on to a basement in nearby Stoke Newington, leaving two brothers named Lambrianou at the club to escort McVitie to the 'party'.

As soon as McVitie entered the room, Reggie Kray pushed him against the wall and pulled the trigger of a revolver. It misfired. As McVitie struggled and fought, the others punched him. Reggie pressed the gun to his head and fired again; nothing happened. He threw away the gun in disgust, and another gang member handed him a carving knife. He jabbed it into McVitie's face, then into his stomach. As Ronald Kray shouted 'Don't stop, Reg. Kill him!' he stood astride McVitie, held the knife with both hands, and plunged it into his throat; the blade came out of the back and went into the floorboards.

The body was wrapped in an eiderdown and driven away in a car. The twins' elder brother Charles was aroused from his bed, and deputed to get rid of it. He took it along to the house of a man called Fred Foreman, who – according to later evidence – had already disposed of one body for the twins. Neither the body nor the car has ever been found.

The twins decided that it might be diplomatic to retire from the London scene for a while. They bought a large house in Suffolk, close to Hadleigh, a village to which they had been evacuated during the war, and there began to live the life of country squires. They provided the parish church with a new roof, bought a donkey for the village children, and generally behaved with discretion and good humour.

The Krays were convinced that no one would dare to give the police information about their activities. They were right. Police investigating the murder of Cornell and the disappearance of McVitie – and rumours that the twins had also been responsible for the disappearance of an escaped prisoner known as 'the Mad Axeman' – met with terrified silence. But the police had time – and manpower – on their side. Commander John du Rose of Scotland Yard decided to form a special team, whose headquarters would be in Tintagel House, a police office block overlooking the river at Lambeth. It was du Rose who had been chiefly responsible for ending the reign of the Messina brothers. He placed Detective Superintendent 'Nipper' Read in charge of the team. They used spies and informers, and even policewomen disguised as charladies. Houses were kept under constant surveillance, and members of the 'Firm' (as the gang was known) were shadowed. In May 1968, du Rose decided they had enough evidence to proceed. At dawn on 8 May a squad of sixty-eight men made surprise raids in the East End. They found Reginald Kray in bed with a blonde girl and Ronald in bed with a youth. Others who were arrested were the Lambrianou brothers, John Barrie (who had been with Ronnie when he shot Cornell), Frederick Foreman and Charles Kray. In January 1969, eleven men stood in the dock at the Old Bailey.

The long list of charges included three murders: George Cornell,

Jack McVitie and 'the Mad Axeman', Frank Mitchell. Mitchell, like McVitie, had simply vanished; but evidence pointed to the Krays, who had arranged his escape from Dartmoor in December 1966.

Frank Mitchell was a simple-minded giant who had started life in a home for sub-normal children, and had been constantly in trouble throughout his life – mostly for burglary. He had escaped several times from prisons and mental institutions; on one occasion, he had tried to attack a magistrate, and although he was manacled, it had taken twelve men to subdue him. After an escape from the Rampton mental hospital, he had stolen two hatchets – hence the nickname. After nine years in Dartmoor, he was a 'trusty', and was allowed out with working parties; he used to stroll into pubs and take bottles back into Dartmoor. Because he was easygoing and good tempered when he was not crossed, the prison authorities found it easier to allow him to do as he liked. But when there seemed to be no prospect of release after nine years, Mitchell decided to escape. This was not difficult, since he was often out all day. By the time his absence was noticed, Mitchell was sitting in front of the fire in a flat in Barking Road, east London, watching the news of his escape on television. The flat had been provided by the Krays. They also provided a pretty club hostess named Liza Prescott to share his bed.

The authorities used newspapers to ask Mitchell to give himself up. Members of the Kray 'firm' cautiously negotiated with the Home Office, on the understanding that Mitchell would be considered for parole if he surrendered. But when Mitchell was consulted, he announced he had no intention of surrendering. He was sick of jail, and he was enjoying freedom and a normal sex life. The Krays became aware that he was going to be a severe embarrassment.

On 23 December 1966, eleven days after the escape, a Kray henchman called at the flat and asked Mitchell to go with him; Mitchell kissed Liza Prescott – who had become fond of him – and left. A few minutes later she heard muffled bangs from outside. The prosecution alleged that Mitchell had got into a van where he had been shot in the head by Fred Foreman, whose gun was equipped with a silencer. At a party soon afterwards, Reggie Kray burst into tears when Mitchell was mentioned, and said: 'This is a tough game.'

With the Krays in custody, many witnesses came forward. The

barmaid who had been present when Cornell was shot – and had insisted she saw nothing – now described the killing and admitted, 'I was too afraid to talk.' And the Krays' cousin, Ronald Hart, described the murder of Jack McVitie. After a forty-day trial, ten of the eleven men in the dock were found guilty. The Kray twins received thirty years each; their brother Charles received ten. The days when London resembled Prohibition Chicago were over.

The study of organized crime underlines the point made by Yochelson and Samenow in *The Criminal Personality*: that the basic characteristic of the criminal is not so much calculated wickedness as a kind of childish wilfulness. We can see this very clearly in the case of Charles Richardson, holding mock trials in his judge's robes. This was not uncontrollable rage; it was the *decision* 'to be out of control'. The same is true of Ronald Kray's shooting of George Cornell. Kray pointed out in court that he had sent fruit to Cornell's son – who was in hospital – only a few days before the killing. It was not rage; it was a feeling that he 'owed it to himself' to avenge this insult, as deliberately as Astyages arranged for Harpagus to eat his own son (see p. 173). He was a judge delivering a sentence, according to a set of laws he had invented himself. Charles Richardson insisted that he had become a changed man in jail; yet he walked out of an open prison because his request for parole had been denied – the gesture of a child suddenly overcome by self-pity. In the last analysis, the criminal is a Peter Pan, a child who refuses to grow up.

Four

POLITICAL GANGSTERISM

At the time the victors of the First World War were quarrelling about the apportionment of the spoils, Russia was divided by a murderous civil war; it ended in 1920. In that year, the year Prohibition came to America, Russia prepared to begin an extra-ordinary experiment: to put Karl Marx's theory of socialism into practice.

From the beginning, the Bolshevists had shown that they had no intention of wasting time on old fashioned democratic procedures. It is true that they had suggested a parliament – a constituent assembly – before the revolution; but when they won only about a quarter of the votes, they used force to break it up. By 1921, most of the people of Russia were sick of the communists and their slaughter of opponents – they had inaugurated a terror like the one that followed the French Revolution – and fourteen thousand sailors on Kronstadt Island – off Petrograd – constituted themselves spokesmen for the peasants and demanded a socialist government without the Bolshevists. Lenin sent in troops, and most of the sailors were killed. In 1922, he re-imposed censorship of literature, its purpose being to prevent publication of counter-revolutionary works. By 1924, with the civil war over and the loyalists – the Whites – defeated, Lenin decided that it would be too much to attempt to impose Marxism – state ownership of all resources – in one swoop. His New Economic Policy declared that only large industries would belong to the state; the small businessmen and farmers could continue to operate as before. Lenin, in fact, showed every sign of being a realist who would apply Marxism cautiously to see how it worked. But he died in January 1924. His place was taken by a triumvirate: Zinoviev, Kamenev and Stalin – the latter being the General Secretary of the Party. Almost immediately, a struggle began between Stalin and Leon Trotsky, the Party's most distinguished theorist (and the man most responsible for winning the civil war) about whether Russia should attempt to spread communism throughout the world, or should be content to try to make it work within its own borders. Trotsky thought the Party should work for international communism; Stalin, more realistic, believed Russia should concentrate on its own problems. Trotsky's expulsion from the Party in 1927, and his subsequent banishment, was a triumph for Stalin. Zinoviev and Kamenev also came under heavy criticism from the Party. Stalin was now virtually the dictator of Russia.

In 1929, the year of Trotsky's exile, Stalin decided to make the Party an instrument for the 'revolutionary transformation of society'. What this meant, in effect, was that everyone of influence was to swallow the Marxist dogmas about 'collectivism'. (Stalin had already ended Lenin's New Economic Policy in the previous year.) There was to be no more backsliding towards capitalism or individualism. According to Marx, the proletariat had to be allowed to take control, to become the true leaders of the new society. The bronzed tractor driver should finish his day's work and go to the local Party meeting to learn about the teaching of Marx and Lenin, or to the local opera house to see an opera about the revolution. Artists and intellectuals had to abandon personal problems and begin to think in political terms. It was their job to educate the masses to recognize their own destiny. Writers who brooded on the nature and destiny of man were wasting their time; when they had achieved mystical union with the proletariat, they would suddenly understand human destiny.

In fact, Russian literature and art had been flourishing since the revolution. The first reaction to the downfall of the tsar was euphoria; the intellectuals saw communism as the defender of freedom. 'Modernism' flourished in art and in the cinema (Eisenstein's *Battleship Potemkin* was the sensation of 1925); the poetry of Mayakovsky and Essenin actually reached the masses; so did Sholokov's *Tales of the Don* and Babel's *Red Cavalry* (the latter containing nightmare descriptions of the cruelty of the civil war). In the theatre, Meyerhold's productions created their own revolution. The first symphony by Dmitri Shostakovich (1925) was soon being played all over the world, while his satirical opera *The Nose* appealed to intellectuals *and* workers. But even at this early stage, many writers expressed their reservations about communism and the 'brave new world' it was trying to force into existence. Olesha's novel *Envy* dramatizes the problem of the old fashioned individualist who feels out of place in this society of commissars and 'comrades'. It seemed to take a critical attitude to the envious individualist; but the underlying feeling is a profound distaste for 'collectivism'. Zamyatin's *We* is an astonishing anticipation of Orwell's *1984*, about a future state in which all freedom has been crushed in the name of collectivism.

By 1930, Stalin had decided that it was time to put a stop to all this individualism, which was basically a longing for the old bourgeois ideals. From now on, literature and art should be political: its aim, to glorify the masses. Experiment must cease, because the masses could not understand experimental works. 'Revolutionary proletarian art' was what was needed. Writers who were willing to glorify the masses, and write about factories and collective farms, became honoured members of the Writer's Union (RAPP); they were presented with country cottages where they could work, and had financial security, since their works were produced in vast editions by the state publishing house. Individualists such as Babel, Zamyatin and Olesha could be ignored and made to feel their isolation. Mayakovsky, who had been made to join RAPP, committed suicide. Zamyatin went abroad. Olesha dried up. Babel finally disappeared into a concentration camp. The same thing happened to Meyerhold, and his wife was brutally murdered soon after his arrest. Shostakovich was criticized for 'formalism', which meant that his work sounded too much like music and not enough like propaganda; he felt obliged to withdraw his Fourth Symphony, his finest work up to that date.

What had happened in Russia is what would have happened in France if Robespierre had been able to stay in power and become dictator. Stalin was not particularly intelligent; but he was cunning and brutal, and became increasingly paranoid. He was also a dogmatic Marxist, and was quite determined that anything that looked like private ownership or private enterprise should be abolished. The small proprietors – kulaks – were forced out, or simply arrested and shot; their farms were forcibly united into 'collectives'. Food production dropped dramatically – although Stalin took care to suppress the figures. Having ordered this forced 'collectivization', Stalin seems to have become alarmed at the resistance it aroused. He announced publicly that his officials were showing 'excessive zeal', and should slow down the process. In this way he managed to appear to be the defender of the peasants against his own officials, the benevolent father figure who was doing his best to keep everybody happy. But the policy of destroying the kulaks continued until millions had been executed or deported. Stalin was committing mass murder on a scale – and with a cool deliberation – that made Genghis Khan and Ivan the Terrible seem benevolent. Another ten million died as a result of the famines that swept the country between 1931 and 1933 because of collectivization. In many areas, there was cannibalism.

All this caused widespread criticism amongst Party members. Some of them were passing the carefully suppressed facts on to Trotsky, whose newspaper quoted them and stated that a 'fundamental change' must soon take place in the leadership. In 1933, Stalin reacted by having thousands of Party members expelled. His former colleagues Zinoviev and Kamenev were exiled to Siberia.

In ancient Rome, Stalin would have been murdered. In Soviet Russia, his secret police were able to surround him with a wall of security. But Stalin's wife, who had become increasingly concerned about the Terror, committed suicide in 1932. Stalin, a typical Right Man, was deeply shaken by this, and at a meeting of the Politburo, offered to resign. There was a long silence – no doubt the members could hardly believe their luck, yet were afraid to show any sign of enthusiasm. Finally, Molotov broke the silence by declaring that Stalin had the Party's full confidence. Stalin never again repeated his offer.

But his paranoia increased. Surrounded by people who wished him dead, he may have felt that the best form of defence was attack. In 1934, the Party secretary, Kirov, was murdered. Stalin decided it was time to get rid of anyone who might harbour the slightest opposition to his dictatorship – particularly older Party members. After the trial of the Kirov assassins, a commission was told to 'liquidate the enemies of the people'. Soon, sixteen leading Party members, including Zinoviev and Kamenev, were on trial, accused of conspiring to overthrow the government. All were found guilty and executed immediately.

What astonished the rest of the world was that many of the accused admitted their guilt in court. And this continued to be true in later 'show trials' that continued for the next two years, until 1938. The 'confessions' seemed absurd – and, in fact, were later shown to be absurdities. The general view was that the accused had been tortured, or kept for long periods without sleep, to induce confession. But in *Darkness at Noon*, Arthur Koestler dramatized a theory that later proved to have some foundation in fact: that these older revolutionaries were caught in a trap of their own Marxism. They had fought for the revolution; now it had come, and they were superfluous. They were being asked to make a final sacrifice for the revolution. If they refused, and went to their death denouncing Stalin, they were handing a weapon to the capitalists and undermining the revolution. In effect, Stalin was behaving like a gunman who grabs a hostage as a living shield; if the old communists dared to shoot, they risked killing communism.

As the show trials continued, there were mass arrests all over the country. Workers, clergymen, civil servants, intellectuals, all were 'interrogated' in the prisons; one authority estimates that between seven and eight million people were executed between 1934 and 1938. These included enormous numbers of Party members – of the 140 members of the Central Committee who had been elected in 1934, only fifteen were still at large in 1937.

In fact, Stalin had struck a greater blow against communism than all its enemies put together. Marxism is basically a theory designed to explain the existence of evil in the world. Its explanation is that evil is due to capitalist oppressors, and that once they have been removed, the oppressed will heave a sigh of relief and live happily ever after. Soviet Russia was a living demonstration that evil has very little to do with economic circumstances, and a great deal to do with human self-assertion.

In the rest of Europe, the lesson was slightly less obvious – at least in the years that followed the Armistice. Long wars always leave behind them a longing for change. When the soldiers returned to their homes and found scarcity and hardship, there was a tendency to look towards Russia, where – according to the socialists – the world's greatest experiment in social justice was taking place. The communist parties of Europe suddenly increased their membership dramatically. In Germany and Italy – where jobs were particularly scarce – it looked as if it could only be a matter of time before the workers took over the means of production. In 1920, the Italian workers anticipated the revolution by taking over six hundred factories. In Germany, Communist Party 'cells' spread over every major city. Everywhere crowds of workers were on the march waving red banners, or listening to socialist agitators outside the factories and docks. Benito Mussolini, a socialist who liked to think of himself as 'the Lenin of Italy', was heavily defeated in elections in 1919, but the riots and strikes of 1920 gave him his chance. His 'combat groups' – *fascio di combattimento* – helped to break the strikes by attacking communists, whom they regarded as unpatriotic extremists. The symbol of these groups was the *fasces*, an axe in the centre of a bundle of rods, an old Roman symbol of power. In 1922, the 'fascists' marched on Rome, and encountered no resistance. The king appointed Mussolini premier. Italian businessmen and bankers preferred a patriotic socialist to a communist.

In Germany, a corporal named Adolf Hitler came back from the war, in which he had served with distinction, and joined the German Workers' Party in Munich. Communist revolutions had already broken out all over Germany, with councils of workers and soldiers seizing power. By Christmas 1918, a revolutionary group called the Spartacists – after the man who had led the gladiators' revolt – had taken over Berlin. They had been formed by Karl Liebknecht and Rosa Luxemburg two years earlier; now the Alexanderplatz was full of workers – two hundred thousand of them – waving red flags. The Free Corps, the German equivalent of Mussolini's fascists, marched into Berlin and crushed the revolution, killing Liebknecht and Luxemburg. In Munich, Kurt Eisner organized a more successful revolution; the king fled, and Bavaria became a republic. Hitler, like Mussolini, detested these communists with their talk of international revolution, and it did not escape his attention that most of the communist leaders – including Liebknecht, Luxemburg and Eisner – were Jewish. He had already acquired a hatred of Jews in the pre-war years, when he was a half-starved art student in Vienna and Munich, and had observed how many Jews seemed to be in influential positions.

16 October 1919 was a turning point in Hitler's life – and in European history. At a meeting of the German Workers' Party in a cellar, Hitler made his first speech, and realized that he was a natural orator. He spoke for an hour; the crowd was fascinated.

The next time he spoke, the audience had doubled. And it went on increasing.

The secret of Hitler's appeal was the emotional force of his delivery, and the clarity of the ideas he put forward. These were as crude and simplistic as Marxist ideology. Germany had been betrayed into defeat by the politicians and the Jews. (There was a widely-held belief in Germany that the army had been strong and undefeated when they were ordered to surrender.) The Jews wanted international socialism because they had no country of their own and were envious of nations with deep roots. But the misery of Germany could be overcome by German courage. The people had only to seize the power from those who had betrayed them, and turn to the great traditions of Germany's past . . .

In November 1923, Hitler attempted a 'Putsch' (uprising) that was inspired by Mussolini's march on Rome. His National Socialists – now called Nazis – tried to march on the war ministry, and were easily scattered. Hitler was arrested and tried for high treason; he used his oratory in court to such effect that his judges found themselves virtually on trial, and sentenced him to a mere five years, of which he only served nine months. In prison he wrote his autobiography, *Mein Kampf*, 'my struggle', outlining his central idea – that the Nordic peoples form a 'master race', and must accept their destiny to guide civilization. 'Non-Nordics' included the negroes, the Jews and the Slavs.

In England and France, there was no danger of communist revolution, since these two countries had gained by the war. But it left behind enough social dissatisfaction to fuel the socialist cause. In both countries, the socialists came to power in 1924. But when it became clear that they were unable to solve the economic problems, their popularity declined.

When Hitler came out of jail he discovered that his audiences were no longer so large and no longer so enthusiastic. When he had led the *Putsch*, inflation had made the German mark practically worthless – four thousand *billion* to a dollar. Socialist governments in England and France took a more moderate attitude towards Germany, and industry began to recover. As prosperity returned, the Germans ceased to look for scapegoats to explain their defeat. The German worker was glad enough to have a job, and promptly lost his interest in politics – a problem that has always been the bane of revolutionar-

ies. But the small farmers and businessmen, whose savings had
vanished during inflation, still felt themselves victimized; Hitler
now became their spokesman rather than that of the workers. And
he began to mix with respectable politicians, who saw him as a
bulwark against communism, and with soldiers – such as General
Ludendorff – who recognized him as a friend of the army. Hitler
quietly consolidated his base, cultivated rich industrialists, and
turned the Nazis into a formidable military organization.

In America, the postwar slump had been brief and, throughout
the twenties, business continued to expand. America was replacing
Britain as the 'workshop of the world', and Britain's own industry
had been undermined by a decision made by Winston Churchill in
1925 – to return to the gold standard at the old pre-war rate. This
was good for national pride but bad for business, since the pound
sterling was no longer worth as much as it had been in 1914. Across
the Atlantic, prosperity engendered confidence and confidence
engendered more prosperity. When Britain, Germany and France
begged America to lower its interest rates, to stop the alarming flow
of gold from Europe to America, the Federal Reserve obliged. Now
money was cheaper to borrow, and in the climate of optimism,
everyone scrambled to borrow it. Everyone was eager to invest.
There were even special companies whose sole purpose was to invest
borrowed money in other companies, which, in turn, would invest in
others. Karl Marx would have been able to point out the weakness in
this system. Profit is produced by labour. And if millions of
investors are all waiting for their dividends, there may not be enough
profit to go round. This is what began to happen towards the end of
the 1920s. The 'land boom' in Florida also demonstrated what could
go wrong with capitalist economy. The newly rich all wanted homes
in the sunshine, so land prices in Florida rose steadily. Finally, areas
of inland swamp were being sold for the price of land by the
seashore, while the investors only knew they were getting 'real
estate' in Florida. Finally, people went to inspect their holdings,
discovered they were almost worthless, and tried to sell at any price.
The result was a slump in the value of Florida land; in 1928 it was
worth only about a sixth of what it had been worth in 1925.

In October 1929, the disaster that Marx could have foretold
overtook the investment companies. For no understandable reason,
the stock exchange in Wall Street suddenly lost confidence on 24

October and everyone began to sell. Brokers realized that this loss of confidence could be a disaster, and united to start buying again. This averted the collapse. But it began again less than a week later, and continued steadily for the next three years. Nine thousand banks failed. At the end of that period, a quarter of America's workforce were out of jobs.

Since all the major industrial nations sold their goods to one another, the disaster spread around the world. Only Russia was unaffected, and this was only because Stalin's Russia was so poor that it had nothing to sell to anyone else.

In Germany, wages were cut and taxes were raised: and the new crisis was Hitler's salvation. In a 1929 plebiscite he had been disastrously defeated, and the government – which had brought back prosperity – received an overwhelming vote of confidence. But in the 1930 elections – with the unemployed now numbering three millions – the Nazis received 107 votes and became the second most powerful party in Germany. The communists ran a close third. In further elections in 1933, the Nazis gained 230 seats – not quite enough to give them the majority they needed. More elections were held, to break the deadlock; the Nazis now lost seats and the communists gained. But finally, when attempts to form a coalition of the other parties failed, the president, Hindenburg, was forced to appoint Hitler chancellor. It was 30 January 1933.

The first thing he did was to ban the Communist Party, hoping this would provoke a rising and provide an excuse for his storm troopers to destroy the communists. He was disappointed; the communists contented themselves with urging the workers to rebel, but avoided presenting themselves as targets. Then, on 27 February 1933, the Reichstag building burst into flames. The culprit was a Dutch ex-communist named van der Lubbe, and subsequent investigation has shown that he acted alone (although most historians still accuse the Nazis of starting the fire). The next day, Hitler persuaded Hindenburg to sign a decree suspending various civil liberties. Then, with an ease that profoundly shocked the communist parties of the rest of Europe, the Nazis stamped out communism in Germany. Van der Lubbe was executed.

The rest of the world felt no particular alarm at the rise of fascism in Italy and Nazism in Germany. The world economy was in crisis, and

USA's NRA — controlled economy

strong leaders were needed to deal with it. Their method was to attempt to regulate the economy through government intervention – a principle that became known as Keynesianism, after J. M. Keynes. Keynes did not believe that 'market forces' – supply and demand – will finally restore prosperity, after eliminating the uncompetitive businesses; he argued that the government can use the nation's taxes to create jobs and get rid of unemployment. Then the new workers will have money to spend, and the great economic machine will gradually begin to work at full capacity again. It was a principle known as 'pump priming'. And to a certain extent, this makes sense. Whether the world is in full production or in recession, there is the same amount of manpower available, the same quantity of raw materials, the same number of mouths to feed. What *is* lacking in a recession is confidence and enterprise. If the government can supply these, then it should only be a matter of time before prosperity returns.

In Italy, Mussolini had made an attempt to rescue the economy with the 'battle of the wheat' – an attempt to double wheat production. It would have been an excellent idea if the world slump had not caused a drop in the price of wheat, so that it could have been imported at half the cost. Nevertheless, the country responded to firm control, and the economy slowly improved. Hitler began an immense programme of public works – such as building motorways (*Autobahns*) – and organized the economic life of Germany into 'national groups' that could turn to the government for guidance or aid. Within three years, unemployment had almost disappeared. In America, the new president, Franklin D. Roosevelt, pursued the same policy with a Civil Works Administration providing work for the unemployed and a Civil Conservation Corps that used the unemployed on natural conservation projects. The NRA, the National Recovery Administration, attempted to rationalize the mad scramble of old-fashioned competition and to fix prices. It also gave all workers a right to join unions. In 1935, the Supreme Court ruled that all this was unconstitutional, and the NRA disappeared. But the workers were now determined to have their unions. The result was that American industry began to suffer from some of the troubles that German and Italian industry had experienced after the war, with clashes between the police and strikers and mass rallies. But since the communists were supporting Roosevelt's 'New Deal', commun-

ism became for a while almost respectable in America. Governor
Huey Long of Louisiana, and Father Coughlin, the 'radio priest' of
Michigan, called for extreme socialist measures; but their rhetoric
sounded ominously like that of Mussolini and Hitler.

And in Germany and Italy, the situation was already beginning to
look dangerous to world peace. Only a few months after Hitler came
to power, the Nazis organized a mass book-burning in German cities
– not only communist literature, but works by writers such as
Einstein, Thomas Mann and H. G. Wells. Hitler's 'brown shirts'
stood outside Jewish-owned stores, advising people not to go in.
Then, in 1934, Hitler discovered that Ernst Roehm, the head of the
storm troopers, was planning to get rid of him. On 30 June 1934, he
flew to Munich, drove out to the Weissee in the early hours of the
morning, and personally supervised the arrest of Roehm and his
chief lieutenants – many of them in bed with young men, since the
SA leadership was largely homosexual. Hundreds of storm troopers
were shot in the 'night of the long knives'. In the autumn of that
year, a mass victory celebration was held in Nuremberg, with
torchlight processions. In the September of the following year – 1935
– the 'Nuremberg Laws' declared that anyone who had more than
two Jewish grandparents was not a German citizen; they also banned
marriage between Jews and non-Jews. The rest of Europe began to
realize that a revitalized Germany could be an uncomfortable
neighbour.

Mussolini was less concerned with abstract issues like race. He
enjoyed posing in front of crowds and making speeches; but at least
he was tolerant of nonconformists. One of his strongest opponents,
the novelist Alberto Moravia, admitted in an interview after the war:
'Mussolini was not a bad man.' But the same could not be said of
many of his lieutenants. The problem of fascism was that it endowed
nonentities with authority and allowed them to indulge their self-
conceit. Hemingway has a short story describing a trip to Italy at
that period – 'Che ti dice la patria?' In it an earnest young fascist
practically orders the Americans to give him a lift, and a corrupt
policeman extorts money from them because their number-plate is
dusty. This was the real problem, both in Germany and Italy.
Prussia under the Hohenzollerns had been a dictator state, but at
least the police and the army were as sternly disciplined as everyone
else, and liable to even stricter penalties. In Germany and Italy, any

stupid bully who wanted to put on a uniform could become a minor dictator. In effect, it was a deliberate encouragement of the criminal element. Hitler had destroyed Roehm because Roehm wanted to 'continue the revolution' and increase the power of the storm troopers. But the increasing power of the Nazi party constituted the same pressure. A healthy army demands to be allowed to fight. In Italy, Mussolini found himself under the same pressure when there was a clash between Italian and Abyssinian troops in December 1934. Thirty-eight years earlier, the Abyssinians had wiped out 20,000 Italian soldiers at the battle of Aduwa. The new incident outraged Italian national pride. And Mussolini, subject to the 'law of expansion' that applies to all successful dictators, was not unwilling to court popularity with a successful war. In October 1935, his troops marched from Italian Somaliland into Abyssinia, and took Aduwa. By May of the following year they had taken Addis Ababa, and the Italian government proclaimed that Abyssinia now belonged to Italy.

Spain, perhaps the most tradition-bound country in Europe, was also undergoing political convulsions. The history of Spain in the first years of the twentieth century reads very much like the history of Russia in the same period: a rigid class structure, a monarchy used to absolute power, a half-starved peasantry, and a steadily growing revolutionary movement. Spain stayed out of the First World War, but its armaments industry grew, and so did the power of the workers. In 1921, a Spanish army was trapped in Morocco and 12,000 were killed. Widespread unrest followed, which was terminated when General Primo de Rivera seized power in a *coup*. Rivera became dictator, with the approval of the king, Alphonso XIII (who introduced him to the king of Italy as 'My Mussolini'). But even a dictator could not hold Spain together; Rivera resigned in 1930, unrest broke out again, and in 1931 the king fled. When a Republican (i.e. liberal communist) government took over, the peasants considered this as an invitation to seize the land from the landowners, and nothing the government did could restrain them for long. They had the bit between their teeth. It was a situation that seems to be recurrent in history. Like the slaves who revolted against Rome under Spartacus, the peasants declined all restraint. The landowners, understandably, objected to being plundered, and turned to the army for help. In 1936, there was an army rebellion, from which General Francisco Franco emerged as the leader. A bloody civil war followed, and continued until March 1939, when Franco became dictator. The war cost three-quarters of a million lives.

In Hitler's Germany, the newly awakened national pride was demanding satisfaction for past humiliations – in this case the losses of German territory suffered at the end of the war; these included the Rhineland, Alsace and the 'Polish corridor'. But the first objective of the Nazis was to unite Germany and Austria. There was a flourishing Nazi party in Austria; it seemed absurd that this German-speaking country, now no longer the heart of an empire, should remain a separate entity. In July 1934, a group of Nazis in Vienna engineered a *coup* and killed the Austrian chancellor Dollfuss. But at this stage Mussolini had no desire to see the collapse of a 'buffer state' between Italy and Germany and moved troops to the frontier; so did Yugoslavia. Hitler quickly disowned the *coup* and temporarily abandoned his plans for Austria. But the incident made him aware of the need for a stronger army; in the following year, in violation of the peace treaty, he reintroduced conscription. In March 1936, he took his first major gamble and ordered his troops into the Rhineland. His generals were nervous; the German army was only 20,000 strong, and if the French had retaliated, they would have been forced to withdraw. But the French did nothing. In November 1936, Hitler signed an anti-communist pact with Japan, and recognized the rebel government that General Franco had proclaimed in Spain. From the beginning of the Civil War Hitler lent Franco armed support.

With Mussolini now a firm ally – a Berlin-Rome-Tokyo 'axis' was formed in 1937 – Hitler turned all his energies to the problem of union with Austria. The Austrian chancellor Schuschnigg was bullied into giving the Nazi party of Austria more freedom. In March 1938, political manoeuvring forced Schuschnigg to resign, and the new Nazi chancellor, Seyss-Inquart, invited Hitler to send troops into Austria.

At the end of the First World War, Austria had lost part of its territory – the Sudeten mountains – to Czechoslovakia. Three million Germans lived there, and they wanted to rejoin the new Germany. Hitler made threatening noises, but he had to proceed cautiously – France, Britain and the Soviet Union had promised to aid Czechoslovakia in the event of an invasion. Then, to Hitler's astonishment, the British prime minister, Neville Chamberlain, proposed to come and see him to find a 'peaceful solution'. This meant that Britain was anxious to avoid war. And after speaking to Hitler, Chamberlain joined with the French premier Daladier to notify the Czechs that they would have to hand over the Sudeten territory. The Czechs were enraged at the betrayal, but could do nothing. In Munich, Hitler, Mussolini, Chamberlain, Daladier and Roosevelt met to discuss the problem, and the Sudetenland was returned to Germany. Chamberlain returned to England and uttered the famous phrase about 'peace for our time'.

In the British parliament, Winston Churchill warned that this policy of appeasement would lead to disaster; he was proved right sooner than even he expected. The Slovakian premier, Tiso, was deposed in a government crisis, and appealed to Hitler for aid for Slovak independence. Hitler responded by taking over most of Czechoslovakia, as well as a slice of Poland that the Czechs had always claimed. At the same time, Mussolini took over Albania. Now the only chance of stopping Hitler was for Britain and France to combine with the Soviet Union. And at this point, in August 1939, the Nazis staggered the world by announcing that they had signed a non-aggression pact with Stalin.

Now all that remained for Hitler was to take back the Polish corridor. Since the Poles would object to losing their link with the sea, this obviously involved invading Poland. On 1 September 1939, his troops marched across the border and his planes bombed Warsaw. Two days later, England and France declared war against Germany.

How had it all come about? Marx would undoubtedly have blamed capitalism – as Marxist historians continue to do; but this crisis had nothing to do with market forces or free enterprise. Tolstoy would have insisted that the 'natural laws' of history are responsible, unknown forces which are as unpredictable as the weather. But we have seen again and again that it is the will of individuals that changes the course of history. A 'great man' – a Julius Caesar, Genghis Khan, Peter the Great, Napoleon, Bismarck – sets out to achieve certain aims, and succeeds to a greater or lesser degree. Lesser men have less of an impact. But the essential clue always lies in the personality of the individual.

The crises of the post-1920s period were the direct result of the First World War. Without that there would have been no Russian revolution, no Italian and Spanish fascism, no German Nazism. And the First World War can be blamed almost entirely on the personality of one man: the Kaiser. And after the Kaiser came Hitler, another hysterical egoist. But if the Kaiser reminds us of Nero, Hitler is more like the adventurous 'loner' Lacenaire or the anarchist Ravachol. There is the same lonely individualism, the same hungry intelligence, the same sense of being an outcast and a misfit. But while Lacenaire and Ravachol blamed the bourgeoisie for all their misfortunes, Hitler found another scapegoat: the Jews. 'Was there any shady undertaking, any form of foulness, especially in cultural life, in which at least one Jew did not participate? On putting the probing knife carefully to that kind of abscess one immediately discovered, like a maggot in a putrescent body, a little Jew who was often blinded by the sudden light' (*Mein Kampf*, p. 60 of the English edition). He had already acquired a profound distaste for Marxism. When he worked as a builder's labourer and listened to his fellow workers using Marxist arguments to disparage patriotism, religion and the law, his dislike of Marxism and his refusal to join a trade union led to threats to throw him from the scaffolding. So when he learned that most of the leading socialists and Marxists were Jews, it was like a revelation. 'My long inner struggle was at an end.' Now he had his scapegoat.

Hitler's problem was the problem of all criminals: lack of self-control. Criticism or opposition drove him to hysteria. His old friend Kubizek wrote in a book about Hitler's youth: 'Adolf was exceedingly violent and highly strung. Quite trivial things, such as a few thoughtless words, could produce in him outbursts of temper which I thought quite out of proportion.' And these rages, so characteristic of the Right Man, did not grow less frequent as he grew older. On both occasions when Neville Chamberlain went to see him, Hitler lost his temper and began to rant and scream. Close associates say that, when this happened, his face became suffused with blood and he seemed like a madman. Wartime cartoons of Hitler on all fours eating the carpet are not far from the truth. A Jewish youth shoots a German diplomat in Paris: Hitler orders a pogrom. An assassination squad kills his SS chief Heydrich; he orders the destruction of a whole village, although it had nothing to do with the killing. Some of his officers attempt to kill him with a bomb; he has dozens of the plotters garrotted with piano wire from meathooks, and orders the whole procedure to be filmed so he can watch it repeatedly.

This insane egoism brought about Hitler's downfall. Two errors were crucial. On 23 August 1940, some German bombers lost their way and dropped their bombs in the centre of London. The British sent their planes to make a token retaliatory attack on Berlin. Hitler flew into one of his blind rages. In a speech he declared: 'When the British Air Force drops two or three or four thousand kilograms of bombs, then we will in one night drop 150, 250, 300, 400,000 kilograms of bombs.' So the Luftwaffe was ordered to destroy London. And the British could hardly believe their luck. The real target should have been the airfields in the south of England and the pathetically small British Air Force. While the Luftwaffe wasted its bombs on civilian targets, British Spitfires fought and won the Battle of Britain, and Hitler had to abandon the invasion he had planned. One error cost him the war in the west.

Another cost him the war in the east. In March 1941, the Yugoslavs agreed to support Hitler; but when the ministers returned to Belgrade, there was a popular rising, and the government was overthrown. The *coup* threw Hitler into 'one of the wildest rages of his entire life'. He screamed about revenge, and ordered that Yugoslavia should be crushed with 'merciless harshness'. Goering was told to destroy Belgrade with a non-stop *Blitzkrieg*. He obeyed; but four weeks spent reducing Belgrade to rubble – 'Operation Punishment', Hitler called it – and smashing the Yugoslav army, delayed the invasion of Russia by four weeks. Those four weeks cost Hitler the war. Like Napoleon, he was caught by the Russian winter before his troops had achieved the shelter of Moscow.

In May 1945, as the Russians fought their way into Berlin, Hitler ordered the flooding of the Berlin underground railway, in which thousands of people had taken shelter. Germany deserved to perish, said Hitler. 'The German people are not worthy of me.' Like the frog in the fairy tale, his ego had swelled until it exploded.

Two weeks later, he committed suicide.

Five

THE CRIME EXPLOSION

At the end of the Second World War, there was the usual sharp rise in crime that has followed every major war in history. By 1946, Britain's crime figures had doubled since pre-war days: twice as many robberies, burglaries, rapes and crimes of violence. Even in America, which had been relatively insulated from the war by distance, crime had risen by two-thirds.

In the early 1950s, the figures began to show a reassuring fall; by 1954, they were actually lower than in 1945. It looked as if the crisis was over and things had returned to normal. But closer examination of the statistics showed a frightening trend. Robbery and burglary *had* fallen dramatically – due to the rise in prosperity – but crimes of violence and sex crimes continued their steady rise; in fact, they had doubled since 1945.

Now crimes are, as we have seen, the most accurate barometer of the stability of a society. Criminals are like the rats who die first in a plague. The criminal is a person in whom the 'T force' – explosive tension – is higher than usual, and tends to sweep away 'force C', the inhibitory function. So when there is underlying social frustration, it is the criminal who provides a measure of that tension. If a new and horrifying type of crime occurs, a type that has never been known before, it should not be regarded as some freak occurrence, any more than the outbreak of a new disease should be dismissed as a medical oddity. For the criminologist, it provides an insight into the total state of the society.

Two crimes from the post-war period provide an example. On 7 September 1949, a French Canadian, Albert Guay, saw his wife on to a plane; twenty minutes later, it exploded in mid-air, killing all twenty-three people on board. Examination of the wreckage revealed the cause of the explosion as dynamite, and investigation showed that Guay had sent his wife on the trip with a bomb disguised as a religious statue; the motive was the $10,000 he had insured her for. Guay and two accomplices were executed. On 1 November 1955, John Graham escorted his mother to a plane at Denver airport; it also exploded in mid-air, killing forty-four people. Again, investigation revealed dynamite as the cause of the disaster, and Graham proved to have detonators concealed in his house; he was sent to the gas chamber. Many men have killed wives or mothers for money, but until 1949 there was no case of the killer destroying so many other human lives to achieve his aim. It demonstrates a peculiar degree of 'alienation' – the kind of alienation that C. R. Carpenter observed in his rhesus monkeys who were deprived of 'territory', or that Colin Turnbull observed in the Ik (see Part One, chapter 2, p. 51).

The same alienation is revealed in the steady rise of sex crime after the Second World War. We have seen that, in Calhoun's 'behavioural sink', the rats responded to overcrowding with cannibalism and rape. Studies of the rising crime rate in America in the 1950s showed that the steepest rise occurred in cities with more than a quarter of a million inhabitants; in the largest cities, the homicide rate was three times higher than in small towns, and rape and violence against the person four times higher. By 1956 it was clear that even the improvement in the larceny figures was only a temporary phenomenon; they also began to rise again. And homicide and rape have continued their steady increase. By 1960 there were approximately ten thousand murders a year in America (mostly by guns). By 1970, the figure had risen to fifteen thousand – that is to say, approximately one every half hour. At the time of this writing (1983) the murder rate is well over twenty thousand per year – about one every quarter of an hour. Rape has risen even more steeply. The 'overcrowded rat syndrome' continues to operate.

Rape has remained the most typical crime of the twentieth century: that is to say, in any list of major crimes, there would be a high proportion of sex murders. We have seen that sex crime began to occupy this prominent position in the second half of the nineteenth century, and that one of the major causes was Victorian prudery, the notion of sex as something wicked and 'forbidden' (although the population increase in big cities undoubtedly played its part). After 1900, this prudery gave way to a healthier sexual realism, and sex crime suddenly became less prominent. But this was deceptive. Sex continued to be the great underlying preoccupation of society – as shown in the case of Mary Phagan (1913), which became a national obsession in America and continued to sell newspapers for years. In England, the most sensational murder trial of the First World War was that of George Joseph Smith, a commonplace swindler who graduated to murder – drowning his newly-married brides in the bath after acquiring their savings. Smith was described by the newspapers as a Don Juan whose basilisk gaze made him irresistible to women; this was enough to keep the courtroom crowded with morbid females. The same was true of the trial of Henri Desiré Landru in 1921; Landru had murdered ten women – whom he first seduced – for their savings, burning their bodies piecemeal in a stove; again, the majority of spectators in the crowded courtroom were women. (When one of them came in late and was unable to find a seat, Landru raised a smile by offering her his own.) It may have been the Landru case that inspired the painter Kokoschka to write a satirical play called *Murderer, Hope of Women*.

Yet not all sex crimes aroused the same morbid interest. In 1916, soldiers looking for petrol at a farm near Czinkota, Hungary, discovered more than twenty petrol drums, each containing the garrotted corpse of a woman preserved in alcohol. The former tenant, Bela Kiss, had apparently advertised periodically for female companions. Prostitutes from the red light district of Budapest described Kiss as sexually insatiable. Like Smith and Landru, Kiss had apparently stolen the belongings of his victims. Then why did the case fail to arouse the same intense curiosity as those of the other 'bluebeards'? It was not simply because it happened in the middle of a war, or because he was never caught. (It was reported that he had been killed in the army, but later discovered that he had stolen the papers of a dead soldier.) This crime was simply a little *too* 'nasty', with its hints of necrophilia. A masochistic woman might conceivably enjoy imagining herself being seduced by Smith or Landru; but being trussed up and preserved in alcohol was too nauseating to be incorporated in anybody's daydream.

The Austrian novelist Robert Musil, writing in the 1920s, made a multiple sex-killer called Moosbrugger one of the central characters in his masterpiece *The Man Without Qualities*. When he remarked: 'If mankind could dream collectively, it would dream Moosbrugger', he was expressing the recognition that figures like Moosbrugger and Bela Kiss are 'plague rats', expressions of the underlying sickness of a society. In post-war Germany, Musil could have found many models for his 'collective nightmare'. Fritz Haarmann, a homosexual butcher of Hanover, made use of the post-war chaos to kill about fifty young male vagrants, whose bodies he sold for meat; Haarmann claimed that he killed them by biting them through the windpipe. During the same period Karl Denke, landlord of a house in Münsterberg, killed more than a dozen vagrants – male and female – who called at his door, and ate portions of their bodies, which he kept pickled in brine. Georg Grossmann, a sadistic sexual degenerate, lived from 1914 to 1921 on the flesh of victims he lured to his room in Berlin; police investigating sounds of a struggle found the trussed-up carcass of a girl on the bed, the cords tightened as if for butchering into neat sections. Peter Kürten, the Düsseldorf 'Ripper', killed nine victims – including a man, women and children – in 1929; he admitted that he could only achieve sexual orgasm through strangling or stabbing, and that he had committed his first murder as a child.

In America in 1926, Earle Nelson – who had spent some time in an asylum – travelled around the northern United States and Canada on a rampage of sex murder, killing twenty-two women. Nelson would go to houses with a 'To Let' notice in the window and, if the landlady was alone, strangle and rape her. Newspapers dubbed him the 'Gorilla murderer', and the trail of violated landladies continued to make headlines until he was caught in Canada. Nelson was hanged in 1927. There can be no doubt that this kind of sensational publicity helped to make everyone more conscious of sex crime, and therefore increased the number of such crimes. In England, on the other hand, the press still observed a rule of gentlemanly restraint. In 1921, a chauffeur named Thomas Allaway answered the advertisement of thirty-one-year-old Irene Wilkins, who wanted a job as a cook; he met her by car at Bournemouth, knocked her unconscious, and attempted rape (which he did not complete). Traced through witnesses who had seen the car, he was tried for her murder and hanged. But although the judge mentioned that Allaway had lured Irene to Bournemouth 'for an immoral purpose', the rape motive was played down. This approach may help to explain why sex crime remained rare in England until the Second World War.

In 1922, the Allaway trial was eclipsed by the enormous publicity given to the trial of Edith Thompson and Frederick Bywaters. The two were lovers, and Bywaters had stabbed Edith's husband to death. Mrs Thompson was accused of inciting the murder, but the evidence was slender; nevertheless, she was also sentenced to death and hanged. The case leaves the impression that she was sentenced as much for adultery as for incitement to murder. In America, the parallel case of the 1920s involved the murder of Albert Snyder by Judd Gray, the lover of Snyder's wife Ruth. Snyder was beaten unconscious with a sashweight, then strangled with picture wire. The police tricked Ruth Snyder into confessing by claiming that Gray had admitted the killing. When she was electrocuted in Sing Sing in 1928, a reporter succeeded in photographing the moment of death with a camera strapped to his leg; the grim picture was syndicated all over the world, and was felt to underline the moral that 'the wages of sin is death'.

But real sex crime continued to increase, and the major cases displayed an increasingly strange element of perversion. In 1932, a Hungarian company director, Sylvestre Matushka, was tried for causing two train crashes and attempting to cause a third. In August 1931 the Vienna express was derailed near Berlin by an explosion, and sixteen passengers were injured; in September, the Budapest-Vienna express was derailed by an explosion and twenty-two people were killed, some literally blown to pieces. Matushka admitted that the thought of trains crashing caused him intense sexual excitement, and that he experienced orgasm when it actually happened. Sentenced to life imprisonment, he escaped and reappeared during the Korean war in 1953 as the head of a unit for blowing up trains.

In New York in 1928, a kindly-looking old man named Albert Fish persuaded the Budd family to allow him to take their ten-year-old daughter Grace to a party; she was never seen again. Six years later, Fish wrote Mrs Budd a letter describing how he had strangled Grace and eaten parts of her body in a stew. The police were able to trace him through the letter, and it became clear that Fish was what Freud called a 'polymorphous pervert' whose sexual oddities including eating excrement and driving needles into his scrotum and leaving them there to rust. The screams of children gave him pleasure, and during the course of a lifetime as a house painter, he had tortured and killed large numbers. Even the idea of

his own electrocution excited him; he told police that it would ̱
'the supreme thrill of my life'. (Peter Kürten had said he hoped to
hear the sound of his own blood running into the basket after
beheading.)

In Germany in 1936 – the year of Fish's trial – a
sixty-three-year-old travelling watchmaker named Adolf Seefeld also
admitted to having spent a lifetime murdering children – in this case,
all male. Seefeld killed by persuading them to drink a poisonous
concoction made of herbs, and the children – a dozen – were found
in an attitude of repose, with no sign of sexual assault. By the time
Seefeld was caught, Hitler was chancellor, and he recognized the
role of publicity in causing imitative crimes. Seefeld was tried with a
minimum of fuss and quickly executed.

In Cleveland, Ohio, a killer who became known as 'the Mad
Butcher of Kingsbury Run' murdered a dozen men and women –
mostly tramps and derelicts – between 1935 and 1938, and left the
bodies in a small pile of dismembered pieces. The heads were usually
missing, and in one case two bodies were found mixed up together.
The 'mad butcher' was never caught.

The world record for sex murder is still held by a German, Bruno
Lüdke, who confessed to eighty-five murders between 1927 (when
he was eighteen) and 1944, when he was caught. In 1936, Lüdke had
been arrested for a sexual assault and castrated on the orders of
Himmler; but it made no difference to his sexual appetite. Again,
because the case took place under the Hitler regime, details are
lacking, but we know that Lüdke was used by the Nazis as a guinea
pig in experiments, and died of an injection.

Let us pause to ask the question: what do such crimes indicate about
the nature of the society in which they take place? It is tempting to
see the crimes of Kürten, Matushka, Lüdke, Seefeld, as a reflection
of the violence of Nazi Germany. That would be a mistake; all were
born in the 'sunset world' of pre-1914 Europe, and all committed
murders long before Hitler came to power. In any case, periods of
violence do not necessarily spawn crimes of violence. Violence is a
reflection of social tension, and this actually diminishes in times of
upheaval and chaos – such as wars – because chaos is at least not
conducive to boredom.

There is usually an evolutionary explanation for violence, and it is this factor that we need to look for. In the animal world, one of the most vicious of all creatures is the shrew, a tiny, mouse-like animal that weighs only a fifth of an ounce. It will kill far larger creatures than itself – like mice – and will eat its own kind. The explanation lies in its size. With a surface area so large in proportion to its volume, the shrew loses its heat almost immediately to the surrounding air; consequently, it has to eat continuously to stay alive. The shrew *has* to be savage, or it would not have survived.

Man's surface area is so much smaller in proportion to his weight that he can at least forget food for several hours after every meal. But during his few million years on the surface of this planet, the climate has been wildly variable, with long ice ages, so survival has been far from easy. One response to this challenge has been intense sexual activity; when faced with a threat to survival, he experiences the urge to copulate; this is his equivalent of the shrew's non-stop eating.

But we have seen that his chief mechanism for survival was the development of a formidable apparatus that allows him to concentrate upon specific problems: a kind of mental microscope. He hurls himself at problems with the same violence that the shrew hurls itself on food. Patience was never one of man's chief virtues. When problems arise that threaten his survival, he experiences an intense desire to solve them *instantly*.

All this explains why man is at once the most creative and the most murderous of creatures. The story of his triumphs cannot be separated from the story of his crimes because they spring from the same source: that specialized instrument for problem-solving. When the novelist Turgenev witnessed the last hours of the murderer J. B. Troppmann, he experienced deep sympathy. Rightly so: Troppmann's downfall arose from his ability at problem-solving, and with a different approach he might have become a famous novelist or scientist.

Because of this 'specialized instrument', man suffers from boredom more than any other creature. Most animals dislike boredom, but man is tormented by it. Chekhov expresses the problem in a play called *The Wood Demon*:

'You've never tasted real boredom, my dear fellow. When I was a volunteer in Serbia, there I experienced the real thing! Hot, stuffy, dirty, head simply

splitting after a drinking bout . . . Once I remember sitting in a dirty little shed . . . Captain Kashkinazi was there too . . . Every subject of conversation was long exhausted, no place to go to, nothing to do, no desire to drink – just sickening, you see, sickening to the point of putting one's head in a noose! We sat in frenzied silence, gazing at one another . . . He gazes at me, I at him, he at me, I at him . . . We gaze and don't know why we're doing it . . . An hour passes, you know, then another hour, and still we keep on gazing. Suddenly he jumps up for no reason, draws his sabre and goes for me . . . Hey presto! . . . I, of course, instantly draw my sabre – for he'll kill me! – and it started: chic-chac, chic-chac, chic-chac . . . with the greatest difficulty we were at last separated. I got off all right, but to this very day Captain Kashkinazi walks about with a scar on his face. See how desperately bored one can get!'
From *Plays and Stories of Tchehov*, Everyman, p. 140. Leader dots are
Chekhov's.

If we combine these two factors – man's violent reaction to boredom, and his sexual response to any survival problem – we have grasped the cause of the rise in sex crime. Boredom creates a sense of unreality. Man's response to a sense of unreality is an attempt to trigger one of his deeper instincts. In a few people – especially women – a sense of unreality can lead to overeating. But in males it is more likely to trigger the urge to sex or violence – or both.

It is interesting to note that Kürten's sadism developed during the boredom of long periods of solitary confinement in prison, when sexual daydreams provided a kind of lifeline. We should also note how many sex killers have been tramps or wandering journeymen – for example, Vacher, Tessnow, Seefeld and Panzram. The life of a vagrant is rootless, and this undermines his sense of identity, and therefore threatens his feeling of reality. Sexual violence re-establishes the sense of reality. For a moment, it is as if some inner-compass started to work again.

This explains another puzzling development in sexual violence. The majority of sex criminals described in Krafft-Ebing are 'degenerates' – like Menesclou and Verzeni, men with some congenital subnormality. In the twentieth century, a large proportion of sex criminals are of average or above-average intelligence: Kürten and Panzram are examples. Here again we confront the 'boredom factor'; people of low intelligence are less subject to boredom than those of higher intelligence. (Under sensory deprivation in a 'black room', intelligent people show signs of distress before the less intelligent;

dogs can last longer than either.) So those of higher intelligence have a lower 'violence threshold', which may manifest itself in crime. This is not to say, of course, that intelligent people are more disposed to violence than others, for other factors are involved – for example, the ability to use intelligence constructively. But it means that, in a percentage of intelligent people, intelligence contributes to instability, which may express itself in violence.

If we wish to get closer to the roots of the problem, we have to recognize that boredom is a feeling that nothing is 'happening inside', and that this springs from a sense of *non-participation* in the environment. Boredom vanishes as soon as we feel 'involved'. But since the mid-nineteenth century, man's opportunities for feeling actively involved in his society have diminished. The result is Marx's 'alienation', and a tendency to try to overcome it by various forms of 'revolt'. In a work as yet unpublished a modern analyst of criminal behaviour, Brian Marriner, has coined the useful term 'reactive man' to characterize the new type of criminal. (I am grateful to Mr Marriner for allowing me access to his typescript.) In the past, says Marriner, criminals may have burgled houses or picked pockets, but they did not feel as if they were making war on society; they were responding to deprivation as a hungry man steals apples from an orchard. The twentieth century has seen the rise of a type of criminal who is *reacting against a society* that he feels is somehow depriving him of the right to feel fully alive; he would like to burn down the orchard.

In a logical sense, 'reactive man' is behaving absurdly. It is not 'society' that is to blame for his alienation; it is social development. Civilization can be defined in terms of labour-saving devices. Even a book is a labour-saving device; it stores information for easy access. Civilization itself is a labour-saving device. But the labour-saving devices inevitably reduce individual participation. And as they improve, participation decreases. The rise of sex crime corresponded to the rise of the motor car, the aeroplane and radio. Radio – which at least demands a certain use of imagination – gave way to black and white television, then to colour television. Each advance demands less and less 'participation'. A supermarket demands less participation than shopping in a village store or the corner grocery. The result of such non-participation is bound to be a certain increase in violence. Chekhov's two soldiers in Serbia are reacting to non-participation.

But we can see that the trouble with Chekhov's two officers is that they lacked imagination. If they had possessed more imagination, they might at least have settled down to reading *War and Peace*. Nowadays, even a soldier with a low IQ could stave off boredom with a comic book or a 'situation comedy' on television. In the past two centuries, man has learned to use his imagination to a truly astonishing extent. And this in itself has contributed to the crime problem. We can see that Frederick Baker had probably spent months imagining killing a child before killing Fanny Adams. In 1867, such crimes were a rarity; a century later, they had become frighteningly commonplace. In 1942, a twenty-three-year-old mechanic named Donald Fearn spent a great deal of time in an old adobe church, about fifty miles from Pueblo, Colorado. It had been one of the last strongholds of the 'Penitentes' religion of the local Indians; during Holy Week they had held religious ceremonies involving torture there (Indians regard the ability to bear pain as a mark of manhood), and these usually ended with a crucifixion of one of their members. Fearn had sadistic tendencies – 'Ever since I was a young boy I have wanted to torture a beautiful young girl' – and the thought of these torments obsessed his imagination. In April 1942, when Fearn's wife was in hospital having a baby, he kidnapped a seventeen-year-old student nurse named Alice Porter at gunpoint, drove her out to the church, and put his appalling fantasies into practice, binding her with hot wires and whipping her. Finally, he raped and killed her. Leaving the area the following day – after throwing the body down a well – he drove off the road and became stuck in the mud; a farmer had to tow him out. It was this farmer's description that later led to Fearn's arrest, and to his execution in the gas chamber.

The role of the imagination can be seen even more clearly in the case of William Heirens, the eighteen-year-old Chicago sex killer who was arrested in 1946. Since the age of thirteen, Heirens had been committing burglaries: his aim was to steal women's panties, which he wore and used for masturbation. Heirens came to associate burglary with sex to the point where he could achieve an orgasm by simply entering through a window. If he was interrupted in the course of his burglaries, he would become extremely violent. In October 1945, a nurse came in as he was burgling her apartment; he fractured her skull. When he found a woman asleep in bed during a burglary, he stabbed her in the throat. After murdering and mutilating a girl named Frances Brown in her bedroom, he scrawled on the wall: 'For heaven's sake catch me before I kill more. I cannot control myself.' In January 1946, Heirens entered the bedroom of six-year-old Suzanne Degnan, and carried her to a nearby basement were he raped her; after this he strangled her, cut up the body, and disposed of it down manholes. He was caught a few months later when police were alerted that someone had been heard breaking into an empty apartment.

It emerged at the trial that Heirens was in the grip of a sexual obsession. On one occasion, he had even put his clothes in the bathroom and thrown the key inside to make it impossible to leave the house; but the urge became so powerful that he recovered them by crawling along the gutter and getting in through a window. The judge who sentenced Heirens ordered that he should never be released.

Cases like this could be classified as 'imaginative possession'; the sexual emotion is amplified by the imagination until it achieves a morbid intensity. In January 1947, a mutilated corpse was found on a piece of waste ground in Los Angeles; it had been cut in half at the waist, and medical examination showed that the woman had been hung upside down and tortured. She was identified as a twenty-two-year-old waitress named Elizabeth Short; she had come to Hollywood hoping to become a film star, but had only succeeded in becoming an amateur prostitute. Her friends knew her as the Black Dahlia, because she wore black clothes and black underwear. Her killer was never caught. The horror of the crime gripped the public imagination, and one result was half a dozen other 'imitative' crimes in Los Angeles in the same year; in one case, the killer scrawled 'BD' (black dahlia?) in lipstick on the victim's breast.

Stranger still, no less than twenty-seven men confessed to the murder; all confessions were investigated and proved false. A twenty-eighth confession was made as long as nine years later. But why should anyone wish to confess to a crime he did not commit? The Freudian view, expressed by Theodore Reik in *The Compulsion to Confess*, is that the criminal is relieving himself *and* society of an unconscious feeling of guilt and hoping for the gratitude of society (p.279). But we can also sense very clearly the element of envy of the murderer's experience, arising out of morbid fascination. Imitative crimes are indeed committed in the imagination. So here is a case in which sexual violence triggered off thirty-four parallel reactions – six murders and twenty-eight false confessions – all in an area about the size of Greater London. One may speculate how many other inhabitants of the same area experienced the same morbid fascination, but confined their imitations to the imagination. In Henri Barbusse's novel *Hell*, the narrator describes the after-dinner conversation of a barrister about a man who has strangled and raped a little girl. He observes the reactions of the others: a young mother with her daughter who has got up to leave the room but cannot drag herself away, the men pretending to be indifferent and trying to hide excitement.

Barbusse, like Freud, is implying that such crimes are the conscious expression of 'monsters' from the unconscious, and that the monsters can be found in every one of us. Such a statement will strike most of us as a partial truth that has been made untrue by gross exaggeration. (For example, if a young mother feels compelled to listen, this is surely because she feels anxiety about the safety of her own child and is trying, so to speak, to forearm herself against disaster.) But this is to overlook the real point: that man has created a civilization *for which he is not fully prepared*. He could be compared to a polar bear placed in a centrally heated cage and suffering from a sense of suffocation. He is 'safe' but uncomfortable. Unless we understand this, we shall not be able to even begin to understand the increase in sheer sadism in so many of the crimes that have taken place since 1960. Civilization increases our mental experience – books, television, conversation – but decreases our physical experience, our contact with nature and with necessity. Most of us have accustomed ourselves to these conditions; but there are a few who would not admit to an obscure sense of 'something missing'. It is as if ordinary experience had become slightly dream-like and unreal. This is one of the basic conditions of civilized man.

A case cited by the Los Angeles psychiatrist Paul De River in *The Sexual Criminal* (p.74) underlines the point. A school guard, aged thirty-two, had lured three children to a ravine and strangled and raped them. The girls were aged seven, eight and nine. The man was married, and had an active sex life with his wife; he had even practised wife-swopping with a neighbour. But he assured De River 'that he had never had a complete fulfilment of his sexual desires'. He was convinced that what he needed for 'complete fulfilment' was

society & hierarchy of needs ~
no clue to evolution
16   The Age of Mass Murder

a narrow vagina, 'something tight and young'. He persuaded the
girls to go with him on a pretence of showing them 'bunnies', and led
them off one by one, claiming that more than that would frighten the
bunnies; then he strangled each child with a rope and committed
rape – and, in two cases, sodomy. He was in a state of intense
excitement and experienced ejaculation in all three cases. Afterwards
he knelt by the bodies to pray for the children's souls, and asked God
to forgive him. But he admitted that, during the attacks, 'he felt that
he was very powerful, and that they were but his slaves, he being the
master'. The next day he felt 'drunk with his own importance'. He
fantasized about the murders as he made love to his wife and
experienced deep satisfaction.

De River comments: 'We must remember that here we are dealing
with a sexual psychopath who has at last achieved his end and
fulfilled his sexual desire, and in this case for the first time his sexual
tension has been reduced to the normal limits.' Yet this is to some
extent contradicted by the killer's own statement that he had
obtained the greatest satisfaction from the eldest girl, who was the
best developed – and therefore closest to a grown woman. This
suggests that his belief that he needed a child for total satisfaction
was a misinterpretation of his urge. What really gave him the
satisfaction, as we have seen, was the sense of *power*, the feeling that
'they were but his slaves, he being the master'. What he wanted was
ego satisfaction; he was misinterpreting Ernest Becker's desire for
'primacy' as sexual desire.

Now we can begin to see why the horrific Black Dahlia case
inspired so many imitative crimes and confessions. It was not
necessarily that these fantasists would have enjoyed such extreme
sadism – in fact, none of the imitative crimes *was* as violent. What
was attractive was the idea of total ego satisfaction, being the
'master'. Barbusse's males were not necessarily lusting to commit a
sex murder; what they – and the mother – were responding to was
the element of ego-satisfaction, of 'primacy'.

We have seen in Part One (chapter 1), that there is a certain
amount of evidence that society, like the individuals of whom it is
composed, passes through the stages of Maslow's hierarchy of needs.
The Victorian age was obsessed by the need for domestic security.
This gave way to the next level of the hierarchy, the sexual level, and
the crimes of Vacher, Pieydagnelle, Jack the Ripper, were a simple

murder & self-assertion

expression of frustration on this level, with the violence sharpened by frustration. This type of sex crime has never disappeared; but it has been increasingly eclipsed by sex crime in which we can sense the element of passionate ego-assertion. In 1946, Britain was shocked by the case of Neville Heath, executed for the sadistic murder of two women, Margery Gardner and Doreen Marshall. Margery Gardner was found in a hotel room in Notting Hill, her breasts almost bitten off, and lacerations of the vagina made by the stock of a riding whip. Doreen Marshall, stabbed and mutilated, was found in a gorge near Bournemouth. What emerged at the trial was that Heath was a born liar and poseur: he liked to use pseudonyms such as 'Group Captain Rupert Brooke', and to talk about his wealthy and aristocratic family background – all imaginary. The sadism of the murders was not simply a matter of sexual desire, but of the need for ego-assertion, a symbolic way of washing himself clean of the humiliations inherent in the life of an unsuccessful confidence man.

This same element is apparent in the case of Dr Marcel Petiot, also tried and executed in 1946. In occupied France, Petiot – who owned a house in Paris – offered to help refugees escape the Nazis. At least sixty-three people came to his house, complete with their most precious belongings and savings; none was ever seen alive again. Petiot gassed them in a specially constructed chamber, then dismembered and burned the bodies. The chamber had a specially constructed periscope through which he could watch his victims die. Petiot was a doctor of exceptional brilliance, but he was another born confidence man, and had been in trouble many times with the police. The murders were not merely a way of making money; they were an act of self-assertion, a declaration that he was not a mere confidence man but a super-criminal, a Professor Moriarty.

We can trace the presence of this element of ego-assertion, the craving for self-esteem, in many of the major murder cases of the 1950s and '60s. In 1953, there was a nationwide manhunt in England when three nude female corpses were found in the cupboard of a flat vacated by John Reginald Halliday Christie in Notting Hill. A fourth woman – his wife – was found under the floorboards, and remains of two more women buried in the garden. It became clear at the trial that Christie was a necrophile; a woman had to be dead – or at least unconscious – before he could achieve an erection; he persuaded several of the victims to breathe in a mixture of Friar's Balsam – for bronchitis – and coal gas to render them unconscious. This sexual problem was clearly a matter of self-confidence, yet Christie was known as an unpleasantly self-assertive man who loved to pretend to a profound medical knowledge; as a policeman during the London black-out, he had been a 'little Hitler', enjoying asserting his authority. The crimes were the outcome of the conflict between the craving for 'primacy' – the desire to be a 'somebody' – and his total lack of sexual self-confidence.

In January 1958, a nineteen-year-old Nebraskan youth named Charles Starkweather lost his temper with the mother of his fourteen-year-old girlfriend Caril Fugate – who believed Caril to be pregnant – and shot her to death; he also killed Caril's stepfather and two-year-old sister. The two then drove across the state, committing seven more murders at random, before he was captured. It emerged that Starkweather was an admirer of the late James Dean – a photograph taken after his capture has the brooding James Dean stare and the cigarette dangling out of the corner of the mouth. Hollywood took him at his word and made a film of his life in which he was represented as a teenage 'rebel without a cause'; it conveniently glossed over the murder of the two-year-old girl and the rape and mutilation of seventeen-year-old Carol King, a college student. Starkweather was executed in 1959.

In January 1959, a truckdriver named Carrol Jackson, out for a Sunday afternoon drive with his family in East Virginia, was run off the road by a blue Chevrolet. A thin-faced man with ape-like arms forced the family – Carrol and Mildred Jackson with their two daughters, Susan, aged five, and Janet, eighteen months – to get into his boot. The Jacksons vanished. Two months later, Carrol Jackson's body was found in a ditch; he had been shot in the skull. Janet had been thrown in underneath him and had apparently died of suffocation. Two weeks later, the bodies of Mildred and Susan were found in a shallow grave. The police investigation had come to a halt for lack of clues when they received a letter from a salesman which named a jazz musician named Melvin Rees as the killer. He quoted Rees as saying: 'You can't say it's wrong to kill. Only individual standards make it right or wrong.' When he had asked Rees point blank if he had killed the Jackson family, Rees had merely evaded the question.

A search of the home of Rees's parents left no doubt that he was the killer. The police discovered the revolver with which Carrol Jackson had been shot, and a kind of diary containing an account of the murders. 'Caught on a lonely road . . . Drove to a selected spot and killed the husband and baby. Now the mother and daughter were all mine.' He described taking them to an empty building, and forcing Mildred Jackson to commit a sex act, probably fellatio. 'Now I was her master . . .' After raping both, Rees killed them.

Rees was arrested at a music shop in Arkansas, where he was working. Like other sex killers already mentioned, he was an itinerant, never staying long in the same place. His friends found it hard to believe that this mild, quietly-spoken, intelligent man could be the murderer of the Jacksons, but investigation also tied Rees to five more sex murders. He was executed in 1961.

The case may be regarded as a turning point in twentieth-century crime. Other criminals – such as Ravachol and Prado – argued that they had a right to kill; but no one had ever used this kind of logic as an excuse for sexual self-indulgence. Dostoevsky's Raskolnikov states that he has a right to kill an old pawnbrokress in order to rescue himself from poverty and be able to lead a fruitful life. Rees was arguing, in effect, that sexual desire blocks self-fulfilment as much as poverty, and that he had a right to commit sex crimes to release his tension and restore a sense of reality. The argument is similar to that of Harry Lime in Graham Greene's *The Third Man*, who looks down from the top of the big wheel in a Vienna amusement park and asks whether the life of any one of those black dots on the ground is really worth twenty thousand pounds. Once this step of the argument – the 'depersonalization' of human beings – has been granted, it is possible to justify anything from cannibalism to genocide.

The problem here, we can see, is that Rees *is* intelligent, and that he is using his intelligence to justify an act – violation – of which every normal male is potentially capable. What has happened could be compared to the situation in the nineteenth century, when the spread of education made it possible for every working man to read Voltaire and August Comte, and rehearse all the standard arguments to prove that religion is a delusion. Whatever our view of religion, it is obvious that this kind of shallow scepticism did as much harm as good. With Melvin Rees we come upon a parallel phenomenon: the man who is intelligent enough to argue that crime is merely a matter of law, and that law is another name for social oppression. A few years later, Ian Brady was using the same argument to justify the sex murder of children; Charles Manson used it to justify the killing of 'pigs' like Sharon Tate and the LaBiancas; John Frazier used it to justify the killing of the Ohta family on the grounds that they were too rich; San Francisco's 'Zebra killers' used it to justify the killing of whites at random, on the grounds that all whites are the enemies of all blacks.

The 1960s, then, are a watershed in modern crime: the decade in which certain social bonds rotted and finally came apart. It *is*, undoubtedly, a matter of social bonds. There are many poor areas in industrial cities that *ought* to have a high crime rate, yet which have, in fact, a very low one. People who have lived in such areas can speak of the concern of neighbours for one another: how, if someone is ill or has an accident, neighbours will take it in turns to do the cooking, wash the clothes, feed the children and send them to school. Such areas obviously differ from the heterogeneous slums in large cities where the poor merely happen to have congregated because they have nowhere else to go. In such slums, most people hardly know the family next door, and the children only know one another because they attend the same school or play in the same street; they follow the lead of their parents, and regard the neighbours with indifference or hostility. Such areas may not even be slums. In modern Los Angeles there is an unprecedentedly high murder rate among Mexican teenagers. In Mexico there has always been a remarkable degree of social stability, even in the worst slums. Transplanted to a 'better' environment, there is nevertheless a sense of boredom and alienation, no feeling of 'belonging'; so a crude territorial urge replaces the old social bonds, and the result is violent hostility to anyone from the next street.

The problem is illustrated by a case that took place in Wimbledon in 1969. The dozen boys who battered to death a man they believed to be a homosexual were not embittered slum dwellers; they lived in an architectural showpiece called the Alton Estate, a huge block of glass and concrete flats set on pillars and surrounded by parkland. But the planners had failed to take account of the psychological effect of transferring working-class families from London slums to this strange, impersonal place in the middle of nowhere. The ringleader of the gang, Geoffrey Hammond, was not a hardened juvenile delinquent; he had been a choirboy, had been in the St John's Ambulance and Royal Marine Cadets, and had appeared in life-saving demonstrations in the children's television programme *Blue Peter*. On 29 September 1969, Hammond led his gang in a hunt for 'queers'; they had been damaging cars belonging to 'pooves', but now their victims parked farther away. They waited by a subway tunnel and ambushed a twenty-eight-year-old clerk named Michael de Gruchy; Hammond shouted 'Charge!' and the boys battered de Gruchy to death with palings. The basic problem was boredom and a sense of rootlessness; picking on 'queers' was their own way of seeking out adventure. ('Charge!')

The same problem – as already noted – is found on many large estates and in blocks of flats: vandalism, mugging, burglary. And an American experiment has shown that when the flat-dwellers are housed in bungalows with individual gardens, the crime rate falls dramatically. The problem is 'territorial'.

Once the social bonds have been loosened, violence seems to become a natural outlet for frustration or boredom. And it is at this point that 'magical thinking' finally comes into its own and provides an 'intellectual' justification for the violence. Werner Boost, a German sex murderer who made a habit of attacking courting couples and raping the women, told police indignantly that he became furious at the immorality of couples having sex in cars, and that: 'These sex horrors are the curse of Germany.' Heinrich Pommerencke, a twenty-three-year-old who had committed twenty rapes and ten rape murders, explained after his capture that he had committed his first murder after seeing a film called *The Ten Commandments* and deciding that women are the cause of all the world's troubles; he then attacked and raped an eighteen-year-old girl in a park, cutting her throat. Patrick Byrne, who raped and decapitated a girl in the Birmingham YWCA hostel in 1959, explained that he was trying to get his revenge on women for causing his sexual tension. Rudolf Pleil, the German rapist who committed suicide in his cell in 1958, liked to describe himself as *'der beste Todmacher'* ('the best death-maker' – he killed fifty women). 'Every man has his passion,' he remarked. 'Some prefer whist. I prefer killing people' – the implication being that murder was an honourable occupation in which a man might feel proud of his excellence.

Yet his suicide seems to be a tacit admission that he was not willing to submit his logic to the mercy of a jury.

It is important to note that 'magical thinking' usually applies to only one department of a man's life; in most ways he may be perfectly normal and logical – as we have seen in the case of so many Right Men who strike their friends and colleagues as perfectly reasonable. In the early 1950s, a 'mad bomber' terrorized New York; bombs exploded in Grand Central Station, Radio City Music Hall, Macy's department store and several other public places; fortunately, no one was killed, although a few were injured. The police tracked down the bomber when he wrote a letter denouncing the Edison Company for causing his tuberculosis; a check of company records revealed that a man named George Metesky had been knocked down by an escape of hot gas in 1931, and had been unsuccessful in his claim for a disability pension. Metesky proved to be a fifty-four-year-old bachelor who lived with his elder sisters, attended church every Sunday, and dressed meticulously in double-breasted suits. He never struck anyone as remotely insane; and, apart from this single streak of paranoid resentment, he *was* apparently quite normal. Metesky was confined in a mental home.

The same point emerges in the case of Richard Speck, the multiple sex killer. When police were summoned to a nurses' hostel in Jeffrey Manor, Chicago, on 14 July 1966, they were convinced that an insane monster was at large. The mutilated corpse of a girl lay on a downstairs couch; upstairs, there were seven more dead women, all naked, all slashed and stabbed. But there was a survivor of the massacre, a nurse named Corazon Amurao, who described how she had opened the door to a pockmarked man who smelt strongly of drink, and who threatened her with a gun. He had tied up the nine nurses, then taken them, one by one, into the next room. Miss Amurao had hidden under the bed, and the killer had overlooked her. When she described a tattoo on the man's arm, with the words 'born to raise hell', the police were able to identify him as a sailor who had applied for a job at a local seamen's union; his name was Richard Speck. Two days later, after his name had been released on television, Speck attempted suicide in a hotel room and the tattoo was recognized by the doctor who tended his slashed wrists.

In spite of a pockmarked face, Speck proved to be a quiet, shy man who gave an impression of gentleness. (One man who met him in Chicago described him to me as a 'charmer'.) A few weeks before the murders, he had been taken into hospital for an appendectomy, and one of the nurses had gone on dates with him; she described him as kindly and considerate, but said that he seemed to be full of smouldering resentment about his divorced wife. The only nurse who had been raped – Gloria Davy (who was found downstairs) – bore a strong resemblance to Speck's wife; Corazon Amurao, who had watched Speck raping her, described how he had said: 'Would you mind putting your legs round my back' – evidence of consideration for a woman he was to murder a few minutes later.

Again and again we encounter this apparent anomaly in criminals. Myra Hindley loved animals. Geoffrey Hammond's father said of him: 'He loves children. He's a sentimental boy.' And in the case of Hammond, we can see that one streak of paranoid resentment – about homosexuals – was enough to lead to violence. It is the 'decision to be out of control' in a particular area. But we can also see that this 'decision' to express resentment as violence depends to some extent on social background, and whether it was kindly and co-operative or hostile and alienated. Richard Speck's home background had been insecure and he became a drifter. Myra Hindley spent her childhood between two homes because – she believed – her parents preferred her sister. Ian Brady was illegitimate and he was farmed out to another 'parent'. Charles Manson's mother became pregnant at fifteen, and went to prison shortly after Manson was born. And so insecure social bonds prevent a capacity for love and affection from being channelled into stable relationships, and the resentment lies dormant, like a volcano, waiting to be detonated into violence by stress.

Albert DeSalvo, the 'Boston Strangler', provides a particularly clear example of this 'balance of forces'. Between June 1962 and January 1964, DeSalvo committed thirteen sex murders in the Boston area; then he stopped killing and contented himself with fondling and rape. He was finally identified as the Strangler only because he chose to confess.

The first four murders were of elderly women, aged between fifty five and seventy-five. DeSalvo, a powerfully built man with a plausible manner and a certain charm, would knock on the door of an apartment and explain that he had been sent to do some work – paint the ceiling, check the windows for leaks, etc. If the women seemed doubtful, he would turn away politely, saying 'I don't want to bother you', and they would usually let him in. When the woman's back was turned, DeSalvo would place his muscular arm round her throat and tighten it until she was unconscious; intercourse usually followed, then the victim was strangled with a belt or some article of clothing. The victim was then left in a deliberately 'obscene' position – perhaps with legs spread apart, wearing stockings and suspender belt, and with a brush handle inserted in the vagina; in one case he tied the victim's ankles to chairs and placed her with the genitals facing the door, so that this would be the first thing that anyone would see on entering the room.

After the killing of the elderly women, there was a lull of four months; the next set of victims were young and attractive girls. The psychiatrist Dr James Brussell propounded the remarkable theory that the killer was actually 'progressing' through murder to greater maturity. The early murders expressed resentment of his mother; then he 'got it out of his system' and turned to attractive girls.

Soon after Christmas 1952, a young student, Patricia Bissette, allowed him into her apartment when he said he was her roommate's boyfriend, and talked to him trustfully as he drank coffee. He strangled and raped her. But – as he later admitted – he felt so ashamed that she had 'treated him like a man' (i.e. like a human being) that he carefully covered the body over before leaving.

In January 1964, DeSalvo talked himself into the apartment of nineteen-year-old Mary Sullivan and ordered her into the bedroom. She pleaded with him, but he hit her and tore off her clothes. After raping her, he bit her all over, then strangled her; then he sat on her chest and masturbated on her face. He explained to the dead girl: 'I can't help doing it . . .' But this was his last murder. Like Patricia Bissette, Mary had made him feel like a human being, and the result was a revulsion from killing.

DeSalvo continued raping; he was sexually insatiable, capable of several orgasms one after another. But the method had changed. He would talk himself into a woman's home, and engage her in casual conversation. At a certain point, he would pull out a knife, force her into the bedroom, and tie her up. He would then kiss and fondle her, taking his time, and usually end with rape. After this he would apologize and leave. If the woman was too distressed, he would omit the rape. DeSalvo claimed to have raped two hundred women between January and October 1964. A description by one of his victims reminded the police of a curious series of sexual offences in 1960, when a man talked his way into women's apartments by asking if they would like to work as a model; he would then take their measurements with tape, but without any attempt at sexual assault. Some of the women complained when his promises of modelling work failed to materialize: DeSalvo was identified as the 'measuring man' and sentenced to two years in jail for assault. The rapist sounded like the measuring man. DeSalvo was arrested and sent to the Bridgewater State Hospital. It was there that he confessed to being the Boston Strangler, and at first no one believed him. Eventually, the exactitude of his descriptions convinced the police that he was telling the truth. In 1973, DeSalvo was mysteriously stabbed to death in his cell, presumably by a fellow prisoner.

Here we have an unusual case of a sex killer whose crimes display paranoid resentment of women, but who slowly outgrows his 'magical thinking' as realism gradually breaks through. Finally, it becomes clear that he craves human relationships as much as sexual satisfaction. The resentment has been finally replaced by a desire to be understood. But, by DeSalvo's own account, it took some two thousand rapes to reach this point.

Psychiatric examination revealed that DeSalvo's childhood had been traumatic; his father was a brute who beat his wife and children – on one occasion he broke his wife's fingers one by one. His mother made no attempt to protect the children. There was an overpowering atmosphere of sexuality in the home; his father would bring home prostitutes and have sex in front of the children, and DeSalvo himself had incestuous relations with his sisters. In the circumstances, it seems inevitable that the resentment would eventually express itself as sexual violence.

It became clear in the 1960s that a generalized social resentment – a hatred of authority – was becoming more pronounced than at any time since the anarchist outrages of the 1880s. After the Second World War there had been a period of social calm – based on relief at seeing the end of fascism. In England it was presided over by a socialist government, but this swing to socialism was not a sign of social unrest – merely of a desire for change after five years of war, and in fact, the national temper was conservative. And this conservatism inevitably caused a reaction in the generation then growing up. The American sociologist David Reisman wrote in 1956 an essay called 'The Found Generation' in which he pointed out that most American students of the new generation possessed the 'organization mentality' to a terrifying degree; that their aims were a wife, a home, a car, and a good job with some large (and therefore 'safe') organization. Such young people, he said, would never drop atom bombs or start world wars. Reisman's famous book *The Lonely Crowd* argued that the American mentality was slowly changing from 'inner-directed' (i.e. self-reliant) to 'other-directed' – conformist. William H. Whyte's book *The Organization Man* made a similar point. Senator Joe McCarthy's anti-communist witch-hunts of the early 1950s seemed to confirm that what the post-war world wanted most was freedom from social upheaval.

By the second half of the 1950s, a new generation was already expressing its distaste for this stability. In England, the 'Angry Young Men' – named after John Osborne's play *Look Back in Anger* – directed their abuse at the 'establishment' – the church, the government, the royal family. In America, the 'Beat Generation' – led by Jack Kerouac and Allen Ginsberg – turned their backs on society in favour of the 'hippie' culture; but the emphasis was still on the iniquity of the establishment. In France, the followers of Sartre called themselves Maoists and called for a communist revolution. In Germany, still numbed by the defeat of 1945, there was as yet no sign of a new literary generation, but the spirit of dissatisfaction was growing.

The revolt against 'stability' received one of its clearest expressions in the manifestos of a group that called itself Situationist International, founded by Raoul Vaneigem and Guy Debord. They argued that the establishment has learned to control the people by turning life into a kind of continuous entertainment – the 'Society of the Spectacle'. Computers, television and all the other 'mod cons' were designed to keep people passive and cow-like. The answer should be 'subversion' in every department of modern life, in schools, universities, factories. Anything that adds to the convenience of modern life should be regarded as a target for attack.

Another increasingly powerful influence on this rebel generation was Herbert Marcuse, a German Jewish sociologist with strong Marxist leanings who emigrated to America after the Nazis came to power. He seems to have detested American society very nearly as much as Hitler's Germany, finding it too obsessed with success, conformity, standardization. As early as 1941 he was expressing deep misgivings about technological society and the tendency of technology to deprive man of his freedom. In 1951, his book *Eros and Civilization* took its starting point from Freud's argument that civilization always seems to involve repression of man's natural instincts. And in 1964, *One Dimensional Man* began with the proposition: 'A comfortable, smooth, reasonable, democratic unfreedom prevails in advanced industrial civilization, a token of technical progress.' At the back of Marcuse's mind lies a vague, misty concept of some ideal 'unrepressive society', a Rousseau-ish dream in which everyone can do as he likes. His hatred of 'repression' became steadily more vitriolic until, in *An Essay on Liberation* (1969), it explodes into a fountain of bilious rage; the rebels of the new generation are advised to cultivate the 'methodical use of obscenity', to refer to President X and Governor Y as 'pig X' and 'pig Y', and to address them as mother-fuckers because they have 'perpetrated the unspeakable Oedipal crime', to take drug trips to escape the 'ego shaped by the established society' and to seize every opportunity for social sabotage. Marcuse was basically an old-fashioned anarchist; but his denunciation of the unsatisfactoriness of modern life aroused an echo in all young people who found modern life frustrating and boring.

The drugs Marcuse was recommending were not opium derivatives, but 'psychedelics' like mescalin and LSD, which are non-addictive. Significantly, these seem to operate by paralysing the normal 'repressive' function of the left brain, and allowing perception to be shaped by our far richer right-brain awareness. In the late 1950s, Timothy Leary, a lecturer in psychology at Harvard, began controlled experiments with 'psychedelics' (he invented the word) and became convinced that they could become the instrument of a new, enriched consciousness. He summarized his doctrine in the phrase: 'Turn on, tune in, drop out.' Sacked from Harvard in 1963, he became a guru of the new generation. He would later be sentenced to ten years in jail for drug-smuggling.

In the autumn of 1966, a number of 'Situationist' students at Strasbourg University founded a society for the rehabilitation of Marx and Ravachol, and printed a pamphlet urging revolt against authority; they were all expelled. This was counter-productive; students all over France took up the protest. They became known as 'enragés'. At Nanterre University, they shouted down lecturers and painted obscene graffiti on the walls. The police had to be called in. In May 1968, the violence spread to Paris; students built barricades and hurled paving stones, while the French police reacted with their customary lack of finesse. For a while, it looked as if de Gaulle's government was about to come crashing down. But, in fact, the workers themselves found all this talk of revolution rather silly, and declined to take over the factories. Slowly, the French revolt faded away. But in England, in West Germany, in America, it smouldered on. When the Shah of Persia came to Berlin in June 1967, students protested about his repressive regime; the police reacted violently, and a student named Benno Ohnesorg was killed. This convinced the young that terror had to be met with terror. Two of the most active organizers of protest were Gudrun Ensslin and Ulrike Meinhof. In London in October 1968, student protesters in Grosvenor Square were treated roughly by the police. Some of them began to speak of founding a more 'active' organization, something along the lines of the French *enragés* – a word they decided to translate as 'Angry Brigade'. In America, a group of 'urban guerrillas' who called themselves the Weathermen were already trying to undermine the capitalist system with bombs placed at military installations, banks and the offices of big corporations.

In San Francisco, this idea of total revolution was taken very seriously by a group of 'hippies' who had formed around a charismatic little guitar player named Charles Manson. Born in 1934, Manson spent his first term in reformatory school at the age of nine. By the time he drifted to San Francisco in 1967, Manson had spent most of his adult life in jail, mostly for such offences as car theft and credit-card fraud. He found himself in the midst of the new 'psychedelic' culture. The hippies of the Haight-Ashbury district took LSD, smoked pot, and called themselves 'flower children'. No one cared that Manson had been a jailbird; on the contrary, it was regarded as being greatly to his credit. Manson was older than most of the 'drop-outs', and girls seemed inclined to regard him as a father-substitute figure. Runaways began to gather round him, and soon the Manson menage in the Haight district seemed to be full of emotionally deprived girls and admiring youths (Manson seems to have been bisexual). If they had never read Marcuse, they never-theless practised his idea that sex could be used as a form of 'unrepressive sublimation' to unfold our higher possibilities.

By 1968, Manson was trying hard to move into the pop music business; Manson's 'family' even moved for a time into the luxury home of a member of a successful group called the Beach Boys. Manson's lack of success seems to have made him increasingly embittered. The 'family', now numbering about thirty (and includ-ing children) moved out to a ranch owned by an old man named George Spahn, and lived there in exchange for cleaning out the stables.

With so much drug-taking, violence was inevitable. In July 1969, Manson shot a negro dope-dealer named Bernard Crowe in the chest; in fact, Crowe recovered and decided not to go to the police. Later that month, Manson and his friend Bobby Beausoleil tried to persuade another drug-dealer, Gary Hinman, to finance a move to Death Valley; when Hinman refused, he was tortured, then stabbed in the chest and left to die. On the wall above his body, Beausoleil wrote 'Political piggy' in blood – intended to lead the police to the belief that the Black Panther movement was responsible.

Manson's plan was to cause a revolution by setting whites against blacks (whom he detested). On Friday, 8 August 1969, four Manson disciples – three girls and a man – drove out to a house in Benedict Canyon which had been rented by a man in the pop music business against whom Manson had a grudge; in fact, it was now occupied by the film director Roman Polanski and his wife Sharon Tate. Polanski was in London, but Sharon Tate had three guests to supper, two men and a woman. Afterwards they took a psychedelic drug and went into various states of dissociation. As the Manson family members entered the drive, they encountered a youth who had been visiting the houseboy; he was shot in the head. Then they went into the house and killed Sharon Tate and her three guests. The men were shot, the women stabbed to death. The word 'Pig' was written on the hall door in blood.

The murders created the sensation Manson had hoped for; the following day, the 'family' watched the television news-casts with satisfaction. By that evening, every gun and guard dog in the Los Angeles area had been bought up by frantic householders. Manson decided to strike again while the iron was hot. That evening, after taking LSD, he led six followers to a house in the affluent Los Feliz district of Los Angeles, the home of a supermarket owner, Leno LaBianca and his wife Rosemary. Manson walked into their bedroom with a gun and tied them up, then sent in three followers, who stabbed the LaBiancas to death. They wrote 'Death to pigs' in blood on a door, and 'Helter Skelter', Manson's code word for the revolt that would occur when the alarmed whites rose up against the blacks.

But the rising failed to occur; Los Angeles was too accustomed to mass murder to over-react. In the following month, the 'family' moved out to the remote Death Valley. When Manson set on fire a bulldozer belonging to the State rangers, the police raided the ranch and arrested all the hippies. And after more than a month in jail, a family member named Susan Atkins, who had taken part in both sets of murders, told her cell-mate about the killings, and word leaked back to the police.

The trial that followed was one of the longest and most expensive in Los Angeles history, and Manson did his best to turn it into an indictment of society and of his judges, explaining that the murders had been committed out of love. Asked if she thought the killing of eight people was unimportant, Susan Atkins retorted by asking whether the killing of thousands with napalm was important. President Nixon denounced Manson even before he and his five co-defendants had been found guilty, and, predictably, Manson became a hero of the west-coast 'underground' network. But the trial had the effect of convincing the rest of the world that the whole movement of social revolt was a form of mindless emotionalism whose arguments defied logic; it produced, in fact, precisely the kind of revulsion against the left that the McCarthy witch hunts had created against the right. In America, at least, the Manson family had discredited 'revolution'.

On the other side of the Atlantic it remained alive, largely as a result of wider social conflicts. The Palestine Liberation Organization had been formed in Cairo in 1964 under the leadership of Yasser Arafat; its aim was to recover Palestine from the Israelis. In 1967, the Arabs, led by Egypt, launched an attack on Israel; but the Israelis quickly went on the offensive, and had virtually won the war within six days. The fading Palestinian hopes of a military victory led to a change of tactics. In July 1968, three members of another

did not; Israel attacked first

Palestinian group – the Popular Front for the Liberation of Palestine (PFLP) – took over an Israeli airliner flying from Rome to Tel Aviv and made the pilot land in Algiers. The Israelis agreed to free sixteen Arab terrorists in exchange for the release of the plane and the Israelis on board. (The old Prohibition term hijacking was soon being used to describe this new form of aerial terrorism.) In September 1970 the PFLP hijacked three planes at once (an attempt on a fourth was frustrated by security guards at Amsterdam) and blew one of them up on the Cairo airport – an American Pan Am jumbo jet costing millions – the terrorist spokesman said that this was to give the Americans a lesson for supporting Israel. Meanwhile, a British VC-10 had been hijacked in Bahrein, and the terrorists demanded the release of the commando woman Leila Khaled, jailed in London for an abortive hijack attempt. The three remaining planes were blown up in Jordan, but not – as the guerrillas threatened – with passengers aboard. Seven terrorists were eventually released in exchange for passengers. These attacks had the initial effect of turning world opinion against the Palestinians; but as the media also allowed a certain amount of space to Palestinian grievances, there was a slowly increasing awareness that the Palestinians had a genuine cause for anger. Over the course of the decade, world opinion swung slowly but surely to the view that the Palestinians deserved a homeland of their own.

1964, the year in which the PLO was formed, also saw a break between the old fashioned IRA (Irish Republican Army) in Dublin, with its Marxist orientation, and the Provisional IRA whose sole aim was the unification of Ireland. In 1968, the dissatisfaction of Irish Catholics with the Protestant Ulster government – which, they alleged, treated them as second-class citizens – led to widespread riots, and the beginning of a wave of terrorism in Northern Ireland. After many violent clashes between Protestants and Catholics, British troops were sent to Ulster in April 1969, at first to defend the Catholics. Within weeks, the troops themselves were under attack from terrorists, mostly 'Provos'. The Provos inaugurated the use of the car-bomb; a bomb placed in the boot of a stolen car and parked in some area in the centre of a city was virtually undetectable until it exploded. Some Catholic districts became IRA enclaves, 'no-go' areas for the police and troops. Belfast became a battleground.

In 1968 there were also an increase in terrorism in South America

– the death of guerrilla leader Che Guevara in Bolivia in 1967 had turned him into a symbolic figure of revolt – new measures in Spain against Basque separatists, riots in Belgium about the Flemish language, and even bomb explosions in Wales by Welsh nationalists. It was also the year that the Russians invaded Czechoslovakia to suppress the liberal regime of Alexander Dubcek. In America, the civil rights leader Martin Luther King was assassinated in Memphis, Tennessee, and Senator Robert Kennedy was shot in Los Angeles. As French students rioted in Paris, it seemed to many that 1968 might well be the start of the revolution predicted by the Situationists. But the outcome of the student riots provided a more reliable pointer to the underlying mood of ordinary citizens; the Gaullists were forced to call a general election, but swept back into power with an increased majority.

Nevertheless, the rise of terrorism encouraged idealistic leftists in Europe and America to hope for the advent of Marcuse's 'non-repressive society'. In England, a group of students – mostly from Essex University – called themselves the Angry Brigade, and began selective acts of 'social sabotage' – such as incendiary bombs in big London stores. In 1971, two bombs exploded at the home of the Conservative employment minister Robert Carr, another at a police computer centre, another at the home of the Secretary for Trade, John Davies, another at the top of the Post Office Tower. No one was injured. The British police tracked down the bombers to a North London commune, and four of them were sentenced to ten years in jail. But in West Germany, a number of bombings attributed to the Baader-Meinhof group, led by Andreas Baader, Ulrike Meinhof and Gudrun Ensslin, killed and injured many people in May 1972. The three leaders were arrested a few months later, and their lawyer, Horst Mahler, was sentenced to twelve years in jail for helping to found the group. But other members of the group continued terrorist attacks. Peter Lorenz, leader of the Christian Democratic Union, was kidnapped in February 1975 and released after the government freed five leftist anarchists. In April 1975, another Baader-Meinhof splinter group took over the West German embassy in Stockholm, demanding the release of all Baader-Meinhof terrorists under arrest, and killed the military attaché. When their demands were rejected, they set off an explosion; after a siege, the terrorists surrendered. In May 1976, Ulrike Meinhof was found hanged in her prison cell; the inquest found that she had committed suicide, but leftists alleged it was murder. In April 1977, the chief federal prosecutor, Siegfried Buback, was assassinated in his car; nevertheless, the three remaining leaders, Andreas Baader, Gudrun Ensslin and Jan-Karl Raspe, were sentenced to life imprisonment later the same month. In July, Jurgen Ponto, chairman of the Dresdener Bank, was killed at his home by terrorists, and in September 1977, an industrialist, Hanns-Martin Schleyer, was kidnapped; the ransom note demanded the freeing of Baader, Ensslin and Raspe. While Schleyer was still held, four Arab terrorists seized a Lufthansa jet airliner and held it at Mogadishu airport, in Somalia, threatening to blow it up with all passengers unless Baader and his companions were released. After five days, West German commandos stormed the plane, killing three of the four hijackers and releasing the eighty-six passengers. A few hours later, Baader, Raspe and Gudrun Ensslin were found dead in their cells in Stammheim prison. An inquest decided that they had committed suicide; but there was widespread speculation that the German authorities had decided that this was the only way to prevent further attempts to free them through terrorism. The body of Hanns-Martin Schleyer was found in the boot of an abandoned car the following day.

In America, the terrorist coup of the decade was the kidnapping of newspaper heiress Patty Hearst, who was abducted from her flat in February 1974. The kidnappers called themselves the Symbionese Liberation Army, and their leader, 'Field Marshall Cinque', demanded that her father, Randolph Hearst, should provide the poor with millions of dollars' worth of free food. The demand was, in fact, unrealistic, since the Hearst newspaper empire had suffered heavy financial losses in recent years. Nevertheless, Hearst distributed two million dollars' worth of food. The SLA promptly announced that this was not enough and demanded far more. But further argument was avoided when the kidnappers released a tape of Patty Hearst in which she denounced her family as capitalist oppressors and declared that she had become a 'freedom fighter' under the name of Tania. When she was photographed by a bank camera during the course of a hold up, carrying a sub-machine gun, she was declared a fugitive from justice. In May, the police traced six members of the SLA to a hideout in the suburbs of Los Angeles; in the shoot-out and fire that followed, all six died, including the leader Donald DeFreeze – 'Field Marshal Cinque'. Patty Hearst was not in the house; she remained on the run for another sixteen months, and was finally arrested in September 1975. At her trial, her defence alleged brainwashing, and it became a point for passionate discussion whether a kidnap victim could be blamed for saving her life by adopting the opinions of the kidnappers. She was sentenced to seven years in jail, but on appeal this was reduced to probation.

The case held the newspaper headlines for more than two years; yet anyone who was in America during that time (as I was) noted a kind of public apathy, a sense of *déjà-vu*. It seemed an oddly out-of-date sort of affair, as if it had been left over from the era of Vietnam protest a decade earlier. By the time Patty Hearst was captured, the North Vietnamese had overrun the south, and vast numbers of Vietnamese took to the sea in boats in an attempt to escape the communist regime. Within months of the communist takeover of Saigon (now Ho Chi Minh City) in April 1975, 150,000 people had fled, many in small boats that disappeared. During the next four years, thousands continued to leave, and the sheer scale of the tragedy slowly became clear. Thousands of children were sent on ahead by parents who hoped to join them later, and ended in refugee camps in South-east Asia. As the refugees flooded in, Thailand and Malaysia – the nearest non-communist countries – began turning the boats back to sea. Thai fishermen became pirates and began intercepting the boats and slaughtering the refugees; survivors told stories of rapes, mutilations, children thrown overboard. Yet the detestation of the communist regime was so great that even four years later, in 1979, another 140,000 fled. Although few of the famous names of the Vietnam protest movement – such as Norman Mailer and Jane Fonda – had the grace to admit that they had been wrong and the US government right about the intentions of the North Vietnamese, the facts spoke for themselves. By the late 1970s, most of the prominent leftist rebels of the 1960s had drifted into respectability, or at least ceased to make public statements about the 'repressive society' that had nurtured them.

By 1980, left-wing terrorism was diminishing in Europe and America, to be replaced to a disturbing extent by right-wing terrorism. In October 1980, a judge indicted eight right-wing terrorists for the bombing of a passenger train in 1974, when twelve people were killed; within hours, an enormous bomb had exploded at the Bologna railway station, killing seventy-nine and injuring more than 160. On 26 September 1980, a bomb in a dustbin exploded outside the Munich Oktoberfest as crowds were streaming from the exit, killing thirteen and injuring more than 200; a young neo-Nazi, who died in the blast, was believed to be responsible. It was an appalling end to the worst decade of terrorist violence in modern history.

The 1970s also set new standards of viciousness in ordinary criminal violence. The worst crimes of the 1970s were characterized by a brutality, an indifference to human life and suffering, that had no parallel in the criminal records of earlier centuries.

In 1971, Juan Corona, a Mexican farmer, surpassed all previous American records for mass murder. A Japanese farmer near Yuba City, California, discovered a grave on his land; it proved to contain the corpse of a male vagrant who had been sexually violated. Further searches in the area uncovered another twenty-four bodies; one of them had in his pocket a receipt signed 'Juan V. Corona'. Most victims were vagrants or migratory workers; the motive was apparently sexual. Corona's brother, a known homosexual, fled back to Mexico, and Corona's lawyers later alleged that he was the real killer. But on the evidence of a bloody machete found in Corona's home, and a ledger containing some of the names of victims, Corona was sentenced to twenty-five consecutive life terms.

In June 1972, following a supermarket robbery in Santa Barbara, California, three members of a family named McCrary were arrested: the father, Sherman, forty-seven, his wife Carolyn, and their nineteen-year-old son Danny. Later, their daughter Ginger was arrested, together with her husband Carl Taylor. It emerged that the family had drifted across the country from Texas, leaving behind a trail of robbed grocery stores and raped shop assistants. The McCrarys had made a habit of stopping by small shops or drive-in groceries in the evening, robbing the till and, if the shop assistant was attractive, taking her along with them. She was then raped by the three men and shot. The family are believed to have committed more than twenty murders. The two womenfolk apparently made no objection, regarding these rapes as the natural 'perks' of males who risk their lives by robbery. Carolyn McCrary commented: 'It may sound crazy, but I love my husband very much.'

On 8 August 1973, a caller to the Pasadena police department, Texas, explained that he had just killed a man. The police went to the home of thirty-four-year-old Dean Corll and found him lying dead in the hallway, with six bullets in his body. Seventeen-year-old Wayne Henley told them that he had murdered Corll in self-defence. Henley had brought a fifteen-year-old girl to a glue-sniffing party. They passed out, and when they woke up found themselves tied up. Henley had 'sweet-talked' Corll into letting him go, promising that he would rape and kill the girl while Corll, a homosexual, raped and killed another teenage boy who was present. Henley had then grabbed a gun with which Corll had been threatening him, and killed Corll.

Under interrogation, Henley admitted that he had procured boys for Corll, and that Corll had been systematically raping, torturing and murdering them. The boys were chained to a plywood board, and sometimes violated for days before being killed. Henley led the police to a boatshed in south-west Houston, and they began digging. Seventeen corpses, wrapped in plastic bags, were uncovered. Henley led the police to other sites where bodies were found; the final total seemed to be thirty-one. Boys had been disappearing from the Heights area of Houston for three years. Another youth, David Brooks, was also implicated, and he and Henley were both sentenced to life imprisonment for their part in the murders. Corll, it emerged, was a morbidly over-sensitive mother's boy who had never really grown up – one recent photograph showed him holding a cuddly toy. Corll was clearly yet another example of Freud's dictum that if a child had the power, it would destroy the world.

In April 1973, twenty-five-year-old Ed Kemper – six foot nine inches tall – crept into his mother's bedroom and killed her with a hammer; the following day he killed her friend Sara Hallett. Then he drove to Pueblo, Colorado, and rang the Santa Cruz police department to confess. In custody, Kemper confessed to six horrific sex murders, all with a strong necrophiliac element. In 1963, at the age of fourteen, Kemper had murdered his grandfather and grandmother, with whom he was living, and spent five years in mental hospitals. In 1972, he picked up two female hitchhikers, threatened them with a gun, and murdered them both; he later dissected the bodies, cutting off the heads. Kemper's usual method was to take the bodies back to his mother's house – she worked in a hospital – and rape and dissect them there; he particularly enjoyed having sex with a headless body. The bodies were later dumped over cliffs or left in remote mountain areas. Kemper was sentenced to life imprisonment.

Another psychopathic mass killer, Herb Mullin, was operating in California at the same time as Kemper. As a teenager, Mullin had been voted by his class 'most likely to succeed', but by the time he was twenty-one – in 1969 – he was showing signs of mental abnormality. In October 1972, driving along a mountain highway, Mullin passed an old tramp, and stopped to ask the man to take a look at the engine; as the man bent over, Mullin killed him with a baseball bat, leaving the corpse by the roadside. Two weeks later he picked up a pretty college student, stabbed her with a hunting knife, and tore out her intestines. In November 1972 he went into a church and stabbed the priest to death. On 25 January 1973, he committed five murders in one night, killing a friend and his wife, then murdering a woman and her two children who lived in a nearby log cabin. In the Santa Cruz State Park he killed four teenage boys in a tent with a revolver. On 13 February 1973, he was driving to his parents' home when a voice in his head told him to stop and kill an old man who was working in his front garden. A neighbour heard the shot, and rang the police, who picked up Mullin within a few blocks. At his trial, Mullin explained that he was convinced that murders averted natural disasters – such as another San Francisco earthquake. But he was found to be sane and sentenced to life imprisonment.

In May 1974, a burglar named Paul John Knowles came out of prison in Florida and flew to San Francisco to join a woman who had become his 'pen pal' in prison, and who had agreed to marry him. At close quarters, she found him rather frightening and, after four days, told him she had changed her mind. That night, according to Knowles's later confession, he went on the streets of San Francisco and killed three people at random. After that, he flew back to Jacksonville, Florida, and went on a rampage of murder and rape that lasted four months and claimed nineteen lives. In Jacksonville he suffocated a woman in the course of a burglary; when two small girls, aged seven and eleven, recognized him, he forced them into his car and killed them both, leaving their bodies in a swamp. He broke into a house in Atlantic Beach and strangled a forty-nine-year-old woman, then murdered and raped a female hitchhiker and strangled another woman in front of her three-year-old son. Then, driving around the country in a stolen car, he continued to commit murders and rapes at random. In Miami, he called on his lawyer and made a tape confessing in detail to fourteen murders (as well as the three in San Francisco), then drove on again. An attractive female journalist named Sandy Fawkes met Knowles in Atlanta, and spent several days with him without suspecting that he was a mass murderer; he made no attempt to harm her. He was finally arrested after a police chase in which he took two hostages and executed them both. The day after his capture, he was killed by an FBI agent when on his way to a maximum security jail when he – allegedly – tried to grab the sheriff's gun.

In April 1974, two blacks, Dale Pierre, twenty, and his friend William Andrews, robbed a Hi-Fi store in Ogden, Utah. The assistants, twenty-year-old Stan Walker and nineteen-year-old Michelle Ansley, were tied up. Cortney Naisbitt, a sixteen-year-old youth, walked into the shop and was tied up. So, later, were Stan Walker's father and Cortney Naisbitt's mother Carol, who came looking for them. The bandits then forced everyone to drink a caustic cleaning fluid, which burned their mouths and throats. Then they were shot. The girl was raped before being shot. One of the bandits pushed a ballpoint pen into the ear of Mr Walker and kicked it into his head. Carol Naisbitt died after being admitted to hospital, but Cortney survived; after many operations, he was able to resume normal life, although badly impaired. The two killers were careless, and were quickly arrested. Both were sentenced to life imprisonment.

In a book about the case, *Victim, The Other Side of Murder* by Gary Kinder (1982), one interesting point emerges. The killers got the idea of making the victims drink cleaning fluid from a Clint Eastwood film called *Magnum Force*, in which a prostitute dies within seconds of being forced to drink cleaning fluid by her pimp; Pierre obviously expected the victims to die immediately. *Magnum Force* is one of Eastwood's 'Dirty Harry' films about a San Francisco cop who, sick of the way that a modern criminal can get away with murder, shoots to kill. Like the Bologna and Oktoberfest bombings, the Ogden case seems to show that a violent reaction against violence can be counter-productive.

In the summer of 1974, three teenage delinquents known as the 'nice boys' gang committed a series of robberies, rapes and murders in Vienna. The leader, Manfred Truber, was seventeen. In late June they kicked to death an elderly man and kicked a seventy-year-old woman unconscious, ripping off her underwear. In July, a twenty-year-old girl was dragged into bushes and raped by all three, being made to sit astride them and move up and down. A Yugoslav construction worker was stabbed twenty-seven times and his nose almost severed from his face. In August, another girl was raped in the park, and then tortured and humiliated for over an hour. On 30 August a sixty-eight-year-old woman was infuriated when one of the boys punched her on the side of the head, and fought back with her handbag. Police arrived and arrested all three. Their score had totalled two murders, two rapes and twenty-two robberies with violence. Under Austrian law, it was possible to pass only short sentences on the gang.

On 2 July 1976, four-year-old Marion Ketter was playing with friends when a mild-looking elderly man persuaded her to go away with him. A few hours later, police searching a nearby block of flats found that a lavatory was blocked up with a child's intestines. In a bubbling saucepan on the stove of a lavatory attendant, Joachim Kroll, the police found the child's hand boiling with carrots and potatoes; the rest of her, wrapped in plastic bags, was in the deep freeze. Kroll admitted that he had been committing rape murders since 1955, and that in most cases he had taken slices of flesh from the victims' buttocks or thighs and later eaten them. The total number of victims is unknown, but Kroll could recollect fourteen. He seemed to have no appreciation of the seriousness of his crimes, and confidently expected to be allowed home after medical treatment.

A case with overtones of a James Bond thriller occurred in California in August 1976. The school bus of Chowchilla, Madera County, was held up by three men, who forced twenty-six children and the bus driver into two vans. They were then driven a hundred miles or so and, in the early hours of the morning, ordered to climb down a shaft in the ground. It led to a large underground room – in fact, a buried truck-trailer. They were given water and potato chips, and left.

When the sun rose, the van became overpoweringly hot. By standing on a pile of mattresses, the driver succeeded in reaching the steel plate overhead, but it refused to budge. Hours later, they succeeded in levering it aside, only to discover that the top of the shaft had been sealed with boards that were apparently immovable. Eventually, in the late afternoon, they succeeded in digging past the boards, and were able to climb out into the blazing heat of a California afternoon. A man working in a nearby gravel pit stared at them in amazement; then, when they explained who they were, rushed off to phone the sheriff. Frantic parents, convinced that they would never see their children again, heard of the escape over the television.

The quarry proved to be in Livermore, and security guards had seen the van being buried – by a bulldozer – and had taken the names of three young men. One of them proved to be Frederick Woods, son of the quarry owner; his companions were two brothers, James and Richard Schoenfeld. In spite of wealthy parents, the three had decided to make five million dollars by holding the children to ransom; the children had escaped before they had time to make the ransom demand.

Between July 1976 and August 1977, New York was terrorized by a series of shooting attacks on young women and courting couples, often sitting in cars late at night. In eight attacks, there were seven killings and eight woundings, many serious. The police began to receive letters from someone who called himself 'Son of Sam', who explained that he was a monster and that his father, Sam, had ordered him to go out and kill.

On 31 July 1977, Robert Violante and Stacy Moskowitz were sitting in a car in Brooklyn when the windscreen shattered; Stacy Moskowitz died later in hospital; Robert Violante recovered, but was blinded. After the shooting, a woman walking her dog saw a man leap into a car and drive away; she had also noticed earlier two policemen putting a parking ticket on the car. A check revealed that the parking ticket had been placed on a car registered to David Berkowitz, who lived in Yonkers. Police located the car and watched it; as twenty-four-year-old Berkowitz approached, a detective stepped forward, and Berkowitz said: 'You finally got me.' He also confessed to two knife attacks seven months before the first shooting. Berkowitz proved to be an inadequate personality who lived in a dream world, and was too shy to approach women. He was sentenced to a total of 365 years in prison.

On 30 September 1978, a fifteen-year-old girl named Mary Vincent set out to hitch-hike to Los Angeles; her third lift was with a heavily built man, who attacked her, raped her, then hacked off both her arms at the elbows and threw her out of the van. His description was broadcast, and brought a tipoff that led to his arrest; he was fifty-year-old Larry Singleton, who admitted to being drunk at the time he attacked the girl; he insisted he had no recollection of harming her. An axe found in his home showed traces of human blood.

In January 1979, two girl students – Karen Mandic and Diane Wilder – disappeared from the small house they shared in Bellingham, Washington State. The following day their bodies were found in the back of Karen Mandic's car. Karen had confided to a friend that she had been offered some kind of 'detective' job by a security guard named Kenneth Bianchi, who had recently moved to Bellingham from the Los Angeles area. And in that area, between October 1977 and February 1978, ten girls had been raped and murdered by a man who became known as the Hillside Strangler.

Bianchi, who was living in Bellingham with his mistress and child, was soon picked up, and at first denied all knowledge of the murders. He was a good-looking young man of twenty-seven, and all the evidence pointed to him as the killer of Karen Mandic and Diane Wilder.

Investigators in Los Angeles discovered that Bianchi and his cousin Angelo Buono – a man in his forties – had been involved in procuring prostitutes. In court in Bellingham, Bianchi confessed to the killing of the two Bellingham girls, and also admitted to five of the Hillside Strangler murders. But, in a surprising development, his defence alleged that his was a case of dual personality, and that the killings had been committed by his alter-ego 'Steve'. In later confessions, Bianchi stated that his cousin Angelo Buono had also been involved in the murders. Police examining the sites where the naked bodies of girls had been dumped in the hills around Los Angeles had, in fact, concluded that two men had been involved.

Psychiatrists were convinced by Bianchi's claim to be a dual personality; nevertheless, at his trial in October 1979, he was sentenced to six life terms in prison. (At the time of writing, proceedings against Angelo Buono are still going on.)

In December 1978, police in Chicago investigating the disappearance of a fifteen-year-old youth, Robert Piest, went to the home of a builder named John Wayne Gacy, who had offered Robert Piest a job. As they searched Gacy's house, the police came upon a trapdoor leading to a 'crawl space' under the house. There was a heavy odour of decaying flesh, and the torch beam picked out human bones and fragments of flesh. In all, twenty-eight bodies were discovered in Gacy's house, all young men. Gacy also admitted to five more murders – bringing his total up to thirty-three, two more than Dean Corll.

Gacy was already known to the police. In March 1978, a young man had fallen into conversation with a fat man in an Oldsmobile, and had accepted an invitation to smoke a joint. The man had clapped a chloroformed rag over his face and driven him to a house; there he had been homosexually raped, flogged and beaten. He woke up in a park, bleeding from the rectum; hospital examination revealed that the chloroform – which had been repeatedly administered to keep him quiet – had permanently damaged his liver. Since the police seemed unable to help, he hired a car and sat by motorway entrances, looking for the Oldsmobile; one day, he saw it, and noted the number. It proved to belong to John Wayne Gacy. Gacy was arrested and charged, but the police had little hope of making the charge stick.

Gacy had already been in prison on a charge of attempted homosexual rape of a youth, and had been twice married. When his second wife left him, in 1976, she had already noticed the peculiar smell that hung about the house. The evidence suggests that Gacy began killing young men – in the course of sadistic homosexual rape – in 1975. He was sentenced to life imprisonment.

On 2 January 1981, police in the centre of Sheffield, Yorkshire, noticed a man and a woman in a parked Rover car; since they had been alerted to look out for the 'Yorkshire Ripper', they asked the man his name. Meanwhile, a check of the car's licence plates revealed they were stolen. The man was taken to the local police station. Once there, one of the policemen admitted that he had permitted the man – now identified as thirty-five-year-old Peter

not surprising in an anonymous mass society

Sutcliffe, a lorry driver – to get out of the car to urinate near a fuel storage tank. A check near the tank revealed a ball-headed hammer and a knife. Soon afterwards, Sutcliffe confessed to being the man police were seeking for thirteen mutilation murders of women.

Most of the attacks had followed the same pattern. A woman walking alone was struck from behind with a hammer and knocked unconscious – sometimes the skull was shattered. The 'Ripper' then raised her clothes and stabbed her repeatedly in the area of the stomach and vagina, sometimes with a knife, sometimes with a screwdriver. In only one case was the victim also raped. Sutcliffe apparently derived his sexual satisfaction from the stabbing.

Eight of the first nine victims – killed between October 1975 and May 1978 – were prostitutes. Sutcliffe explained later that he had a grudge against prostitutes after one of them had swindled him, then made him a laughing stock in a pub. But after the ninth victim he attacked women and girls at random, killing four more and injuring two. One of the biggest police hunts in British criminal history was totally unsuccessful – although Sutcliffe was interviewed several times during the enquiry, his car having been observed in the red light area of Leeds. He was caught by a fortunate accident.

Sutcliffe was a shy, introverted man with few friends; his relationship with his wife Sonia was close but stormy. In the cab of his lorry police discovered a card that read: 'In this truck is a man whose latent genius, if unleashed, would rock the nations, whose dynamic energy would overpower those around him. Better let him sleep?' Again, we observe the element of frantic ego-assertion that is the characteristic of so many modern killers.

Sutcliffe's defence was insanity – he claimed that, when working as a gravedigger, he heard a voice speaking to him from a tombstone, ordering him to kill prostitutes. The jury chose to disbelieve him, and he was sentenced to life imprisonment.

Perhaps the strangest – and most characteristic – case of the 1970s was that of Ted Bundy. When Bundy was first arrested, in August 1975, he was suspected of a dozen sex murders that had taken place over the past year, the first eight in Seattle, the rest in the area of Salt Lake City. Bundy, an intelligent, personable young law student, had moved from Seattle to Salt Lake City. The events of 14 July 1974 seemed typical of the killer's method. A polite young man with his arm in a sling approached a girl at a picnic table near Lake

Sammanish and asked her if she would help him lift his boat on to a car. She accompanied him, but when he told her the car was at a house up the hill, changed her mind and went back. She saw the young man accost another girl, Janice Ott; he introduced himself as Ted. Janice Ott went with him, and vanished. So did a girl named Denise Naslund on the same afternoon. Their skeletons were found months later on a hillside near Lake Sammanish.

In November 1974, a polite young man accosted a girl named Carol DaRonch in a shopping centre in Salt Lake City, introduced himself as a police officer, and told her there had been an attempt to break into her car. She went with him to inspect it, and agreed to go with him to view a suspect at police headquarters. Once in his car, she was handcuffed, and he tried to knock her out with a crowbar. She managed to jump out, and the man drove off as another car approached.

During the next nine months, more violated corpses were found. In August 1975, Bundy was arrested for acting suspiciously late at night, and Carol DaRonch identified him as the man who had tried to abduct her.

Bundy insisted that his presence in the area where corpses were found was an unfortunate coincidence, and his plausibility and intelligence supported that view. He was a popular prisoner, and conducted his own defence brilliantly. On 30 December 1978, he hoisted himself through a hole in the ceiling and escaped.

Two weeks later, a man walked into the student sorority house in Tallahassee, Florida, and violently attacked four girls with a heavy piece of wood; one was shot and raped, and the man also bit her. Another girl was strangled. These two died; two others survived the beatings. In a nearby house, another girl was attacked and her skull fractured. The attacker fled when the phone rang. A few blocks away, Ted Bundy was living in a students' lodging house, using a false name and stolen credit cards. Shortly afterwards, he left Tallahassee in a stolen car; the car was recognized a few days later, and he was arrested.

At his trial, Bundy remained as charming and plausible as ever, and it was generally agreed that he was an unlikely sex killer, and that most of the evidence against him was purely circumstantial. But the clinching evidence against him came from a dentist, who testified that the teeth marks on the buttocks of one of the Tallahassee victims were identical with Bundy's dental imprint. The judge who sentenced him said: 'Take care of yourself young man . . . You went the wrong way, pardner.'

The key to Bundy's career of sex crime has been provided in a book called *The Only Living Witness* by Stephen G. Michaud and Hugh Aynesworth (Linden Press, 1983). In his interviews with Stephen Michaud, Bundy insists that he is merely 'speculating' about the motives of the killer, but the precision of his descriptions makes it clear that this is far more than guesswork. Bundy – who was born in 1946 – was an illegitimate child, who was spoilt by his grandparents, and who was deeply resentful when his mother married a cook in Seattle. He grew up to be a 'loner' with a streak of bitterness and resentment. Like most healthy young men, he was highly sexed: 'But this interest, for some unknown reason, becomes geared towards matters of a sexual nature that involve violence. I cannot emphasize enough the gradual development of this. It is not short-term.' Sexually shy and repressed, he indulged in fantasies of rape. One evening, walking down a street, he saw a woman undressing in a lighted room. He became a voyeur, and prowled the neighbourhood for hours every night. He tried disabling women's cars by pulling out the rotor arm from the distributor, or deflating the tyres, but there were always helpful males in the area to help the intended victim get started. His fantasies – like those of Melvin Rees – were of kidnapping a woman and having total control over her. After drinking heavily, the need to play the Peeping Tom became obsessive.

One evening, after heavy drinking, he saw a woman leave a bar and experienced a compulsion to follow her. He found a heavy piece of wood, and stalked her for several blocks. He managed to get ahead of her and wait in a dark corner. But she arrived at her front door and went in before she reached him.

The need to attack a woman became stronger. On another evening, he walked up behind a woman who was fumbling for her keys, and struck her on the head with a piece of wood. When she screamed, he ran away.

He followed one woman home regularly and watched her undressing. One evening, he got into the house through the basement and attacked her in bed; when she screamed, he fled.

He began to feel that there was another 'being' inside him, which he referred to as the 'entity', the 'disordered self' or the 'malignant being'.

Bundy described the first murder. He found a front door open and wandered around the house after dark. Lynda Healy, a twenty-one-year-old student at the University of Washington, was strangled into unconsciousness, and taken to a remote place where she was raped. At this point, Bundy realized that he would have to kill her because he couldn't let her go. Asked by the interviewer whether there was any conversation, Bundy replied: 'Since this girl . . . represented not a person, but . . . the image, or something desirable, the last thing we would expect him to want to do would be to personalize this person.' The victims were merely depersonalized females.

After this, the need to rape became an obsession that allowed him no peace. According to Bundy's account, on the day the two girls were abducted separately from Lake Sammanish, the first girl was kept tied up in his room until he brought the second one back, and so witnessed the rape of Denise Naslund. He had become a man possessed by a need that absorbed his whole life. He is a terrifying example of a type of killer that has only existed since Jack the Ripper.

The total number of Bundy's murders is unknown; police suspect that it could be in excess of those committed by Dean Corll or John Gacy. But in any case, Gacy no longer holds the American murder record; by 1980, unknown men known as the Freeway Killers had murdered forty-four teenage male hitchhikers, dumping their sexually abused bodies around California's highways. (In 1981, William Bonin confessed to twenty-one of the murders and was sentenced for ten of them; three other men were charged with him, one of whom committed suicide in prison.)

The most obvious point to emerge from this survey of crime since 1945 is that, as the figures have continued to rise, the nature of the crimes themselves has become steadily more horrific. It is as if some basic inhibition in human beings is finally beginning to break down. Like the Ik, many criminals seem to have lost all capacity for fellow feeling. But the Ik had an excuse: starvation and the disruption of their traditional life. The worst criminals of the past twenty years have been the product of a comfortable welfare society.

As the nature of the crimes becomes more brutal, they cease to produce a shock effect on society. In 1913, the murder of Mary Phagan made headlines all over America; today it is doubtful if it would achieve more than local coverage. The following three items were collected from newspapers over the New Year period of 1983. In Manchester, a youth of fifteen was sentenced to life imprisonment for a sexual attack on his music teacher and stabbing her fifteen times. In San Francisco, two men were arrested and charged with kidnapping a three-year-old girl and an eleven-year-old boy, and keeping them as 'sex slaves' in a van for almost a year; when arrested, one of the men was in bed with the girl, both naked from the waist down. In Bolton, Lancashire, a seventy-eight-year-old woman was mugged by three children, aged six, eight and nine, and left bleeding on the ground. Three weeks before that, her eighty-one-year-old brother, partially blind, was attacked by an intruder in his home and had to spend two weeks in hospital recovering from his injuries. The woman commented: 'I feel very bitter and angry. I don't know what is happening these days.'

After this survey of the criminal history of mankind, we are at least in a slightly better position to answer that question.

lack of empathy

Six

THE SENSE OF REALITY

In 1750, a traveller in Haworth, Yorkshire, was puzzled to see men jumping out of the windows of a public house and scrambling frantically over walls. The reason, he discovered, was that someone had seen the parson coming with his whip. The vicar of Haworth (where the Brontës would live a few years later) was the Rev. William Grimshaw, a man who spread terror throughout the district. When the church service had started and the congregation were singing hymns, he used to slip out to the village and use his whip to drive any truants to the church.

In this permissive age, we find it difficult to imagine just how powerful was the religious and moral code of a few centuries ago. Men like Grimshaw were by no means uncommon, for Sabbath breaking was regarded as the most shocking of sins. A prison chaplain remarked that men sentenced to death often began their confession with Sabbath breaking before they went on to robbery or murder. When Dr Johnson visited the death bed of the painter Sir Joshua Reynolds, he made him swear never to paint on Sunday. Even humming a merry tune on Sunday was regarded as scandalous. As Gordon Rattray Taylor has shown in *The Angel Makers* (chapter 2), many people attended church four times a day, even on weekdays. Sermons sold better than novels – Sterne said he made more money from his volumes of sermons than from *Tristram Shandy*.

If we can grasp the sheer rigidity of the religious observances of our ancestors – of their total acceptance, for example, of the idea of damnation, and that God was watching them every moment of the day – we can begin to understand why the disappearance of this outlook has caused such moral chaos. A cultural historian would probably date the decline from the rise of the novel. This was the equivalent of taking a hot bath instead of a cold shower; it was the

rise of self-indulgence [handwritten annotation]

beginning of a slide into self-indulgence. We have seen how the rise of the novel was accompanied by the rise of pornography, and how Victorian pornography laid more emphasis on the perverse and the forbidden. The Victorians were so fascinated by the 'forbidden' because most people still clung to the religious outlook of Parson Grimshaw and his flock. We have also seen how this 'morality of prohibition' gave rise to sex crime, and how this has finally become the most characteristic crime of the twentieth century. Dr Johnson would have characterized the whole process as, quite simply, the rise of self-indulgence.

What has happened is clear. Man created civilization for his own protection. But civilization, as Freud pointed out, involves one considerable drawback: frustration. A man who is economically deprived naturally covets his neighbour's wealth. A man who is sexually deprived lusts after his neighbour's daughters. To deal with these inclinations, society has had to set up a system of laws and moral prohibitions. While these remain strong, society remains healthy. When they disintegrate, civilization begins to show signs of breakdown. *need for personal limits, ego limits* [handwritten annotation]

It was towards the end of the eighteenth century that political philosophers began to break down the economic prohibitions. They argued that, if most men are poor, this is because the social system is unjust. Karl Marx dotted the i's and crossed the t's. The economically deprived have a *right* to seize their neighbour's wealth, for the neighbour would not be wealthy if he were honest.

The sexual revolution took longer to gather momentum – largely because, while a society is economically deprived, sex remains a secondary issue. Once a society is affluent, sex becomes the major issue. Our society has a very high level of sexual stimulation. The result is that most healthy males would like to undress every girl they pass in the street. There has been no sexual equivalent of Karl Marx to argue that women have no right to withhold their bodies from sexually deprived males, and ought to be raped. Yet every rape could be regarded as 'propaganda of the deed' for this point of view. The sex killer Melvin Rees came close to putting it into words when he said: 'You can't say it's wrong to kill. Only individual standards make it right or wrong.' So did Patrick Byrne, the YWCA killer, when he explained that he was trying to get his revenge on women for causing him sexual tension.

We can see, then, that sex crime is basically a form of 'magical thinking'. The 'decision to be out of control' may be purely emotional, as in the case of Paul Knowles, who goes on a murder rampage because his girlfriend has jilted him, or it may be a 'logical' decision, as in the case of Ted Bundy, who decides to satisfy his sexual desires through rape and risk the consequences; in either case, the criminal feels he has a *right* to make such a decision, and that if society disagrees, then society is trying to deprive him of his rights. The same analysis applies increasingly to crime in general. The individual concentrates on his frustration and resentment, and feels that his robbery or burglary is a legitimate way of expressing his sense of social grievance. If society doesn't like it, then it should take notice and treat him better . . .

If, then, we cast our minds back to the days of Parson Grimshaw, then forward to modern California, we can see precisely what has gone wrong. California has a pleasant climate, an excellent social welfare system, a tolerance of social rebels and a thriving drug traffic. Taken together, these elements combine into a powerful acid that can dissolve most of the prohibitions that society has set up for its own protection. The result is bound to be an increase in 'magical thinking' and in the violence that springs from it. And it is difficult to see how such a trend could be reversed, or prevented from gradually spreading across the whole of our civilization.

If this description of the situation is correct, then the outlook certainly seems bleak. The problem seems to be man's deep-seated assumption that he has a right to 'freedom', and his inability to make use of it when he has it. The philosopher T. E. Hulme expressed it when he remarked that man habitually overrates his capacity for freedom. In our muddled romanticism we believe 'that man, the individual, is an infinite reservoir of possibilities; and if you can so rearrange society by the destruction of oppressive order then these possibilities will have a chance, you will get Progress . . .' But the truth, said Hulme, is the reverse. 'Man is an extraordinarily fixed and limited animal whose nature is absolutely constant. It is only by tradition and organization that anything decent can be got out of him' (*Speculations*, p. 116). Or, to put it another way, human beings go to pieces without discipline. And, according to Spengler's *Decline of the West* and Toynbee's *Study of History*, this explains the breakdown of civilizations. They become powerful as hardship

true

much of society at Maslow esteem
level in the hierarchy

drives them to self-discipline. Then they become successful, the need for discipline vanishes, and they slide into decadence. The history of crime in the past century suggests that our civilization has now reached this stage.

There is obviously a great deal of truth in this analysis, but is it the whole truth? Hulme, for example, is obviously going too far when he says that man's nature is 'absolutely constant'. We know that man has, in fact, evolved faster than any other creature on earth. Spengler and Toynbee are clearly correct when they say that all civilizations go through the same cycle of rise and decline; but this does not mean that all civilizations are fundamentally alike – otherwise we would be literally repeating the history of ancient Sumeria. If man evolves, then so does civilization. To grasp what is really happening, we need to look at the problem from an evolutionary perspective: not merely the history of civilizations, but the history of man himself.

We can begin from the observation that there have been a number of watersheds in human history: events so important that they have created a basic variation in human behaviour. These include the beginning of agriculture, the building of the cities, the invention of writing, the rise of astronomy, the founding of the great religions, the creation of the drama, the discovery of philosophy, the triumph of Christianity, the rise of science and the development of the novel. A glance at the list reveals that most of these are intellectual. Man has evolved faster and farther than any other animal because he has learned to use his mind.

We have seen that this depended on the development of a kind of mental microscope, the ability to examine problems with precise attention. But this ability, which assured man's survival, also turned him into a criminal, for it narrowed down his consciousness so that he became a bad-tempered obsessive. Man exchanged the bird's eye view, which is natural to all animals, for a worm's eye view. He developed the left-brain ego, with its craving for esteem and respect. The earliest tyrants murdered out of a ruthless egoism. And civilization is now faced with an acute crime problem because it has now reached the self-esteem level – the ego level – of Maslow's hierarchy, and there are millions of ruthless egoists.

The worm's eye view has introduced another complication: it has made man far more 'hypnotizable'. We hypnotize an animal by narrowing its attention. Man's attention is almost permanently narrowed. Hypnosis is basically a loss of the sense of reality (clinically speaking, this is known as schizophrenia). Man spends most of his life in a semi-hypnotized state. And this, as we have seen, explains a great deal of violent crime. The hypnosis makes us feel trapped in triviality. Rupert Brooke welcomed the First World War, and compared it to the experience 'of swimmers into cleanness leaping'. Violence usually has this effect – like a thunderstorm that clears the air. Violence is the snap of the hypnotist's fingers.

It begins to look, then, as if the development of 'double consciousness' was one of man's greatest mistakes. For crime is basically an attempt to escape the narrowness of left-brain consciousness. This applies particularly to sex crime. There is a passage in *My Secret Life* in which Walter describes picking up a middle-aged woman and a ten-year-old girl. Back in her lodgings, he persuades the woman to allow him to penetrate the girl. Then he stands in front of the mirror, holding her against him, so he can actually *see* himself doing it. He is trying to make himself realize it is *actually happening*. Some couples have mirrors attached to the bedroom ceiling for the same reason.

Let us look more closely at the mechanism involved here. The philosopher A. N. Whitehead pointed out that we have two 'modes' of perception, which he called 'presentational immediacy' and 'causal efficacy'. 'Immediacy' could be described as 'close-up perception', the worm's eye view. But we have another mode of perception which corresponds to the bird's eye view. As you read this paragraph, you take it in sentence by sentence. If the argument is too complicated, or badly presented, you will remain in this state of 'worm's eye' perception. This could also happen simply because you are very tired, and fail to make the act of *connection* between the sentences. This act of connection – of linking them together in a sequence of cause and effect – allows a *leap* from the worm's eye view to the bird's eye view. This is what Whitehead calls 'causal efficacy'. It would be simpler to call it 'meaning perception'.

Sartre's novel *Nausea* is about a man whose perception is always collapsing into the 'worm's eye view'. Reality suddenly seems stupid and meaningless. Sartre argues that 'nausea' is *truer* than 'meaning perception', because we *add* the meaning to life by a kind of act of faith – or delusion. A man falls in love with a girl, and believes that she is the most exquisite and desirable creature in the world. He marries her and they go on honeymoon. That first night is not a disappointment – in fact, it is very enjoyable. Yet it is not quite the rapture he expected; it is somehow too real. And a year after they are married, he makes love to her as a matter of routine; sometimes he even allows his mind to wander and pretend it is somebody else. If he recalls that early adoration, he smiles wryly; it seems to be based upon a lack of insight into her actuality.

Yet what of those occasions when the delight suddenly returns – when, for example, he comes back from a long business trip, finds her looking radiant, and falls in love all over again? If this is illusion, it must be a singularly persistent one to triumph over experience.

What has happened, in fact, is simply that the two modes of perception have once again combined; immediacy perception and meaning perception have fused together.

In *The Dam Busters*, the story of the wartime RAF squadron, Paul Brickhill explains how they succeeded in destroying the Moener dam. The bombs were spherical, and had to bounce along the surface of the lake to strike the dam from the side. But in order to do this, they had to be dropped from an exact height above the water. The altimeters were not accurate enough, and any form of measuring device suspended from the plane – like a rope of the right length – would blow backwards. Then the inventor Barnes Wallace came up with the solution – to place two lights in the nose and tail of the plane, focused so that their two beams would blend into a single circle at the correct height. When a single circle appeared on the water, it was time to release the bomb.

In moments of excitement, our two modes of perception also focus into a single point, and we experience a sense of total reality. The bird's eye view and the worm's eye view combine. When a man is feeling tired, he is flying at the wrong height; so although he is holding his wife in his arms, he is not aware of her *reality*. His immediacy perception is focused, but his meaning perception is blurred.

If, on the other hand, he is talking to a friend about his wife, he may experience a sudden recognition of how much he loves her. His meaning perception has focused – but then, she is not present, so there is no immediacy perception.

This is the problem of most human beings for most of the time. We are flying at the wrong height. So, as Walter stands in front of

positive function of war

The Age of Mass Murder

the mirror, he is trying to focus the two beams into a point. This is also why he enjoys making women describe what he is doing. Most of his sex life had been a blurry perception of immediacy. The writing of *My Secret Life* was an attempt to restore meaning perception. A simpler way of putting it would be to say that it restored *objectivity*.

And now we can begin to see the problem in historical perspective. Human evolution was first of all a response to the challenge of survival. Man created civilization for his own protection. But living in cities created territorial problems. Man went to war about boundaries. Because of this sense of the 'alienness' of his neighbour, robbery and piracy became part of his way of life.

War forced man to grow up. The great dinosaurs had died out of sheer laziness, because there was no challenge. Man was faced with the opposite problem. He had created civilization for security, and found that his fellow human beings were a far worse menace than wild animals and bad weather. War and natural disasters obliged him to become more vigilant than he had ever been as a Stone Age hunter. He was forced to develop the 'microscope' – left-brain perception. One result was cruelty and inhumanity. Another – more important – was increased efficiency in survival.

Then man began to discover that there were enormous compensations in left-brain consciousness. Language is a left-brain function, and he could use language to store his past experience instead of forgetting it. He could even pass it on from generation to generation. Homer was not alive at the time of the Trojan war; but the whole experience had been preserved in language, and Homer was able to write it down two centuries later, so that Greeks in the time of Aeschylus and Sophocles could elaborate it into great dramas.

Moreover, Plato discovered that thinking was man's natural instrument for problem-solving, rather than old-fashioned trial and error. *Any* problem could be solved by thought. A slave who had never heard of geometry could be made to solve geometrical problems by reason alone. His pupil Aristotle inaugurated an ambitious project for applying these new techniques of thought to every department of human knowledge – and very nearly succeeded. Man had a breath-taking vision: the notion that he might not be merely human after all, but a close relative of the gods.

The Roman experiment seemed to reveal that this was wishful

thinking. The Romans were the most remarkable left-brain thinkers so far; they revelled in problem-solving, but they encountered all the disadvantages of left-brain awareness: its narrowness, its tendency to become bogged down in trivialities, its inherent pessimism. Roman civilization seemed to prove that, in spite of the intellect that distinguishes him from the brutes, man is a hopeless weakling. It is not surprising that the Christians laid so much emphasis on Original Sin, man's innate wickedness; they had the Romans in front of their eyes as living examples.

These Christians, when they took over Roman civilization, proved to be very little better. But at least they transcended Roman pessimism. They returned to a vision that was closer to that of Plato. Man might not be a god, but at least he had an immortal soul, and could be 'saved'. Unfortunately, they insisted that he could only be saved by ceasing to use his mind, and leaving his salvation in the hands of the Church.

The Muslims were more sensible; their Prophet had nothing against the use of reason. The result was that science and philosophy eventually came back to Europe as a gift of the Arabs. There followed the great surge of medieval invention, the revival of learning, the rebirth of science. When Plutarch taught his contemporaries to appreciate archaeology, he was demonstrating that man can use the two 'beams of perception' simultaneously, that he can look at a broken statue and suddenly *grasp* the fact that this was made in Greece nearly two thousand years ago, or in the Rome of Marius and Sulla.

This new confidence in the power of the human mind reinvigorated science. The results were spectacular: new knowledge of the heavens, of the laws of nature, of the mechanisms of living creatures. The men of the eighteenth century had good cause to be proud of human reason and contemptuous of superstition. Science had transformed human life, and there was every reason to believe that it would continue to do so. Bacon's New Atlantis was not really such an impossible dream.

This was also the period of the rise of the novel – from which we can date our modern age of violence. There was an increasingly strong feeling that man *ought* to be free, and that being free means to do what he likes. Novelists such as Monk Lewis and Maturin explored this theme of human freedom – and wickedness – with

freedom too often defined as caprice

pleasant shivers of apprehension, while de Sade instantly carried the idea to an extreme that seemed to demonstrate that man is capable of becoming the wickedest creature alive. But romantics such as Wordsworth, Goethe and Hoffman were preoccupied with another problem: if man is capable of these breath-taking glimpses of freedom – what Maslow was to call 'peak experiences' – then why do they vanish so quickly? Why can he not revive them at will? This problem caused a great deal of agonized heart-searching, and was responsible for the high number of suicides and early deaths among the romantics, who concluded that life is a cheat.

We can see precisely where they were mistaken. They experienced moments in which the two 'beams of perception' became focused, and they felt an overpowering sense of delight and optimism. In such moments, the old 'split' was healed; for a moment, man ceased to be a 'bicameral' animal and experienced a new sense of unity – no longer the simple, instinctive unity of the cow or the drunken man but the intenser unity of a higher level. We could say that he was using the two modes of perception as stilts that raised him far above most human beings. But, being unaccustomed to walking on stilts, he soon found himself lying flat on his back, convinced that the 'glimpse' had been some kind of delusion.

We have also seen that the nineteenth century was characterized by a surge of pornography. This could, in fact, be regarded as the underbelly of romanticism. Pornography derives from the romantic notion that sex is infinitely delightful and infinitely forbidden. We can also see that pornography is an attempt to achieve 'objectivity', a combination of immediacy perception and meaning perception. A man who is in bed with a girl in the dark is trapped in mere sensory impressions; in such a situation there is very little difference between Cleopatra and the fat girl next door. The experience needs to be completed by a sense of reality – meaning perception. This is so feeble in human beings that it tends to switch off when we are in the dark. Yet the human imagination is such a remarkable faculty that a written description of the sexual act can be more 'real' – more intense – than the experience of an actual girl in the dark. It is the 'forbiddenness' that produces the surge of intensity, and the momentary experience of 'focusing'. The poet Swinburne affords an interesting example. He was obsessed by flogging and by punishment, and some of the best of the *Poems and Ballads* dwell on pain.

His friend Monckton Milnes was a collector of pornography, so Swinburne had access to a great deal of it. His interest in pornography – like the alcoholism of his middle years – was an attempt to revive the intensity of the poetic vision – to clamber back on his stilts. What he craved was 'objectivity', the moment of focus. In fact, neither pornography nor alcohol could get him back on his stilts, and his poetry became depressingly dull.

So we can see that the upsurge of sex crime in the second half of the nineteenth century was not simply an expression of human depravity, a result of the wicked self-indulgence that began with the rape of Clarissa Harlowe; it was a clumsy attempt to focus the two beams of perception, a form of perverted romanticism. It is, in fact, the attempt of the individual to evolve at the expense of society.

By 1900, romanticism was dead; it had died of despair. The romanticism of Wordsworth and Goethe is vigorous and optimistic; the romanticism of Verlaine, Dowson and Trakl is tired and sad. The poets of this 'tragic generation' had come to accept that the 'moments of vision' were an illusion, and that there was no point in struggling. Better to accept that life is a cheat and a fraud and turn your face to the wall . . .

But the vision of freedom was not dead. It revived in a new form in the twentieth century, calling itself 'existentialism'. Kierkegaard, the founder of existentialism, had observed that a schoolboy can experience a curious feeling of freedom by concentrating on a fly in the inkwell or the drip of rain from the roof. Hermann Hesse observed that it is when we give our attention to *small* things that we feel renewed and invigorated. Sartre observed the paradox that he had never felt so free as under German occupation, when he was likely to be arrested. Camus recognized that Sisyphus can be free even when condemned to roll a rock uphill for ever. All had recognized that freedom is an inner state in which we cease to *leak energy*. It is true that man is being continually undermined by boredom. Yet in flashes of insight, he becomes aware of the paradox that *anything upon which he concentrates his full and total attention becomes interesting*. A blank wall would become fascinating if you could put into it the same interest you put into an absorbing book. When Dostoevsky stood in front of a firing squad, he was overwhelmed by the revelation that *nothing* is boring.

These 'new romantics' – for existentialists were precisely that –

more mode

were less pessimistic than their forebears. They believed that human existence is meaningless; but they also accepted that man has the power of free choice. They also had access to the most important philosophical insight of the twentieth century: Edmund Husserl's recognition that *consciousness is intentional.* That is to say, consciousness is not simply a mirror that reflects reality; it is more like a hand that has to reach out and *grasp* the things it apprehends.

Now this was, in fact, the answer to the problem that had driven the romantics to despair. They had observed that in 'moments of vision' the world seems self-evidently fascinating and delightful, but that for most of the time it seems dull and exhausting. They tried to reconcile the two perceptions, and decided that the 'moments of vision' were probably some kind of illusion. With Husserl's recognition that consciousness is intentional, the problem vanishes. If you look at your watch without paying attention, you fail to see the time. If you look at a blank wall with total attention, you become aware of 'meanings' that normally go unperceived. Consciousness participates in perception; it reaches out and *attacks* reality, as the teeth of a mechanical digger tear up the earth.

This recognition is of incalculable importance. Ever since he developed 'divided consciousness' – with one side of the brain acting as a microscope, the other as a telescope – man has felt alienated from existence, a passive spectator. What was so exhilarating about the rise of science and technology was that they made man aware that the mind is not really passive – that it can help him transform reality. Husserl's insight goes deeper still; it is the recognition that consciousness itself is the transformer of reality. At the moment we use it crudely and clumsily, as a baby reaches out to grab at some shining object. But if consciousness is a kind of hand, then it could be trained and developed for as many subtle uses as the hand: for grasping, for striking, for lifting, for caressing, for fashioning, for creating.

The yogis of India caught a glimpse of this truth. In fact, we all recognize it when we experience moments of excitement or absorption. Setting out on a holiday, we experience a delight that goes beyond the satisfaction of our desire for change. There is somehow a recognition that the world is a bigger and more interesting place than we gave it credit for, and that if we could now grasp this insight, it need never again be lost.

a vast serial exploration of freedom

mastery

Hulme was clearly wrong. Man is *not* a 'fixed and limited animal whose nature is absolutely constant'. He changed drastically when he developed 'divided consciousness' to cope with the complexities of civilization, and he has been changing steadily ever since. His greatest problem, the problem that has caused most of his agonies and miseries, has been his attempt to compensate for the narrowing of consciousness and the entrapment in the left-brain ego. His favourite method of compensation has been to seek out excitement. He feels most free in moments of conquest; so for the past three thousand years or so, most of the greatest men have led armies into their neighbours' territory, and turned order into chaos. This has plainly been a retrogressive step; the evolutionary urge has been defeating its own purpose.

But the past three centuries have seen an interesting development. Newton demonstrated that the human mind can grasp the secrets of the heavens, and that in this respect at least, man resembles a god. In the following century, man began to show a desire to explore this problem of freedom, to test its limits. And it is in this light that we should view that apparently catastrophic change from the age of Parson Grimshaw to our own age of violence. It was far from being a mere decline into self-indulgence and 'magical thinking'. It was also man's most determined attempt so far to understand his own nature and possibilities. And, in the evolutionary sense, it has been an astonishingly successful experiment.

Let us try to understand precisely what has happened: Man's chief problem has always been his tendency to feel that life is something of a cheat and a disappointment – 'vanity of vanities'. Desire drives him to enormous efforts; then the experience seems to run through his fingers like fairy gold, leaving a sense of 'So what?'

But if we observe closely what happens in such experiences, we can see that it is the mind itself that fails. When we feel that something is within our grasp, the mind *automatically relaxes*. It is as if we habitually dropped food a moment before it reached the mouth. But then, babies who are learning to feed themselves *do* drop most of their food before it reaches the mouth. Human consciousness is still in its infant stage. Like a baby's hand, it has not yet learned to make proper use of itself.

In the past half century, human consciousness has shown an interesting tendency to explore its own possibilities: to learn to use

itself. Some of these manifestations have been thoroughly negative –
the drug culture, for example, or the attempt of a Dean Corll or Ted
Bundy to explore the limits of self-indulgence. Our age has also seen
the appearance of an unprecedented number of messiahs and gurus,
from Wilhelm Reich and L. Ron Hubbard to Meher Baba and the
Maharishi; most of these cults have their positive aspects, although
their disciples are inclined to claim too much for them. Aldous
Huxley's recognition, in the 1950s, that certain drugs such as
mescalin and LSD could amplify the 'intentionality of consciousness'
and reveal the infinity of meaning locked in every common object, was
an important step in the exploration of perception (even though the
psychedelic cult of the 1960s reduced it to another form of self-
indulgence).

Other disciplines, like split-brain psychology and bio-feedback
control, were almost wholly free of such drawbacks. The two are
closely connected; indeed, bio-feedback control could be regarded as
a method of exploring right-brain awareness. Bio-feedback machines
enable the subject to see or hear his brain rhythms or the electrical
impulses of the skin, and to recognize those connected with relaxation. When we relax deeply, we sink into an inner-armchair, and the
left-brain ego ceases to patrol up and down in front of consciousness.
The result is a sense of richness and multiplicity, as the right brain
adds its own voice to the dialogue of perception. This is what happens
when we set out on holiday; we relax in the armchair, sense
impressions flood the senses, and the right brain adds its commentary
– memories of other times and places. (It might be better to speak of
the 'right-brain complex', for we now know that memory is stored all
over the brain.) So bio-feedback is a method of reminding the ego that
it is only the façade of consciousness, and that it can call for support
upon a far more powerful ally; it is a practical method of contacting
Wordsworth's 'other modes of being'. If the romantics had possessed
such a technique, many tragedies would have been avoided.

In this mechanism of 'enrichment' lies the whole secret of human
evolution. Let us look at it more closely.

When I open my eyes in the morning, I become conscious. I also
begin to perceive. But my consciousness is far more than mere
perception. A man with amnesia would 'perceive' the same bedroom
that I see; so would a baby or a dog. But there is obviously a great
difference between their consciousness and mine.

The difference lies in what I *add* to perception. My brain is a storehouse containing millions of memories, and I use these memories to 'fill out' my perceptions. When I look at a photograph of my house, I see a quite different house from some stranger to whom I am showing the photograph, for I *complete* the photograph with all my memories of the house, while he has nothing to 'complete' it with except his own memories of similar houses.

This mechanism called 'completing' is the most important of all functions of consciousness. Without it, the world would be meaningless. I glance across the room and see something lying under the table; for a moment I cannot decide what it is. Then I realize it is a child's toy seen from an odd angle. I have 'completed' it.

Consider what happens if I come home from a long journey. I am delighted to be back in my own sitting room. I pour myself a glass of wine, toss a log on the fire, put my feet on the footstool and sigh with contentment. The room is somehow *realler* to me than usual. Why? Am I not 'completing' it in the same way as usual?

Not quite. Because I am pleased to be home, I am *paying more attention* to everything, putting more energy into perception. The result is that I am actually seeing more. That sounds absurd – surely I am seeing the same room I always see? But no. Because my mind is more awake, I notice that my wife has changed the curtains, that the lampshade is lopsided, that one of my children has left his shoes where someone can fall over them . . . On a normal evening, I notice none of these things; my perception limits itself to a few crude basic facts, like a simple sketch. Because I am wide awake, my mind has added all kinds of new details to the sketch.

The reason I enjoy setting out on holiday is that the sketch becomes far richer than usual, more detailed. I am 'completing' perception with more care and attention.

We have a name for this more-complete perception. We call it happiness.

And how do we 'cause' happiness? By what process do we enrich perception?

A simile will help to make this clearer. Think of the mind as a lake. Consciousness is the surface of the lake. All our memories and experiences lie below the surface of the lake – some in its very depths, some floating around just under the surface. When I have any new experience, I 'complete' it by calling up memories from below the surface. So when I set out on holiday, I relax into a state of contentment, and all kinds of memories come floating to the surface. These memories may bring a surge of delight, and the delight causes more memories to surface. And suddenly, there are so many memories bobbing around on the surface that I can hardly see the water. The more consciousness is 'enriched', the more I experience delight. The more I experience delight, the more memories break the surface. And these are the moments in which I want to shout 'Of course!' as it suddenly dawns on me that life is infinitely marvellous and exciting, and that most of us waste it by allowing consciousness to remain a mirror, a flat surface of water.

The next morning, I wake up, and consciousness is once again a smooth watery surface. I make an effort; a few memories bob up, float around for a few minutes, then sink again. And suddenly I can see the basic problem of human existence. It takes *energy* to bring objects to the surface. I can 'summon' this vital energy to a certain extent. But if I am to experience 'holiday consciousness', the sense of enrichment, I must start a process of 'feedback', whereby my delight releases more energy, and the energy causes more delight. And this seems to be the problem. It is not difficult to cause flashes of 'delight' – in fact, as Maslow pointed out, most healthy people have them. But it is far more difficult to start the 'feedback process'. My mind is usually like an old car with damp spark plugs; I can press the starter until the battery is flat, and the engine still shows no sign of life.

Of course, physical stimulus helps a great deal. This is why I may experience 'enrichment' setting out on a holiday, and why children experience it on Christmas day. If I can relax in some new and interesting place, with a glass of wine and the prospect of a good meal, my chances of achieving 'feedback' are very high indeed. And here we have the motivation of crime. Haigh, the acid-bath murderer, hankered after fast sports cars, good clothes, expensive hotels. He clearly believed that 'enrichment' lay in obtaining these by any possible means. Bundy's crimes could be translated into the belief that no ordinary man can have as much sexual experience as he wants, and that this unfulfilment is a permanent obstacle to enrichment of awareness; he decided that the simplest solution to the problem was rape and murder.

Then why do such methods never seem to succeed? Anyone who

has any dealing with criminals – any policeman, lawyer, psychiatrist – will verify that, far from being happier than the rest of us, most of them seem to be gnawed by a permanent dissatisfaction. The Boston Strangler may have worked a few of his problems out of his system; but it took him two thousand rapes and a dozen or so murders, and he paid for these with his freedom and his life. As a method for the enrichment of consciousness, crime is a failure.

The reason should be obvious. Enrichment depends upon focusing the two 'beams of perception'; and 'meaning perception' must be as powerful as 'immediacy perception'. Meaning perception is a power of the mind; it depends upon a certain mental energy. And this mental energy is precisely what all criminals lack. They lay far too much emphasis on the physical stimulus in the process of 'enrichment'. Carl Panzram committed his first burglary at the age of eleven: he was reaching out for the physical stimulus; so was Steven Judy, who committed his first rape at the age of twelve.

The poet Shelley, on the other hand, recognized from an early age that the answer lay in strengthening meaning perception. In the 'Hymn to Intellectual Beauty', he wrote:

> I vowed that I would dedicate my powers
> To thee and thine – have I not kept the vow?
> With beating heart and streaming eyes, even now
> I call the phantoms of a thousand hours
> Each from his voiceless grave . . .

Shelley grasped that the real answer to enrichment of awareness lies in that action of 'summoning' memories to the surface of consciousness, the 'phantoms of a thousand hours' which lie inside us. Proust made the same discovery when he tasted a cake dipped in herb tea and was flooded with memories of childhood. Proust also experienced the paradoxical sense that man is really a kind of god: 'I have ceased to feel mediocre, accidental, mortal . . .'

The poet also experiences the odd conviction that the physical world around us is not as real as it looks. Shelley writes:

> The awful shadow of some unseen Power
> Floats, though unseen, amongst us . . .

and Wordsworth describes how he rowed a boat on to Lake Windermere by night and was overwhelmed by a sense of 'unknown

a childish materialism

...es of being'. The man who has once experienced these insights is never likely to become a criminal, for he never makes the criminal's mistake of believing that the physical world is the only reality. He now knows intuitively that the answer lies in a hidden power behind the eyes.

In fact, even the criminal grasps this, in his own muddled way. As the author of *My Secret Life* observes himself in the mirror, he is trying to add a final element of *realization* to the experience; that is, he is attempting to bring his mind to a *focus* it does not normally achieve. And this, we can see, is the motivation behind all sex crime. Frederick Baker attempts to achieve it in the rape of a child, Jack the Ripper in his orgy of sadism, Paul Knowles in his rampage of violence. The Boston Strangler deliberately arranges his victims in obscene postures so that he can, so to speak, photograph the scene, engrave it on his consciousness, to be able to 'summon' it later to enrich his awareness. And this element of sharpened perception explains the addictive element in crime. The Chicago rapist William Heirens began to experience orgasm as he climbed in through a window. The French gangster Jacques Mesrine turned from fighting rebels in Algeria to armed robbery; the sharpened awareness produced by danger had become a drug.

So crime is not, as Wells suggested in *The Croquet Player*, some horrible legacy of our cave-man ancestry. It is an attempt to compensate for the narrowed awareness produced by split-brain differentiation; and, in that sense, it springs from the same source as human creativity. Shakespeare said that the lunatic, the lover and the poet 'are of imagination all compact'; he could have added the criminal to the list. It is a mistake to think of the criminal as inhuman – notwithstanding some of the examples in the previous chapter. He is, on the contrary, more human than the rest of us; he is more enmeshed in the basic fallacy that makes most human life an unsatisfactory pursuit of will o' the wisps. We are all victims of the 'passive fallacy', the failure to grasp that, where happiness is concerned, it is the mind itself that provides that final convulsion of achievement.

Crime is, then, a completely mistaken solution to a problem that accompanies all of us from the cradle to the grave: the problem of personal evolution. But then, as we have seen in the course of this book, most human solutions tend to be mistaken – from the paradise of the religious fanatic to the simplistic materialism of the Marxist. The criminal simply goes farther than most of us in embracing the wrong solution; and, in doing so, provides the rest of us with a flash of insight into our own stupidity – the recognition that *we* are making the same mistake, but – fortunately – on a smaller scale. *This* is the real justification for the human interest in crime.

We have seen that this is an evolutionary problem. All animals are trapped in physical immediacy. Man is lucky to have succeeded in achieving some degree of detachment from it. Instinctively he has concentrated on developing the power of the mind – meaning perception. His problem is that his very success has retarded his progress. Civilization has enabled him to 'rest on his oars'. He needs challenge or crisis to get the best out of him, but he built civilization to protect himself from challenge and crisis.

Is there a way out of this vicious circle? Consider again this basic problem of the 'dual self'. Our inner-being may be divided, but we still have the two halves inside our heads, and they are perfectly capable of co-operation – in fact, they do it all the time. As I write these words, my right brain provides the insights, my left translates them into language. Of course, when I perform some simpler function – like eating my breakfast – the left hardly plays any part at all; I can even read a newspaper as I butter my toast.

And this explains how the problem comes about. For if I happen to be eating my breakfast in a hotel, and there is a noisy and irritating child at the next table, I cease to function quite so smoothly. What happens is that the child's noise distracts my attention from the newspaper, and 'I' – the left-brain self – begin to get angry. I cease to enjoy my breakfast and may even develop indigestion. My left brain has interfered with the smooth functioning of my right brain, my 'robot' and my digestion.

And what exactly happens when it interferes in this way? It causes *an internal leak of energy*. When I am relaxed and interested in what I am doing, my energies are 'funnelled' quietly and without waste into the effort I am making. The moment my left brain is distracted by some anxiety, I begin to 'leak'. And this is civilized man's basic problem. He 'leaks' all the time without even noticing it. And the leakage keeps his consciousness at a far lower pressure than it is capable of attaining.

If his anxiety increases sharply, he suddenly notices how badly he is leaking. He may experience a continual unpleasant queasiness in the pit of his stomach, and anything that reminds him of his anxiety causes a 'sinking feeling' – a bigger leak still. The reverse can also happen. He has a second martini, becomes interested in the conversation, and suddenly realizes that he is no longer leaking. But these delightful states of mind only make us aware of how much we normally leak without even noticing it.

Anything that makes you *self-conscious* causes a 'leak' – for example, someone staring intently at your feet as you sit on the train and making you wonder whether you have odd socks on. But man's whole evolution has been the evolution of self-consciousness. It is hardly surprising that 'leaking' has become the major characteristic of the human animal. We have only to look at a cat to see that its lack of self-consciousness protects it from 'leaks'.

Anything that arouses our interest, that makes us *focus* intently, seals the leaks. It does this by encouraging the two halves of the brain to collaborate without fuss. This explains the disproportionate part that sex plays in human existence. We can imagine, let us say, a man who is suddenly confronted by a girl who believes she is alone, and who is hitching up her skirt to examine a ladder in her stocking. Within a split second, all his 'leaks' are sealed, and his attention is undivided – which is another way of saying that his brain is undivided. All kinds of physical functions can produce this state of undividedness – eating, drinking, yawning, walking, even excreting. But few of them do it as instantaneously as sex.

And it is because sex can instantly repair the leaks of divided consciousness that human beings are so prone to sexual deviation – which, as we have seen, is closely connected with crime. John Christie was too self-conscious to enjoy normal sexual intercourse – in his home town he had been known as 'Can't-do-it Christie' and 'Reggie No-dick'. But if he reduced the girl to unconsciousness, then his self-consciousness disappeared and he could enjoy sex to the full. This, in other words, was the only way in which he could unite the two beams of perception, and it turned him into a mass murderer. 'Forbiddenness' would add a new dimension of excitement, and therefore of *objectivity*. It is not surprising that he experienced a deep sense of peace after a murder, and told the police: 'I had no regrets.'

The same analysis applies to a man who needs to get prostitutes to dress up as nursemaids or schoolgirls. His meaning perception is so weak in proportion to his immediacy perception that normal sex crushes his vitality. He feels feeble, inadequate, 'contingent'. The sight of a schoolgirl uniform arouses a kind of inner demon; it rubs its hands and chuckles wickedly as it prepares to lift her skirt; he is no longer feeble and inadequate, but bold and defiant. And this, we can see at a glance, is the basic psychological mechanism of crime. This is why Knowles went on a crime rampage after being jilted; he was asserting: 'I am not a weakling, a social reject. I have the power to *do*.' Through criminal aggression, he was asserting self-respect. The journalist Sandy Fawkes, who became Knowles's mistress for a few days, described him in her book *Killing Time* as an interesting and intelligent person. It was precisely because he was an intelligent person that he was racked by the 'identity crisis' to which the violence was a response. This explains the whole phenomenon of the 'high IQ criminal' which has become so characteristic of our time.

We can also see that the 'identity crisis' is due to the distress the left-brain ego feels at the belief that it is 'on its own'. It is unaware that it possesses a powerful helper only a few centimetres away. This also explains why no poet, artist or composer in history has ever committed a calculated, first-degree murder. The artist may also suffer an identity crisis, a sense of 'Who am I?' Yet the fact that he *is* an artist means that he can never be wholly unaware of the 'invisible helper'.

We are beginning to see our way towards a solution of the problem – not just of crime, but of the 'bottleneck' in human evolution.

The problem – it should now be clear – is that the left-brain ego is unaware of its powers. But then, awareness is something that can be cultivated.

Consider what happens when a hypnotist orders a man to do something that he would normally find very difficult – to stop smoking, or to lie rigid across two chairs while someone jumps up and down on his stomach. What the hypnotist has done is to immobilize the left brain – to stop it from 'interfering'. But if we are capable of these unusual feats, why can we not order ourselves to do them? Because, as we have seen, the left-brain ego *does not believe it has the power*. It is unaware of its own capacities.

But this seems absurd. Every time we become deeply interested in something, every time we experience 'holiday consciousness', every time we perform some difficult action easily and unselfconsciously, the ego realizes that it has a powerful 'backer'. There are even times, when we are feeling very relaxed and optimistic, when this backer seems to be able to foretell the future, to prevent our making stupid mistakes, even to arrange interesting coincidences. It is presumably this right-brain 'backer' who quite gratuitously tells us to expect a letter from someone we haven't heard from in years. In any case, most normal and healthy people have plenty of experience of the 'invisible backer'. So it seems preposterous to say that our chief problem is that the left brain is unaware of its powers.

But then, experience is one thing, awareness another. I may be able to drive a car without knowing the first thing about internal combustion engines. I may be able to use a mathematical formula to solve a problem without knowing why it works. I may be able to solve the Rubik cube without knowing why a certain sequence of twists rearranges the sides. But in each of these cases, a certain mental effort can enable me to understand what I am doing, to see precisely why it works. Paying attention to the moments of close collaboration between the right and left brain can endow us with conscious awareness of some of the powers of the left brain.

Abraham Maslow discovered that, when he talked to his students about peak experiences, they began to recall peak experiences which they had had in the past, but had *not noticed at the time*, flashes of that deep sense of well-being. He also discovered that, when his students began to talk and think about peak experiences regularly, they began to have more peak experiences. The left brain was beginning to recognize the 'invisible helper' and its power to induce those sudden moments of supreme well-being.

And now, at last, we can see the outline of the solution to this problem of human criminality and human evolution.

Once we are aware of some fact, we can begin to absorb it into consciousness until we know it instinctively. And in the past century, we have slowly become aware of the basic facts about consciousness. Freud's insight into the unconscious, Husserl's into intentionality, Adler's into the will-to-power, Maslow's into the peak experience, Frankl's into the law of reverse effort, Sperry's into the double brain: all these have revolutionized our knowledge of human psychology. What has emerged is the recognition that consciousness is not a passive mirror that reflects experience. It is a hand that grasps reality. The tighter it grasps, the 'realler' the world becomes. And any sudden 'clenching' of this fist induces the flash of the peak experience. This is why, as Dr Johnson says, 'the knowledge that he is to be hanged in the morning concentrates a man's mind wonderfully'. It is because he is at last using consciousness for its proper purpose, to *grip*. It is because we so seldom use it for its proper purpose that the hand remains so feeble. When Maslow's students began to think and talk about the peak experience, this knowledge dawned on them instinctively, and they began to induce peak experiences *by a simple clenching of the fist*.

'Clenching' has the effect of closing the leaks, and closing the leaks has the effect of suddenly increasing the 'pressure' of consciousness. This, as Hesse says, is why concentrating on small things revitalizes us; it closes the leaks. And 'clenching' does it instantaneously, bringing a flash of insight. In the same way crisis so often brings the sense of 'absurd good news'. It causes consciousness to 'clench', convulsively, making us aware that it has 'muscles', and that these muscles can be used to transform our lives.

Nothing is easier than to verify this statement. All that is necessary is to narrow the eyes, tense the muscles, make a sudden powerful effort of 'clenching' the mind. The result is an instantaneous twinge of delight. It vanishes almost instantly because the 'muscle' is so feeble. But we know that any muscle can be strengthened by deliberate effort.

We can also observe that as we 'clench' the mind, it produces a sense of 'inwardness', a momentary withdrawal into some inner fortress. This is clearly what Kierkegaard meant when he said 'Truth is subjectivity'. It is, in fact, a sudden flash of contact with the 'source of power, meaning and purpose' inside us.

And what relevance has all this to the problem of crime? The answer can be seen if we consider again Dan MacDougald's cure of 'hard core psychopaths' in the Georgia State Penitentiary. A criminal, as Sartre pointed out, is a man who has become accustomed to thinking of himself as a criminal; he feels himself to be a *victim* – of society, of bad luck, of his own violent impulses and lack of purpose. MacDougald 'cured' his criminals by making them recognize that their problems lay in their own mental attitudes. When he intervened in the case of a prisoner who was planning to kill another

will to power / will to meaning
2 sides / one coin
670 *The Age of Mass Murder*

prisoner with an iron bar – to avenge an insult – the convict invited his enemy to have a sandwich and a coffee, and the situation was resolved; MacDougald had taught him that he was not trapped in some inevitable fatality, some murderous destiny. He had taught him the secret that has transformed man from a naked tree dweller to the most highly evolved creature on earth: that man's *controlling force* – 'Force C' – is the most important thing about him. As Wells's Mr Polly discovered: If you don't like your life, you can change it.

At the moment, society shares the assumption of the criminal: that nothing much can be done. But then, all the major transformations of society have started with the few who know better. The conclusion is inescapable. Only when society recognizes that it possesses the power to control crime will crime be controlled.

Looking back over three million years of human history, we can see that it has been a slow reprogramming of the human mind, whose first major turning point was the moment when the mind became aware of itself. When man learned to recognize his own face in a pool and to say 'I', he became capable of greatness, and also of criminality.

But if this history of human evolution has taught us anything, it is that 'criminal man' has no real, independent existence. He is a kind of shadow, a Spectre of the Brocken, an illusion. He is the result of man's misunderstanding of his own potentialities – as if a child should see his face in a distorting mirror and assume he has changed into a monster.

The criminal is, in fact, the distorted reflection of the human face, the 'collective nightmare of mankind'. And this insight is in itself a cause for optimism. As Novalis says: When we dream that we dream, we are beginning to awaken.

SELECTED BIBLIOGRAPHY

Ardrey, Robert, *African Genesis*. Collins, London, 1961.
——*The Territorial Imperative*. Atheneum, New York, 1966.
——*The Social Contract*. Collins, London, 1970.
——*The Hunting Hypothesis*. Collins, London, 1976.
Barbi, Michele, *Life of Dante*. Cambridge University Press, 1954.
Birkenhead, Earl of, *Famous Trials*. Hutchinson, London, 1926.
——*More Famous Trials*. Hutchinson, London, 1928.
Braudel, Fernand, *Capitalism and Material Life 1400–1800*. Weidenfeld & Nicolson, London, 1973.
Bury, J. B. *A History of Greece*. The Modern Library, New York, 1900.
Calder, Ritchie, *After the Seventh Day – The World Man Created*. New American Library, 1961.
Coon, Carleton S., *The Story of Man*. Knopf, New York, 1954.
De Coulanges, Numa Denis Fustel, *The Ancient City*. Doubleday, New York, 1975.
Fox, Robin and Tiger, Lionel, *The Imperial Animal*. Granada, London, 1974.
Gaute, J. H. H. and Odell, Robin, *The Murderer's Who's Who*. Harrap, London, 1979.
Godolphin, Francis R. B. *The Greek Historians*, Vols. 1 & 2. Random House, New York, 1942.
Griffiths, Major Arthur, *Mysteries of Police & Crime*, Vols. 1 & 2. Cassell, London, 1898.
Hays, H. R. *In the Beginnings – Early Man and his Gods*. G. P. Putnam's Sons, New York, 1963.
Hazlitt, Henry, *The Conquest of Poverty*. Arlington House, New York, 1973.
Kennedy, Ludovic, *A Book of Railway Journeys*. Collins, London, 1980.

Lorenz, Konrad, *On Aggression*. Methuen, London, 1966.

McNeill, William H. *The Rise of the West*. University of Chicago Press, 1963.

Mommsen, Theodor, *The History of Rome*, Vols. 1–5. Richard Bentley & Son, London, 1894.

Morris, Desmond, *The Naked Ape*. Jonathan Cape, London, 1967.

——*The Human Zoo*. Jonathan Cape, London, 1969.

Nash, Jay Robert, *Murder America – Homicide in the United States from the Revolution to the Present*. Harrap, London, 1981. Simon & Shuster, New York, 1980.

Pelham, Camden, *The Chronicles of Crime or the Newgate Calendar*, Vols. 1 & 2. Reeves & Turner, London, 1886.

Pike, Luke Owen, *A History of Crime in England*. Smith, Elder & Co., London, Vol. 1, 1873; Vol. 2, 1876.

Plutarch, *The Lives of the Noble Grecians and Romans*, translated by John Dryden, The Modern Library, New York.

Reade, Winwood, *The Martyrdom of Man*. Watts & Co., London, 1961.

Shew, E. Spencer, *A Companion to Murder*. Cassell, London, 1960.

——*A Second Companion to Murder*. Cassell, London, 1961.

Suetonius, Caius Tranquillus, *The Lives of the Twelve Caesars*. Henry G. Bohn, London.

Tacitus, Works of, Vol. 1. *The Annals*. George Bell & Son, London, 1877.

Vol. 2. *The History, Germany, Agricola and Dialogue on Orators*. Henry G. Bohn, London, 1854.

Thomas, Hugh, *An Unfinished History of the World*. Hamish Hamilton, London, 1979.

Thorpe, W. H., *Animal Nature and Human Nature*. Methuen, London, 1974.

Toynbee, Arnold, *A Study of History*, Vols. 1–12. Oxford University Press, London, 1934–61.

——*Hannibal's Legacy*.

(Vol. 1) *Rome and Her Neighbours Before Hannibal's Entry*. Oxford University Press, London, 1965.

(Vol. 2) *Rome and Her Neighbours After Hannibal's Exit*. Oxford University Press, London, 1965.

Unesco, under the Auspices of, *History of Mankind: Cultural and Scientific Development*.

Vol. 1 (i) *Prehistory* by Jacquetta Hawkes, Allen & Unwin, London, 1963.

Vol. 1 (ii) *The Beginnings of Civilization* by Sir Leonard Woolley, Allen & Unwin, London, 1963.

Vol. 2 *The Ancient World* by Luigi Pareti assisted by Paolo Brezzi & Luciano Petech.

(i) *1200 B.C. to A.D. 500.* Allen & Unwin, London, 1965.

(ii) *From about 500 B.C. to the Christian Era.* Allen & Unwin, London, 1965.

Vol. 3 (i, ii and iii) *The Great Medieval Civilizations* by Gaston Wiet, Vadime Elisseeff, Philippe Wolff, Jean Naudou. Allen & Unwin, London, 1975.

Wilkinson, George, *The Newgate Calendar*. T. Werner Laurie, London, 1774.

Yochelson, Samuel and Samenow, Stanton E., *The Criminal Personality*, Aronson, New York, 1977.

Zinsser, Hans, *Rats, Lice and History*. Atlantic Monthly Press, USA, 1935. Bantam, 1971.

ACKNOWLEDGEMENTS

Many people have helped in the making of this book. I am grateful to my old friend A. E. Van Vogt for supplying me with the basic material for the second chapter and allowing me to quote from unpublished radio talks. Dr James Rentoul drew my attention to Völgyesi's book on animal hypnosis. Veteran crime writer John Dunning went to considerable trouble to get me information on the Sala case. My friend Ted Harrison pointed out to me Defoe's connection with spying. And I also wish to thank Dan MacDougald, Alfred Reynolds, Ludovic Kennedy, Stephen Spickard, Dennis Stacy, Kenneth Moyer, Pat Bruneni, Jerome Drost, Joe Gaute, A. L. Rowse and Jacquetta Hawkes (for their advice on historical points) and finally my friend and collaborator Donald Seaman for endless suggestions. The final form of this book owes a great deal to the patience and suggestions of Mark Barty-King.

Gorran Haven, 1983

INDEX

creativity, 5, 6, 160, 174
Crete, 170–71
crime: change in types of, over time, 11, 106; counterbalances to, 214; as a miscalculation, 420; shock effect of, 647
criminal character, the, 104
Crippen, Dr, 15, 515
Cristobal, M., 506
Cro-Magnon man, 46, 112, 115, 120, 122, 126, 159
Croix, Sainte, 390–91
Cromwell, Oliver, 527
Cromwell, Thomas, 370
Crook, Japhet, 410
Crowe, Bernard, 629
cruelty: cities and, 108; impersonal, 63; innate, 61; stress and, 134 *see also* sadism
crusades, the, 277–90, 292, 393, 441
Culley, Robert, 468
Culpepper, Thomas, 370
Cyrus, King, 175, 254
Czechoslovakia, 449, 600, 632
Czolgosz, Leon, 525

Dagobert, 268
Daladier, Édouard, 601
Damiens, 410
Danes, the, 272
Dante Alighieri, 328–9
Danton, Georges, 434
Darius, King, 147, 249, 250
DaRonch, Carol, 644
Dart, Raymond, 47–8
Darwin, Charles, 52
Davy, Gloria, 623
Dean, James, 618
death, 316

death wish, 63–4
Debord, Guy, 626
Decembrists, the, 445
Decianus, Catus, 202, 203
Decius, 241
Defoe, Daniel, 415–21, 425, 466
DeFreeze, Donald, 634
Degnan, Suzanne, 614
Delhi, 331
Delhomme, Eugenie, 509
delusions, 505
democracy, 172
Demuth, Hélène, 450
Denke, Karl, 607
Denmark, 453
depersonalization, 619
depression, 91
deprivation, 649
Dereham, Francis, 370
De River, Paul, 615–16
de Sade, Marquis, 22, 23, 102–3, 105, 153–7, 433, 435, 438, 497, 656
DeSalvo, Albert *see* Boston Strangler
Descartes, René, 394
desire, satisfaction of, 154–6
D'Este, Alfonso, 354
desynchronization, 136–7
detectives, 482
Dewey, Thomas E., 558–9, 561
Diamond, Legs, 555
Dias, Bartolemeu, 334
Dickens, Charles, 166, 412, 455, 482, 483, 514
Dimes, Albert, 577
Diocletian, 227–8, 229, 230, 393
DiPalermo, Joe, 565
discipline, 650–51
dissenters, 416

694　　　　　　　　　　　　*Index*

702 *Index*

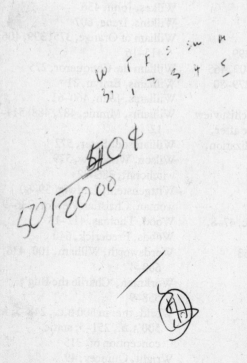